A History of the University of South Carolina
1940–2000

A HISTORY OF THE UNIVERSITY OF SOUTH CAROLINA

1940
2000

HENRY H. LESESNE

UNIVERSITY OF SOUTH CAROLINA PRESS

Published by the University of South Carolina Press in cooperation with
the University of South Carolina Bicentennial Commission

UNIVERSITY OF SOUTH CAROLINA *BICENTENNIAL*

© 2001 University of South Carolina

Published in Columbia, South Carolina, by the
University of South Carolina Press

Manufactured in the United States of America

05 04 03 02 01   5 4 3 2 1

Library of Congress Cataloging-in-Publication Data

Lesesne, Henry H.
  A history of the University of South Carolina, 1940–2000 / Henry H. Lesesne.
    p. cm.
  Includes bibliographical references and index.
  ISBN 1-57003-444-3 (hard : alk. paper)
  1. University of South Carolina. I. Title.
  LD5033 .D47 2001
  378.757'71—dc21   2001005099

CONTENTS

ILLUSTRATIONS

All illustrations are courtesy of the University of South Carolina Archives,
South Caroliniana Library, Columbia

TABLES

PREFACE

The origins of this book lie in the mind of Walter Edgar, who realized that as the University of South Carolina began preparing for the two hundredth anniversary of its chartering in 1801, the published history of the institution needed updating. The most recent of the University's three institutional histories, Daniel Walker Hollis's two-volume work titled *University of South Carolina*, was published on the occasion of Carolina's sesquicentennial and brought the institution's history up to that date.[1] Hollis's history, though published in the 1950s, has stood the test of time well and deserved the acclaim it received as one of the South's monumental institutional histories of a college or university. However, at the time he finished his second volume, Professor Hollis could see only faintly the sweeping changes World War II and its aftermath would bring to the institution and the state. Since his volumes were published, the University of South Carolina, like other southern institutions of higher education, was remade by the forces unleashed by the second World War. Though many of its core values remain the same, in many ways the University of South Carolina in the 1990s is fundamentally a different place than it was in 1940. It is the post–World War II transformation of the University of South Carolina that I have set out to trace in this volume.[2]

As a successor to Hollis's volumes, this book was conceived as an institutional history of the University of South Carolina, in the genre known among historians of higher education as the "house history." Historians of higher education have noted some weaknesses associated with this genre of institutional history, primarily due to the fact that most college and university histories have been written by older graduates and incorporated only incidental connection to regional and national themes. House histories overwhelmingly dominate the historiography of southern higher education in particular, and generally these works have tended to be narrow, insular, preoccupied with the events of a particular campus, and little concerned with the social, political, and cultural contexts within which colleges and universities operate.[3] However, more recent years have seen a flowering of more broadly conceived house histories of southern universities, and the best of these works avoid provinciality and are genuine contributions to the historiography of the entire American South and nation rather than to a narrow genre.[4] While most of these look at the entire sweep of the history of their institutions—some beginning as early as the eighteenth century—the vast changes of the twentieth

century have recently garnered special attention among historians of southern higher education.[5]

I have attempted to place this book firmly in the line of the broadly conceived "house history." It is an institutional history, not an intellectual history; the complex and far-reaching changes that have taken place in nearly
every field of intellectual inquiry since 1940 are beyond its scope. Nonetheless, I have tried to put the institutional development of the University of
South Carolina in state, regional, and national contexts, connecting the development of this institution to the broader themes of the history of twentieth-
century South Carolina and the American South. As much of the material I
have dealt with is still a part of the living memory of many readers, it presented a special challenge. Vanderbilt University historian Paul Conkin wrote
in his monumental history of that university, "Any institutional history has
its pitfalls and limits. It cannot capture and express the unique experiences
of those who make up a university community."[6] From the perspective of the
many thousands of students, faculty, staff, and friends of the University of
South Carolina whose personal histories converged with the institution over
the years, there are any number of University of South Carolinas. Though
this is primarily a history of institutional development, I tried to write the
story of Carolina in such a way that those who were there will recognize my
description as accurate. It is not an uncritical homage to Carolina. While
some might disagree with my interpretations, I hope that those who took part
in the making of this history will, at some level, recognize themselves and
their experiences.

The remarkable breadth of the changes that took place in nearly every
aspect of the University during more than half a century presented another
challenge. The book is organized chronologically by decade, and a postscript
deals briefly with the last decade of the twentieth century. At this writing, the
historical perspective necessary for a more lengthy treatment of this final
decade does not yet exist, but I am hopeful that the future historian who
writes of this decade might find this postscript to be a useful introduction. I
chose a chronological arrangement and a narrative form simply because the
many stories of change are intertwined throughout the post–World War II
history of Carolina. Change went in many directions and keeping track of it
is difficult. Thus, I selected a number of themes that cut across the decades
of the University's twentieth century history and examined them as they
reappeared through time. The reader should be aware of these themes and
keep them in mind; recognizing them will make the work more coherent.

Among the themes addressed, perhaps the most important is the interaction between state politics and state-funded higher education. As Merle Curti
and Vernon Carstensen wrote of state universities in their landmark history

of the University of Wisconsin, "the American state university is a public institution and—like a state prison, a state hospital, or a highway system—its success or failure in winning appropriate authority or procuring adequate funds from the legislature has seldom rested exclusively on its merits. A host of politically pertinent but often educationally irrelevant elements have usually helped determine the success or failure of the University with the legislature and the state."[7] Such has been the case with the University of South Carolina, located only one city block from South Carolina's State House complex. For USC administrators, faculty, and students, at times that location has been a blessing, at other times a curse. Nonetheless, the history of the University is intertwined with the history of politics in the state, and the interaction of the two is a key theme. Likewise, the organization and operation of the state's overall system of public higher education has been a continuing issue in these fifty-plus years. Debates over issues such as the state's role in making higher education available to its citizens were, and are, ongoing.

Closely related to state politics is the theme of chronic underfunding of public higher education in South Carolina, which hampered the development of the University for much of the period under study. For most of the twentieth century, Carolina struggled with a level of funding well below that of its peers. As Daniel Hollis observed in his own history of the University, "While no one can deny that it takes more than money to establish a first-class university, it is equally true that no great university has been created in America without it."[8] While at times the story of Carolina's struggle to cope with a lack of funding may seem repetitive, it is at the heart of the story of the development of this university and cannot be overemphasized.

As Hollis's books have shown, at several key times in its history, the University of South Carolina has struggled with the vital question of whom it was to serve. In the post–World War II period, USC continued to struggle with that question. That war set in motion forces that ultimately democratized access to higher education for South Carolina's blacks and whites alike. The single most important development at the University of South Carolina in the post–World War II era was desegregation. Desegregation was closely related to state politics, and issues of race, segregation, the civil rights movement, and the expansion of the African American student body at Carolina is a reoccurring theme in these chapters. Like underfunding, racial segregation hampered Carolina's institutional development. However, in the years after desegregation began in 1963, the University launched a drive for modernization and status as a full-fledged research university. The story of the desegregation of the University of South Carolina appears in thematic sections throughout the volume and is closely bound to other developments at the University in the respective decades.

Also vitally important to the development of the University of South Carolina in this era were the vast economic changes in post–World War II South Carolina. Like politics, the University was closely tied to the changing economy, and economic change directly influenced reoccurring themes such as the "nationalization" of faculty standards, the growth of a wide range of graduate and undergraduate programs, and the development of a comprehensive research program funded by both internal and external sources. Another important theme associated with economic and political change has been the tremendous physical growth of the institution, both in Columbia and on "extension" campuses across the state. Each chapter addresses these themes as they relate to institutional developments in that period.

World War II had a tremendous and long-lasting impact on the University of South Carolina. During the war, the U.S. Navy used the campus to train sailors. After the war, veterans used the GI Bill to attend college and changed the nature of the institution permanently. The 1960s and 1970s brought their children, the baby boom generation, to college. The challenge of educating the baby boomers helped transform the institution from a small regional university to the large national research university we know today. The growth and change that was a direct outgrowth of World War II is another important echo in these chapters. One consequence of the astounding growth of the institution was significant change in the character of student life. Between 1940 and 1990, the system of strict rules governing student life in loco parentis (literally, "in place of the parent") that had been an integral part of the institution since its founding dissolved, and that decline was accompanied by a corresponding loss of the very personal character of student life as Carolina became a "megaversity." By the 1990s, there was no longer a common "Carolina experience" for its students. These vast changes in student life are another important recurring theme.

Among the most important public faces of the University of South Carolina in the state is its athletic program. No one can deny the important role "big-time" university athletics plays in shaping institutional image. This book addresses the most significant people and events that have helped shape the athletic program that has such an important role in shaping the public's perception of the University of South Carolina.

With this list of themes in mind, the reader should be able to navigate the complex story of the development of the University of South Carolina into a modern research university.

This book would have been impossible without the help of a great number of friends and supporters. My primary debt is to Walter B. Edgar. At his suggestion, I undertook this topic as my doctoral dissertation. As my graduate advisor, dissertation director, and friend, his patience, guidance, and encouragement made this book a reality. The fact that he consistently made time to confer with me while he was in the midst of writing his land-mark history of the state of South Carolina is a testament to his dedication as a genuinely committed teacher as well as scholar.

Credit should also go to USC president John M. Palms, who foresaw the need for an updated scholarly history of the University and was willing to support my effort. Thomas L. Stepp, Othniel H. Wienges Jr., and Thorne Compton also provided me with the time and resources to complete this project. Alexander Moore at the University of South Carolina Press was ever patient and helpful, reading and correcting numerous drafts and contribut-ing valuable advice that made this a far better book. Barbara Brannon's care-ful editing was also a tremendous help. Among others in the USC family who deserve thanks are Lacy Ford, Thavolia Glymph, Dean Kinzley, Tom Brown, Connie Schulz, Mary Alice Spoone, Marcia Synnott, Sally McKay, and Jill Grantz.

My friends on the staffs of the South Caroliniana Library and the Univer-sity Archives helped me endure the long hours of research, offering advice and an unceasing willingness to keep retrieving yet another round of requests from the stacks. Elizabeth C. West and John Heiting of the University Archives generously shared their knowledge of the University's history and the holdings of their repository. To Allen Stokes, Henry Fulmer, Beth Bilder-back, Laura Costello, Robin Copp, Herb Hartsook, Thelma Hayes, Mark Herro, and the rest of Caroliniana's staff go my heartfelt thanks. Tammy Hyatt and Ruth Jenkins in the office of the Board of Trustees always cheerfully accommodated my research requests, despite the hardship I caused. Tibby and Homer Steedly in the Institute for Southern Studies always offered coopera-tion, expertise, and encouragement. Keith McGraw and Becky Wilson gave invaluable help with the illustrations. All those who agreed to share their knowledge of the University's history with me in interviews and memoirs deserve credit for many of the insights in this book.

My family played the central role in my love of history and of South Caro-lina. My grandfather Joab Mauldin Lesesne (Ph.D. USC, 1948), did not live to see me earn my doctorate or finish this book, but he was always present in my mind and his example inspired me in the love of history.

To my wife, Kim, I dedicate this book. She endured many frustrations (both mine and hers) in the course of the research and writing. Without her love, support, and ability to force me to keep the ultimate goal in mind, I am sure I would never have completed it.

A History of the University
of South Carolina
1940–2000

Prologue | THE UNIVERSITY OF SOUTH CAROLINA

1801–1940

The transformation of the University of South Carolina in the post–World War II decades reflected the pace of change in a state that moved haltingly into a new world brought about by the development of an industrial economy. The story of the University's postwar transformation is but part of one of the most interesting histories of any state university in the United States. Historian Daniel Hollis has written that "few institutions of higher learning have had a more tragic history than has South Carolina's state university."[1] At the beginning of the period under study, the University of South Carolina suffered from the effects of that tragic history and was well below the level of quality established within the first six decades of its founding. The state had originally established the South Carolina College in 1801 as part of an effort to unite South Carolinians in the turbulent wake of the American Revolution. South Carolina's leaders saw a new college as a way to bring together the sons of the elite from the upcountry and the lowcountry, in order to promote, as they said, "the good order and harmony" of the state. Such was a break from the past, for in the colonial period South Carolinians frequently went abroad for their education. Although South Carolina's population was relatively small, the Palmetto State sent more of its sons to England to study at the Inns of Court than did any other English colony.

The founding of a state college in South Carolina at the beginning of the nineteenth century was also a part of the southern public college movement spurred by Thomas Jefferson. Within twenty years of one another, Georgia, North Carolina, South Carolina, and Virginia established state-supported colleges, keeping many of the region's best minds at home. In the antebellum era, the Palmetto State generously supported the South Carolina College with regular appropriations, and the institution could boast of a cosmopolitan faculty that included such noted scholars as Europeans Francis Lieber and Thomas Cooper, as well as renowned American scholars such as John and Joseph LeConte. Offering a staunchly traditional classical curriculum, the South Carolina College became one of most influential institutions in the

South, earning a reputation as the training ground for South Carolina's influential antebellum white elite. With a distinguished faculty, up-to-date scientific equipment, and liberal state support, the antebellum South Carolina College ranked among the leading institutions of higher education in America and was a leader in the South.[2]

Then disaster struck. South Carolina's secession in 1860 unleashed the devastation of civil war; the state and the South Carolina College paid dearly. The institution closed for want of students, and throughout the next century it struggled to regain the leading role in the region it had held during the antebellum era. State leaders revived the institution in 1866 with ambitious plans for a diverse university, but with a nearly empty state treasury, the institution that emerged was barely a shadow of its former self.

The good intentions of its alumni had revived the institution in the immediate aftermath of the war, but soon the political controversies of Reconstruction buffeted the newly established University of South Carolina, and during Reconstruction the institution entered a revolutionary era. In 1868, the newly elected, Republican-dominated General Assembly elected the first black members of the board of trustees (Francis L. Cardozo and Benjamin A. Bozeman). In 1873, when Republicans insisted that black students be admitted, influential faculty members resigned and the state's white elite abandoned the institution. Under the patronage of South Carolina's Radical Republicans, the University of South Carolina became the only southern state university to enroll and grant degrees to black students during the Reconstruction era. Black and white students lived and attended classes side by side, a concept that was anathema to the old white elite. Though politically controversial, Carolina's first desegregation provided an extraordinary opportunity to both white and African American students in an era when the opportunity for higher education for anyone was rare.[3]

Following the turmoil of "Redemption" in the Palmetto State, South Carolina's white conservative leaders, led by Governor Wade Hampton, closed the institution to purge it of Radical influences. They reopened it in 1880 as a whites-only Morrill Land Grant institution: the South Carolina College of Agriculture and Mechanics. This institution thereafter became caught in the political upheaval of the last two decades of nineteenth-century South Carolina. It went through several reorganizations in which the curriculum frequently changed and its status shifted from college to university and back again.[4]

The height of uncertainty came in the early 1890s when Benjamin R. Tillman harshly attacked the institution. Tillman was the champion of those in South Carolina who thought the state should support an agricultural college, not a comprehensive liberal arts university. In 1889 he convinced the state to establish Clemson Agricultural College as an alternative to the University of South Carolina, and in 1890 South Carolina elected him governor. Tillman and his political allies made attacking the University a central part of their program, calling it "the seedbed of the aristocracy" and promising to close it forever. Although they never followed through with their threats, their attacks crippled the institution. Enrollment fell to just sixty-eight students in 1893–94, and in 1895, the entire book budget was only $71 ($1,145).[5]

By the late 1890s, as Tillman's movement lost momentum, the institution, once again known as the South Carolina College, began a slow recovery. The school's leaders admitted the first women in 1895, and they gradually broadened the curriculum in the first decade of the twentieth century. Enrollment rose, and the state rechartered the college as a university in 1906. Since that time, the institution served the state as a university, at least in name.

Although its leaders no longer had to worry about whether their institution would continue to exist, the University of South Carolina struggled to compete for funding with three state colleges established by the Tillmanites (Clemson Agricultural College and Winthrop College for white students, and the Colored Normal, Industrial, Agricultural and Mechanical College—later known as South Carolina State—for black students), as well as two previously existing institutions, The Citadel and the State Medical College. Clemson and Winthrop were the strongest of the state's colleges and led all others in enrollment, state appropriations, and general popularity. However, a small, poor state like South Carolina simply could not afford to support a total of six separate colleges and maintain a high standard of scholarship at any of them. William H. Hand, USC professor of education, said in 1910 of the duplication among the state's colleges, "However unpalatable and unpopular the statement, it is but plain truth that the state has blundered badly" in establishing four competing institutions of higher learning for whites. When the Southern Association of Colleges and Schools (SACS) was founded in 1895, not a single college in South Carolina—public or private—qualified for membership. USC became the first of South Carolina's state-supported institutions to qualify for SACS membership, in 1917.[6]

Because of the intrastate competition, the University of South Carolina also suffered in comparison with state universities in other southern states. As Daniel Hollis observed, in the early decades of the twentieth century, at a time when the major universities in North Carolina and Texas were laying the foundations to build leading American institutions, the University of South Carolina was one of the weakest state institutions in the South and not even a leader within the Palmetto State.[7] As a result of the attacks of the Tillman era, the overall poverty in South Carolina, and the competition for higher education dollars, the University of South Carolina suffered through what Hollis called "troubled years" of "general malaise" during the first two decades of the twentieth century, years that put it far behind in the effort to build a leading university.[8]

In the 1920s however, with an improving state financial situation, reforms in the state's secondary schools, and the arrival of an energetic new president, the University of South Carolina began a sustained recovery. The new president, William D. Melton, brought renewed optimism, arguing forcefully and successfully for greater appropriations. As confidence and state funding increased, enrollment increased as well. Between 1921 and 1925, the student body more than doubled, growing from 621 to 1,419. By 1930, the University of South Carolina equaled or surpassed both Clemson and Winthrop in the levels of appropriations and enrollment for the first time in the twentieth century. New academic programs in music, art, and electrical engineering, Ph.D. programs in history, English and education, and new schools in pharmacy and journalism all expanded the offerings of the burgeoning University.[9]

For all the successes of the 1920s, however, serious problems remained. As it had since the Civil War, the state provided inadequate resources for higher education. For example, in 1925, the annual appropriation for University of North Carolina exceeded that for all of South Carolina's state colleges put together.[10] The financial depression that plagued the state and nation in the succeeding decade did nothing to improve the University of South Carolina's financial situation, ending the brief period of promise of the 1920s and delivering a cruel setback to the institution. State appropriations plummeted from a high of $454,680 ($3,613,042) in 1929 to a Depression-era low of $156,355 ($1,572,337) in 1933–34.[11] In 1933, the hard times forced the state to pay faculty salaries, which were already woefully inadequate, in scrip. The administration raised student tuition (from $20 to $30 [$210 to $315] per semester for in-state students, and from $40 to $100 [$420 to $1,051] for out-of-state students), curtailed graduate programs, and eliminated the Ph.D.[12]

By the late 1930s, although the state's economy had not completely recovered, the University began to adjust to the hard times and pull out of its Depression woes. Enrollment increased from 1,421 in 1934–35 to 2,051 in 1939–40, while state appropriations, at $168,450 ($1,693,858) in 1934–35, had risen to $301,025 ($2,936,345) by 1939–40. An energetic and popular man assumed the presidency in 1936: former dean of the USC school of journalism J. Rion McKissick. McKissick brought renewed confidence as he sought to improve the institution's public reputation. The brief interlude between the depths of the Depression and the outbreak of World War II brought a return of optimism to Carolina. New departments, including political science and an Extension Division, as well as an expansion of courses in fine arts and music, were evidence of the University's tentative steps toward growth.[13]

Although state appropriations had not returned to the level of the 1920s, an influx of federal spending from the New Deal helped contribute to a sense of momentum. Federal funding sparked a badly needed building boom on the campus, helping the University refurbish old buildings and build five new dormitories, a library, a new football stadium, and an indoor swimming pool. Programs such as the National Youth Administration and the Works Progress Administration aided students and provided work for faculty as well.[14]

By 1940, the University was a secure institution, a long way from its precarious position at the beginning of the century, but also a long way from its antebellum status as a leading American institution of higher education. With better economic times, there was little reason to doubt that the fortunes of the University of South Carolina would continue to improve, and someday it might even hope to regain its pre–Civil War reputation. At the time, the war clouds of Europe still seemed far removed from South Carolina, and the University of South Carolina was poised for growth.

1 | "ON THE BRINK OF A NEW ERA"

1940–1945

I do not see that we shall make any radical change in this community . . . in generations, perhaps centuries.

James McBride Dabbs, 1940

In the coming days, and probably soon, [the South] is likely to have to prove its capacity for adjustment far beyond what has been true in the past.

Wilbur J. Cash, 1941

In such times, men find their measure. Out of such times, progress will emerge or the world will collapse. Your University, your State and your Country expect you to do your full part—and you cannot do that unless you take full advantage of the educational opportunity you have at Carolina.

J. Rion McKissick, 1941

In a 1934 essay, H. Clarence Nixon, Vanderbilt University political scientist and "Southern Agrarian" turned New Dealer, surveyed of the status of higher education in the American South. Nixon noted that colleges and universities of the region had made significant improvements since 1900, and he pointed especially to developments at universities in Chapel Hill, Durham, Nashville, and Charlottesville.[1] His essay also gave a telling hint of the perception of the University of South Carolina in the eyes of its regional peers in the fourth decade of the twentieth century. In a discussion of the antebellum colleges of the American South, Nixon ignored the South Carolina College. In any list of the leading southern colleges of that era, the college in Columbia surely deserved mention. However, Nixon's oversight was probably more indicative of the relative significance of the institution in his own day rather than of its standing seventy-five years earlier. In an article that included discussions of numerous contemporary southern state universities and faculty, athletics, trends in finance, and the overall low standing of higher education in southern society, Nixon never once mentioned anything about the University of South Carolina, in either a positive or negative light. It was as if USC did not exist.[2]

It is unlikely that H. Clarence Nixon held any special grudges against the University of South Carolina. It was simply that during the 1930s USC was not an integral part of the considerable social and intellectual ferment taking place in the leading universities of the South. Led by sociologist Howard Odum at the University of North Carolina, many southern intellectuals of the 1930s had begun searching for solutions to the seemingly intractable problems of the region that the Great Depression had made so obvious.[3] Scholars at the University of South Carolina however, were largely outside of the circle of those involved in the "regionalist" reform movement.[4] The University's status relative to other southern universities was in large measure a legacy of the problems that had plagued the institution and state since the Civil War. As USC historian Daniel Hollis wrote, "In 1850 the South Carolina College [the forerunner of the University of South Carolina] and the University of Virginia were the two most influential institutions of higher learning in the South; in 1906, while Virginia still held much of its former distinction, the University at Columbia was one of the weakest state institutions in the region and not even preeminent in South Carolina."[5] Despite significant improvements made since 1906, and though the University offered a good quality undergraduate education to those who sought it, at the end of the 1930s USC was decidedly among the middle ranks of southern higher education.

This situation would begin to change in the years after the Second World War. World War II was the twentieth century's watershed event, one that led to dramatic changes within the nation, the state of South Carolina, and ultimately, South Carolina's state university. As historian James C. Cobb saw it, World War II was the "final act" in a protracted drama that marked a great turning point in southern history.[6] For southern higher education as well, World War II was such a watershed. Clarence Mohr has written, "World War II constituted a turning point for both American higher education and for Southern colleges and universities . . . setting in motion forces that would permanently reorder their priorities, remake their institutional culture, and alter their relationship with society at large."[7] For the University of South Carolina, World War II and the forces it unleashed finally helped it overcome the obstacles, primarily poverty and racism, that had crippled its development since the Civil War. In the coming decades, the University took steps that would radically transform it from an institution primarily concerned with undergraduate education to its current status as a comprehensive research university.

On the eve of the Second World War, the University of South Carolina was a racially segregated, small, sleepy southern college with a few limited graduate programs, primarily serving a state and regional constituency. This condition was due in part to South Carolina's grinding poverty, but also to its insistence on defending racial segregation, which stunted the state's economy and required it to fund costly duplication of educational institutions. While the war brought the U.S. Navy, the GI Bill of Rights, and an onslaught of the war's veterans to the campus, racial segregation meant that South Carolina denied nearly 43 percent of the state's population access to its state university. The 1940s would be a decade of transition, a time when the University of South Carolina established itself as the largest comprehensive university in South Carolina, but it was also a time when it was forced to face squarely the issue of racial segregation, a question with which it would wrestle through the early years of the 1960s.

For the first four decades of the twentieth century, Clemson Agricultural College had stood as the University of South Carolina's chief in-state rival for students and appropriations. Starting about 1930, the University maintained relative parity with Clemson in state funding for educational purposes. However, USC had a decades-long legacy of trailing Clemson in the competition for favor among South Carolinians, and it lagged in general popularity with the people of South Carolina, as measured by enrollment—which was a primary funding yardstick. In 1940, Clemson's enrollment surpassed Carolina's, as it had thus far throughout the entire twentieth century. The 2,051 students at Carolina in the 1939–40 academic year ranked as an all-time high for the school, but it still trailed Clemson's 2,334.[8] Overall, in 1939–40 South Carolina spent just over 6 percent of its total revenue for the operation of the six colleges and universities in the state (in 2000, it spent just over 15 percent of its budget on thirty-three institutions of higher education).[9]

In 1940, USC could barely be called a university. The institution offered an almost exclusively undergraduate education. Of the 2,051 students in 1940, graduate students made up less than 4 percent (78 students). These graduate students were all master's-degree candidates, primarily in education and the arts and sciences, and there was no money available for graduate fellowships.[10] Even though the University of South Carolina's graduate school was small, no other college in South Carolina offered as many graduate programs-—a sad commentary on the state's attitude toward advanced education. Most South Carolinians seeking graduate education had to go outside of the state to find it, causing a "brain drain" that led many of the state's brightest minds to leave South Carolina, never to return.[11]

Compared to its regional peers, USC ranked well behind the leading public universities in other southeastern states in many objective measures. It trailed all southern universities except the University of Mississippi in the categories of enrollment and total budget. In graduate enrollment, it led only the University of Mississippi and Clemson. It was the only university in the southeast without a private endowment fund. The objective measures indicated how far USC had to go to reach parity with its peers.

As Table 1.1 makes clear, while the University of South Carolina struggled with small budgets, it was not alone. Throughout the South, colleges and universities suffered as a result of the poor economic conditions of the post–Civil War era and a set of values that did not place a premium on higher education.[12] In 1934, an American Council on Education survey identified only seven southern institutions, public or private, with the staff and equipment adequate to offer doctoral-level work.[13] In 1940, The Association of American Universities (AAU), the organization of the nation's top thirty-three graduate

Table 1.1   Comparison of selected state universities in the
                1938–39 academic year

STATE UNIVERSITY	TOTAL ENROLLMENT	GRADUATE SCHOOL ENROLLMENT*	TOTAL BUDGET 1939–40†	ENDOWMENT‡	Ph.D.s GRANTED
South Carolina	1,845	97	$725,000	$0	0
Clemson	2,150	0	$1,127,852	$164,439	0
Mississippi	1,382	42	$413,089	$733,808	0
Georgia	3,735	153	$1,310,610	$928,051	0
Alabama	5,409	122	$1,777,522	$4,875,123	0
Tennessee	4,758	337	$3,009,172	$480,833	0
Virginia	2,934	281	$2,658,604	$11,028,877	28
North Carolina	3,842	585	$4,010,319	$2,121,758	32
Louisiana State	8,550	817	$6,481,233	$320,313	15
Texas	11,444	816	$4,066,653	$32,280,804	41
Wisconsin	12,134	1,520	$9,319,884	$1,510,000	141
Illinois	15,074	1,502	$8,532,397	$1,341,046	106
Michigan	12,434	2,873	$10,870,299	$14,356,133	83

Source: Clarence Stephen Marsh, ed., American Universities and Colleges, 4th ed. (Washington, D.C.: American Council on Education, 1940).

* This figure excludes law, medical and other professional schools.
† This figure includes expenditures for non-educational and auxiliary functions such as agricultural research and extension services. The figure for the University of Michigan is for 1938–39.
‡ This represents total endowment, from both private and state endowment funds. Texas, for instance, had a non-state endowment of $3,342,824, and a state endowment fund of $28,937,980, made up primarily of the proceeds of oil and gas royalties and mineral lease bonuses on a two-million-acre tract in West Texas.

universities, had only four southern members: Duke University and the state universities of North Carolina, Virginia, and Texas.[14]

Despite the unfavorable conditions, the University of South Carolina had several internationally respected scholars on the faculty. Best known was probably Wilfred H. Callcott of the department of history, a Columbia University Ph.D. who published four influential books between 1926 and 1942 in Latin American history. He was recognized as one of the top historians in the world in that field. The level of interest in Latin American history boomed in the United States during and after World War II, and Callcott's books were widely read. In great demand as a lecturer on campus and as a public speaker nationwide, in 1942 he delivered the prestigious Albert Shaw lectures on diplomatic history at the Johns Hopkins University. Other outstanding professors at Carolina were Reed Smith, professor of English and dean of the Graduate School, who held a Harvard University Ph.D. and was renowned for many books, including works on Shakespeare, books on South Carolina Gullah culture, and textbooks on writing. Geologist Stephen Taber (Ph.D., Virginia) was internationally known for his research in earthquakes,

Table 1.2   Comparative 1938–39 budget and endowment figures, in 1991 constant dollars

STATE UNIVERSITY	TOTAL BUDGET, 1939–40 IN 1991 CONSTANT DOLLARS	ENDOWMENT, 1938–39 IN 1991 CONSTANT DOLLARS
South Carolina	$7,114,608	$0
Clemson	$11,067,897	$1,585,036
Mississippi	$4,053,747	$7,073,214
Georgia	$12,861,348	$8,945,533
Alabama	$17,443,273	$46,991,570
Tennessee	$29,529,766	$4,634,775
Virginia	$26,089,554	$106,307,932
North Carolina	$39,354,275	$20,451,738
Louisiana State	$63,601,979	$3,087,514
Texas	$39,907,095	$311,156,389
Wisconsin	$91,458,380	$14,554,970
Illinois	$83,730,571	$12,926,414
Michigan	$106,672,994	$138,379,531

Source: Figures from table 1.1 were converted using the tables in John J. McCusker, "How Much Is That in Real Money? A Historical Price Index as a Deflator of Money Values in the Economy of the United States," *Proceedings of the American Antiquarian Society* 101, pt. 2 (October 1991), 297–373.

tectonics, frozen soils, and the geology of the coastal plain. Education professor Patterson Wardlaw, biologist W. E. Hoy and chemist Guy F. Lipscomb (the latter two holders of Princeton University Ph.D.s), and English professor Joseph E. Norwood, a Rhodes scholar, all possessed scholarly reputations that brought esteem to the institution.[15]

While these and other outstanding professors called Carolina home, the generally poor condition of southern graduate education left a short supply of highly trained scholars as potential faculty. Of 103 full-time faculty members at USC in the 1938–39 academic year, only 30 held the doctorate; 26 held only a bachelor's degree.[16] In 1945, the average faculty member at the University of South Carolina had studied on the graduate level less than two years. In their careers, USC faculty members had published an average of only 0.3 books each.[17] In addition, competition for higher education dollars within South Carolina limited faculty salaries and further hampered the University's ability to compete. Overall, faculty salaries at the University of South Carolina ranked at or near the bottom in comparison with all other southern state universities.[18] While the earned doctorate was not required as a minimum scholarly credential for employment in most of the southern universities, the University of South Carolina still ranked near the bottom of its peers in the numbers of faculty with this level of education. The University of

Table 1.3 Proportion of faculty holding the earned doctorate at selected state universities, 1939

STATE UNIVERSITY	TOTAL FACULTY	PERCENTAGE HOLDING PH.D.
Clemson	134	21
South Carolina	103	29
Georgia	192	30
Alabama	300	37
Tennessee	216	44
Texas	442	46
Mississippi	100	47
North Carolina	312	58
Virginia	243	72
Wisconsin	1,039	46
Illinois (Urbana)	784	52

Source: Clarence Stephen Marsh, ed., *American Universities and Colleges,* 4th ed. (Washington, D.C.: American Council on Education, 1940).

South Carolina had a lower proportion of Ph.D.-holding faculty than any other flagship southern state university.

Possession of a Ph.D. or a degree from a prestigious northern university did not represent a foolproof measure of the quality of a professor, however, especially when the degree was not widely available in the South. Many "old guard" faculty at the University without the doctorate discounted the degree's significance; they had taught at Carolina for decades and hailed from the older tradition of the gentleman-scholar. They judged the Ph.D. a superficial measure of an individual's worth. In 1932, former dean of the School of Journalism William Watts Ball (then editor of Charleston's *News and Courier*) wrote to longtime history professor Yates Snowden that "the practice of sardining universities and colleges with oafs, upstarts, and anile asses because they are 'doctors' is uncivilized."[19] This attitude was a holdover from an era from which the University of South Carolina was only just beginning to emerge. In the years before World War II, the University of South Carolina remained committed to what historians of American higher education have called "the college ideal," a remnant of the institution's nineteenth-century heritage. The University's faculty largely concentrated on the inculcation of character in students, rather than serving the interests of narrow academic fields. In such an atmosphere, the primary consideration in choosing faculty was moral character rather than evidence of scholarly research. Increasingly, however, in the early decades of the twentieth century the Ph.D. became more and more important in the South as a badge of professional competence among college educators. In the late 1930s, USC was in the midst of an inexorable transition from the older "college ideal" toward national standards and a "research ideal" that valued specialized scholarship over character education.[20]

In 1940, the University of South Carolina was a small community still largely committed to the collegiate ideal, and the faculty and students had a tightly knit, family-like relationship. Many professors lived in one of the sixteen on-campus faculty residences or in nearby neighborhoods surrounding the campus along Senate, Pendleton, College, and Greene Streets. Most students lived on campus. The *Garnet and Black,* the student yearbook, boasted that "relations between students and faculty at the University are intimate and friendly. . . . Living on or near the campus as many of the professors do, their homes are easily accessible to students and the professors welcome their visits for advice or consultation." Faculty, staff, and students developed a close bond that extended outside the classroom. People such as YMCA director R. G. Bell and dean of women Arney Childs acted as surrogate parents to students. Before World War II, the University of South Carolina more closely resembled a small liberal arts college than the modern research university of later years.[21]

Despite the fact that a majority of the faculty did not hold the Ph.D., many were excellent teachers and dedicated their lives to the school and its students, despite the low salaries the state paid them. Former students frequently recalled the interest faculty took in their personal development. Among the favorite professors on campus was English professor Havilah Babcock, whose vocabulary-building course "I Want a Word" was always full. Other favorites on campus were Wilfred Callcott and Robert Wienefeld of the history department, Grace Sweeny in foreign languages, Bruce Coleman in mathematics, and Frank Herty in engineering.[22]

Another student favorite was University President J. Rion McKissick, who exemplified Carolina's historic commitment to a collegiate experience stressing moral and character education of undergraduates over a research ideal that stressed faculty achievement in specialized fields. Though he lacked the doctorate, McKissick excelled as a teacher and mentor to students; one recalled that he was "one of the kindest, most thoughtful men I knew." A 1905 graduate of the South Carolina College, McKissick had earned a law degree from Harvard and then entered a career in journalism, serving as the editor of both of the leading newspapers of Greenville, the *News* and the *Piedmont,* where he earned acclaim for his writing. Active in the University of South Carolina's alumni association, he was elected by the state General Assembly in 1924 to a seat on the University's board of trustees.

In 1927, administrators persuaded McKissick to join the faculty as dean of the School of Journalism. Having learned the art of oratory as a student at the South Carolina College, he was renowned for his eloquent speeches addressed to "the men and women of Carolina." McKissick had a friendly, informal manner and was known to his students as "the Colonel."[23] Chosen president in late 1935, McKissick was devoted to the University of South Carolina. He wrote in 1942, "I would rather be president of the University than hold any other position in this state and country. . . . If I could live my life over, I would give much more of it to Carolina."[24]

McKissick's love of the institution led him during his administration to attempt to change the perception of the University of South Carolina among the state's citizenry, a reputation springing from the institution's turbulent history. McKissick declared that the University had long been the target of "unjustifiable criticism" and discrimination in state appropriations because of its "poor moral reputation." This reputation had lingered from the bitterness of the Tillman era and earlier, dating back as far as the 1820s when critics scorned the South Carolina College under President Thomas Cooper as a den of irreligion and blasphemy. The University of South Carolina's enemies (presumably the friends of Clemson, Winthrop, and the state's denominational colleges) had carried out a century-long "whispering campaign" against

Carolina, McKissick claimed. They had "maliciously" and "outrageously" slandered the institution by insinuating that the students and faculty were somehow corrupt and immoral.[25] In addition, the impression still persisted that the University of South Carolina, coeducational and nondenominational, was the college of the state's elite and was a "playboy" or "party" school.[26]

Seeking to earn the good will of South Carolina's citizens, Rion McKissick combated popular doubts by promoting the high character and purposes of the institution and the "morally clean," religious student body. As one of his first initiatives, McKissick established a public relations office (the University News Service), under the direction of journalism professor Frank Wardlaw, to get the University's message out to the people of South Carolina. McKissick's annual reports to the General Assembly consistently highlighted the moral uprightness and religious activities of the University's student body. He told legislators in 1940, "In conduct, attitude, good habits, and moral and religious character our student body is equal to that of any other institution of higher education anywhere in the world. Our students are more interested in and concerned about religion than in many years past." Religious Emphasis Week, begun in 1939 by the Federal Council of Churches, was a major annual event that attracted a considerable following among students. The centrality of the YMCA and R. G. Bell in campus life also exerted moral influence on the lives of Carolina's students, and along with regular (though not compulsory) chapel services, religious influences were an integral part of the character education provided at Carolina.[27]

In McKissick's time, the University comprised eight colleges and schools. In 1939–40, they were the College of Arts and Science (42 percent of total enrollment), the School of Commerce (22.5 percent), the School of Engineering (10.5 percent), the School of Law (6.5 percent), the School of Education (6 percent), the School of Journalism (5 percent), the Graduate School (3.5 percent), and the School of Pharmacy (3.5 percent). There was also an Extension Division that offered off-campus classes around the state, most frequently to public school teachers.[28] The General Assembly elected fourteen members of the institution's board of trustees, one each from the state's judicial districts. There were four additional members ex officio: the governor, the state superintendent of education, the chairman of the state senate's education committee, and the chairman of the house education committee. A small administration served at the pleasure of the board. In addition to President McKissick, former USC president Leonard T. Baker served as chief academic officer, holding the titles of vice-president and dean of the faculty. Baker, along with the deans of the individual colleges and schools, continued to teach and maintained a teaching schedule nearly as heavy as that of other faculty members.[29]

The University and its faculty offered a good quality undergraduate education and enrolled many exceptional students. One indication of the caliber of the undergraduate program was the presence at the University of a chapter of the prestigious national honor fraternity Phi Beta Kappa, which it gained in 1926 (the first in South Carolina).[30] The nation's top graduate schools recognized that qualified Carolina graduates could excel in their graduate programs. The Association of American Universities (AAU) included the University of South Carolina on its approved list, which meant that USC graduates could directly enter AAU graduate programs without having to take additional courses. Many did just that.[31]

However, uneven quality characterized the student body as it did the faculty. South Carolina's high schools had improved since the early 1900s, but continuing problems meant that some students entered the University unprepared for college. The 1940 undergraduate admission standard admitted any white student who could pay the fees and who had completed a four-year course at an accredited high school. But a 1940 diploma from a South Carolina high school did not necessarily mean a student was prepared for college-level work. Failure rates at the University were high. Dean Leonard T. Baker wrote that the presence of unprepared students at the University was "a drag on the progress of the more ambitious and competent students, [tending] to pull down the standards to the level of mediocrity."[32] The generally poor quality of South Carolina's high school system made it difficult to sustain across-the-board excellence in university classrooms.[33]

Another reason for the low quality of some students' academic work was the rich nature of student life at Carolina, where, according to students, "there was a smorgasbord of things to do." Extracurricular activities were a primary focus of their energies. Carolina was still an intimate university of about 2,000 students, almost all of whom lived on campus, and alumni recall that "everybody knew everybody."[34] The national Depression of the 1930s hit the state's elite and common people alike and in effect democratized the student body. Few students had much money, and not all could afford to attend Carolina continuously without a semester off to work for tuition money. Fraternity members and independents alike worked their way through school with the help of $15-a-month National Youth Administration work-study scholarships or other part-time work both on and off campus. Daniel W. Hollis, a student during the late 1930s, described the situation: "With students from the antebellum aristocracy, the Tillmanite farm group, the new business class, the Low Country, and the Up Country all rubbing elbows in the same economic boat, many of the old prejudices disappeared."[35]

Some elitism survived however, embodied in the Greek-letter fraternities and sororities that represented the center of college life for many students.

Fraternities were "a bit of snobbery mixed with close friendships . . . and a lot of fun for the campus as a whole," remarked a writer for the campus yearbook, the *Garnet and Black*.[36] In the late 1930s, the University board of trustees began requiring all students to live on campus unless administrators granted a special exemption. Thus, the social fraternities and sororities, many of which had acquired off-campus housing since their legal reinstatement at Carolina in 1927, moved back on campus in the late 1930s and early 1940s. Students speculated that the trustees had forced the move because they were concerned about the effect of unchaperoned off-campus behavior on the University's reputation. Alcohol was expressly forbidden on campus, though sometimes-rowdy fraternity men bent this rule. Fraternities took over entire sections of the "tenement" dormitories on the Horseshoe, while the sororities moved into the Wade Hampton and Sims dormitories. Other popular student activities were student government, intramural athletics (including boxing), student publications like the *Gamecock* and the *Garnet and Black,* and the honor fraternities like Phi Beta Kappa, Blue Key, and Omicron Delta Kappa (ODK).[37]

Enrollment of female students at Carolina rose after the General Assembly removed restrictions on their entrance in 1936. Freshmen and sophomore women were then allowed live on campus, and females no longer paid higher tuition than males. In the 1939–40 academic year, nearly 35 percent of the student body were women.[38] They remained under the University's social restrictions in loco parentis, which closely governed their extracurricular lives with strict curfews, dress codes, and sign-out procedures from dormitories. University officials were intent on preserving traditional behavioral norms toward sex. History professor Arney Childs, in her dual role as dean of women, stood as the "champion defender" of the virtue and reputation of Carolina's women and enforced with an "iron hand" University regulations regarding their personal lives.[39]

Traditional gender roles for women at Carolina survived: most women were enrolled in the College of Arts and Science (not professional schools), and R. G. Bell, director of the University Y.M.C.A, reported that even after their graduation "a fair number of girls don't want and are not seeking employment."[40] This attitude reflected national norms. *Fortune* magazine reported in 1936 that some 60 percent of women college students "wanted to get married within a year or two of graduation," and 50 percent wanted children soon after marriage.[41] A Gallup poll in the same year revealed that 75 percent of American women believed that wives should not work. Thus, after graduation, although a woman might work for a year or two after college, most women would choose marriage and family as their career.[42] In an earlier era, educator and Carolina alumnus John Andrew Rice had called Columbia "not only a seat of learning but also the principal matrimonial agency of the state." Evidence and anecdote suggest that this held true through mid-century and beyond.[43]

On campus, the center of social life revolved around the University's chapter of the YMCA, located in Flinn Hall. "Y" director R. G. Bell was a fixture on the Carolina campus, taking under his wing many of the young students fresh to Columbia from South Carolina's rural towns. The campus policemen, known as "judges," also developed close relationships with students and kept the sometimes-unruly men in line. The highlights of the student social calendar were formal dances put on by the campus social cabinet or by the Greeks and two exclusive social dance organizations, the German and Damas clubs. One student recalled that "there were dances at Carolina from the first minute of Sorority rush the week before school began to the June German," which took place around commencement. The dances of the social cabinet were open to all students, while German Club (male) membership was selective, and the Damas Club included 60 percent of each sorority as well as fifteen independent women.[44]

In a state just emerging from the Depression, few students owned cars, and all were prohibited from parking on campus. University regulations stated that "the University does not encourage possession of automobiles by students." The few who did have them attended shows at Columbia's new drive-in theater, which opened in 1941 at the corner of Garner's Ferry Road and Fort Jackson Boulevard and featured the largest movie screen in South Carolina. Students without cars walked to the restaurants and theaters downtown, including the Palmetto Theatre and the Ship-Ahoy Restaurant on Main Street, the Toddle House on Gervais, and the College Shop on Sumter Street. On campus, students passed their spare time shooting pool in the YMCA or hanging out in the canteen in the basement of Maxcy College. In retrospect, campus life at Carolina in the late 1930s and early 1940s seemed a haven in a nation emerging from the Depression but as yet largely unaware of the chaos about to be unleashed in Europe and Asia.[45]

The Carolina campus itself covered a mere forty-six acres, not much bigger than it had been in antebellum days. Bounded on the north by Columbia's Pendleton Street, on the east by Pickens Street, on the south by Devine Street (which in those days ran from Pickens Street to Main Street), and on the west by Main Street, the USC campus was by far the smallest of any state university in the South.[46] Many buildings dated from the antebellum period and were in dilapidated condition. Dean Leonard Baker described them as "old, poorly constructed and not adapted to modern educational needs."[47]

In the 1930s, the University of South Carolina's campus benefited greatly from the largesse of the New Deal, receiving about $800,000 ($7,850,602) in federal construction grants to improve the physical plant.[48] Despite the New Deal funding, the University lacked adequate academic resources and buildings for a state university. In 1936, Dean Baker called the problems with the institution's library the "greatest from which the university is suffering."[49] Through the late 1930s, the building on the Horseshoe now known as the South Caroliniana Library housed the main library collection. The 1840 structure, though in its day the first freestanding college library in the nation, by the modern era lacked sufficient space to accommodate both book storage and space for study.[50] In the late 1930s, the federal government stepped in to help solve the library problem, with the Works Progress Administration providing a portion of the funds for a modern building. Completed in 1940, the new $560,000 ($5,430,000) library occupied the earlier site of the president's home at the head of the Horseshoe. Designed by prestigious architect Henry Hibbs (who designed an identical building at Davidson College and another at Vanderbilt University), it had an impressive facade, which the *Garnet and Black* called a "poetry of stone and steel."[51]

The new library alleviated the seriousness of the University's library problem and should have been a long-term solution, but it was not. The large number of small rooms in the building made it expensive and cumbersome to operate, and as a functional library, the new building proved unsuccessful.[52] To make matters worse, the state underfunded the library's operating and book budgets, so the general library collection remained inadequate. In the early 1940s, the University of South Carolina ranked at the bottom of all eleven southern state universities in annual expenditures for books and periodicals, and the size of the library collection ranked next to the bottom (see table 1.4). The poor library collection limited the University's ability to support a broad range of graduate programs.[53]

As much as any other single factor, the state of the University's library collection in 1940 revealed how far the institution had fallen since its antebellum heyday. Until the completion of the new library, the main library building on campus was the building now known as the South Caroliniana Library. It had been completed exactly a century earlier. In 1838, President Robert W. Barnwell had stated that "it is necessary that an extensive library should be created to which men of letters may resort with the certainty of finding whatever book their researches might require." As a result, in 1839 the board of trustees spent $4,000 to purchase books ($6,286 in 1941 dollars, $58,179 in 1991 dollars), and thereafter spent some $3,000 annually on books ($4,714 and $43,634). By 1858, the library boasted 21,400 volumes, and, according to Daniel Hollis, the South Carolina College library was one of the two best college libraries in the South and ranked among the best in the nation. It was the equal of the University of Virginia's, and larger than either Princeton's or

Columbia's. The outstanding library helped to establish the antebellum reputation of the South Carolina College.[54] In the intervening years, however, the state had not maintained the library collection at a level with the University's peers, and the condition of the library in 1940 contributed as greatly to the University of South Carolina's low reputation as it had to its luster a century before.

In 1940, a new science building constituted Carolina's other urgent physical need. Built in 1910, LeConte College (now known as Barnwell College) served as the University's main science building. It represented a serious fire hazard and was terribly overcrowded. In addition, its scientific equipment was badly outdated. For example, the department of biology, located on the top floor of the un-airconditioned building, was in such urgent need of laboratory space that department head W. E. Hoy converted a classroom into a laboratory and stored preserved specimens in boxes stacked around the walls

Table 1.4 Average annual book, periodical, and binding expenditures, and total volumes in library collection for selected university libraries, 1939–40 to 1942–43

UNIVERSITY	AVERAGE ANNUAL EXPENDITURE	VOLUMES
South Carolina	$10,781 ($96,232)	166,264
Mississippi	$16,015 ($142,950)	97,018
Arkansas	$23,853 ($212,912)	192,578
Tennessee	$26,763 ($238,887)	230,858
Alabama	$29,249 ($261,077)	278,250
Florida	$31,938 ($285,079)	218,590
Kentucky	$33,004 ($294,594)	337,011
Georgia	$35,981 ($321,167)	172,834
North Carolina	$38,095 ($340,037)	434,020
Virginia	$50,331 ($449,256)	405,145
Louisiana State	$71,759 ($640,522)	351,865
Texas	$113,282 ($1,011,158)	702,429
California (Berkeley)	$122,147 ($1,090,287)	1,170,738
Illinois	$141,865 ($1,266,290)	1,306,561
Princeton	$62,106 ($554,360)	990,657
Columbia	$168,098 ($1,500,447)	1,887,034

Source: Public Higher Education in South Carolina (Nashville, Tenn.: George Peabody College For Teachers, 1946), 385–86.

of the room. The decrepit condition of the building and its facilities made it nearly impossible to conduct modern scientific research and hindered the development of graduate programs. The ominous world situation in 1940 demanded more citizens trained in the sciences, and further intensified the need to replace the inadequate science facilities.[55]

While the University's condition left room for improvement, it nonetheless faced the 1940s with optimism spurred by an improving economy, an energetic president, a dedicated faculty, a vibrant student life, and a record enrollment. Soon however, foreboding developments overseas tempered the optimism and the storm clouds of war seized the attention of the University community. Even before the Second World War directly involved the United States, the University of South Carolina mobilized to help the nation prepare for war. Students led in demonstrating their patriotism. Enrollment dropped from the prewar high of 2,051 in 1940 to 1,734 in 1941 as the draft began to draw students into the armed forces. The federal government made enlistment easier when, with the help of James F. Byrnes, in the summer of 1940, the University of South Carolina secured a Naval ROTC detachment (one of eight in the nation), and immediately the maximum number of student midshipmen enrolled in the program. The following year, over two hundred freshmen applied for ninety vacancies in the Navy's ROTC program. Women students got into the act as well, organizing a women's rifle team to train in the use of weapons, and forgoing silk stockings to free up more of the fabric for Army parachutes. Students raised money for the Red Cross to benefit the English during the Battle of Britain, and some five hundred signed a petition calling for a repeal of the neutrality act that prevented the United States from protecting lend-lease shipping.[56]

Faculty joined in early war preparations. By mid-1941, the Army had called to active duty several faculty members who were officers in the South Carolina National Guard. In addition, two professors, T. F. Ball (electrical engineering) and Robert D. Bass (English), took leaves of absence to teach at the Naval Academy. Other professors formed the Faculty National Defense Committee to coordinate the University's resources to help build the nation's "arsenal of democracy."[57]

In addition, in 1940, cooperation with the federal government led the University to start two training programs to help prepare the state for war. One was a program of defense-related training courses in engineering, science, and management that would help defense industries meet their urgent need for skilled workers and managers. The other was a civilian pilot training program that provided initial ground instruction to students interested in joining military aviation units. Hundreds of regular University students and adults from the Columbia community took courses in these programs in their spare time.[58]

Despite the war fever, opinion among some students typified the strain of isolationism in the nation in the period just before Pearl Harbor. When several professors circulated a petition calling for Congress to unilaterally declare war on Germany in September 1941, the editor of the *Gamecock* protested. He chastised them for "subscribing to a petition designed to kill students they now teach how to live" and suggesting alternatively a petition asking Congress to keep American troops in America.[59]

Much of the student trepidation about the war disappeared following the surprise Japanese attack at Pearl Harbor. After recovering from the shock of the attack, students declared their willingness to fight. The *Gamecock* editor wrote that there was "no question that the students of the University of South Carolina are ready to serve, yes, and to make the supreme sacrifice."[60] Uncle Sam obliged their willingness by setting up a draft registration table in the new library for all eligible male students and faculty.[61] The *Gamecock* immediately urged the administration to abandon all university holidays and move to an accelerated academic calendar in order to speed up the students' education and allow them to more quickly serve the nation in the expanding war effort.[62]

President Roosevelt responded to the rush of college student volunteers for the armed forces by urging them to stay in school. He reminded them that it was the "patriotic duty" of college students to continue with their education until they were drafted, so that they would be "well prepared for greatest usefulness to their country."[63] Thus, in the early part of the war, many male students stayed in school until their draft call, despite suffering from guilty consciences as siblings and friends were drafted. While they remained on campus, they faced serious questions about their future, such as those enumerated in the *Garnet and Black*: "What is my draft number? Will I go in as a private? What will I do with my 'steady' when the army nabs me—will she remain true to me or fall in love with a uniform and bars? Is it worthwhile to retain my life dreams if the conflict allows me to survive?" Many volunteered for some form of reserve duty, allowing them to assuage their consciences, receive military training, and avoid the draft, all while completing their education.[64]

The University community responded to the crisis by mobilizing for the war effort. Students served as air raid spotters, firefighters, and first-aid helpers in a campus civil defense program, and the Carolina community learned how to react to air raid sirens.[65] Women students began wearing what they called the "defense haircut," a hairstyle that did not require the use of bobby pins, which were in short supply because of the need for metal in defense industries. Student organizations conducted scrap metal drives, salvaging items such as toothpaste tubes and razor blades. The University's chapter of the Red Cross and the women student's organization, the Co-Ed

Association, coordinated war fund drives such as the selling of war stamps. Wartime rationing caused Steward's Hall, the University cafeteria, to reduce the amount of meat it served to students and to restrict the amounts of coffee and sugar they could use.[66]

Beginning in early 1942, Carolina began admitting high school students who performed well on aptitude tests. The early admission program sped up the higher education process and provided more trained men and women for the war effort.[67] Despite the relaxing of admission standards, the enrollment of civilian male students plummeted. The draft drew more and more men into the armed forces, and the booming war economy made good jobs available in the civilian sector. Between the fall of 1941 and the spring of 1944, civilian male enrollment at the University of South Carolina dropped from 1,117 to 277, a decline of 75 percent. This reflected a nationwide trend, as U.S. civilian male college enrollment dropped 68.7 percent between the 1939–40 and 1943–44 academic years.[68] Graduate training ceased nearly entirely. By the fall of 1944, there were only 25 full-time graduate students at the University.[69] The war drew away professors as well. Some 23 members of the faculty took leaves of their jobs to serve in the armed forces.[70]

While male students and faculty left the campus to serve in the war, the numbers of female students remained nearly constant. In the fall of 1941, there were 617 females enrolled, and in the fall of 1943, there were 646. However, women made up roughly 60 percent of civilian students on the campus during the war.[71] Amy McCandless, a historian of the college experience for women in the South, has concluded that "the outbreak of World War II . . . had a profound impact on Southern College women." The rising proportion of women on campus accompanied wartime propaganda that stressed an integral role for women in the nation's war effort. In short order, women who had previously been discriminated against on the USC campus as recently as 1936 (in the form of admissions restrictions and higher tuition) became a central part of the University's contribution to the war effort.[72]

By late 1942, an overall shortage of students and their tuition fees had become an acute problem. In January 1943 the federal government came to the rescue, when the U.S. Navy began operating the first of three training programs, in addition to Naval ROTC, on the USC campus. Most of the campus community were overjoyed to have the influx of trainees and their federal dollars, but fraternities and sororities were forced to vacate their housing in the "tenements" and in Sims and Wade Hampton colleges. When President McKissick announced that the naval programs would be coming to the University, students and faculty responded with a standing ovation.[73]

McKissick insisted that "the Navy is not taking over the school, but is simply using a part of its facilities and staff."[74] However, it was hard to tell the difference. University historian Daniel Hollis wrote that during the war the University was "from all outward appearances a naval base."[75] Robert E. McNair, an undergraduate at the time of Pearl Harbor, remembered that "almost immediately, the University was transformed from a small very happy group of civilian students to a military school. There were naval trainees here from all over the country. The place was overrun by people in the service."[76] In December 1943, there were some 1,034 civilians enrolled at the University, but about half lived off campus. Of the 1,917 young people living on campus, nearly 73 percent (1,392) were Naval trainees. Carolina was four institutions in one, as three Naval programs operated alongside civilian courses. The *Garnet and Black* commented: "Last year sailor suits were entirely alien to the Carolina scheme of life—today they are as much a part of the historic campus as the Colonel's cigars." Cadence calls in the wee hours of the morning began awakening civilians on campus.[77]

The Naval programs required an accelerated academic calendar (and the Navy paid for one), so administrators abolished all holidays except Christmas, and the University offered classes year-round beginning in early 1943. Three full semesters per year offered students the opportunity to earn a bachelor's degree in two and a half years of full-time work. Classes began before dawn and ended late in the evening. The University held four commencements a year, one at the end of each semester and one at the end of a short summer term.[78] Anyone who has suffered through the heat of a Columbia summer can appreciate the misery of students and trainees as they hurriedly struggled to complete summer course requirements in the days before air conditioning.

The first of the naval programs to come to Carolina was the flight preparatory school (a part of the Navy's V-5 program). Operating from January 7, 1943, to August 18, 1944, the flight prep school occupied seven buildings on campus. Davis College served as the headquarters and classroom building. Aviation cadets filled five nearby dormitories and took over Steward's Hall, the University's main cafeteria.[79] The school involved 650 cadets at a time in a fifteen–week course that was the first stage of naval aviation training. Cadets were active-duty sailors, not university students. They did not participate in university activities or earn university credit.

However, fifteen members of the regular University faculty taught in the flight prep school. Men such as Clyde Ferrell (history), Joseph Norwood (English), and Julian J. Petty (geography) switched from their usual fields to instruct courses in subjects such as basic navigation, communications, and physics. The Navy also used teachers from local high schools and other colleges. Instructors in the flight prep school taught anywhere from 24 to 30 hours a week in classes averaging 108 students each, making for a heavy teaching load.[80]

The second and smallest of the Navy training programs was the Civil Aeronautics Administration–War Training Service (CAA–WTS). This course represented the second stage of naval aviation training. In operation from April 1, 1943 to August 25, 1944, the CAA–WTS involved about 120 trainees at a time in a two-month course. Instructors hired by the Navy taught all the classes, and like the flight prep trainees, the students were not considered University students. In addition to advanced flight instruction, the trainees received actual flight training at Columbia's Owens airfield.[81]

The last and most important of the naval programs was the Navy college training program (V-12). Operating from July 1, 1943 through the summer of 1946, the V-12 program included about 650 trainees per term, with the purpose of preparing officer candidates for commissions in the Navy, Marine Corps, and Coast Guard. Unlike the flight prep school, V-12 trainees earned full university credit and attended regular university classes alongside civilian students, although they were on active duty and wore uniforms. A standard V-12 curriculum included mathematics, foreign languages, English, history, physics, engineering, and physical training alongside specialized naval courses like navigation, gunnery, and chemical warfare. Trainees specialized in programs leading to sixteen different types of officer commissions. Among them were the Navy's medical corps and chaplain corps, and seven types of engineering specialties. The full V-12 program took two and a half years to complete.

The V-12 program foreshadowed the later GI Bill in that it allowed many students who otherwise could not have afforded college to attend or stay in school. It also allowed the University to continue offering classes that otherwise would have been canceled for lack of civilian students. Several departments hired additional faculty to meet the increased demand for classes, and by the war's end the University had hired 14 temporary instructors. A number of these new teachers were women, reflecting the expanded role for women on the campus during World War II. Even with the faculty additions, wartime classes were large, averaging 82 students each. The V-12 trainees worked hard, spending as much as 55 to 60 hours in class and study per week.[82]

Those in charge of the naval training programs immediately realized what the University's administrators had known: that the University's campus buildings were inadequate to meet the needs of a student body numbering more than 2,000. Officers complained about the insufficient facilities for their trainees to spend spare time. Captain R. C. Needham, the commander of the University's V-12 unit, described the canteen in the basement of Maxcy College as "a most unsuitable and unsightly place for V-12 students to spend their recreation hours. It is dark, crowded, small and very seldom clean."[83] The Works Progress Administration helped pay for the construction of

Hamilton College and a new naval armory, completed in 1943. Hamilton housed the School of Engineering, the Naval ROTC, and the V-12 program.[84]

Since the Navy programs filled so many of the university's buildings, space was at a premium for naval trainees as well as civilian students, faculty, and staff. Students crowded three or four to a room in dormitories. Because of a shortage of classroom space, professors held some classes in their homes. When on-campus faculty homes became vacant, they were converted to general university use. University offices were moved into previously unused attics and basements.[85]

The war altered the regular rhythms of student life. "Everyone seemed to realize that the Carolina of old was gone for the duration," recounted the *Garnet and Black*.[86] Gas rationing and a shortage of automobile tires made it difficult for commuting students to get to class and prevented other students from going off-campus for their socializing. A shortage of camera film limited the number of photographs in the yearbook, the *Garnet and Black*. Since most civilian students were women, isolation on campus, the space problem and the presence of so many Navy men presented a challenge to the house mothers (each dormitory had one), charged with enforcing the University's regulations in loco parentis.[87]

The Navy encouraged the V-12 trainees to participate in extracurricular activities, and many became heavily involved in campus life. They dominated fraternities, honorary societies, student publications and student government since they outnumbered civilian males nearly two to one. V-12s served alongside women on the staffs of publications like the *Gamecock* and the *Garnet and Black* (who struggled mightily to keep producing issues during the war), but frequent transfers of the naval trainees disrupted the continuity of student organizations. For example, the student body president elected in the spring of 1943, Bill Jones, was transferred during the summer, and vice-president M. T. Pitts finished out the term as president.[88]

The women's Co-Ed Association held biweekly dances for the cadets in the flight prep school, and in the summertime, V-12 trainees attended outdoor dances on the Horseshoe and the women's quad. As much as possible, the social fraternities and sororities continued their peacetime schedule of social events, including rush, formals, and dances. Other festivities, like the German Club balls and the crowning of the May Queen, continued as well, and students did their best to maintain a semblance of normalcy. But the annual German Club June Ball, once the grand finale of the school year, was overshadowed by the dance sponsored by the Compass and Chart Society, the Naval ROTC social organization.[89]

The seriousness and urgency of wartime campus life disrupted many of the traditions of the old institution. Class of 1944 member George C. Caughman remembered that the war "turned student life around in a lot of instances because of the rush to try and get a degree before you went and got drafted."[90] Before the war, the University had been a small community where students had followed campus politics with enthusiasm, but by 1942, they lost interest in such pursuits. Football star Louis Sossaman won an uncontested election for president of the student body that year when Connie Morton, the opponent everyone assumed would run against him, joined the Army Air Corps instead. The *Garnet and Black* reported that the vote total was the lowest in history, and that the election was "the first time in Carolina history only one aspirant sought the presidential toga."[91]

Civilian students complained that many naval trainees did not care to become part of the University community. "Some students entered campus life and became true sons," remarked the *Garnet and Black;* "others muttered reminiscently and proudly of previously attended schools."[92] The naval students endured intense pressure because if they did not perform well, they would be removed from officer training and sent overseas as enlisted men. Most took their work very seriously. As a result, some civilian students lamented that the Carolina tradition of campus friendliness had disappeared. One female student complained that "when I speak to a V-12, he looks at me as though I were being fresh!"[93]

One campus tradition that did not disappear, however, was the frenzy surrounding the University's athletic teams. Students greeted games with prewar enthusiasm. Festivities surrounding athletic events, such as homecoming floats and parties as well as the annual bonfire and "shirt-tail" parade down Main Street before the Big Thursday game against Clemson, continued throughout the war.[94]

The war nonetheless curtailed intercollegiate athletics. Prior to the war, college football had become big business at the University and in the state, causing Dean Leonard Baker to remark that the sport had become so commercialized and professionalized that "intercollegiate athletics constitutes a serious obstacle to the realization of the aims and purposes of higher education."[95] Nonetheless, the condition of the Carolina football program of the 1930s was as poor as the nation's economy, and head football coach Rex Enright inherited a perennial loser in 1938. By 1941, he had succeeded in turning the program around, when his Gamecock team broke a seven-year losing streak to Clemson with an 18-14 victory. Just as he had the program headed in the right direction, however, the draft and declining enrollments of 1942 drew away some of the University's best athletes, including star running back "Manly" Stanley Stacia. The football team won but one game that season, despite the standout performance of Louis Sossaman, who later played professional football in New York.[96]

By late 1942, the war reduced the football coaching staff to one-third its peacetime size. Rex Enright joined the Navy, where he became a physical training instructor and coached football in the University of Georgia's Navy preflight school. Statewide, organized athletics such as professional baseball and the Carolina Cup steeplechase at Camden went on hiatus. Serious questions arose about whether the University of South Carolina could continue its athletic program through the war. The varsity boxing team disbanded in 1942 for want of participants; the tennis team faced a similar problem, as well as a lack of tennis balls (because of a rubber shortage). However, in 1943, Solomon Blatt, chairman of a new board of trustees athletic committee, vowed to continue fielding a football team "within the means available."[97]

The naval programs provided the means to save Carolina's athletics, although the teams were a shadow of what they had been in peacetime. Naval instructors served as the wartime coaches (such as 1943 football coach James P. Moran and 1944 coach William "Doc" Newton, a former head coach at North Carolina State), and the Navy provided athletic financing. The Navy encouraged the V-12 trainees to participate in sports, and they assigned to USC some outstanding athletes, several of whom had played on teams at other colleges (football player Buck Williams, for example, was a transfer from Davidson College; R. M. Hodges had played for the University of Tennessee; "Curley" Culdell had lettered at Virginia). V-12 trainees made up the entire roster of the 1943–44 basketball team and the 1944 baseball team. Other wartime teams were a motley combination of freshmen too young for the draft, men not physically qualified for the armed services, and V-12 trainees. With frequent transfers of the V-12s, players, coaches, and fans never knew who would be on the team from week to week.[98]

This situation led to the unusual case of Cary Cox, whose naval career led him to Carolina and who had the distinction of serving as captain for both Carolina and Clemson football teams. Cox played for Clemson in 1942, but early in the following year, he signed up for the V-12 program. Assigned to USC in 1943, he was ordered to football practice by naval instructors. He performed so well they named him Carolina's team captain for the Big Thursday Clemson game. Cox had second thoughts about playing against his old teammates, but when he voiced his reservations to the V-12 coach, the coach responded unequivocally, "Cox, I can't promise you'll get a Navy commission if you play Thursday, but I can damn well promise that you won't get one if you don't play!" Cox swallowed his pride and played in the game, leading Carolina to a 33–6 victory. After the war, he returned to Clemson, and in 1947 served as team captain for the Tigers in that year's Big Thursday matchup.[99]

The V-12 trainees saved the Carolina athletic program during the war. The University fielded some pretty good teams as well. The 1943 football team compiled a 5–2 record; the 1943–44 basketball team, led by Bob Baggot, won 13 of 15. Baggot's performance earned the team an invitation to the 1944 Southern Conference basketball tournament in Chapel Hill, but Navy authorities declined the invitation since the date conflicted with the University's exam schedule. Most importantly for the Carolina community, the University's athletic program provided a morale boost and an outlet to take minds off the stress of war.[100]

In general, the naval programs were a godsend for the University. The federal money more than doubled Carolina's total expenditures. In 1939–40, the budget had totaled $561,009 ($5,472,357), but at the height of naval involvement in 1943–44, the budget was $1,561,813 ($12,173,174). Of this 1943–44 total, some $377,460 ($2,942,020) was state-appropriated money, while revenue from the Navy equaled $990,382 ($7,719,293). Trustees set up a rainy-day reserve fund using rent money the Navy paid to use classrooms and other buildings that normally earned no income at all. The University also gained two new buildings, Hamilton College and the Naval Armory, from wartime federal involvement.[101]

The University operated at full capacity throughout the war. Naval trainees filled the cafeterias and classrooms and created demand for staff workers and instructors. Full-time faculty temporarily received 30 percent pay raises.[102] The exigencies of war also altered the academic curriculum. The requirements of the V-12 program created an increased demand for basic courses in engineering, mathematics, and the sciences. Administrators scaled back graduate courses and advanced subjects such as chemical engineering. There was also a decided decline in students majoring in the liberal arts. As might be expected, the courses least relevant to the war effort were the least popular. For example, the department of ancient languages, under the direction of Edwin L. Green (who taught ancient Greek and Latin), suspended all classes because of a lack of student interest.[103]

The administration also made a conscious effort to develop classes directly applicable to war service. President McKissick asserted that the University "must establish new courses essential for more effective preparation for the service." Alongside the civilian pilot training program and the defense science, engineering, and management courses, the University offered special courses in wartime safety and first aid, and a program to train laboratory technicians. In early 1942, the University received recognition for organizing the nation's first Red Cross nurse's aide course, which quickly evolved into a program leading to a bachelor's degree in nursing, preparing graduates for commissions in the Army Nurse Corps. The University even offered a French class that emphasized everyday speaking vocabulary and military terms.[104]

As the University community's wartime attention focused on the urgent tasks at hand, leaders began to think about the shape of the University in the postwar world. The changes World War II brought to the University were significant, but many were only temporary. Peacetime would bring even more sweeping, and this time more lasting, changes to USC. The student editor of the *Gamecock* wrote in early 1944, "The University is on the brink of a new era—an era in which the cataclysmic upheavals of war will work revolutionary changes in . . . educational systems and institutions."[105]

South Carolina's Preparedness for Peace Commission spurred the University to begin a rational approach to developing postwar plans, and in mid-1943 President McKissick appointed a special faculty postwar planning committee charged with evaluating the university's facilities and academic programs to identify problem areas and suggest improvements.[106]

The committee's first recommendations included several additions to the curriculum. In 1944, the University established three new departments: nursing, homemaking, and retailing.[107] These departments represented modest expansions of the University's course offerings, with two aimed primarily at women. However, the faculty committee realized that the demands of the postwar era would require the University to expand its mission much further. With wartime growth of government and business, the state urgently needed to expand its ability to conduct research and to offer advanced degrees within South Carolina.

As it stood in 1945, the University of South Carolina's understaffed, underequipped Graduate School simply could not fill this role. The Graduate School repeatedly turned away qualified applicants because of staff shortages and inadequate facilities. Thus, expansion of the graduate and research programs became one of the faculty's most sought-after goals late in the war and in the immediate postwar period. To improve the University's ability to offer graduate education and research, the institution would have to improve the overall quality of staff, equipment, and facilities—a tall order in 1940s South Carolina.[108]

To expand the Graduate School, in late 1944 the faculty planning committee requested that the state establish a $31,500 ($244,350) endowment fund to support graduate fellowships, faculty chairs, research grants, and the publication of research findings. The General Assembly failed to comprehend the state's urgent need for research capabilities, though, and declined to establish such an endowment. Nonetheless, the University moved forward. In 1945, it began funding graduate fellowships out of its operating funds.[109]

Research programs also began a slow growth that reflected the direction of postwar expansion. In 1944, the University founded the University of South Carolina Press under the leadership of its first editor, Wilfred Callcott.

The Press's first books, such as *South Carolina: Economic and Social Conditions in 1944* and G. Croft Williams's *A Social Interpretation of South Carolina,* demonstrated a desire to contribute useful research to solving the state's postwar problems.[110] In 1945, the University established the Bureau of Public Administration with the help of grants from Tennessee Valley Authority and the Rockefeller-financed General Education Board. The bureau provided research services to state government. Its first major study, *South Carolina's Natural Resources* (published by the USC Press in 1947), benefited both state government and businesses.[111]

Improvements in the condition of the University's library facilities made it possible to reopen candidacy for the Ph.D. beginning in 1944. The new library housed the University's general book collection, freeing the old building on the Horseshoe to serve as a repository for an ever-growing collection of South Carolina–related books, manuscripts, newspapers, photographs, and artifacts, known as the South Caroliniana collection. Trustees renamed the old building the South Caroliniana Library. The Caroliniana collection had begun in 1906, but administrative emphasis helped it grow quickly in the 1930s. Under the direction of Professor Robert L. Meriwether (head of the history department), by the mid-1940s it had become comprehensive enough to support a Ph.D. program focused on southern history.[112]

This was the only doctoral program the University had the resources to support, however, and the new dean of the Graduate School, historian Wilfred Callcott, at first limited the University's Ph.D. offerings to this single field. Continuing shortcomings of the general library collection, scarcity of adequately trained staff, and the condition of scientific equipment and facilities prevented the University from offering a broad range of doctoral programs.[113]

South Carolina's preoccupation with its turbulent past helped the South Caroliniana Library and a doctoral program get on their feet, but the sciences were a victim of other relics from the past—the University's dilapidated academic resources. LeConte College, the only science building, still desperately needed renovation. The Columbia fire marshal rated the building "a firetrap." The postwar planning committee recommended that the state immediately address the problem by refurbishing LeConte and constructing two new buildings to house the departments of chemistry, biology, and pharmacy. It also recommended that the University build five other new buildings, including a student activities building, to meet general campus needs.[114]

The University's physical facilities limited the institution's growth when the peacetime student body stood at 2,000, but college administrators knew that peacetime would bring "revolutionary changes" in the form of enrollment increases. Pent-up demand for college education among veterans who had deferred their college educations would likely swell student bodies across the nation. Indeed, a wartime survey of 6,500 South Carolina soldiers indicated that nearly one-half wanted assistance in improving their level of education after the war. Their wishes were granted on June 22, 1944, when President Franklin D. Roosevelt signed the Servicemen's Readjustment Act, better known as the "GI Bill of Rights." Championed by the American Legion and the American Council on Education, the bill offered generous education aid for all veterans with more than ninety days of service, including the payment of all tuition, fees, and books and a $50 ($388) per month stipend ($75 [$582] if married) at any college to which they qualified for admission.[115]

Initially intended to ease the adjustment of veterans to civilian life and to help the nation avoid a postwar depression, the GI Bill intensified veteran demand for higher education in postwar South Carolina, especially at the University of South Carolina. Even though forty percent of South Carolina soldiers surveyed who wanted to attend college said they wanted to do so out of state, some 3,200 indicated they intended to enter the University of South Carolina. University officials predicted a postwar enrollment peak of 4,500.[116] Administrators and faculty knew their facilities were entirely inadequate to handle a student body of such size. The enrollment forecast portended a time when the University would have to cope with large numbers of students in lieu of improving academic quality. To prevent such a situation from developing, the state had to quickly address the University's needs for adequate buildings if it were to handle the anticipated enrollment boom while offering quality education.

President J. Rion McKissick died on September 3, 1944, before he could begin a lobbying campaign to make such a building program a reality. During a time of too much death overseas, the loss of the beloved University president shocked the campus. Students and faculty showed their respect by petitioning the University's board of trustees to allow McKissick to be buried on campus, an honor bestowed upon no other University of South Carolina president. After a solemn funeral service in which his body lay in state in the new library and the University's naval units attended in full dress, students laid McKissick to rest in front of the South Caroliniana Library. A flat marker there bears the inscription, "I have kept the faith." A few months later, students and faculty asked the board of trustees to name the new University library for McKissick, and they readily agreed. Students also began a McKissick memorial scholarship fund to help worthy students.[117]

Under McKissick's leadership, the University made concrete strides: through the help of the New Deal, the University built a new library, added five dormitories, and refurbished the campus. The University's curriculum expanded to include departments in homemaking, retailing, nursing, political science, and music, as well as a revitalized Extension Division and courses in medical technology, predentistry, and library science and expansions in the fine arts. He had led the institution through tumultuous times, presiding during the Great Depression and World War II. A bibliophile fascinated with the institution's history and the history of South Carolina, McKissick donated his personal collection of more than 5,000 books, manuscripts, and papers to the South Caroliniana library and helped that collection become the leading public repository for private historical records in South Carolina.[118]

Perhaps McKissick's greatest achievement came in public relations, where he did all in his power to combat the University's poor "moral reputation" and elitism to make the University of South Carolina "the University of all the people of South Carolina."[119] The editor of the *Pee Dee Advocate,* W. G. Hazel, wrote that before McKissick became president, "Winthrop or Clemson could put across any program that they set their wills to, but just let the University start something and opposition developed from every side." As a result of McKissick's efforts, wrote Hazel, "there is no such spirit today, or if there is there is very little of it. Carolina has made vast gains in popularity, and most Carolinians today have a certain affection for their state university. We believe that this is due almost entirely to J. Rion McKissick."[120]

The University's board of trustees appointed dean of the faculty and former president Leonard T. Baker to serve as acting president while they searched for McKissick's permanent successor. In November 1944, Baker went before the State Budget Commission to request funding for the University's urgently needed physical expansion plans. At the same meetings of the Budget Commission, however, a far more ambitious plan emerged to expand the University's facilities. University trustee and South Carolina House Speaker Solomon Blatt conceived and championed a proposal that called for the state to help finance an entirely new campus for the University of South Carolina, outside the confines of Columbia. The urban landscape surrounding the campus had long restricted the University's growth, and the campus was already the smallest of any southern state university. To relieve campus crowding and accommodate the impending wave of students, Blatt suggested that the University sell its Columbia campus and move all its operations to a 1,200-acre site just beyond Columbia's Veterans Hospital, or to a smaller site overlooking the Broad River, both in the Columbia area.[121]

In Blatt's ambitious vision, the new campus was to be the basis for a great modern university in South Carolina. The proposal, which he called the "new and greater university" plan, would cost a total of $12.8 million ($99,291,429), would comprise more than forty new buildings, and would draw funds from several sources. Blatt expected that the federal government would pick up half of the cost through a bill pending in Congress that would provide matching funds to pay for buildings needed to accommodate college expansion brought by the GI Bill. He proposed that state and local governments finance the other half, with the state's portion to be drawn from a budget surplus that had accrued due to the booming wartime economy. Blatt argued that the University's board of trustees must act quickly to seize the unique opportunity given South Carolina by proposed federal aid to higher education and the state's wartime windfall. In so doing, they could secure for the University nearly unlimited room for physical expansion and the money for new buildings. A new campus would give the University of South Carolina modern facilities and the momentum to establish itself as a great American state university.[122] Such a move was not unprecedented in the South. As a result of the "greater university" movement in the region, Louisiana State University in 1925 had moved its campus from downtown Baton Rouge to a location outside of town on the banks of the Mississippi River. With a new campus and the generous patronage of Governor Huey Long, by the 1940s that institution had made strides toward becoming a leading southern university.[123] It is not difficult to imagine Sol Blatt envisioning a similar renaissance of the University of South Carolina as a result of a new campus. The fate of his proposal is an object lesson in South Carolina's ambivalence toward modernization at the dawn of the post–World War II era.

Blatt claimed that when he first presented the proposal for a new campus at hearings of the State Budget Commission, he had secured the support of the other key political figures in South Carolina, including Governor Olin D. Johnston, Governor-elect Ransome J. Williams, Senator Edgar Brown (chairman of the Senate Budget Committee) and Morris Tuten (chairman of the House Ways and Means Committee). Among the board of trustees, J. C. Long of Charleston and Harry Hughs of Walhalla were leading proponents, and almost the entire nineteen–member board supported it as well. Only board chairman Edwin G. Seibels of Columbia and Frank M. Samrill of York expressed reservations. Seibels argued that the proposal had sketchy details and that board members had been given little time to think about the matter. He instead preferred to expand on the current site, an option Sol Blatt considered too costly. Blatt demanded quick action to secure a portion of the state surplus, and at their December 1944 meeting, the board of trustees immediately approved Blatt's sweeping "new and greater university" proposal with only two dissenting votes (Seibels and Samrill). They made their decision with little apparent debate or study, and no opportunity for public comment. They then hired a full-time architect, J. Carroll Johnson, to draft plans for the new campus, and prepared to lobby the legislature for financial support.[124]

In late 1944, Sol Blatt was one of the most powerful politicians in South Carolina, and if he pushed an ambitious proposal to build a new University campus, people listened. Blatt loved the University of South Carolina, where he had graduated from the School of Law in 1917. The son of Russian Jewish immigrants who ran a mercantile firm in Blackville, he became one of the state's leading political figures in the late 1930s when the South Carolina House of Representatives elected him Speaker. Blatt soon became linked in state political lore with fellow Barnwell County legislators Edgar Brown and Winchester Smith. These men formed the core of the so-called "Barnwell Ring," a group of like-minded politicians from rural counties who formed an entrenched legislative establishment. In a state where the rural-dominated legislature controlled all the critical sectors of government, Blatt and Brown were the chief power brokers. Blatt served as House Speaker, and Brown held the chairmanship of the Senate Finance Committee (probably the most powerful position in state government at the time).[125]

If any plan to move the University campus was to succeed, it needed Edgar Brown's support. Brown's principal power lay in control of the state's finances: he had a seat on the State Budget Commission, but even more important, as Senate Finance Committee chairman, he tightly controlled the channel through which all state appropriations bills passed.[126] These two positions made him more powerful than the governor and, according to political scientist V. O. Key, his function in state government was akin to that of a prime minister.[127] This made Brown's support for a new university campus critical.

Securing Edgar Brown's support for Blatt's "new and greater university" plan was another matter. Blatt and Brown, even though linked together in popular perception as the "Barnwell Ring," often bitterly disagreed.[128] One of their chief disagreements was over spending priorities for the state's colleges: Blatt ardently supported the University's interests in the legislature, while Brown, though not a Clemson graduate, was a staunch Clemson partisan. The General Assembly had elected each man to a seat on the board of trustees of his favorite college, Brown to Clemson's board in 1934 and Blatt to the University's in 1936. Thus, each was able to influence the cause of his favored school in the legislature and exercised decisive influence in internal college affairs as well. Blatt, for instance, chaired two of the USC board's most politically important committees, the buildings and grounds committee and the athletics committee.[129] As chairman of the Senate Finance Committee, Brown held the key to the final passage of any spending legislation, and Blatt's costly proposal to move and expand the University of South Carolina's campus was sure to draw Brown's close attention.

In late 1944, Sol Blatt began to prepare the way for passage of a bill to finance the state's portion of the "new and greater university" plan. With Leonard Baker serving in limited capacity as acting president, however, the General Assembly was unlikely to pass such sweeping legislation. The University of South Carolina needed stable, permanent leadership, and the final choice of a new president demonstrated the extent of Sol Blatt's vision and his decisive voice in University affairs. Blatt, a member of the board of trustees' presidential search committee (along with Edwin Seibels and Olin Johnston), sought a candidate with close ties to both the South Carolina political establishment and the federal government, a candidate who could help secure funding for Blatt's plan.[130] Their ultimate choice, retired Navy Rear Admiral Norman Murray Smith, closely matched Blatt's criteria.[131]

Smith had close ties to the Washington, D.C. establishment. Known as the "father of the Seabees," he founded the first of the famous naval construction battalions during World War I. In the early 1930s, Smith directed the building of several of the Navy's West Coast bases, including San Diego, and was responsible for the construction of the dry docks at Pearl Harbor. He rose to the rank of rear admiral and served as the Navy's chief civil engineer before retiring in 1938. During World War II, Smith returned to active duty, but saw no combat, serving instead as the commander of a small base in California and handling other administrative duties.[132] To Sol Blatt, he seemed a logical choice to help seek both federal money for its expansion plan and to maintain its close ties with the Navy after the war. In addition, Smith's vast experience as a construction engineer would help to ensure the successful realization of Blatt's "new and greater university."

Sol Blatt liked Norman Smith for another reason as well. A native of Williston in Barnwell County, Smith had been a high school classmate of former South Carolina governor Emile Harley and was the brother of former state legislator Winchester Smith. Both Emile Harley and Winchester Smith had at one time been considered influential members of the Barnwell Ring. Winchester Smith served as chairman of the powerful House Ways and Means Committee from 1939 until 1942, while Sol Blatt served as House Speaker. Winchester Smith lost his legislative seat in 1942 when reapportionment reduced the size of the Barnwell County delegation. The county's two house seats became one, and because Sol Blatt occupied the Speaker's chair, Winchester Smith chose not to contest the remaining seat. He remained active in state politics, however, and in 1944 served as chairman of the executive committee of the South Carolina Democratic Party and as a member of the powerful Public Service Commission.

Many observers saw the selection of Norman Smith for the Carolina presidency as quid pro quo for his brother's quiet retirement from one of the most powerful posts in the General Assembly. The admiral's connections to South Carolina's entrenched political establishment certainly helped secure him the presidency, because he had not lived in the state since leaving for the Naval Academy as a teenager, nor had he sought the job. Despite his lack of experience in higher education, with high expectations Smith assumed the office of University president on February 1, 1945, and prepared to carry out Blatt's ambitious plans for the Carolina campus.[133]

However, between Smith's selection as president in December 1944 and his taking office in February 1945, Sol Blatt's plan to build a modern university on the outskirts of Columbia had collapsed. Blatt failed to anticipate the intense opposition that his plan to move the University from its venerable old campus would arouse. The announcement that the University board had approved the plan generated a flood of letters in newspapers across South Carolina, attesting to the southern attachment to place. Alumni reacted with horror to the idea of destroying the traditions of the antebellum campus, whose buildings dated to 1805, by selling it off and moving.[134] One opponent of the plan, W. Perry Brandenburg, penned a poem titled "On Moving Carolina!," to express his outrage. The first verse read:

> Oh, let her stand on sacred sod,
> I pray her friends and cry to God!
> I'd almost wish her drowned at sea,
> Than moved, one inch, from where she be.[135]

A population weary from years of disruption and sweeping change during war was nostalgic for the stable traditions of peacetime. The "new and greater university" plan struck many in South Carolina as a wanton abandonment of one of the legacies of the state's antebellum past. Others complained of the excessive cost of the move and of the quick approval of the plan before alumni could express their opinions. Mary Graydon Ariail of Columbia wrote that it was an idea that "smacks . . . of a political scheme made public only a few weeks before it is to be rail-roaded through the legislature."[136]

South Carolina's newspaper editors roundly condemned Blatt's proposal. The (Columbia) *State,* representing Columbia's business interests, argued that South Carolina should provide for expansion on the current site and spend University appropriations on higher faculty salaries, not a new campus.[137] The *Sumter Daily Item* criticized the proposal as simply a way for trustees with "hungry eyes" to "relieve" the state treasury of its budget surplus.[138] Charleston's *News and Courier* remarked that the plan showed that "the university's board of trustees is fully in step with current trends and beliefs in politico education." That newspaper's conservative editor, W. W. Ball (former dean of the USC School of Journalism turned harsh critic of the University), also thought that the University might spend money on improving faculty salaries instead of "glittering" new buildings. The editor concluded sarcastically that "perhaps it will be better to spend the money on palatial halls rather than waste it on brains."[139]

On campus, students expressed dismay that trustees would want to move the campus. The *Gamecock*'s editor, Harry Jenkins, wrote that "students are averse to the moving of the institution because it will mean the destroying of the 140-year old tradition and atmosphere of the nation's oldest state-supported University." Jenkins continued, "The buildings of the school, old and outmoded as they are, embody in them the ghosts and spirits of former students, scholars and gentlemen that serve as an inspiration of other scholars." The editor suggested that the University build a skyscraper instead.[140] In a later editorial, Jenkins criticized the board for exaggerating the cost of expanding the existing campus and underestimating the cost of a new one. He, like most of the state's newspaper editors, supported raising faculty salaries and expanding on the current site.[141]

Four hundred students attended a special December 20, 1944, meeting in the University chapel to debate the issue. Law student Jerry Sindler expressed doubt that trustees could secure the money to move the campus. J. B. Heatherly of Greenville supported the move to a new campus, arguing that "all this idea of a school being based on tradition is a bunch of bunk." After an extended debate, the students passed a resolution authored by Bill Hutchinson opposing the move, declaring that moving the University to another site "would inevitably destroy many of the traditions which have for more than a century endeared it to those who have entered its portals."[142]

A group of some of the University's most distinguished faculty members wholeheartedly supported the effort to build a greater university but believed that the expansion should take place on the current campus. The group, which included dean of the College of Arts and Sciences Francis W. Bradley, English professor Havilah Babcock, geologist Stephen Taber, historian Robert Meriwether, and law professor J. Nelson Frierson, expressed their opinion in an open letter to the board of trustees, published in the *State*.[143] University trustee chairman Edwin G. Seibels, an influential Columbia insurance executive, also spoke out publicly against the plan, but declared that South Carolinians should understand that Sol Blatt and the supporters of the proposal were only doing what they believed was best for the University.[144]

The state's political leaders had, at best, a lukewarm attitude toward the plan. The entire Richland County legislative delegation opposed it. Sol Blatt had assured the trustees that Governor Olin Johnston supported the move, but the governor declared neutrality to the idea, as did new governor Ransome Williams, who assumed the office in January of 1945.[145] While the public attacked Blatt's proposal, municipal boosters from around the state lobbied to bring the new campus to their towns. Spartanburg, Sumter, Camden, Kershaw

County, Manning, Cheraw, Georgetown, and Oconee County all expressed interest in having the University move to their locality.[146]

Reacting to the statewide uproar, Blatt retreated.[147] Realizing that there was virtually no support to move the campus, in February 1945 he agreed to a compromise that would enlarge the downtown Columbia campus—a plan that gained the support of students and alumni. It cost just over $7 million ($54,173,721), with local, state, and federal governments again sharing the cost. The proposal envisioned that the campus would expand to the south four blocks on an additional twenty-one acres of land. It called for the construction or renovation of twenty-five buildings.[148]

Gamecock editor Harry Jenkins wrote, "The Gamecock reverses its field editorially and gives its most laudatory commendation to this new plan." The student body met once again, and this time passed a resolution favoring the new proposal.[149] The president of the University Alumni Association, James E. Leppard, supported the new plan as well, and wrote to the organization's members that the proposal was "necessary to preserve the finer elements of the present University, and at the same time adjust a great state institution to a changing society."[150]

As might be expected in South Carolina, the supporters of other state colleges lined up to propose similar programs for their campuses. Clemson's friends offered a $8,465,000 ($64,137,140) proposal for their institution, and Winthrop's president floated a $3,750,000 ($28,412,791) plan for his campus. With the backing of Sol Blatt and Carolina's supporters, in 1945 the House of Representatives approved a total appropriation of $8,550,000 ($64,781,163) from the state budget surplus to be shared by all South Carolina's public colleges for a building program. Of this appropriation, the House allocated some $3,450,000 ($26,139,767) to the University, while the other state schools were to receive smaller amounts.

However, the bill bogged down in Edgar Brown's Senate Finance Committee, which did not act on it in the 1945 legislative session. The following year, the bill came up again, but this time the Finance Committee completely rewrote it, slashing Carolina's share to $350,000 ($2,651,860) (and the shares of other state colleges to a similar amount). This bill became law. However, Brown's legislation stipulated that the University's money could be used only to build an infirmary, and only in conjunction with matching federal funds, which never materialized.[151] Sol Blatt's ambitious vision in the final analysis netted virtually nothing for the University or any other state college. The state's colleges, and the University in particular, therefore faced the postwar era with physical plants unprepared to handle the great numbers that the GI Bill would bring to the campuses.

The ultimate fate of Blatt's proposal stands as a barometer of the structural problems the University of South Carolina faced as it moved into the pivotal postwar period. The failure of the "new and greater university" plan in the General Assembly demonstrated South Carolina's fixation with its past, its peculiar legislative politics, the effects of a structure of public higher education that prevented any one school from benefiting above the others, and the low overall priority of higher education. Local interests and the internecine fight for scarce South Carolina higher education dollars doomed Blatt's ambitious proposal for a "new and greater university." South Carolina was not yet ready to embrace wholesale modernization of its institutions, especially if it meant a rejection of the symbols of its past. The compromise plan that emerged attempted to reconcile modernization with tradition, but even that proposal was not acceptable to the state's leaders.[152] With the failure of the expansion plan, the state missed an opportunity to give South Carolina the momentum to create a modern university for the postwar decades, when ever-growing numbers of young people would seek higher education and universities would become a vital engine of economic development.

2 | "THE G.I. IS THE FINEST THING THAT COULD HAVE HAPPENED"

1945–1949

At present we are in the backwash of World War II. South Carolina, as the United States in general, is fluctuating in all parts of its life. Population is intensely mobile, labor is restless, the cost of living is high and rising, many economic developments are taking place, religion and moral standards are in transition, new political ideas are spreading and many of our cherished state ways are receding before them. . . . Yet new life springs from the old. Tomorrow's shape is emerging from today's.

G. Croft Williams, 1946

Conversion to peace-time operation has proved even more hectic than the war-time program. . . . The University has had to lift itself by its bootstraps.

Norman M. Smith, 1948

In November 1944, twenty-one World War II veterans were students at Carolina. However, rapid demobilization of the armed forces after V-J Day combined with the GI Bill to produce a college enrollment explosion. Between the spring of 1945 and the fall semester of 1947, the University's enrollment ballooned from 1,420 to 4,614, an increase of 225 percent in just two and a half years. Of the 1947 total, some 2,743, or nearly 60 percent, were veterans (forty-four of whom were women). There were more veterans at the University in 1947 than there had been students before the war. The veteran enrollment boom masculinized the student body, and the proportion of women on campus dropped from nearly 35 percent in 1939–40 to about 20 percent in 1947–48. Likewise, colleges and universities across the nation also saw unprecedented enrollment growth in the wake of the war. Between 1939 and 1947, national college enrollment jumped nearly 72 percent, with World War II veterans making up 69 percent of all male college students in 1947.[1] The mushrooming enrollment presented daunting challenges to the University of South Carolina in the period between 1946 and 1950.

The University of South Carolina enrolled far more World War II veterans than any other college in South Carolina. They came to Carolina for several reasons. Of South Carolina's public colleges, the State Agricultural and Mechanical College was segregated for black students, and Winthrop for white women. Both The Citadel and Clemson were military schools (although Clemson did not require veterans to participate in military training); the prospect of returning home to attend a military college was distasteful for the older men leaving the military after fighting the largest war in world history.

The University, on the other hand, welcomed veterans, actively recruiting them through informational mailings.[2] President Smith declared, "No qualified South Carolina veteran who wishes to enroll will be turned away." The University's location in urban Columbia provided a ready market for both part-time work and for off-campus housing that became a necessity as veterans overflowed the dormitories. The University's curriculum with its professional schools appealed to veterans as well, with the schools of law, engineering, and business administration attracting large numbers.[3] The GI Bill made Carolina the largest university in South Carolina and foreshadowed decades of growth when "bigness" on the Carolina campus would become the norm.

The campus of the state's other large public college, Clemson, was in a rural area, and the institution had only a few programs attractive to veterans, such as the schools of engineering, textiles, and agriculture. In addition, Clemson's leaders decided not to throw open their doors to all qualified students. Such an open-door policy, they argued, would provide veterans with an inferior education because classes would fill quickly and it would take students too long to finish their degrees. Clemson president Robert F. Poole claimed that Clemson only would admit only the number of students who could be educated "properly," so Clemson's leaders capped enrollment at around 3,200. Ironically, Carolina and Clemson swapped their traditional reputations in the postwar era: Carolina had long had a reputation for elitism, while Clemson had been the founded as the college for the common man. After the war, Carolina opened its doors to all eligible white South Carolina veterans, while Clemson limited its enrollment. Consequently, while the University's student body increased 125 percent between 1939–40 and the fall of 1947, Clemson's enrollment increased only 39 percent in the same period.[4]

The University of South Carolina established special programs in an attempt to accommodate the wave of veterans, programs that foreshadowed the modern conception of student services. In cooperation with the Veterans Administration, the registrar established a special veterans' guidance office to

offer vocational counseling and to handle veterans' benefits. A new placement bureau acted as a liaison between businesses seeking employees and
veterans and other students seeking off-campus employment. The University
offered veterans degree credit for military training received during the war,
and loans and grants to help them pay for the costs of education not covered
by their GI Bill benefits. Through the Extension Division, it offered training
to veterans who had not graduated from high school as well as refresher
courses to older veterans.[5]

The University shouldered much of the load of educating South Carolina's
World War II veterans even though its physical plant was overwhelmed. As
the postwar student body boomed, President Smith wrote that "student
enrollment has far surpassed the capacity for which our forebears designed
our buildings."[6] Carolina provided housing for only 1,720 students, while
there were well over 4,000 enrolled. It provided eating facilities for only one-
third of the student body. Of the 1,300 veterans attending Carolina in the
spring of 1946, some 800 had to find off-campus housing because of the
shortage of dormitory space.

Students, faculty, and administrators struggled to meet the challenge the
enrollment boom presented. They converted basements, attics, garages, brick
stores, servants' quarters, carriage houses, and even an old firehouse on Main
Street (which served as the chemical engineering laboratory in the immediate postwar years) into dormitories, classrooms, and offices. Four or five students squeezed into dormitory suites on the Horseshoe that were designed to
accommodate two; bathroom facilities were overwhelmed. A special office
helped students and new faculty find off-campus housing. The board of
trustees asked retiring professors with decades of service to quickly vacate
faculty residences so the University could convert them for use as dormitories and classrooms. The administration altered class schedules to make use
of the available space for as long as possible during the day. Because of the
overwhelming number of white male Carolinians seeking higher education
at the University, the board of trustees temporarily suspended the acceptance
of civilian women and all out-of-state students during 1946 and 1947.[7] President Smith wrote of the crisis, "By begging, borrowing, altering, improvis-
ing, doubling up, and by keeping our facilities in use from early morning
until late evenings we have been able to accomplish our objective—that is,
to see that every qualified South Carolinian desiring higher education may
enroll in the university."[8]

World War II veterans who came home to South Carolina wanted an education, but they also wanted to change the status quo in their state and were
generally impatient with the slow pace of change.[9] Their first direct postwar
experience with the entrenched and conservative nature of South Carolina's

leadership came in their college experience. Veterans were highly critical of the University's leadership, the state's political leaders, and the haphazard system of governing public higher education. Exasperated over the crowded conditions at their University, in April 1946 students pleaded with the General Assembly to pass the massive campus expansion bill pushed by Sol Blatt, but the legislature declined. When the plan failed, veterans at an increasingly crowded Carolina became more and more agitated over conditions at their school.[10]

President Smith proved to be a lightning rod for veterans' complaints about the slow response to their needs. Before his arrival at the University, Smith had had no experience in higher education, having spent his entire adult career as a naval construction engineer. His connections with the Barnwell Ring were well known, and critics charged that the board of trustees put politics before academics when they named him president. In addition, Smith had something of a gruff, cold personality, and his military style seemed out of place in an academic environment—an environment he did not entirely understand. Upon his arrival on campus, Carolina's student body president William "Willy P." Horton (who was also a V-12 trainee) went to Smith's office to welcome the new president to the campus. Instead of accepting the welcome, however, Smith scolded Horton for not going through his V-12 chain of command to get an audience with the president. The story quickly made its way around the campus, and Smith became unpopular with students from the beginning. His manner was a striking contrast to that of his predecessor, the gregarious and affable J. Rion McKissick.[11]

Veterans returning to college after wartime service were in no mood to continue submitting to military-style authority. Weary of war, they were anxious to put their wartime experiences behind them, complete their education, and get on with civilian lives that would allow them to take part in the economic opportunity unleashed by the war. They resented the fact that Smith was a career naval officer, and many viewed their university president with disdain. Ernest F. "Fritz" Hollings, a veteran who enrolled at the law school in late 1945, recalled that "as veterans, we had seen admirals and generals who exhibited real leadership, and we'd seen some that were rather dormant. He [Smith] was on the dormant end of things."[12] At a student convocation marking the beginning of an early postwar school year, Smith began his remarks by welcoming "all hands" to the campus. The veterans in the audience took offense at the greeting and began to whistle and stomp their feet. That set the tone for the veterans' opinion of their university president.[13]

Smith did little to endear himself to the veterans. He readily admitted that the Naval ROTC was his "pet program" at the University, and he sought a greater role for the military on the campus, a position sure to anger veterans anxious to leave the military behind. Smith claimed that he tried to run the institution as he would a naval unit. "I can't see anything different in being in uniform and wearing a cap and gown," he said. He hired retired naval officers to serve as top administrators, including assistant to the president Captain (Ret.) Fred Elder. Smith named Captain (Ret.) Ralph C. Needham, former commander of the Carolina V-12 unit, as the University's registrar, a position whose responsibilities included the administration of all GI Bill benefits and veterans programs. Needham soon became a target of veteran ire when GI Bill payments were delayed.[14]

Veterans were dissatisfied not only because of crowded physical conditions at the University, but also because they believed that the administration, especially Smith and Needham, were insensitive to their needs. Veterans loudly complained about the administration's decision to convert from the wartime accelerated academic calendar of three full terms per year back to the old peacetime regimen of two semesters and a summer session. In December 1945, Norman Smith suggested this conversion, and the board approved it. However, a large group of freshmen veterans in the School of Law strongly objected, since this less rigorous schedule would mean that it would take them longer to complete their schooling, which they were anxious to finish as quickly as possible. In addition, veterans received their GI Bill benefits only when school was in session, so a shortened school year meant they would miss their benefits during the summer.

When Smith refused to reconsider the issue, the young veterans took their complaints to the General Assembly, and in early 1946 legislators unanimously approved a nonbinding resolution directing the University to stay on an accelerated schedule. Smith continued to resist the veterans' pressure, arguing that to continue the third term would cost the University an additional $260,000 ($1,817,768) a year. Taking a hard line, he claimed that he did not want to set a precedent of "undesirable appeasements" of veterans, nor did he want to encourage them to take their complaints over the heads of the administration and the board of trustees to the General Assembly. The veterans persisted and lobbied the legislature for binding legislation requiring the University to stay on the accelerated schedule. A meeting of 500 student-veterans voted nearly unanimously to maintain the three-semester-per-year schedule. In the aftermath of their agitation, the most influential trustee, Sol Blatt, sided with the veterans. When it began to appear that the General Assembly would indeed pass a law requiring a third session, in March 1946 the board overruled President Smith and approved a continuation of the accelerated academic calendar that included an extended summer term. The University continued this schedule until mid-1949.[15]

The second half of 1946 was a time of further discontent among veterans. During the summer, they demonstrated their disenchantment with the administration when they hanged President Smith and registrar Ralph Needham in effigy. Not only was the campus literally overflowing with students, but the administration continued to give the impression that it was unresponsive to their needs. Students continued to assert that Smith paid them little attention when making University policy. The young veterans felt that through their service they had earned the privilege of having a greater degree of control over student life than had previous generations. *Gamecock* columnist Dick Breland wrote in the fall of 1946, "This is a time of understandable unrest on the campus. After a war-imposed period of somnambulation, the university is in the throes of a great awakening." The unrest, he explained, "springs from . . . a fundamental difference between student leaders and officers of the administration on a point of the greatest importance: does the voice of the students have any influence on University policy?"[16]

Students indeed questioned whether Smith paid any attention to them when making decisions. For example, local musicians refused to play at University dances because Smith would not honor a student-negotiated deal to pay unionized musicians the union wage rate. Student dances thus could not attract professional entertainment. Student body president Fred Brogdan said of the situation, "It has long been a question as to the effect of student opinion . . . on the president's administrative policies. Now we have our answer." Smith retorted that he was "glad to get student opinion on anything, but if it is contrary to what the Administration . . . feels [is] best for the University," then he would make his own decisions.[17]

Students further charged that Smith was a tool of the Barnwell Ring, or more accurately Sol Blatt, who they claimed singlehandedly controlled the University board of trustees. Political involvement in their education had gotten out of hand, they argued. A *Gamecock* editorial read, "We, the younger generation, . . . resent this state University being a political football. . . . The University of South Carolina was conceived in education and brought forth in political iniquity."[18] Student R. A. Culbertson wrote that Smith was the "product of a political machine. . . . The significance to me is that a corrupt political machine places undesirable men in important places. . . . Mr. Smith is as much at sea here as a retired professor would be if in command of a battleship." Culbertson concluded that "the Admiral's feet will never grow large enough to fit the shoes of the late President J. Rion McKissick."[19] Students filled the *Gamecock* with critical editorials and letters demanding Smith's ouster, and veterans derisively nicknamed Smith "Snuffy" (referring to the diminutive cartoon hillbilly).[20]

Indeed, in the fall of 1946, the Barnwell Ring, which veterans charged controlled President Smith, was a hot topic in South Carolina. That fall, Strom Thurmond, a forty-five-year-old war veteran from Edgefield, was running for governor. Thurmond ran on a platform that promised modernization and reform of state government, including the expansion of the state's college facilities—a political position ready-made to appeal to discontented student-veterans. John Carl West, a veteran and then–Carolina law student, recalled that as Thurmond was the only World War II veteran in the race, "We were all pulling for Strom." The Barnwell Ring received the lion's share of the candidate's scorn. In a one-party state like South Carolina, the 1946 race was unusual for its bitterness, and foreshadowed the more partisan campaigns of the late twentieth century. Thurmond claimed that the ring was a clique of "cunning, conniving men" who blocked reform. In a bold speech in Barnwell he attacked this "ring," declaring, "so long as this ring and its henchmen dominate this state you won't get the reforms people want."[21] His negative campaigning and scathing attacks on the Barnwell Ring paid off, for he was the top vote-getter in the August primary and won the September runoff.[22]

Thus, student dissatisfaction and accusations that Norman Smith was the tool of the Barnwell political establishment took place in the context of an acrimonious political campaign that was felt even more acutely on college campuses overwhelmed with veterans. The student outcry against Smith during the fall of 1946 drew notice in the state's newspapers. When students booed the president at a football game, the *Greenville Observer* declared that there was a spirit of rebellion in the air. "It seems," the editor wrote, "that no one wishes to respect authority any more."[23]

In response to the veteran-led controversy over Smith's administration, in late 1946 the board of trustees appointed a special committee to investigate the causes for student agitation. In early January 1947, they reported that they found no evidence to sustain the rumors against Smith, except "idle and unwarranted gossip." They then passed a resolution of "complete confidence, endorsement and appreciation" of the president.[24]

The board's action did not appease disgruntled veterans. The day after the vote of confidence, students hanged an effigy of President Smith and University trustees Sol Blatt and Edwin Seibels in the University post office lobby in Maxcy College. The president of the freshman class (which included many of the veterans), Pete Hyman of Florence, announced that the effigy "was just the beginning of student demonstrations." Hyman concluded that "the effigy was done by students desiring to have their voices heard concerning University affairs." Characteristically disdainful of student opinion, Smith replied that "if the students want an effigy of me, I'll have one made and they can hang it up every morning, if they get a kick out of it."[25]

The spirit of discontent prevalent at the University of South Carolina in 1946 was not an isolated event. Across the South, citizens emerging from the war looked to modernize the region and its political and economic institutions by overturning entrenched elites that had dominated since the Civil War.[26] Strom Thurmond's 1946 election victory occurred as part of an anti-incumbent election year and accompanied the election of many political newcomers and young reformers to the South Carolina General Assembly. Bruce Littlejohn, a Spartanburg veteran and USC alumnus, recalled that 1946 was "the day of the young veterans, and there was to be a new way of thinking in the General Assembly." Of the 124 members of the House elected in 1946, 44 were veterans. Their average age was thirty-one. Both John West and Bruce Littlejohn remembered that veterans had "the political bug." "It was a part of a service mentality that we got during the war," said West. "We had served our country, now we wanted to serve our state." Among the idealistic young veterans elected to House seats in 1946 were eight University of South Carolina students.[27]

One of these newly elected student-legislators vowed to use the power of the General Assembly against President Smith. Twenty-two-year-old representative Joseph Wise Jr. of Charleston, a USC journalism student, demanded an immediate investigation of the University's administration. He claimed that the University's administration was "shot through and through with politics." Veterans, Wise believed, had no confidence in the board of trustees to oversee the institution. "The veterans feel that the board is a political setup from top to bottom," he declared. Representative Wise said that "there has been so much dissension at the University that only a full legislative investigation would be satisfactory."[28]

Almost immediately, Wise submitted a resolution for just such an investigation, and when it came up for debate in a House education subcommittee, it brought the complaints of veterans against President Smith and his administration into the open. Testifying before the committee, veteran and Carolina student R. A. Culbertson of Greenville summed up the feelings of many Carolina vets: "One half of the student body is made up of veterans who gave up the best days of their lives in the service and feel they deserve the best in education. We can't have the best in education when the president is not the best to be had." Reflecting the nastiness of the 1946 political campaign, he raised the charge that Smith had been made president only because of his political connections. He continued, "The unrest is an indication of how the people of the state feel towards political education. So long as men control education for their own selfish motives and not for the good of the state, education cannot be free and if not free then it is not worth a tinker's dam." Culbertson concluded, "The President, I believe, is the product of a political machine, and veterans and non-veterans are fed up with not having the best man available."[29]

The debate turned to larger issues than Norman Smith when Representative Hugo S. Sims Jr. of Orangeburg, a highly decorated war hero and Carolina law student, questioned the utility of an official investigation. Although critical of Smith and his administration, Sims believed that the charges and complaints against Smith were essentially based on his personality and that an investigation would therefore accomplish nothing. He alternatively claimed, "Our problem is deeper than the University; it is to take politics out of education in South Carolina." Sims's proposed reform of state-funded higher education was twofold: first, the state must eliminate all members of the General Assembly from membership on the boards of trustees of state institutions. Second, it should establish an overall board of regents to govern state-supported colleges. The education subcommittee tabled the Wise resolution for an investigation of the University and approved Sims's substitute proposal.[30]

Sims's proposed solution to political involvement at the University reflected a bitter political power struggle in the General Assembly following Strom Thurmond's election—with the University caught in the middle. In the wake of the divisive 1946 election, Blatt announced that he would not seek another term as House speaker, as he said, "in the interest of peace and harmony in the state." Thurmond supporters, including new House Speaker Bruce Littlejohn of Spartanburg, then took over the most powerful seats in the House of Representatives from members of the Barnwell Ring.[31]

One of the new governor's central attacks on the ring in his campaign had been the practice of "dual office holding" (when members of the legislature also held positions on the boards of trustees of state institutions). Not satisfied with having forced Blatt from his seat as House Speaker, Thurmond attacked dual office holding in his inaugural address, quoting Article VI, Section 24 of the Constitution of South Carolina, which reads in part: "No person shall be eligible to a seat in the General Assembly while he holds any office or position of profit or trust under this State."[32] Thurmond and his supporters called for enforcement of the provision, which had long been ignored. The governor and his allies aimed their attack directly at Sol Blatt and Edgar Brown, "ring" legislators with seats on college boards of trustees. The state attorney general and the state supreme court resolved the acrimonious dispute in March 1947, when they both held that dual office holding was indeed unconstitutional. Blatt subsequently resigned his seat on USC's board of trustees, and three other Carolina board members who also held state offices declined to run for reelection to the board. Dual office holders on the boards of other state colleges, including Edgar Brown, resigned their seats as well.[33]

Sol Blatt artfully dodged the provision of the constitutional provision by putting forth his son, twenty-five-year-old Sol Blatt Jr., as a candidate to be his replacement on the board. The General Assembly then elected the younger Blatt to the seat, and a group of dissatisfied Carolina students responded to the news by hanging an effigy of the elder Blatt from the Maxcy Monument. A placard identified the effigy as "King Sol Blatt," and an attached poem read, "King Sol: Through my son I shall rule, with house members as my tools."[34] Edgar Brown managed to escape the provisions of the law when the Clemson board named him as a life trustee the following year.

With the question of dual office holding apparently resolved, the second part of Representative Hugo Sims's proposed reform that would divorce the University from state politics involved the creation of a board of regents to govern public higher education in South Carolina. Supporters of this reform pointed to the precedent set by Georgia, which instituted such a system in 1932.[35] Proposals to do so in South Carolina had come up several times during and after World War II as citizens looked to modernize their institutions and prepare for postwar growth.[36]

The most important of these proposals had been a 1946 consultant's survey of the state's public colleges, prompted by the state's Preparedness for Peace Commission and conducted by Nashville's highly respected Peabody College for Teachers. The Peabody consultants concluded that South Carolina should establish a higher education commission to plan and coordinate public higher education. As of early 1947, however, the General Assembly had not acted on the Peabody recommendations.[37]

After the election of a reform-minded governor and legislature, the Peabody plan received new life. The House subcommittee charged with writing the regents plan into legislation included Carolina student-veterans Sims and Wise as well as USC alumnus and war veteran Thomas H. Pope of Newberry, and they used the Peabody Report to draft their legislation. The measure called for an overall governing board that would receive a single lump appropriation annually and would then apportion it among the state's six colleges. The measure passed the House, where Thurmond's reformist supporters held sway, but like the "greater university" expansion bill in the previous legislative session, it bogged down in Edgar Brown's Senate, where it died.[38]

Thus the uproar concerning political involvement in higher education ousted Sol Blatt Sr. from the Carolina board, but it did nothing to bring long-term reform to the state's haphazard college appropriations process. Veteran agitation culminated in an effort to modernize public higher education as a result of Hugo Sims's proposal, but it ultimately changed little in South Carolina's highly political system of providing for higher education. In turn, the crisis of space that had been one of the catalysts of the entire episode persisted at the University.

As it had done in World War II, in the postwar years the federal government again stepped in to alleviate a crisis at the University. At the end of 1945, the U.S. Congress passed a measure to provide relief to colleges that had acute veteran student housing problems by paying to move and reconstruct surplus war housing on their campuses. Under this program, the University of South Carolina received 228 emergency housing units for married veterans and their families. Between 1946 until 1948, the Federal Public Housing Authority sporadically assembled sets of these prefabricated buildings one mile north of the campus along Bull Street near the State Hospital. Dubbed the Carovet (Carolina Veteran) Apartments, the temporary housing provided veterans a small one- or two-bedroom apartment, a bathroom, a living room, a kitchen, and modern conveniences like an electric refrigerator. The University built a playground and clubhouse for the community of married veterans, which also supplied child care services. Because of the shortage of housing in postwar Columbia, new faculty lived in the Carovet Apartments as well.[39]

Along with helping meet the student housing shortage, the federal government provided relief for the critical shortage of classroom, laboratory and office space. Another congressional measure passed in August 1946 empowered the Federal Works Agency to transfer surplus military buildings to colleges with acute classroom shortages. Called the Veterans Educational Facilities Program, it paid to move, re-erect, and outfit the buildings while the University had to pay only for preparing the site and connecting utilities. By the end of 1947, the Federal Works Administration had put up nine of these unattractive one-story wooden structures on the campus, most near the McKissick Library on Gibbes Green. Several of the buildings contained laboratories for the departments of chemistry, pharmacy, biology, and engineering. Others housed classrooms for fine arts, psychology, philosophy, political science, journalism, and music, while still others served as offices for student publications and the extension division. The buildings, which students dubbed "termite halls," helped to relieve the crisis of space, albeit in a temporary fashion.[40]

While the federal government acted quickly in response to the space crisis in the nation's colleges, South Carolina's leaders finally proceeded to action. For the 1947 legislative session, Smith resubmitted the University's earlier plans for expansion on twenty-one acres south of the campus. The first priorities on Smith's building list were a naval engineering laboratory and a naval science building. The long-needed building to house the sciences (chemistry, biology, geology, pharmacy, and physics) was fifth on his priority list, an indication of the emphasis Smith placed on naval programs vis-à-vis the academic core of the University. The overall building proposal still depended on yet-to-be-approved federal financing to match the state's appropriation.[41]

In 1947 the reform-minded General Assembly approved a $10,260,000 ($62,597,528) state institution construction bill, with an allocation of $1,450,000 ($8,846,629) for the University's building program. The money came from the state's wartime budget surplus, and it appeared the University's urgently needed postwar expansion program might finally get off the ground. However, an overly cautious University leadership refused to spend the money. An agreement between Governor Thurmond, President Smith, and the University board of trustees provided that they would delay the start of the University's construction program until construction prices, which had risen sharply in the years since the war, began to drop. President Smith also wanted to wait until matching federal funds were approved by Congress before beginning the building program, hoping to double the amount of funding available. Finally, the legislation appropriating Carolina the money contained no authority to buy land. Since there were few building sites available on the existing campus, Smith and the trustees wanted to wait until they could secure an appropriation to purchase land.[42] However, neither federal matching funds nor declining building prices ever materialized, and the University did not begin a general building program to relieve the facilities problem until 1950, after the bulk of World War II's veterans had completed their education.

Nonetheless, crowded conditions in the law school and a lawsuit over racially segregated education in the late 1940s led the South Carolina Bar Association to prompt the University to alleviate that school's overcrowded facilities. Smith wanted the University's Navy ROTC to get the first new buildings the University constructed under a building program. But the law school's enrollment had grown exponentially since the end of the war, going from 16 in the spring semester of 1945 to 275 in the fall of 1947 (94 percent veterans). Accordingly, the school had far outgrown its building (today's Currell College). The state's lawyers became more and more concerned that the quality of legal education in South Carolina was slipping, citing a report from the Association of American Law Schools that had criticized the law school's crowded facilities. At the same time, as a result of a lawsuit brought by a black student who sued to enter Carolina's law school, the General Assembly appropriated $200,000 ($1,131,250) to build a law building for a new law school at South Carolina State College (see the account of the lawsuit later in this chapter). The state bar association pleaded with the University to build its own law school a new building with the newly appropriated money, even offering to buy a site if the University's leaders would commit to spending the appropriated funds. The board of trustees agreed to study the situation, leaving open the option of simply adding on to the existing law school building when they began a general building program at some time in the future.[43]

In the late 1940s, the USC board of trustees represented an interesting mix of personalities. Board chairman Edwin G. Seibels and J. Arthur Knight, a former state legislator from Chesterfield, had both served on the board since the 1930s. However, in the wake of the dual-office-holding controversy, five new members came on to the board in 1947. Among them were Sol Blatt Jr. (A.B. '41), a man with an interest in University athletics, Donald Russell (A.B. '25), the bookish protégé of James F. Byrnes who would go on to be one of Carolina's finest presidents in the modern era, A. C. Todd (A.B. '01), a prominent Greenwood attorney, and Rutledge L. Osborne (A.B. '16), who would go on to serve as the board chairman and driving force at Carolina until the mid-1970s. Some trustees, such as Frank Samrill of York, were said to care only how an issue affected the Athletic Department and to vote accordingly. It was men such as these on the board of trustees who would make the decisions about the University's direction in the late 1940s.[44]

While the board had decided to study the law school issue, the South Carolina Bar Association (with Edgar Brown serving as its president), forced the board to act. Not to be accused of spending more on legal education for blacks than on that for whites, in the spring of 1948 they convinced the General Assembly to pass an additional $1,302,000 appropriation ($7,364,438) (again from the state budget surplus) for state college buildings. The legislation required the University to use its $250,000 ($1,414,063) share of the appropriation to construct a new law school, to be completed by 1 September 1949. Ironically, Edgar Brown, the man who had torpedoed the University's earlier plans to expand, now forced an unwilling University administration to construct a new building for the state's white law students. If Carolina were to use the money at all, it had to spend it immediately.[45] The trustees acted, and after considering several off-campus sites, they chose an open space on the edge of Gibbes Green for the site of the new law building (today's Petigru College). In early 1950, the law school occupied the new building. It was the first building constructed at the University in the post-war years, and the first financed entirely with state funds since Sloan College in 1927. Trustees renamed the old law building (formerly Petigru) Currell College for Carolina's fifteenth president, William S. Currell, and turned it over to the history department. This freed up classroom and office space in Legare College, the former home of the history department.[46]

Through the end of the 1940s, President Smith and the board of trustees would not spend the $1,450,000 ($8,846,629) the legislature appropriated in 1947, citing their agreement with the governor. Through the early 1950s, they continued to submit additional requests for money to carry out the massive expansion program first proposed in 1945, but the General Assembly repeatedly refused to give more money since the institution had not yet spent what it had already been appropriated.[47] In 1948, the University received additional funds to renovate some older dormitories on the Horseshoe and LeConte College, the science building.[48] However, the renovations did not relieve the overall campus crowding problem. Nor did they satisfy students who wanted a major program to expand the campus. At the end of 1948, the Carolina student body made a well-organized effort to revive the plan for a totally new campus outside of downtown Columbia. The University board of trustees politely ignored their request.[49]

While the General Assembly made limited amounts of money available for University construction projects in the immediate postwar period, it skimped on annual maintenance and operational appropriations that supported the academic programs. In South Carolina in the 1940s, the annual appropriations process reflected the style of politics that had allowed the Barnwell Ring to monopolize power. A "friends-and-neighbors" style rewarded local interests and crippled the state's colleges by pitting them against one another in a fight for scarce education dollars. Under the haphazard appropriations system, the legislature individually debated and passed the annual budgets for the six publicly-supported institutions (The University, Clemson, The Citadel, Winthrop, State College and the Medical College). There was no general coordinating body, like a board of regents as suggested by the Peabody Report, to distribute revenues rationally or equitably.[50]

As a result, a college's annual appropriation depended largely on the ability of its administrators and friends to argue its case effectively before the General Assembly. Such an arrangement primarily benefited those institutions with well-connected supporters and popular, persuasive presidents. Carolina and Clemson had the most influential and well-connected supporters in the state in Sol Blatt and Edgar Brown. Even with the support of these men, however, the state provided inadequate budgets for its public colleges.[51] For example, in fiscal year 1947–48, the state spent less than 6 percent of its total revenue on all of its public colleges (in 2000, it granted some 15 percent of state general funds to higher education).[52]

After the war, the University of South Carolina's financial situation went from bad to worse. The Veterans Administration paid the University an out-of-state tuition rate for all veterans on the GI Bill, regardless of their residency. To take full advantage of this policy and to reduce the burden of higher education on the state, in 1946 the General Assembly mandated a tuition increase from $30 ($210) to $40 ($280) per semester for in-state students, and from $100 ($699) to $125 ($874) for out-of-state students.[53] Consequently, with a tuition increase and the veteran-driven enrollment boom, the University's income from student revenues skyrocketed. However, the General Assembly accompanied the tuition hike with a cut to the University's state-appropriated operating funds (as it had done during the war). Thus, federally-paid student fees largely supported the University during the late 1940s.[54] The state contributed far less money per student than it had done even in the 1920s. The proportion of operating revenue provided by the state fell from 89 percent in 1924 to 52 percent in 1939–40, and to just 17 percent in 1947–48, the height of veteran enrollment (table 2.1). For much of the 1940s, the University could more nearly be called a federally-supported university than a state-supported one.

As veteran enrollment and federal GI Bill payments declined after 1947, state government was forced to assume more of the cost of operating the institution, but state funding remained well below the prewar level. The University's expenditures exceeded its revenue in the final three years of the 1940s, but it made up the difference with a surplus built from GI Bill payments. In the late 1940s, *Gamecock* editorialist Carroll Gilliam wrote of the University's financial dependence on the GI Bill: "This part of the game has not been too harsh on South Carolina while Uncle Sam was the party being

Table 2.1 State appropriations to the University of South Carolina for
maintenance and operation in selected years, 1924–1950

(Figures do not include appropriations for construction or permanent improvements)

YEAR	AVERAGE ENROLLMENT	NET STATE APPROPRIATION	PER STUDENT COST TO STATE	TOTAL FEES FROM STUDENTS*	PERCENT OF REVENUE FROM STATE	PERCENT OF REVENUE FROM STUDENT
1924	909	$412,025	$453	$52,158	89	11
1939–40	2,051	$301,025	$141	$282,000	52	48
1943–44	2,000	$334,000	$167	$1,310,000	20	80
1944–45	1,767	$274,000	$155	$971,935	22	78
1945–46	2,600	$612,496	$235	$1,162,270	35	65
1946–47	4,152	$785,500	$189	$1,848,482	30	70
1947–48	4,497	$403,741	$90	$1,930,170	17	83
1948–49	3,943	$487,690	$124	$1,772,318	22	78
1949–50	3,651	$761,945	$209	$1,537,685	33	67

Source: "Report of the University of South Carolina," 1947–48, 12; 1949–50, 12; contained in *Reports and Resolutions of the General Assembly of the State of South Carolina,* 1949, vol. 2; 1950, vol. 2.

* Includes receipts from Navy Training Programs and Veterans Administration for GI Bill benefits.

soaked, but those days are ending and Mr. and Mrs. Parent will be paying through the nose. The General Assembly has evaded the responsibility of the state for maintaining an adequate state university."[55]

The state's accounting procedure helped camouflage this reality. Beginning in the 1947–48 fiscal year, the state required the University and other state institutions to remit to the state treasurer all income from tuition and fees, then it reapportioned the money out again to the various state colleges.[56] Since the University had so many veterans with their fees paid by the federal government, Carolina came out the net loser under this scheme even while the state's total appropriation appeared to grow markedly. For instance, between 1946–47 and 1947–48 (the year of peak veteran enrollment), the gross state appropriation to the University increased from $785,500 ($5,118,318) to $2,293,500 ($13,487,767), but the University paid the state some $1,889,759 ($11,113,420) in fees in the latter year, so the net appropriation in 1947–48 was but $403,471 ($2,372,759), a 49 percent decrease from the previous year.[57]

While the General Assembly deserved much of the responsibility for the University's woeful financial condition in the late 1940s, the administration shared some of the blame. For instance, it badly underestimated the costs of operating the institution during the peak enrollment year of 1947–48. The state's appropriation was only 3.2 percent less than the administration requested, but because of enrollment increases, the actual appropriation per student dropped 49 percent from the previous year.[58] In addition, Clemson and Winthrop "out-hustled" Carolina in the annual political battle for appropriations. As table 2.2 shows, Winthrop made out best during the late 1940s, and for the next decade, it attracted far more money from the legislature on a per-student basis than any other public college in the state.[59] Clemson's per-student appropriations also exceeded USC's in every year from 1945–46 to 1948–49.[60]

President Norman Smith lacked the political savvy that Sol Blatt had hoped he would bring to the job, and as a result the University of South Carolina suffered during the late 1940s. The residue of bitterness from the 1946 election and the 1947 battle over the makeup of the University's board of trustees lingered, straining communication between University officials and Governor Strom Thurmond. For example, on the board of trustees (where Thurmond, as governor, was president ex officio), the governor technically had the power to appoint committees, but in the years since the governor had ceased to be the board's chairman in 1936, the state's chief executive had not chosen to take an active role on the board, and the University president had traditionally made the appointments. Midway through his term, however, in 1949, Thurmond decided he wanted to exercise his appointment power and claimed that the board had treated him rudely by not allowing him to do so

Table 2.2 Comparative net state appropriations to the University of South
Carolina, Clemson College, and Winthrop College, 1947–48

INSTITUTION	ENROLLMENT*	NET STATE APPROPRIATION†	PER STUDENT APPROPRIATION
University of SC	4,614	$403,741 ($2,374,346)	$88 ($518)
Clemson College	3,251	$491,339 ($2,889,499)	$151 ($888)
Winthrop College	1,616	$730,161 ($4,293,979)	$452 ($2,658)

Source: "Report of the University of South Carolina for 1947–48," 12, 47; "Fifty-Eighth Annual
Report of the Board of Trustees of The Clemson Agricultural College, 1947," 7; "Report of
Winthrop College for 1947–48," Winthrop University Archives; "Report of the Comptrol-
ler General of South Carolina, 1947–48," 9–11. These reports are contained in *Reports and
Resolutions of the General Assembly of South Carolina*, 1948, vol. 2; 1949, vols. 1 and 2; *Acts
and Joint Resolutions of the General Assembly of South Carolina*, 1947, 621–22.
* This figure represents the fall 1947 session.
† This figure is computed by subtracting the total fees remitted to the state from the gross
state appropriation. In Clemson's case, the gross appropriation figure was for collegiate
activities only.

prior to that time. He told the board, "There is a cool atmosphere to me [at
the University] as far as I am concerned. . . . I am saying this to your president's face; I am against him when he is wrong, and I will be with him when
he is right." Thurmond continued, "I want to help this University; I can help
it or I can hurt it. It seems to me the attitude of this administration down here
has not been what it ought to be. There is not the cordial relation there ought
to be." He assailed the administration's approach toward him, complaining,
"I don't like the attitude down here. I am telling you now, I think the attitude
here has been wrong. There has been too much picayunishness—too much
jealousy—too much secrecy."[61]

This unfortunate exchange pointed out the University's political difficulties at this critical time. President Smith failed to provide vigorous leadership in
public relations with the state—one of the implicit duties of a public university president. The man chiefly responsible for his being named president, Sol
Blatt, repeatedly urged Smith to organize a statewide publicity campaign to
help sell the University to the General Assembly. Blatt wrote to Smith of his
own frustrated efforts to secure greater appropriations for the University:
"Heretofore, I have carried the load and I am getting a little tired because of
the lack of cooperation on the part of others who should be interested in the
University." Blatt believed that the University's lobbying effort was weak, and
the levels of state support reflected that. Blatt wrote, "We need help and we
need it badly. We are never going to make the progress we should until we
get active and organize. . . . We need someone to go out into the state and
preach the cause of our University and its needs."[62]

Norman Smith was not suited for such a campaign. Blatt later wrote that his many requests to Smith had "fallen on deaf ears." "It hurts me," Blatt wrote, "that the Administration does nothing in order to get the necessary appropriations in order to properly operate the University."[63] Clemson, on the other hand, used its board of trustees members to persuasively lobby the General Assembly. Blatt wrote, "Clemson always makes a better showing than we make and the result is, that institution gets what it wants. . . . Politicians are afraid of the Clemson group but are not afraid of us."[64] The superior political positions of Winthrop and Clemson, along with the general low level of South Carolina's state funding for higher education, doomed the University of South Carolina to low appropriations in the late 1940s and early 1950s at a time when it was shouldering the disproportionate burden of educating South Carolina's World War II veterans.

The consequent financial crisis threatened the quality of the University's academic programs. Smith reported to the General Assembly in 1949: "The reduction in appropriations . . . has been severe, and the accumulative effect over a period of years is startling. . . . We have maintained and operated the University as best we could with the funds appropriated, but only at a sacrifice of high standards that should be maintained at the University."[65]

The administration's decision to throw open the doors to all qualified veterans had an impact on the quality of education the University offered. Indeed, the University's accrediting body, the Southern Association of Colleges and Schools (SACS), questioned the school's academic standards. Because state appropriations did not match enrollment increases, the University failed to meet the SACS minimum standard for per-student expenditures for graduate students, $250 ($1,414). The University spent but $205 ($1,159) per graduate student in 1948–49. In addition to low per-student expenditures, SACS representatives cited Carolina's paucity of graduate programs, low level of research work, and poor library facilities. Because of the threat to the University's accreditation, the legislature initiated a small spending increase for the 1949–50 fiscal year, but the levels of state funding and overall spending per student remained precariously low.[66]

In the postwar years, the University's largely veteran student population crowded courses in the professional schools. Enrollment in the School of Law increased from 16 in the spring of 1945 to 314 in the fall of 1948. The renamed School of Business Administration (formerly the School of Commerce) surpassed the College of Arts and Sciences to become the largest academic unit at the University. In the fall of 1948, it enrolled 1,190 students, while the College of Arts and Sciences had 888. In addition, the School of Engineering grew to enroll nearly 20 percent of all male students at the University.[67]

Despite significant problems, there were some decidedly positive developments in academics. The University began offering a major in music education, improved its department of fine arts with the addition of Edmund Yaghjian as department head, established a separate department of anthropology and sociology under the direction of Harry Turney-High, and won provisional accreditation for the School of Social Work. The Navy ROTC became a permanent part of the University in 1945, and in 1949 the Air Force established its own ROTC program on the campus.[68]

The outlines of a modern university began to appear in the late 1940s, however faintly. The Graduate School awarded its first post-Depression Ph.D. in 1948, to J. Mauldin Lesesne in the Department of History.[69] By 1949, in the five years since its founding, the University of South Carolina Press had published eighteen scholarly books.[70] With improvements in laboratory facilities (in temporary buildings and in the remodeled LeConte College), in 1948 the department of chemistry under chairman Willard Davis began a master's degree program and sought full accreditation from the American Chemical Society. As Dean Bradley pointed out, such a move was imperative since South Carolina was one of only two states in the nation without an accredited chemistry department (the other was Wyoming).[71]

Overall Graduate School enrollment increased along with the undergraduate, and between 1945 and 1949, full-time graduate enrollment rose from 35 to 134. These students were concentrated in the fields of history, English, economics, biology, chemistry, and education. In 1949 alone, the Graduate School awarded 147 degrees, a 445 percent increase over the 33 graduate degrees given in the 1939–40 academic year.[72]

Despite these developments, the financial difficulties of the late 1940s stunted any sustained drive to broaden graduate degree offerings. Doctoral programs continued to be limited to history. The department of geology was a strong candidate for expansion, boasting an outstanding faculty led by professors Stephen Taber and Lawrence L. Smith, and was home of the Colburn Mineral Collection, one of the southeast's finest geological collections. Because of the shortage of laboratory space, however, the department was forced to maintain the valuable collection in packing crates, where it could not be used by students. The geology department granted only three master's degrees in 1949.[73]

The continuing weakness of the graduate and research program made it difficult to attract increasingly important contract research dollars from outside of the state. In 1950, the federal government spent over $150,000,000 ($848,437,500) per year on contract research at American colleges and universities, but these grants were concentrated at a small number of universities, mostly outside the South. The University of South Carolina received only one federal research contract in the sciences during the late 1940s, a $500 ($2,828) grant to the department of geology.[74]

One of the chief problems facing dean of the faculty Francis W. Bradley was the heavy teaching load on professors in almost all departments. While student enrollment increased 104 percent between the end of 1945 and the end of 1948, the ranks of teaching faculty increased by only 54 percent. In 1947–48 the average teaching load per instructor was 146 students (with no teaching assistants), and the recommended load was but 100. A single professor of education taught fifteen hours a week and had 193 students, including 42 graduate students, all without the aid of a graduate assistant. Such heavy loads made it nearly impossible for most professors to engage in research. The teaching loads were also a restraint on the national standing of academic programs. For example, the department of music had a well-qualified staff, but was denied membership in the National Association of Schools of Music in part because of heavy teaching loads.[75] Likewise, in 1949 the American Chemistry Society denied the department of chemistry's first attempt to earn accreditation primarily because of the department's heavy teaching loads.[76]

Such a situation was bound to be detrimental to the morale of faculty members, but it was just one of the difficulties that faced the University's postwar professors. In the immediate postwar period, colleges and universities all over the country hired new instructors in unprecedented numbers to cope with the enrollment boom. Competition for qualified faculty was intense. As a result of USC's financial problems, its faculty salaries were among the lowest in the southeast among state universities, and recruiting well-qualified faculty was very difficult. As a result, in the 1948–49 academic year, only 19 percent of the faculty held the Ph.D., and more than one-third held only the bachelor's degree.[77] Several departments, including chemistry, used their best senior undergraduate students to teach overloaded introductory-level courses to freshmen and sophomores.[78]

The University's salaries had never rebounded from the reductions of the Depression era, and the salary scale was 7 percent to 8 percent lower than that of other southern state universities. In the late 1940s other southern state universities with their higher salaries lured away some of the University's best young faculty members.[79] A 1947 petition to the Carolina board of trustees by a committee of deans and department heads told of the impact low faculty salaries had on the University. They wrote, "Perhaps we shall never be able to compete with the larger universities of the North and West in the matter of salaries, but today we find ourselves unable to compete with even those of the South." The situation was dire, they believed: "[U]nless salaries are materially increased, the University will not only continue to lose some of its most valuable staff members, but will have to be content with inferior replacements." In the long run, they feared that on account of low salaries "the University of South Carolina will never be a research institution, nor can it maintain its high standards unless it is placed in a position where it can attract competent men and women to its faculty."[80] Most departments largely sought South Carolinians and southerners for their faculty during the 1940s, partly out of a desire for homogeneity and partly of necessity.[81] Despite small bonuses for faculty in the later years of the 1940s, the University's salary scale remained at the bottom of all southern state universities, mainly because the General Assembly repeatedly rejected the administration's requests for across-the-board salary increases.[82] In the decade of the 1940s, faculty salaries rose 25.6 percent, while the cost of living rose 84 percent. Consequently, President Smith's failure to vigorously address the faculty salary problem earned him their enmity.[83]

Smith's communication problems, evident with the governor and General Assembly, extended to USC's faculty. Dean Samuel Prince of the law school wrote of a "most detrimental gulf between the Administration and Trustees on one side and the faculty on the other."[84] Prince wrote to the president about the faculty, "[N]early all are low and discouraged. This discouragement among your best faculty material comes from a feeling on their part that the Administration and Trustees neither understand them, their activities, ambitions, and performances; nor are particularly interested."[85] Because of his lack of academic experience, Smith had trouble relating to professors.[86] He sometimes refused to hire prospective faculty who lacked uniformed military service during the war, no matter their professional qualifications.[87] A faculty colleague told of an episode involving geologist Stephen Taber that hints at Smith's attitude toward institutional advancement. In 1945, Taber worked for months in competition with several universities, including the University of North Carolina, to try to buy the valuable Burnham S. Colburn mineral collection from the Colburn family of Asheville. The collection would be a boon to teaching in the geology department. Finally, Taber managed to interest the Colburn family in USC, and he convinced a member to meet with Smith. After listening to Taber negotiate for the purchase of the collection, Smith got up from his desk, put his hands behind his back, paced a bit, looked at the Colburn representative, and said, "Didn't you say that the University of North Carolina wanted these rocks?" "Yes sir," was the answer. Smith then replied to the family member, "Well why don't you sell 'em to them and quit bothering us?" Despite Smith's disinterest, Taber nonetheless secured the prestigious collection for USC.[88]

While Smith worked hard, he was uniquely ill-suited for the University's presidency, failing to provide direction and leadership in either the political or the scholarly arenas. In a state where a public college's fortunes depended so much on the ability of its leaders to gain the support of the general public, Smith was unable to generate excitement about the good things happening at the University, such as the education of the state's veterans or the modest growth of graduate programs. In the words of Dean Prince, the University was "the poorest-sold institution in the State."[89]

Smith failed to develop and articulate a vision for the University at a critical time in its history. Dean Prince wrote that "the faculty has no idea as to what the long-view planning of the Administration and the Trustees is, and they don't know whether they even have such [a thing]."[90] To Smith and many of the trustees, the massive building program submitted to the legislature each year *was* their long-range plan. The lack of vision at the highest levels of the University was all the more striking considering what comparable institutions in other states were doing at the same time. For example, in late 1945 at the University of Georgia (an institution that suffered from problems similar to USC's), President Harmon Caldwell advanced a comprehensive plan to expand that university's teaching mission as well as its physical plant. Georgia's leaders realized that their university was much more than bricks and mortar.[91]

The result of Carolina's lack of direction was a muddled mission for the University as it tried to be all things to all people. Smith believed that the University existed mainly to offer professional training, and that it should offer courses in whatever subjects showed sufficient student demand. He said that the University was no longer a "gentlemen's college" that existed to train "teachers, lawyers and preachers" as it had been before the war. "Today," he said, "it is necessary that men and women train themselves to make a livelihood in this competitive world."[92]

The Peabody committee of 1946 recommended a higher education commission to coordinate the state's resources and prevent undirected growth, but the General Assembly ignored the report.[93] Likewise, trustee Donald Russell questioned USC's direction: "We are not going to make progress at the University until we definitely determine what is the character of this institution as opposed to Clemson, the Citadel and Winthrop." Russell sought a more focused mission. "We must determine what is to be our place in the overall picture of education in South Carolina," he observed. "Where are we to excel? What is our primary responsibility to the state?" Under the system in place in 1948, Russell claimed that he was "struck by the fact that . . . we are covering entirely too much and that we don't have an overriding philosophy of the function of this institution."[94] Despite Russell's objections, Smith and the other trustees did not provide a philosophy, and the uncertainty continued until Russell himself became the University's president in 1952.

The University's confused situation in the late 1940s was a legacy of a dilemma it had faced often in its post–Civil War history, a dilemma between mass professional education and high scholarship. In the decentralized system of higher education in South Carolina in the 1940s, playing such a dual role was impossible to do while maintaining high quality in both. The 1952 question of Robert M. Hutchins, former Chancellor of the University of Chicago, applied to the postwar University: "If we attempt to educate everybody, shall we end by educating nobody?"[95] Neither Norman Smith nor anyone else had a clear vision of what the University's unique place in the system of public higher education in South Carolina should be.[96] The consequence was that educational quality slipped, and the ship that was the University was adrift in the Admiral's hands.

As trustees and administrators struggled with Carolina's postwar problems, for the University's students, life in the second half of the 1940s was largely shaped by war veterans. The attitudes of student-veterans toward their education became a concern to faculty around the nation as soon as the GI Bill became law. College educators were uncertain about what to expect from having war-hardened men in their classrooms instead of the inexperienced teenage undergraduates to whom they were accustomed. Some predicted that the veterans would be exceptional students because of their added maturity, greater initiative, and wider experience. Others worried that veterans would come home from the war restless and would rebel against authority.[97] At the University of South Carolina, World War II veterans demonstrated the accuracy of both predictions.

The veterans' 1946–47 rebellion against President Smith and the status quo in South Carolina higher education showed their determination to change things in their home state. However, nationwide, anecdotal and empirical evidence showed that veterans were indeed more mature and better students than non-veterans. They adjusted quickly from the military to an academic lifestyle.[98] USC professors reported that in general, veterans showed more seriousness and a more genuine interest in classroom work than non-veterans, and that they expected excellence from their instructors. President Smith asserted that they were an asset to the University. He wrote, "As a whole, they are a splendid group of men, serious about getting an education and setting a higher standard of scholarship."[99] Fritz Hollings, a law student who enrolled in the school only one day after mustering out of the army in late 1945, recalled the heavy workload that veterans assumed as they rushed to complete their degrees and get jobs: "We were hungry for knowledge, and we were all playing 'catch up ball,' trying to hurry up and get out of there." He and other veterans worked through holidays to finish courses, and the faculty obliged by working with them. "Everybody was for the veteran," especially faculty, Hollings remembered.[100] Veterans raised the level of academic performance at the University. In general, they had better grades than non-veterans, earning themselves the nickname "D.A.R.s" (Damned Average Raisers).[101] Carolina's veterans were not surprised at their better-than-average performance. One wrote, "That is to be expected. We are older, more mature, and moreover, we know what we want."[102] Veterans wanted simply to be college students and not considered a special class. A University of Texas study concluded that the veteran wanted "to be a civilian and to be treated like one; to get an education, a job, marry and live a normal life." At Carolina, veterans insisted that "as soon as possible we want to forget that we are veterans. We are college students."[103] Most veterans had one primary idea in mind, as Robert E. McNair remembered; "most of us were married, most of us were interested in one thing, and that was getting through school and making a living."[104]

John Carl West, a veteran who entered the USC School of Law in the spring of 1946, remembered that Carolina in the years just after the war had "a very invigorating, very refreshing, very challenging atmosphere that permeated the whole university. We had come out of a difficult war and had lost a lot of our friends, but we had won. The world was now our oyster." Despite the fact that veterans simply wanted to be normal civilians, they realized that were not the average college student. West described himself and his classmates:

> We were full of ambition, full of pride and full of the desire to make something of ourselves and the state. I've often thought that our generation had a unique experience that molded both character and motivation. The war forced us into a situation in which we were involved in something bigger than ourselves, an unselfish crusade, we thought, to save the world as well as to save our own lives, and that gave us an unselfish commitment to goals that were bigger than we were. Our individual selfish goals were put in a wider perspective because when we came out, we were all very thankful to be alive. And coming back to college, we were thankful that we were getting an education, because many of us could not have afforded it [without the GI Bill].[105]

The presence of these older students, many with families, at least temporarily changed the "cliquish" student culture of the University. For many veterans, a college education was not a family birthright. They came to college to earn a degree that would land them a well-paying job upon graduation. Some 60 percent of them held part-time jobs.[106] The GI Bill made a University education accessible to all South Carolina veterans who were high school graduates, and they helped further democratize an institution formerly perceived as elitist. A *Gamecock* columnist writing under the pseudonym "Jane W. Dowe" wrote of the impact of war veterans at Carolina, "The G.I. is the finest thing that could have happened to an institution that had become more social than educational before the war." She continued, "Today . . . young people realize that intellect, culture and hard work are more important in college life than 'knowing the right people' or 'joining Dad's fraternity.' And the veteran is responsible."[107] Fritz Hollings remembered rejecting a fraternity bid outright. As an ambitious law student, he simply did not have time for such frivolity.[108]

Nonetheless other veterans did take part in student life, and as their tweed jackets replaced the Naval uniforms of V-12 trainees, veterans dominated campus organizations such as the social and honor fraternities. However, many took a different approach to college life. Older and more experienced than most other students, they admitted that many older campus traditions seemed "a little puerile."[109] For instance, many refused to be subject to the traditional hazing of the fraternities, or to wear "rat-caps," the garnet-and-black beanies required of all freshmen. Barbara McSwain wrote in the *Gamecock* that "no matter how hard they tried and wanted to, most of [the veterans] could not regain the enthusiasm and desire for college life they had before they went away."[110] The seriousness with which some veterans took their studies affected the campus community. Manning Harris commented in 1948, "Since the end of the war and the return of civilians to the campus, things are still amiss. The average age of the men students is greater than it would ordinarily be. Many students are married and have children." He expressed the main focus of many Carolina's veterans: "They are . . . obsessed with one idea . . . to get a degree and get out of school. They don't have the time for extra curricular activities, nor the patience."[111]

This characterization did not apply to all of Carolina's veterans, however. Despite their reputation as serious students, some veterans, especially the single ones, used their opportunity to return to college to "blow off steam." Most had been children of the Depression and were accustomed to scarcity. Coming of age during the war, they had never had the chance to enjoy the collegiate lifestyle of their prewar predecessors. Even if they had been to college during the war, their lives had been tightly restricted and they had experienced little of the freedom experienced by the typical collegiate. Veterans returned to college with wartime experiences that made them seem older than their years. Moreover, some had saved money during the war, and with the GI Bill stipend, a few men who had never had much money before felt flush with cash. Some remembered all-night poker games that sprang up whenever Veteran's Administration checks came. As a result, at least a few single veterans were as concerned with having fun in college as getting a degree.[112]

As college students will do, veterans and non-veterans alike managed to make Carolina an enjoyable place to be in the latter half of the 1940s. Veterans took over leadership positions in campus organizations, including the fraternities, which after the V-12 program disbanded moved back into the "tenements," the dormitories around the Horseshoe. Non-Greeks had their own campus organizations: the Men's and Women's Independents. Some students jokingly claimed to be majoring in "canteenology," and spent much of their leisure time around the soda fountain in the canteen in the basement of Maxcy College. Students continued to go to the "Y" in nearby Flinn Hall for a game of pool, ping-pong, or cards. They overflowed the two cafeterias on campus, located in Wade Hampton College and Steward's Hall (at the corner of Sumter and Greene Streets). Since these two facilities could not handle the huge enrollment, students often ate off-campus, frequenting the restaurants and boardinghouses that surrounded the campus, such as Mrs. McGregor's on College Street.[113]

Students did their best to revive the traditions of the prewar university that had disappeared during the tumult of the war and its aftermath. The student council tried to encourage campus friendliness by sponsoring "Hey, How You" week and insisting that students greet each other as they passed on the campus.[114] The exclusive dance clubs, the German, Damas, and Cotillion Clubs, continued to sponsor two formal balls a year for their members. Since University social regulations prohibited the individual Greek organizations from holding more than one formal event every two years, the German and Cotillion Club dances were even more important to their members. The annual festivities surrounding May Day and Homecoming were more democratic, and afforded all Carolina students an opportunity to put on their best and take part in old Carolina traditions.[115]

Students also developed new traditions in the postwar period. One was the annual "Powder Bowl," a flag football game played between the Delta Delta Delta and Pi Beta Phi sororities to raise money for charity. Another was the campus radio station, WUSC, which began regular broadcasting in 1947.[116] Two student organizations achieved national recognition for their excellence in the late 1940s. The debate team, under faculty coach Merrill Christophersen, consistently placed among the nation's leaders in forensics, and the team of Robert Bates and Robert Hirch (both naval trainees) won the national title in 1946.[117] In 1948, 1949, and 1950, the *Gamecock* received an All-American rating from the Associated Collegiate Press, rating it in the nine top student newspapers in its class in the nation.[118] Students greeted these outstanding performances with pride.

One University program continued in vain to try to reach national prominence: football. In 1939, the board of trustees took control of the athletic program, which had run up debts of $120,000, failed to make tuition payments for some student-athletes, and failed to pay other outstanding bills—forcing the University to make up the difference. In 1942 the board created a special committee to govern the athletic department, supported by a new Gamecock booster club known as the B.A.M. ("Buck-A-Month") Club, which had been organized in 1939 and 1940 to raise private money to benefit the cash-strapped Carolina athletic program. Sol Blatt led the board's move, and he became chairman of the new athletic committee, which became the final authority in athletic matters at the University. The committee never really functioned as a committee, however, and for all intents and purposes Blatt controlled Carolina's athletic program. Through his son (who succeeded his father on the athletic committee), Blatt maintained a strong influence on the athletic program even after leaving the board of trustees. In a situation similar to that at other southern state universities, the administration had little authority over athletics. The trustees minutes record that President Smith complained that "in general he was seldom consulted or kept informed of athletic activities."[119]

In the wake of the war, Blatt received board approval to keep all athletic department financial reports secret and to pay the head football coach $7,500 ($54,300)—the same salary drawn by President Smith. In addition, the board established a special $2,000 ($14,480) football recruiting fund which, in his words, Blatt could spend "without accounting to anyone, in order to secure good football material."[120] Blatt was trying to position the University for a run at greatness in collegiate football (or at least consistent wins over Clemson).

His efforts to achieve gridiron success appeared to work initially. The 1945 Gamecock football team, under the direction of first-year coach Johnny McMillan, managed to earn the Gamecock team its first-ever bowl bid. They traveled to the 1946 Gator Bowl in Jacksonville, where the Gamecocks lost to Wake Forest 26–14.[121] Despite better offers from other schools, in late 1945 prewar athletic director and head football coach Rex Enright returned to the University along with his entire prewar staff.[122]

In 1946, the Gamecock football team met with early success, setting the stage for a memorable "Big Thursday" game with Clemson. The students celebrated the annual October clash by continuously ringing the chapel bell for twenty-four hours prior to the game, a campus tradition. After building a bonfire on the campus, students paraded up Columbia's Main Street and burned a tiger effigy in front of the Jefferson Hotel, where the Clemson team was staying.[123] The game itself produced even more of an uproar. Out-of-state operators printed 4,000 counterfeit tickets to the game, for which all 26,000 legitimate tickets were sold well in advance. The result was chaos. The Carolina stadium, with 17,500 seats, was filled with 30,000 people, many who crashed the gates when their tickets were ruled forgeries. The only unoccupied space in the stadium was the playing field itself, which had to be cleared several times during the game when the crowd spilled onto the field. U.S. Secretary of State James F. Byrnes attended the game, and because the throng blocked the view from his box seats, he joined them on the sidelines. Carolina won the bizarre affair, 26–14.[124]

The 1947 season was another winner for the Gamecocks, who accepted a bid to play in the Dixie Bowl in Memphis, but the game was canceled because of a national coal shortage.[125] The Big Thursday game continued to be the big attraction, with the postwar years witnessing an increase in the intensity of the Carolina-Clemson rivalry. In 1947, the Blue Key honor fraternity and student government worked to try to smooth the increasingly hostile relationship between the schools by encouraging the two sides to "bury the hatchet" and reduce the ill feelings generated in the state by the festivities surrounding Big Thursday.[126] Despite their efforts, the rivalry continued to prove attractive to South Carolinians. In response to the infamous "gate-crashing" game and continued high attendance at the Big Thursday game, in 1948 the legislature approved a $175,000 ($989,844) appropriation to nearly double the size of the fairgrounds stadium to 32,000 seats.[127] While Carolina's students and faculty lived and worked in overcrowded dormitories and classrooms, the state found the money to build a stadium filled for only a few hours each year. By 1949, the athletic department's $326,000 ($1,863,347) budget, supported by B.A.M. Club donations, was more than three times larger than that of the University's libraries. The money did not generate much of a return, however, for the 1949 team finished with a 4–6 record.[128]

That South Carolinians would spend large sums for football scholarships and a stadium while neglecting academics demonstrated attitudes prevalent in the state. Students noticed. General morale suffered as they realized that Carolina was not providing them the best education available. Tired of hearing over and over about the institution's past glories while living with present problems, students became disillusioned with contemporary conditions on the old campus. Editorials in the *Gamecock* reflected the sentiment. One particularly cynical student editorial read: "It is the height of shortsightedness and absurdity to pour money into this rat-hole of hired education, the Puniversity of South Carolina. After the shiny wrapper of tradition is removed, only a mass of crumbling walls and antiquated equipment remains." The writer maintained, "Not only do we have the poorest state school in terms of quality, but it is the smallest in the South. Thank God for Guam. (Mississippi is ahead of us.)"[129] On another occasion, *Gamecock* editorial writer Carroll Gilliam wrote of South Carolina's paltry appropriations to the state's six institutions of higher education, "We're knocking ourselves out trying to spread a teaspoon of jam on six pieces of bread while the youth of South Carolina goes hungry for a modern education in the twentieth century."[130]

Through the late 1940s, the *Gamecock* continually editorialized for the General Assembly to do something about the conditions at their school. The second attempt to move the University's campus was a part of the student reaction to the poor state of the campus.[131] Because of a shortage of general maintenance funding, the buildings themselves were literally crumbling. It was a common occurrence for large chunks of the plaster ceilings in older buildings on the Horseshoe to fall on their inhabitants—a condition indicative of the state's unwillingness to provide quality facilities for public higher education.[132]

Elsewhere, the campus looked "bedraggled." The *USC Alumni News* reported that in the immediate postwar years, "behind practically every building on the Horseshoe were little shacks full of assorted supplies, tools, even junk. . . . The central campus needed regrassing, shrubs needed careful pruning, new plantings were required."[133] In the spring of 1949, the *Gamecock* summed up the overall feeling on campus: "There is much dissatisfaction among those who attend the university and among those who instruct the students when they find their facilities for instruction crippled."[134]

One reason for the low fortunes of the University in the late 1940s, in addition to the competition for funding with other state colleges and athletics, was the state's determination to maintain racial segregation. Racial segregation drained energy and resources from any efforts to improve the state's educational system. It was a constant, if not always obvious, accompaniment to the debates about higher education in South Carolina, especially in the late 1930s and 1940s. The New Deal and World War II set in motion forces that ultimately desegregated South Carolina's colleges and universities—another watershed event in the postwar history of the University of South Carolina.

Led by Charles Hamilton Houston and his assistant Thurgood Marshall, in the 1930s the National Association for the Advancement of Colored People (NAACP) began a campaign to challenge the legality of Jim Crow in the South. They focused their initial efforts on higher education, where southern states made few provisions for graduate and professional training for blacks and where the principle of separate but equal was most egregiously violated. Houston's efforts culminated in the 1938 *Gaines v. Canada* ruling. In that case, the U.S. Supreme Court required Missouri, which had no law school for blacks, to admit a black applicant to the white law school at the University of Missouri unless the state provided a school for blacks that was "substantially equal" to the one provided for whites.[135] In the wake of this ruling, in 1938 and 1939, two black South Carolinians, Charles B. Bailey and Rollin P.

Green, applied for admission to the University of South Carolina's law school and graduate school, respectively. The University board of trustees referred the issue to a special committee, headed by Sol Blatt. The board stonewalled the two men, prevented publicity, and took no action on the applications, apparently hoping the issue would go away on its own.[136]

In this case, the issue did go away, but the issue of racial segregation subsided only temporarily. During the early 1940s, black Carolinians became increasingly active in their attempts to abolish Jim Crow restrictions in South Carolina, and their attempts to change the segregated system of higher education focused on South Carolina's state university. In 1944, the state legislature, fearful that attempts to enter the University would become more frequent and aggressive, gave the State Agricultural and Mechanical College (the state college for black Carolinians) authorization (but no money) to establish a law school, a medical school, and other graduate programs.[137] The following year, the state commissioned Wilfred Callcott, the dean of USC's Graduate School, to determine the feasibility of opening a graduate school at State College to alleviate the legal pressure on USC's graduate programs. When black Carolinian Cleveland M. McQueen applied to the University's graduate program in education in 1946, the legislature quickly acted on Callcott's recommendation and appropriated $20,000 ($139,828) to open a similar graduate program in education at the Orangeburg school. It also appropriated $5,000 ($34,957) to fund tuition payments for black Carolinians who wanted to enter graduate programs not offered at South Carolina State. The funds would be used to send these students to out-of-state universities that would accept black students.[138]

In spite of these preemptive efforts to hold off racial desegregation, a direct challenge to South Carolina's system of racially segregated higher education came in June of 1946, when John Wrighten, a black World War II veteran from Edisto Island who had earlier tried unsuccessfully to gain admission to the College of Charleston, applied for admission to the University of South Carolina Law School. Registrar R. C. Needham flatly refused to admit him. In July, another well-qualified African American veteran, Daniel George Sampson, tried to apply to the law school, but was denied as well. John Wrighten refused to accept the denial and sued in federal court for admission, with the NAACP supplying him legal assistance from Harold Boulware of Columbia and Robert Carter and Thurgood Marshall of the national NAACP office. The NAACP lawyers based their case on the precedent set by the *Gaines* decision, arguing that the University should either admit Wrighten or the state should provide a separate law school for African Americans. In trial testimony, President Smith maintained that the University refused Wrighten admission because to admit him would violate the state constitution, in which Article XI expressly prohibited whites and blacks from attending the same schools. Furthermore, the University's lawyers argued that the state had made "ample provision" to establish a Jim Crow law school for blacks, referring to a $60,000 ($454,950) state appropriation for a law and graduate school at South Carolina State, passed in 1946 just after Wrighten filed his suit.[139]

The federal judge in the case, J. Waties Waring of Charleston, gave the state three options: admit Wrighten to USC's law school, provide him adequate legal education elsewhere in the state, or close the University's law school altogether. South Carolina chose the second option, and quickly made plans to open the new law school in the fall of 1947.[140] However, Wrighten continued to press his case, arguing that the Orangeburg law school was not "substantially equal" to the University's (as required by law and Wrighten's decision), and he refused to attend it.[141] The lawyer for the state, T. C. Callison, argued that South Carolina was not discriminating at all and that it had never provided legal education for black Carolinians simply because there had never been an applicant. This legal argument seemed to invite black activism and was difficult to square with that of James K. Price, the University's attorney, who told the judge, "We want the Negroes to be educated. . . . But if they'll just leave us alone we'll work these things out with friendship and love between the two races."[142]

In September 1947, South Carolina State College opened a law school with a dean, three faculty members, and four students. Judge Waring ultimately ruled that it was "almost impossible to intellectually compare" the University's law school, with 342 students, and South Carolina State's, with four.[143] The General Assembly, however, was committed to separate-but-equal education and continued to pour money into the Orangeburg law school.[144] They appropriated $200,000 ($1,131,250) for a law building and $30,000 ($169,688) for a law library at South Carolina State in 1948. In addition to this money, at the same time it appropriated $250,000 ($1,414,062) for a similar building in Columbia. Judge Waring expressed dismay at the state's sudden spending frenzy for legal education, done only "to prevent the meeting of whites and Negroes in classrooms."[145] Dean Samuel Prince of the University's law school explained to legislators inquiring into the high costs of maintaining the two law schools and two graduate schools, "Gentlemen, well I'll tell you, the price of prejudice is very high."[146] Paying this high price, Judge Waring decided, was the South Carolina General Assembly's decision to make, and he dismissed Wrighten's case against the University in June of 1948. The state, he ruled, had complied with his order by creating a separate law school for African Americans.[147] Separate but equal higher education had been vindicated in South Carolina.

Because of the state's determination to maintain segregated institutions, the University of South Carolina and its students suffered. The effort to fund a new law school, a new graduate school in education, and a program to pay out-of-state tuition for graduate programs drew funding away from the University's other cash-strapped programs. For example, the student-faculty ratio in the University's law school remained high. The South Carolina State law school had four faculty members for an enrollment of some eight students, while the University had five full-time and nine part-time faculty for an enrollment of 342.[148]

Some USC students insisted that the state was sacrificing the quality of their education at the altar of Jim Crow. Carroll Gilliam, writing for the *Gamecock*, called for the state to stop pouring money into duplicate programs. "To continue dual education is to continue throwing tax money into too many needless drains," he wrote. "This is not sensible! Yesterday's solutions are not today's answers." He continued with a scathing indictment of the state's policy: "South Carolina, as everyone knows, needs better educational facilities . . . yet duplicity of institutions robs us of the full opportunities of the sums of money spent for these purposes. . . . It is time to look at the calendar. The date is 1948, not 1868!"[149] Despite Gilliam's pleas, the majority of University alumni, students, and the state's white citizens agreed with the administration when it continued to flatly deny the applications of black students, even though maintaining racial segregation clearly put a burden on the University and hindered its development.[150]

Rutledge L. Osborne, who was elected to a seat on the board of trustees in 1947 and served until 1975, later summed up the conditions at the University in the immediate postwar era: "At the end of World War II, the University was in a rather poor and run-down condition. . . . The academic curriculum was not what it should have been. The physical plant was not in good order and salaries were ridiculously low. The problem was, and always has been, one of inadequate finances. One result was that many of our professional schools were not nationally accredited. In the immediate postwar period the University's situation was all but impossible—obsolete physical plant, overcrowded, understaffed, underpaid."[151] For South Carolina's decision makers, higher education was clearly not a top priority. Maintaining white supremacy was. While most state institutions made do with inadequate budgets, the cost of the duplicate law school at South Carolina State and other programs designed to safeguard segregated higher education in South Carolina may have been the margin needed to improve salaries, lower teaching loads and improve overall academic quality in academic programs at all of the Palmetto State's public colleges, including the University of South Carolina. However, quality in its state university was not a prominent issue in late 1940s South Carolina, and the University of South Carolina paid the price of prejudice.

In late September 1940, workers demolished the University of South Carolina's first president's house, which had stood at the head of the Horseshoe since 1807. The demolition made room for the University's new library (now McKissick Museum).

At 46 acres, the University of South Carolina campus—seen here in a 1941 aerial photograph—was the smallest of any state university in the South. The dome of the University Library (completed in 1940 and today serving as McKissick Museum) is clearly visible at the head of the Horseshoe. Wardlaw College and the old Field House stand in the foreground.

President J. Rion McKissick (1884–1944) was one of the most beloved figures to ever serve at Carolina. His grave in front of the South Caroliniana Library is the only one on the USC campus. Students gave him the bicycle in 1942.

Arney R. Childs (1890–1957) served as professor of history and dean of women from 1935 to 1957.

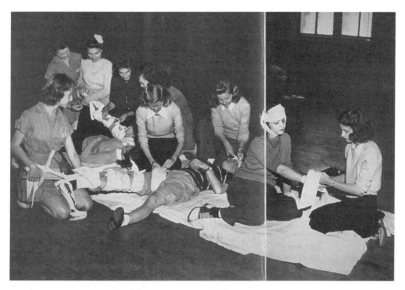

USC women participate in first aid training, 1942. The Red Cross sponsored first aid classes for students as a contribution to the war effort.

The "Corsairs," the Naval ROTC drill platoon, march in front of the new University Library, 1942.

Norman M. Smith (1883–1968), twentieth president of
the University of South Carolina, 1945–1952.

Frustrated with their overcrowded campus, USC students (many of them World War II
veterans) protested in the rain on the steps of the state House in 1947. They demanded
increased state appropriations to improve conditions on the Carolina campus.

The "Carovet" Apartments (short for "Carolina Veterans") were located along Bull Street about a mile north of the campus. These war surplus buildings housed married students and their families from 1948 to 1960, when they were demolished.

Students relax in the popular canteen in the basement of Maxcy College, 1948.

The 1946 Big Thursday game between Carolina and Clemson at the State Fairgrounds was as memorable for what happened off the field as on it. In the infamous "gate-crashing" game, counterfeiters sold 4,000 tickets beyond the sellout of 26,000 legitimate tickets, and the resulting crowd overwhelmed the capacity of the stadium. On several occasions, the game had to be stopped to clear the field of spectators. On this play, Bobby Giles (39) scampered for a 62-yard touchdown to give Carolina a 6-0 first-quarter lead. Carolina won the game, 26-17.

To help ease the overcrowding brought by the GI Bill and World War II's veterans, the federal government paid to install these war surplus buildings on Gibbes Green in 1948. The wooden buildings held classrooms, laboratories, and offices. This view of Gibbes Green was taken near the corner of Pickens and Greene Streets, c. 1948.

Students in Professor Francis Townsend's biology class prepare to conduct a dissection in old LeConte College, 1948.

Donald and Virginia Russell revived morale at Carolina during his tenure as USC's twenty-first president, from 1952 to 1957, bringing a sense of style and renewed optimism to the campus.

Chester C. Travelstead, dean of the School of Education from 1953 to 1956, was dismissed after advocating compliance with the U.S. Supreme Court's integration decision in *Brown v. Board of Education.*

Coleman Karesh (1903–1977) was a 1925 graduate of the USC School of Law and, after joining the school's faculty in 1937, was one of its best-loved teachers until his retirement in 1972. In 1957, he received the first Russell Award for Distinguished Teaching, Carolina's highest faculty award.

Havilah Babcock (1898–1964) served as professor of English from 1926 to 1964. A writer of outdoor fiction and one of the University's most popular teachers, his vocabulary building course called "I Want a Word" often filled classrooms to overflowing.

Senator John F. Kennedy delivers the commencement address on the Horseshoe, June 1957.

Elaborate May Day festivities were a rite of spring on the USC campus from the early twentieth century until the 1970s. Here, the May Court weaves its way around the Maypole, 1957.

The Russell House, the long-awaited student union building, under construction, 1955.

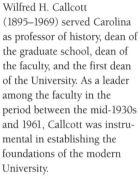

Wilfred H. Callcott
(1895–1969) served Carolina
as professor of history, dean of
the graduate school, dean of
the faculty, and the first dean
of the University. As a leader
among the faculty in the
period between the mid-1930s
and 1961, Callcott was instrumental in establishing the
foundations of the modern
University.

Robert L. Sumwalt, dean
of the School of Engineering,
1943–1957, served as acting
president from 1957 to 1959,
and the University's twenty-
second president from 1959
to 1962.

The University's first extension campus opened in the basement of the Florence County Public Library in 1957. USC Florence became an independent institution in 1970 under the name Francis Marion College (now University).

The University of South Carolina's Beaufort campus opened in 1959 with 82 students. The administration building was completed in 1852 and served as the center of Beaufort College, a private college formerly located on the site.

USC (in white) tips off against North Carolina State in the old Field House along Sumter Street, 1958.

Carolina Stadium (pictured here in 1959) at the State Fairgrounds was the home of the Big Thursday football matchup between Carolina and Clemson through 1959.

The Zodiacs entertain at an off-campus dance, 1961. Despite the University's ban on black performers at on-campus events, students wanted rock and roll bands to perform at their parties, and African-American artists were in high demand.

The controversial January 11, 1963, issue of the *Gamecock*, featuring a photograph of Henrie D. Monteith, brought complaints that the newspaper had given publicity to a "negro publicity seeker and agitator." However, it signaled that the exclusion of African American South Carolinians from the University of South Carolina would soon end.

Surrounded by SLED agents and reporters, Robert Anderson, Henrie Monteith, and James Solomon walk past McKissick Library on the day they desegregated the University of South Carolina, September 11, 1963.

An aerial view of the USC campus, looking north, circa 1962, shows the expansion of the campus in the years following World War II. In the foreground is Blossom Street, which represented the southern boundary of the campus in the early 1960s.

Air Force ROTC on parade in front of the Undergraduate Library, 1965. The Air Force ROTC program was established on the USC campus in 1949. The Undergraduate Library, completed in 1959, was substantially enlarged and renamed the Thomas Cooper Library in 1976. In the background, the third set of Honeycomb dormitories is under construction.

3 | AN EDUCATIONAL RENAISSANCE

1950–1959

If South Carolina is to maintain its accelerated momentum in progressive growth and development, it must equip its own leadership through education and training in our own institutions of higher learning on a level equal with the best anywhere.

South Carolina Fiscal Survey Commission, 1956

The university is the focal point for educational progress in our state. . . . If you want to build education, you have to start with the college.

Donald Russell, 1952

■

In the life of the postwar University of South Carolina, the year 1950 saw the institution in the midst of a transition period. This pivotal year saw a marked decline in the enrollment of World War II veterans, most of whom had completed their degrees in the five years since the end of the war. There was also a consequent falloff in general enrollment that coincided with the outbreak of war in Korea. The year also saw the long-awaited beginning of a broad construction program to relieve campus overcrowding. Finally, 1950 marked the election of James F. Byrnes as governor of South Carolina, an event that had a significant impact on the future of the University of South Carolina.

The level of veteran enrollment at the University in the immediate post–World War II years peaked in the fall of 1947 at 2,743, and the overall enrollment that semester also peaked at 4,614. A slow but steady decline followed, but the number of veterans remained over 2,000 until 1949, while overall enrollment stood at more than 3,800. In 1950 however, veteran enrollment dropped precipitously, and by the fall of 1951 there were only 574 vets at Carolina. Also, in the spring of 1951 overall enrollment fell below 3,000 for the first time since 1945. The decline in the numbers of veterans on campus accompanied a rise in the proportion of females in the student body, which reached over 26 percent. The veteran enrollment at Carolina dwindled until the mid-1950s, when a second wave of vets, this time from the Korean War, began returning to college using federal benefits provided by their own version of the GI Bill.[1]

With the departure of the veterans, University life began a return to "normalcy," and officials predicted that such reduced levels of enrollment would continue indefinitely.[2] The academic calendar reflected the return to peacetime stability. In mid-1949 the administration abandoned the twelve-week summer term that had operated in 1946, 1947, and 1948 for the benefit of veterans and reverted to the prewar schedule of a single nine-week summer term.[3] Students who came of age after the war rejoiced that the serious veterans were being replaced on campus by young freshmen direct from high school, who would be "ready for the full college life" and have the youthful spirit to participate in extracurricular activities. These students longed for an idyllic college career. A *Gamecock* editorialist wrote, "Carolina has revived. The population has completed its evolution from a mass of weary and mature people who have seen and tired of the world. Now an eager group whose main ambition in life is not to graduate and support a family forms the majority. . . . Spirit is high; the long awaited day has arrived."[4]

Campus spirits may have been high in 1950 as students looked to the future, but the return to normalcy was not complete. The changes that World War II had brought lingered on, and the outbreak of the Korean War brought armed conflict to a new generation. The war mobilization of the early 1950s, while it did not transform the University or evoke patriotic fervor as had World War II, did bring the reality of war to some USC students. Men in the upper half of their classes could defer the draft until graduation, creating an important incentive to do well academically. Many men not drafted joined local reserve units or one of the University's two ROTC programs as another strategy to defer active service. By late 1951 some 70 percent of Carolina's males were either veterans or were serving in one of the armed forces' reserve components.[5]

Meanwhile, in 1950, the University's board of trustees at last decided to proceed with a postwar building program to modernize the institution's inadequate academic facilities. Since 1947, Norman Smith and the board of trustees had not spent the nearly $1,500,000 ($9,151,685) that the General Assembly had appropriated for construction. They were waiting until construction prices dropped, the University received additional funds to purchase land, and the federal government provided matching funds. By 1950, however, construction prices showed no signs of decline and the much-anticipated program of federal matching funds failed in Congress. Even more importantly, some members of the South Carolina General Assembly threatened that if the University did not spend the funds it had been allocated, they would rescind the appropriation.[6] Thus, in March 1950, the board of trustees decided to begin the building program using all unspent appropriations (a total of some $1,735,000 [$9,813,594]), despite the objections of President Smith.[7] Students rejoiced that the delayed postwar building program would finally get under way.[8]

The first buildings on the University's wish list were a long-needed science building, an engineering building, and an administration building. Since the University lacked the authorization to buy new land with the available funds, the trustees chose sites on existing University property for the three newest buildings. Manpower shortages and difficulties in obtaining building materials, caused in part by the massive construction at the new Savannah River Plant, delayed the progress of construction, but by mid-1951 all three projects were under way.[9]

The new science building was the biggest project, and when completed in 1952, it was the University's largest building. Built on the eastern edge of Gibbes Green along Pickens Street, it offered the departments of chemistry, biology, geology, geography, and pharmacy much-improved facilities. The trustees transferred the name of the old science building, LeConte (named in honor of John and Joseph LeConte, renowned scientists of the antebellum faculty), to the new building and renamed the old science building Barnwell College in honor of Robert W. Barnwell, former U.S. senator and twice chief executive of the South Carolina College and University (1835–1841 and 1866–1873).[10]

The second project was the engineering laboratory, also completed in the summer of 1952. Built on the south side of Greene Street midway between Main and Sumter Streets, the facade of the new College of Engineering contrasted with the other buildings constructed during the Smith administration (which were designed by University architect J. Carroll Johnson). The Columbia architectural firm of Lyles, Bissett, Carlisle and Wolff designed the new engineering building, and it reflected a modern design with an exposed brick face, smooth lines, and a boxlike appearance. The new College of Engineering was the first University building to break with the traditional architecture of the old campus. It provided much-needed space to the school, which had been located in Hamilton College since World War II.[11]

The last construction project of Smith's administration was an administration building, which offered a centralized location for University offices that had been scattered across the campus in places like DeSaussure College (the location of President Smith's office) and other dormitories, as well as in former faculty residences and the basement of the McKissick Library. Designed by Carroll Johnson and completed in July 1952 just north of McKissick, the new administration building reflected the traditional lines of the old buildings of the Horseshoe. The new construction allowed the University to demolish four of the war surplus buildings on Gibbes Green that had served as administrative offices.[12]

The 1950 decision to proceed with a construction program came while James F. Byrnes, former congressman, U.S. senator, U.S. Supreme Court justice, "assistant president," and U.S. secretary of state, was campaigning for the office of governor of South Carolina. Byrnes' election in the fall of 1950 proved to be a significant event not only for the University of South Carolina, but for all the schools of the state. Byrnes assumed office promising an "educational revolution," and he vowed to improve all of the state's schools. Like Strom Thurmond before him, "Jimmy" Byrnes promised to improve the state's colleges, in addition to its elementary and secondary schools. The difference was that Byrnes, with a worldwide renown greater than that of any South Carolinian since John C. Calhoun, could unite the disparate factions of South Carolina politics, and he delivered on his promise.[13]

Shortly after Byrnes's inauguration in January 1951, rumors began to swirl in South Carolina that President Smith would resign his post, to be replaced by Byrnes's protégé, Donald S. Russell, a Spartanburg attorney and member of the University's board of trustees.[14] The rumors ultimately proved true. In October 1951, Smith submitted his resignation to the board of trustees (effective June 1952). The board immediately accepted Smith's resignation.[15]

Reflecting the general malaise at the University in the late 1940s and early 1950s, some Carolina students rejoiced at Smith's resignation. In an editorial entitled, "Let's Not Have Any More Snuffies!," *Gamecock* editor Mordecai Persky responded to the news with a brutal appraisal of Smith's tenure as president. "Since he was rushed in under the wings of shifty state politicians, Smith and his administration have been the acme of failure," wrote the editor. "In all fairness to this man, he has tried in his inadequate way to do his job. He has spent up to fourteen hours a day working at being a college president. For various reasons, these 14-hour days have resulted in monumental bungles and a continuous loss of prestige for the university." Persky concluded, "In retrospect, the Admiral's term of office can serve as a criterion for selecting the next president. Smith has shown us what we do not want." Widely criticized for the frankness of his editorial, Persky offered a mild retraction the following week, but the editorial seemed to accurately represent the opinion of a significant portion of Carolina students.[16]

Others in the state were a bit more measured in their evaluation of President Smith, offering traditional goodwill farewells. The *State* praised him for his hard work and his ingenuity in overcoming the difficulties presented by World War II's veterans.[17] The board of trustees bestowed on him the honorary title of president emeritus, a title they had also given former Leonard T.

Baker upon his retirement in 1945. They praised Smith for laboring "long hours over the trying problems of the University, taxing his energy unsparingly and unstintingly," and expressed a "sincere gratitude and appreciation for his devoted services" during the challenging postwar period.[18]

Despite the many criticisms he had endured while president, Smith pointed with pride to the four major buildings constructed during his tenure, and to developments such as the expansion of the graduate school, accreditation of programs in engineering, chemistry and social work, and to the development of a program to encourage junior faculty to complete advanced degrees.[19] He left behind a sum of over $30,000 ($154,164) in the University's treasury, accumulated as a result of his refusal to accept many of the perquisites of office (including an automobile and a $2,500 ($14,289) raise in 1949). After 1951, Smith refused to accept his entire $10,000 ($51,388) a-year salary, working for only $1 during his final year as president. With these funds, the board of trustees established the Norman Murray Smith Scholarships, given to a junior undergraduate who exhibits leadership, integrity, and high scholarship.[20]

Smith departed with a final request to the trustees on behalf of the next president, whoever it might be. He asked that the board furnish the University president a home somewhere in Columbia, a provision he had done without. William S. Currell (president from 1914–1922) had been the last Carolina president to live in the University's original president's home, built in 1807 at the head of the Horseshoe. After Currell, most Carolina presidents had lived off-campus, and the University demolished the old home in 1940 to make room for the McKissick Library. J. Rion McKissick lived in the Wauchope House, a faculty duplex on the Horseshoe (built in 1854 and now the President's Home), as result of his tenure as dean of the School of Journalism. As president, Smith lived at two different locations in Columbia. For his first three years he lived in the Columbia Hotel; he then rented an apartment on College Street for the remainder of his tenure. In response to Smith's request, in October 1951 the board of trustees allocated $100,000 ($525,484) to secure a permanent president's home.[21]

The question as to who would occupy the new home was nearly a foregone conclusion the moment President Smith announced his resignation. Trustee Donald Stuart Russell was the leading candidate, and many, including faculty, students, and alumni, urged his selection.[22] However, others in the state saw such a choice as a reflection of the same forces that brought Admiral Smith to Columbia: the overbearing influence of South Carolina's leading politicians. The *Charleston News and Courier* and the *Greenville News* both decried the possibility that politics would again determine the choice of the University's next president and continue to hamper its progress. "No

Politics, Please!" asked the *News,* while the *News and Courier* stated that "the greatest need of the University of South Carolina is independence from political influences and pressures."[23] "[Russell's] appointment would bear out the original reports that the politicians intended to continue political rule over the University," wrote the *News and Courier's* editor.[24] Some South Carolinians insisted that Russell had his own political aspirations, having an eye on the governor's chair or a U.S. Senate seat, and were reluctant to have an office-seeker take over the University.[25]

However, despite these scattered reservations, when Governor Byrnes proudly announced that the trustees had indeed chosen his longtime friend and protégé as the University's next president, the campus community and its friends greeted the news with nearly unanimous acclaim.[26] The *Gamecock* wrote of the December 20, 1951, announcement, "We of the University— faculty, alumni and students—received a premature Christmas gift this year in the form of an acceptance of the presidency of our beloved institution by Mr. Donald Russell." The appointment and the charges of political involvement in the choice drew the attention of *Time* magazine, which compared Russell's selection to that of Admiral Smith. As in the choice of Smith, *Time* wrote, with the appointment of Russell "the odor of politics arose again. But the scent was false. Students, alumni and facultymen had been consulted, and all agreed that Russell was a good choice." *Time* continued, "In both size . . . and stature, the university still ranks far below such Southern campuses as Virginia and Chapel Hill. Both able and powerfully connected, Donald Russell might prove to be just the man to bring it up to par."[27]

The widespread acclaim for the selection of Donald Russell came with good reason. In South Carolina, Russell was a known and highly respected individual. Described by colleagues as "brilliant" and "intellectually gifted," Russell brought a sharp mind, gentlemanly manner, and quiet confidence to a campus that had stagnated since the end of World War II.[28] A native of Mississippi, Russell moved to Chester, South Carolina, after the death of his father (when Russell was four). He entered the University at age fifteen, and while a student put himself through school by pumping gas in a filling station. He soon became a favorite of president William D. Melton, with whose administration Russell's would later be compared. Russell graduated from Carolina in 1925, first in his class. He then entered the University's law school and helped pay his way through that program by teaching undergraduate history. Russell graduated first in his law class in 1928.[29]

After leaving Carolina, he entered the practice of law in Union and soon thereafter joined James F. Byrnes's firm in Spartanburg. Following the Japanese attack on Pearl Harbor, Russell went to Washington, where he joined Byrnes when the latter became director of economic and war stabilization in the Roosevelt administration (a post often referred to as "assistant president"), with Russell serving as assistant to the director. After a short tour in the army, where he served in Europe's Supreme Allied Headquarters during 1944, Russell returned to Washington to serve as deputy director of war mobilization and reconversion (again serving under Byrnes, who was director). When Byrnes became U.S. secretary of state under Harry Truman, Russell was named assistant secretary for administration.[30]

Russell served in this high-level position at a formative moment in the nation's history, when the U.S. dropped the atomic bomb on Japan and a cold war developed with the Soviet Union. When Byrnes resigned as secretary of state in early 1947, Russell followed him to the lucrative Washington law firm Hogan & Hartson. In addition to the law practice, Russell capitalized on his Washington network and investment expertise to enter several businesses, and soon became well-off financially. In the meantime, in 1947 the General Assembly elected Russell to a seat on the University of South Carolina's board of trustees in the wake of the dual-office-holding controversy. Russell quickly became a leading trustee, demonstrating a level of vision, political acumen, and clear thinking that later characterized his administration. With Russell's acceptance of the University's presidency, the institution's friends believed they finally had a man who could lead them out of the educational wilderness.[31]

In a sense, Russell's acceptance of the University presidency reflected a path he followed throughout his early career: serving under James F. Byrnes. However, at the University, Donald Russell emerged as a prominent state figure in his own right. Despite the apparent similarities between Russell and Norman Smith (political ties, Washington experience, and the lack of an earned doctorate), Russell was everything Smith was not. First, he had the respect of faculty. According to Rutledge L. Osborne, when the board of trustees began a search for a new president and they consulted the faculty, no man other than Russell was suggested or considered. "The choice was unanimous," said Osborne.[32]

Russell earned this respect not only because of his vast experience in the highest levels of government, but because many faculty remembered him as an exemplary student. In addition, he was extremely well read (especially in history and literature) and described by contemporaries as a "bookish" intellectual with a penchant for collecting first editions of the classics. At forty-six, Russell was young in comparison to the sixty-nine-year-old Smith. Along with his attractive wife, Virginia (a former May Queen at Carolina, class of 1927), and their four children (ranging in age from fourteen years to seven months), the Russells projected a youthful, vigorous image and were a striking contrast to Norman Smith.[33]

Almost immediately, the Russell appointment and the prestige it brought to the University generated a new sense of enthusiasm. The arrival of the new president on campus represented the onset of springtime at an institution mired in a long, cold winter since World War II. *Gamecock* columnist Lowell Ross wrote that the change of administration brought "the biggest boost to student morale that I have witnessed on the Carolina campus."[34]

The newly renovated president's home served as a visible symbol of the new spirit. Donald and Virginia Russell wanted to live on campus, and the vacant Wauchope House dual faculty residence on the Horseshoe seemed a logical choice. This 1854 faculty home served as a dormitory for women after the death of J. Rion McKissick and housed the Alpha Delta Pi and Pi Beta Phi sororities for a time in the immediate postwar period. Since 1949, it had been vacant and in disrepair. With the $100,000 ($525,484) designated for the purpose and a personal donation of $5,000 ($26,274) from President-elect Russell and his wife, in March 1952 the trustees decided to renovate the Wauchope House as the new University of South Carolina president's home.[35]

The 1952 renovation transformed the decrepit duplex into an elegant home designed to be both a center for entertaining as well as a home for the president and his family. The large downstairs rooms designed for official functions were lined with bookshelves to house Russell's large personal book collection. Decorated by Virginia Russell in cooperation with renowned New York City interior designers, the home and its occupants projected a sense of charm and good taste. The Russells strived to make their new home a welcome place for the students and faculty whom they frequently entertained. For example, the family invited every Carolina senior to dinner in their home at least once during his or her final year.[36]

Fortunately for the University community, there was even more substance than style to Donald Russell. He assumed office in September 1952, taking over from Francis W. Bradley, the dean of the faculty who served as acting president after Norman Smith's retirement in June. Immediately, Russell articulated a clear vision of where he wanted to take the University, and then provided the leadership necessary to get it there. His dream for the institution, he said upon his introduction as president, was simply "a great university—one for which we'll have to apologize to no one." "Soon," he said, "we're going to quit apologizing to the University of North Carolina. We're going to build an institution that is as good as North Carolina's."[37]

Donald Russell wanted to make the University of South Carolina fully a part of the "renaissance" in education that was the centerpiece of Jimmy Byrnes's term as governor. He recognized that for South Carolina to advance, it had to utilize its human capital in a way it had never done before. "In population, wealth, income, and industrial activity South Carolina is athrob and on the march," Russell told the State Budget and Control board. "But the momentum of that progress . . . can only be sustained by an enlightened public policy which will assure to every talent the full exploitation of its mental potential." He continued, "Public education . . . is not a luxury; it is, in truth, the imperative of this dynamic age of which we are a part."[38]

As a trustee in the late 1940s, Russell had been the chief advocate of focusing the University's mission vis-à-vis the state's other public colleges. "We should not try to operate . . . a school which will enable a student . . . to get any course he wants," he told the board in 1948. "You could just as well assure a boy who goes to Clemson that he will be able to get any course he wants there," he added.[39] Russell believed that the University of South Carolina should be the liberal arts college of South Carolina, as distinguished from Clemson, The Citadel, and Winthrop. When President Smith declared that the University was no longer "a gentleman's college," which produced only "teachers, lawyers and preachers," Russell responded that "an institution dedicated to turning out lawyers, teachers and preachers performs one of the most essential functions of our university system."[40] Russell thought that the University had the primary responsibility for leadership of South Carolina's entire educational system. The University, he believed, "should be the capstone of the whole educational firmament of South Carolina. It should radiate leadership to the public educational system and to the other colleges."[41] Thus, in the mid-1950s Russell envisioned USC as the "capstone" in the arch that was the state's system of public education.

Building the faculty was the means Donald Russell would use to reach the desired end—a great university for South Carolina. As a trustee, he had remarked to the board in a comment that was an implicit criticism of the earlier administration, "The University consists not in buildings, but in faculty. I think too many colleges have been destroyed because the Board of Trustees tried to build a monument to themselves in the way of buildings rather than build faculty."[42] Thus, the first requirement for a great institution, he said shortly after becoming president, was a "faculty adequate in numbers and soundly qualified in scholarship, professional competency and integrity."[43] "My supreme objective," he said, "is the development of a great faculty."[44]

The faculty needed improvement in both quality and quantity, and the new administration looked to provide both. In the first year alone, Carolina added twenty-eight new professors, lightening the teaching loads of an overburdened staff. It also managed to increase salaries for a few new professors.[45] To provide quality, Russell sought "star" faculty with national reputations and looked to hire young professors with doctoral degrees, preferably from prestigious universities outside the South. "We have got to bring in real educational leaders, recognized as such over the nation," he said. Such a prospect was difficult considering the overall low level of faculty salaries, but with Russell's personal credibility he convinced scholars from the world's top universities that good things were happening at Carolina. He took a personal interest in every faculty member hired and made the final hiring decisions. He went to some lengths to hire those he most wanted. Dean Francis Bradley told the story of a physics professor from Canada whom Russell wanted to hire in the face of competition from other colleges. Russell got him to come to Carolina by using his contacts in the State Department to get the man a visa within twenty-four hours, something none of his competitors could do. Russell attracted numerous quality professors to the University's largely understaffed departments, raising the standard of excellence at the institution.[46]

Among the host of outstanding new faculty were DeLos F. DeTar in chemistry (Ph.D., University of Pennsylvania), Wade T. Batson in biology (Ph.D., Duke), Tomlinson Fort in mathematics (Ph.D., Harvard, and former head of the department of mathematics, University of Georgia), and Robert W. Paterson in economics (Ph.D., University of Virginia, and former vice consul of the U.S. State Department). In the humanities, Russell attracted scholars such as James C. Haden in philosophy (Ph.D., Yale), George C. Brauer, Ennis S. Rees, George M. Reeves, and John L. Kimmey in English (with Ph.D.s from Princeton, Harvard, the Sorbonne, and Columbia, respectively), and Charles W. Coolidge and George C. Rogers Jr. in history (with Ph.D.s from Trinity College, Dublin, and the University of Chicago, respectively).[47]

The list of institutions from which the newly hired faculty earned their doctoral degrees included almost every leading university in America, and some from all over the world. Among those drawn to Carolina's faculty included those with Ph.D.s from Princeton, Yale, Harvard, Chicago, Johns Hopkins, Stanford, Columbia, Pennsylvania, Duke, Northwestern, Wisconsin, Cambridge, Oxford, Berne (Switzerland), and the Sorbonne (Paris). Russell's faculty recruitment initiative improved academic quality across the board, for between 1951 and 1959, the percentage of the University's faculty holding the doctorate increased from 23 to 48 percent. Although not all of these scholars remained at the University of South Carolina for their entire careers, many did, becoming faculty leaders and ranking among the most outstanding professors in the history of the institution (several continued teaching at Carolina into the 1990s). The remarkable group that Donald Russell recruited during his relatively short tenure as president was of unprecedented quality for the twentieth-century University and became the foundation of the modern University of South Carolina.[48]

Faculty enhancement went hand in hand with progress in academic programs, and Russell's overall strategy was to target areas vital to the University's success in serving the state and nation in the postwar world.[49] The basic sciences had long been a glaring weakness, owing to the lack of adequate facilities and an insufficient number of properly trained faculty. Russell noted that "South Carolina ranks almost at the bottom in the production of physicists and chemists."[50] The imperatives of the emerging cold war and its emphasis on "keeping up with the Russians" drove Russell to concentrate much of his effort in the early years of his administration to improving science programs.[51] "National necessity," he declared in 1953, "demands that training in the pure sciences be stimulated."[52] The new LeConte science building helped alleviate the facilities problem, and the efforts to recruit quality faculty addressed personnel shortages in the sciences.

For example, the physics department required drastic changes because its entire 1952 staff of four lacked doctoral-level training. The department head, Charles F. Mercer, held the master of arts degree, earned in 1926 from USC.[53] At a modern university in the atomic age (and in a state that was the site of the new Savannah River Atomic Energy Commission Plant), weakness in such a fundamental academic department was untenable. "Without a strong and up-to-date physics department," Russell said, "the university can have no adequate science school."[54]

In short order, he attracted an outstanding physics faculty. In 1953 he hired as the new department head Fred T. Rogers, who held a Ph.D. from Rice University and came to the University after heading the U.S. Navy's weapons testing laboratory in China Lake, California. Rogers then attracted Anthony P. French, an eminent British nuclear physicist with experience on World War II's Manhattan Project and a degree and teaching experience earned at Cambridge University. By 1958, the physics department had three Cambridge-trained physicists (Ernst Brietenberger and R. D. Edge, in addition to French), and one each with doctorates from MIT (E. C. Lerner), Harvard (Paul H. Pitanken), and the University of Illinois (F. H. Giles), among others. In addition to the new faculty, the department modernized its course offerings and updated its facilities with new equipment to study nuclear physics. Students recognized the dramatic improvements in the department, and enrollment in physics courses more than doubled in the period between 1952 and 1957.[55]

Similar improvements, though not as dramatic, occurred in other essential but understaffed departments such as English, philosophy, foreign languages, and mathematics. In addition to the enhancements of individual departments, some entire University divisions required compete revamping to bring them up to existing national standards. The program that received the most initial attention was the School of Education. The "education revolution" of James F. Byrnes's administration as governor, initiated for the single purpose of precluding a court order mandating racial desegregation by attempting to make "separate but equal" schools more than just a legal abstraction, produced vast improvements in the state's elementary and secondary schools. However, for the most part, the colleges that supplied the state's public school teachers had been left out of the improvements.[56]

Donald Russell claimed that if the state were to sustain the desired progress in its public education system, the University's School of Education had to be improved. "The quickest way of improving the schools of the state is to improve the training of teachers," he said.[57] Russell told the state Budget and Control Board: "The commendable endeavor to improve our public schools will be seriously handicapped unless there is contemporaneously built up a sound School of Education where . . . the quality of teachers and school administrators is improved to meet the requirements of the new public school program."[58]

The School of Education faced several problems in the early 1950s, not the least of which was an understaffed, undertrained, demoralized faculty. In 1951, there were only five full-time faculty to handle an enrollment of 405 undergraduates and 306 full and part-time master's candidates. Only two of the five full-time faculty held doctorates, and there was considerable dissension among faculty within the school.[59] The University of South Carolina had the state's only graduate school in education for whites, and South Carolina was the only state in the South without a doctoral program in the field of education.[60]

Russell was determined to build the School of Education to the highest modern standards. To that end, in the fall of 1952, he and Orin F. Crow, dean of the School of Education, secured the services of a team of consultants from the University of Chicago's highly esteemed department of education, and the two schools established a close working relationship in developing a new program.[61]

The recommendations of the University of Chicago's educators led to radical improvements. The faculty of five in 1951 expanded to sixteen by 1954.[62] They included a new dean, Chester C. Travelstead, formerly assistant dean of the College of Education at the University of Georgia, who accepted the position in the fall of 1953. The deanship had become vacant when Russell promoted Orin Crow to the University's top academic post (dean of the faculty) upon the retirement of Francis Bradley. Another new faculty hire in the School of Education was former University of Chicago professor Newton Edwards, a 1910 USC graduate with a doctorate from Chicago. He was the author of a widely read and timely book on school law titled *The Courts and the Public Schools*. Other new faculty included Lawrence Giles (Ph.D., University of Minnesota) and others trained in the most modern fields of education.[63]

Significantly for the state, many in the newly revamped school were experienced with desegregation issues, as the main issue facing the educational community was the impending decision by the U.S. Supreme Court in the landmark *Brown v. Board of Education* case. The USC School of Education faculty would be intimately involved with this issue in one way or another for the next thirty years.[64]

The expanded education faculty that Travelstead and Russell hired developed a new curriculum and new programs to better serve the state's public school teachers and students. For example, the school added a new library science program to train librarians.[65] The Chicago team recommended a remedial reading clinic for public school children, and it opened in 1954.[66] A doctoral program in education constituted the primary need of the school, as it would help build all other programs. The developments in faculty and curriculum allowed the school to begin offering the Ph.D. in education in the fall of 1954, as well as a limited number of fellowships to help students pay for the additional training. The development of the education program brought a turnaround in faculty morale and an increase in the school's enrollment.[67] The University's School of Education could now play a significant role in the state's "education revolution."

Once the new program in education was well launched, in late 1954 Russell turned his focus to another academic division that needed a major overhaul, the School of Engineering. South Carolina and the nation faced a critical shortage of trained engineers, and if the University was to contribute to the state's burgeoning industrial growth and the cold war, the engineering program needed major changes. Two of the four divisions of the school were unaccredited, and, as in the University's other schools, there was a shortage of faculty members, which made the teaching loads heavy and research nearly impossible.[68] The curriculum was outdated as well, with courses such as "Mechanics of Machinery," "Internal-Combustion Engines," and "Direct Current Machinery and Storage Batteries" stressing narrow, practical learning.[69]

As in the case of the School of Education, Russell sought the advice of the top program in the nation to reorganize the school. This time, he and a group of leading faculty (including chemist Willard Davis, physicist Fred Rogers, and dean of the School of Engineering Robert Sumwalt) convinced a team of consultants from the Massachusetts Institute of Technology to evaluate the University's engineering program and help them develop a new one.[70]

The nationally respected consultants recommended a complete restructuring of the School of Engineering. The MIT committee called for "far reaching changes in course requirements to provide broader theoretical foundations, more modern ideas and applications, and increased emphasis upon basic scientific training."[71] The new program stressed mastering theory over developing technical skills. It required students without proper backgrounds in the humanities, physics, and mathematics to enroll in the College of Arts and Sciences until they made up deficiencies. Some 19 percent of the new required courses were in the humanities and social sciences, among them English and philosophy. The School of Engineering's curricular prerequisite standard became the highest of any in the South.[72]

The effort to improve the University's engineering education included attracting eminent faculty, and the school added men such as Rufus G. Fellers (B.S., USC; Ph.D., Yale), Warren G. Ferris (D.Eng., Brooklyn Polytechnic), John Taylor (D.Sc., Harvard) and Admiral (Ret.) W. L. Anderson, a decorated World War II hero and respected engineer. The new program represented a pioneering step in engineering education in the South, and the MIT committee report became the basis for standards used by the American Society for Engineering Education to accredit all the nation's engineering schools.[73]

One additional existing University program also faced a major reorganization. When he first evaluated the University's nursing program (begun during World War II), Donald Russell declared that it would have to be either "substantially changed or eliminated."[74] The administration chose the former, largely because of a shortage of adequately trained nurses in the state. Again, Russell brought nationally known consultants to evaluate the program (this time from the Kellogg Foundation), and in 1957, the department of nursing was removed from the College of Arts and Sciences and redesignated as the School of Nursing. The Kellogg consultants recommended an overhaul of the curriculum, and the previous two-year, pre-nursing training was expanded to provide a full four-year baccalaureate degree program.[75]

The across-the-board improvements in the University's departments and schools led to a broadening of academic degree offerings and programs. Expansion of the Graduate School had long been an essential need if the University were to take its place among its peers in the South and the nation. "No progressive state," said Donald Russell, "can be without competent professional and graduate schools."[76]

With improvements in faculty, a more broadly based graduate curriculum was possible. For example, the proportion of faculty teaching graduate classes who also possessed the earned doctorate rose from 52 percent in 1950 to 70 percent in 1955.[77] At the beginning of 1950, the University offered the Ph.D. only in history. In 1950, the department of English introduced a Ph.D. program focusing on southern literature. Faculty enhancement in the early 1950s allowed the University to quickly add several doctoral programs in its strongest departments, reflecting Russell's desire to develop the state's leading arts and sciences program.[78] Under the leadership of chairman Willard Davis, chemistry became one of the University's most outstanding departments, and improvements in faculty and equipment allowed that department to begin a doctoral program in 1953.[79] Similar developments in biology led to the opening of a Ph.D. program in that department in the same year.[80] The School of Education's doctoral program began in 1954.

The expansion of graduate work required administrative changes, and in 1955 the University established the graduate faculty and graduate council to help dean of the Graduate School Wilfred Callcott administer the advanced programs.[81] However, even with the significant growth of doctoral programs, in the 1950s the University of South Carolina and the state continued to lag far behind its neighbors in the numbers of Ph.D.s it produced (see table 3.1). For example, the University of South Carolina granted but one Ph.D. in 1949–50, in the field of history. In 1954–55, USC granted two Ph.D.s, one each in history and chemistry. In 1959–60, it granted seven Ph.D.s, three in chemistry, two in biology, and one each in history and English.[82]

Table 3.1 Average doctorates awarded per year, 1953–1962, and number of doctoral fields in the arts and sciences awarding degrees 1953–62, at selected southern institutions

UNIVERSITY	DOCTORATES PER YEAR 1953–1962	DOCTORAL FIELDS ARTS & SCIENCES
South Carolina	4	4
Mississippi	5	2
West Virginia	7	6
Georgia	9	6
Alabama	17	8
Kentucky	30	11
Vanderbilt	37	11
Virginia	45	12
Tennessee	45	11
Oklahoma	49	12
Louisiana State	58	13
Duke	73	14
Florida	79	11
North Carolina	93	16
Texas	152	16

Source: Allan M. Cartter, "Qualitative Aspects of Southern University Education," *Southern Economic Journal* 32, no. 1 (July 1965), part 2, tables II, IV.

In addition to the expansion of doctoral degree offerings at Carolina, Donald Russell's vision of a great university included some entirely new academic departments. As a result of World War II and the tensions brought by the Cold War, there was a growing awareness of global problems in the United States. Russell's experience in the U.S. State Department convinced him that the study of international problems and foreign policy should be an integral part of a modern liberal education. The University's existing political science department largely focused on domestic politics, so he decided to create a new department and undergraduate degree devoted exclusively to international studies.[83]

To that end, in 1957 Russell induced Richard L. Walker to come to Carolina as chairman of a new academic unit, the Department of International Studies. Walker came to USC from Yale, where he had earned his Ph.D. and taught for seven years. A specialist on communist China, he came to the University in part because of a $1,000 ($4,848) salary supplement that Donald Russell himself provided from a personal gift to Carolina. Richard Walker soon became Carolina's first holder of an endowed chair since the Civil War (the James F. Byrnes Professorship of International Studies), made possible by another gift to the University from Donald and Virginia Russell.[84]

After Walker's arrival in Columbia, he recruited an outstanding faculty for the new department, which included Raymond A. Moore (M.A., Columbia University). The new program was one of the first specialized programs in international studies in the nation to incorporate the study of the entire world into a general undergraduate curriculum. Among the courses Walker offered was a survey entitled "The United States and World Problems," designed for the major and non-major alike. It drew students from diverse backgrounds (such as those in the School of Engineering) and helped them gain an understanding of U.S. foreign policy and the forces affecting it around the world. The course featured regular guest lectures by eminent figures from both government and academia, and the department sponsored an ongoing lecture series that brought leading foreign policy thinkers to the campus.[85]

Russell's emphasis on internationalism led him to expand foreign language programs as well. Because of the ongoing cold war with the Soviet Union, Russell believed that "it behooves all modern-day universities to acquaint themselves with Russia, the Russian people, and Russian thinking." Thus the University began offering courses in Russian under Professor W. C. Zeigler in 1953.[86] The foreign language program received another boost when it became one of the first universities in the nation to use a "language lab" for beginning-level language study.[87]

Russell emphasized international exposure for Carolina's students and introduced an unprecedented program of visiting lecturers and professorships.

During the mid-1950s the University began to bring highly esteemed scholars from the best universities in the United States and the world to Columbia for short stays of up to one year. This program was funded partly through
federal and foundation grants (from such funds as the Fulbright program,
the Smith-Mundt Act, and the John Hay Whitney Foundation), and partly
through internally budgeted funds. Visiting professors such as Heinz W.
Arndt in economics (from Canberra University, Australia), Francis W. Coker
in political science (a South Carolinian who taught at Yale), Zaki N. Moham-
med in philosophy (from the University of Cairo, Egypt), Joseph Miller in
chemistry (from the University of Western Australia), and Ernst Cloos in
geology (from the Johns Hopkins University) gave University of South Carolina students exposure to top scholars from throughout the nation and
world.[88]

The most successful visiting professor program was in the department of
history, at that time the University's strongest department in graduate work.
In 1955 the department began a program of distinguished visiting professorships with Oxford University and leading American universities. Looking
back on the Oxford exchange, Russell remarked, "We got the real cream of the
crop from the English historical community" to teach at Carolina. He added,
"The fact that Oxford was exchanging professors with us gave us credibility
that we didn't have before. Frankly, as I look back on it, I can't believe they
did it; they could have done it with Columbia University, Harvard, Yale, or
any of those schools. This was something that those schools normally tried
to nurture and develop themselves, but they didn't have it, we did."[89]

Through the respect with which the University's own history department
was held in the field, Carolina attracted many of the world's top historians.
In 1955, medieval historian Thomas Van Cleve from Bowdoin College and
diplomatic historian Bernadotte Schmitt, a former Rhodes scholar and professor at the University of Chicago, both taught at Carolina. The following
year, the first visiting scholar from Oxford University came to the University
of South Carolina: David Ogg, a historian of seventeenth-century England. In
following years, the University annually hosted at least one world-renowned
historian for undergraduate teaching, and the department nearly always had
at least one from Oxford. Among those who taught at Carolina in subsequent
years were Civil War historians Avery Craven of the University of Chicago
and William B. Hesseltine of the University of Wisconsin and Latin American scholar J. Fred Rippy of the University of Chicago. Oxford historians
Martin Gilbert (the official biographer of Winston Churchill and renowned
historian of the twentieth century), Henry Bell (medieval Europe), and
Michael Brock (modern British politics) all taught at Carolina in the 1950s
and early 1960s.[90] In addition, some Carolina history professors spent a year

as visiting professors at Oxford, including George Curry in 1959–60 and Wilfred Callcott in 1961–62.[91] The visiting professor program in history helped raise the profile of a department already recognized as one of the University's leaders, and the agreement with Oxford continued until the early 1990s, giving Carolina students access to many of the world's top historians.[92]

While the 1950s saw Carolina strengthen many of its academic programs, those years also marked the beginning of a research program that had direct benefits for graduate and undergraduate students. In the years after World War II, the federal government had drastically expanded its role as a funder of university research. In the 1950s, annual federal support for contract research in the nation nearly tripled; in addition, large private corporations and foundations increasingly funded university research. However, a handful of major universities in the United States received the lion's share of the funding. The University of South Carolina received a far smaller share of external funds than even other southern universities, but in the 1950s scholars at Carolina did begin to attract some federal and private research dollars. A faculty research committee parceled out a small amount of state-appropriated funds for research. Research and publication became more and more common at a university that was struggling to enter the national mainstream.[93]

The University's nascent research program spanned many disciplines. For example, through the support of the National Historical Publications Commission, in 1952 the University of South Carolina Press began to publish the papers of John C. Calhoun, a project first edited by Robert L. Meriwether of the history department.[94] In 1955, enhancements of the School of Education (which included the addition of a Bureau of Educational Research), brought a $39,000 ($198,534) grant from the W. K. Kellogg Foundation to improve public school administration.[95] In 1953, the School of Business Administration began the Bureau of Business and Economic Research, which featured a monthly magazine, *University of South Carolina Business and Economic Review,* edited by professor Robert W. Paterson. The magazine and bureau reported on research and trends of interest to the business community of the state.[96]

However, the bulk of funded research at the University took place in the sciences, much of it related to the activities of the federal Atomic Energy Commission. For example, in 1950, an effort spearheaded by chemistry department chair Willard Davis resulted in the acceptance of the University as a member of the Oak Ridge Institute for Nuclear Studies. This allowed USC scientists in fields such as chemistry, chemical engineering, physics, and biology to use the modern federal laboratories at Oak Ridge.[97] That same year, the biology department (under the direction of William E. Hoy) received a major Atomic Energy Commission grant to study the flora and fauna of the Savannah River project area and record their status before the nuclear work began. The department later expanded this research project to include the entire state, in order to record the same kind of information before large-scale industrialization began in South Carolina.[98]

In addition to these and other contracts with the Atomic Energy Commission, University scientists attracted contracts with federal agencies such as the U.S. Army and Air Force, the Coast and Geodetic Survey, the National Science Foundation, and the National Institutes of Health. Between 1950 and 1960, outside research funds for science and engineering increased from $2,980 ($16,856) in two departments (chemistry and physics), to $230,972 ($1,062,863) in nine departments (biology, chemistry, geology, mathematics, physics, and four fields of engineering). The department of chemistry attracted the most outside funding, including a prestigious $40,000 ($188,324) grant from the American Chemical Society to professor Delos DeTar in 1958. Of the University's 1960 total for outside funding, chemistry brought in 45 percent.[99]

Despite the real advances in research, because the University began the decade so far behind, at the end of the decade it placed near the bottom of a ranking of southern universities in total income for contract research and services (see table 3.2). A faculty committee charged with evaluating the University's research efforts admitted that "it is true that there has been a notable growth in research activity in the past five years, but this should not blind us to the fact that we have a very long way to go."[100] Only one-third of USC's faculty were actively engaged in research, and more than half were skeptical of the value of rigorous research. USC's accrediting body, the Southern Association of Colleges and Secondary Schools, commented that compared to other southern universities, Carolina was on a "near-starvation diet of faculty research."[101]

While much of Donald Russell's plans for improving the University consisted of strengthening or adding programs, he realized almost immediately after taking office that some of the University's programs needed not improvement, but elimination. He commented, "Second-rate departments do not improve a college and represent an unjustified 'drag' upon the general program of the University."[102] Thus, in the spring of 1953, he appointed a faculty advisory committee to analyze curriculum offerings. Among the recommendations they made was the discontinuance of the program in social work and elimination of the department of homemaking. In 1954, the board of trustees cancelled both programs. In 1957, believing that the University's mission lay in higher education, not in giving makeup high school work, USC eliminated all remedial courses.[103]

These were a few examples of the evolving administrative structure at Carolina. In addition to the revolution in faculty and academic programs,

Table 3.2 Total income for contract research and services, all disciplines, 1958–59

UNIVERSITY	TOTAL INCOME FOR CONTRACT RESEARCH AND SERVICES	
Clemson Agricultural College*	$308,995	($1,450,585)
University of South Carolina	$322,053	($1,511,886)
University of Mississippi	$732,966	($3,440,927)
University of Georgia	$827,016	($3,882,447)
University of Virginia	$1,055,648	($4,955,765)
University of Florida	$1,259,219	($5,911,434)
University of Alabama	$1,343,433	($6,306,779)
University of North Carolina	$1,448,144	($6,798,348)
Florida State University	$1,661,715	($7,800,962)
University of Tennessee	$2,067,529	($9,706,066)
Emory University	$2,794,027	($13,116,628)
University of Texas	$5,973,149	($28,041,094)
Duke University	$6,054,848	($28,424,632)

Source: Mary Irwin, ed., *American Universities and Colleges,* 8th ed. (Washington, D.C.: American Council on Education, 1960), 168, 291, 295, 304, 317, 587, 763, 780, 950, 959, 994, 1033, 1068.

* Clemson's figures are skewed in part because the institution had been forced to turn down an Atomic Energy Commission grant worth a possible $350,000 ($1,696,875) in June of 1957. South Carolina's governor, George Bell Timmerman Jr., threatened to sue Clemson because he believed a nondiscrimination clause in the grant would open the door to "integration and communism." Robert Muldrow Cooper, chairman of Clemson's board of trustees and the director of the state development board, argued without success that South Carolina's future was tied to nuclear education programs and that the state was entitled to "her fair share of such industries as they develop." Timmerman only saw the racial question, and Clemson was forced to rescind the grant. See Marcia Synnott, "Federalism Vindicated: University Desegregation in South Carolina and Alabama, 1962–1963," *Journal of Policy History* 1, no.3 (1989), 301–02.

there was significant turnover in the University's leadership. Chairman of the board of trustees Arthur Knight of Chesterfield died in June 1952 and was succeeded by Rutledge L. Osborne of Orangeburg. With the retirement of John A. Chase as dean of administration in June 1952, William H. Patterson, formerly assistant to the president, became the new dean of administration and business manager. Subsequently, in 1953 Carter L. Burgess, a former special assistant secretary of state and close friend of Russell, became assistant to the president, before leaving Carolina in 1955 to become an assistant secretary of defense under President Eisenhower. In August of 1954, dean of the

College of Arts and Sciences Joseph Norwood retired, and Robert H. Wiene-feld, history department chair, replaced him as dean. In 1955, dean of the fac-ulty Orin F. Crow died, and Wilfred Callcott succeeded him as dean of the faculty while continuing to serve as dean of the Graduate School.[104]

Despite the many encouraging developments at Carolina in the mid-1950s, the financial crisis of the late 1940s persisted. The legacy of underfunding was compounded by the accounting policy that required the University to remit all tuition and fees to the state, which substantially reduced the net amount of annual state financial support for operations. For example, in 1950–51, the state appropriated $1,500,000 ($8,145,000) to the University, but the University had to return $433,944 ($2,356,316) in tuition and other fees, so the net appropriation was but $1,066,056 ($5,788,684).[105]

Donald Russell saw that his principal challenge was to figure out how to spend that tuition money before the state could take it away. With the sup-port of Governor Byrnes, in April of 1953, Russell and the state's other col-lege presidents convinced the General Assembly to approve a plan by which public colleges could issue revenue bonds, with student tuition fees pledged in advance to amortize the loans. Then, in May of 1953, the General Assem-bly passed another bond bill, this time authorizing the University and other state schools to issue bonds payable out of dormitory room rent revenue, with the proceeds of these bonds to go toward the construction of new stu-dent housing. These two bond bills gave the University a total of $8,000,000 ($40,725,000) of credit for the construction of classrooms, laboratories, offices, and dormitories. In addition to the bond bills, in the 1953 legislative session the General Assembly directly appropriated $800,000 ($4,072,500) to the University for the purchase of land, and in 1954 it designated $200,000 ($1,014,953) for dormitory renovation. With the help of a friendly and influ-ential governor, in the first legislative session since he became president, Donald Russell managed to equip the University with a supply of self-liqui-dating borrowing power and $1,000,000 ($5,074,766) for new land and ren-ovations that transformed the institution's financial condition and began to expand the University's crowded campus.[106]

The unprecedented physical expansion program of the second half of the 1950s was nearly as impressive as the improvement of its faculty and aca-demic programs; it continued nearly unbroken for more than two decades. In 1953, the first priority was to expand the campus by buying nearby land, since it was crowded into the smallest area of any southern state university: just 46 acres. President Russell appointed an advisory committee of local citizens, including B. M. Edwards, Susan Guignard, R. Beverly Herbert, and Joseph Walker, to help negotiate for the purchase of adjacent property. In 1953, the University bought the Kirkland Apartments at 1611 Pendleton Street (which then served as a women's dormitory), and the white section of the racially segregated University Terrace housing project along Devine Street (which became a new "freshman center" and later gave way to a parking garage). In 1958, USC acquired the other half of the University Terrace housing project—the African American section—along Blossom Street.

Since the end of World War II, officials had purchased nearly all the lots not already owned by the University in the block bounded by Greene, Main, Devine, and Sumter Streets (the block containing the Engineering building and the old fieldhouse). In 1953, the board began to purchase lots in two other blocks south of the campus, bounded by Devine, Main, Blossom, and Marion Streets, occupied by what was described as "slum" housing. By early 1954 the University owned nearly all of both blocks, an area that expanded the campus by nearly 25 percent. In addition, construction in the area of Melton Field (the present site of the Russell House) meant that the University needed new athletic fields, so Carolina purchased twenty-one acres along Rosewood Drive and South Marion Street at a distance of about a mile and half from the campus, which later formed the nucleus of the University's modern athletic complex. These land purchases gave the University the *lebensraum* so long needed for physical expansion.[107]

New land was only a small part of the physical expansion of the 1950s. The first phase of major construction projects to utilize funds from the new bonds began in 1954 with a $230,000 ($1,167,196) addition to and renovation of the buildings making up the School of Education. This construction was a vital part of the overall improvements to the school in the mid-1950s.[108]

The first completely new construction project of Russell's building program was a long-needed student union. Such a building had been proposed as early as 1938, and students had suffered without adequate buildings for their activities ever since—many having their offices in the temporary structures placed on the campus just after the war. A student union was a favorite topic of *Gamecock* editorialists and student politicians, and Donald Russell placed it at the top of his agenda. Preliminary plans called for a location on the Horseshoe (on the site of McCutchen House), and the $1,075,000 ($5,472,422) building was to have a classical design matching the other buildings of the historic area. But new architects (Lyles, Bissett, Carlisle and Wolfe) gave the building a new location (on the site of Melton Field) and a totally new look that set the standard for the architectural style of the new campus south of Green Street. The modern building contained dining and assembly halls, recreational rooms, and offices for student and alumni organizations. Completed in mid-1955, the facility so pleased the student body that they petitioned the board of trustees to name the building in honor of Donald and Virginia Russell. The board obliged the students of their wish, and

Governor Byrnes dedicated the building as "Russell House" on October 16, 1955, as a symbol of the progress the University had made in the three years since Donald Russell assumed office. Students gushed that the new building was their "dream come true," and the *Gamecock's* editor wrote, "We vote the Russells the most popular people at the University, and the student union as the most popular building. What could be better than to bestow the name of the first upon the second, thus uniting our most prized possessions."[109]

Meanwhile, other construction in the first phase of the massive building program began in earnest. In addition to the Russell House and the new addition to the School of Education, in 1954 and 1955 the University was in the midst of a frenzy of new construction, including a building to house the School of Business Administration (today's Callcott Social Sciences Center), McClintock women's dormitory, the McBryde Quadrangle housing, an addition to the relatively new College of Engineering building, and extensive renovations to Rutledge Chapel and the old dormitories on the Horseshoe. All told, the first phase of improvements to the University in this one-year period cost nearly $6 million ($30,543,750)—almost all of it financed through tuition and dormitory revenue bonds.[110]

Russell did not slow down. The year 1956 saw the construction of a new athletic facility on the recently purchased property along Rosewood Drive. The new fieldhouse, known as the "Roundhouse," was later named in honor of longtime athletic director Rex Enright. The athletic facility also included a baseball diamond, a track, and three football practice fields.[111] Enrollment increases necessitated the planning of additional student housing and eating facilities. In 1958, a new dormitory consisting of two seven-story towers (distinguished by a "veil-block" exterior that lent the compound its nickname, the "Honeycombs") and designed in part by world-renowned architect Edward Durrell Stone of New York, was completed in 1958 at the corner of Devine and Main Streets. Also in 1958, the Russell House was enlarged to include two new cafeterias (this addition was also designed with help from Stone and featured a "veil-block" exterior).[112] State officials deemed the Wade Hampton dormitory for women, built in 1924, to be too small and decrepit. Russell proposed to demolish the building and replace it with a modern residence with more space. The new building, also named for Wade Hampton, was completed on the same site as the old dormitory in 1959.[113]

In October 1955, Russell proclaimed that "the most pressing need of the University . . . is for a remodeling of our existing library." A bibliophile, Russell intensely disliked the closed-stack system of the McKissick Library, in which "students do not come into contact with the books and do not get that feel of books so essential at a college or university." He told the board of trustees, "If we are to continue . . . developing a stronger academic atmosphere, it is necessary to remodel our library in a manner that will make . . . [it] one of the vital spots on our campus, attractive in every detail to the students and opening them up freely to the books of learning which are part of a university education."[114]

Initially, administrators proposed to extensively remodel McKissick, but later decided that such a renovation would be unsatisfactory. They chose instead to build a completely new facility. After the state granted the University the deed to the 1300 block of Devine Street, the University built a new $900,000 ($4,237,283) library partly on the old street and partly on the south end of Davis Field. The distinctive, ultra-modern Undergraduate Library was completed in 1959. Modeled on the famous Lamont Library at Harvard and designed in part by Edward Stone (who described it as the new "center of gravity of the campus"), it featured 60,000 volumes geared toward undergraduates. With its self-service book stacks, the library was the first separate undergraduate library in the South. In 1963, the design of the new library won the First Honor Award of the American Institute of Architects, the American Library Association, and the American Book Committee, the highest distinction available for library architecture.[115]

The other architecture of the "new campus" south of Green Street drew mixed reviews. The modern design of the Russell House created the most controversy. Virginia Russell and several members of the board of trustees (including Leonard L. Long of Charleston), wanted the new student union to have a design matching the old campus and a "country club-like appearance."[116] The board of trustees minutes record that when the modern design of the architectural firm Lyles, Bissett, Carlisle and Wolfe was presented, "several [board] members expressed the opinion that the exterior facade was not particularly attractive," and they requested that the architects redesign the building.[117] In the face of opposition to the modern design, Russell hired a neutral consultant, Michael Hare of New York, to give the board guidance as to the appropriate style for the new building.[118]

Hare responded with mild rebuke to the board and a lesson on trends in architectural design. He wrote that "pre-determining the appearance of a building . . . paralyzes artistic expression and the result will be portentious [sic] and sterile." While many wanted to preserve architectural uniformity, Hare declared that on the University's old campus, "Some of the architecture is very distinguished . . . and some can charitably be described as mediocre . . . [and] the mediocre has been hallowed by time and sentiment. . . . A student union poured into a colonial mould would be peculiarly anachronistic and uneconomical." He continued, "As the South converts to an industrial economy varying greatly from the earlier agricultural economy so well expressed by the colonial, the opportunity arises for fresh and valid architectural expression."

Hare believed that the solution did not lie in enforced conformity, rather that "the best architecture of today is compatible with the best architecture of the colonial period in that both . . . were designed to express the problems of their eras. History will explain their juxtaposition and time will soften their transition." Despite the fact that several board members agreed with trustee J. D. Kerr of Spartanburg that the modern design was "too drastic a change in comparison with other university buildings," Hare's arguments swayed enough members, and they endorsed the modern design by a vote of seven to five.[119]

While many in Columbia still view the facade of the Russell House as an abomination, its design was in tune with architectural fashion of the day. Contemporary style stressed the abandonment of master building plans for college campuses and the belief that "no building should depend for its character upon its relation to another."[120] Several of the University's new buildings, including the Undergraduate Library and the new "honeycomb" dormitories, were prominently featured in national architectural magazines such as the *Architectural Record*.[121] However, in South Carolina, approval of the architecture was not universal. Columbia's *Record* noted that "there was some understandable deploring of the sharp departure [the Russell House] made from the traditional lines of the architecture of the old campus."[122] The *News and Courier* derided the new buildings, declaring that the honeycomb dormitory "resembles nothing so much as a giant air-conditioning unit. Sometimes we believe that architects get their ideas by studying the designs of air filters under the hoods of their automobiles."[123]

Like it or not, the frenzy of new construction at Carolina in the 1950s revolutionized the campus. An extensive landscaping program accompanied the construction, beautifying all areas, especially the Horseshoe. The completion of the modern buildings meant that the University said good-bye to older ones. With the completion of the Russell House, students rejoiced as the last of the temporary World War II surplus buildings around the campus (nicknamed "termite halls") were demolished at the end of 1955. The Carovet Apartments, also war surplus, began to be razed in 1958 (although they were not completely gone until 1960).[124] The new cafeteria in the Russell House allowed the University to tear down Steward's Hall (built in 1901 at the corner of Green and Sumter Streets) to make room for an expansion of the School of Engineering.[125] Finally, the five faculty houses lining Sumter Street between College and Greene Streets were demolished to open up the facade of Wardlaw College.[126]

The overall enhancement of the University's physical plant, faculty, and academic programs during Russell's administration truly brought an "educational renaissance" to the University, an institution that had lacked direction since World War II. English department head Havilah Babcock wrote to President Russell in early 1954, "The esprit de corps now obtaining among faculty, students and administration is finer than I have known it during the 27 years I have been at the University. You have enkindled a sense of pride and achievement which we sorely lacked."[127] The new enthusiasm for the institution was reflected in popularity with the state's students and led to rising enrollments that soon surpassed the levels of even the peak years immediately following World War II (1947–48).

In the early 1950s, administrators had predicted that declining enrollments would continue (Carolina's enrollment hit a postwar low of 2,860 in the spring of 1951), but with the return of good morale, the student body's size defied predictions. Enrollment rose about 10 percent per year in the mid-1950s, prompting the General Assembly's fiscal survey commission to comment in 1956 that "the University is experiencing an unprecedented popularity, which, in our opinion, will continue." By 1959, the University's enrollment stood at 5,019, a 75 percent increase over the 1951 low. The proportion of female students rose from 26 percent in 1951 to 33 percent in 1959. Donald Russell claimed that even with the increases, inadequate dormitory space deterred many prospects from applying and that enrollment was "well below what it would have been had the University had enough modern dormitory facilities."[128]

The surge in the numbers of students at Carolina was not simply a matter of demographics. Some of the rise can be attributed to the return of veterans from the Korean War. Nonetheless the rate of enrollment increase at Carolina was not matched equally by other state schools. At Clemson, enrollment increased 40 percent between 1951 and 1959 (from 2,788 to 3,890).[129] High school seniors, faced with the draft when they graduated from college, were less than enthusiastic about attending a school where students were military cadets, wore uniforms, and enforced military discipline. Single-gender education decreased in popularity as well. While all-male Clemson had its problems in the 1950s, at all-female Winthrop, enrollment continued to decline as it had since the 1930s. From a peak of about 2,000 in 1929–30, the student body fell to around 1,600 in 1946 and stood at approximately 1,000 in 1956. Carolina grew partly as a result of Clemson's slower growth and Winthrop's declines.[130]

Winthrop had plenty of space to handle a much larger student body: only 913 of 1,444 dormitory beds were occupied in 1956. Meanwhile USC was building new dormitories as fast as it could, and the expansion still could not keep up with student demand. In the spring of 1956, all 2,209 of Carolina's dormitory beds were filled, and there was a waiting list of 200 for the men's dormitories and 150 for the Carovet Apartments. To better balance the utilization of state-owned facilities, a state task force recommended that Winthrop and the University merge to reduce state costs, declaring that "South Carolina should not build new dormitories and classrooms elsewhere if those now at Winthrop can be utilized." However, the General Assembly declined to take such a politically difficult step.[131]

While tuition and dormitory revenue bonds helped to expand and modernize the University's physical plant, the state's support of regular operations and maintenance continued to lag. The appropriation continued to be of paramount importance since it made up about 70 percent of the University's operating revenue in the last half of the 1950s.[132] The University's state appropriation increased from $1,500,000 ($8,145,000) in 1950–51 to $3,132,849 ($14,539,633) in 1959–60, but because of ongoing enrollment increases, the per-student appropriation for the University increased only slightly during the decade, and compared with the South Carolina's other public colleges, every year it was the lowest in the state.[133]

In the South as a whole, state operational support per student at public colleges averaged $653 ($3,223) in 1956–57, while the national average was $709 ($3,500).[134] The University's appropriations fell well below both averages, while support for other South Carolina state institutions generally exceeded them. A committee from the Southern Association of Colleges and Schools noted that USC's per student appropriations were "reasonable for a limited undergraduate program." "They are not adequate," the committee continued, "for a program that includes science, engineering, pharmacy, law, and graduate studies. . . . The nature of the educational program in the University suggests that it should receive higher per student appropriations . . . than any other state-supported institution." Instead, it received less.[135]

In addition to the low levels of per student funding for the University in comparison with other South Carolina institutions, the levels of overall state spending for higher education in South Carolina trailed other states in the South (see table 3.3). Even while all of South Carolina state colleges (save one—USC) enjoyed funding above the national average, the state trailed its neighbors in overall spending. The University of South Carolina bore the brunt of South Carolina's penchant for funding higher education "on the cheap."

The combination of enrollment increases and appropriations that failed to match them had several detrimental effects on the University. First, the student-faculty ratio and teaching loads skyrocketed in the 1950s. As part of its program of general improvement, the University increased the number and variety of course offerings, and tried to increase the size of the faculty.

Figure 3.1 South Carolina Institutions of Higher Learning State Appropriation per Student per Annum Information from South Carolina Budget and Control Board Reports

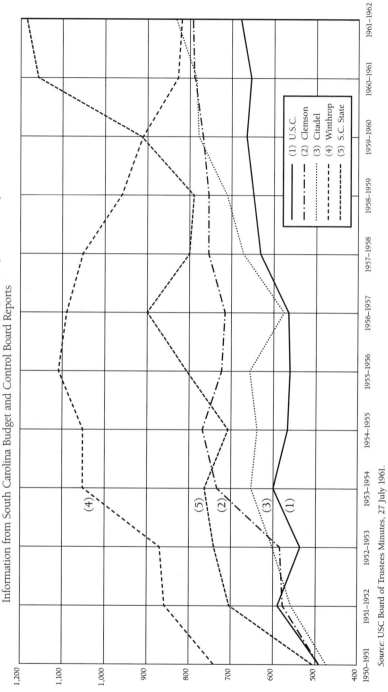

Source: USC Board of Trustees Minutes, 27 July 1961.

Between 1951 and 1958, the faculty (both full- and part-time) grew from 235 to 271. However, enrollment increases far offset faculty growth, and the student-faculty ratio went from 11.7:1 in 1952–53 to 18:1 four years later. In the biology department, the faculty increased from 6 full-time teachers in 1952–53 to 9 in 1956–57, but the student load per faculty member increased from 88 to 105. In English, the department increased from 12 to 21, but student load still increased from 105 to 117. Carolina's 18:1 student-faculty ratio in 1956–57 was far higher than that of its peers, including Duke, North Carolina, and Virginia, all with 8:1 ratios, Alabama, with a 10:1 ratio, and Tennessee and Florida, with 12:1 ratios. The student-faculty ratio at Carolina was the highest in the state as well, despite the fact that, as Russell said, "with our graduate programs, it should, by all normal standards, be the lowest." In response, the University hired part-time instructors, but these only met the University's needs temporarily.[136]

Table 3.3 State operational appropriations for higher education, as a percentage of tax revenue, 1959–60

STATE	STATE SUPPORT AS % OF TAX REVENUE
South Carolina	5.1
Tennessee	5.6
North Carolina	6.2
Kentucky	6.5
Georgia	6.5
Florida	7.7
Mississippi	7.8
Alabama	7.8
Arkansas	8.6
Virginia	8.8
Louisiana	8.8
Texas	9.0
West Virginia	9.4
Oklahoma	9.8
U.S. Average	7.8
Southern Average	7.7

Source: E. F. Schietinger, *Fact Book on Higher Education in the South, 1968* (Atlanta: Southern Regional Education Board, 1968), 52.

Low appropriations also meant that faculty salaries, already among the lowest in the South, remained depressed. South Carolina provided adequate funding for physical facilities, but not for scholars. In the latter years of his administration, President Smith had tried to convince the General Assembly to raise salaries, but it had refused.[137] Donald Russell emphasized decreasing administrative costs and applied the savings toward instruction. Between 1951 and 1957, spending on faculty salaries nearly doubled, going from $822,000 ($4,319,477) to $1,610,000 ($7,805,625). However, the increased spending on instruction was more than offset by inflation and the steady, consistent growth of the student body.[138] Instead of raising overall faculty salaries, new faculty had to be hired. Faculty salary increases that the University could afford went to younger professors, leaving more experienced faculty in the upper ranks behind.[139]

USC's faculty salaries were low in comparison to other universities even in an era in which nationwide, as one observer noted, "college teachers were scandalously underpaid."[140] By the mid-1950s, the relative economic condition of USC faculty members had declined markedly. Between 1940 and 1954, the income (in real terms) of physicians and lawyers increased 80 percent and 10 percent respectively, but the buying power of college teachers nationwide decreased by 5 percent. To make matters worse, University of South Carolina faculty suffered a 24 percent decline in real income in the same period. In comparison with 11 other southern state universities, at the end of 1956, USC ranked last in average salary paid to professors, and second to last in payments to associate professors and assistant professors. In the words of history professor Daniel Hollis, these numbers put Carolina's average salaries at "virtually rock-bottom among state universities in America." While morale was high and the University was widely recognized as being "on the move," a study of its salary situation concluded that without an adjustment to the pay scale, "it will be impossible to obtain new staff members and many of its present teachers will surely leave to accept positions elsewhere."[141]

The chronic underfunding of higher education in South Carolina owed not only to the poverty of the state but to the competition for higher education dollars. Consequently, one of Donald Russell's first initiatives was to try to end this competition. He believed that the University had a responsibility for leadership among the state's colleges, and that they should work together. He said, "Our state will progress as its educational system progresses. The University should act as a senior partner and work with other educational institutions to provide the best possible training for the people of South Carolina." [142] Led by Kenneth M. Lynch, president of the Medical College, the state's college presidents attempted to form a voluntary association among state-supported institutions (a "South Carolina Council of Higher Education"), to "promote a program of cooperative . . . effort among the institutions for their mutual benefit in preserving and progressively continuing a university system of the highest standards."[143]

This voluntary organization was to be formed in lieu of a legislated higher education commission, and Lynch envisaged that through it, state colleges could submit joint budget requests and work together to eliminate duplication in course offerings. The move to establish such an organization played a role in securing passage of the 1953 bond bills, which all state college presidents jointly supported. But judging by the level of appropriations for the remainder of the decade, the voluntary attempt to end state competition clearly failed.[144]

On numerous occasions between the end of World War II and the mid-1950s the General Assembly considered legislation to create a formalized state university system with a single board of control. In 1956, the state's fiscal survey commission made the most detailed study of South Carolina's public colleges since 1946. Their report concluded that South Carolina lacked a rational system of higher education. "[South Carolina] has no university system—its university is merely one of six institutions," the report read. It recommended that the state create a board of higher education to coordinate and give direction to state colleges.[145] As in previous years, the General Assembly declined to act on its own study.

Despite the financial inequities, morale at the University remained high. Havilah Babcock of the English department wrote, "The old University is undergoing a renaissance. 'The most progressive University in the South,' they are calling us." The achievements in faculty, research and academic programs and physical plant improvement were concrete examples of the renaissance. Another example was the series of special convocations and commencement addresses featuring high-profile national and international speakers—a part of Donald Russell's emphasis on international awareness. Among the speakers were poet Carl Sandburg and historian Arthur Schlesinger Jr.

Using his experience in the State Department, Russell also attracted the top men from the U.S. political, military, and foreign policy establishment of the mid-1950s to speak at Carolina. They included Secretary of State John Foster Dulles, former president of General Motors and then-secretary of defense Charles E. Wilson, former commander of U.S. armed forces in Europe General Lucius Clay, and under-secretary of state Walter Bedell Smith. Others were distinguished foreign diplomats, including former French prime minister and minister of defense René Pleven, and British ambassador Roger Matkins. Perhaps the most well-known of the speakers Russell brought to campus was then-senator John F. Kennedy, who delivered the commencement address in

May 1957. These speakers brought world attention to the University and did wonders for the institution's self-esteem.[146]

Student morale had made a startling turnaround since the early 1950s. *Gamecock* columnist Bill Leggitt wrote in 1954, "A couple of years ago, this school would have made a pretty poor impression on anybody. . . . Students, new and old, weren't proud of their school. Frankly there was little to be proud of. . . . Carolina today is different."[147] Students pointed to the outstanding professors, improved curriculum, the presence of world leaders, and especially the new buildings as evidence of the progress the University was making. Herbert Bryant wrote in 1955, "This is a truly good time to be at Carolina. A transition is taking place. The school is progressing from a great background to a greater future in the ever progressing modern world."[148]

The students of the 1950s were considerably different than their counterparts of the previous decade, and their general complacency was typical of the times. While the veterans of the late 1940s came to college determined to change the status quo in their home state, the students of the 1950s generally considered themselves conservative. Nancy Fox of the *Gamecock* commented that "Carolina has been described as 'the most conservative of the conservative schools'. . . . We tend to feel the observation is correct." She continued, "the apparent conservation is, in a way, rebellion against the rebelliousness of the last generation."[149] College students of the era earned the label "the silent generation." Observers noted the students' general "indifference to public affairs, their preoccupation with the present, their lack of conviction and curiosity, their sense that life had no deeper meaning than securing a career, their fear of involvement in anything other than the frivolities of a fraternity or sorority . . . and their acceptance of the status quo—in two words, their complacency and their conformity."[150]

Indeed, a 1957 nationwide survey of college students concluded that "a dominant characteristic of students in the current generation is that they are *gloriously contented* both in regard to their present day-to-day activity and their outlook for the future."[151] Another described the college student of the 1950s this way: they "saw no evil, spoke no evil, heard no evil."[152] One Carolina student compared the student of the 1950s with his counterparts in earlier decades, such as those of the early nineteenth century, whose rebellions presented South Carolina College administrators with major headaches. "Today's students usually limit themselves to such enterprises as hanging in effigy, mutilation of elevators and telephones, swiping megaphones, pennants and such from the opposition cheerleaders and bombing the basketball court with paper cups, pennies, etc. when they want to misbehave."[153] Nancy Fox expressed the students' contentedness and satisfaction: at Carolina, she said, "conservatism is plainly comfortable."[154]

The students of the 1950s reveled in college life. They revived the prewar tradition of freshman initiation and orientation, complete with "rat week"— which featured a scrubbing of the Maxcy Monument with toothbrushes.[155] The monument itself was the subject of several pranks during the decade; on one occasion students painted it bright pink. Later, students replaced the gold ball with a flaming torch, which was only to be replaced again with a 100–pound hitching post statue.[156]

The most notorious pranks of the decade were the "panty-raids," a nation-wide phenomenon. The panty raids began at the University of Missouri in the spring of 1952, and within weeks they swept the nation. At Carolina, the first of what newspapers called "lingerie raids" took place on the night of May 19, 1952, when, with exams and the summer break approaching, a crowd of 350 rowdy men stormed Wade Hampton and Sims dormitories on the women's quad in search of "unmentionables." Authorities called out a force of University and Columbia police, who prevented the raiders from overtaking the women's dorms. For the most part, the crowd (which included towns-people and servicemen as well as students) milled about the quad, but several students did enter girl's rooms and make off with their underwear. They got into the room of one girl through a window and emptied the entire contents of her dresser drawers out the same window. The sense of chaos spread when a prankster pulled a fire alarm in one of the buildings, bringing three fire trucks to the scene. One woman student reportedly doused a city policeman with a bucket of water poured from a window. A middle-aged woman was stopped by police as she attempted to let the air out of the tires of a patrol car.[157]

The following day, President Smith released a statement announcing, "The university deplored the behavior of some of our students last night in the women's dormitories. The matter is being thoroughly investigated, and subsequent disciplinary action . . . will be taken."[158] After a one-day investigation, the University's discipline committee suspended six male students for terms varying from three months to one year. The student body responded to the suspensions with a petition to the board of trustees, signed by some 500 students, declaring that the panty raid was "an outgrowth of like demonstrations which have spread from Colleges and Universities throughout the United States as of late. It was not designed or intended as a malicious or vandalistic demonstration but rather . . . [was] prompted by an amassing of school spirit." They appealed, arguing that the suspensions were "grossly inconsistent with the degree of the violation." However, the board, seeking to make an example of the perpetrators, upheld the suspensions. The University then reimbursed one female student $48 ($247) (drawn from Student Activities funds) for clothing lost during the raid.[159]

Once the idea for panty raids had started, they were difficult to prevent. In the spring of 1955, anonymous phone calls to the fraternities organized a raid of nearly 1,000 men on Sims dormitory, but the mob was unsuccessful in entering the building. The *Gamecock* reported that women taunted the men from their windows, calling them "chicken," and dumped water on their heads after luring them near the building by tossing panties out of the window. Columbia police and University vice president W. H. Patterson restored order. The following night, authorities dispersed another attempted raid before it could start. The students involved apologized to the administration, and no one was suspended.[160]

To prevent more raids, in 1956 the University declared the entire city block surrounding the women's quad off limits to males after 11 P.M. But the following year, another raid on the women's dorms drew 500 men, and this time, they managed to get into the dorms and make off with the coveted undergarments. This raid drew President Russell as well as police. When some women egged on the crowd by throwing their underwear from the windows, the crowd grew unruly and attacked police. Fifteen students were arrested but none prosecuted. In 1959, two more raids provoked suspensions of several students.[161]

While they were the target of the decade's most notorious pranks, Carolina's women students largely followed traditional courses in their choice of degree program. For example, in the fall of 1953, women made up 52 percent of students in the School of Education and 33 percent in the School of Journalism. However, the School of Engineering had only 2 women out of 519 students, and the School of Law 3 of 122.[162] Women were subjected to a strict dress code on campus. Dean of Women Arney Childs insisted that "the human knee is never an attractive sight," and prohibited women from wearing short pants outside of the women's quad. Enforcement of the in loco parentis policy in the dormitories continued with a double standard that had far stricter rules for women than men. Any on-campus social function had to be approved by the director of student activities four days in advance and required an approved chaperone. Men were allowed only in the lobbies of women's dormitories and were banned from the women's quad after 11 P.M.[163]

While the University of South Carolina community enforced such rules, they reflected postwar cultural trends that proscribed the roles of women in society.[164] The annual crowning of a homecoming queen and May queen (students chose the winners in elections) were only two examples of the beauty competitions held on campus that reinforced a traditional role for women. The yearbook, the *Garnet and Black,* chose an annual "Miss Garnet and Black," judged for "the features and contours of the face, expression and apparent personality, and feminine charm." The winners and runner-ups were featured in full-size photographs in the yearbook.[165]

By modern standards, the Derby Day festivities of the Sigma Chi fraternity, featuring a beauty contest that crowned a "Miss Venus," were the most offensive. In contrast to the Miss Garnet and Black contestants, women competing for Miss Venus were judged for qualities other than their faces. The contest consisted of female students, dressed in tight blouses, short-shorts, and high-heeled shoes, their heads covered by a paper bag, parading in front of a crowd of ogling fraternity men and college administrators who acted as the "judges."[166]

In an era of conformity and social conservatism, the fraternities and sororities enjoyed a heyday. In 1953, the interfraternity council pushed a plan to allow the organizations, housed in the tenements along the Horseshoe, to build new houses or rent nearby off-campus houses. Because of the overcrowded dormitories, the board of trustees approved the plan—provided the fraternities remained subject to existing dormitory rules (including the presence of a housemother). Two fraternities, Pi Kappa Phi and Sigma Nu, began renting homes on Pendleton Street in 1954. However, preferring to keep the fraternities on campus, the University soon offered an alternative to off-campus houses: it would build them their own dormitories, complete with separate social and chapter rooms, as well as a room for a housemother. By the end of 1955, the first of the University's thirteen fraternities moved into the new housing on McBryde quad, and when the entire facility was complete, the others followed.[167]

That the University would build fraternities their own housing was indicative of their relative standing in campus affairs. In his novel *Beach Music,* Pat Conroy wrote of the University in the mid-1960s, "The Greek system was paramount and unchallenged in its authority over all aspects of campus life."[168] His description was apt for 1950s student culture as well. Fraternity members controlled leadership positions in the important student organizations such as the honor fraternities and student government; Floyd Spence, a Kappa Alpha, for example, was elected student body president in 1951 and Bob C. McNair, a Sigma Chi, president in 1957. Fraternity parties were a center of social life. The exclusive formal dances held by the German and Cotillion Clubs continued as a highlight of the social calendar. Prospective fraternity brothers could go through the ordeal of rush only once, so the pressure on freshmen to receive a "bid" from a fraternity was intense. The facts of fraternity life would later be accurately portrayed in fiction: a character in Conroy's *Beach Music,* Jack McCall, is bewildered by the intricacies of rush and the social milieu of Greek life at Carolina. McCall's friend Capers Middleton explains that the choice of the proper fraternity at Carolina "was the most significant selection a man would make before his engagement to a proper young woman."[169] For those men not selected to join a fraternity, the independent organizations of the 1940s evolved more formal structures, becoming the Maxcy and McBryde Brotherhoods, both independent social fraternities.[170]

For women, the choice of what sorority to join was at least as important as the selection of a fraternity was to men. The gender role conditioning that Betty Friedan would later describe as the "feminine mystique" was a powerful force at the University of South Carolina, as at most southern colleges, in the 1950s. For the young woman at Carolina, special curfews, dress regulations, and social organizations saw to it that she remained a southern "lady" in the traditional understanding of that term. Her sorority membership might also be a highlight of her life as an independent person, for as soon as she was married, she was often expected to submerge her own identity to that of a wife and mother.[171]

In general, the Carolina students of the 1950s reflected the prosperity and complacency of the decade. Alumni noted that "students have far more money than formerly and drive big new automobiles."[172] Historian Daniel Hollis called them the "automobiled, suit-coated, allowance-supported, draft-ridden, hydrogen-bomb-worried students of the 1950s."[173] In a 1955 speech to the staff of the *Gamecock*, Hollis assailed the student body for their "anti-intellectuality." He criticized the fraternities and sororities for their pursuit of campus status, and unfavorably compared USC to Columbia University, where Hollis, a holder of a Carolina bachelor's degree, had attended graduate school. A *Gamecock* editorial described the thrust of Hollis's remarks: "the Columbia [University] library was a big student attraction and the scene of much student competition. Nobody called Bellevue if you read a book. At USC things are not quite the same. Joe College is being overdone and beat to death."[174]

Carolina's active extracurricular life remained the focus of student energies and reflected the close community of the relatively small University. Nonetheless, the nature of the institution underwent considerable change and growth in the 1950s, and one important element was the establishment of permanent extension centers outside of Columbia as way to expand the availability of higher education in the state. The University had offered limited extension work as far back as 1897 and had established a permanent extension division in 1915. The division offered several programs: a series of "field courses" in the high schools of the state, correspondence courses, an audio-visual aids library, and a magazine, all primarily designed to offer continuing education to public school teachers.[175]

However, in the fall of 1956, Dr. J. Howard Stokes and a group of the leading citizens of Florence began to work to establish a full-fledged junior college there. They pointed out that while the state had over twenty colleges, in the 30,000-square-mile area east of a line drawn from Rock Hill to Columbia to Charleston, there were only two colleges: Coker College in Hartsville and the Coastal Carolina Junior College in Conway. In early 1957, Florence legislators convinced the General Assembly to charter the Florence County Higher Education Commission, and in August, discussions with University officials, including dean of the faculty Wilfred Callcott and dean of arts and sciences Robert H. Wienefeld, produced an agreement with the Commission to establish a two-year college in Florence. In the fall of 1957, the new extension center opened to 52 freshman in the ground floor of the Florence County Library.[176]

Donald Russell stressed that the new extension center was "not a makeshift operation" but was "of University calibre." Students were subject to the same admission standards, grading system, and regulations as students on the Columbia campus and were considered full-fledged members of the Carolina student body. Regular University faculty taught the classes (such as biology professor W. R. Kelley, history professors George Curry and Wilfred Callcott, English professors George C. Brauer and George Reeves, and mathematics professor Robert Vause), who commuted to Florence twice a week.[177]

Other communities, anxious for their own two-year colleges, soon followed the Florence example. A 1959 movement by Beaufort citizens managed to have the existing USC "field courses" taught there transformed into a permanent extension campus, with John Duffy as resident director. In that same year, Lancaster citizens won legislative support for a two-year campus in their city. In late 1959, the University assumed control of the Coastal Carolina Junior College in Conway, in existence since 1954. In 1961, Aiken added a campus. The rapidly expanding regional campuses were initially designed to be strictly two-year institutions. They were to provide education entirely equivalent to the first two years of baccalaureate work in Columbia, and upon completion students could then transfer to the main campus in Columbia or to another college, with a minimum of inconvenience.[178] The University maintained control of the extension campus's academic programs, while the local board of higher education provided buildings and grounds and state and local taxpayers provided funding for capital improvements. From the University's perspective, these extension campuses not only expanded the availability of higher education in South Carolina, but they broadened the University's political constituencies to communities outside of Columbia, thus strengthening its hand in the General Assembly.[179]

The establishment of the regional campuses was a new development at the University, and one that came while the institution was in the middle of an important transition. Amid widespread speculation that Donald Russell would make a run for governor in 1958, on October 25, 1957, he saddened the campus community when he submitted his resignation effective December 1, 1957. The resignation was indeed the prelude to a gubernatorial candidacy, which Russell announced in December of that year.[180]

The board of trustees reluctantly accepted Russell's resignation, suggesting a list of essential qualifications for the University's next president. Among them: "Unquestionable character, scholarly interest, Southerner (South Carolinian if possible), Married—attractive wife—children—ambitious, Reasonably Dry, Proven Executive ability, Public Speaker—Diplomat, Democratic, Able to make decisions, Financial Genius who can do things that require money without the money, Thorough understanding of Traditions, History, and Customs of South Carolina."[181] Rutledge L. Osborne, chairman of the board, added, "We just lost the above described man. Where do we look for another one?" Speaking for the entire board of trustees, Osborne said of Russell's resignation, "It is doubtful that the University has ever sustained a greater loss in the one hundred and fifty-five years of its existence. No man ever accomplished so much in so short a time as Donald Russell."[182]

Faculty and students also expressed profound regret at the news. One anonymous faculty member admitted to a reporter, "I could cry over this."[183] Student Madeline King wrote to the *Gamecock*, "Donald Russell pulled Carolina up by its bootstraps, gave it a fatherly smack on the bottom, and put it back in the race for school progress, a race in which it had been scratched for a long time."[184] Bob Talbert wrote that Russell's "entry onto the Carolina scene was the rebirth, or maybe the birth of South Carolina as a great university."[185]

Russell later claimed that his years at the University were the "happiest of his life." Not only had he put the University "back in the race for school progress," but his unselfish giving materially benefited the University in an era when it received virtually no private financial support at all. He served without pay for his entire five-year stint as president, and he and Virginia Russell quietly made substantial personal financial contributions to the University. They spent a considerable sum on the renovations of the president's home (perhaps as much as $67,000 [$344,300]). Shortly after he became president, Russell made a gift worth more than $50,000 ($254,531) to the University, which he hoped would attract other private gifts to be used to endow special professorships. He set the example with his establishment of the James F. Byrnes Professorship of International Studies in 1959. In addition, upon his resignation, Russell made a "parting gift" to the University of some $26,000 ($124,205) in stock. The proceeds from these gifts funded not only the Byrnes chair, but also the Russell faculty awards for teaching and research.[186]

After Russell's resignation, the board of trustees immediately named Robert L. Sumwalt, Dean of the School of Engineering, acting president. A native of Baltimore, Sumwalt had been a faculty member since 1926 and dean since 1943. He had been intimately involved with the planning and construction of all of the new buildings at Carolina in his tenure and had overseen the reorganization of the curriculum of the School of Engineering during Russell's administration. In these roles, he had developed close relationships with key figures, including board chairman Rutledge L. Osborne and Sol Blatt Sr.[187]

In the wake of Russell's resignation the faculty worried over who would be appointed as his successor, and the appointment of Sumwalt as acting president raised some eyebrows on campus. Traditionally, acting presidents named after presidential resignations had been the chief academic officer. Wilfred Callcott, the dean of the faculty in 1957, was a highly respected scholar and administrator, but was not a man to seek the spotlight. He had been instrumental in the academic progress of the Russell administration, including the expansion of the graduate program and the extension centers. Sumwalt, on the other hand, made his mark as an overseer of the high-profile construction projects at the University rather than in scholarship or teaching. Thus, having personal friendships with influential figures and a more outgoing personality, Sumwalt was the board of trustees' choice over Callcott. Dean of the College of Arts and Sciences Robert H. Wienefeld, upon hearing that Sumwalt had been named acting president, is said to have exclaimed, "Sumwalt? What an insult to Callcott!"[188]

At the time Sumwalt was named as acting president, the appointment was expected to be temporary. Promptly upon Russell's resignation the board named a five-man search committee to select a new chief executive.[189] However, their work dragged on for months, and after Donald Russell's gubernatorial bid failed in the summer of 1958, some students and faculty began a movement to bring Russell back as president. In September 1958, a *Gamecock* editorial and a student petition with 600 signatures urged his return. A group of the University's leading administrators met with Russell at his Spartanburg home hoping to entice him back, and newspapers reported that he was "receptive" to the idea of returning.[190]

However, the exceedingly bitter 1958 political campaign, in which Russell tried to use the Barnwell Ring issue against his opponent Ernest Hollings, alienated influential Carolina supporters (such as Sol Blatt Sr.) and split the board of trustees. Furthermore, student and faculty opinion about bringing Russell back was far from unanimous, for some felt that Russell had attempted to use the presidency as a stepping stone to the governor's office and would do so again if the opportunity arose. Furthermore, they believed that the bitter words exchanged in the campaign would harm the University in the legislature. In the meantime, rumors began to circulate that former congressman

James P. Richards or former governor George Bell Timmerman Jr. were being considered for the University's top job.[191]

Through the fall of 1958 and the spring of 1959, the board of trustees remained deadlocked between Russell supporters (led by board chairman Rutledge L. Osborne) and opponents. The faculty was becoming restive over the lack of permanent leadership and wanted the University's affairs removed from the political arena.[192] The *Gamecock* declared that the matter of choosing a new president "has been left hanging far too long."[193] In April 1959, the board announced its intention to name a president by the end of the year, but in May, they agreed on a compromise that removed "acting" from Robert Sumwalt's title. They unanimously chose him president nearly eighteen months after he assumed the duties of the office.[194]

When Sumwalt assumed the position of acting president on December 1, 1957, his theme was one of continuity with the successful Russell years. He stressed sustaining the "momentum of progress." He said, "The University has . . . lost much through Mr. Russell's resignation, but the progress—academic, physical and spiritual—made under his leadership must not come to a halt."[195] As a former faculty member who understood a professor's problems and priorities, Sumwalt, with the help of Wilfred Callcott, continued a strong push Donald Russell had begun in the last year of his tenure to raise overall faculty salaries.[196]

For example, as a part of a general salary increase given to all state employees, Russell secured funds to raise the median salary 3.8 percent in 1957–58. However, this raise did not apply to all faculty, and as a whole, USC still lagged behind other southern universities. Dean Callcott wrote of the salary situation, "Thanks to the splendid progress made in recent years the University can properly boast that it is traveling "first class" with regard to its plant and many other fine facilities. Thanks to the splendid effort made to increase salaries over the past few years," he concluded, "we are now in position to consider making the final step which will take us from our position . . . *at the foot of the list* to one where we can stand with first class neighboring institutions."[197]

Toward this end, during the first legislative session of Sumwalt's acting presidency, the administration convinced the General Assembly to appropriate funds raising the median faculty salary 8.3 percent for the 1958–59 academic year.[198] This represented the largest annual salary increase most faculty had seen since World War II, and they appreciated it. English professor Hubert Spigner wrote to Sumwalt of his raise, "There's only one part of your title of which I do not approve: the word *acting*. You've been most zealous in your outgoing concern for all of your colleagues."[199] Between 1956–57 and 1960–61, the median salary for all faculty ranks at USC rose from $5,250

($25,837) to $6,850 ($31,345). Despite these real gains in income, elsewhere salaries were rising as well, and USC's raises, while unprecedented for the institution, were more than matched by other universities. An American Association of University Professors (AAUP) survey of faculty salaries gave USC an "E" rating (on an AA to F scale, with AA the highest score) for average faculty salary during the 1959–60 academic year. This compared to a "B" rating for the University of Virginia, a "C" rating for the University of North Carolina, and "D" ratings for the Universities of Alabama and Florida.[200]

Hence, at the end of the decade, the top-flight faculty recruited during the mid-1950s were still vulnerable to being lured away by other schools. Dean Callcott pointed out to Sumwalt that "the University has recently emerged as an institution that is 'doing things.' Accordingly, we are being watched. Unfortunately, this also means that our men are understood to be good, hence are being sought after throughout the nation." He cited many examples, among them: "A dean here at a proposed salary of $11,400 ($53,364) was offered $16,000 ($74,897) in New York State. A Professor of Education at a proposed salary of $8,700 ($40,725) was offered $15,000 ($70,216) in private industry. A professor of Economics went to Missouri at $12,000 ($56,172). His salary at University of South Carolina was $8,200 ($38,384)." Callcott stressed that several faculty members had been granted one-year leaves of absence to teach at schools such as the University of California, the University of Wisconsin, Duke University, and the University of North Carolina. He asked, "Having tasted the flesh-pots abroad, will they return?"[201] As 1959 came to a close, while still recognized as an institution "on the move," the University faced a salary situation that without improvement, in the words of Robert Sumwalt, would cause "mediocrity" to prevail.[202]

Sumwalt directed the "momentum of progress" in other directions as well. He declared that the University had to place continuing emphasis on graduate training and research if it was to realize its ambition of becoming one of the leading institutions of higher education in the United States.[203] Carolina still ranked far behind other southern universities in the size and number of doctoral programs (see table 3.1). However, in 1959, the University added a doctoral program in physics and became one of four institutions in the nation to receive Federal Education Act funds for graduate fellowships in physics.[204] In that same year, USC began offering master's degrees in business administration and journalism, and in 1960, it added a Ph.D. program in mathematics.[205]

The dictates of post-Sputnik America in the late 1950s demanded ever-increasing emphasis on scientific research. The Sputnik crisis led to massive federal aid for schools and universities and increasing federal involvement in university research. As Sumwalt said, "It is only too clear in these days of earth satellites, guided missiles, H-bombs, and nuclear-powered submarines that our nation must push to ever higher levels of scientific and technological development."[206] However, because of its high teaching loads and comparatively poor research facilities, the University of South Carolina was well behind its peers in attracting outside research funds in the sciences.[207] In response to Sputnik and the University's need to better coordinate, mobilize, and focus its scientific resources, the University established the Institute of Science and Technology in March 1958 under the direction of chemist Willard Davis. The institute aimed toward encouraging fundamental research programs in pure and applied sciences, and improving the teaching of science and technology in both colleges and schools. In the year following the establishment of the institute, outside funds for research and teaching institutes in the sciences and engineering increased nearly 29 percent.[208] The post-Sputnik hysteria also extended to efforts to improve America's public schools, and Carolina's school of education received funds from the landmark National Defense Education Act (1958) to help establish an education guidance and counseling program.[209]

While the new institute helped attract outside research contracts, the University had long had a dire need to attract private money for the general support of academic programs. The alumni of the University had never been generous with their money, instead preferring to let the state and student fees fund the institution almost singlehandedly. In fact, Carolina alumni had been accused of caring only for the fortunes of the football team, not academic programs. History professor Daniel Hollis wrote to alumni of this charge: "We wish that we could state categorically that it was false. In all candor, however, it must be admitted that there is some truth to the allegation. Compared to other universities in the region and nation, USC alumni have indeed done little to support their alma mater."[210] The University of South Carolina was the only state university in the South without a private endowment fund to benefit academics.[211]

In 1956, however, a group of active alumni began to consider forming of a private eleemosynary foundation to supplement Carolina's academic programs. Donald Russell told them that "some type of foundation, with the additional revenue that it can provide, is a necessity if the University is to serve as an intellectual dynamo for future state leadership."[212] Under the leadership of alumni T. Eston Marchant, Charles W. Knowlton, Jeff B. Bates, and William S. Brockington, the University of South Carolina Educational Foundation was officially established on May 3, 1958. The foundation's main goal was to build a fund of sufficient size that its income could be used along with a newly established annual giving program to supplement academic activity. With the University's existing alumni association acting as a partner by soliciting its members, the USC Educational Foundation raised nearly $108,000 ($507,009) from industry, private institutions, and 424 alumni in its first year.[213] At last the University had an alternate source of funds with which it could support faculty through salary supplements and grants for research and publishing, as well as student scholarships and library improvement.[214]

While a private endowment fund for academics was just beginning, alumni had long supported the Carolina athletic program, which underwent changes during the 1950s. In the late 1940s, the National Collegiate Athletic Association (NCAA) adopted the so-called "sanity code," their first attempt at putting restrictions on "cut-throat" competition for student-athletes by limiting how scholarships were awarded and what they could cover.[215]

In 1950, the University of South Carolina challenged the new rules. The NCAA threatened to suspend the University and five other schools (including Clemson) for operating "training tables" for athletes—a violation of the code, which limited athletic scholarships to tuition and one meal a day. The University made no attempt to abide by the rule, and it threatened to leave the NCAA if the organization enforced the code. Carolina then joined with other southern schools protesting the sanity code, schools that were in favor of only voluntary compliance with NCAA rules (a plan that had failed previously—hence the need for the sanity code). At the 1951 NCAA annual convention, the entire organization was slated to vote on the suspension of the University of South Carolina. Instead, Carolina and its allies succeeded in fatally weakening the entire sanity code, and thus the University escaped its first brush with NCAA rule violations.[216]

Meanwhile, the Gamecock football team was enjoying excitement on the field, part of it provided by one of the first true superstars in Carolina history, running back Steve "the Cadillac" Wadiak. A student favorite, Wadiak was Southern Conference player of the year in 1950 and a top candidate for numerous All-America teams. Tragically, Wadiak died in a car accident in the spring of 1952, just before the end of his fourth year as a Carolina student.[217] In 1954, the Gamecocks got their first-ever All-American football player, Frank Mincevich. And on the basketball court, Grady Wallace led the nation in scoring with a 31.3 points per game average; Wallace became the Gamecock's first-ever basketball All-American in 1957.[218]

When Donald Russell became president in August 1952, he was committed to not only to building a first-class academic program, but he was a sports fan and recognized the public relations potential of athletics. He was committed to a successful, well-rounded athletic program that was fully integrated into campus life. To reach that end, in early 1954, the board of trustees granted athletic director and head football coach Rex Enright faculty tenure, a move designed to remove him from the pressures of alumni hungry for victories and give stability to the athletic department. Russell believed that "if a coach represents a man of character, integrity, and recognized ability . . . then he ought to be given tenure the same as a professor." He reasoned that if a coach must depend on winning seasons to keep his job, "then you can expect nothing other than for him to take a better job when he has a winning season."[219]

Enright had indeed delivered postwar football success. His teams were 5–0–1 against Clemson between 1949 and 1954, and they went four years without a losing season in the early 1950s. However, the year after he gained tenure, his 1955 team was 3–6, and Enright resigned the head coaching position following the season. When he retired, he had served as Gamecock head coach longer than any other man in Carolina history. Enright remained athletic director and hired Warren Giese, a former assistant at the University of Maryland, to coach in his stead. Giese's first season was a success, including a victory over Orange Bowl–bound Clemson and an overall 7–3 record. In 1958, Giese compiled another 7–3 season, and Alex Hawkins was named ACC player of the year. Rex Enright continued as athletic director until his death in 1960, and after the 1960 football season, Giese resigned as head coach and took over the athletic director position. He assumed leadership of a department that in 1960 cost the University $151,000 ($694,856) per year to operate—double the amount it spent on library books.[220]

The 1950s saw another important development in the Carolina athletic program. In 1953, the University of South Carolina was among the leaders of seven southern universities (Clemson, North Carolina, North Carolina State, Wake Forest, Duke, and Maryland, along with Carolina) who left the Southern Conference and formed the Atlantic Coast Conference (ACC). Carolina biology professor James T. Penney served as the conference's first president. Scheduling problems in the seventeen-member Southern Conference was the key factor precipitating the split, and conference rules could be more easily enforced among a smaller, more homogenous group than in the much larger Southern Conference.[221]

At the end of the decade, one of the nation's unique annual sporting events, the "Big Thursday" Carolina football game with archrival Clemson, came to an end on October 22, 1959. Beginning in 1960, the game was moved to the end of each team's schedule and alternately played at each team's home field rather than at the fairgrounds stadium in Columbia. Clemson head coach Frank Howard had wanted the change for years, since the Columbia site essentially gave Carolina a home field advantage every year. After negotiations with Rex Enright, the two schools agreed to play every other game in Clemson, and Carolina lost the final Big Thursday game in Columbia 27–0.[222]

Carolina's athletic teams drew public attention to the University like no other activity. However, during the 1950s, the public's attention focused on universities in the South for another reason: racial segregation. The increasing success of the civil rights movement during the 1950s, especially as it related to public education, forced white supremacists in South Carolina to continually adjust to the changing landscape of human rights. As in the late 1940s, in the early years of the 1950s civil rights activists seeking to overturn "separate but equal" education in South Carolina focused some of their effort on the state's graduate schools, primarily those at the University of South Carolina. Two landmark U.S. Supreme Court cases decided in June 1950 had a direct impact in Columbia. In *Sweatt v. Painter,* the court ordered a black applicant admitted to the University of Texas law school when it decided that the state's black law school did not offer a legal education equivalent to that offered at the University of Texas. In *McLaurin v. Oklahoma,* the court ruled that the University of Oklahoma had to stop putting humiliating restrictions on the attendance of elderly student George W. McLaurin in graduate school.[223] In South Carolina, the *Wrighten* case had shown that the state's black law school at Orangeburg, despite massive state funding, was nowhere near equivalent to the school of law at Carolina, and the USC law school was an obvious target for those seeking to overturn South Carolina's segregated system.

Recognizing the legal implication of the *Sweatt* and *McLaurin* rulings, almost immediately Jacob Joseph Martin, a twenty-one–year old graduate of Allen University, applied to the USC law school. His application was quickly followed by those of applicants to two other USC undergraduate programs that had no equivalent at South Carolina State: Cleveland Stevens, a student at South Carolina State College, applied for advanced standing in journalism, and Samuel Herman Rubens applied to the pharmacy school. The administration and board of trustees began a quiet search of the men's backgrounds to see if they could deny them admission on the grounds of "moral character," which had become a University entrance requirement as a way to deny black applicants. Finding no moral deficiencies, the board nonetheless denied them admission, responding to all three men simply, "Your application . . . has had proper consideration and it is declined." Publicly, the University claimed the men were denied admission on the grounds that the state provided "equally comparable facilities in all lines of college activities" at South Carolina State. Despite that fact that this was not the case, in the absence of a legal challenge, the denial stood.[224] The following year, the University again flatly denied admission to a black candidate for no other reason than his color. This time the student was Edward Allen Dantzler, an applicant to the graduate school in business administration. Dantzler appealed the denial, but later joined the Air Force and dropped his lawsuit.[225]

The law school continued to be a primary target of those fighting "separate but equal" education. In 1951, the Association of American Law Schools

(AALS) began putting pressure on southern schools of law that practiced racial segregation, but AALS threats to expel discriminating schools were replaced by a plea that member schools voluntarily comply with an antisegregation statement, to which Carolina refused to agree.[226] The University continued to flatly decline the applications of black applicants. Soon, however, the high failure rate of graduates of the South Carolina State law school on the state bar exam became a concern. As of January 1952, only one of three graduates of the Orangeburg law school who had taken the South Carolina bar exam had passed it (he was future federal judge Matthew J. Perry). The South Carolina State law faculty were concerned that few of their graduates would pass in the future, and dean of the USC school of law Samuel Prince said that "the effect of this will probably mean [law]suits against the University on the grounds that the work done at Orangeburg is not equal to that at the University." Prince himself claimed to believe in the quality of the South Carolina State instruction and was confident that Thurgood Marshall, the NAACP counsel leading their antisegregation effort in the courts, would not back lawsuits in South Carolina directed toward university-level education.[227]

When one of the South Carolina State graduates who had failed the bar exam, Frank Edward Cain, applied to the USC law school in late 1951, he was denied admission. Cain threatened to expose the failures of the Orangeburg law school graduates and the general tendency of the South Carolina bar to fail black examinees. However, Dean Prince was apparently right about Marshall's reluctance to bring suit in South Carolina, for no black applicant sued for admission to the University in the 1950s, despite ongoing applications and consistent denials. The General Assembly continued to spend large sums to keep the races apart in the state's colleges. For example, in 1961 it cost the state $100 [$455] per semester hour taught in the South Carolina State law school as opposed to $17 [$77] at the USC School of Law. The out-of-state tuition payment program that paid for black Carolinians to attend graduate schools grew from 15 students receiving about $6,000 ($35,285) in 1947–48 to 239 students receiving some $55,000 ($263,128) a decade later. Whatever the cost, these expenditures achieved the purpose for which they were intended, for through the end of the 1950s South Carolina avoided court orders to desegregate state higher educational institutions.[228] Despite the lack of court orders, at least one black student quietly enrolled at the University in the fall of 1951. To the horror of state legislators, a black member of the integrated military briefly took classes at an extension division program that taught courses at Shaw Air Force Base in Sumter. The General Assembly quickly cancelled the extension program.[229]

The absence of landmark court cases in South Carolina higher education did not mean that the University avoided the racial issue in the 1950s. In fact, throughout the decade, and especially after the May 1954 *Brown* decision, racial segregation was *the* issue in South Carolina, and the University and its students reflected it. For example, in late 1953, the Hypatian Literary Society, a women's debating organization, passed a surprising resolution supporting the admission of black students to the University.[230]

A few weeks later, the *Gamecock* ran a series of student editorials discussing the institution of racial segregation, and several took the minority position. Gus Manos declared, "Segregation is wrong. Its practice is sinful, hypocritical and backward. It represents the antithesis of the great concept of the brotherhood of man." In another issue he wrote, "Segregation has been perpetuated through the years by minds that have become stagnant."[231] Flynn Harrell spoke for the majority of Carolina students when he responded that segregation was essential to the "peculiar southern way of life," writing that "We who live in the South . . . are far better able to cope with our particular problems than are the NAACP agitators who occupy office suites in downtown New York and who base their opinions on the distorted stories appearing in the Negro Press and the Daily Worker."[232]

The editorial series drew such active student responses that the *Gamecock* polled them about their opinions of racial segregation: 74 percent supported it. One student attacked the editorials, stating "Segregation has been the accepted pattern for thousands of years, and now a bunch of 19-year old college sophomores are trying to change the world in an attempt to be intellectual." Another attacked "yankees," claiming that "Both the whites and Negroes in the South were satisfied with our system until some yankees, duped by communist propaganda, came down to 'set us straight.'" Other students simply felt that black Americans were inferior, and thus segregation was natural.[233] The *Gamecock's* series demonstrated both the lack of historical perspective among students and their high level of interest in the racial situation, even before the *Brown* decision.

In late 1950, *Briggs v. Elliott,* the landmark civil rights case that originated in Clarendon County (and ultimately became a part of *Brown v. Board of Education*) began to make its way through the federal courts. The South Carolina General Assembly recognized the danger the case presented to their system of racially segregated schools. They responded by casting about for ways to preserve racial segregation. One strategy, supported by James F. Byrnes, was the introduction of a one-penny state sales tax whose proceeds would be used to provide black schools with improved facilities, so that the state could argue that "separate but equal" was indeed a reality. The General Assembly also created a special fifteen-man committee, headed by Senator Marion Gressette, to recommend other measures to prevent desegregation.[234]

As a part of the state's preparations for the defense of racial segregation in higher education, in the spring of 1950 the South Carolina College Association (SCCA, the organization of white colleges in the state, both public and private), set up a committee to study the feasibility of requiring examinations of applicants to its member schools. In addition, Governor Byrnes, committed to maintaining segregation, requested a ruling on the duty of state-supported institutions to admit all graduates from accredited high schools. The state attorney general declared that there was no legal duty to do so. He also determined that the respective institutions' boards of trustees could limit admissions by whatever means they chose. As a result, in May 1951, the SCCA committee recommended that its member institutions adopt a policy of requiring all candidates for admission from South Carolina to take aptitude tests. In the words of the University's registrar, H. O. Strohecker, such a program would "be a valuable safeguard should the Supreme Court fail to uphold segregation in state schools."[235]

However, although member schools generally agreed that entrance exams were a good idea, Strohecker and President Smith persuaded the board of trustees that the University should delay implementing such a program. First, they argued the University could not begin such a program unilaterally. To do so would put Carolina at a recruiting disadvantage vis-à-vis the state's other colleges, who declined to act immediately. While Governor Byrnes wanted the state to administer the tests in high schools, there were other obstacles: How would out-of-state applicants take the tests? What would the University do about prospective athletes, many of whom might fail examinations? By the end of 1952, the proposal for statewide entrance exams as a safeguard against desegregation appeared dead.[236]

However, the progress of *Briggs v. Elliott* in the federal courts led Donald Russell to revive the proposal. In fact, even before the court's decision, Russell believed that the desegregation of the University was inevitable and that it would probably occur at some time during the 1950s. He advocated a plan of gradual desegregation, beginning first with the law school and proceeding slowly toward the total desegregation of the institution.[237] As a court decision loomed, his primary concern was to prevent any court ruling from interfering with his progress in improving the academic programs. Knowing that a court ruling was on the way, in the weeks and months prior to the ruling Russell worked feverishly to convince the state's other colleges to act in concert to institute a program of entrance exams. On the USC campus, he set up a special faculty committee, chaired by Dean Robert H. Wienefeld, to develop a workable system to implement such a plan. Just three days before the court announced its ruling, Russell set up a June meeting of all the SCCA college presidents to discuss acting on the entrance exam plan.[238]

On May 17, 1954, the U.S. Supreme Court ruled on the *Briggs* case in its landmark *Brown v. Board of Education* decision, declaring that "separate but equal" education was unconstitutional. When the Court handed down its ruling, the University administration's aversion to acting unilaterally on the issue of entrance exams disappeared. On May 27, just ten days after the ruling, at a general faculty meeting the special committee recommended that "the admission of all new students to the University . . . shall be by examination." Faculty realized that the proposal was directly related to the *Brown* decision. One professor asked Donald Russell, "Let's face it Mr. President. Is it not true that these entrance examinations are, in reality, being introduced as a means of keeping out Negro applicants?" Russell is said to have replied, "Certainly not! As far as I am concerned, if a qualified Negro applies for admission to this institution and passes these proposed entrance examinations, he can and will be admitted." This position was in line with Russell's earlier "gradualist" position. The faculty then approved a motion that entrance examinations be adopted. The following day, the board of trustees approved the faculty decision, and entrance exams became University policy. USC was the first southern state college or university to institute such examinations, but it is hardly the point of pride that University boosters in later years tried to portray it.[239]

The rationale behind the entrance exams was twofold. First, they would allow the University to continue its program of overall academic improvement by raising the caliber of students. The academic performance of students produced by South Carolina's public high schools had long been a problem. For example, since 1927, the University had required entering freshmen to take standardized placement tests, and the resulting scores were below national averages. The use of standardized entrance exams and merit-based admissions was becoming increasingly common at colleges and universities nationwide in the postwar era as a new ethos stressing individual ability and upward mobility over wealth, family connections, or ethnicity began to shape some colleges' admissions policies.[240] But second, USC's reasons for considering the entrance exam ironically constituted a way to maintain some admissions restrictions rather than to break them down. Foremost in the minds of state leaders, entrance exams would give administrators a way to prevent the graduates of black high schools from flooding the University. Russell admitted of entrance examinations, "This matter, in frankness, was academic until the recent action of the Supreme Court." The exams would, he said, allow them to legally exclude students "who might retard the progress of the University." He continued, "We feel that we must establish a system of entrance examinations that are not based on racial standards but on social standards. If we deny access to particular students we would be discriminating[,] and this can be avoided if we do not admit anyone without examinations." He concluded, "If we have an impartial entrance examination we would be reasonably sure that all students admitted would be able to measure up to college work."[241]

Reaction to the plan was mixed. Many, like George C. Rogers Sr. (the superintendent of Charleston City Schools) approved, pointing to the benefits for the state of raising academic standards.[242] Most of the state's major newspapers approved on similar grounds, arguing that, in the words of the *State,* entrance exams were "a move in the direction of higher scholarship."[243]

However, others decried the examinations, declaring that high academic standards were antidemocratic. South Carolinian John R. Williams wrote to the *State,* "In a democratic country a state institution should be established for the average intellect. If not—there is no democracy."[244] Many of the University's staunchest supporters, such as Sol Blatt Jr., worried what impact the examinations would have on the athletic program. Russell admitted that "our entrance examinations may eliminate some football talent," but he believed that exams would strengthen the football program in the long run since coaches could now have a reasonable expectation that athletes who were admitted would pass their classes and stay in school.[245] Rex Enright agreed and supported the examination program.[246]

With only a few exceptions, public comments about the new examinations avoided the racial issue, instead focusing on overall academic standards. However, John R. Williams wrote to the *State,* "Your editorials have not even mentioned the real reason for the University adopting this policy. You know it as well as I do."[247] Russell later admitted the reason for the exams openly. In his 1958 campaign for governor, he claimed that the entrance examinations had been administered so as to preserve segregation. He boasted that the University had "pioneered in protecting our Southern way of life and in taking a necessary precautionary step."[248]

Charleston's *News and Courier,* never a timid observer of state events, went to the heart of the matter and expressed the thinking of most state leaders. The editor remarked, "State colleges and universities will be the immediate target of those seeking mixture of the races in tax-supported institutions." In case white colleges might be forced to admit black students, entrance exams would ensure that "there would be no danger . . . that the academic standards of our colleges—already none too high—would be pulled down to fit the lowest common denominator." The editor concluded that entrance examinations would not completely solve the "segregation problem" in the state's colleges, but at least they would "be an immediate guarantee that tens of thousands of diploma-bearing Negro high school graduates would not show up next autumn or in the autumn of 1955 at the gates of our white colleges."[249]

In the years after *Brown*, the University's administration continued its practice of denying admission to black students in accord with state policy, and the entrance examinations worked to head off black attempts to enroll. Through 1954 and 1955, white politicians throughout the South began championing massive resistance to the *Brown* decision, denouncing the NAACP and the Supreme Court. White Citizen's Councils made diehard opposition to "integrationists" a litmus test for their support in elections and branded any whites who advocated compliance with the *Brown* decision as traitors— assuming them to be in favor of communism, atheism, and "mongrelization." To many white South Carolinians in the mid-1950s, maintaining segregation became more important than improving education.[250]

At the University of South Carolina, this poisoned atmosphere led to the disappearance of the ability to openly and critically discuss the controversial issue of racial segregation. University faculty felt legitimate threats to academic freedom, especially the professors in the recently revamped school of education. Less than a month after the announcement of the *Brown* decision, newly hired education professor Newton Edwards, a recognized authority on school law, gave a speech at Duke University in which he outlined the significance of the court's decision. The Associated Press ran a story about the speech that began, "A University of South Carolina professor says, 'Race segregation in the public schools is in itself a denial of the equal protection of the law.'"[251] The AP story portrayed Edwards's talk as an attack on segregation, and it aroused a minor furor in South Carolina. In a letter to Donald Russell, trustee Sol Blatt Jr. demanded that "if [Edwards] feels this way then he certainly should not make speeches as our representative or while connected with the University."[252] In truth, Edwards's speech was no attack on segregation at all. In it, he merely attempted to summarize the court's decision.[253] In the atmosphere of hysteria among some white South Carolinians, however, simply explaining the meaning of the *Brown* decision in public was enough to draw criticism in a society that had resolved to resist the decision of the nation's highest court. To advocate compliance with the court was deemed by most white South Carolinians to be akin to heresy.[254]

Dean of the School of Education Chester C. Travelstead soon felt the full force of white South Carolina's rage over the *Brown* decision and its consequent abandonment of the principle of free speech. Travelstead had been hired at USC in 1953 as a part of the reorganization of the School of Education. A Kentucky native, he later claimed that even before he was hired, he had been open with Donald Russell in his belief that southern universities should not discriminate. He immediately became a critic of the way South Carolina ran its educational system and a reformer dedicated to improving it.[255]

On the job, Travelstead was highly successful in shaping the new School of Education that was a priority to Donald Russell. [256] However, Travelstead believed that with the stifling of free speech, South Carolina was "fast becoming an autocratic police state." He wrote of conditions in the Palmetto State, "One no longer hears in this state the opinions of those who advocate even a gradual process of desegregation. Their voices have been silenced."[257] To challenge this development, in May 1955 Travelstead sent a long letter to South Carolina Governor George Bell Timmerman, an ardent segregationist who in his inaugural address and in a major speech to the South Carolina Educational Association (SCEA) had denounced the U.S. Supreme Court and strongly condemned attempts at integration. In his SCEA speech, Timmerman said, "It is cowardly to advocate gradualism in this matter of integration. There will be no compulsory race mixing in our state." In his reply to Timmerman's speech, Travelstead emphatically disagreed with the governor's positions. The dean challenged the governor's views on the state's school attendance laws, his criticism of the Supreme Court, and his announced policy of noncompliance with the *Brown* decision, among other educational issues. He asked the governor about the example he was setting for the state's children, "Can we on Monday tell them to obey the law . . . and then on Tuesday tell them they don't need to obey the law, that it is right to circumvent the law as long as they don't get caught?" [258]

Timmerman responded by writing to Donald Russell, charging that Travelstead's opinions were contrary to "established State policy and the expressed wishes of the public." The governor concluded that Travelstead was "a bad influence at the University," claiming that "few parents of University students in this state would want their children under the influence of his thinking."[259] Russell summoned the maverick dean to his office and calmly beseeched him to cease writing letters such as the one he had sent to the Governor, advising him, according to Travelstead, that "such controversial matters make politicians mad. . . . You don't change a governor's opinion on such a matter by writing him a letter." Despite the controversy, with Russell's recommendation in late July 1955 Travelstead received a reappointment as dean and a substantial raise.[260]

Just as the uproar over the Timmerman letter died down, Travelstead spoke against segregation again, this time in a public lecture to Carolina's summer session students. In it, he directly attacked segregation at length, stating, "It is my firm conviction that enforced segregation of the races in our public schools can no longer be justified on any basis—and should, therefore, be abolished as soon as practicable."[261] After the lecture, the audience clapped politely (though not enthusiastically), and no one present challenged Travelstead on its contents.[262]

Nonetheless, his lecture elicited a storm of criticism. Marion Gressette, chairman of the house education committee and ex officio member of the USC board of trustees, wrote to Governor Timmerman, "This man's attitude is definitely wrong. The State of South Carolina should not continue to employ him at the University in any capacity. I do not think it is fair to our young people to expose them to his personal opinion on this important subject, which is in conflict with the overwhelming sentiment of the white and colored people of the State." As a result, Russell again called Travelstead to his office and warned the dean that such comments would "cut our throats" in the General Assembly (and in an implicit message, damage Russell's own political future). Russell tried to persuade the dean to publicly recant his statement, but despite Travelstead's refusal took no action against him.[263]

However, two weeks after the speech, the executive committee of the USC board of trustees summarily fired Travelstead, claiming that it was "not in the University's best interest" to renew his appointment, and that he would be dismissed in the summer of 1956. After they informed the dean by letter, Travelstead asked them to discuss his dismissal with him. The committee eventually met with the dean, and though they were initially evasive about why their reasons for firing him, they made it clear, according to Travelstead, that university employees were not to publicly discuss "controversial issues." When the dean responded that no such written policy existed, he claimed that the board told him, "A person should have enough common sense to know what he should and should not discuss—without any clear-cut policy in such matters."[264] In the months following his dismissal, Travelstead accepted the position of dean of the school education at the University of New Mexico. William W. Savage, a man said to have "impeccable segregationist credentials," replaced him as dean of the school of education and was given the job of running the school in accord with the state government's position on racial segregation.[265]

The Travelstead dismissal did serious damage to the newly reorganized School of Education. One of the most important of Donald Russell's vaunted efforts to improve the University fell victim to the state's commitment to paying the price of prejudice. Three promising instructors resigned in protest (Margaret Rauhof, Sarah Drayton, and John Bachelor) despite Donald Russell's efforts to convince them otherwise. They followed Chester Travelstead to the University of New Mexico. Another faculty member hired at USC by Travelstead, Herbert Rudman, resigned soon after as well.[266] Other members of the faculty in the school of education expressed support for Travelstead, and a committee of faculty from across the University conferred with the board of trustees on the matter, seeking a statement on academic freedom. Despite the support of Donald Russell, who confidentially told the board that they could not "undertake to tell faculty members what they may or may not discuss." He continued, "As I see it, the University has an opportunity here of taking a forthright, unequivocal, and historic stand" in favor of academic freedom, but the board declined to issue such a statement.[267] The American Association of University Professors (AAUP) looked into the matter, but because the USC board took the position that Travelstead had been speaking as an administrator rather than as a faculty member, and because he had already secured employment elsewhere, the AAUP let the matter drop.[268]

On campus, students reacted strongly to the firing. In the *Gamecock,* many editorials and letters opposed the decision. Editor Carolyn McClung called the dismissal "a hard and definite blow to the University." If University officials took upon themselves to squelch persons with unpopular ideas, it was "no place for students with intellectual curiosity," wrote McClung.[269] Jack Bass read Travelstead's offending speech and declared it "very appropriate and an extremely fine analysis of the segregation problem facing South Carolina's schools." He called the decision to fire Travelstead a "rash and shortsighted" act that was "a damaging blast at the very basis of the foundation of this or any other university—intellectual integrity."[270]

On the other hand, James K. Sanders wrote, "I think that the University of South Carolina did exactly what the people of South Carolina . . . wanted and expected." He asked, "Why don't the people who like to go to school with, or teach, the Negro people go where segregation is not enforced?"[271] Billy Mellette supported the firing as well, writing, "I . . . believe that before a man speaks he should think about what he is and where he is." He concluded, "You say the policy is not written, and how then are you to know what to say? Use your damned head, that's how you know."[272]

Like most of South Carolina's newspapers, the *News and Courier* of Charleston supported the firing, declaring that the academic freedom question had two sides—"the freedom of the professor to speak his mind" and "the freedom of a university to choose the lines of education it wishes to follow." Travelstead, believed the editor, was out of step with both the people of South Carolina and university policy. Hence, wrote the editor, "He can easily exercise his academic freedom elsewhere." The Travelstead story was picked by the wire services and carried in newspapers across the country, eliciting quite a different response outside South Carolina. The *Fresno (California) Bee* asked of the University of South Carolina, "What kind of educational institution is it which makes discussion of controversial subjects taboo, with expulsion for those who dare to violate the rule? What is left of even a semblance of free speech under such circumstances?"[273]

The Travelstead firing and the resulting controversy over academic freedom damaged the University and its reputation, but the board of trustees and the state's leadership held firmly to their position. The atmosphere in South Carolina as it related to free speech on the issue of segregation had reached a nadir. Camden Episcopal minister Stiles B. Lines summed up the situation in January 1957: "Fear covers South Carolina like the frost. Men are afraid to speak. Freedom of speech is almost extinct in South Carolina, except for those who wish to speak in favor of and in accord with the policies of the pressure groups who self righteously assume that they, and only they, have the answers."[274] It was in this atmosphere that the powers in South Carolina forced the University of South Carolina to fire another professor who dared to take a public stand against segregation.

The next victim of the anti-integration hysteria was Joseph Margolis, an untenured assistant professor in the department of philosophy and psychology with a Ph.D. from Columbia University. In December 1957, Margolis published an article in the *Bulletin* of the American Association of University Professors (AAUP) titled "The Role of the Segregationist," in which he theorized that the anti-integration drumbeat by southern segregationists was more "play acting" than real, more a symbolic gesture of defiance than a real threat of rebellion. "The 'resistance' of the South is *not* wholehearted resistance," he wrote, ". . . because it is not really *hopeful;* it is not so much actual resistance as the enactment of a role of resistance." Margolis further attacked the southern segregationist position, claiming that in its treatment of black citizens the South was "suffering from a moral embarrassment that it cannot easily overcome." He struck at the heart of white southern identity when he wrote that white southerners relish such "lost causes" as segregation because "it is in defeat alone that the South is persuaded it has an identity it can cherish."[275]

When correspondent William D. Workman publicized the article in the *Charleston News and Courier,* the state's newspapers immediately attacked Margolis. The *Barnwell People-Sentinel* declared, "We haven't read . . . Margolis's article, but from what we have seen in the way of excerpts it appears he would be much happier were he to quit the South as a place of residence and return to a northern state."[276] Referring to the Travelstead incident, the *Summerville Scene* wrote of the Margolis article, "A dean at his university lost his job for saying less along this line, and surely an associate professor can't expect to get off easier than a dean."[277]

The *Scene* was correct, for the state's power structure quickly mobilized against Margolis. Sol Blatt Sr. wrote to acting president Robert Sumwalt, declaring, "It is my judgment that he [Margolis] should not be allowed to remain on the faculty at the University." He continued, "If this professor continues to express himself as he did in this article, the University is going to be in terrible shape and we might run into trouble with the legislature."[278] Blatt suggested that Sumwalt contact Donald Russell for advice on how to handle the situation (since he had handled the Travelstead matter as president) and recommended to Sumwalt that "something be done to relieve this man of his employment before the beginning of the second semester [spring 1958]." Though Blatt recognized that firing another professor for antisegregation speech might get the University censured by the AAUP, he was in favor of taking action "even though we might be blacklisted."[279] James F. Byrnes and Governor George Timmerman expressed similar opinions about Margolis to Sumwalt.[280]

On February 12, 1958, the head of the department of philosophy and psychology, Kershaw Walsh, did the requested deed and reported that Margolis did not fit the needs of the department. He recommended that Margolis's annual contract not be renewed. Walsh claimed that Margolis could not get along with his fellow department members.[281] Immediately, a group of faculty members, many of whom were among the "stars" hired by Donald Russell, came to Margolis's defense. Delos DeTar of the chemistry department (head of the local AAUP chapter), Anthony French of physics, Tomlinson Fort of mathematics, and Rufus Fellers of engineering led the opposition to the firing, insisting that the AAUP guidelines for the dismissal of a professor were violated, even though Margolis had no tenure. They saw the issue as a grave threat to the University, a danger that threatened the progress made since the arrival of Donald Russell. If blacklisted by the AAUP, the University would be unable to hire quality professors, and several top members of the chemistry and physics departments threatened to resign if the dismissal stood.[282]

Sumwalt, on the other hand, believed that Margolis had known what he was doing all along and that he should pay the consequences.[283] Sumwalt promised Margolis that he would consider holding a hearing, but before the dismissal was officially approved, William D. Workman reported in the April 13, 1958, News and Courier that "Prof. Margolis will not be at the University next year."[284] This led Margolis to claim to the AAUP that his firing was preordained and not in line with University nor AAUP regulations. Ultimately, the University let him go without a hearing.[285] An AAUP investigation of the incident was inconclusive. Meanwhile, the threatened resignation of other professors never materialized, since the University's AAUP standing was not seriously in jeopardy.[286] In May 1958, Margolis requested a leave of absence to take a position with the University of California, and in June, the board of trustees approved his dismissal.[287] Academic freedom at the University of South Carolina suffered another blow.

Faculty were not the only people at the University punished for speaking out on the segregation issue during the high tide of massive resistance during the late 1950s. In the midst of the so-called segregation session of the 1956 General Assembly, student R. L. Morton, a state house page, wrote a

Gamecock editorial in which he criticized the legislature for their obsession with the segregation issue. He wrote that members of the state legislators were closed-minded and that, "arrested by the decision of 'nine evil old men' on the United States Supreme Court, they are intent on circumventing movements which would abolish segregation of races in our state. . . . I am ashamed to be called a 'Southerner.'"[288] One week later, Morton was fired from his page's job; a petition with 85 student signatures made its way to the state house congratulating the legislators on their decision.[289]

White South Carolina's determined defense of segregation and its aggressive hounding of opponents nearly backfired, however. In the summer of 1957, Governor Timmerman pressured the Reverend Frank Veal, the president of Allen University (a private, historically black university in Columbia), to fire three professors whom Timmerman considered racial agitators, two of whom were listed in the files of the Un-American Activities Committee of the U.S. House of Representatives. When Allen's board of trustees refused to fire the men, Timmerman convinced the State Board of Education to revoke the accreditation for Allen's teacher training program.[290]

The revocation of Allen University's teacher accreditation gave black students a legal reason to apply to the School of Education at the University of South Carolina, and the resulting episode presented the most serious threat to racial segregation at Carolina during the 1950s. In January and February 1958, students from Allen and nearby Benedict College (a private, historically black college in Columbia that had also been threatened by Timmerman) sought to apply to take the entrance examinations at the University of South Carolina. On January 15, eleven Allen students visited the office of W. C. McCall, the director of USC's Examination and Counseling Bureau, where McCall refused to issue them application forms. The following day, five Allen students showed up at McCall's office with completed forms, but McCall refused to accept them as well. The next day, January 17, McCall's office received three applications from Allen students in the mail. The applying students declared that "upon rejection of our applications for entrance examinations for the spring semester, we will take legal steps. We plan to see this thing through."[291]

While the black students were treated sternly but politely by University officials, white students on the campus were not so restrained. One USC student is said to have leaned out a window and shouted "Here come the niggers!" The night after the first Allen group came to campus, a cross was burned on the USC athletic fields and a black effigy hanged on campus.[292]

On January 20, W. C. McCall wrote to the three students who applied by mail, Christine Thomas, Mary Alston, and Thelma McClain, "I am not in a position to give you the entrance examination which you requested. I am, therefore, returning the ten ($10.00 [$47]) dollar money order which was enclosed with your application."[293] Two days later, McCall turned away four Benedict students asking for application forms.[294] On February 12, two more Benedict students applied by mail.[295]

University officials took seriously the sudden flurry of black applications, which came at the same time the administration was also dealing with the Margolis situation, and initiated lengthy consultation about how to handle them. The day that McCall refused applications to the first group of black students (January 15), the University Council, a representative group of faculty members, passed a resolution stating that the University would accept no more applications nor would they consider those initiated after January 15, 1958, thus denying the applications of most of the applicants.[296] Acting President Sumwalt repeatedly conferred with Marion Gressette (the head of South Carolina's "special school committee" and ex officio member of the University board of trustees), Governor Timmerman, and Donald Russell, and gave explicit instructions to McCall about the exact wording he should use to address black applicants. University attorney David Robinson drafted the letters declining to accept the applications received by mail.[297]

In the meantime, seven of the rejected students approached the NAACP about supporting their case for admission in the courts. The students initially chose Charleston attorney John H. Wrighten, who had been denied entry to USC's law school a decade earlier (and who had subsequently finished the law school at South Carolina State), to represent them. Wrighten contacted the NAACP for legal assistance, but protracted discussions between the students, their representatives, and local, state, and national NAACP representatives brought no legal action. Internal confusion, misunderstanding, and dissension among members of the NAACP was the cause, and it appeared to the students and their supporters that state NAACP president James M. Hinton and Allen president Frank Veal were working to thwart their efforts to enroll at USC, over the objections of other prominent members of the South Carolina NAACP. The students claimed that Hinton resented the fact that they had acted on their own, applying to USC without first consulting him. Hinton in turn claimed these applicants were not acceptable candidates to be the plaintiffs in a high-profile desegregation lawsuit, citing their class standing, their residency, or their vulnerability to white economic reprisals as chief reasons. Whatever the reasons, the NAACP's inaction left the students high and dry. When the organization failed to come to the students' aid, South Carolina's black community missed what Columbia civil rights leader Modjeska M. Simkins called "a long-awaited, God-sent opportunity to make a driving wedge toward entry into the state-supported higher institutions." The damage to the NAACP's credibility and to its organization in South Carolina as a result of their dissension and failure to vigorously pursue this highly publicized case was significant, and it would be years before another opportunity to make a "driving wedge" for African American admission to USC would present itself.[298]

Despite black students' attempts to enroll, as a result of the NAACP's internal problems and the intricate legal safeguards built by South Carolina's white leaders to maintain segregation, the threat to segregated higher education in South Carolina did not go to the courts in 1958. The entrance examination served one of the purposes for which it was designed—it created a level of bureaucracy that intercepted black applications before they were unwittingly accepted. In addition, another deterrent to the black students pursuing their right to attend the University was a 1956 law stating that any public college was to close "upon any pupil being ordered admitted . . . by the order of any court" and to remain closed until the court order was revoked. Moreover, South Carolina State College would be forced to close if a court ordered any black student into any white public college.[299] Despite the failure of the NAACP to press this case in the courts, Governor Timmerman's incautious actions had opened the door for the very type of lawsuit that University of South Carolina officials had long feared. While most newspapers in South Carolina supported the governor's actions and vilified the students, at least one newspaper recognized the difficult situation Timmerman created for the University. The Palmetto State's last remaining anti-massive resistance newspaper, the *Cheraw Chronicle,* called the governor's actions "a tactical error of massive proportions."[300] In this case, USC and South Carolina narrowly avoided a situation that, according to state law, would have required state-supported colleges to close. To have shut down even a portion of the state's higher education system would have been a severe test of white South Carolina's commitment to segregation.

For the remainder of the decade, the racial issue continued to simmer at the University of South Carolina. In late 1958, a former USC history professor, Howard H. Quint, published a highly critical book about South Carolina's race relations. *Profile in Black and White: A Frank Portrait of South Carolina,* based on a master's thesis written by USC graduate student Idus A. Newby, used extensive research in local newspapers to document the state's racial problems. The book's publication created a minor sensation on campus and across the state, although Quint had left USC for a position at the University of Massachusetts shortly before it came out. The editor of the *Gamecock* recognized that Quint was a "brilliant student of history," but, unaware of the long-term damage racial segregation had inflicted on the institution, lamented that Quint "was dissatisfied with the operation of the University and the state government to the extent that he felt compelled to write a book denouncing our segregational system."[301] The *News and Courier* was not so kind. Its editor, while noting that much of Quint's research was based on his own newspaper, opined that "Prof. Quint seems not to have learned much in the 11 years he lived in South Carolina. . . . On at least one point Prof. Quint and The News and Courier agree, and that is the advisability of his departure from the University of South Carolina."[302]

As the decade drew to a close, racial segregation continued to be the central issue in the civic dialogue of South Carolina. Students at the University of South Carolina took their racial views with them when they left the state, and USC delegates to the National Student Association (NSA, a national organization of college and university students), created a minor controversy when they attempted to pass a pro-segregation resolution at the organization's national meeting in August 1958. Delegates Mike Osborne and Fred LeClercq sponsored a resolution decrying racial integration, but it failed to get more than 10 votes out of the more than 600 cast.[303]

The following year, after John Bell Williams, a member of the U.S. House of Representatives from Mississippi and an ardent segregationist, attacked the NSA for harboring communists, the USC student council voted to withdraw from the organization. The NSA was in actuality a moderate organization, and during the 1950s and 1960s it maintained a relationship with the CIA, receiving funding in exchange for supplying information on foreign student activists. However, in 1959, the NSA launched the Southern Student Human Relations Project in Atlanta to promote interracial understanding among students, headed by Constance Curry (who would soon become a leader in the civil rights movement). One of USC's NSA national delegates, Jimmy Trusdale, said that the NSA was "eager to force integration on the South" and that the University of South Carolina could not, therefore, remain a member.[304] USC student John A. Hagins claimed that the views of the NSA on communism and integration were "classic examples of their ultra-liberalism, left-wing, and native [sic] idealistic thought."[305] After pulling out of the NSA, in February 1960 the USC student council joined an all-southern student organization organized to counter the NSA, the Southern Universities Student Government Association (SUSGA). The SUSGA stressed "that local student government is more capable of truly representing its own students and also solving its own problems."[306] As the decade of the 1960s opened, it appeared that Carolina's students, like their elders, were preparing to resist any attempts to introduce racial integration to their campus.

The 1950s saw the state of South Carolina continue to toe the white supremacist line. The decade nonetheless witnessed a dramatic transformation of the University of South Carolina. In many ways, the institution was playing catch-up with its peers. Nonetheless, at the end of the decade, it could now take a position squarely alongside other state universities in the South. It had substantially improved its faculty, its academic programs, and its physical plant and had widened the availability of higher education in a state that desperately needed it. It was recognized as an institution "on the move." The state's determined defense of white supremacy threatened the University progress compared to its peers outside of the South, however, as racial segregation was increasingly viewed nationally as reactionary and was considered a moral problem that signified the South's backwardness. But USC had nonetheless become a university that in the next decade could legitimately strive to become one of the leading public institutions in the South. Whether or not it achieved this, that USC's leaders could even profess such a goal would have been almost unthinkable in 1950, when Carolina was so far behind its peers. In the 1950s, the foundation was laid for the modern University of South Carolina. In the following decade, the institution would complete a transition into a university that could fully serve all the people in the new South Carolina.

4 | THE GREAT
TRANSFORMATION
1960–1969

South Carolina must have a renaissance in education if the State is to achieve its proper place in the life of the nation. Multiplication of educational mediocrity by preserving the status quo in state-supported education . . . will deny to the coming generation the opportunities that should be their heritage. The increasing value and importance of education in today's complex society is recognized by business and educational leaders alike. The task of educational leadership is to burn this message into the public consciousness. There must be brought home to the people of the State the brutal fact that there is no place in today's economy for the uneducated, the untrained, the unskilled.

The Governor's Advisory Committee on Higher Education, 1962

The University of South Carolina is the State University. Because it is basically dependent on the state's economy, it is sensitive and responsive to needs throughout the state and can be counted on for friendly and enthusiastic cooperation with government, industries and business. . . . It is our intention and determination to develop and maintain a cultural and educational atmosphere in the university community which will attract and hold creative people in all fields.

Thomas F. Jones, 1963

■

In the South Carolina of the 1960s, the post–World War II changes that swept the state came to a head. Decades-long trends such as the decline of rural areas and agriculture along with a corresponding rise of industry and cities were accompanied by a power struggle over who would control South Carolina. The rural county elites—characterized by men such as Sol Blatt Sr., Edgar Brown, and Marion Gressette—which had dominated the state (and the University of South Carolina) since the end of Reconstruction were locked in a struggle with the emerging metropolitan elites of the state's growing cities for leadership of the state. As historian Walter Edgar has written, the old rural elite of South Carolina was "on the defensive in a three-front war (economic, social, political). . . . The Old South Carolina . . . was giving way to a New South Carolina." But as Edgar also observed, "this New South Carolina was not yet complete. There were too many unanswered questions."[1] In working out these answers, the pace of change in South Carolina quickened in the 1960s, and as the state's economy became increasingly tied to industrialization, the chief concern of the state's leadership shifted from maintaining white supremacy to promoting economic development. The role of the University of South Carolina in the state reflected the changing priorities. The institution's response to the civil rights movement, an ever-increasing emphasis on developing the institution's research capacity and graduate education, and new demands for widely accessible higher education were the most important facets of the important transition for the University of South Carolina in the 1960s.

In American higher education, in the years after 1960 the forces unleashed by World War II came to a head as well. The year 1960 saw the beginning of a twenty-year era that Clark Kerr has called the "great transformation" of higher education in the United States, an era that revolutionized the nation's conception of what a university was. As Kerr put it, spurred by the Cold War, the university became "a prime instrument of national purpose." Swelled by the children of the baby boom, enrollment in American colleges and universities that numbered 3.5 million students in 1960 had reached some 12 million by 1980. The nation's higher education system was approximately half private and half public in 1960, but by 1980, 80 percent of American students attended public universities and colleges. The nation's professorate grew from 235,000 to 685,000; universities that awarded 10,000 Ph.D.s in 1960 conferred 33,000 in 1980. Enrollment in community colleges grew from 400,000 to over 4 million. Federal expenditures on student aid rose (in 1980 dollars) from $300 million to $10 billion. These decades witnessed the dismantling of de jure segregation, the greatest student unrest in American history, and the widespread politicization of college campuses. They saw a wave of attempts at academic reform, followed by the widespread failure of that reform. They saw a vast extension of bodies to coordinate state-level higher education, such as South Carolina's Commission on Higher Education; 24 states had such bodies in 1960, while 46 had them in 1980. As Kerr wrote, "This was, in its totality, a particularly critical epoch in the life of American higher education." Alumni from earlier eras who visited their alma mater in the late 1960s hardly recognized their old campuses.[2]

At the University of South Carolina in the 1960s, these two historic trends—the rise of a "New South Carolina" and the "great transformation" of

American higher education—were intertwined. More than any other single post–World War II decade, the 1960s were a defining era for the modern University of South Carolina. In these years, South Carolina's leaders made decisions that transformed Carolina into a research university and set state policy that determined how South Carolina would meet the needs of its citizens for broadly available higher education. It was in this decade that the University of South Carolina finally threw off the yoke of racial segregation that had so long impeded the development of the institution. In a time of burgeoning industrial growth, the institution's leaders sought to transform the University into an institution measured by national rather than regional standards in faculty, research, and graduate education. The decade saw tremendous growth—and brought complicated problems.

That these years would be crucial was a fact not lost on the leaders of the University of South Carolina in the previous decade. Highly publicized demographic studies by John K. Folger of the Southern Regional Education Board (1954) and Robert W. Paterson of USC's Bureau of Business and Economic Research (1955) both predicted an "impending tidal wave" of college students in South Carolina as a result of the postwar baby boom. Folger wrote that "between 1960–1970 college enrollment will . . . rise to unprecedented heights." He expected South Carolina's college enrollment to more than double between 1952 and 1970, with the bulk of the rise occurring after 1960. Paterson predicted that South Carolina's college enrollment would increase 50 percent between 1954 and 1960, 90 percent between 1960 and 1970, and 50 percent between 1970 and 1980. Between 1954 and 1980, college enrollment in the state would increase 334 percent, Paterson expected.[3]

Such drastic increases had serious implications for South Carolina's colleges. "Quite possibly," wrote Paterson, "the pressure of the impending tidal wave of prospective students will bring about a wide-open discussion in South Carolina and the Nation . . . as to whether the college or university experience for all should automatically be the goal of educational policy." He concluded that public colleges and universities would have to step in to provide higher education for the majority of young people wanting it. "In the absence of any thoroughgoing revision as to the function and goals of collegiate education," he wrote, "this will be a tremendous undertaking."[4] With the civil rights movement and South Carolina's industrial awakening occurring at the same time that this enrollment bulge hit college campuses, the debate over how to meet the challenge was exceedingly complicated.

Paterson's warning did not fall on deaf ears. These reports, combined with the Sputnik crisis in 1958, were a call to arms for policymakers and educators. President Robert Sumwalt saw the challenge facing the state and the University, and in mid-1958 he appointed a special faculty committee on long-range development to plan for the University's growth. Sumwalt declared, "We must anticipate the future development and needs of our institution in order to continue our 'momentum of progress.'" The committee soon reported that the University could expect to grow from its enrollment of about 4,800 in 1958 to a conservative projection of 10,033 in 1970.[5]

The student body growth of the coming decade ultimately surpassed even the highest projections of demographers. Enrollment expansion was completely unprecedented. USC's Columbia campus student body, which had averaged 4,307 in the 1950s and stood at 5,661 in 1960, grew to 9,150 in 1965 and to 14,484 by 1970.[6] Robert Paterson's prediction that public colleges would have to assume more of the burden of educating South Carolina's young people was correct. The proportion of South Carolina's college students attending public colleges rose from 54.9 percent in 1960 to 65.9 percent in 1969 (despite this growth, South Carolina's public colleges and universities enrolled the lowest proportion of its college students of any southern state).[7] The ways in which South Carolina's leaders coped with this astounding growth while at the same time trying to build academic excellence and adjust to a changing state was the most important challenge of the decade.

Even though the projected numbers available to University and state leaders in 1960 were lower than they would turn out to be, they nonetheless called for action. Along with dean of the faculty Wilfred H. Callcott, President Sumwalt developed a list of six major tasks which the University needed to tackle immediately. They included preparing faculty and facilities for the increased enrollments on the horizon, increasing faculty salaries, placing more emphasis on research and graduate training, and developing scholarship programs and regular private support. In large measure, reaching these goals remained the University's central task throughout the 1960s. "There can be no delay. We must take the initiative and we must have the courage and wisdom to face these six tasks *right now.*"[8] On the eve of the new decade, Sumwalt warned of a coming crisis unlike any in his more than thirty years in higher education.[9]

While the crisis Sumwalt had identified referred to the problems presented by the impending tidal wave of students, at the dawn of the 1960s another crisis dominated civic dialogue in the Palmetto State: the issue of racial desegregation of public institutions. The state and University leadership would finally face this crucial issue head-on in the 1960s, and the manner in which they did so set the stage for much of the institutional advancement that took place during the coming decades. Racial segregation was a major obstacle in the overall advancement of the institution, as it consumed energies and resources that could be so much better used furthering knowledge. It also burdened the University with a liability that limited its ability to serve

South Carolina's citizens and its ability to compete with other institutions outside of the South. With the obstacle of desegregation finally addressed and overcome, Carolina's leaders could focus on the development of their institution as a full-fledged research university. Their achievement was a significant accomplishment for the state, and one that was reached in an atmosphere of considerable intransigence among South Carolina's whites. Typical of this resistance was the move in early 1960 of Carolina student leaders, who made a defiant statement against integration by withdrawing from the National Student Association and joining the Southern Universities Student Government Association (SUSGA)—composed of twenty-two colleges and universities from throughout the South.[10]

Like other state universities in the deep South, South Carolina's colleges and universities remained completely segregated in 1960. In border states and the upper South, limited desegregation had taken place in the 1950s. In North Carolina, for example, the first black students entered the University of North Carolina law school in 1951, and a suit by three Durham students, upheld by the U.S. Supreme Court, led to the desegregation of the undergraduate programs at UNC in 1955. By that year, black students had enrolled at all of the previously segregated state universities and land-grant colleges in Delaware, Maryland, West Virginia, Kentucky, Missouri, and Oklahoma. In North Carolina, Virginia, Tennessee, Louisiana, Arkansas, and Texas, black students were attending at least a few programs on previously segregated state campuses by the late 1950s. The deep South was another matter. In 1960, an observer said of colleges in South Carolina, Georgia, Alabama, and Mississippi, "For all practical purposes, the institutions of higher education in these four states are still tightly segregated, and the prospects for desegregation in the near future are extremely dim."[11]

In the fullness of time, South Carolina's day would come. In March and April of 1960, three black students, Lloyd Williams and Raymond Weston of South Carolina State University and Gertrude Boatwright, a high school graduate from Darlington, were denied USC application blanks after requesting them from the University registrar.[12] In the fall of 1960, the University again denied applications from two black students, Julie A. Wright, a Claflin College graduate and Youth Field Secretary for the NAACP for the Southeast Region, and Essie Anne Duncan. In what was becoming a familiar response to these applications, the students were told: "Under the laws of the State of South Carolina the University of South Carolina cannot process an application for admission from you." Wright worked with NAACP legal committee member Matthew Perry to bring a case for admission to the courts, but it never proceeded.[13] Carolina's denial of applications reflected general University policy toward black Carolinians: for example, the University's administration officially refused to allow black artists in Carolina's artist series or bands with black members to play at Student Union-sponsored dances, despite student assertions that they wanted black bands "very badly."[14]

Meanwhile, as the sit-in movement begun by black college students in Greensboro, North Carolina, in early 1960 spread throughout the South in the first years of the decade, to the consternation of University administrators a few USC students expressed support when black activists brought the lunch counter sit-in movement to Columbia in February of 1961. The brief participation of two white USC history graduate students (Selden Smith and Hayes Mizell) in Columbia's sit-ins earned them a reprimand from deans Callcott and Wienefeld, who warned the two that Carolina wanted "agitators of neither stripe" on its campus. State Law Enforcement Division (SLED) agents had spotted the two at the sit-in and had reported them to the deans.[15]

Smith and Mizell were among a small group of USC students (most of whom were South Carolina natives) who were involved in efforts by the South Carolina Council on Human Relations (SCCHR, an interracial group committed to furthering racial understanding) to foster communication between white and black students in South Carolina's colleges in anticipation of the desegregation of higher education. In 1960 and 1961, Elizabeth Ledeen, a volunteer at USC's Presbyterian Student Center and a SCCHR official, organized the South's only statewide biracial meetings of college students interested in improving understanding between the races. Held in Columbia and at the Penn Center in Frogmore, these meetings featured speakers such as Ella Baker and James McBride Dabbs and established the South Carolina Student Council on Human Relations (SCSCHR), whose first chairman was Charles Joyner, a graduate student in USC's history department. Though small at first, the SCSCHR demonstrated the commitment of a few of Carolina's students, such as Hayes Mizell, Selden Smith, Dan Carter, and faculty such as Raymond Moore of the department of International Studies, to work with students of other colleges to improve race relations.[16] *Gamecock* editorialist Tom Marchant reflected the sentiments of these Carolina students when he wrote, "Integration is going to be, Klu Klux [*sic*] or no Klu Klux. . . . I venture that perhaps it is time that we Southerners stop acting like a covey of scared ostriches."[17]

Though administrators considered them "agitators," this small number of USC students remained involved with the state's growing civil rights movement. In a demonstration linked to the downtown Columbia sit-ins, on March 3, 1961 a group of 189 college students, all but one of them black, were arrested for disturbing the peace on the state house grounds after quietly marching around the building. The lone white student arrested was Frederick Hart, a Conway native and USC freshman. Hart claimed to be merely observing the march, but when asked by a local policeman if he agreed with the black students, Hart replied, "Yes, I sympathize with them." He was promptly arrested, and the episode was reported in local newspapers. After the incident, his landlady asked him to stay away from his apartment because of harassing telephone calls. When he showed up at class the next day, dean of students George Tomlin asked him to leave school. Under intense pressure (including death threats from the Ku Klux Klan), Hart withdrew from Carolina two days later. A friend of Hart's wrote President Sumwalt, "It is disgusting to discover that a student has been requested to withdraw from a university because of his intellectual convictions. . . . The entire University community should be ashamed by the outcome of this affair."[18] Indeed, Frederick Hart's intellect proved to be quite sharp, and his dismissal from Carolina became yet another loss for the state and University as a result of the persistence of prejudice. Hart left Columbia for Washington, D.C., and later became a leading American sculptor whose designs include the elaborate west facade of the National Cathedral in Washington. One of the best-known sculptures in America, the *Three Soldiers* statue at the Vietnam Veteran's Memorial on the national mall, is Hart's work.[19]

University administrators continued to put pressure on white students who participated in civil rights demonstrations through the early years of the decade, revoking the graduate fellowships of at least three students in the history department who had been involved in the SCCHR student group. A few USC students remained committed to the civil rights movement however, for in 1962, the SCSCHR mailing list showed thirty-four members from the University of South Carolina, nineteen of them women.[20]

In the whole of USC's student body, this was a small number, and some Carolina students were also active on the other side of the desegregation issue. After the sit-ins led Columbia businesses, including Woolworth's and Eckerd's, to introduce limited desegregation in their lunch counters in August 1962, a group of USC alumni and students, led by Farley Smith (son of former U.S. Senator "Cotton" Ed Smith and longtime executive secretary of the Citizen's Councils of South Carolina), organized a series of counter demonstrations to protest desegregation. Complaining that local media outlets had imposed a "blackout" on coverage of desegregation, in late August two USC students, Lake Erie High and Eddie Hightower, picketed the desegregated lunch counters of both Eckerd's and Woolworth's to bring media attention to their cause. The *Charleston News and Courier* published a photograph of High holding a sign that read, "MONEY SPENT AT ECKERDS & WOOLWORTHS IS MONEY SPENT FOR RACE-MIXING."[21]

The possibility of racial desegregation in higher education swirled around the University of South Carolina in the early 1960s, but the failure of any black students to sue for admission left USC and South Carolina isolated from the mainstream of change, even within the deep South. A South Carolinian, Due West native Charlayne Hunter, took her application case to the University of Georgia, enrolling there in January 1961 amid rioting.[22] Similar developments were expected at USC if and when a black student decided to press the courts for admission. As of early 1962, however, none had done so.[23]

Barely four weeks after Thomas F. Jones took over from Robert L. Sumwalt as USC's twenty-third president in July 1962, rumors began to circulate that a black student or students would indeed sue for admission to Carolina.[24] Jones began consulting his colleagues around the South about how to handle an integration crisis, particularly seeking the advice of President Edwin Harrison of the Georgia Institute of Technology, who had managed desegregation at that school quietly and without incident. Georgia Tech's experience dealing with the press became a model Jones would follow in Carolina's inevitable desegregation crisis.[25]

The desegregation of Carolina came a step closer to becoming reality on October 31, 1962. Seventeen year-old Henrie Dobbins Monteith, a Columbia native and niece of local civil rights leader Modjeska Monteith Simkins, filed suit in federal court asking for admission to USC, represented by pioneering NAACP legal counsel Matthew J. Perry, Lincoln C. Jenkins, Donald Sampson, and others from the NAACP's legal committee in South Carolina. Monteith filed suit primarily because she wanted an education. The University of South Carolina, she said, "was close to my home" and "it offered the courses I wanted to take." But she was also committed to expanding civil rights. She told reporters that she brought suit against USC "to correct this social wrong —prejudice." Her mother, also a Columbia civil rights activist, had vowed that she would open the University to African Americans "if it was the last thing she did." Monteith had finished at the top of her class at St. Francis de Sales High School in Powhatan, Virginia, in 1962, but she had nonetheless been turned down for admission to Carolina in May, and had since enrolled at Notre Dame College in Maryland. University officials openly admitted that she had been denied admission only because of her race. Thirty-seven years later, she recalled that if the University had simply had the courage to admit her without requiring a court's intervention, she probably would never have pushed the issue and tried to attend the University. However, as she later wrote, "The power of family and the African-American church, coupled with an irrational 'no' from the University or State power structure . . . propelled me across the threshold." Along with her family and a network of supporters in the civil rights community, black and white, she had decided that the time had come to directly challenge South Carolina's segregated higher education. She recalled that they realized it was time to "shift the paradigm of business as usual in South Carolina." As she put it, "Wanted or unwanted, I decided that 'we' had a right to be at the University of South Carolina." The ensuing court battle that followed took nine months to complete.[26]

Meanwhile, at precisely the same time Monteith was contemplating her lawsuit, events at the University of Mississippi were unfolding that would have a profound impact on students at the University of South Carolina. After James Meredith had attempted to integrate that school in October 1962, violence erupted with the tacit endorsement of Mississippi Governor Ross Barnett. Some 700 Carolina students reflected the feeling of many white South Carolinians when they signed a telegram addressed to the governor supporting his stand and declaring, "White Rights for the South!"[27]

The *Gamecock* devoted a special section to the Mississippi violence, and its reporter Dennis Myers traveled to Oxford, gained entry to the closed campus, and wrote an account of the riots. His act earned him a dismissal from the newspaper staff, but the William Randolph Hearst Foundation rewarded him with a $500 scholarship. In response to the Mississippi disorder, *Gamecock* editor Joan Wolcott wrote a widely quoted editorial in which she asked, "What comes next?. . . . Is segregation's last stand inevitably set for the Palmetto State?" She answered that it was her "fervent hope that if integration comes to the USC campus, it will be met with rationality and wisdom on the part of those concerned. We are not peacemakers but we desire no scars to mar our beautiful campus or to blemish the heart. . . . We want no hotheads stirring up trouble at our state university." Her call for moderation was reprinted in newspapers all over the region and received television coverage as well. The *Gamecock* was deluged with letters about the article, much of it supportive of Wolcott. Creed C. Burlingame of Mount Pleasant wrote that the editorial "was like a breath of fresh air. . . . [I]t took a young fresh mind to point out the plain simple, unvarnished truth—integration is inevitable, much as we disapprove of it." Wolcott received other letters accusing her of membership in such organizations as the NAACP and the Communist Party.[28]

Some students agreed with Wolcott, with Virginia Glymph saying that the Mississippi incident was "a shame and a disgrace, both to the State of Mississippi and to the nation as a whole!" Many students who opposed integration nonetheless abhorred Mississippi's tactics, and the Mississippi situation seemed to burn into the University community's consciousness that violence in the face of court-ordered integration would disgrace both the University and the state.[29] Indeed, in an article titled "They Don't Want Riots," *Time* magazine reported that South Carolina was committed to have order, and Tom Jones said that USC would take desegregation "in our stride."[30] Local newspapers, including the *Columbia Record*, began preparing citizens for integration with pleas for calm, declaring, "Now, as seldom before in its history, South Carolina demands responsibility."[31]

At the beginning of 1963, the issue of desegregation in South Carolina's public higher education seized the state's attention. However, the spotlight was directed on Clemson, where on January 28 Harvey Gantt became the first black student to enter a white college in South Carolina since 1877. The change was accomplished peacefully and "with dignity," as Governor Ernest Hollings had urged in a much-publicized January speech.[32] However, the day after Gantt's admission to Clemson, the state's new governor, Donald Russell, vowed to continue the legal fight against desegregated education, despite the forced integration of Clemson. After the University of Alabama desegregated in June 1963, the University of South Carolina was the last flagship southern state university that remained racially segregated[33]—an ironic status, considering that it had been the only southern state university to desegregate during the Reconstruction era, some ninety years earlier.

The issue of racial integration remained at the center of public dialogue on the Carolina campus and in the state in early 1963, as evidenced by a controversy that erupted when the *Gamecock* published Henrie Monteith's photograph and a story about her court case on its front page. Readers assailed the newspaper for giving coverage to what they called "a negro publicity seeker and agitator."[34] In April, the University received another barrage of criticism when the local AAUP chapter invited U.S. Attorney General Bobby Kennedy to speak on campus. Kennedy told the group that "the practical needs of the world today would compel our national government . . . to do everything possible to eliminate racial discrimination."[35] An alumnus wrote to President Jones complaining that "Mr. Kennedy is an avowed enemy of the South, he is determined to do away with our way of life, and his very presence in the state will cause useless bitterness and resentment by thousands of honorable South Carolinians."[36] Frank B. Best of radio station WDIX in Orangeburg commented, "Only on the grounds of academic freedom could the University professors entertain Attorney General Kennedy. This promotion of integrated schools is not academic freedom. It is academic prostitution. The University of South Carolina has some explaining to do to the South Carolina General Assembly."[37]

Such sentiments reflected a significant body of vehement opposition both within and without the University community toward racial desegregation that administrators feared could lead to violence. John H. Martin, an African American employee of the University who had worked on campus since 1938, said of desegregation, "I expected trouble . . . I was sure blood was going to be shed." In May 1963 a group of about 200 Carolina students protested integration on the campus. They burned a cross in front of the president's home and marched to the state house chanting "Two, four, six, eight, we don't want to integrate!"[38]

The attitude of a few student leaders suggested a somewhat more responsible approach. Student body president Todd Wilson wrote in a *Gamecock* editorial that while "we do not want integration . . . neither do we want to be blamed for the loss of dignity and integrity." He vowed that student government would do all it could "to insure peace and rationality" if desegregation were ordered.[39] Keith Elliot, president of USC's chapter of the prestigious honor society Blue Key, also committed to help maintain calm in the event of a desegregation order.[40] In the aftermath of the University of Mississippi violence, the small number of white students that had been involved with the efforts of the South Carolina Student Council on Human Relations to foster interracial cooperation and communication organized a local group called the Student Committee to Observe Order and Peace (SCOOP). According to its statement of purpose, the committee "was established for the sole purpose of promoting the peaceful observance of any future court decisions" regarding the desegregation of the University of South Carolina.[41]

Meanwhile, Monteith's case was making its way through the federal courts. On July 10, 1963, Judge J. Robert Martin of Greenville ordered USC to admit her in the fall semester. A USC appeal was flatly denied. On July 25, Robert G. Anderson of Greenville, a transfer student from Clark College of Atlanta, and James L. Solomon, Jr. of Sumter, a graduate student, also applied for admission, bringing to three the number of black students seeking fall 1963 admission. The University of South Carolina had run out of courts. Desegregation would be a reality.[42]

Even prior to Judge Martin's order, USC administrators had begun making detailed plans to accommodate, rather than resist, black students. On April 18, 1963, President Jones appointed an ad hoc faculty committee, chaired by dean of the School of Engineering Rufus G. Fellers, to plan the details of what they called "I-Day" (integration day). A Columbia native who grew up in the neighborhood adjacent to the campus, Fellers himself represented University history: his great-grandfather, Maximilian LaBorde, was a member of the South Carolina College faculty from 1840 to 1873 and wrote the institution's first published history. LaBorde was briefly a member of the faculty during the University's first period of racial integration during Reconstruction. Fellers, as a "good southern boy" with an impeccable background, was an important symbol on the University's committee to plan the institution's desegregation. On July 26, 1963, Jones issued a confidential memo stressing that the University intended to control media coverage and maintain open communication on campus. The ad hoc committee would carefully script the registration of the black students down to the last detail and allow the South Carolina Law Enforcement Division (SLED) to prevent outside interference.[43]

While careful behind-the-scenes planning went on between the administration and SLED, four days after the federal court order the University board of trustees made an important symbolic decision and unanimously endorsed a statement of compliance drafted by the members of the Fellers committee. Their statement read in part: "In the interest of the preservation of the dignity of the orderly processes of education at the University of South Carolina, the Board of Trustees is forced to direct compliance with the order of Judge Martin, unless it can be lawfully modified or rescinded."[44] It concluded, "The full cooperation of students, faculty, and administration of the University in its determination to maintain law and order on the campus and in the community is expected by the Board. With the support of its devoted alumni and with the encouragement of the people of South Carolina, the University will be able to continue undeterred in its progress toward greatness and in its service to the State."[45] With all legal remedies exhausted, white South Carolina would reluctantly accept the desegregation of its flagship state university as the law of the land and enforce it as such. There would be no defiant "last stands."

Preparations for the impending desegregation of the University included riot-control exercises by the South Carolina Army National Guard and detailed plans for handling the expected deluge of reporters. Carolina officials sought to limit and control press coverage as much as possible. The University also erected a low iron fence around the portions of the campus that were not surrounded by the University's old brick wall to help control any crowds that might try disrupt registration.[46] In early August, USC officially notified Monteith, Anderson, and Solomon that they had been accepted. University officials and USC students of the SCSCHR met with the three to prepare them for what might face them at Carolina. Dean of students Charles H. Witten wrote to all students in late August, informing them of the court's decision and the University's commitment to legal compliance. Witten gave the students guidelines for their behavior on campus, directing them to carry their identification cards at all times; in the event that disorder occurred, they were to remain where they were until notified otherwise. He told them that "the faculty and administration have faith that the intelligence and maturity of our students will enable them [to] exercise the necessary judgments so that our university will come through this difficult period with its reputation unsullied."[47]

University officials, including Fellers and Witten (who wrote the University's desegregation plans), were reasonably sure they could keep the peace on the campus; they had prepared students and law enforcement agencies and had limited press access to the campus. However, they could not control events off campus. On August 27, several sticks of dynamite exploded in the yard of Henry and Martha Monteith, Henrie Monteith's uncle and aunt, in Columbia. No one was injured, and Henrie Monteith courageously told reporters, "There's no point in becoming afraid. I'm going to enter the university next month just as planned."[48] The families also received hateful, harassing telephone calls. Henrie Monteith Treadwell later recalled that the dynamite "did nothing to deter us. We saw this assault as yet another truly misdirected and uninformed attempt to stop the move to the future. The hate phone calls were viewed as a nuisance, not a deterrent. In fact, the dynamite, the phone calls . . . all strengthened my resolve."[49]

In spite of these disturbances, after the University finalized its elaborate plans and briefed reporters on the procedures the institution would use in registering the three new students, officials believed they were prepared for the historic desegregation of the University. President Tom Jones told the people of the state that with all legal options exhausted, the University would admit the black students and tolerate no disturbances. Appealing to state and institutional pride, he insisted, "We will make this transition with honor and dignity worthy of the great state that provides the University of South Carolina as the capstone of its educational system."[50] Students also appealed to local pride in expressing support for a peaceful transition. Contrasting South Carolinians with Mississippians, one freshman woman told a reporter that natives of the Palmetto State were a "'better breed' than to allow anything untoward to develop concerning Miss Monteith's admission." Referring to Harvey Gantt's peaceful admission to Clemson, she appealed to Gamecock pride as well, declaring that "If Clemson can, Carolina can."[51]

On the morning of September 11, 1963, while about sixty curious white students looked on, Henrie Monteith, Robert Anderson, and James Solomon were driven to the front steps of the Administration Building by their attorneys, Matthew Perry of Columbia and Donald Sampson of Greenville. The three students quietly entered the building, where they received advisement in their respective dean's offices, and then proceeded to the Naval Armory, where they registered for fall classes. The entire process took only about twenty minutes. Soon thereafter the three attended a news conference in Hamilton College. The only tempers that flared were those of the photographers and reporters who missed the students' initial arrival while USC officials held them in a briefing room. Reporters described Monteith, Anderson, and Solomon as "poised, affable and generally relaxed" during the registration and news conference. The following morning, Henrie Monteith attended her nine o'clock physics class, and the color line at USC was broken for the first time in the twentieth century—entirely peacefully.[52]

Thorough preparation paid off. SLED had stationed a car on nearly every block surrounding the campus and had undercover agents disguised as students all over campus.[53] A *Gamecock* photograph showed a long line of police cars parked in a nearby lot, ready to respond to the first sign of trouble. The newspaper noted of the USC campus, "It's all quiet, and that is the big part of the story."[54] In a speech twenty-five years later, Monteith recalled the "orchestrated calm" with which she, Anderson, and Solomon entered Carolina.[55] African American USC employee John H. Martin said of Carolina's desegregation, "Everything went through as smoothly as anyone would ever expect it to go. I had no idea, no dream that the change-over would be as smooth as it was."[56] Because of the complete preparation, the most significant event in the modern history of the University came as an anticlimax to the defiance and racial tension of previous years. Though their reporters were on the scene, the national press gave little attention to Carolina's desegregation. Paul Turk, editor of the *Oakland (Michigan) Observer,* noted of the low-key nature of the event, "Apparently, 'no violence' means 'no coverage.'"[57] The University of South Carolina, the last flagship southern state university to desegregate, had recognized the inevitable and achieved desegregation with dignity.

White students on campus had responded the way USC officials had asked; although most may not have supported racial integration, they realized it was going to happen no matter what they did. They reluctantly accepted the situation. One student took it philosophically, reasoning that three black students in a student body of over six thousand mattered little to him: "As long as the odds are the way they are now, integration won't make much difference. . . . They'll just get lost in the crowd."[58]

For most Carolina students, the remainder of the 1963 school year went much the way of earlier years. However, for Monteith, Anderson, and Solomon, as for the institution, it was a watershed year. Both Anderson and Monteith lived on campus—he in Maxcy College, she in Sims. They occupied single rooms with private bathrooms and specially installed telephones that allowed only outgoing calls. University police kept close tabs on their safety. Solomon, a thirty-three-year-old Air Force veteran and mathematics graduate student who taught math at Morris College, commuted from his home in Sumter. The undergraduates, Monteith and Anderson, remembered that for the most part white students were indifferent to them. Monteith noticed subtle harassment. "I saw myself as just a student." she said. "Yes, I noticed the security. Yes, I endured harassing phone calls on campus. Yes, I endured little parcels left at my dormitory door. I enjoyed knowing that those who planned the harassments took more time planning to bother me than I spent eliminating the acts of hate, or disrespect, from my mind." There were supporters, however, especially the South Carolina Council on Human Relations. In addition, she realized that "many of my professors did not embrace the principles of segregation. . . . So the classrooms were safe, if not always extremely nurturing places." Ironically, for her the most "nurturing" place on campus was the cafeteria, "even though I ate alone most of the time. The cafeteria help were mainly African-American and they looked after me. . . . The men and women who prepared and served the meals, and who cleared the tables, were my friends and supporters."[59]

Robert Anderson had a far more difficult time. Like Monteith, he recalled that his life at Carolina was lonely and isolated. A Greenville native, he had grown up in a family and community that had protected him from prejudice; Carolina was his direct first experience with raw racism. "Some of my experiences at Carolina were funny, others painful, and some leave bitter memories and scars," he recalled twenty-five years later. He most often ate alone, and he commonly endured racial epithets from white students who would not confront him directly. He recalled several incidents very clearly. For the first month or so, white students would take turns bouncing a basketball outside his dorm room at night. Just after the assassination of John F. Kennedy a little more than two months after he entered, Anderson was walking down the Horseshoe, and a white student with a broomstick leaned out a window, pointed it at Anderson, and pretended to shoot, calling, "Nigger, we got you now!" On another occasion, a student in Anderson's dormitory committed suicide. When police and an ambulance arrived on the scene to take away the body, Anderson solemnly recalled that he "could tell that everyone was a little disappointed. They all seemed to hope that it had been me." Though most students ignored Anderson, a few "unconventional" ones did befriend him, such as the students of SCOOP and the South Carolina Student Council on Human Relations. He recalled several faculty and staff members who befriended him as well, including debate team coach Merrill Christophersen and Methodist chaplain Don Bundy. Nonetheless, Anderson found his experience at Carolina so traumatic and painful that after his graduation in 1966 he did not return to the campus again until 1988.[60]

James Solomon, as an older student and a Ph.D. candidate, had a different experience. He received a "warm welcome" in the mathematics department, especially from fellow students and department head Wyman Williams. He recalled that a few faculty "had a problem with race" and he never felt completely accepted, but he was always treated fairly. His experiences with racism at Carolina, he said, were "nothing" compared to the discrimination he had faced earlier in his life. As a safety precaution however, the administration asked all three students not to attend football games, a request with which they complied. They were refunded the University's eight-dollar ($35.61) student activity fee.[61]

Alumni were generally congratulatory toward the administration for their handling of the potentially explosive situation. USC Educational Foundation official Charles W. Knowlton wrote to President Jones that although the University would probably have gotten more positive publicity had there been a period of unrest leading up to the event, "greater praise is due because there was in fact no crisis and no incidents."[62]

There were some unhappy alumni. One graduate wrote to the Alumni Association to express her indignation and requested that they cease any correspondence with her. "I did not graduate from an integrated school, and I have no interests in the activities of one," she wrote. "Any communications, if received by me in the future, will be burned immediately." Tom Jones responded to her personally, writing, "The University is becoming integrated through no fault of her own. How should a son or daughter act toward a parent who has fallen into misfortune through no fault of his or her own? Should the parent be disowned or given more love and support than ever to offset the misfortune?"[63] There is no indication whether or not the addressee read this correspondence before putting it to the torch.

In August 1965, Henrie Monteith became the first black student to earn a degree from USC in eighty-eight years and the first African American female graduate in the institution's history. She finished the degree requirements in pre-medicine in two years at Carolina. Upon her graduation, she told reporters, "In general, the past two years were enjoyable. I like the way things turned out. Nothing sticks in my mind as a bad experience." However, years later, she recalled that the atmosphere for her and other black students was not ideal.[64]

The entry of Monteith, Anderson, and Solomon began the process of desegregating the University of South Carolina. The following year, eleven more black students entered, including the first black student in the School of Law, Paul Cash. The desegregation of the University's law school, which had long been a gate of entry into South Carolina's circles of political power, was especially significant. The dean of USC's School of Law, Robert McC. Figg Jr., had helped argue South Carolina's side in the *Briggs v. Elliott* case (trying to prevent desegregation) and despite the desegregation of the University in the 1960s he discouraged blacks from applying to the law school. Nonetheless, they came. While Paul Cash did not finish his degree, in 1967 Jasper M. Cureton and John Lake, who had both transferred from the South Carolina State School of Law in 1965, became the first African American graduates of USC's law school since Reconstruction. I. S. Leevy Johnson was the first twentieth-century African American to complete the entire USC program in the School of Law, doing so in 1968.[65]

By late in the decade, the desegregation of the University of South Carolina was well begun. In 1970, there were some 279 black students at USC, making up less than 2 percent of undergraduates and less than 1 percent of graduate students on the Columbia campus. Although black students were few in number and there was still significant support for segregated education in the state, on the Carolina campus black students were, if not actively welcomed, accepted as a fact of life. Carla Smalls George, who came to Carolina as an undergraduate in 1966 and became the first black student to earn a master's degree from the College of Humanities and Social Sciences, in 1971, did not recall overt racism on campus. However, she remembered feelings of alienation, invisibility, and a sense of exclusion from the majority of white students and some white faculty. Other students recalled similar feelings and experienced subtle racism. For example, the photos of black students rarely appeared in the *Garnet and Black*. However, black students participated in a range of activities. Robert Anderson was a member of Carolina's debate team and Henrie Monteith sang in the University Choir. Monteith was also active in the South Carolina Student Council on Human Relations, and in her senior year was the organization's state coordinator for "Operation Search," a project designed to encourage African American students to apply to desegregated colleges. In the fall of 1964, Karen Deas became the first black cast member in a major theatrical production at USC, and A. P. Williams III became the first black member of the Gamecock marching band. Also in the fall of 1964, there were two black reporters on the staff of the *Gamecock,* and a few black students participated in intramural athletics. In 1969, Betty Anne Williams of Orangeburg became the first black student to win a prestigious Carolina Scholarship.

In other areas the University was slow in adapting to a desegregated environment. Prior to 1969 no varsity sport at Carolina had any black participants, and the lily-white nature of Carolina's teams became controversial. Football coach and athletic director Paul Dietzel adamantly denied that the department discriminated. However, since coming to Carolina in the mid-1960s, Dietzel, basketball coach Frank McGuire, and their staffs had not recruited a single black athlete, even when highly regarded and academically qualified recruits lived in the Columbia area. However, in 1969, in the aftermath of a controversy, they began recruiting black athletes. In that year Carlton Heyward (football), Ansel E. "Jackie" Brown (baseball and football), and Casey Manning (basketball) became the first black athletes to play in Gamecock uniforms. Harold White became the university's first black coach when he joined Dietzel's staff in 1971. Likewise, the University's teaching faculty remained all-white until 1968, when African American Earline Cunningham joined the department of chemistry, coming from the University of California at Berkeley. Later that year, James Luck from Harvard joined the College of Education and Thomas Davis joined the new Graduate School of Social Work.[66]

With desegregation under way, University leaders could devote energy and resources to the goal of joining the national mainstream and developing Carolina into a modern research university. However, at the beginning of the 1960s the internal structure of the institution was not prepared to develop and lead such a transformation, as it was still by and large a small teaching institution. State leaders such as Governor Ernest Hollings recognized the need for a comprehensive evaluation of the functions and goals of the Palmetto State's public higher education system. He urged the University's board of trustees to hire a team of outside consultants to conduct a comprehensive management survey to help prepare the University for future growth. He had recommended to Clemson that they hire the New York firm of Cresap, McCormick and Paget (CMP) to do a similar survey of its structure in 1955. The CMP report had recommended drastic changes at Clemson, including a sweeping administrative reorganization and the transition from a single-sex military college to a civilian and coeducational one.[67] Governor Hollings urged the USC board to contract with the same firm to evaluate Carolina. Despite the objections of some board members who opposed bringing in a northern firm to evaluate the University, in July 1959 they agreed. They commissioned CMP to prepare a comprehensive report covering the University's organizational structure, long-range planning, and the effectiveness of nonacademic activities.[68]

Cresap, McCormick and Paget found an administrative structure that had evolved to direct the small university that existed before World War II, but had not modernized to cope with postwar growth and was inadequate to handle the anticipated growth of the next decade. They noted that the University had no formal organizational plan and lacked clear lines of authority and responsibility. "The President," they observed, "is faced with an impossible supervisory task." There were at least thirty-one organizational entities reporting directly to the President.[69] The consultants also noted that since 1922, there had been nine acting or permanent presidents of the University, serving an average term of 4.6 years each. "This rapid turnover," the report stated, ". . . has left the University in an almost constant state of adjustment to a new administration."[70] As they saw it, the lack of continuity in the University's leadership was a severe handicap on long-range planning and inhibited the achievement of excellence.[71]

To modernize the University's organization and prepare it for the "impending tidal wave" of students, CMP proposed an overhaul of the administrative structure, highlighted by a formal organizational plan. They recommended the University consolidate its various activities under four broad divisions, each with a "line officer" who reported directly to the president: a dean of administration, a dean of the university, a dean of students, and a director of development. Within this structure, the president was to function as the "chief executive officer of the University," and the division of administrative tasks provided appropriate delegation of responsibility.[72]

The University administration responded positively to the CMP reform recommendations and adopted the proposed administrative reorganization, which became effective July 1, 1960. Dean of the faculty Wilfred H. Callcott became the first dean of the University; William H. Patterson continued as dean of administration; dean of men George W. Tomlin became the dean of students; and C. Wallace Martin became the first director of development.[73]

Paired with the extensive reorganization of the academic programs under Donald Russell, the CMP report and the changes it recommended gave the University hope that it could adequately and efficiently cope with the expected growth and change of the 1960s. One positive sign was that the administrative reorganization created an internal entity responsible for coordinating private fund-raising—the development office, under C. Wallace Martin. The development office worked closely with the still-new USC Educational Foundation to map a new approach for obtaining private financial support. The June 1960 announcement that beloved English professor Havilah Babcock would receive the Educational Foundation's first professorship (in the form of a $2,000 [$9,203] per year salary supplement) demonstrated the potential of private giving to aid the educational advancement of the University. President Sumwalt told alumni that although state appropriations could "take the University a long way toward its destination of excellence," they could not provide "the margin of excellence" the University needed in the form of scholarships, fellowships, salary supplements for distinguished professors, or programs needed by the libraries. Private funds, he said, were the way to provide this margin.[74]

To meet these additional needs, in June 1961 the University announced a major capital funds drive, the first in its history. Called the "Greater University Fund," this campaign set a goal of $2,250,000 ($10,238,128) to be raised from private sources to support distinguished professorships, undergraduate scholarships, graduate fellowships, and the purchase of library books. The fund drew the support of alumni, faculty, staff, and students along with major gifts from business and charitable foundations (such as $50,000 [$227,514] in gifts from the Citizens and Southern Bank and the Richardson Foundation).

Through the leadership of Jeff B. Bates, the president of the USC Educational Foundation, the campaign dramatically increased alumni financial support, which had been virtually nonexistent a decade earlier. Non-athletic annual alumni giving to the University increased from $7,286 ($35,324) in 1957 to $146,000 ($641,061) in 1964 and to $214,700 ($798,507) by 1969. By the time of the USC Educational Foundation's tenth anniversary in 1968,

it had provided eight National Merit Scholarships, eight endowed professorships, salary supplements to twenty-two faculty members, numerous graduate fellowships, supplements to departmental budgets, gifts for library
acquisitions, and grants for faculty sabbaticals.[75] As a part of the anniversary,
the Educational Foundation established a prestigious new undergraduate
scholarship to compete with programs such as the Morehead Scholars at the
University of North Carolina: the Carolina Scholars, which provided a four-
year, $5,000 ($19,579) scholarship to ten outstanding incoming freshmen.[76]
The advances in fund-raising boosted USC's endowment totals and substantially contributed to the improvement of University students and programs,
but USC's permanent endowment still trailed that of most of its peers in the
South.

The Cresap, McCormick and Paget report also helped the University
forecast long-term physical plant needs. Long-range planning in this area
began in the 1950s, and a report completed in 1958 by the City of Columbia's
Department of City Planning identified areas for further campus expansion,
most notably the two blocks on either side of College Street adjoining the
campus to the east.[77] The CMP recommendations echoed these plans to a large
degree, and in September 1960, the board of trustees approved a sizable two-
year, $8,480,000 ($39,022,373) construction and land acquisition program
based on their recommendations. Among the new projects were two 500-bed
"veil-block" honeycomb dormitories just south of the two existing towers
between Main and Sumter Streets. The program also included a ten-story

Table 4.1 Market value of endowment assets, selected southern state
universities, 1962–63, 1970–71

(in millions; 1991 constant dollars in parentheses)

STATE UNIVERSITY	ENDOWMENT 1962–63	ENDOWMENT 1970–71
South Carolina	$1.35 ($6.04)	$2.00 ($6.87)
Clemson	$0.52 ($2.33)	$0.87 ($2.98)
Georgia	$3.07 ($13.74)	$4.40 ($15.12)
Tennessee (Knoxville)	$2.56 ($11.46)	$5.68 ($19.52)
Alabama	$11.04 ($49.40)	$12.83 ($44.09)
North Carolina	$10.7 ($47.88)	$20.99 ($72.14)
Virginia	$70.41 ($315.10)	$91.55 ($314.63)

Source: Allan M. Cartter, ed., *American Universities and Colleges*, 9th ed. (Washington, D.C.:
American Council on Education, 1964); W. Todd Furniss, ed., *American Universities and
Colleges*, 11th ed., (Washington, D.C.: American Council on Education, 1964).

women's dormitory (first known as South Building, today Patterson Hall), an addition to the College of Engineering building, a science building on the northeast corner of Greene and Sumter Streets (originally built to house the departments of biology and pharmacy, now known as the Health Sciences building), a sixty-apartment married student housing complex (the University Terrace apartments), an addition to Currell College, and a neutron generator for nuclear research. The new construction increased USC's student housing capacity by 50 percent. This phase of construction, paid for in part with state institution bonds and partly by federal loans that were increasingly available in the 1960s, ended in September 1962.[78]

The massive construction program complemented the University's ongoing land acquisition program. The University purchased McMaster College, formerly a public school, in the area to the northeast of the old campus in 1960. In the previous year it began the process of acquiring six city blocks to the south of campus in the Wheeler Hill neighborhood through the federal government's "urban renewal" program. Under this program, the federal government paid two-thirds of the cost of purchase and clearing of what it called "blighted slums" in a thirty-three-acre area. Described by outsiders as a "seedy, rundown section of sagging wooden houses," it covered the city blocks south of Blossom Street, east of Main Street, north of the Southern Railway, and west of Pickens Street. Before their removal, the area was home to 42 businesses and 210 families, mostly African American. While some described the section as a slum area, to its residents it was a vibrant community, and many resented that their neighborhood was to be destroyed without their consent. The project compounded ill will toward the University within Columbia's black community, already angered over the University's long refusal to admit black students. It was Columbia's first-ever urban renewal project, and those in charge had a great deal to learn about involving those who were to be displaced. According to former residents, the project "tore the heart out" of the closely knit Wheeler Hill community. Nonetheless, within five years the University obtained the entire area, cleared of its residents, worth more than $1 million. Columbia Housing Authority head John A. Chase (the former dean of administration at the University) called the project "the largest-ever gift to the University." Plans called for the area to be used for the construction of a physical education center.[79]

Once the University had completed this phase of planning and physical expansion, two key elements of the brain trust that had guided the University in the postwar era retired. Dean of the University Wilfred H. Callcott, who came to USC as a faculty member in 1923 and had served as either dean of the Graduate School or as the University's chief academic officer since 1944, retired from his administrative post in 1961. In addition to his significant scholarly achievements in history, Callcott had guided much of Carolina's academic improvement since World War II. He was also instrumental in the development of extension campuses in other South Carolina communities. Callcott retired as dean in 1961, but remained on the faculty until 1968—a total of forty-five years of service at Carolina. During the 1960s he taught in visiting professor programs at the University of Texas and Wofford College, earned accolades as a Fulbright professor at Oxford University in 1963–64, and later served as acting president of Coker College in Hartsville. The University memorialized him by renaming the former business administration building (which now houses the departments of geography and sociology) Callcott Social Sciences Center.[80] William H. Patterson, formerly dean of administration, replaced him as dean of the University.

In 1962, President Robert L. Sumwalt retired from the University as well. While his initial appointment as acting president had come with some doubts among the faculty, his performance soon quieted critics. Sumwalt's efforts to modernize the University administration and physical plant, as well as preparing the institution for future growth, earned him their respect.

His most popular initiative among the faculty was a concerted drive to raise their salaries. In the late 1950s and early 1960s, Sumwalt lobbied hard for higher salaries. In 1961 he told the State Budget and Control Board that "the major problem facing the University of South Carolina now and for the foreseeable future is to catch up, and then keep up, with comparable institutions in the matter of faculty salaries." With the support of Governor Hollings (who made a 10 percent increase in faculty salaries a prominent proposal in his 1960 "State of the State" address) and backed by the recommendations of the CMP report, Sumwalt secured across-the-board pay raises for faculty— especially in the higher ranks, where USC salaries were weakest. While USC continued to trail its peers in salary levels (and continued to lose outstanding young faculty to schools with higher salaries), the gap began to close during Sumwalt's tenure as president.[81]

Faculty praised his efforts. Wyman L. Williams, longtime head of the department of mathematics, said that of the seven presidents he had served under at USC, Sumwalt "had had the faculty more at heart than his predecessors." A 1962 legislative committee studying higher education in South Carolina noted the high morale of both faculty and students at Carolina under Sumwalt's leadership. The board of trustees honored Sumwalt by naming the College of Engineering building for him and giving him the title of president emeritus. After a career spanning thirty-six years at Carolina, Sumwalt retired in June 1962.[82]

In choosing Sumwalt's replacement, the board of trustees had the luxury of time. When Sumwalt accepted the presidency in 1959, he initially intended to retire in 1961. However, the board requested that he stay an additional year while a search committee looked for a suitable replacement. They wanted a young president who could give them a sustained period of service and continuity in leadership. They also sought a nationally respected leader who could bring the University of South Carolina into the mainstream of research universities in the United States and provide dynamic leadership in devising creative solutions to the new challenges facing the University and the state in the 1960s. Governor Hollings, president ex officio of the board of trustees, played an active role in the search, consulting with the presidents of universities throughout the South for potential candidates. T. Marshall Hahn Jr., an up-and-coming young physicist then serving as dean of arts and sciences at Kansas State University, was the first choice of the board of trustees. The thirty-five year-old Hahn accepted the position at Carolina in early 1962 after an interview with the board of trustees. While staying at the South Carolina Governor's Mansion the night after he accepted the position, however, Hahn received a late telephone call notifying him that he had been simultaneously chosen president of Virginia Polytechnic Institute. Hahn, who had been a faculty member at VPI prior to moving to Kansas State and whose wife was a Virginia native, ultimately declined the position at USC to accept the presidency of VPI.[83]

The board's next choice for president was Thomas F. Jones Jr., then serving as dean of the School of Electrical Engineering at Purdue University. A native of Henderson, Tennessee, Jones grew up in his father's newspaper offices in Arkansas and Mississippi. After graduating from Mississippi State College with a degree in electrical engineering, Jones went to the Massachusetts Institute of Technology, the nation's premier engineering school, where he earned his M.S. and Ph.D. degrees in the same field. He spent the World War II years at the prestigious Naval Research Laboratory in Washington, D.C., where he helped develop sonar technology and held several patents in the field. In 1947, Jones joined the pioneering electrical engineering faculty at MIT, there contributing to the development of new teaching methods that set the standard in technological education, as well as conducting research in missile systems technology, analog computers, and nuclear instrumentation. After eleven years at MIT, in 1958 he accepted the deanship at Purdue. While there, he earned a reputation as an educational innovator, revising the curriculum and greatly expanding the graduate and research programs.[84] His experiences in the critical field of electrical engineering at the Naval Research Laboratory, MIT, and Purdue put him on the leading edge of change among the circle of the nation's top research universities.[85]

In addition to his impeccable credentials as a scholar, educator, and administrator, Jones brought special qualities and skills that made him attractive to

South Carolina's leaders. A native southerner, he would possess the credibility in the state's white community to handle sensitive racial issues (issues that indeed would dog the University in the coming decade). Jones also had experience with business—an attribute that appealed to leaders like Hollings who were interested in attracting outside industry to South Carolina. For example, Jones was involved in the establishment of McClure Park, a research park at Purdue aimed at bringing the expertise of academia and research-oriented industry into a closer relationship.[86] He also served on the board of directors of several high-tech electronics firms (General Electronics Laboratories, CP Electronics Company, and Hemotheritrol Corporation).[87] Only three months after Jones came to Carolina, Governor Hollings excitedly told how Jones had helped him woo a prospective industry to South Carolina. Hollings and Jones had been meeting with an industry representative, and Hollings admitted that he himself was unable to understand the technical aspects of the industry—in this case, watch manufacturing. Jones and the representative, however, understood each other. Hollings bragged, "It is with tremendous pride that we can bring industrialists to the state and know that Dr. Jones can speak their language."[88]

Thus, on July 1, 1962, "Tom" Jones, a forty-six-year-old father of five, took the reins of the University of South Carolina, saying, "My job here is to do everything possible to develop higher education in the state through the University of South Carolina." His attitude reflected the optimism that state leaders exuded in the early 1960s. He was determined that USC would, in his words, "be the pace-setter, the capstone of higher education in our state." "We will—we must—provide an opportunity for the optimum intellectual development of every young man or woman of our State who can profit from higher education," he said.[89] Tom Jones became a pivotal figure in the post–World War II development of the University of South Carolina, leading the racial desegregation of the University, leading its development as a national research university, and encouraging the development of innovative educational programs, allowing the University of South Carolina to confidently take its place alongside its peers among American universities.[90]

Upon taking office, Jones immediately stressed world-class academic excellence as his primary vision for the institution. Southern universities, he said, were equal to their northern counterparts in athletics, but "let's face it, they haven't met the competition scholastically." Although Carolina was "a healthy, thriving university," nonetheless it lagged behind even its southern peers. Thus he intended to place his emphasis on improving and expanding graduate and research programs. The economy of the space age would be geared to a high degree of specialization in science, technology, industry, and culture, he believed, and the University of South Carolina in 1962 was simply not staffed or financed to meet the increasing demands of the future. If USC was to meet these challenges, he said, it "must develop graduate study and research programs far beyond present levels in all areas." Like his predecessor Sumwalt, Jones saw that raising faculty salaries, in which the University had "hardly kept pace" with its peers, was a key to improving academic standards.[91]

Also like Donald Russell when he was USC's president, Jones recognized that to improve academic quality, the place to start was with the faculty. Upon taking office Jones declared his intention "to do everything within my power to see that adequate resources are available to attract talented personnel. . . . I will personally engage in a campaign to provide the university with top-flight professors."[92] In his first budget request, Jones laid out his plan for what it would take to build academic excellence at Carolina. He asked for $200,000 ($900,000) to hire twenty new faculty members that would help meet needs brought by enrollment increases; $300,000 ($1,350,000) to grant merit pay raises to deserving faculty; $125,000 ($562,500) to fund a sabbatical leave program for twenty-five faculty; and raising of the maximum salary ceiling for USC professors, at that time $12,000 ($54,000).[93]

However, his most revolutionary proposal and the top priority of his new administration was an ambitious plan to hire an elite corps of ten "prestige" professors for graduate instruction and research, each earning $20,000 ($90,000) per year (a sum equal to Jones's salary as president and more than the governor's salary), using a special state-appropriated $200,000 ($900,000) fund. The prestige professors would serve as "seed corn" to attract private and government grants, as well as outstanding graduate students who would be more likely to remain in South Carolina after earning their degrees. "Right now—this year—the University needs to leapfrog forward," Jones said. "The key to a university's progress is research," he felt, and these professors would attract the abundant research funding available for truly outstanding students and faculty. Jones would seek scholars of "international stature and competence . . . who can do creative kinds of work" for the program. Without it, South Carolina would continue to suffer what he called "intellectual evaporation," because so many of its bright minds would continue to leave the state for better educational opportunities elsewhere.[94]

The plan received support in area newspapers, with the *Charlotte (N.C.) Observer* calling Jones' proposal "one of the most exciting ideas to touch S.C. education since 'Pitchfork Ben' Tillman put Clemson on the map." The newspaper's editor remarked, "If the idea is carried out successfully, the unimpressive state of graduate education at USC would be given powerful impetus for the better."[95] State Development Board director Walter W. Harper declared that he was "100 per cent behind the program." For South Carolina to attract the types of "space age" industries it wanted, he said, then it desperately needed "a colony of top research men on our campuses." The state was missing out on recruiting many industries because of its lack of scientific research, he said.[96]

Governor Hollings gave Jones's bold proposal a boost when he strongly endorsed it, devoting most of his gubernatorial farewell address to describing the merits of a program to catapult USC into the ranks of the nation's research universities. In an important speech remembered more for the brief concluding paragraph in which he declared that South Carolina should, if ordered by federal courts, accept racial integration "with dignity," Hollings spent most of his address discussing South Carolina's "last shot" to join the quickly emerging space age. His speech represented a prominent example of the developing shift in South Carolina's white leadership from a concern with maintaining white supremacy to promoting economic development. It also demonstrated the central role the state's leaders envisioned for the University of South Carolina in the state's emerging industrial economy, in contrast to its rather peripheral role in the state's dying agricultural one. If South Carolina were to play a part in the new era, Hollings said, it meant "taking a tremendous leap forward now to prevent forever being relegated to the 50th state."

"What is the one shot we are going to use?," Hollings asked rhetorically. His answer: "A college professor. . . . You say we have lots of these . . . but we don't have one with a National Aeronautics Space Agency [sic] grant. We don't have one with a space science grant. We don't have one internationally famous [one] who will attract leading scholars and professors. You say that's Harvard thinking. South Carolina can't afford it. Any money available should go to the [public school] teachers, not these 'ivory-tower' professors. But I disagree. We can't afford not to do it."[97] He continued, "Let's talk money. Suppose we had a faculty budget of $60,000 for five professors. The ordinary way, the South Carolina way, is to hire five professors at $12,000 each. But the space age approach is to retain an outstanding one at $20,000 and hire the other four at $10,000 a piece. The $10,000 ones are just as good, perhaps better than the original $12,000 professors, for this type will sacrifice to associate with the outstanding. And you haven't spent any more money. In fact, you've made money. For the grants and contracts that the outstanding professor can attract will bring a fortune to the campus."[98]

Hollings then recounted the story of Professor John Gibson at Purdue, a former colleague of Tom Jones. Internationally known before going to Purdue in 1957, Gibson soon secured $300 ($1,412) to start a computer research program there. By early 1963, Gibson's research team consisted of seven other professors and sixty graduate students, with an annual budget of $300,000 ($1,335,246). "Recently, his team's work on computers has received national fame—and further grants. . . . This one shot—the outstanding professor—has a snowballing effect," said Hollings. It was this kind of "snowballing" that Hollings and Jones wanted to bring to South Carolina in the early 1960s. "First you have the professor, then his associates, then talented students, then contracts, then grants, then quality education, then leadership. Multiply this by five or ten professors and it's easy to see the effect." Hollings urged legislators to make the proposal a reality: "Similar endeavors are underway in Alabama, Texas, Florida, Virginia and Georgia," he said. "And the place to start is with that one nationally prominent professor."[99]

With such strong backing from a successful governor, the prospects for the proposal's success seemed good. Hollings's successor in the governor's office was to be Donald Russell, who as USC president had concentrated on building his own version of a prestige faculty, and he could be expected to support further efforts in this direction. In arguing the case for the first budget request of his own presidency—exactly ten years earlier—Russell had said, "My supreme objective is the development of a great faculty."[100] "We have got to bring in real educational leaders, recognized as such over the nation," he had said in 1952.[101] Russell made improving South Carolina's education the centerpiece of his 1962 campaign for governor, and observers predicted that he would likely become known as the "education governor."[102] Tom Jones's "prestige professors" program looked as if it would fit perfectly with the theme of Donald Russell's new administration.

However, less than two weeks after Hollings's January 9, 1963 farewell address, the *Observer* wrote, "For all practical purposes, the 'prestige' professors are dead." Jones's proposal went nowhere in the General Assembly.[103] What happened? For one thing, the legislature was in no mood to undertake bold new programs to improve education. The *Observer*'s editor commented that it seemed that the legislators, though they wanted improvements in education, felt that "no 'big push' and no extraordinary effort, such as Governor Terry Sanford initiated in North Carolina two years ago, are either necessary or desirable." As state senator Edgar Brown put it, "We don't want the budget to get out of kilter."[104] Another stumbling block was the strained political relationship between Ernest Hollings and Donald Russell (a legacy of the bitter 1958 gubernatorial campaign), which left Russell unlikely to support an initiative begun by his rival.[105]

A final reason for the proposal's failure was that, as so often has been the case in South Carolina's post–Civil War history, the specter of race reared its head and overwhelmed every other issue on the table. The prestige professors proposal became lost among the last-ditch efforts to address the issue of racial segregation in the early months of Donald Russell's term. Following Hollings's farewell address, Senator Marion Gressette issued a terse "no comment" to the press primarily because of Hollings's moderate stand on segregation. The speech, by and large, was unpopular with South Carolina politicians, not because of the "seed corn" faculty plan, but because of Hollings's statement that South Carolina must have "a government of laws rather than a government of men"—a reference to the state's continuing battle to avoid compliance with the Supreme Court's *Brown* decision.[106]

Less than three weeks later Harvey Gantt entered Clemson University.[107] The integration of Clemson was paired with a racially integrated post-inaugural barbecue picnic on the grounds of the Governor's Mansion hosted by the new governor, Donald Russell, and it appeared that a new day might be dawning in South Carolina's race relations. But, in an example of the complexity of the times, days later that same governor vowed to continue to fight school integration "by every lawful means."[108] The means became clearer as Russell's administration unfolded, and it was clear that the new day in race relations would have to wait.

In Russell's inaugural address (the day after Hollings's farewell speech), the new governor pointedly ignored the prestige professors proposal, going so far as to say, "let us not . . . falsely assume that we can have a sound educational structure by merely building at the top." He instead emphasized that to improve education in South Carolina, "We must begin at the bottom and work methodically up, step by step." This approach was a far cry from Hollings's and Jones's "top-down," "great leap" idea. Russell's education improvement proposals included a $3,000,000 ($13,352,459) plan to raise public school teacher salaries, and an even more notable $1,000,000 ($4,450,820) tuition grants program to provide state funds for any public school student who wanted to withdraw from public school and attend a private one—widely understood to be an anti-desegregation measure. Despite the fact that the state budget was expected to run a $5,000,000 ($22,254,098) surplus in the 1962–63 fiscal year, Russell made no mention of the $200,000 ($900,000) faculty improvement program. The tuition grants proposal—which later turned out be an utter failure—became the marquee educational legislation passed by the General Assembly that year.[109]

South Carolina's leaders had determined to continue paying the price of prejudice, and the University of South Carolina continued to suffer because of it. Tom Jones's prestige professors proposal could very well have been the "great leap forward" that the University of South Carolina needed to put it among the ranks of the region's leading research universities. Instead the plan failed, in part as a result of being ignored by the one person who, up until that time, had done the most to improve the University's faculty in the post–World War II era—Donald Russell. In the words of historian Ron Cox, 1963 was South Carolina's "year of decision" as it dealt with the question of desegregation, and the state finally began to address that issue head-on in 1963. However, with the failure of the prestige professors plan, that year was an equally important year of decision for public college and university faculty as well.[110]

With the failure of the prestige professors plan, Tom Jones and the USC administration introduced a fall-back position that imitated a plan used by Stanford University administrators in their own drive for institutional advancement. Jones would build on Carolina's existing strengths by using regularly budgeted and endowment funds. Instead of a broad "great leap forward," he planned to focus on upgrading a few departments at a time. By skewing resources into a few carefully selected departments, he believed that the University could achieve what he called "localized leaps." He chose the departments that would receive proportionately more resources based on two factors: the department should already have a strong base from which to "leap" to excellence, and the development of the state must be directly enhanced by having that department strong. The departments selected were history, English, chemistry, and physics.[111]

Through the remainder of the decade, these departments received proportionally more support, and it showed. The department that made the biggest leap was English. During the 1960s the department added several noted faculty members to an already strong department, including poet and writer-in-residence James Dickey and F. Scott Fitzgerald scholar Matthew J. Bruccoli. Dickey's national reputation preceded him at Carolina and Bruccoli's presence on campus paid off soon and handsomely for the department, for in 1971 he earned a prestigious Guggenheim Fellowship, a first for a departmental member at Carolina. Other outstanding English professors added in the 1960s were Frank Durham, Morse Peckham, John Guilds, James B. Meriwether, W. B. McColly, William H. Nolte, G. Ross Roy, Donald Greiner, and Benjamin B. Dunlap. Dunlap was a Columbia native and Rhodes Scholar who quickly became one of the University's most innovative and popular professors. The growth in the department of English was reflected in numbers as well. With 26 faculty members in 1962, the department grew to 51 by 1970.[112]

In history, traditionally one of the University's strongest departments, the department hired scholars such as Richard D. Mandell, Owen S. Connelly, Thomas L. Connelly, Edward Beardsley, Richard Rempel, Thomas Terrill, John P. Dolan, and Walter B. Edgar. Chemistry added professors James R. Durig, Elmer L. Amma, Robert Cargill, Thomas T. Tidwell, Jerome D. Odom, and Benjamin Gimarc, who attracted large research grants to the University and further improved one of the University's leading departments. In physics, a new department head, Oswald F. Schuette, attracted prominent scholars such as Charles P. Poole and Frank T. Avignone to a department that had improved markedly since the early 1950s.[113]

In many respects, the efforts of Tom Jones to achieve "localized leaps" paid off. In a 1964 national assessment of graduate faculties and programs, not one USC department was considered among the nation's best. By 1969, a new rating named Carolina's English department among the nation's top 64, and the chemistry department barely missed a similar ranking.[114] Overall, the quality of the faculty continued to improve, and the proportion of Carolina's faculty holding the Ph.D. rose from 47 percent in 1958–59 to nearly 63 percent in 1970–71.[115]

One reflection of the tremendous growth of the institution was that by the end of the 1960s, the faculty was considerably younger than it had been at the beginning of the decade. In 1970, over 60 percent of the faculty had come to the university within the previous five years. Only a quarter had more than twenty years of teaching experience.[116] Carolina continued to face the challenge of holding on to these professors, but many of the promising professors recruited in the 1960s stayed on to become University leaders as well as leaders within their respective fields. Those hired during Tom Jones's tenure as president became the critical mass of teaching and research faculty at the University through the 1990s.[117]

Nonetheless, the University's salary situation made the task of attracting "prestige" faculty difficult. In evaluating faculty salaries, the American Association of University Professors (AAUP) had given USC an "E" rating (using an AA through F scale, with "AA" the highest rating) as recently as 1961, and USC's average salary ranked only above that of the University of Mississippi among southern state universities. By 1965, average faculty salaries had made real improvements, rising to a "C" rating. However, in the critical area of full professor salaries (the rank most "prestige" faculty would hold), USC's average trailed the University of North Carolina by some $3,295 ($14,313), and the University of Georgia by $2,995 ($13,010). As the University of South Carolina's own 1971 self-study remarked, "These comparisons suggest that the University can compete with many smaller colleges and those universities which do not yet push doctoral programs, but this institution is not in a very competitive position respecting graduate faculty." Despite the fact that USC's salaries made substantial gains in the decade, building a "prestige" faculty at the University of South Carolina was difficult in the midst of fierce competition (see table 4.2).[118]

During Tom Jones's first year as USC's president, the institution reached an important milestone—full accreditation of all seven of its professional schools.[119] Such a step was essential if Jones's primary goals, overall academic excellence and an expansion of graduate programs and research, were to

Table 4.2 AAUP index grade for average faculty compensation, 1961–62 and
1969–70; average faculty compensation, 1961–62, 1969–70
(1991 constant dollars in parentheses)

STATE UNIVERSITY	AAUP INDEX GRADES		AVERAGE FACULTY COMPENSATION (IN DOLLARS)	
	61–63	69–70	1961–62	1969–70
Mississippi	E	E	6,863 (31,229)	11,765 (43,756)
South Carolina	E	C	7,170 (32,626)	13,528 (50,313)
Kentucky	D	B	7,322 (33,317)	15,190 (56,494)
Clemson	D	C	7,397 (33,658)	13,083 (48,658)
Alabama	D	C	7,934 (36,102)	13,812 (51,369)
Georgia	D	B	8,003 (36,416)	14,517 (53,991)
Florida	D	B	8,075 (36,744)	13,919 (51,767)
Tennessee	D	C	8,233 (37,462)	13,305 (49,483)
Louisiana State	C	C	8,408 (38,259)	12,903 (47,988)
North Carolina	C	B	9,564 (43,519)	15,345 (57,071)
Virginia	C	A	10,263 (46,700)	16,805 (62,501)

Source: "The Economic Status of the Profession, 1962–63," AAUP Bulletin 49, no. 2 (summer
1963), 141–87; "Rising Costs and the Public Institutions: The Annual Report on the Economic Status of the Profession, 1969–70," AAUP Bulletin 56, no. 2 (summer 1970),
175–239.

become reality. He considered a high level of graduate activity an essential
element of quality higher education. "Graduate programs and accompanying
research," said Jones, "largely determine the intellectual environment of a
university." Even more importantly, they were "the natural response of a state
University to the unfolding needs of a dynamic, forward moving economy."[120]
To meet the demands of the new economy, Jones said, "we must have the
leadership, the technicians, and the specialists to meet and conquer the many
new and complex problems that will arise. This leadership can and will come
from our graduate schools."[121]

Indeed, as the "old South Carolina," largely rural and agricultural and
concerned with white supremacy, gave way to a "new South Carolina," largely
urban and industrial and concerned with economic development, South
Carolina's leaders increasingly realized the potential benefits of a broad graduate program for the state's economy. In 1965, Governor Robert McNair
declared that South Carolina "must commit itself to the development of a
comprehensive and far-reaching program of graduate training." The state's
universities must concentrate, he believed, on the types of graduate and
research programs that would make the state a leader.[122] In later years,

McNair recalled that "the state had begun to attract firms like the DuPonts, the G.E.s, and the BASFs, and so we began to see a need for raising the overall level of education from kindergarten through graduate school."[123]

USC officials saw that graduate education could remove the "psychological ceiling" on the ambitions of South Carolina natives and provide homegrown human capital to develop significant industry in the Palmetto State.[124] Although the University's graduate programs grew substantially in the early part of the decade, in late 1965 USC was, according to Jones, falling short of its potential because of underfunding. Tom Jones recognized that for University programs to advance, the institution must tie its fate to the emerging political concern with economic development. Thus, in that year USC requested its first special appropriation to expand the graduate school. As a result, the General Assembly granted $250,000 ($1,049,613) for the purpose and thereafter gave special funding to expand graduate offerings. It was the first-ever recognition by the state that graduate education cost more than undergraduate education and was an indication that the state's leaders were beginning to understand the fundamental importance of advanced education to South Carolina's industrial economy.[125]

Under the direction of dean of the Graduate School Robert H. Wienefeld, who held the position until 1966, and later James A. Morris and Willard Davis (who both served as vice-president for advanced studies and research—an administrative position created in 1966), the 1960s witnessed growth in the Graduate School that far outpaced the growth of the overall student body (see table 4.3). Carolina's graduate programs substantially benefited from the abundant federal funding, resulting from the Sputnik crisis, that aimed to increase the numbers of college and university professors. The National Defense Education Act, the National Science Foundation, and the National Aeronautics and Space Administration were a boon, providing graduate scholarships and fellowships in unprecedented numbers and supplementing scarce state fellowship dollars. Graduate programs such as chemistry, English, history, physics, engineering, and education grew most quickly.[126]

There was a commensurate increase in the number of graduate programs available for Carolina's students (see table 4.4). As Tom Jones wrote, "never before have we offered so many courses in such a variety at the master's and doctoral levels."[127] New schools, departments, and degree programs broadened the number of academic subjects students could pursue at an advanced level, thereby strengthening the University's ability to serve the state in new ways. Among them were a revived Graduate School of Social Work (reestablished in 1969 and led by Dean Joseph Hungate Jr.), new departments in fields such as computer and library science, and new master's degree programs, such as the Master of Arts in Teaching, Master of Transportation, and

Table 4.3 USC Overall Columbia campus enrollment compared with
Graduate School enrollment, 1960–61, 1965–66, 1970–71

YEAR	OVERALL ENROLLMENT	% CHANGE, OVERALL. ENROLLMENT	GRAD. SCHOOL ENROLLMENT	% CHANGE, GRAD. SCHOOL	GRAD. SCHOOL ENROLLMENT AS % OF OVERALL ENROLLMENT
1960–61	5,661	–	318	–	5.6
1965–66	9,150	+62	841	+164	9.2
1970–71	13,358	+46	2,006	+138	14.8
% Change, 1960–1970		+136		+531	–

Source: Caroline Denham, ed., The University of South Carolina Statistical Profiles, 1991–92, 4; Annual Report, 1970–71, 8.

Table 4.4 University of South Carolina graduate degree offerings and degrees
conferred, 1960–61 to 1970–71

DEGREE TYPE	DEGREE PROGRAMS OFFERED, 1960–61	DEGREE PROGRAMS OFFERED,1970–71	DEGREES CONFERRED 1960–61	DEGREES CONFERRED 1970–71
Master's*	19	71	84	414
Ph.D.	7	29	7	81

Source: Catalog, 1960–61, 276; Self-Study, 1971, iii, 418–20; Annual Report, 1960–61, 8; 1970–71, 8; Furniss, ed., American Universities and Colleges, 11th ed., 1465.
* Includes the Master of Arts, Master of Science, Master of Arts in Teaching, and professional Master's in Accountancy, Business Administration, Education, Fine Arts, Engineering, Mathematics, Music, Music Education, Public Administration, Social Work, and Transportation.

Master of Public Administration programs. In addition, the University introduced new doctoral programs in fields such as psychology, business administration, economics, international studies, geology, and linguistics, as well as in several sub-fields of engineering and education.[128]

By the end of the decade, thanks in large part to federal aid for scholarships and research, South Carolina had finally begun to offer a broad array of programs leading to the Ph.D. It could now claim legitimate status as a research university. However, even while USC made significant progress in expanding graduate programs, other universities in the South were undergoing their own transformations, and it would take time for the University of South Carolina to catch up (see tables 4.5 and 4.6).

If increasingly available graduate education was evidence of Carolina's transformation, faculty research was the other sine qua non of the research university. At Carolina, research had traditionally not been a faculty priority. The SACS visitation committee of 1961 noted that the weakest characteristic

Table 4.5 Earned doctorates conferred, 1961–70, and 1970–71 academic
years, in selected southern state universities

UNIVERSITY	PH.D.S GRANTED 1961–70	PH.D.S GRANTED 1970–71
Univ. of South Carolina	274	81
Clemson University*	159	42
Univ. of Mississippi	356	77
Univ. of Alabama	743	156
Univ. of Georgia	870	256
Univ. of Virginia	975	226
Univ. of Tennessee	1,155	262
Louisiana State Univ.	1,257	207
Univ. of North Carolina	1,637	278
Univ. of Florida	1,815	293
Univ. of Texas	3,018	443

Source: Furniss, ed., *American Universities and Colleges*, 11th ed., 1779–83, 1809–32
* Clemson granted its first Ph.D. in 1960. *Greenville News*, 29 September 1965.

Table 4.6 Earned doctorates conferred by state, 1959–60, 1969–70;
percent change, 1960–70

STATE	PH.D.S 1959–60	PH.D.S 1969–70	PERCENT CHANGE 1960–70
South Carolina*	14	115	721.3
West Virginia	6	143	2283.3
Mississippi	12	178	1383.3
Alabama	33	221	569.7
Virginia	73	306	319.2
Georgia	47	345	634.0
Louisiana	101	348	244.6
Tennessee	104	452	334.6
North Carolina	202	634	213.9
Florida	136	668	391.2

Source: *Fact Book on Higher Education in the South*, 1971 and 1972 (Atlanta: Southern
Regional Education Board, 1972), 69.
* Doctorate-granting institutions in South Carolina were the University of South Carolina,
Clemson University, and the Medical University of South Carolina.

of Carolina's faculty was the relatively low level of interest and achievement in research. Only about a third of faculty were actively involved in research in 1960. Between 1960 and 1962, only 11 percent of USC's faculty received any independent research funding. Faculty complained that heavy teaching loads, inadequate salaries, poor research facilities, too much committee work, and lack of leadership had long hindered their ability to do research.[129]

However, a substantial increase in research accompanied the expansion of USC's graduate program during the 1960s; demonstrated ability and interest in research became a primary criteria for new faculty appointments.[130] The recognition that the University was an institution that could and should provide essential research services to an industrializing state grew as well. The concern of state leaders with economic development led the General Assembly in 1961 to begin to encourage the University's research capacity. It appropriated $250,000 ($1,150,423) (to be to be divided between USC and Clemson) to conduct research related to the emerging industrial economy in South Carolina. The research was designed to develop information that could be used to attract outside industry.[131] Research got another boost with the purchase of an IBM 1620 computer in early 1962, the first such computer in a college or university in South Carolina. Another IBM computer was added in 1964, and in 1965 William J. Eccles, a former electrical engineering colleague of Tom Jones at Purdue, became the computer center's director. In 1966, an upgrade to an IBM 7040, the largest and most modern computer IBM made at that time, gave the University additional computing power. These early computers aided the administrative support of the institution through registration as well as for student and faculty research in engineering, physics, and other fields. They were evidence of USC's new commitment to a research agenda.[132]

The 1960s saw a dramatic increase in federal funding for university research, but southern universities continued to receive proportionately less external research funding than non-southern institutions. Nonetheless, USC was committed to expanding its share of the national research pie, and ever-increasing federal spending on basic and applied research complemented state funding and contributed to a boom in research-related income. By 1965, outside research funding at USC grew to over $1,000,000 ($4,320,955) per year, and to better coordinate applications for grants, contracts and special institutes on campus, the University established the position of associate dean for research in the office of dean of the University (F. Phillips Pike served as the first head of the research office.) By 1969, Carolina annually received research and training grant funding of nearly $4.5 million ($16,736,301).[133]

In the late 1960s state boosters increasingly saw the University's research potential as tool to help contribute to South Carolina's economic development.

The state development board considered Tom Jones "one of South Carolina's best salesmen," and he was a regular participant in discussions among the state's leaders as to how to improve South Carolina's economy.[134] In his inaugural address in early 1967, Governor Robert McNair declared that "grants and other resources are going to those institutions which are capable of generating modern research. We also know that industries looking to the future are gravitating toward those states which recognize this relationship." In an era that has been called the "golden age of academic science," the University of South Carolina was becoming one of those institutions. The vast majority of the University's grants in the 1960s came from the federal government's largest funders of research, such as the National Science Foundation, the National Institutes of Health, the U.S. Office of Education, and the National Historical Publications and Records Commission, but others came from state agencies such as the South Carolina Highway Department or the Water Resources Commission, and from private foundations such as the Belle W. Baruch Foundation and the General Electric Foundation. Chemists Elmer Amma, James Durig, and Thomas Tidwell, botanist Wade T. Batson, and education professor M. I. Freidman all attracted sizable grants for basic and applied research. These research grants allowed the University to continually upgrade the quality of both graduate and undergraduate education.[135]

In 1969, two leading programs attracted the University's largest federal and private grants for academic programs to that date. The department of chemistry received a prestigious $500,000 ($1,859,589) grant from the National Science Foundation to upgrade the department and create a "Center of Excellence." The grant funded the addition of a biochemistry program that brought scholars such as Bruce Dunlap, Thomas Bryson, and Paul Ellis to Carolina's chemistry department. The NSF grant was instrumental in helping build the department into one of the University's finest. In the social sciences, the Scaife Family Foundation awarded grants in 1966 and 1969 totaling $210,000 ($881,675) and $359,000 ($1,335,185) respectively to improve the research efforts of members of the department of international studies. USC's international studies program had come to be known as the leading program as its kind in the southeast, and soon boasted prominent scholars such as Donald Weatherbee, Bruce Marshall, and Paul Kattenberg. USC's international studies program trained a large number of the U.S. military's foreign service officers.[136]

The development of several new service bureaus and research institutes increased the ability of the University's faculty to provide research services to the state and its government, industry, and cultural institutions, strengthening the ties between the University and these entities. The existing bureaus of Governmental Research and Business and Economic Research enlarged their operations through special state appropriations. New centers such as the Environmental Research Institute, the Bureau of Urban and Regional Affairs, the Institute for Estuarine and Littoral Sciences, the Institute for Research on Problems of the Underprivileged, and the Institute of Archaeology and Anthropology generated useful research to help ease the state's transition from an agricultural to a industrial economy. A new Institute of International Studies, established in 1961 under the leadership of Richard L. Walker, capitalized on the strengths of the existing department of international studies. Through the efforts of English professor Matthew Bruccoli, in 1969 the University became the home of the Center for Editions of American Authors (CEAA), a program of the Modern Language Association that published definitive texts of the works of great American authors—further evidence of the emergence of Carolina's Department of English to national prominence.[137]

As a result of the expanding research and service mission of Carolina, in the spring of 1966 President Jones announced a major reorganization in which the top-line deans became vice presidents over their respective areas, and created the "second in command" position of senior vice president. A reflection of the expanding importance of research and graduate programs, he created a new top-line position, vice president for advanced studies and research (with authority over both the Graduate School and all research programs, institutes and bureaus). Filling the new positions were senior vice president William H. Patterson (formerly dean of the University); vice president for academic affairs H. Willard Davis (formerly dean of the College of Arts and Sciences); vice president for advanced studies and research James A. Morris (formerly dean of the College of Business Administration); vice president for business affairs Harold Brunton Jr. (formerly dean of administration); vice president for student affairs Charles H. Witten (formerly dean of students); and vice president for development C. Wallace Martin (formerly director of development). Geologist Bruce W. Nelson replaced Davis as dean of the College of Arts and Sciences. Two years later, James Morris left the University to become head of the South Carolina Commission on Higher Education. After his exit, the senior vice president title was changed to provost and the vice president for academic affairs position abolished. William H. Patterson then became the University's first provost, and H. Willard Davis moved to head Advanced Studies and Research.[138]

The administrative reshufflings at the top levels were not the only organizational changes in the 1960s, nor were graduate and research programs the only areas that underwent a transformation. Undergraduate programs adjusted to the tremendous growth as well. In 1961, the College of Arts and Sciences created "Upper" and "Lower" divisions, with the Lower division primarily responsible for freshmen and sophomores who had not declared a major or met the requirements for entry into the professional schools. The Lower

Division was to provide better counseling and guidance for younger students.[139] Other organizational developments in the College of Arts and Sciences concerned the fields of geology and geography. Long combined in one department, the two fields became separate departments in 1963. Likewise, the department of psychology and philosophy was separated into two departments in 1964. These developments improved the curriculum for majors in all four areas.[140]

Another development in the College of Arts and Sciences was the establishment of an honors program for the University's best undergraduate students. Faculty worried about the impact on undergraduates as a result of the University's tremendous growth and emphasis on graduate education, and they called for an honors program in the University's 1960 self-study. They wrote of an honors program: "The Need is Great and Immediate. . . . The superior student is the member of a small minority in the University community and is in serious danger of receiving something less [than superior education]." The self-study committee noted that the University's increasing enrollment and larger classes made individual attention difficult, noting that "superior students will suffer from this . . . more than the average student, unless they are rescued by a special program designed to stimulate their intellectual powers."[141]

After four years of planning, in 1965 Carolina began its honors program, which, said Tom Jones, offered "a rare opportunity for superior students to attain an education of the highest quality no matter how large our university becomes." The program initially offered special introductory courses in the departments of English, history, political science, philosophy, biology, chemistry, and physics, taught by the most distinguished professors in the departments. They were not part of a separate curriculum but were designed to supplement existing departmental programs. The classes were kept small, usually between ten and twenty students, and encouraged classroom discussion and close student-professor relationships. For entry into the honors program, entering students had to have at least an SAT score of 1200 and rank in the top quarter of their high school class. Professor Benjamin Dunlap, who had taught five years at Harvard before coming to USC, commented that the level of work done in the honors classes was "surprisingly comparable to the work at Harvard." The program attracted excellent students, and Dunlap noted that two of his students had been accepted at Harvard but had come to Carolina in part because of the honors program. The first class in 1965 consisted of 36 freshmen; the program grew to include about 120 students (total enrollment) by 1970.[142]

While the honors program attracted superior students, the University became more selective about who it admitted to its regular undergraduate programs on the Columbia campus. In 1960, some 30.9 percent of entering freshmen were in the top quarter of their high school class, while 8.2 percent were from the bottom quarter. Throughout the 1960s the university consistently raised the standards of admission to its regular degree programs, and by 1969 some 42.4 percent were from the top quarter, while only 3.22 percent were from the bottom quarter. The average SAT score for entering freshmen rose from 896 in 1960 to 992 in 1969. The University also raised the bar for enrolled students, requiring higher grades of those who wished to continue in school.[143]

Among other significant improvements in the College of Arts and Sciences in the 1960s was a new emphasis on the visual and performing arts. In the late 1950s, the University had discontinued the department of dramatics, and the music and art programs had long struggled with inadequate budgets and general administrative neglect.[144] However, Tom Jones made the development of strong cultural arts programs an important facet of his administration. They were vital to society and USC could not be a complete university without them, he said.[145]

The effort to improve USC's programs in the arts started with the department of music, once described by an observer as "the neglected stepchild of the University." Arthur Fraser took over as department head in 1963 and immediately launched a reform program. He began a chamber music series in his first year, and in the next initiated a concerto-aria competition. He took steps to form an orchestra, which began performing in 1963 with student, faculty, and community musicians. In 1966, the department added two new degree offerings to the existing B.A. in music: the Bachelor of Music, and the first graduate music degree at USC, the Master of Music Education. In 1971, the Master of Music was added as well. Enrollment in music classes increased from 46 in 1963–64 to 151 in 1969–70, while full-time faculty increased from 10 to 17. Arpad Darzas, a young Hungarian choral director of international fame, came to USC in 1966 and revived USC's choral programs; in 1969 the concert choir toured Europe. In that same year, the USC music department earned full accreditation from the National Association of Schools of Music, capping the revival of music at USC in the 1960s.[146]

In the art department, a new era began when graphic designer and art historian John C. Benz took over as department head in 1966. Edmund Yaghjian, who had been department head since 1945, then became the university's first artist-in-residence. Within two years, the faculty of four had grown to include 10 full-time and 8 part-time teachers, all of whom were producing artists. The curriculum expanded to include four degree programs (B.A.s in art education, studio art, and art history, and the Bachelor of Fine Arts), and instruction in fields such as painting, advertising design, printmaking, sculpture, art history, and ceramics. In 1967, the department established the highly successful Summer School of the Arts at Hilton Head Island, which exposed students to leading southeastern artists.[147]

The University's efforts in theatre, defunct since 1959, revived with the efforts of John Guilds, the chairman of the emerging English department who came to the University in 1964. The following year, Guilds brought Russell Green, a Carolina alumnus with an M.F.A. from Yale, to Columbia to direct the University theatre. That same year, the University established an academic major in theatre, and the following year, it established an M.F.A. program. By 1968, the theatre program performed four major faculty-directed productions, two full-length graduate thesis productions, and eleven one-act undergraduate-directed plays. The curriculum grew from two to nineteen undergraduate courses and included five graduate courses. The theatre program became an autonomous department in 1969, completing a real renaissance of the arts at USC.[148]

In the College of Engineering, fast-moving developments in the field brought about by the age of nuclear energy, space exploration, and computers meant that the college had to constantly revise its curriculum to stay current. In 1963, the college adopted a new curriculum, the culmination of revisions that began with the MIT study of 1955. The college began to move away from departmentalizing its curriculum into the traditional fields of civil, mechanical, chemical, and electrical engineering. "There has been a rather rapid disappearance of boundaries between conventional engineering departments," said engineering dean Rufus Fellers. They instead began to emphasize an interdisciplinary approach to engineering education. The "engineering science" curriculum allowed majors to be more flexible in their course selection and specialize in newer fields such as chemical systems, electronics, thermo-mechanical systems, materials, structures and mechanics, and transportation. Modeled on cutting-edge programs at universities such as Case Institute of Technology, UCLA, the California Institute of Technology, Harvard, and Yale, Tom Jones declared that the revisions would "prepare young South Carolinians to be major contributors in the fantastic new endeavors of man and to give technical strength, leadership and direction to our most important industries." Throughout the decade, the college continually refined its curriculum to keep up with the latest scientific developments.[149]

The new programs in the College of Arts and Sciences and the revisions of curriculum in the College of Engineering provided outstanding new programs to the most gifted of Carolina's undergraduates. However, one of the great challenges of the 1960s was providing access to post–high school education for all of the "tidal wave" of baby boomers who wanted it, not only the superior students. Despite desegregation of the University and of the colleges in the state, South Carolina's high schools remained largely segregated, and the students who would come to Carolina would thus be the products of a segregated school system. As one way of addressing this challenge of integrating the Carolina student body, in 1968 Carolina launched the Opportunity Scholars, a program which allowed the admission of a select group of low-income and minority high school graduates who were unable to meet the University's entrance requirements but otherwise showed potential for success. A counterpart to the honors program, the Opportunity Scholars offered these students special class sections and counseling services in the freshman year to prepare them for regular University classes in the second year. Beginning with a group of 26 students, the program was judged a success. The retention rate of students in the program moving on to a sophomore year was similar to that of a typical freshman class at Carolina. One student remarked that the program "has given me the first break to really do what I want."[150]

A counterpart to the Opportunity Scholars was a federally funded program known as Upward Bound. Funded by the Office of Economic Opportunity (a part of Lyndon Johnson's "Great Society"), Upward Bound brought underprivileged high school students that showed promise to the campus during the summer to expose them to the academic experience and inspire them to strive for higher education. Tom Jones took a personal interest in it, and USC was the first southern state university to begin an Upward Bound program. In the words of Charles Witten, vice president for student affairs (who supervised the program), it was one way the University could "ease the cultural shock by preparing students to function in the University culture before they actually enter it." More than 90 percent of the Upward Bound graduates went on continue their education beyond high school.[151] Upward Bound and the Opportunity Scholars were but two of the new ways the University sought to serve a far broader range of students during the 1960s (both continue into the twenty-first century as a part of USC's TRIO Program).

As Robert Paterson had predicted in 1955, the arrival of the baby boom on college campuses brought a heated discussion about how the state should go about providing educational opportunities for the mass of its citizens.[152] The Opportunity Scholars and Upward Bound were relatively small pilot programs, and the state had yet to address in a systematic way how it was going to meet the challenge of educating all of the baby boomers, black and white. Without an overarching body to coordinate the state's higher educational institutions, the debate about the future took political overtones. South Carolina's resolution of that discussion would have a long-term impact on the University of South Carolina.

One early indication about how the state would resolve the challenge of providing access to postsecondary education was the 1961 creation of the

Technical Education Centers (TECs), created in part to give industrial workers specific technical job training tailored to industries who located in South Carolina.[153] But such industrial training, though of important significance for the state at large, was geared more toward attracting outside investment to the state by offering industry-specific training, not providing educational opportunity for the masses of young people seeking general higher education.

South Carolina's attempts to formulate a policy to deal with the inevitable rise in college enrollments began in 1960, when the General Assembly appointed a special joint committee to evaluate the need to establish a system of two-year colleges. The committee made its report in May 1961, and while it admitted that it could not suggest any concrete plans for establishing a junior college system without a broad study of higher education in the state, it did make an important preliminary recommendation. The committee suggested that the state establish a system of comprehensive two-year colleges, offering both general academic courses on the freshman and sophomore level and vocational courses such as those given at the state's new TECs.[154]

Before this committee had even made its report public, however, Governor Hollings took the initiative to begin making a more detailed survey of South Carolina's existing system of higher education. First, in early 1961 he appointed the Governor's Advisory Committee on Higher Education to make a thorough study of the state's overall system of higher education and recommend ways for South Carolina to both improve the existing state colleges and meet the challenge of booming college enrollments. The committee, chaired by A. L. M. Wiggins of Hartsville, immediately recognized that they needed a professional study to provide the kind of in-depth information necessary to make informed decisions. Consequently, the Wiggins Committee hired Cresap, McCormick and Paget to conduct a comprehensive survey of South Carolina's higher education. The 1962 CMP report, *Higher Education in South Carolina,* was the most comprehensive look at the state's public colleges since the Peabody Report of 1946. The Wiggins Committee incorporated many of CMP's recommendations into their final report. Issued in March of 1962, it reflected the growing recognition of the centrality of higher learning in the future economy of South Carolina.[155]

The Wiggins Committee report went to the heart of the problems South Carolina's public colleges had faced in the post–World War II era, declaring, "In the past decade, higher education in South Carolina has not kept pace with the progress of other states in the Southern region nor in the United States generally. This is shown by the comparatively low level of the financial support of the state's institutions of higher learning, their lack of accreditation in many subjects, the limited development of their graduate schools and their meager programs of basic and applied research."[156] The committee called for much stronger programs in graduate study and research, and in the coming decade Tom Jones and the University of South Carolina would begin to address some of these notable shortcomings in the state's higher education. From the perspective of the University of South Carolina, another important recommendation of the Wiggins Committee was that the state should develop a comprehensive system of two-year, nonresident colleges within commuting range of most citizens. They recommended that the extension branches of the University of South Carolina should be removed from University jurisdiction and converted into comprehensive junior colleges, offering not only college academic requirements but also other local community needs such as adult education. The TECs would expand and remain independent. The committee also recommended the establishment of a coordinating body for the state's colleges. Their recommendations framed the debate over the future of higher education in South Carolina for the next decade.[157]

Almost immediately, the oft-called-for body to coordinate higher education in South Carolina became a reality. By the end of March 1962, the General Assembly passed legislation creating the State Advisory Commission on Higher Education. The commission was not a board of regents but an advisory body with relatively weak powers. Nonetheless, it was a step in the direction of coordinating state-supported higher education in South Carolina.[158] However, after Hollings left office in early 1963, the new governor, Donald Russell, essentially ignored the new commission and the other recommendations of the Wiggins Committee, and in the absence of an overarching state policy USC further developed its extension campuses.[159]

Carolina had continued to develop the five two-year extension campuses that it had begun in the late 1950s (at Florence, Conway, Lancaster, Beaufort, and Aiken). Through the early 1960s, the University opened no new extension campuses, and the two-year centers continued to provide academic courses equal to the standards at the Columbia campus. However, as the decade progressed Carolina's leaders changed the nature of the extension campuses in response to calls for more widely available and accessible higher education. Their number grew and USC's branch campuses began to lower entrance requirements. As a result, the University's extension campuses remained at the heart of a debate that raged throughout the 1960s and early 1970s over the creation of a community college system in South Carolina. Many felt that the extension campuses should be merged with the state's TECs to create all-purpose community colleges. Others emphatically disagreed, stressing that the TECs and the USC branches had such divergent but important missions that they should be kept separate. Thus, in response to the Wiggins Committee's call for junior colleges that could provide community service as well as academic education, in 1962 the University began to make plans to offer technical courses, terminal "associate" degrees, and adult education in a wide-ranging curriculum that included credit and non-credit courses. University leaders were determined that Carolina could provide a complete range of educational services, thus making a community college system unnecessary.[160]

To reflect the new emphasis on the expanding responsibilities of extension work, in 1962 the name of the Extension Division was changed to the Division of General Studies and Extension. In 1964, the board of trustees authorized another name change, and the Division was renamed the School of General Studies, and in late 1965, the School became known as the College of General Studies—commensurate with its new status as an equal with the University's other major divisions. The director of general studies, Nicholas P. Mitchell, assumed the title of dean.[161]

The name changes mirrored the broader mission of General Studies and the extension centers. In 1963, the University began offering graduate education courses outside of Columbia. Between 1964 and 1966, the University's board of trustees also authorized General Studies to offer two-year associate degrees and one-year certificate programs in nursing, secretarial science, commercial science, and preschool education. These programs had lower admission standards than regular degree programs. In 1966, the University lowered admissions standards to all degree programs on the extension campuses and in the College of General Studies on the Columbia campus in order to make higher education available to a broader range of students; Carolina thus established a "two-tier" admissions policy—one for its extension campuses and the College of General Studies, and one for regular degree programs on the Columbia campus. Tom Jones argued that by doing so, the University extended the opportunity for higher education to more students at a lower per-student cost. Though this policy was successful in creating more educational opportunities, it also created problems, for it lowered the academic credibility of the work done in the College of General Studies, and consequently some of its coursework would not transfer to the other schools and colleges within the University.[162]

However, the state of South Carolina desperately needed to expand the availability of affordable higher education to its citizens. As a result, state leaders made plans to expand extension campuses to more locations. In January 1965, Clemson announced plans to begin its own two-year center in Sumter, only forty-four miles from Columbia. Thereafter began an effort to establish additional regional campuses throughout the state that could not only expand the availability of higher education but also extend the political reach of the two universities into new communities, which were eager to establish local colleges. Sol Blatt Sr., still Speaker of the South Carolina House, wrote to Tom Jones in response to the Clemson venture in Sumter, "I think the University should build as many two year colleges over the State as rapidly as possible to prevent the expansion of Clemson Schools for the Clemson people."[163]

As a result, in the spring of 1965, the state chartered new USC extension centers at Union and in Lieutenant Governor Robert McNair's hometown of Allendale (the Salkehatchie Regional Campus). Soon after, Carolina began to make plans to offer graduate studies in Charleston. In 1967, Spartanburg business leaders convinced the legislature to establish an extension campus there, primarily to offer nursing education in addition to the first two years of baccalaureate work.[164] USC board of trustees chairman Rutledge L. Osborne asserted, "We are meeting the needs of the state and regional campuses are being established as quickly as possible." He insisted that the University was not lowering its academic standards in opening so many regional campuses and adopting two-tiered admissions. Instead, he said, through the extension centers, it was "merely trying to take care of those who merit post-high school education but cannot meet the University requirements."[165]

Making higher education available in South Carolina was indeed a real challenge, and one the state had not systematically addressed at the state policy level since the recommendations of the Wiggins Committee. In early 1965, as it became apparent that USC and Clemson were intent on expanding to additional campuses, Governor Donald Russell began to devise a response to the sudden rush. In March, a study committee made up of Russell, President Jones and Dean Patterson from USC, and other representatives from the General Assembly, Clemson, and the state's TECs made a trip to California to observe that state's three-level system of higher education. In 1960, California had established a comprehensive network of community colleges (offering both academic and technical courses), four-year colleges, and a multi-campus state university, which provided universal access to higher education while ensuring high academic quality. Russell returned from the trip convinced that a California-type system was right for South Carolina. In a widely publicized address to a special joint session of the General Assembly, he asserted that "the key to the future for both the individual and state lies not in better education for a few, but in more and better education for all. And it is the responsibility of the state to make available to all—to those of many talents and to those of few talents—these educational opportunities."[166]

Russell and the study committee asserted that the increasingly complicated system of public higher education was not meeting the needs of South Carolina. "The situation will worsen," they wrote, "unless adequate steps are taken to bring academic order out of what is almost academic chaos."

They offered a three-part plan for a modified California-style system which included higher admissions standards and specific areas of specialization for the state's existing senior colleges and universities; a system of comprehensive community colleges that would combine the types of instruction offered at the USC branch campuses and the Technical Education Centers (the USC branches would be absorbed by the new system, which would be independent and governed by a state-level board of trustees for two-year colleges); and a State Board of Regents to coordinate the activities of the state's senior public colleges and universities.[167] The plan aimed at giving South Carolina the best of two worlds: providing efficiency and expanded access to higher education while maintaining quality at the state's existing colleges and universities.

Russell's plan was widely praised, with both USC president Tom Jones and Clemson president Robert Edwards giving it their hearty endorsements. Jones declared to the study committee as they put the finishing touches on their report, "Gentlemen, this may well have been the most significant afternoon in South Carolina's educational history." In addition to the crucial support of Jones and Edwards, it appeared that there was substantial momentum for passage of the plan in the General Assembly.[168]

However, only four days after Russell presented his California-style plan to the General Assembly, an unexpected shakeup of South Carolina's political leadership occurred, brought on by the death of South Carolina's longtime U.S. Senator Olin D. Johnston on April 18, 1965. Four days after that, on April 22, Governor Russell resigned his office in expectation of a Senate appointment. Lieutenant Governor Robert C. McNair then assumed the governor's office and appointed Russell to Johnston's Senate seat. By mid-May, McNair let it be known that he opposed Russell's plans and would not support action on the community college plan in the 1965 legislative session. The General Assembly then set up yet another special legislative-citizens committee, chaired by pro–community college Senator John C. West of Kershaw, to study the feasibility of establishing such a system.[169]

In the interim, without an advocate in the governor's office, momentum evaporated for legislation combining the USC branch campuses and the TECs as community colleges. McNair believed that the California-style plan was not the right one for South Carolina. Sol Blatt Sr. also favored maintaining University control over the extension campuses. By August, Tom Jones, once a strong supporter of Russell's plan, had reversed course and declared his opposition to community colleges. Edgar Brown emerged as an opponent as well.[170]

At hearings of the West Committee in January 1966, Tom Jones declared his resolute opposition to any plan that combined the USC branches with the TECs to form a system independent of University control. While at Purdue,

Jones had seen the effect of a junior college system on large state universities, the small independent campuses using their wide, combined political base to drain funding away from the central campus. The University, he believed, should maintain control of its extension campuses. He insisted that while the state should do its best to provide higher education to all its people, the TECs and USC system campuses should remain separate.[171] In speeches around the state he praised the existing system, arguing that the USC campuses best met the needs of the state's students who sought a general education. "The University has set the entrance requirements to all programs on the regional campuses at a level which guarantees most high school graduates an opportunity to pursue a degree," he said.[172]

Despite Jones's efforts and the opposition of the state's most influential legislators, when the West Committee released its report in March 1966, it echoed the recommendations of Donald Russell's plan and endorsed comprehensive community colleges. The committee called for the state to establish three pilot community colleges in Greenville, Sumter, and Conway, using the existing USC and Clemson branches or local TEC schools as a base to begin combining the two systems. It also recommended that the previously defunct State Advisory Commission on Higher Education be closely involved with the details of establishing the community college system.[173]

In the meantime, Governor McNair revived the State Advisory Commission on Higher Education, appointing the powerful executive director of the South Carolina Textile Association, John K. Cauthen, as commission chairman. Soon thereafter, in the 1967 legislative session, with McNair's support the General Assembly created a much stronger body to coordinate state-supported higher education, the Commission on Higher Education (CHE), an independent state agency with regulatory and policy-setting powers (including the review of institutional budgets and degree programs) as well as a full-time executive director and staff (the first director was Frank E. Kinard). McNair appointed Cauthen as the first chairman of the new commission, and the new CHE began work on an overall master plan for state-funded higher education.[174]

However, Governor McNair, who favored keeping the TECs and USC extension centers separate, requested that the new CHE cease work on their educational "blueprint" while consultants from Moody's Investors Services made a thorough study of the state (including its higher educational system). The 1968 Moody report, the landmark study *Opportunity and Growth in South Carolina, 1968–1985,* represented the vision of the McNair administration and recommended that the University turn the operation of the two-year extension campuses over to a board of trustees to be created for the state's two-year and four-year colleges. In the spring of 1969 the General Assembly created this board, and the newly independent Francis Marion College, formerly the USC branch campus in Florence, was brought under its jurisdiction. USC's other branch campuses remained under University control. Otherwise, the Moody report said nothing of combining the USC branches and the Technical Education Centers or a comprehensive system of community colleges, and provided support for those who wanted to keep the Technical Education Centers and USC branches separate.[175]

Differences between McNair and Cauthen over the structure of post–high school education soon led to Cauthen's resignation as chairman of the Commission on Higher Education. Under Cauthen's leadership, the CHE had produced its master plan, the so-called "Thomas report" (named for committee chairman Glenn G. Thomas of the Medical College), which it released just after the Moody report. It recommended taking two-year colleges away from USC and Clemson and strongly endorsed comprehensive community colleges. The Thomas report angered McNair, and Cauthen and Frank E. Kinard, the full-time CHE director, left their positions after McNair's rebuke. McNair replaced Kinard with James A. Morris, USC's former vice-president for advanced studies and research. Morris was committed to carrying out the Moody recommendations, including divesting the University of its branch campuses. However, the legislature rejected his recommendations in 1969 and again in the early 1970s. Thus the University maintained control over its various regional campuses, despite efforts by some of the state's most prominent leaders to establish an independent, comprehensive community college system. Despite a decade of political wrangling and the expansion of USC's extension campuses, availability and access to higher education in South Carolina remained a major problem. In 1950, 35 percent of students who received high school diplomas in South Carolina went to college. Despite a decade of fantastic growth in the size and number of state colleges, by 1968 that number had fallen to 31 percent— the lowest proportion in the nation.[176]

The establishment of a Commission on Higher Education with the power to review institutional budgets held potential benefits for the state and the University, giving hope that longtime inequities in funding with the other public colleges might come to an end. Since the end of World War II, the University's per-student appropriation had substantially trailed that of South Carolina's other colleges (see figure 3.1). This trend continued into the 1960s. To help make up the difference and continue to raise faculty salaries and build new facilities, in 1960 and 1961 Carolina raised tuition and fees for the first time since 1946 (annual tuition went from $80 in 1959 to $150 in 1961 for in-state students [$368 to $683], and from $250 to $350 [$1,150 to $1,611] for out-of-state students). Tuition remained the same for in-state students for the remainder of the decade, but other fees increased.[177]

Faced with ever-increasing enrollments on the horizon, Tom Jones insisted that state appropriations "must grow as the student body grows."[178] They did not. For example, in the 1963–64 academic year, USC's per-student appropriation, $704 ($3,107), was $160 ($706) less than that of any other public college in South Carolina. The situation grew worse in 1964–65. When enrollment increased 13.2 percent from the previous year, the University's per-student appropriation dropped to $693 ($3,018), while Winthrop's was $815 ($3,549), Clemson's was $953 ($4,150), and the Citadel's was $1,011 ($4,403). This represented the lowest per-student appropriation for USC in ten years.[179]

When the *Record* began to criticize the General Assembly for allowing such a situation to exist, the *Greenville News* and the *Charleston News and Courier* criticized the *Record*, and by extension the University, for "waving the flag of sheer numbers" of students in arguments for higher appropriations. The *News* in particular pointed out that using total enrollment figures was not a proper way to measure per-student funding, but instead "full-time equivalent" (FTE—the number of credit hours being taught divided by the normal full load per student) was the right way to measure appropriations. The *Record* responded that even using FTE-adjusted enrollments, "the University has by far the largest number of additional students—no matter how you figure it." Furthermore, it claimed, "It still receives the lowest per capita support for any state-supported institution—no matter how you figure it." The *Gamecock* responded to the *News*, "Perhaps the doubters would like to come count us ourselves."[180]

In response to the debate, the University began to submit its budget requests based on FTE calculations, and began to receive special supplemental appropriations for expanding graduate programs. Per-student FTE funding rose from $804 ($3,328) in 1966–67 to $902 ($3,441) in 1968–69. The graduate student supplement rose from $202 ($836) in 1966–67 to $687 ($2,621) in 1968–69. Despite these increases, USC trailed many of its peers, such as the University of Georgia, where total funding per FTE graduate student was about $6,400 ($25,553) in 1967–68 (as compared to a USC total of $1,469 [$5,865]).[181]

Such numbers reflected the state's legacy of underfunding its public colleges, particularly the University. Despite the talk about the importance of higher education in the new economy and making higher education available to more of its citizens, funding that education remained a low priority in South Carolina (see table 4.7).

Consistently low operational funding, while it hindered the University's academic program, did not limit the University's building program, which relied on tuition bonds (for academic and administrative buildings), room rent revenue bonds (for dormitories), and other federal grants or loans for financing, instead of direct state appropriations. The Higher Education Facilities Act of 1963 was an especially important piece of legislation, representing the federal aid for campus construction that Carolina administrators had hoped for since the days of Norman Smith. The 1960s and early 1970s saw a building boom as unprecedented at USC as the enrollment increases, much of it relying directly on partial federal financing. In the thirteen-year period between 1961 and 1974, the University added some 59 new buildings; to a total of about 1.5 million square feet of physical space, 3.5 million were added.[182] This dramatic construction required an extensive administrative structure to manage contracts, contractors, and plans for the buildings, as well as maintenance and upkeep after they were completed. Dean of administration Harold Brunton presided over the new bureaucracy, overseeing the University's sprawling physical plant.

Between 1963 and 1966 the University built and acquired additional student housing to keep up with the tremendous enrollment growth. The housing crisis on campus during the mid-1960s was reminiscent of the one during the late 1940s: three and four students were crowded into rooms designed to

Table 4.7 State appropriations for higher education per $1000 of personal income, 1960, 1967; state operational funding for higher education per college age person (ages 18–21), 1967–68; state operational appropriations for higher education as a percentage of state tax revenue, 1967–68

STATE	APPROP. PER $1000 PERS. INCOME 1960	1967	FUNDS PER COLLEGE AGE PERSON, 1967–68	APPROP. AS A % OF TAX REVENUE, 1967–68 (%)
South Carolina	$2.78	$6.24	$160	8.5
Virginia	$3.48	$5.90	$209	10.2
Tennessee	$3.08	$6.99	$229	11.2
Alabama	$4.36	$7.59	$231	11.0
Mississippi	$5.74	$8.25	$204	11.4
North Carolina	$3.98	$8.84	$271	11.8
Georgia	$3.71	$7.71	$257	11.9
Louisiana	$7.42	$10.40	$368	12.6
U.S. Average	$3.51	$7.04	$330	12.1

Source: E. F. Schietinger, Fact Book on Higher Education in the South, 1968 (Atlanta: Southern Regional Education Board, 1968), 49, 58; Fact Book on Higher Education in the South, 1970 (Atlanta: Southern Regional Education Board, 1970), 54.

hold two, and kitchens in some apartments were converted to bedrooms. The University purchased the Wales Gardens Apartments from the Columbia Housing Authority in 1963 (along Pickens Street to the south of the campus —later renamed the Carolina Gardens Apartments) and bought the Woodland Terrace Apartments in 1965 (on South Beltline Boulevard, several miles from campus). On campus, USC built South Tower, a twenty-story women's residence hall, and the final pair of veil-block (or more popularly known as "honeycomb") dormitories along Blossom Street, both of which opened in 1965. To alleviate a critical housing shortage in 1966, the University bought the Hotel Columbia, a twelve-story hotel at the corner of Gervais and Sumter Streets in downtown Columbia.[183]

The year 1965 marked a significant year in the University's plans for physical growth. In May, Tom Jones, Harold Brunton, and C. Wallace Martin chartered the Carolina Research and Development Foundation (CRDF), a private corporation designed to promote Carolina's physical expansion. The CRDF was established to buy property the University was interested in, hold it until the University could secure funding, then sell or lease it to the University at a bargain price. Supported by loans from local banks and led by president David Robinson, a prominent Columbia attorney, the CRDF gave Carolina flexibility in expanding the limits of its campus by allowing administrators to move quickly to secure available property.[184]

With the support of the CRDF behind USC, in May 1965, Hal Brunton announced a twenty-year long-range physical development plan, prepared in cooperation with Richard Webel, an internationally recognized landscape architect whom Donald Russell had first consulted in the 1950s. The plan represented a further evolution of plans laid down in the late 1950s and called for campus expansion in three directions: east, south, and west. To the east, Brunton and Webel planned to extend the academic campus in a six-block area bounded by Pendleton, Gregg, Greene, and Pickens Streets. They envisioned a "second horseshoe" along College Street with a Humanities Center, a School of Nursing, and Capstone House. To the south, the plan envisioned an expansion of student housing, physical education facilities, and parking on land that would eventually link the Carolina Gardens Apartments and the Rex Enright Athletic Center to the main campus. To the west, plans centered around a new coliseum to be built along Blossom Street, and other land to be secured through urban renewal between Main and Lincoln Streets. The campus development of the 1960s and early 1970s largely followed the outlines of the 1965 long-range plan and determined the shape and look of the modern University campus.[185]

After the founding of the CRDF and the finalizing of the campus long-range plan, construction on several major projects began in earnest. In January

1966, crews broke ground on a new physical sciences building along Main Street (in the works since 1962). Tom Jones called the $5,735,000 ($23,414,323) building "the biggest academic move USC has made in a generation." It was partly financed with federal funds, with $550,650 ($2,414,959) from a National Science Foundation grant and $1,303,850 ($5,633,877) from the National Higher Education Facilities Act of 1963. When completed in 1967, the eight-story, 185,000-square-foot science center symbolized the University's emergence as a center for modern scientific research, housing the departments of chemistry and physics as well the computer center. Today it is appropriately known as the Thomas F. Jones Physical Sciences Building.[186]

The transformation of Carolina from a small, intimate college into a research university meant physical growth, and this growth ran headlong into problems directly related to the confined nature of the urban campus. Despite the approval of the University's long-range plan to extend the campus into the neighborhood east of the campus, the plan ran counter to the best available advice on expanding an urban university. In advising the rapidly expanding universities of the 1960s, Julian H. Levi of the University of Chicago wrote that to foster a university's well-being, an essential element was a strong surrounding community that was compatible with the university's character. "A university is more than a collection of scholarly commuters," he wrote. "It is, rather, a community of scholars living with one another and with their work. The relationship of student and faculty is disrupted if the community around the university cannot attract and hold faculty members as residents."[187] The eastward extension of the campus and subsequent disruption of the historic residential neighborhood in the College Street area caused consternation among the area's residents, who included Carolina professors and students and some of Columbia's most prominent families. It permanently damaged a neighborhood critical to the long-term health of the University community.

Carolina began acquiring land in the area in the early 1960s, and in late 1963 it bought nearly half a block between Barnwell and Gregg Streets (including the Spigner House, a spacious home that became offices for the University's continuing education programs). Administrators assured residents that the University would acquire property in the neighborhood in a "slow, piecemeal" fashion over a period of twenty years, and told landowners that since there was no immediate demand, there were no foreseeable problems with the land acquisition.[188]

However, even as these words were spoken, increasing enrollment led administrators to begin planning an eighteen-story dormitory and conference center in the midst of the neighborhood—without first consulting the area's residents. An uproar ensued when furious residents learned of plans to construct a high-rise building next to their one- and two-story homes, two blocks away from the nearest University building. A distraught Mary L. McGeary (a Carolina alumna) of Gibbes Court wrote to Tom Jones, "Needless to say, I was most distressed to learn by word of mouth . . . what was to happen to the neighborhood in which I live. . . . Certainly it seems to me that the University officials who thought of this idea could have at least notified the property owners on Gibbes Court that they were going to ruin this neighborhood. As one of the property owners, I thoroughly disapprove."[189] Residents protested bitterly, citing noise, traffic, and parking problems that a dormitory would bring to their quiet neighborhood. It was in the University's interest, they argued, to preserve the old, upscale neighborhood so close to the heart of the campus. However, as in the University's earlier urban renewal projects, the thirst for *lebensraum* overrode the strong objections. The citizens' effort to halt construction was to no avail, for though the board of trustees directed the administration to cooperate with residents, the project continued.[190]

The modern 600-bed, eighteen-story dormitory-conference center, oddly out of place among the stately homes, opened in 1967 complete with a revolving restaurant on the top floor, 175 feet above ground level. Tom Jones had become fascinated with revolving restaurants, and the administration found a platform and mechanism for such a facility that had originally been built for the 1964–65 New York World's Fair. Through a gift from Greenville businessman Robert G. Wilson, the University became home to the only revolving restaurant at a U.S. university: the Top of Carolina. The high-rise dormitory was named "Capstone House," because it was designed to house upper-level and graduate students, who were the "crowning stone of the University," according to Tom Jones.[191]

The University's heavy-handed efforts to expand eastward into the College Street neighborhood continued as the "second horseshoe" between Capstone and the old campus began to become a reality—again over the objection of the residents whom the development displaced. Because of the refusals of many neighborhood residents to sell their homes, the CRDF resorted to condemnation proceedings to secure their property. Far ahead of the twenty-year time frame initially announced, in early 1969 Carolina opened a new Humanities Center at the corner of Pickens and College Streets, which included a ten-story office building and a five-story classroom building, home to the departments of English, Foreign Languages, and Philosophy. Among the homes sacrificed for the humanities complex was a century-old farmhouse located at 832 Pickens Street.[192]

To the south, the search for *lebensraum* displaced more longtime residents. In this area, the federal urban renewal program was used to clear another section of the Wheeler Hill neighborhood. "The urban renewal project will wipe out a slum area and give the people that live there decent living quarters," said Hal Brunton. There were 84 homes housing 63 families in the project area. Forty-three of the families were white and twenty were black, while 61 of the houses were classified as "sub-standard," thus justifying their removal. Through both urban renewal and CRDF purchases, this project cleared away the community in the area and connected the first urban renewal project with the Rex Enright Athletic Center. By 1969, the University had built a ten-story residence hall (Bates House—named for Jeff B. Bates) and a dormitory for athletes ("the Roost") on this newly acquired property.[193]

Controversies over the University's relations with the communities it displaced as it expanded continued with plans to move to the west. In 1965, University officials began planning for expansion in the area that would house a new Coliseum. They envisioned acquiring some five-and-a-half city blocks through a larger City of Columbia urban renewal project. This project would encompass the entire city block now occupied by the USC Law Center between Main and Assembly Streets, as well as blocks surrounding the new Coliseum.[194] Urban renewal programs, by definition, were designed to "re-develop" areas "where deteriorating conditions and community requirements justify clearance"—a euphemism for clearing poor neighborhoods. The area west of the campus included homes that met the federal guidelines for "sub-standard" housing as well as the 114-year-old Green Street Methodist Church (a white congregation), which was not a deteriorating property.[195]

Green Street pastor C. Murray Yarborough and church members protested the pending forced relocation of their congregation and asked that the church be removed from the urban renewal area. When the Columbia City Council refused (as it had done for black congregations in other urban renewal areas adjacent to the University), the Green Street Church began a grass-roots campaign to fight the plans. Church leaders claimed that forced removal would destroy their small congregation, which relied heavily on student support. "We exist to serve the University community," said Yarborough. Bumper stickers proclaiming "Save Green Street Methodist Church!" began appearing around the campus and city, and the congregation circulated petitions objecting to the plans to take the church property. "Green Street Church," said Yarborough, "has become a symbol for little people everywhere . . . who need to know that just because something is little, it does not have to be blotted from the face of the earth."[196]

The USC board of trustees reconsidered the question in mid-1969 but reaffirmed their intent to take the church property, stating, "The block in question is considered of prime importance to the growth and continuity of community service by the University of South Carolina."[197] However, after further lobbying, federal authorities agreed to allow the church to be removed from the urban renewal plans, provided USC officials also agreed. Soon thereafter, the board consented, and the church stands today, surrounded by the USC Law Center.[198]

Meanwhile, one block to the west, the Carolina Research and Development Foundation was in the process of buying and clearing the neighborhood on the site of the Carolina Coliseum. In what was becoming a familiar refrain, University officials were criticized for insensitivity to the needs of residents of the area, who were mostly African American. Student Harold Kirtz used the Student Senate to voice complaints about the University's lack of concern for the people it was relocating in the Coliseum area and in the other urban renewal areas—such as failure to find them decent homes. The University, Kirtz said, should "allow the present neighborhoods surrounding the campus to continue to exist alongside the University as communities. . . . The University can go only so far before the community will not support it. We hope the University will never be burned, but [it] keeps moving people."[199]

The long-needed Coliseum project continued, a need made more urgent when the old University Fieldhouse was destroyed by fire during Coliseum construction. The nearly $10,201,544 ($39,947,873) Coliseum building (a total that included both the building and site development), with a 12,400-seat arena and more than 100,000 square feet of academic space (housing the College of Journalism and the College of General Studies), opened in the winter of 1968 as workers completed the arena only hours before the tip-off of the first basketball game held there. When completed, it was believed to be the largest building in South Carolina and the largest arena in the Southeast.[200]

The construction of such a structure for the athletic program indicated the level of interest in Carolina athletics, which during the 1960s made its strongest push since World War II to reach national prominence in college sports. But first Carolina endured a period of controversy and mediocre seasons in both football and basketball. Head basketball coach Frank Johnson resigned in 1958 after a sixteen-year career. He was followed by Walt Hambrick, a USC assistant coach who brought All-American Grady Wallace to the Carolina campus. However, after a 4–20 season in 1958–59, Hambrick resigned, and the athletic committee of the board of trustees hired Bob Stevens, a former assistant at Michigan State University. After two losing seasons, Stevens's team, led by Art Whisnant, improved to 15–12, and Stevens was named Atlantic Coast Conference coach of the year in 1961–62. However, the brief success backfired on the Gamecocks, as Stevens left Carolina for a position at the University of Oklahoma after his most successful season.[201]

Carolina filled the vacancy with Chuck Noe, a former head coach at Virginia Military Institute and Virginia Tech. In his first season, the Gamecocks finished 9-15, and midway through his second season (1963–64), personal problems led Noe to step down as coach. The athletic committee then named Dwane Morrison, a twenty-six-year-old Carolina alumnus and Noe assistant, as interim head coach. Although Morrison did a respectable job as coach, compiling ACC wins over Clemson, North Carolina State, Virginia, and Maryland, he was not what Gamecock supporters were looking for in a head coach. Mirroring Tom Jones's plans for the faculty, they wanted to hire a "prestige" head coach. They at last got their man in Frank McGuire.

McGuire, a New York native, had coached ACC archrival University of North Carolina for nine seasons, compiling a .739 winning percentage and winning the 1957 NCAA Championship. After leaving UNC and coaching in the National Basketball Association for one season, McGuire left coaching. Even before Noe's resignation, Carolina alumni had sought McGuire. As a result, in February 1964 McGuire made a trip to Barnwell to meet with Sol Blatt Sr. and Sol Blatt Jr.—who wanted McGuire badly. While there, McGuire accepted their offer of the Carolina job, contingent on the University's building a new Coliseum. The news of his hiring shocked the East Coast sports world, who could not figure out why Frank McGuire would go to South Carolina, a school with a notoriously poor basketball program. McGuire himself promised to make South Carolina "the basketball capital of the world," but despite bringing in three prized New York–area recruits (Skip Harlicka, Jack Thompson, and Frank Standard), his first team (1964–65) finished with a 6–17 record.[202]

Meanwhile, the football program was going through its own period of turbulence. After Warren Giese stepped down as head coach in 1960, the board of trustees hired Marvin Bass, a former Giese assistant, as head coach. In 1962, Giese resigned as athletic director (and since, like Rex Enright, he had been granted faculty tenure, he remained on the faculty as head of the department of physical education). Marvin Bass then took over the athletic director position. As head football coach for six seasons, Bass was loved by his players but never had a winning record, and his tenure as athletic director proved to be as difficult. He compiled back-to-back four-win seasons in 1961 and 1962, but halfback Billy Gambrell earned ACC player-of-the-year honors in the latter year. Bass's next team went 1–8–1, one of the worst Carolina records in the twentieth century; they followed that with a 3–5–2 season in 1964. In 1965 the Gamecocks went 5–5 but nonetheless managed to tie for the ACC Championship. The brief on-the-field success came with a price, for just after the 1965 season, the ACC fined the University $2,500 ($10,496) and five football scholarships for violating a rule against having more than 140 athletes on scholarship. Poor oversight of the athletic program caused the University considerable embarrassment.[203]

In March 1966, shortly after Carolina received the ACC's penalty, Marvin Bass resigned his positions as USC head coach and athletic director to take the head coach's job with a professional football team in Montreal. To clean up the problems in the athletic department, Gamecock athletic supporters wanted another "prestige" coach, and they did everything it took to get one. Tom Jones, Sol Blatt Sr., and Governor Robert McNair found that they could secure the services of Paul Dietzel, the then-West Point head coach who had compiled a .630 winning percentage in seven years at Louisiana State, including a national championship and coach-of-the-year honors in 1958. The board of trustees agreed to the contract Dietzel asked for, and the Army coach was Columbia-bound. His contract was Carolina's first real entry into the emerging "big-time" world of college football. He received a ten-year deal that paid him $25,000 ($104,961) a year—the same salary the state paid Governor McNair. The contract also included a guarantee of a television coaches' show that would pay him at least $10,000 ($41,985), an expense account of $2,000 ($8,397), and the use of an airplane for the athletic department (which the CRDF bought for University use two years later). Dietzel's responsibilities included the athletic director's position, despite the efforts of many Carolina alumni to get Frank McGuire promoted to that job.[204]

Thus Sol Blatt and other Carolina athletic boosters got Carolina its prestige coaches. With the hiring of Frank McGuire and Paul Dietzel, Gamecock fans felt that the athletic program had finally reached the promised land. Tom Jones received letters from alumni declaring, "By a very wide margin, you get my vote for the *best president* we have ever had at USC!" Of Paul Dietzel's hiring, Rhett Jackson of Columbia wrote to Jones, "If I had been told to hire a coach at USC, and anyone in the United State was available, your choice would have been the same as mine. I think you got us the best!"[205] Hampton Davis of Camden wrote, "I commend you on the acquisition of Mr. Paul Dietzel. His presence along with Mr. McGuire's gives us a powerful combination in the two major sports. . . . I see USC on the move academically and athletically. I now feel that the state will rally around USC and this will start us toward the place we should have as the state university."[206]

Not all alumni were so happy with the moves in athletics. Henry R. Wengrow commented that while the USC Educational Foundation was soliciting him for donations to academics, "I read in the paper that my University can afford '$25,000 to $35,000 per year with fringe benefits' to an extra-academic person." Wengrow concluded, "I cannot reconcile my social conscience to the moral injustice of high paid coaches and low paid scholars."[207]

Optimism among the Gamecock faithful was soon tempered when Dietzel discovered that the problems he found in the athletic department, left over from Marvin Bass, were far deeper than administrators had known. In the summer of 1966, the ACC hit the football program with even more serious penalties than it had issued after the 1965 season. Wanting to start out with a clean slate, Dietzel had revealed that three USC athletes had received scholarships even though they did not meet the ACC minimum of 800 on the College Board exams. Carolina thus forfeited all of its ACC football games from the 1965 season, as well as the conference co-champion trophy.[208] Dietzel vowed that from then on, the athletic program would "be run in accordance with both the letter and the spirit of the rules of the ACC and the NCAA."[209]

However, these penalties were just the beginning of controversies that would cast a shadow over the successes of Carolina's athletics boosters. In October 1966, as Carolina approached what many believed would be Carolina's breakthrough season in basketball, Duke athletic director Eddie Cameron questioned the eligibility of Mike Grosso, a highly prized Carolina recruit who had averaged 22.7 points and an amazing 26 rebounds on the freshman team at USC. Although Grosso had not met the ACC minimum SAT score for scholarship eligibility, in 1965 the Conference had ruled him eligible for competition since his family was ostensibly paying his tuition. However, at Cameron's urging, the following year the Conference changed its minimum College Board rule, declaring that any athlete who failed to make 800 on the exam, whether on scholarship or not, was ineligible for ACC competition. There was no mention of the rule's being retroactive.[210]

Nonetheless, just before the beginning of Grosso's sophomore season, the ACC's executive committee ruled that he was now ineligible for ACC play. A furious Frank McGuire reportedly had to be restrained from physically attacking a member of the committee when it announced the Grosso decision. The ruling ignited a furor in South Carolina, with USC supporters claiming that Duke and the University of North Carolina were jealous of Frank McGuire's recruiting success and that Eddie Cameron was dominating ACC policy. Robert C. Thames Jr. wrote of the ACC ruling, "The odor from such a decision makes a load of week old mackerel smell like Chanel #5 in comparison."[211]

McGuire claimed that the move was a "spite vendetta" by Cameron and publicly called those who ran the ACC "skunks." Edward Saleeby, a member of the USC board of trustees, suggested that USC take the case to the federal courts. Alumni began to circulate petitions demanding that USC secede from the ACC. President Jones quickly squelched such talk, reprimanded McGuire, and apologized to ACC officials for the coach's remarks. In response to the ill will created by the situation, the ACC, in an unprecedented ruling, declared that any conference team who wished could reschedule its games with USC on a neutral court. Duke then announced that they had canceled all their games with USC for the following season.[212]

Louis Chestnut, a sportswriter for the *News and Courier,* called the Grosso situation and the uproar it caused "the most mixed up state of affairs, the most mis-handled, botched-up mess ever to hit college athletics in our part of the country." A *Gamecock* editorialist wrote in December 1966 that the controversy threatened USC's reputation and that "the complexity of this situation attests to its seriousness. However, one fact stands out above all others in the mass of confusion: the University is in trouble, serious trouble, and all that has gone before may pale before what is to come."[213]

Indeed, the University's standing sank lower when the NCAA reviewed the case. This more neutral body found that Duke had been justified in its complaints against the University. In January 1967, the NCAA leveled a humiliating probation against USC, citing six major rules violations.[214] Both the football and basketball programs were put on probation and barred from television and postseason play for two years. Among the reasons the NCAA cited for the probation was that "the [USC] Administration had yielded to outside pressures far beyond acceptable limits in the running of its own athletic department." They made it clear that if USC did not clean up its act quickly, the University might be suspended from the NCAA.[215]

The scandal was a hard blow the University's credibility, both academically and athletically. One alumnus, John Hamilton of Charleston, wrote, "South Carolina has many handicaps. We are poor. We are benighted. But I used to hold my head high, saying that wealth and learning are not everything. We South Carolinians still had our honor and our good name. Now that is gone, and I am badly shaken."[216] Tom Jones and athletic director Dietzel vowed to take firm action, with Jones declaring, "We have the sins of the past to clean up, and we must begin the job now." The NCAA "ruled we were out of bounds," he said. "And we'll never come close to the line again."[217]

On the court and on the field, even with the effects of probation, USC teams improved markedly over their counterparts earlier in the decade and rewarded the Gamecock faithful. Led by the "four horsemen," Gary Gregor, Skip Harlicka, Jack Thompson, and Frank Standard, by 1968 the Gamecock basketball teams under Frank McGuire emerged as a national power. In 1968–69 the program arrived, filling the seats of the new Carolina Coliseum, compiling a 21–7 record and finishing thirteenth in the Associated Press poll. They took regular-season wins from both Duke and North Carolina, the acknowledged basketball powers of the ACC. They also traveled to the National Invitational Tournament, Carolina's first trip to postseason play in school history. The combination of John Roche, Tom Owens, Bobby Cremins, Billy Walsh, and John Ribock on this team formed the core of a group that would remain national championship contenders into the early 1970s—the first national success ever for a Gamecock athletic team.[218]

In football, by the end of the decade Paul Dietzel brought success as well. His first season, 1966, was disastrous, with a 1–9 record that surpassed even 1963 as the worst in school history up until that time. In his second season, the Gamecocks improved to 5–5, and two-sport star Bobby Bryant was named ACC athlete of the year (he pitched on the baseball team as well). After a disappointing 4–6 season in 1968, in 1969 the Gamecocks put together their first winning season since 1958. Led by quarterback Tommy Suggs, receiver Fred Zeigler, first team All-America fullback Warren Muir, and halfback Rudy Holloman, Carolina had a 7–3 season complete with USC's first-ever outright ACC football championship. The football team's perfect conference record in 1969, combined with the basketball team's own perfect record later that academic year, was the first and only time in the history of the ACC that both the football and basketball teams from the same school went through their entire regular seasons in an academic year without a conference loss. It seemed that football, like basketball, had arrived in 1969, and that prestigious coaching staffs could promise a bright decade in the 1970s. With the addition of former New York Yankee great Bobby Richardson as Carolina's first full-time baseball coach in 1969, Paul Dietzel brought on board another nationally known coach who added further respectability to the Gamecock athletic program. Master promoters, Dietzel, McGuire, and Richardson managed to generate tremendous excitement for Carolina athletics, raising money and improving facilities markedly.[219]

The newfound athletic success seized the attention of Carolina students, for whom athletics had long been a primary diversion. As the desegregation of the student body had demonstrated, the lives of USC students of the 1960s changed significantly. In fact, the 1960s witnessed a revolution in student life unlike any in the institution's history. However, at the outset of the decade students were for the most part like their counterparts of the 1950s. The college experience of Carolina students in the first half of the 1960s were very similar to that of the 1940s and 1950s, a world of "bobby socks and button-down collars," as former student John Gregory recalled. The 1960 *Garnet and Black* declared that they came to USC from all over South Carolina, "eager to be assimilated—ready to conform."[220] The paternalistic relationship between the University and the student that had existed since the institution's beginnings continued; the institutional rules that governed their lives in loco parentis continued as well. The most pressing disciplinary issues that faced the administrators of student life early in the decade were drinking and profanity at social events like football games and dances. As a faculty subcommittee concerned with student discipline declared in 1962, "Many [students] are immature and indeed attend the University in part to develop maturity. . . . The University's role is not simply to separate the sheep from the goats but to make sheep of as many candidates as possible." The University saw itself as the upholder of societal norms, and its regulations reflected growing challenges to those norms as the 1960s unfolded. In 1964 such challenges led the board of trustees to approve a policy on student behavior declaring, "Persons who exhibit behavior which deviates from the normal to the extent that their habits and practices are generally unacceptable to society will not be acceptable as students of the University." Such decrees indicate that the level of "deviance" from norms was increasing as the decade proceeded.[221]

Early in the decade, fraternities and sororities continued to dominate the social life of the campus, which included control over campus organizations such as student government.[222] To those who criticized the Greeks as elitist, *Gamecock* columnist Carl Hendricks asserted that the fraternities and sororities were "a wholesome influence on this campus." "These organizations produce many outstanding leaders," he wrote, ". . . and alumni who care about the institution."[223] However, despite such "wholesome" influences, the popularity of Greek organizations served as a barometer of the dramatic changes in student life during the 1960s, and their popularity waned later in the decade. By 1965, student government noted the existence of considerable anti-Greek attitudes among students. Even as the number of undergraduates at the University nearly doubled between 1963 and 1970 (from 6,029 to 11,827), the number of freshmen pledging fraternities stagnated (fraternities pledged 298 in 1963 and 313 in 1970). Such a trend simply reinforced the notion of Greek elitism. "The Greeks are in a very difficult situation," said Interfraternity Council president Pete McCausland in early 1970. "It is very difficult to establish individual identities. Part of this is due to the traditional categorizing of the 'frat man' image."[224] Such a "frat man image" was at odds with the emphasis on individualism and self-fulfillment in late 1960s student culture and contributed to declining influence in campus affairs for both fraternities and sororities.

Nonetheless, despite their decline, throughout the decade Greek life maintained a powerful hold on a significant proportion of Carolina's students, and campus traditions such as the elaborate May Day and Homecoming festivities, Sigma Chi's Derby Day, Cotillion Club dances, and other annual parties remained staples of Carolina's social life. Fraternity parties contributed to Carolina's reputation as a party school.[225] In 1965, Kappa Sigma member Karl Beason commented that "I came to Carolina expecting to see people falling down all over the place because I had heard so much about Carolina being a drinking school."[226] In Pat Conroy's novel *Beach Music*, the character Jack McCall describes the parties this way: "We drank bathtubs full of a ghastly concoction called 'purple Jesus,' composed of unfermented grape juice and cheap vodka. Silver kegs of beer enthroned in melting ice sat in royal attendance at every campus event. Drunkenness was a condition of choice among a high percentage of the student body."[227] While certainly this percentage was a minority, there is no dispute that alcohol played an important role in the social lives of a significant portion of the student body, Greeks included.[228] In 1965, dean of women Elizabeth Clotworthy observed that Carolina students did not "frown on one who drinks now as they once did. It seems to be more accepted now. This drinking problem of course is not peculiar to Carolina," she added, "It's happening all over the country."[229]

The expansion of open drinking at Carolina reflected a youth rebellion among baby boomers of the 1960s that deeply concerned those of the older generations. To them, trends such as the rock and roll music that was popular among young people represented a threat to social order. They saw rock and roll as gratuitous noise that set young people into frenzied new dances. The fact that rock and roll grew out of rhythm and blues, a musical style made popular by urban blacks, suggested to some white conservatives that the music might be a plot to sway young people toward integrationist thought.[230] In 1960, Carolina officials barred the Student Union from hiring black bands to play at campus dances, expressing a fear that to do so would lead to "racial incidents." Other USC officials were loath to allow black performers to play at University functions for fear of giving the impression that Carolina endorsed integration. Nonetheless, students were eager to hear the kind of rock and roll played by black bands.[231] An example of these conflicting attitudes occurred in 1961, when the Carolina Homecoming Dance at the Township Auditorium erupted into a riot. A report by President Sumwalt described a party that featured a rock-and-roll "orchestra" (made up of black performers) attended by between 4,000 and 6,000 students. The report read that at about 11:15 "several persons went to the stage . . . and there began to dance a currently popular innovation called 'The Twist.'" Police escorted the dancers from the stage, but others took their places. When stagehands attempted to close the curtain, students ripped a hole in it. Other guests began throwing cups and bottles onto the auditorium floor. After lowering the curtain, police cleared the auditorium. The president blamed the riot on the music, concluding, "The Rock and Roll music provided for the students at this dance was in response to the students' wishes. Unfortunately, it is almost impossible to obtain white orchestras who play the kind of music the students want."[232] Indeed, students wanted to hear the rock and roll of black performers, regardless of the wishes of the administration.[233] Sumwalt's approach to the changes in Carolina student culture foreshadowed a decade when the generation gap between students and senior administrators would widen to a chasm.

Another nationwide trend that reflected significant changes in youth culture began to affect Carolina as the 1960s wore on: illegal drug use. Three students were suspended in 1966 for selling amphetamines, the most common drug of the mid-1960s. By 1968, drug use was becoming more widespread. In February of that year, the *Charleston News and Courier* ran a series of exposé articles detailing drug use at both Clemson and USC. Although the articles contained sensational charges—such as an allegation that some 25 percent of the USC student body had tried marijuana—none could be proven. After making several arrests, Columbia police blamed USC students for the city's increasing drug traffic. USC and SLED officials denied that drug use was out of control on the campus. While the charges were likely blown out of proportion, it was clear that drugs such as amphetamines and marijuana were gaining a foothold at Carolina as they were on other campuses across the country.[234]

These developments demonstrated the changes in youth culture, but for interested students the intellectual atmosphere at Carolina enjoyed a heyday. The growth in graduate programs and the recruitment of outstanding faculty quickened the pace of academic life on campus. The civil rights movement and growing involvement in Vietnam brought stepped up political activity and debate among students. Graduate students particularly recalled that Carolina, as an advancing institution "on the move" in so many areas of study, was an intellectually exciting place during the 1960s.[235]

However, among some undergraduates, anti-intellectual attitudes that Professor Dan Hollis had noticed in the 1950s persisted. In 1964 Carl Hendricks wrote, "At the University of South Carolina there is no real intellectual atmosphere—no concern of the great majority of students for academic pursuits, just a desire to have a good time and get the heck out."[236] Later in the decade, history professor John Scott Wilson commented that the typical USC undergraduate "sits through the required courses, satisfies the various degree requirements, in short, endures x hours of tedium and at the end of a fairly pleasant ordeal is awarded a degree. Both the student and society mistakenly believe . . . that the student has been educated. In actuality, he has only been processed."[237]

Some students blamed the faculty for this state of affairs, citing their lack of caring for students, while others blamed the growing emphasis on research. Hendricks asked, "What has happened to the teaching teacher?" He concluded that "there seems to be quite a vogue in many of the nation's colleges and universities (including the University of South Carolina) to place greater value on faculty members who do research and publish than those who place greater emphasis on teaching."[238] Indeed, the University's own self-study report of 1970 noted that the objectives of the College of Arts and Sciences seemed to have changed since 1960, when most of the faculty were deeply committed to good undergraduate teaching. Because of the emphasis on graduate education and research, faculty noticed a significant decline in the emphasis on effective undergraduate education.[239]

These kinds of complaints by students and faculty were common at Carolina as they were at other quickly expanding universities in the 1960s.[240] Many of the problems on the Carolina campus could be traced to the ill effects of the tremendous growth of the student body. "The University has grown very fast in recent years and the resulting 'bigness' is a major factor in the impersonality of the University," wrote Carl Hendricks.[241] Many students complained about the computer record-keeping that seemed to compound the loss of community and identity. "The average student comes to the University and right away becomes a student number, a hole in an IBM card," Hendricks wrote.[242] Craig Hammond vividly described the effects of the computer on the student's life: "With the advent of the IBM system, the USC 'Joe College' became a number on card and file. He can not eat the magnificent varieties of left-overs in the Slater System [the University food service], stuff his face with a cheese omelet in *The Gamecock Room*, attend the Artist Series presentation, obtain a blue book in class, or even cash a certified fifty cent check in the Campus Shop without first showing the number."[243] President Tom Jones responded to talk that Carolina was too big by arguing that growth had brought the University (now a "multiversity" in 1960s parlance) better education for more people at lower cost. He nonetheless admitted that "the modern university has difficulty having the personal touch that we would all like it to have."[244]

It was clear that the increasing impersonality of the institution was becoming a significant problem. The close-knit, intimate student body of an earlier era was a thing of the past. As the student body surpassed 10,000, there was distinct loss of community feeling on campus, and a principal victim of the loss was the relationship between student and teacher. The mother of one student who was having academic problems wrote to President Jones that "I am sure that this is of no interest to the college . . . as there are many pupils and no one individual is given special attention." She insisted that all her son needed was personal attention: "Just one minute of an instructor's time with a pupil – might just save a pupil."[245] Other evidence that the University was losing much of what it had made it such a special place to earlier generations was the decline of institutions such as the YMCA. The "Y" had once been a primary student organization on campus, combining moral and spiritual education with the functions of a latter day student affairs office. However, in 1964, the "Y" deeded to the University its Bell Camp, the recreation area in northeast Richland County that it had long operated for the benefit of students, because it could no longer afford the upkeep. The following year the "Y" ceased sponsoring the University's freshman orientation program that had been one of its primary responsibilities. After 1965, the YMCA no longer received any funding from the University, and the expanding student affairs division gradually took over the work it once did. Likewise, Religious Emphasis Week, a tradition that dated to 1938, ended in 1967.[246] Another move that demonstrated the increasing bureaucratization of the student life was the administration's takeover of student publications like the *Gamecock*. Since its founding in 1906, the *Gamecock* had been independently operated by the Euphradian and Clariosophic Societies, debating organizations that dated to the earliest years of the South Carolina College. Concerned that the *Gamecock* had aired controversial opinions, in 1964 the administration created a board of student publications that placed the *Gamecock* under the jurisdiction of the student affairs office.[247]

Another old tradition that became a casualty of the 1960s was the University's honor system. Historian Daniel Hollis noted there had been a strict honor code at Carolina until 1930, when a less stringent, voluntary honor system was adopted. But mushrooming enrollments led that system to weaken that as well. By 1960, a special student-faculty committee released a report showing "deliberate and persistent malpractice on the part of a minority" of students, which led to a "loss of confidence" on the part of all students in the workability of an honor principle. A 1960 revision of the honor system placed the responsibility for enforcement within each individual college, but by 1964, this plan appeared to have failed to strengthen the system. Student Ruth Henderson reflected the views of most Carolina students when she said, "The understatement of the year is to say that Carolina has an honor system." In 1965, the Honor System was again revised. Freshman and sophomore courses no longer operated under the system at all, and all exams were to be proctored. Junior- and senior-level classes would continue to operate under the honor system provided that 90 percent of the students in each class agreed to abide by it. The ultimate responsibility for enforcing the honor system lay with students, and with the depersonalization of campus life students became increasingly hesitant about "making waves," instead preferring to let cheating go unpunished.[248]

Another important change in student life in 1960s was the decline of University rules that functioned in loco parentis, as well as a relaxing of some academic requirements. These trends grew out of increased student demands for more control over their lives and their academic programs. Students, especially females, had long been subject to strict curfews, dress codes, class attendance rules, and dormitory rules that allowed room searches at any time. But these rules began to weaken as social mores changed and students pressed for more freedoms. Soon after becoming president, Tom Jones recommended dropping class attendance requirements for upperclassmen, reasoning that "after a year at school a student should be on his mental enough to meet his classes in order to pass."[249] By 1968, class attendance in upper-level undergraduate courses was completely voluntary. In that year as well, students were given the option to take up to 24 hours of elective course credit on a pass-fail basis.[250] In 1969, the University experimented with shorter class times (for example, forty-five-minute instead of fifty-minute classes) and reduced the language requirement in the College of Arts and Sciences. In the spring of 1970, the administration abolished Saturday classes.[251]

In addition to less stringent academic requirements, student housing regulations became more liberal as the student body expanded rapidly and pressed for more control over their personal lives. Throughout the 1960s, on-campus housing was at a premium as administrators struggled to build (or purchase) dormitories. The University maintained a rule that all undergraduates not living with their parents were required to live on campus, but juniors and seniors could apply to live off-campus. Dormitories were nearly always filled to (or beyond) capacity, and roughly half of the student body had to live off-campus.[252] For male students on campus, dormitory regulations governing their lives were gradually relaxed during the decade.[253]

For women—who made up about one-third of Columbia campus students—the double standard of strict curfews and dress codes continued for most of the decade but declined by 1970. In the early 1960s, these rules did not present much of a problem, for student norms and the desire to conform meant that most did not resist the codes. However, changing clothing styles and social norms in the middle and late 1960s made enforcement of the dress code difficult. The popularity of knee socks, pantsuits, and miniskirts presented a challenge to traditional dress codes. In early 1967, the Association of Women Students (AWS), a women's organization dedicated to abolishing the University's restrictive regulations on women, challenged the University's ban on women's wearing of slacks and shorts in academic buildings. In a letter to the *Gamecock*, two anonymous students wondered if the University were going to "revert to witch burning" of coeds found breaking the rules. Defenders of the regulations, such as Jean Johnson, said that they were intended ensure that Carolina women would "present a good appearance to those within and outside our University life—it should be the appearance of ladies. It is my opinion that females do not look like ladies" in slacks or miniskirts, she said. The Student Senate reacted by passing a resolution declaring the rule against these clothes an infringement on the rights of individuals.[254] As clothing styles continued to change, the dress code became unenforceable. By 1970, a *Gamecock* survey indicated the extent of the changes in norms towards women's clothing during the previous decade. Nearly 20 percent of women students admitted that they occasionally went without bras in public.[255]

Curfews in women's dormitories—another double standard for women—began to disappear as well. Through the requests of AWS, when Capstone House opened in the fall of 1967, it was designated as an "honor dorm" for women. Juniors and seniors who met grade criteria, as well as the graduate students who lived there, were free from any curfew rules. The *Gamecock* called this development "USC's first acknowledgment of the advent of the twentieth century." By 1969, the less stringent rules applied to all women's dormitories: with parental permission, any female student with two semesters as a full-time student could live without curfew restrictions. Room inspections remained a fixture, however, and freshmen women were still subject to a midnight curfew during the week and a 1:00 A.M. curfew on weekends—though even this rule allowed much more freedom than earlier regulations.[256] Nonetheless, the late 1960s witnessed the steady emancipation of students, both male and female, from the regulations imposed in loco parentis.

Changes in the University alcohol policy also reflected student demands that they be treated as adults. As late as 1969, USC regulations stated, as they had for many decades, "Students may not use or have in their possession any alcoholic beverages on any property owned or used by the University." In response to student demands, in May of 1969 the board of trustees voted to reword the regulation to "The drinking of alcoholic beverages is discouraged." Students were still prohibited from drinking in public, but they were thereafter allowed to drink in residence halls, provided of course that they were of legal drinking age (then eighteen years old). However, despite calls by the Student Senate, the trustees declined to allow beer sales on campus.[257]

By and large, the majority of students at the University of South Carolina during the 1960s could be classified as socially "conservative," just as their predecessors of the 1950s had called themselves. Some noted that Carolina students were reluctant to get involved on campus. The enormous growth of the University coincided with the national movement toward student activism on college campuses, and activism at USC increased as the decade wore on. However, even during the late 1960s, when student radicalism was vocal and visible, most Carolina students remained aloof from the controversies. John Gregory recalled a student friend who, while observing an antiwar rally in the late 1960s, responded to the activist's message with the statement, "I don't want to knock the establishment, I want *in*."[258] Student support for the presidential candidacies of Barry Goldwater and Richard Nixon, as well as an active chapter of Young Americans for Freedom (YAF), a conservative student organization sponsored by William F. Buckley, indicated that Carolina was home to a considerable number of political conservatives.[259]

The major political issue on campus in the late 1960s was the war in Vietnam, and early in the U.S. involvement, most USC faculty and students stood

solidly behind the United States' effort. In July of 1964, the National Committee for Sane Nuclear Policy had circulated a petition among faculty members of colleges and universities across the country, calling for neutrality and
an international peacekeeping force in Vietnam. Only three USC professors
signed it (Edmund Yaghjian, Douglas Bub, and W. C. McCall). Richard Walker
of USC's department of international studies, an expert on foreign policy in
the East, claimed that contrary to U.S. policy, the neutrality petition constituted "a . . . naïve assessment and lack of understanding of the political
organization of the communists in Viet Nam."[260] Tom Jones, noting the lack
of student protests in early 1965, wrote that USC was "fortunate in having no
leftist-inspired uprisings." He added however, that such activities on other
campuses had made administrators "skittish."[261] While anti-Vietnam feeling
was growing on other college campuses across the country, Tom Laughlin, a
writer for the *State,* commented that "the 'peace-nik' movement spreading
across college campuses in the U.S. does not seem to have much support at
Columbia's institutions of higher learning." In November 1965, the USC
Student Senate passed a resolution supporting U.S. policy in Vietnam by a
vote of 31–9.[262] Pat Conroy's *Beach Music* character Jack McCall makes the
observation—quite likely accurate—that USC students in the mid-1960s
were largely unconcerned about the war: "While other colleges in America
seethed and boiled during the nationwide debate in the Vietnam War, we students of the University of South Carolina drank." To mid-1960s USC students,
"the war was overwhelmingly popular."[263]

While student activism was not widespread at Carolina in the mid-1960s,
a 1965 incident showed the campus a glimpse of things to come. In the
wake of the dramatic free-speech movement at the University of California
at Berkeley and a state-imposed ban on controversial speakers on state-
supported campuses in North Carolina, USC had its own free speech controversy that marked a beginning of organized student activism on campus. In April,
students Martin Price, president of the University's YMCA, and Brad Poston,
president of USC's Unitarian Universalist Fellowship respectively, invited
Carl Braden, a member of the National Committee to Abolish the House Un-
American Activities Committee who had been cited for contempt by refusing
to tell that House committee whether or not he was a communist, to deliver
a speech on campus. A resulting controversy led the South Carolina General
Assembly to consider a law like North Carolina's 1963 "Act to Regulate Visiting Speakers," which prohibited speakers with ties to the Communist Party
from state-supported college campuses. Poston and Price later charged that
pressure from the administration had forced them to cancel the Braden
speech. USC students, faculty, and even some administrators signed a petition protesting the denial of free speech. Braden ultimately spoke in a private

home in Columbia, rather than on campus, and Jones was congratulated by the conservative organs such as the *News and Courier* and a White Citizen's Council in Tennessee. In the wake of the controversy, the University issued carefully worded guidelines regarding campus speakers; among the rules were that "no person who advocates the overthrow of constituted government by violence shall be a guest speaker or otherwise sponsored in any University appearance." However, the proposed law to ban controversial speakers on state campuses failed in the General Assembly. President Jones concluded of the affair, "We want our young people to be able to know the facts about what's going on in the world, but we feel the campus is a place for scholars rather than a place for agitators!"[264]

Brad Poston, who had been a member of the South Carolina Student Council on Human Relations, wrote Jones that though he would like to pursue the free speech matter further, the pressures of school prevented him from "creating a ruckus" over the issue. He concluded, "Maybe in the future USC will become a place where students will be educated in the true sense of the word rather than indoctrinated with the same old ideas that have been floating around for years."[265] To that end, student and faculty activism on the subject of free speech led to the founding of a free speech newspaper, the *Carolina Free Press*, and an organization called AWARE, both designed to further the cause of free speech issues on the USC campus. In late 1966, the board of trustees clarified the University's policies regarding visiting speakers. An outside speaker had to be approved two weeks in advance, and the policy granted the president wide discretion in deciding the ground rules for a speech.[266] Students continued to challenge the speaker policy. In January 1967, the Student Senate passed a resolution objecting to the policy, claiming that it "smacks of censorship and thereby limits academic freedom."[267]

Throughout the spring of 1967, the free speech movement at USC gained steam as students pressed demands for freedom of political activity on campus. AWARE brought controversial speakers to Carolina such as prominent anti-Vietnam War figures Julian Bond (civil rights leader and Georgia state legislator) and Wayne Morse (U.S. senator from Oregon), amply demonstrating that speakers from outside of the mainstream could gain a hearing at Carolina. Despite having the administration's approval, these visits aroused the ire of prominent University supporters such as trustee Sol Blatt Jr., who, confusing opposition to the war with opposition to the soldiers fighting it, wrote Tom Jones that "To allow Julian Bond to speak at the University with the Administration's approval, is . . . an insult to our entire State and . . . to the graduates and former students of the University who are now fighting and dying in Viet Nam." "The University is going to suffer irreparably," he wrote. Jones replied to his critics that although he despised Bond's views, free speech laws nonetheless protected Bond's right to speak on campus.[268]

The free speech issue again merged with anti-Vietnam War sentiment when General William Westmoreland, a Spartanburg native and commander of U.S. troops in Vietnam, came to the USC campus in April 1967 to receive an honorary degree. During a special convocation in Rutledge Chapel, President Jones granted Westmoreland the degree. Just before Westmoreland was to make his remarks, a young assistant professor of chemistry, Thomas Tidwell, stood up, shouted "I Protest: Doctor of War!," and held up an anti-war sign before leaving the chapel. Outside, a small but vocal group of about thirty-five student protesters peacefully picketed the ceremony, displaying antiwar signs reading "Stop the War!" and other slogans. Along with police and SLED agents, a crowd of about five hundred onlookers gathered, but the relative peace was broken when at least one student attacked a protester. Police intervened and escorted the demonstrators off campus.[269]

Thus the first significant expression of public antiwar feeling on the USC campus came not from a student, but from a faculty member. While Senator Edgar Brown demanded that the University dismiss Tidwell, at the urging of Tom Jones and other faculty members the board of trustees voted to "vigorously" censure the young professor "in the harshest possible terms" but stopped short of summarily firing him. Later in the year, they denied Tidwell a raise, and he was ultimately denied tenure despite a commendable record as a researcher and teacher.[270]

The protest of Westmoreland and the forced removal of the demonstrators from the campus galvanized the small number of student members of AWARE. The organization immediately pressed for a revision of the University's speaker policy and a statement affirming the constitutional rights of students to demonstrate on campus. Leaders of AWARE, including president James A. Torgeson, Trina Shali, and faculty advisor Robert B. Patterson, met with President Jones, and soon thereafter he issued an interim regulation which reaffirmed the students' right to assemble and guaranteed protesters police protection. AWARE had earned a significant victory.[271]

AWARE's challenge to the administration was a symptom of the rapid change in student life in the years between 1966 and the end of the decade. John Gregory, who was both an undergraduate and law student from 1964 through 1971, recalled that his first years at Carolina were almost a stereotype of the "traditional" southern college experience. However, in his latter years he witnessed a revolutionary change in student culture. "It was like two different worlds," he remembered. The speed of the change, remembered alumnus Thorne Compton, was remarkable. The civil rights movement and activism over the questions of free speech, the Vietnam War and the rights of young people led students to question many of the fundamental assumptions of their upbringing. While only a handful became activists, few students could avoid the serious questions that were being asked about the place of young people in American society.[272]

In the years after 1967, as students at Carolina and all over the nation became more and more radicalized, AWARE became the central organization for the small group of activist students on the Carolina campus who wanted to expand student rights. The group became increasingly aggressive in its challenges to University authorities. They pressed for a formal "Statement of Student Rights and Freedoms Within the Academic Community," which would codify student rights on campus, and the Student Senate passed a version in December 1967. The USC faculty repeatedly rebuffed the bill, which several characterized as "all rights and no responsibilities." However, after months of controversy, they passed it a year later, and the board of trustees approved it, thus finally guaranteeing student political and constitutional rights.

As the student movement moved from concern with free speech to opposition to the Vietnam War, AWARE sponsored frequent teach-ins, speeches by antiwar activists, a voting boycott of the 1968 presidential election, peace demonstrations, and a "military resistance fair." In the fall of 1968 the group affiliated with Students For a Democratic Society (SDS) and its Southern Students Organizing Committee. AWARE soon became closely allied with the quite active antiwar movement in Columbia. Some students, including the Interfraternity Council, the Clariosophic Society, and the Young Americans for Freedom called on the University to revoke AWARE's charter because of its SDS affiliation. The administration and board of trustees became increasingly concerned about AWARE and its activities, and SLED infiltrated the group and fed reports of its activities to University officials.[273] Likewise, alumni became more and more uncomfortable with the presence of "radicals" on the campus and blamed the administration for allowing the situation. One wrote Tom Jones, "As head of the University, it is your responsibility to keep it as an institution of education, not as a festering ground for unshaven, unwashed cruds as have been seen and heard from as late. . . . If for some reason you are afraid to take a stand openly, and denounce such un-American organizations as AWARE/SDS . . . then you should consider retirement."[274]

Meanwhile, as issues of free speech and America's involvement in Vietnam had captured the attention of student activists, events at a college campus elsewhere in South Carolina had a tremendous impact on the Carolina community. The February 8, 1968, killing of three South Carolina State College students by state troopers in Orangeburg brought home the seriousness of the state's simmering racial problems, which up until that time had seemed, at least on the surface, relatively peaceful. The deaths struck close to home, and many asked themselves, "Could this happen at Carolina?" In the week after the "Orangeburg Massacre," the USC campus played host to a speech by George Ware, campus coordinator for the Student Nonviolent Coordinating Committee (SNCC), who called for "Black Power." In the wake of the killings at South Carolina State, administrators and student leaders came together to discuss continuing racial problems, and the USC student government and the Association of Afro-American Students combined to sponsor a memorial service for the dead at South Carolina State, which some 300 Carolina students attended.

USC student body president Sammy Drew, who had called the memorial service, drew criticism from a few white students who rejected the reasons for the student demonstrations in Orangeburg. While he was careful to state that by conducting the memorial service he was not choosing sides, nonetheless the Student Senate moved to censure him for acting without their approval, claiming that in doing so he was condoning the reasons behind the demonstrations. He responded that he had made an executive decision and that Carolina needed to face its racial problems. "It is too easy to *ignore* that we have problems," Drew said. "What is needed is a step *away* from clash *toward* cooperation." Ken Price, president of the Association of Afro-American Students (AAAS), said of the overall racial climate in South Carolina, "This state has a serious problem, and it is time for each and every person to react by saying to himself that I will do everything in my power to correct this problem."[275]

The remarks of George Ware demonstrated the growing influence of the black power movement on Carolina's small contingent of African American students. SNCC sent organizers (including Cleveland Sellers, later a member of the USC faculty) to the USC campus in the fall of 1967 to help black students organize into groups that could promote black awareness. The Association of Afro-American Students was chartered that fall as an official student organization, with Ken Price as the first president.[276] The Orangeburg incident galvanized the AAAS into action. The organization resolved "to eliminate racial injustices in all aspects of university life." As a first step toward their goal and "in the interest of avoiding a resort to extraordinary measures," the AAAS drafted a thirteen-point plan which they submitted to the administration; among the points were requests that the University increase the hiring of black faculty, increase the proportion of black students at USC, and recruit black athletes. Their most prominent request, however, was that Carolina develop courses in African American history and culture.[277] In response, in the fall of 1968, the University began offering a history course titled "The Negro in American History," taught by USC history professor

Thomas Terrill—the first offering of an African American-oriented course in the University's history.[278]

The discord of the spring of 1968 continued following the April 4 assassination of Martin Luther King, Jr. Throughout Columbia, some thirty fires broke out in protest of the killing, one of them in the University's Hamilton College, causing $40,000 ($156,635) in damages. Another fire at the USC Field House completely destroyed the building, which had been partially damaged by fire only three weeks earlier. A USC student was shot in the leg in Five Points, and car and dormitory windows were broken on campus. President Jones dismissed students two days early for spring break when the rioting began, allowing students to leave town in case the situation became dangerous.[279]

When the student government suggested a memorial service in honor of King, AAAS leaders called the idea "hypocrisy." They asked why whites wanted to hold a memorial service for King when a white fraternity had held a party celebrating his death. Instead, they asked for a more lasting memorial. Along with Methodist chaplain Robert Alexander, AAAS leaders such as Harry Wright proposed a comprehensive program to ease the strained race relations in Columbia. Two days later, at the urging of Sammy Drew, the Student Senate adopted the AAAS proposal and unanimously approved the establishment of the Metropolitan Education Foundation (MEF), an organization aimed at providing educational, recreational, and work opportunities in Columbia's poor neighborhoods.

The MEF became a biracial volunteer effort of students, faculty, staff, administrators, and local business leaders to improve race relations in the city and relations between the University and the local community. It received a charter from the state and cooperation from the Columbia City Council and Chamber of Commerce, as well as Richland County. Through fund-raising that included a performance by native Carolinian and soul star James Brown, the organization raised $15,000 ($58,738) and operated summer programs for children in some of Columbia's poorest neighborhoods, including Camp Fornance and Liberty Hill. Black law student Franchot Brown, one of the MEF's student directors, said that the program helped "reach young people and direct their anger, frustrations and energies into constructive channels." White student director Tom Salene said, "I knew after King's death that words and apologies were not enough any more. . . . I know it is time to get myself personally involved, to do something about [the state's racial problems]." A year later, the University set up the Office of Volunteer Services to help coordinate volunteer activities by students involved in projects such as the MEF.[280]

The MEF program represented a positive outcome from the racial strife of 1968, but racial tension on the USC campus did not disappear as a result.[281]

Instead, in the spring semester of 1969, a series of related events led race relations at USC to nearly reach a point of open conflict. In early February, increasingly radical AWARE sponsored "White Awareness Week" to inform white USC students about the black power movement. The week concluded with a memorial service on the Russell House patio to commemorate the one-year anniversary of the Orangeburg massacre. The service gave black student activists, such as Sidney A. Moore and the self-styled "Redfern II," an opportunity to demonstrate to the University community the anger among young blacks who were dissatisfied with the slow pace of change in South Carolina. A sign behind the stage read, "The Only Thing Non-Violence Proved is How SAVAGE Whitey Is."[282]

As a part of the memorial service, the AAAS requested permission to burn a Confederate flag. Administrators denied the request because it violated state law and because of a University rule that forbade actions which "offend or outrage normal sensibilities." AAAS then asked University officials to ban flying the Confederate flag and playing the song Dixie on University property, because as "a tribute to the peculiar institution that enslaved human beings," they "offend normal sensibilities." Nothing came of their request.[283] Next, the actions of AWARE leader Brett Bursey raised the tension level on campus even further. At a scheduled meeting of AWARE, Bursey showed up with a Confederate flag and a bottle of rubbing alcohol. A group of sixty students then proceeded from the Russell House to the front of the President's Home on the Horseshoe, where they burned the flag.[284]

In the wake of the flag burning, racial tensions began to heat up on campus among the most radical groups on both the right and the left. An organized debate on the Confederate flag issue on the Horseshoe broke up after speakers were unable to talk over the shouts of the crowd. Confederate flag wavers held a rally afterward, then marched to the Confederate monument on the state house grounds, where they sang "Dixie" and the national anthem. Flag supporters began passing out lapel pins bearing an image of the battle flag. Two days later, black students burned another Confederate flag between the Russell House patio and the front of the main library, before a crowd of jeering white onlookers. As the two groups taunted one another, SLED agents and administrators had to intervene to maintain order.[285]

Amid rising tempers, University officials tightened security on campus and called for students to "cool off." President Jones stated that the situation had "polarized the Carolina family" and that the emotional climate could result in violence. The *Gamecock's* editor wrote of the incidents, "The blacks are frustrated and angry, and the whites are scared and proud. These two forces will come into open conflict unless there is some sober thought given to the situation on campus."[286] Letters in the *Gamecock*, almost all of which derided the actions of AWARE and the AAAS, attested to the high level of tension. One writer sarcastically suggested banning the national anthem, since "it could possibly offend the Chinese, Japanese, Indians, Italians, Lebanese or other such MINORITY groups on campus."[287]

The Carolina community had reached the brink of racial conflict. Several University buildings received bomb threats.[288] The AAAS, which had accumulated grievances in the year since the Orangeburg Massacre, was further alienated. White students had broken into their offices and destroyed their files, they claimed; bricks had been thrown through the windows of black students; white University administrators had driven hundreds of nearby black residents from their homes through urban renewal. They asked, "What do we do now, Brothers?" An AAAS publication answered,

> The showdown has come: To be on the campus of the University of South Carolina is to place your life at the mercy of the man—the white man. The atmosphere is one of tense hostility and threatening danger. Antagonism has been aroused among the so-called liberal and the southern conservative. It must be understood that this antagonism was stimulated by a group of white—not Black—students. But the showdown has come. The line has been drawn. The war has been declared. Where are the white liberals now!!!![289]

However, instead of violence, AAAS leaders called for black students to avoid confrontation, stating "The lives of black folk are too precious to lose in another massacre."[290]

Tempers eventually cooled without significant violence, but not before the faculty appointed a committee to study the racial situation at Carolina. Their report, written by Professor Thomas Terrill in May 1969, demonstrated that race relations on campus left much to be desired. The report suggested several ways of improving the climate: it called for further curriculum revisions, better orientation programs, and better training in the "handling of student dissent" by law enforcement officials. The report also noted the detrimental effect of the University's land acquisition program on community race relations.[291]

President Jones then released a statement to students addressing the crisis, saying, "I . . . challenge each and every one of you to carefully re-examine your personal attitudes toward your fellow Carolinians. . . . We cannot allow continuous polarization of our campus." He continued, "We must refrain from participation in group activities that would . . . polarize segments of this academic community; and we must resist the use of thoughtless gestures or other symbols of prejudice." Jones concluded, "I ask, I plead, that all students, regardless of race, color, or creed give your utmost efforts to practice

The Golden Rule of all great faiths—'Do unto others as you would have them do unto you.'"[292] The incident was indeed a catharsis for the University, for as black law student John Roy Harper recalled, "USC from that moment on was never the same." While some 65 percent of Carolina students still supported waving the Confederate flag at USC events, lapel pins disappeared and open racial conflict on the campus faded away as well.[293]

Thus a decade that had begun with USC student government withdrawing from a national student organization because of its "liberal" racial views ended with another racial controversy—but notably, the decade ended without significant racial violence on campus. However narrowly, Carolina escaped the discord that plagued some other southern state universities in the 1960s. That kind of tumult was rare on the USC campus. Even the initial desegregation of the University in 1963, an event fraught with potential for widespread campus unrest, had proceeded nearly without a hitch. The most vocal student activist groups in the late 1960s—AWARE and AAAS—represented the views of only a small minority of Carolina's 13,000 students. For most, Carolina was about more conventional collegiate social life and student organizations, even as the specter of the Vietnam War hung over them while they prepared for their futures.

The 1960s was a decade of profound change for the University of South Carolina, one that witnessed desegregation, unprecedented campus physical expansion, academic advancement, the decline of in loco parentis, the transformation of student culture, and foremost, enormous enrollment growth. At the beginning of the decade, in many ways USC still resembled the intimate, primarily liberal arts university it had been in the early 1940s. By end of decade, it was well on its way to becoming a modern research university, with all the attendant advantages and problems that came with such status. *Gamecock* editor Sally Zalkin commented in 1968, "Signs of growth are everywhere—the Coliseum, Capstone, the Roost, the Humanities complex, a pass-fail system, an honor dorm for women, new academic programs, an increase in qualified faculty members." But she saw even more significant changes, noting, "We have made changes in the 'mind' of [the] institution. The University has done what it must do if the school and the state of South Carolina are to progress to the top: it has discarded the baggage of the past and placed itself in the mainstream of the modern world."[294]

By the end of the decade, the University of South Carolina was no longer the small, tightly knit southern university it had been in the 1940s. It had become much like other large, comprehensive universities across the nation, institutions that University of California at Berkeley Chancellor Clark Kerr called "multiversities." By seeking to serve a wide range of South Carolina's population (honors as well as marginal undergraduates, graduate students, state government, and industry—to name only a few), the University of South Carolina sought to offer something to everyone. In its astounding growth it had doubtless improved its quality, but by the end of the decade it was beginning to lose much of the sense of community that had bound it together in earlier years, and the growing depersonalization was reflected in the strife in the last years of the decade. In many ways USC fit the description of the modern university put forth by Robert M. Hutchins, president of the University of Chicago: "a series of separate schools and departments held together by a central heating system."[295]

This change was a part of the "Americanization of Dixie" that has occupied observers of post–World War II Southern history. Writing in the 1960s, Allan M. Cartter of the American Council on Education saw the post–World War II "nationalization" of southern universities as inevitable, arguing that southern universities had to raise their aspirations to meet national standards of accomplishment.[296] Indeed, as burgeoning industrial growth in South Carolina contributed to an emphasis on graduate programs and research in the 1960s, the University of South Carolina increasingly began to measure itself against national standards rather than state or regional ones. Released from the restraints that racial segregation had placed on the institution, the University was free to pursue a research ideal that led it to emulate an ideal type of research institution established by universities outside the South in the years after World War II.

However, the drive for growth and excellence measured by national standards produced tension, and the University had yet to adjust the torrid growth of the 1960s. While Carolina had taken important steps toward entering the mainstream of education, events in the first months of the 1970s demonstrated how fractured the University community had become in the previous decade and how alienated the institution had grown from even its own students.

Capstone House, an eighteen-story dormitory that would eventually be topped with a revolving restaurant, under construction in the east campus neighborhood, 1967.

History professor Charles Coolidge was recognized as one of Carolina's great teachers in the post–World War II era. The recipient of the Russell Award for Distinguished Teaching in 1961, Coolidge spent thirty-six years on the Carolina faculty and mesmerized generations of students with his lectures on English and European history.

USC historian Daniel Walker Hollis, whose two-volume work on the University of South Carolina established him as the foremost authority on the institution's history from its beginnings until the 1950s, joined the faculty in 1947. He remained as a professor of history until his retirement in 1986.

H. Willard Davis, longtime professor of chemistry, served in a number of administrative positions and helped manage the tremendous growth of the University from the 1940s to the 1970s.

Dean of administration Harold Brunton unveils the University's long-range campus development plan in 1965. Note the bounds of the campus in 1965 (left map) and the three major areas targeted for growth in the east, south, and west (right map).

Football coach Paul Dietzel, trustee Sol Blatt Jr., basketball coach Frank McGuire, and House Speaker Sol Blatt Sr. introduce Dietzel as USC's new head coach at a 1966 press conference.

In the first basketball game in the Carolina Coliseum, November 30, 1968, Billy Walsh goes up for a shot while John Roche (that season's ACC player of the year) looks on. Head coach Frank McGuire is seated on the bench. Carolina defeated Auburn 51-49 on Roche's last-second shot. The 1968–69 Gamecock basketball team finished with a 21–7 record and made the school's first-ever trip to postseason play.

The 1960s witnessed an awakening of the women's movement and the weakening of in loco parentis for Carolina's female students. Here, members of the campus honor society Mortar Board post a banner publicizing "Feminine Focus '69," an event that addressed women's issues in society.

Banksia Mansion, the original campus of USC–Aiken, circa 1963.

USC–Lancaster's first campus opened in 1959 in a private residence in
downtown Lancaster.

USC's campus in Union opened in 1965 and today serves students in Union County
and surrounding areas.

Opened in 1965 in Allendale, USC's Salkehatchie campus today serves a five-county area united by the Salkehatchie River.

USC's Spartanburg campus opened in 1967 in the first floor of the Spartanburg General Hospital. In 1969, it moved to its new campus outside of Spartanburg.

On May 5, 1970, USC students protest the killings at Kent State University
the day before.

Through a haze of tear gas, South Carolina national guardsmen and SLED officials
attempt to subdue crowds of student protestors during the disturbances of early May
1970. The tear gas quickly spread over the campus, driving previously uninvolved
students out of dormitories and buildings and into the streets.

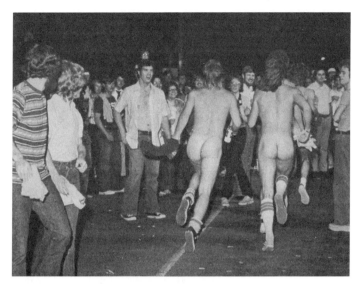

Responding to a challenge from students at the University of North Carolina, on March 3, 1974, more than 500 USC students ran naked across campus in the nationwide streaking craze. Thousands of students and Columbians showed up to watch, and the mass "streak" was covered on the national television news.

From left: T. Eston Marchant, chairman of the USC board of trustees, 1970–1978; Rutledge L. Osborne, member, board of trustees, 1947–1975 and chairman, 1952–1970; and Thomas F. Jones, twenty-third president of USC, 1962–1974.

William H. Patterson (1913–1996), assistant to the president, 1950–1952, dean of administration, 1952–1961, dean of the University, 1961–1966, senior vice president, 1966–1968, provost, 1968–1974, and twenty-fourth president of the University, 1974–1977.

Leading F. Scott Fitzgerald scholar Matthew J. Bruccoli came to the University of South Carolina in 1969 and quickly became recognized as one of the University's most outstanding scholars. A one-man publishing juggernaut, Bruccoli brought worldwide recognition to the scholarly activities of USC's outstanding department of English.

One of America's distinguished modern poets, James Dickey came to the University of South Carolina in 1968 to serve as poet-in-residence and professor of English. A charismatic teacher, he wrote the majority of his published poetry, and his most popular work, the novel *Deliverance,* while a faculty member at USC.

USC's Sumter campus opened in 1966 as a branch campus of Clemson University. In July 1973, it became a USC regional campus.

The USC School of Medicine, located on the outskirts of Columbia, admitted its first class in 1977 and soon became a leader in primary-care medical education.

James B. Holderman (left), president of USC from 1977 to 1990; President Ronald Reagan (third from left); Judge Donald Russell (sixth from right); and Senator Strom Thurmond (second from right) on the USC Horseshoe, September 1983. In front of a special convocation, Russell awarded Reagan an honorary degree, the first the University had ever awarded to a sitting U.S. president.

The 1980s saw more consistent success for USC's football program than any previous decade. Here, Johnnie Wright scores against Clemson in 1981.

USC president James B. Holderman and Jihan Sadat, widow of assassinated Egyptian president Anwar Sadat. In 1985, Sadat began teaching a course at USC titled "Women in Egyptian Culture"; when a 1986 Freedom of Information Act suit forced the University to reveal the amount Sadat had been paid to teach the course, she resigned. The controversy launched a series of scandals that led to Holderman's resignation in 1990.

The Koger Center for the Arts and the Carolina Coliseum, two of the University's most visible buildings in Columbia, serve the Midlands region by hosting sports and cultural events.

Connecting the South Campus to the main campus area, the Bates Ramp was a major student thoroughfare on the sprawling USC campus, which expanded south of Blossom Street beginning in the early 1960s.

As a result of federal laws, women's sports received increased emphasis in the 1970s and 1980s. The Lady Gamecock sports programs, including the 1989 volleyball team (shown here against North Carolina State), were a far cry from the rudimentary athletic program in place for women in the 1940s and 1950s.

A panorama of Williams-Brice Stadium during a 1985 football game demonstrates the phenomenal growth of the USC campus in the post–World War II era. From Capstone House on the right to the Cliff Apartments on the left, the Carolina campus expanded far beyond the borders of its Horseshoe beginnings.

Pope John Paul II (in white), on a dais in front of the President's Home, greets the crowd of some 8,000 on the Horseshoe during his historic September 1988 visit. USC President James B. Holderman stands behind the Pope.

USC's twenty-sixth president, John M. Palms, opens the University's Bicentennial celebration on January 10, 2001. As president from 1991 to 2002, Palms stressed continual improvements in the quality of a Carolina education. The year-long Bicentennial celebration focused on reconnecting the University to the people of South Carolina. It culminated on December 19, 2001, the 200th anniversary of the University of South Carolina's initial chartering.

5 | ADJUSTING TO LIFE AS
A "MULTIVERSITY"
1970–1979

The time has arrived when South Carolina for all time must break loose and break free of the vicious cycle of ignorance, illiteracy and poverty which has retarded us throughout our history.

John Carl West, 1971

We are on our way to greatness. Nothing can prevent that except our own reluctance.

James B. Holderman, 1979

■

The 1970s were a decade of turbulence for the University of South Carolina unlike any seen since the 1940s. As South Carolina became a part of the prosperous and optimistic "Sunbelt South," the University of South Carolina played an increasingly important role in the state's development. Three different presidents led Carolina, which continued the torrid growth that had begun in the early 1960s. Passing the 10,000-student threshold in 1966, within six years the University's enrollment doubled. A 1970 enrollment of 14,484 grew to 25,908 by 1979. The number of full-time equivalent faculty doubled from 812 in 1970 to more than 1,600 in 1979. The University's budget grew from $37,063,556 ($130,121,838) in 1970 to $123,071,544 ($203,536,594) in 1980, a nearly 56 percent increase (in constant dollars).[1] The remarkable growth, which reflected the continuing economic expansion in South Carolina, brought serious growing pains to the campus. Student unrest reached a height not seen since riots in 1856. A concerted effort to introduce innovative educational techniques to help the University adapt to changing student culture largely failed. The University's mission continued to expand, with the development of its branch campuses and the establishment of new colleges and schools in Columbia. The circumstances surrounding the years in which presidents Tom Jones (1962–1974) and William H. Patterson (1974–1977) led the University meant that during the period prior to 1977 the University focused primarily on adjusting to its new form—that of a racially integrated large state research university that attempted to offer a broad range of programs and services to an industrial economy, while at the same time endeavoring to hold on to traditions of value. These programs and services varied from its undergraduate program, programs for disadvantaged and honors students, graduate work, and research for industry and government. After 1977, led by James B. Holderman, the University of South Carolina entered a new era in which it ambitiously sought national prominence and recognition as a leading American university.

A series of related incidents in the spring of 1970 had a profound impact on the University's direction during the next decade. As the University grew into a large "multiversity" in the late 1960s, students and faculty grew increasingly dissatisfied with the impersonal nature of the institution. Students, many of whom were already distressed over the war in Vietnam, demanded more personal freedoms on campus, an education more relevant to their lives, and a greater role in determining the institution's direction. Faculty, dissatisfied in part with what they perceived as priority given to USC's athletic programs over its academic ones, also demanded a greater role in directing the University. They requested enlarged decision making powers, assurances of free speech, the authority to appoint faculty committees, and greater access to information on funding for academic buildings, libraries, and athletic facilities. The board of trustees responded to the dissatisfaction in late 1969 by establishing student and faculty liaison committees to discuss problems with its members, and the administration established an ombudsman's service to act as a conduit for information between students and the administration. However, none of these piecemeal attempts to lessen the impersonal nature of the nearly 15,000-student university really succeeded. Smoldering student and faculty dissatisfaction with University affairs in the winter of 1969–70 preceded an unprecedented explosion of unrest in the spring of 1970.[2]

The spring of 1970 was a tense time on college and university campuses across the country. While there was student unrest on hundreds of college and university campuses that spring, Carolina's disturbances of 1970 were the result of a complex series of factors and events, including antiwar, antidraft sentiment and dissatisfaction with the University administration's response to student activism, but a substantial part of the responsibility for the outbreak of violence lies with local pressures from outside the University that raised the already high level of campus dissatisfaction.

In January, Columbia law enforcement officials closed down the "UFO Coffeehouse" at 1732 Main Street, one of a chain of "New Left" establishments (with no relation to the University) located near military posts that provided soft drinks, coffee, and anti–Vietnam War literature and discussion to disgruntled soldiers. In addition to hosting soldiers from Fort Jackson, the UFO Coffeehouse became a popular hangout for counterculture "hippies" in Columbia and for those looking for alternative points of view on current issues. Local law enforcement officials, most prominently Fifth Circuit solicitor John Foard, were convinced that the coffeehouse was a center for disseminating illegal drugs, pornography, and radical political thought.[3]

After local officials closed the UFO Coffeehouse in January 1970 and prosecuted its owners, many Carolina students and faculty alike were outraged. They felt "the UFO" was unfairly targeted because of the political views it represented. In the wake of the closing, Columbia's anti-establishment activists moved their operations to the USC campus, particularly the Russell House, where they began to operate a so-called UFO in Exile. Informed by students who infiltrated residence halls, local police also began to target Carolina students in drug raids, raising the ire of a small pro–drug use organization on the campus called FREAK (Freedom to Research Every Aspect of Knowledge). After one student and two ex-students were arrested on drug charges, on April 13 some 250 FREAK members marched on the President's Home and later staged a brief takeover of the Russell House. FREAK leaders such as Wayne Hembree charged that law enforcement officials were abusive in their treatment of students and that political influence from the legislature in an election year was pressuring the board and the administration to harshly discipline them. In response to rising tensions, President Jones took a reasoned approach, meeting with Hembree and other FREAK members and issuing a letter to all students in which he expressed concern over illegal arrests, searches, and seizures, and by student suggestions that there had been "strong arm" tactics by local police. Jones stressed that he understood student grievances, but while expressing sympathy for their point of view, he also emphasized his administration's commitment to law enforcement, stating that USC was no sanctuary for lawbreakers. Meanwhile, he and other University officials met with local officials, including Solicitor Foard and SLED chief Pete Strom, to ensure that student rights were protected while local laws were enforced on campus.[4]

Despite Jones's cooperation with Strom and Foard, these two men soon lashed out at the administration for what they called its "weak" handling of anti-establishment activists. On April 29, Solicitor Foard—who was running for reelection in the fall of 1970—publicly assailed USC administrators, charging that they had failed to live up to promises to clear the Russell House of radical activity. He called the law enforcement problem at the University "very serious." The solicitor also suggested that transcripts from the trial of the operators of the UFO Coffeehouse should be used against USC faculty members who had testified for the defense in the case. He recommended that such faculty, who in his opinion harbored radical, communist sympathies, should be dismissed from their jobs. According to Jones, Foard's statements brought "highly agitated" calls to his office from the state house. Some of the calls, Jones said, "proposed actions that would be outside the bounds of my ethics." Later that day, SLED officials gave the administration an ultimatum: "Put your police in Russell House," they said, "or we'll take it over."[5]

The following day, USC police barred the former UFO operators from the campus, and plainclothes officers began patrolling the Russell House, checking identification cards amid verbal abuse from students. The local chapter of the AAUP sharply criticized Foard's remarks about USC faculty. Student body president Mike Spears, representing a hastily formed "Student Emergency Coalition for Academic Freedom at USC," presented the University board of trustees a resolution for their approval which stated, "The University community is disturbed, dismayed and distressed by the brazen attempts by a few ill-informed local politicians to exercise unjust and dictatorial control over the University of South Carolina." He requested that the board of trustees resolve in favor of unqualified support for students' academic freedom, freedom of association and freedom from police or political restrictions in the use of University buildings. On May 2, the board referred the resolution to their Student-Trustee Liaison Committee without action, further alienating students.[6]

Two days later, with tensions already rising on the USC campus, Ohio national guardsmen killed four students at Kent State University during a demonstration protesting the American invasion of Cambodia. Campuses across the nation reacted in shock and anger; repercussions at USC included a protest at the University's annual awards day ceremony on the Horseshoe and the disruption of an administration news conference that addressed the University's status in the Atlantic Coast Conference. A complex of smoldering resentment on campus only needed a spark to set the situation afire.[7]

The University community was awash in grievances, among them drug arrests, SLED's ultimatum, Foard's attack on the University's faculty and administration, police patrols in their student union, the board's refusal to support rights to academic freedom, the U.S. invasion of Cambodia, the senseless killings at Kent State, the University's heavy-handed clearing of minority neighborhoods near the campus, and a general sense on the part of students that the administration and board of trustees did not recognize or defend their constitutional rights as adults. In protest, a coalition of students and faculty representing a broad spectrum of campus life, including members of the AAUP, AWARE, FREAK, the Student Emergency Coalition for Academic Freedom, the Inter-Fraternity Council, the Association of Afro-American Students, the student union, and even the normally staid Student Senate called for a voluntary student strike to begin on Thursday, the seventh of May. The strike coalition was chaired by former AWARE leader Brett Bursey, who had been barred from the campus.

When May 7 arrived, morning class attendance was near normal. However, a scheduled midday "strike rally" of about 500 protestors surrounded the flag-pole on the Horseshoe to begin the student strike. The crowd demanded that the U.S. flag be lowered to half-staff in memory of the dead at Kent State. A smaller group of students, opposed to the strike, also gathered and were equally adamant that the flag should remain where it was. As the rally proceeded, the two groups began taunting one another. Tempers flared, and the situation became more intense than the 25 student marshals who had been recruited to maintain order could handle. The possibility of bloodshed loomed.

Student leaders frantically called President Jones, who dispatched four University policemen to surround the flagpole and keep the peace. Student leaders soon called Jones again, telling him, "The police are being cursed and abused. The crowd is getting out of hand. Please order the flag lowered, please!" Jones, again trying to mediate a tense situation, relented and ordered the police to lower the flag to half-staff, momentarily diffusing the protest. After a group of students protested Jones's action, he admitted, "I agreed in principle [with students who wanted the flag to remain]. But . . . a free-for-all fight on the Horseshoe would have been blood on my hands." Despite the intentions, his actions merely postponed the crisis.[8]

At about 2:00, the crowd of some 400 moved from the Horseshoe to the Russell House, where they assembled in the auditorium and announced a takeover. Strike leaders seized the keys to the building, expelled all University officials, and locked or tied the doors shut. Several student leaders who had earlier been supportive of the strike coalition, including student body president Mike Spears and other members of student government, disavowed the takeover and urged their fellow students to leave the building. Throughout the afternoon, the occupying students repeatedly ignored pleas and demands from fellow students, faculty, and administrators to give up their takeover and leave the Russell House. Meanwhile, President Jones went to Governor McNair's office to consult on the situation, and a crowd of well over 1,000 curious students began to gather outside the Russell House.[9]

At 5:15, State Highway Patrolmen and SLED agents arrived, greeted by both cheers and abuse from the gathering crowd. After the students inside again refused to leave the building voluntarily, police stormed up the ramp and into the building, herding the occupying students into a prison bus waiting at the rear of the Russell House. The outdoor crowd then surrounded the bus, and amid rock- and bottle- throwing, sat down on the pavement and refused to allow it to move.

At about 6:15, South Carolina national guardsmen arrived. The troops formed a wedge in front of the police bus and forcibly removed those sitting in the way. The bus, the National Guard troops, police, and SLED agents then left the scene, chased away by a rock-throwing crowd.[10]

In the wake of the takeover, 42 people were arrested, and all the arrested students were temporarily suspended from the University. The next day, with rumors of violence swirling on campus, a disorganized "strike rally" of about 1,000 students gathered at the flagpole on the Horseshoe and marched to the steps of the state house, demanding amnesty for the arrested students. The rally ended peacefully, but a petition signed by 723 students and faculty evidenced the sentiments of that crowd. The petition stated that the Russell House takeover was the result of a "lack of a responsive channel of communication." To punish these students, it said, "would both undermine their non-violent precedent and jeopardize the development of effective communication on this campus." Nonetheless, the same day, the executive committee of the board of trustees met to plan the disciplining of the suspended students, an action they scheduled for May 11. Their response brought complaints from the faculty that the board was violating the University's normal disciplinary procedures, which left student discipline up to a faculty committee. The board was undeterred, citing a state statute that gave them the authority to act in case of a threat to University property.

After a quiet weekend, the uneasy calm disintegrated on the afternoon of Monday, May 11 (Confederate Memorial Day, a holiday for most city police). The board of trustees' executive committee began their disciplinary meeting in the administration building at 2:30. At about the same time, students began to rally on the Horseshoe, and talk began to spread about a peaceful sit-in to be staged in the administration building. Student leaders demanded amnesty for the suspended students, but the board refused to meet their demands. By 3:15, the group of some had 300 moved to the front of the administration building, and the raucous crowd grew as curious students gathered to watch the action. Various speakers either cajoled the crowd or urged calm. Soon the mood turned ugly, and a few in the crowd began to vandalize cars parked in front of the building.

Inside, the trustees tried to continue their hearings, despite their increasing concern about the unruly crowd outside. First-floor offices were cleared and staff ordered out of the building. Just after 4:00, with students outnumbering the contingent of University police four to one, the crowd rushed the doors of the building. Trustees and administrators huddled on the second floor, guarded by a small police force, while the mob ransacked the offices on the first floor, concentrating on the records of parking tickets in the treasurer's office. They also destroyed furniture and equipment, chanting "Power to the People!" and scrawling slogans such as "Up the revolution, Pig!" on the walls. Some student activist leaders such as Rita Fellers (daughter of dean of the College of Engineering Rufus Fellers) later claimed that the crowd had turned violent at the instigation of agent provocateurs. She insisted that the students had intended for the administration building takeover to be peaceful. Trustee Eston Marchant recalled that "everyone on the second floor was in a state of absolute disbelief," and feared for their safety. Marchant, who was also a senior officer in the South Carolina National Guard, immediately called the state adjutant general, Frank Pinckney (Governor McNair was in Washington—ironically attending a White House conference on student unrest), and requested that he send National Guard troops to the campus. However, since there had been no warning of trouble, there was no standby force available. National Guard troops did not arrive for another three and half hours.[11]

Meanwhile, students occupied the offices on the first floor and barricaded the doors. They tried to storm the second floor, but SLED agents held them off. Negotiating in the stairwell, students continued to demand amnesty for the suspended students. Outside, a small city police force arrived, greeted by rock-throwing students. A bomb threat to the building further added to the disruption.

When National Guard troops arrived at about 8:00 P.M., the occupying students immediately fled the building. Along with a large crowd of onlookers, they moved to the Horseshoe. Guardsmen and police followed, and with them, still more chaos. After warning the crowd of about 2,000 to disperse, the troops began to clear the area. Moving from the crest of the Horseshoe in ranks, they fired tear gas into the crowd, effectively breaking it up. Some in the crowd threw rocks and bottles at officers; television news footage broadcast nationwide showed city police hurling them back at students. Meanwhile, authorities fired tear gas at demonstrators along Greene Street. The tear gas seeped into nearby dormitories and the library, sending previously uninvolved students into the streets to enter the melee. Rock- and bottle-throwing battles with authorities lasted through the night.[12]

The next day, the tension did not abate. Governor McNair, by then returned to Columbia, declared a state of emergency and had SLED and the National Guard patrol the campus, forbidding non-students from entering and also setting a 9:00 P.M. to 6:00 A.M. curfew. A recorded message from President Jones, urging students to "keep cool," played every hour on WUSC. The faculty held a special meeting at Town Theater and passed a resolution affirming the rights of students to academic freedom, but they condemned violence and vandalism and declared their determination to keep the University open and functioning. They set up a rumor control center in the Russell House, and many devoted a portion of their classes to discussing the disturbances. Others, such as Donald Weatherbee and Bruce Marshall, organized "rap sessions" with students in every dormitory between 6 and 8:30 P.M. Later, many credited the faculty who visited the dormitories with keeping the disorder on campus from escalating into lethal violence.[13]

However, the situation was beyond anyone's ability to completely control. While faculty met at Town Theater, a student rally in Maxcy Gregg Park attracted a large crowd which then moved to the state house steps, where five dissident student leaders (Barbara Herbert, Steve Martin, Cantey Wright, Ray Pressley, and Wayne Hembree) met with Governor McNair. They continued to demand amnesty for the previously suspended students as well as removal of all police and guardsmen from the campus. The governor held to his previous position.

While faculty and student government leaders tried in vain to calm the situation, as night descended violence and vandalism followed the state house rally, partly as a result of the governor's refusal of the student's demands. Rioting was heaviest around the Honeycomb dormitories, and police again called for National Guard reinforcement. Upon their arrival, officers and troops drove the rock-throwing students into the buildings. Some students alleged that police pursued students into the dormitories, clubbing those in the halls whether or not they were involved in the riot. Police again used tear gas to clear the area, and just as they had the previous night, the gas spread through the building and forced many occupants into the streets. The second straight night of disruption ended with numerous arrests, injured students, and charges of arbitrary arrests and police brutality.[14]

The following day, rumors swirled that outside agitators such as the Weathermen were coming to the campus to burn it. The administration and Governor McNair received numerous calls urging them to close the University, but they instead put on a flurry of activity to attempt to maintain calm and avoid closure. President Jones met with five different student groups, assuring them of his determined commitment to keep the school open. The *Gamecock* issued a special edition on the situation to reassure students of the safety of the campus. Campus ministers set up a first aid station to care for those beaten during the riots, tending to hundreds of students, many of whom had head wounds. Fifteen faculty members volunteered to spend the night in the dormitories to continue the rap sessions. Jones assured worried parents and students that the campus was safe, with his wife telling them that their own children were still on campus. "When we are fearful for our own children," she said, "my husband will send everyone else's sons and daughters home." Jones and the USC administration directed police and National Guardsmen to avoid responding to student provocation with violence. As a result, though another student rally in Maxcy Gregg Park attracted a crowd of 500, the night passed with relative calm.[15]

The next day, students planned yet another rally for Maxcy Gregg Park, this one featuring antiwar activist Jane Fonda. The presence of such a celebrity on campus created a stir among curious students. However, just before the rally was to start, Columbia law enforcement officials arrested two of the principals in the administration building riot, Barbara Herbert and Paul Gumm. News of the arrests quickly spread through the gathering crowd, as did the breaking news that two students had been killed in demonstrations at Jackson State University in Mississippi, further heightening tensions. This potentially explosive combination of factors led University officials to fear a renewed outbreak of violence. Fonda's antiwar message, however, proved to be one of nonviolence—she urged students to "get political" and stage a peaceful sit-in at the state house. Tom Jones commended her for helping cool the volatile situation.[16]

Over the next several days, more than 100 faculty members visited the dorms, some spending nights there. After several quiet nights, the governor lifted the curfew and the military presence on May 16. Students planned yet another rally for Gregg Park on May 18, this one led by USC basketball star Bobby Cremins. Cremins urged President Jones and other administrators to participate and to reassure frightened students of the safety of the campus. On the same day, Governor McNair agreed to remove police from the Russell House—one of the initial grievances that had started the chain of events leading to the disturbances. Significantly, McNair gave student government leaders the responsibility for policing their student union. The next day McNair lifted the state of emergency, and the period of unrest drew to a close. The University remained open throughout the episode and its commencement exercises took place in June as scheduled, unlike many other university campuses that spring.[17]

In the wake of the affair, state politicians attacked Jones for allowing the situation to get out of hand and for failing to deal harshly enough with student activists. A citizen's petition he received attested to the strong opinions of many in the state about what they perceived as lawlessness at Carolina: "If the presidents and administrators of our colleges and Universities are not able to control the subversive activities of the faculty and students, they should resign or be fired and replaced by those are capable of doing so."[18] Sol Blatt Sr. demanded that the board of trustees be given more authority to mete out student discipline.[19] Solicitor Foard charged the president with "terrific weakness" in dealing with the student dissatisfaction—citing Jones's failure to clear the Russell House of the "UFO in Exile" and his decision to allow the flag to be lowered to half-staff during the early hours of the student strike. In

July, Foard appeared before the board of trustees and for two hours appealed to them to fire Jones. However, reacting to Foard's attempts to bully the board, some 2,800 students and faculty signed a petition supporting the president. Local newspapers rallied to Jones's defense, and even Sol Blatt Sr. publicly defended the president's handling of the affair. The board of trustees unanimously approved of Jones's actions during the disturbances and endorsed him as president, issuing a resolution of support for him. While Foard continued to hold forth for months in a personal vendetta against Jones—even threatening to convene a grand jury to investigate affairs at the University—most in the state discounted his rantings as those of a political opportunist.[20]

While the disturbances at USC occurred at the same time as a wave of student rioting swept the nation's research universities, at Carolina the immediate causes emerged from local factors. Although anti-establishment activists were key figures in inciting resistance to authority, the widespread nature of the disturbances was largely a result of student dissatisfaction with the administration and the blunt tactics of men such as Solicitor Foard and SLED chief Pete Strom. The police they sent to the campus overreacted to the situation and alienated students who were normally apathetic toward radical activity. According to most accounts, when authorities first arrived on campus during the Russell House takeover, the majority in the crowd of students outside cheered their presence. But following constant checking of ID cards, tear gassings, arbitrary beatings, and random arrests, these students turned on the authorities. An unidentified student protestor said of his involvement, "I don't know too much about the war in Vietnam because I don't read the newspapers that much. I don't know the circumstances at Kent State that led to the shootings. What I do know for certain is there is a cop in the Russell House. . . . That's why I'm in the streets." Julianne Still, student body treasurer and student leader, said of the disorders: "The Kent State deaths weren't the only reason, in fact I think they were at the bottom of the list of reasons for unrest at Carolina." Instead she blamed the fact that Carolina was a "political puppet" in an election year—a direct reference to the calls for a hard line against anti-establishment students. Student government leaders and members of fraternities and sororities—in more normal times conservative influences on campus—became involved in the resistance to outside policing. As historian John Hammond Moore wrote of police behavior during the USC disturbances, "Those in uniform may not have won friends, but they certainly influenced people."[21]

Significantly, in spite of the chaotic nature of the rioting and the numerical superiority of the students to police in the various confrontations, no gunshots were ever reported fired by either side, and there were no deaths. Carolina avoided the lethal bloodshed of similar disturbances at campuses such as South Carolina State, North Carolina A&T, Jackson State, and Kent State.

Over the summer of 1970, the board of trustees acted as judge and jury for the students arrested in the Russell House takeover and the administration building riot. They exonerated four students, put four on probation, suspended thirty-three in lengths varying from six months to indefinitely, and permanently expelled thirteen. Eventually however, the University readmitted all of them when the board learned that the suspensions would not hold up in court. Additionally, six students—Barbara Herbert, Paul Foxworth, G. P. Sammon, Paul Gumm, Lynn Zorak, and an unidentified minor—were tried in state court and convicted for trespassing during the Russell House takeover. Authorities later dismissed the charges when the South Carolina Supreme Court ruled that one could not trespass in a public building. In the wake of that ruling, charges against over thirty other defendants were dropped as well.[22]

The impact of the disturbances went far beyond the immediate end of the crisis period. Relations between the board and faculty remained strained as the board, not the faculty's discipline committee, handled the cases of the students involved in the disturbances.[23] Student-faculty relations improved as a result of the role of faculty in calming students during the worst of the rioting. The nature of the board itself changed in the wake of the strife. In September 1970, longtime board chairman Rutledge L. Osborne of Orangeburg (affectionately known as "Mr. Rut") announced he would step down as chairman. The seventy-five-year old alumnus had been a guiding force at the University for decades—he had served on the board since 1947 and as board chairman since 1952. In his place, the board elected T. Eston Marchant, a Columbia attorney and trustee since 1965, as its new chairman. Osborne remained on the board until 1975, and in the meantime, in 1973, the board named the University's administration building for him.[24]

The student riots laid bare the problems on the University campus—primarily related to its explosive growth and the failure to address the problems and needs of individual students. Tom Jones later admitted that while barricaded on the second floor of the administration building, he realized that something was obviously amiss. "This is Carolina," he told himself, not Berkeley or Columbia University. "For this to happen here, something must be wrong." The University of South Carolina had grown too impersonal. It was not *humane* enough, Jones decided, and he set about trying to find innovative ways to address that central problem. He declared that his idea of the ideal university was "one that fit the student instead of the student having to fit the University."[25]

Such talk should not have surprised those familiar with Tom Jones. He came to Carolina with a reputation as an innovator, and though at first he concentrated on building USC into a research university, by the late 1960s he became more and more concerned with looking for solutions to the problem of impersonality on the rapidly growing campus. Dean Hal Brunton, a close associate of Tom Jones for nearly his entire presidency, described Jones as "an idea man." He remembered that Jones would "come up with ten different ideas every day."[26] Jones had introduced a number of unconventional programs like Upward Bound, mostly aimed at addressing the challenge of offering "relevant" education to the large number of students, including the under-privileged, that had flooded USC since the early 1960s. He had declared 1968 as a "Year for Innovation" and asked faculty to reevaluate USC's entire edu-cational approach. In that year he founded the Institute for Research on Prob-lems of the Underprivileged and discussed the possibility of starting an "experimental college" where nontraditional learning concepts could be tested. He hired an assistant to the president for special projects, educator Laurence Flaum, who set about developing plans to make Carolina's educational expe-rience more accessible and relevant, less impersonal, a place where students were free to inquire about intellectual topics that interested them, and where they were released from tradition-bound institutional constraints. With the support of the Ford Foundation, by the summer of 1972, Jones established a special office to handle the University's myriad innovative undergraduate pro-grams, the educational development office headed by Jay C. Smith. One col-league said of Jones's commitment to innovative education in the late 1960s and early 1970s, "He came in as an electrical engineer, but the 1960s changed him into a social engineer."[27]

Among the most significant of the innovative programs USC developed in the late 1960s was the so-called Contemporary University (CU) program. Supported by a Ford Foundation grant, the University of South Carolina was one of three universities in the country to participate in an initial trial of CU in the fall of 1969 (the University of Massachusetts at Amherst and Federal City College in Washington, D.C., also participated). Of the three schools, USC was the only one to continue the program after its first year.[28]

The Contemporary University was an independent study program designed to give students the opportunity to design their own curriculum for a semes-ter's work (fifteen hours of credit) under the guidance of a single professor, completely free of the traditional curriculum structure. With the support of such faculty as Richard Rempel, Donald Weatherbee, and Robert Heckel, the administration committed substantial resources to CU and earned a renewal of the Ford Foundation grant. They saw the program as a way to encourage undergraduate research, bring students and faculty closer together, and most of all motivate students who had become fed up with traditional degree pro-grams.[29]

Later, in the midst of the student disturbances, Tom Jones decided to try an even more radical independent study–style program called the University

Without Walls (UWW). Begun in the fall of 1970, this experimental program for alternative undergraduate education was tested by a loose consortium of some eighteen colleges and universities and administered by the Union of Experimenting Colleges and Universities of Antioch College, Ohio. Supported by a $20,000 ($70,215) Ford Foundation grant and the U.S. Office of Education, UWW at USC was specifically designed to attract disadvantaged, unmotivated, and underachieving students who had not been successful in traditional academic programs.

While Contemporary University was only a one-semester hiatus from Carolina's traditional curriculum, UWW was a complete break from it. The student designed his or her entire undergraduate program of study and courses, with guidance from UWW staff (frequently adjunct faculty) who used a variety of alternative teaching methods including tutorials, "learning facilitation groups," independent study, and group projects as well as off-campus learning experiences such as travel and internships. Students enrolled in USC's UWW program could not earn a bachelor's degree and had to reenter the normal curriculum at some point in their undergraduate careers, though this point was never well-defined.

Conrad Lodziak, UWW assistant director at USC, described the typical student volunteering for the UWW as one who "does not want to be in school . . . has drifted here because his friends do or is avoiding the draft." Lodziak continued, "He is a student who is seeking the line of least resistance on his path to becoming a college graduate. He is looking for an 'easy way out,' he does not want to be hassled, and does not want to do too much which would upset his style. He would much prefer to be left alone in his subculture, which for a majority of these students . . . appears to revolve around smoking marijuana, listening to rock music and being cool."[30] Self-direction was the hallmark of the UWW program, and students were given as long as they wanted to complete course requirements. They routinely submitted their own grades (if grades were even required); in some cases, everyone in a class was simply given an A. One student earned UWW credit for hiking across the country.[31]

In their purest forms, the lifespans of the innovative Contemporary University and University Without Walls programs were relatively short. While faculty from USC's traditional colleges and schools such as John Duffy, Charles Coolidge, and F. H. Giles wholeheartedly backed the alternative programs, others saw them as easy ways of earning credit without academic legitimacy or rigor. The programs never attracted students in large numbers. CU had about 30 participants per semester in its early years, but by the fall of 1974 its numbers had dwindled to 12. UWW attracted 36 students in its first year and grew to 415 by the fall of 1971. However, the latter program was discontinued in 1972 amid serious questions about its academic integrity. Contemporary University survived with a new name—Interdisciplinary Independent Study—and higher academic standards.[32]

In response to the failure of the University Without Walls, Tom Jones, still committed to developing a permanent program of alternative undergraduate education at Carolina, sought approval for a similar degree program, the Bachelor of General Studies (later renamed the Bachelor of Arts in Interdisciplinary Studies). Like the UWW, the program had no set curriculum and students designed their own course of study. However this program, administered by the College of General Studies, had far more structure and faculty oversight than the UWW. In addition, students in the program had to meet USC's minimum entrance requirements and the teaching faculty were to be drawn from the University's regular departments—not adjuncts. Despite significant faculty disagreement about the need for such a program, they approved it in the spring of 1972.[33]

Following the outbreak of violence in May 1970, Tom Jones and the administration sought out student advice to discover how they and the faculty could go about making the entire University community more "humane." "No one segment of our academic community has a leasehold in new ideas or how best to make old ideas work better," Jones said. Student government leaders such as Mike Spears and Julianne Still set up a series of off-campus retreats or "think tanks," where small groups of students, faculty, and administrators met in an informal atmosphere to discuss University problems and suggest solutions. Culminating at Camp Gravatt near Aiken in October 1971, the think tanks allowed students a chance to voice frustrations about the academic atmosphere at Carolina. Among the significant problems they cited were weak University community communications, a feeling of alienation among black students, little genuine enthusiasm for learning among the undergraduate student body, little opportunity for close student-faculty relations, and an excessive number of large classes which hampered faculty-student relations. All of these were directly related to the explosive growth and changes of the previous decade to which the institution had not yet adjusted.

Students stressed ways in which the University could improve its academic atmosphere, including higher standards, better advisement, improved teaching methods (including fewer graduate teaching assistants, smaller classes, and more "team teaching"), increased student opportunities for living-learning and informal experiences with faculty, and emphasis on curriculum reform and innovative programs. The faculty saw the solutions to the University's problems as lying chiefly with lower-division undergraduate teaching. They suggested better recognition for outstanding, innovative teachers, better counseling, and a better library as ways to improve the academic atmosphere. The Gravatt conference and its aftermath had a significant impact on the direction of the University during the following years.[34]

The most lasting and successful outcome of the "think tanks" was University 101, an experimental program designed to provide alternative learning experiences while making the University more humane and relevant to students. The report from the Gravatt conference recommended that the University overhaul its freshman program to include a semester-long orientation to ease the student's transition from high school to university life. A faculty committee chaired by philosophy professor Robert Mulvaney put together a plan with three chief aims: to familiarize freshman with the meaning of higher education, to acquaint them with their roles as individuals at the University, and to introduce them to the University's offerings and resources. All this would be offered in a structured, small-group seminar setting using innovative teaching methods called "University 101, The Student in the University."[35]

The program was judged a success. Beginning in the fall of 1972 with 239 freshman volunteers, after two years it became institutionalized as a permanent course. Initially under the direction of J. Manning Hiers and later John N. Gardner, by the 1975–76 academic year it enrolled nearly 1,300 freshmen in 62 classes. Not only did University 101 improve the college experience for Carolina students, but the training programs set up to prepare faculty to teach the seminars were cited as excellent opportunities for professional development. USC's program has been used as a model for hundreds of similar freshman seminars across the country in the decades since. In 1983, USC began offering annual national seminars in the freshman year experience to interested institutions. The program may be safely considered the most influential educational innovation ever to emerge from the University of South Carolina.[36]

University 101 owed part of its success to the University's emerging reputation as a center for innovative education. In 1971, the Ford Foundation awarded the University a $250,000 ($841,425) venture grant to be used by President Jones as a discretionary fund to improve undergraduate teaching by seeding worthwhile projects. University 101 received vital startup funding via the venture fund. Jones used the fund to aid numerous other experimental programs as well, including the educational development office, under Jay C. Smith, a series of teaching/learning seminars to improve faculty teaching methods, led by John L. Kimmey, and audio-tutorial courses in biology and geography.[37]

While a key part of Jones's drive to reform the University was the introduction of innovative programs, his administration moved to bring change in other areas as well. One was a revision of the curriculum in the College of Arts and Sciences. As Jones was committed to closely involving students in designing their education to increase its relevance, in April 1969 he and the dean of the College of Arts and Sciences, Bruce Nelson, set up a joint committee of students and faculty to study the college's curriculum and "suggest innovations and changes that would be more consistent with student interests and needs." Over the next year, the committee studied University history, student questionnaires, and curricular reforms at universities such as Duke, Stanford, Brown, and Yale. Led by student government vice president Scottie Barnes, the committee found that the basic curriculum in the College of Arts and Sciences had changed little since the early 1900s in teaching methods or degree requirements. In July 1970, the College of Arts and Sciences faculty substantially revised basic degree requirements, allowing students more options in their curriculum and more flexibility in academic programs.[38]

Another significant change was a revision of the University's undergraduate grading system—something colleges and universities all over the nation were doing as calls for innovative, "relevant" education reached their height. Amid considerable faculty opposition, in 1971 the University changed to a "non-prejudicial" grade scale with a "forgiveness clause": the grades of D and F were abolished and replaced with NC (for no credit). Technically, it became impossible for a student to fail a class. The faculty made this move in part because of intense pressure to pass male students who, if they failed out of school, were likely targets for the draft and service in Vietnam.[39]

The period of rapid changes also encompassed several significant organizational reforms. A faculty senate, seriously considered since 1962, became a reality in May 1970. It provided that some 18 percent of the faculty (with proportional representation for all faculty ranks) would form a representative body for decision making. This made it more efficient for faculty to exercise their responsibilities over curriculum and academic matters.[40]

New degree offerings also accompanied this period of growth and change at the University. A new school of librarianship, an undergraduate program in health science, new master's degrees in music, fine arts, and nursing, and an entire program in marine science from the bachelor's to the Ph.D. were but a few of the new offerings at the University.[41] In the summer of 1970, the faculty approved an Afro-American studies program under the direction of its first director, Willie L. Harriford, offering an interdepartmental major that responded to the requests of USC's growing number of students for courses relating to African American culture and development. When Afro-American studies classes, such as history courses taught by Grace J. McFadden, began in the fall of 1971, they proved popular with both black and white students. During the 1973–74 academic year the University also began offering its first courses in women's studies; by 1979 a formal women's studies program, under the direction of English professor Paula Feldman, was under way.[42]

With the ever-growing list of degree programs, administering the bureau-cratic apparatus designed to manage them had become increasingly complex. In the summer of 1972, Provost William H. Patterson presided over a reor-ganization of the academic affairs division, which was now to include five vice-provosts, one each for advanced studies and research, health sciences, liberal and cultural disciplines, professional schools, and regional campuses. Because of the continued growth of the College of Arts and Sciences, that division, first established in 1912, was divided into three separate colleges: the College of Arts and Letters, the College of Science and Mathematics, and the College of Social and Behavioral Sciences.[43]

One of Tom Jones's desires had long been to establish an experimental college to administer USC's myriad nontraditional programs; one of the rec-ommendations of the Gravatt retreat had been that the University should establish a center to encourage creative scholarship and teaching on campus and cooperation among students, faculty, and laypeople in the community. Thus, in the summer of 1973, John C. Guilds, vice-provost for liberal and cul-tural disciplines, announced the creation of the Center for Cultural Develop-ment, which was to serve as a home for innovative programs, support research, and attract noted scholars to Carolina with a particular expertise that could contribute to the cultural life of South Carolina. Under the aegis of the Cen-ter for Cultural Development (to be directed by Bert Dillon, assistant dean of the College of Arts and Letters) it would include both senior and junior scholars as well as special academic programs such as Afro-American and women's studies, the honors program and Contemporary University. Other programs such as the Center for Shakespeare Studies and the Center for Edi-tions of American Authors (both research arms of the English department) were also to be affiliated with the center. John Guilds described it as "a focus for intra- and extra-mural intellectual growth and innovation." The proposed Cultural Center represented the culmination of the innovative effort of the Jones administration to foster the academic and cultural life of the Carolina campus, and was also an attempt to end the intellectual isolation of the Uni-versity community from the state.[44]

With the continuing growth of the undergraduate student body (it grew 21 percent between 1969 and 1971 alone), in the fall of 1971 Tom Jones announced a shift in the administration's philosophy of enrollment growth. Carolina would now seek status as a "senior" institution and limit new fresh-man admissions to approximately 2,500 students per year. USC made this move voluntarily in the wake of a CHE recommendation that the University limit its enrollment to 16,000 students—approximately the level in 1971.

Many in the state had begun to view Carolina's continued growth with suspicion, perceiving that it was out of control.

Jones stressed that USC could slow its growth because South Carolina had largely addressed the issue of the availability of higher education. "South Carolina High School Graduates now have several alternatives—they can attend many private or public colleges, including the two new state colleges, Francis Marion and College of Charleston. They can also attend one of the eight USC Regional Campuses or one of the two Clemson Regional Campuses," he wrote. While South Carolina still trailed the nation in the number of its high school graduates who went on to college, more then a decade of unchecked growth at USC brought about some notable improvements in faculty, equipment, and facilities. Rather than continuing to grow indiscriminately, Jones asserted that it was appropriate to slow down enrollment growth on the main campus and concentrate on improving quality. Carolina would now look to grow graduate programs (which in 1971 made up about 16 percent of the main campus student body). By 1975, while enrollment in undergraduate programs had slowed considerably, graduate programs continued growing at the fast pace of the late 1960s. Carolina made progress toward becoming a more "senior" institution (see tables 5.1 and 5.2).[45]

Table 5.1 Growth of USC undergraduate and graduate programs, 1965–1980

YEAR	UNDERGRAD. ENROLLMENT	% CHANGE, UNDERGRAD. (FROM PREVIOUS FIGURE)	GRAD. SCHOOL ENROLLMENT*	% CHANGE, GRAD. SCHOOL (FROM PREVIOUS FIGURE)	GRAD. SCHOOL ENROLLMENT AS % OF OVERALL ENROLLMENT
1965	7,962	–	841	–	9
1971	13,248	66	2,625	212	16
1975	16,028	20	7,420	182	30
1980	18,969	18	6,274	(15)	24

Source: Denham, ed., *The University of South Carolina Statistical Profiles*, 1991–92, 4.
* The Graduate School figures exclude law and medical enrollment.

Table 5.2 Degrees awarded at the University of South Carolina,
1969–70, 1975–76, 1979–80

YEAR	MASTER'S	PH.D. & ED.D.
1969–70	303	73
1975–76	1,742	146
1979–80	1,423	146

Source: USC Annual Report, 1969–70, 21; 1975–76, 10; 1979–80, 28.

Tremendous physical growth accompanied the growth in enrollment. Because of the seemingly never-ending construction on campus of the late 1960s and early 1970s, Carolina earned a reputation as "the empire in which the concrete never sets." The major construction project of the decade was a new library—which eventually became the largest such project ever undertaken by the University of South Carolina. In 1967, the board of trustees had made a new library their number one priority because of overcrowding in the McKissick Library (designed to accommodate 360,000 volumes, it held 500,000). With seating space for only 10 percent of the student body, McKissick was called by Kenneth Toombs, director of USC's libraries, "one of the most inadequate major university libraries in the world." By late 1969, plans were complete for a large new four-story library to be built directly behind McKissick on Gibbes Green.[46]

However, when Tom Jones unveiled to the public the University's plans for 1970s expansion, he revealed that the board had put the library project as "co-equal" with a proposed enlargement of the football stadium. The announcement caused an immediate firestorm of protest both on and off campus since it appeared to put desperately needed academic improvements like the library and new law and nursing school facilities behind stadium enlargement. Governor McNair declared that the University needed to "get its thinking straight." Law students, whose own new facility was fourth on the board's building priority list (where it had slipped from first since March of 1969), flailed the plan as "incomprehensible, arbitrary and without any regard to prior commitments to academic progress." Rumors began to circulate that 40 percent of the faculty would resign if stadium expansion remained a number one priority. The faculty unanimously resolved that any stadium enlargements should be postponed until after new academic facilities were funded. Governor McNair then left both the library and stadium projects out of his proposed capital bond issue, threatening to delay the project for another five years. The controversy badly strained student and faculty relations with the board of trustees and administration in the months before the 1970 disturbances.[47]

Through the efforts of Tom Jones, William H. Patterson, and Sol Blatt Sr., the legislature eventually restored funding for the $9,200,000 ($32,299,138) library project. In the meantime, planners had concluded that the Gibbes Green area was too small for a large addition to McKissick. Instead, they decided to dramatically expand the Undergraduate Library and rename it for Thomas Cooper, the controversial second president of the South Carolina College. They would triple the size of the three existing floors and build an additional four floors underneath, increasing the size of the building by some 615 percent. Working closely with Kenneth Toombs and other librarians, architects managed to preserve much of the character of the original building while expanding it into a major research facility. When it opened on June 4, 1976, the building included 286,000 square feet, 40 miles of shelving, and seating for 2,500. It represented the coming of age of Carolina's library, which had caught up with its peers since the late 1940s and grown into a major research library (see table 5.3). The new facility included the most modern library technology, including a light-pen/bar code circulation system—the first in the nation. The "new" Thomas Cooper Library gave Carolina a facility compatible with its dreams of academic excellence.[48]

While this major addition to the campus was in planning and construction, many other physical additions went forward. The University of South Carolina Law Center, located in the urban renewal area between Main and Assembly Streets, opened in 1973. In the east campus, University expansion into the College Street neighborhood continued with the addition of a new dormitory, Columbia Hall, opened in 1971 just north of Capstone House. The next year, the Carolina Research and Development Foundation acquired the stately Flora M. Barringer home (later the Alumni House) at 1731 College Street. Private fund-raising by the USC Business Partnership Foundation

Table 5.3 Size of library collection in selected southern university libraries, 1949–50, 1962–63, 1976–77

UNIVERSITY	1949–50	VOLUMES IN COLLECTION 1962–63	1976–77
Duke University	–	1,592,672	2,764,348
Univ. North Carolina	557,189	1,349,584	2,274,173
Univ. Virginia	835,794	1,214,625	2,143,226
Univ. Georgia	254,340	549,258	1,719,178
Univ. Florida	407,436	1,017,405	1,703,006
Louisiana State	395,628	1,100,889	1,659,549
Univ. Kentucky	497,550	1,003,158	1,640,420
Univ. South Carolina	255,579	530,105	1,558,797
Univ. Tennessee	324,067	742,032	1,332,782
Univ. Alabama	357,010	–	1,135,847
Univ. Mississippi	159,951	–	703,760

Source: College and Research Libraries 12, no. 2 (April, 1951), 180–81; U.S. Office of Education, Library Statistics of Colleges and Universities, 1962–63: Institutional Data (Washington, D.C.: U.S. Government Printing Office, 1964), 6–46; James R. Mingle, ed., Fact Book on Higher Education in the South, 1977 and 1978 (Atlanta: Southern Regional Education Board, 1978), 29.

(established in 1970) contributed $1.5 million ($5,266,164) to help build a new nine-story business administration building along College Street in the east campus area, opened in 1973 (along with a second phase completed in 1983, the complex was later named the Close-Hipp Building). Vice president for business affairs Hal Brunton and director of campus planning Thomas B. Faris forecasted continuing expansion in the east campus area (as far north as Gregg Street) until 1985—despite the continued objections of residents of the neighborhood.[49]

A part of this expansion included widening and depressing Pickens Street and building a pedestrian bridge over the street, thus uniting the new east campus with the older Gibbes Green and Horseshoe. In the spring of 1972, when Hal Brunton announced these plans, students objected strongly. They complained that the popular lawn in front of the Humanities Classroom building would be cut in half and that noise from the street would interfere with classrooms on either side. They directed much of their resentment at Brunton, who had become a controversial figure because of the continual construction. Student government, led by president Mike Spinazzolo, led a fight against the Pickens Street plans. Students picketed meetings designed to discuss the plan, carrying signs declaring "Don't make Carolina a concrete campus—save our grass," and "Stop Brunton Before He Spreads." Despite vehement student opposition, the plan went forward and the pedestrian walk-way has been a resounding success.[50]

In the south campus area, land purchases by the CRDF continued, as did construction. In 1973, the new Thompson Student Health Center, located behind the Russell House, replaced the Thompson Infirmary that dated to 1908. The Sol Blatt Physical Education Center on Wheat Street opened in 1971. New dormitories along Whaley Street, Bates West and the Cliff Apartments, opened in 1974, housing Carolina's growing population of upperclass-men and graduate students. Also in 1974, the University bought a Columbia landmark, the Booker T. Washington High School complex, along Blossom Street.[51]

Carolina's continued physical expansion mirrored its expansion in an area most South Carolinians identified with the University of South Carolina—athletics. The early 1970s were the golden age of Gamecock basketball, with Frank McGuire's teams piling up wins and generating "hoop-mania" in a state that had long been preoccupied with football. McGuire's 1970 and 1971 teams were among the nation's best, combining for a record of 48 wins versus 9 losses; however, they never won the national championship many national prognosticators predicted. Led by Bobby Cremins, John Roche, and Tom Owens, the 1970 team romped through the fourteen-game regular-season ACC schedule undefeated—earning the ire of fans throughout the conference, especially at Duke and North Carolina. Frank McGuire, who had coached a North Carolina team to a national championship in 1957, called his 1970 season "probably the greatest that I have ever had as a coach." It ended after an ACC tournament loss to North Carolina State, one of the most bitter defeats in Gamecock sports history. The Gamecocks thus missed out on the NCAA tournament (the ACC sent only its tournament champion) and a chance to compete for a national championship.[52]

Nonetheless, Carolina fans adored McGuire and his New York–imported players. One writer commented that McGuire was "easily the most popular man in the university and state." "McGuire for Governor" bumper stickers were a common sight in Columbia. The overwhelming support McGuire earned allowed him to sign the first black basketball player to play at Carolina, Casey Manning, in 1970. The 1971 team was named a preseason number two pick in the nation and was strengthened by the addition of Kevin Joyce, but it ended the regular season in second place in the ACC. That ACC season was marred by several free-for-all fights and constant jeering and abuse from the notoriously tough ACC crowds, with whom USC had become an attractive target. The Gamecocks answered their hostility with an ACC tournament championship, won over North Carolina on Tom Owens's last second-shot. The season ended with another bitter defeat—to Pennsylvania in the NCAA tournament—but John Roche was named first-team All-America. McGuire's stock at Carolina had never been higher, and he received a nine-year contract extension through the 1980 season.[53]

While McGuire's basketball program produced enthusiasm across the state, football still ruled within the University's athletic power structure. The 1969 ACC football championship (with a perfect 6-0 conference record) signaled that Gamecock football had also arrived, but the ACC success was not enough for athletic director and head football coach Paul Dietzel. He wanted national prominence, and in his view, ACC rules inhibited his ability to recruit "blue-chip" football players. NCAA rules stated that an athlete had to have a projected 1.6 grade point ratio (GPR) to be eligible for competition, but the ACC added an additional requirement, a minimum 800 score on the SAT.[54]

Just after the 1969 football season, Dietzel submitted to the ACC a proposal to eliminate the additional stipulation. The ACC executive committee agreed to study the proposal and report on it at its May 1970 meeting. Speculation on the campus and throughout the state had it that USC would secede from the conference if the proposal were not accepted—despite the vehement opposition of USC faculty. The USC board of trustees athletic committee agreed to leave the decision up to Dietzel and Tom Jones, shutting out the faculty from any advisory role and angering the members of the faculty athletic committee.[55]

After the ACC's executive committee refused to act on the proposal to eliminate the conference's SAT standards, on May 2, 1970, the USC board of trustees met to consider its course of action. Despite rumors to the contrary, friendly overtures from ACC officials persuaded the University to remain in the conference for the time being.[56]

However, the ACC rule continued to chafe at coach Paul Dietzel. Of ten blue-chip prospects he recruited in the fall of 1970, only two met the ACC's SAT requirement, while all met the NCAA's criteria. Of the ACC non-qualifiers, five were black and all were from South Carolina. Dietzel wrote that the ACC rule meant that "all 5 of these black athletes can attend most other universities, but they can't go to school at their own state [university]." He continued, "They will be playing for Notre Dame, Southern California, the Big Ten, the Southeastern Conference, or the Southwestern Conference. This means we cannot sign a single black athlete from the State of South Carolina this year."[57] By October 1970, such arguments led Tom Jones to support Dietzel's position, and the board of trustees' athletic committee unilaterally abandoned abiding by the ACC's SAT requirement, authorizing Dietzel to sign players who met the NCAA's criteria regardless of their SAT scores. They vowed to work to overturn the ACC's rule, calling it "educationally unsound and athletically unwise." Their action was an ultimatum to the ACC. It created a September 1971 deadline for ACC action on the issue, a date when the players recruited under the NCAA guidelines (and who would be ineligible for ACC competition) would take the field in Gamecock uniforms.[58]

At their pivotal December 1970 meeting, the ACC executive committee again upheld the 800 minimum SAT rule, but added a corollary: prospective student-athletes who scored between 700 and 799 on the SAT but had a projected GPR of 1.75 would be eligible as well. This compromise failed to satisfy either Paul Dietzel or Clemson's leaders, and both vowed to continue recruiting under NCAA standards only.[59]

USC's relations with the ACC had deteriorated sharply for several reasons, including the Mike Grosso incident in the mid-1960s, the failure of the 1970 basketball team to make the NCAA tournament, the intense hostility of ACC athletic directors such as Duke's Eddie Cameron as well as ACC fans toward Frank McGuire and the Carolina basketball program, and now the controversy over eligibility standards. The hope of satisfying Paul Dietzel with a compromise on the eligibility question was beyond reach, and Frank McGuire, who was not a leader in the move to leave the conference, nonetheless acquiesced as a result of his own differences with conference members. Thus, in March 1971, the USC board of trustees voted to secede from the ACC, an athletic conference of which it was a charter member.[60]

Most members of the board believed that their secession was temporary. Board chairman T. Eston Marchant remarked, "Because USC has enjoyed and hopes to continue to enjoy its relationship with fellow conference members, we hope that this separation will be of a temporary nature and for a minimum amount of time."[61] They also believed that Clemson would be joining them in secession, but just after USC's action, Clemson president Robert Edwards announced that the school would stay in the conference. Ironically, as a result of a federal lawsuit filed by two Clemson athletes whom the ACC had ruled ineligible, the conference abolished the 800-minimum-SAT rule just over a year after South Carolina withdrew over the issue. Ongoing discussions between USC and ACC officials left the door open for USC's reentry into the conference sometime in the future.[62]

The University's withdrawal from the ACC demonstrated the influence of extra-academic influences on the institution, but the political fate of Tom Jones in the wake of the spring 1970 disturbances demonstrated it even more vividly. While the board had unanimously supported Jones in the face of political attacks and demands for his resignation by Solicitor John Foard, privately, several members of the board (such as Sol Blatt Jr.) had also objected to his handling of student activism on campus. As a result of the on-campus turmoil of the late 1960s and early 1970s, Tom Jones's and USC's political effectiveness in the state slipped.[63]

Almost exactly one year after the May 1970 riots, another event brought negative attention to the University. Without notifying faculty advisors or the administration, on April 28, 1971, the *Gamecock* deviated from its normal format and devoted three full pages, including the cover and a sympathetic editorial from editor Charles Beebe, to a statement from Brett Bursey, the former USC student and activist leader who had been arrested and convicted for his role in vandalizing the Columbia Selective Service office but who was at the time a fugitive. The *Gamecock* issue, which gave favorable press to a man South Carolina's elite viewed as an enemy of the state, received wide coverage in the state's newspapers and angered many, including legislators, alumni, and some students, embarrassing University leaders.[64]

The incident infuriated Sol Blatt Sr. He called the *Gamecock* a "red sheet" and declared that he had "no regard for anyone who puts his stamp of approval on things published in it." It was "a disgrace," Blatt said. "I wouldn't let anybody stay at the University who had anything to do with publishing it." However, because of first amendment protection, there was little he or the University could do to silence the newspaper or its editors. Amid rumors that they were to close the newspaper, the board of trustees conducted an in-depth investigation and concluded that it needed tighter oversight from faculty.[65]

However, damage had been done to Tom Jones's credibility. Sol Blatt squarely blamed Jones for the *Gamecock*'s controversial issue. He wrote the president a blistering letter in which he declared that he was "disgusted" with affairs at the University. It appeared that the students and faculty were running the institution and "telling the President . . . what to do." Blatt insisted, "The time has come that somebody must take charge of the University. Legislators are disgusted . . . and the University would have a hard time getting any funds for any purpose at this moment. . . . Some changes must be made and made now."[66]

The situation was only one in a series of political problems for Tom Jones. Within a few months, for a variety of reasons Jones was at the center of a political vortex. Julio Bartolozzo, who briefly served as head of the state's TEC system, strongly criticized Jones and USC for putting up roadblocks to merging the state's TEC system and Carolina's regional campuses. Governor John West had brought Bartolozzo to South Carolina from California specifically to accomplish this task. Another political battle within the state over the establishment of a new medical school at the University increased the political heat on Jones, whose statements in favor of the school raised the ire of interests in Greenville, Clemson, and Charleston. Sol Blatt Jr.—who was about to step down from the his seat on board after receiving a federal judgeship—met with the president privately and recommended that he resign, citing Jones's loss of credibility and lack of effectiveness within the state, particularly with members of the General Assembly.[67]

In the fall of 1971, Sol Blatt Jr. took his opposition to Jones's continued presence at USC to the board of trustees. He told the board of his advice to Jones that he step down. The board at first demurred, but then passed a vote of confidence in Jones, citing his "imaginative and progressive administration" and criticizing the "unwarranted public suggestions that the board's attitude toward Dr. Jones and his administration is something less than approval." Students generally liked Jones (a turnaround from their opinion of him during the late 1960s) and the student senate endorsed him in the wake of Blatt's moves, as did the University's Alumni Council. Sol Blatt Jr.'s effort to convince Jones to resign failed, but served notice that influential Carolina supporters were looking for a way to ease the president out.[68]

The uproar from this controversy had barely subsided when the *Gamecock* stirred up another political hornet's nest. In early February 1972, it ran a series of articles detailing rampant drug use on campus, including quotes from an anonymous faculty member who claimed that he gave better grades to students who used drugs.[69] The sensational article again brought negative public attention to affairs on campus—with Tom Jones drawing more fire from his growing list of political foes. Governor John West vowed to have

SLED investigate the drug situation on campus. Fifth Circuit solicitor John Foard appointed a grand jury to investigate. He subpoenaed *Gamecock* writers to testify before the grand jury, but they refused to answer Foard's questions on the grounds that their sources were confidential.

While the *Gamecock* eventually won a legal victory, the story had nonetheless inflicted more damage to Carolina's reputation in South Carolina. A year later, authorities under the direction of Solicitor Foard arrested a twenty-nine-year-old philosophy professor on serious drug charges, and most assumed he was the faculty member quoted in the article. USC was becoming known as a home for radical political thought and out-of-control drug use—even by faculty members—not a good political reputation in South Carolina. As a result of these controversies, Tom Jones appeared to be unable to control events on the University campus.[70]

Despite the fact that events seemed to be conspiring against him, Jones managed to hang on to his job. By early 1974 however, sentiments among the state's leadership led to a final push to unseat him. Most powerful Carolina supporters acknowledged that he had fallen behind in the in-state political battle with Clemson, outmaneuvered by Clemson president Robert Edwards. In spite of Sol Blatt Sr.'s retirement from the House speakership, the former Speaker still had tremendous power among the state's political elite, and his opposition to Jones was common knowledge in South Carolina. In late 1973, Blatt made another move to oust the president. While most of those involved denied that there was anything "sinister" with Jones's resignation, it is clear that powerful Carolina supporters, including Sol Blatt Sr., Governor John West, and board of trustees chairman T. Eston Marchant had concluded that the time had come for Jones to step down. In late January 1974, Marchant let Jones know that the sentiments of a majority of the board were against him.[71]

No one factor drove Tom Jones out of the presidency; instead it was an aggregation of incidents over the years that gave opponents the critical mass to convince him to step down. Reflecting on his tenuous position, Jones concluded in a memorable quotation, "Friends come and go, but enemies accumulate."[72] Tired of fighting seemingly endless political battles, on January 22, 1974, Jones resigned, effective June 30. In spite of his well-known political troubles, the decision shocked many on the campus. Jones said of the political nature of the last days of his presidency, "There was pressure against me in the State House and on the Board. . . . Rather than continue, it was time for me to [go]. Twelve years is about long enough." He remained magnanimous in the wake of the ouster, refusing to criticize those who eased him out of office—instead citing his love of the institution and his desire to continue serving it in a teaching capacity. Likewise, those who presumably forced

Jones out refused to criticize him as well, praising his accomplishments as president instead.[73]

Tom Jones's years as Carolina president witnessed extraordinary growth and change unlike any the institution had experienced in its 175-year history. The faculty attracted during his tenure made tremendous strides toward establishing national standards of excellence and became the basis for the research university of the late twentieth century. The Columbia campus enrollment grew from 6,699 in 1962 to nearly 22,000 by the end of his presidency. The Graduate School grew from 487 students to nearly 6,000. Some $60 million ($223,467,701) in buildings were added to the campus, while another $24 million ($66,264,407) were under construction at the time of his resignation. The University's overall budget grew from $6,936,299 ($31,213,346) in 1962–63 to $57,574,805 ($158,965,012) in 1973–74. A small, weak state university just after World War II, the University of South Carolina under Thomas F. Jones's leadership grew into a full-fledged research institution with a wide range of degree programs on both the undergraduate and graduate levels. Carolina emerged as a quality regional university with a reputation for innovative education, and had a vision that it could be a leader. Jones originally planned to stay at USC indefinitely after his resignation, and the board of trustees awarded him the title "distinguished professor of the University." However, in the days after he stepped down, he accepted a visiting professorship at MIT, and a year later took a permanent position as vice-president for research there, ending a thirteen-year association with the University of South Carolina.[74]

The board of trustees named his successor immediately after accepting Jones' resignation. Their choice of Provost William H. Patterson was a surprise to outsiders. It appeared that Patterson's selection was a foregone conclusion. At the January 30, 1974, board of trustees meeting at which they decided to officially accept Jones's resignation, the board was to announce the process for selecting a successor. Instead, they named Patterson USC President outright, without forming a search committee or giving the new head an "interim" or "acting" title. The faculty senate's steering committee had already endorsed Patterson; there were preprinted biographical statements available for the press, and Patterson gave a prepared speech at the meeting's conclusion.

This apparently engineered process immediately brought charges that Governor West and the board had, in secret, replaced Jones with a puppet president who would be amenable to their wishes. With the resignation coming in the wake of the Vietnam War and in the midst of the Watergate controversy, both of which had heightened distrust of "the establishment," many people viewed such behind-the-scenes dealings with suspicion. Patterson was a true insider—he had served in the inner circle of USC presidents and the board of trustees for nearly thirty years—and got along well with men such as Eston Marchant and Governor John West. The student senate disapproved of the board's tactics of naming the president "behind closed doors," and passed a resolution condemning their action. As a result of the method of his selection, charges that Patterson was acting as a yes-man for powerful political figures in the state dogged his administration for the next three years.[75]

However, Patterson's good relations with these figures came as a boon for the University, which, after all, relied on state politicians for its funding. A Charleston native, Patterson held three degrees from USC (he was the first USC president to hold three USC degrees—B.A. 1934, M.A. 1948, Ph.D. 1951, all in history) and had served as the University's chief academic officer since 1961 and as secretary of the board of trustees since 1964. Before that, he had served as assistant to the president or dean of administration under Presidents Smith, Russell, and Sumwalt. While not known as a scholar or teacher (he had been in the administration since 1950), Patterson had a reputation as a master administrator with good political instincts and a knowledge of how to get things done.[76] In the wake of the campus troubles of the early 1970s, it was common for American universities to promote from within the institution those who were already familiar with existing problems and personalities. Nationwide, provosts in particular seemed to be a popular choice for institutions choosing new presidents in the mid-1970s.[77]

It soon became clear that Patterson's assumption of the presidency would bring sweeping changes to Carolina. At the same meeting at which the board named him president, they established a committee to study a major reorganization of the University's administrative structure.[78] In the first weeks of his administration, Patterson subsequently announced such a reorganization, putting his own imprint on the University and marking a distinct departure from the Jones years.[79]

Patterson declared that the theme of his administration would be consolidation of the University's sprawling growth. Enrollment, physical plant, and academic programs had grown continually in since the early 1950s, but the leveling off of the college-age population led Patterson to declare in 1974, "We have reached the end of that era." "I think we have been so busy rushing from 5,000 students to 20,000 that we might not have looked back," he said. "It is a good time to see whether the road we took was the best one." Patterson concluded that Carolina was "going to have to look toward consolidation and—just as important—towards constant improvement of what we have rather than take for granted the fact of expansion."[80]

The clearest area in which Patterson broke from the past was his approach toward the physical expansion of the campus. He established a "good neighbor" policy toward the neighborhoods surrounding the campus, seeking to "trim the rough edges" of campus expansion by placing firm limits on its boundaries. He acknowledged the acrimony that physical growth had caused among nearby residents, and he sought to ease concerns in these neighborhoods. With Harold Brunton declaring that "the era of large expansion is over," in mid-1975 the board of trustees reduced the boundaries of the 1965 master plan in two respects: they eliminated one block (the Gibbes Court block) from the proposed East Campus expansion, and they eliminated from long-range expansion plans a six-block area south of Blossom Street and east of Pickens Street in the Wheeler Hill neighborhood. Faculty and President Patterson strove hard to "mend fences" with the residents of these neighborhoods, establishing a "Town-Gown" advisory committee (chaired by historian Richard Rempel) who worked to revitalize the communities, which had deteriorated since the University began accumulating property there. The board of trustees directed the CRDF, which owned most of the individual lots involved, to stop buying land in both areas and to sell lots outside of the new campus expansion boundaries back into private hands. In the Wheeler Hill neighborhood, University officials cooperated with the city and urban planners to redevelop the area, but the prices asked for the lots ensured that the area would become an upscale residential area. The fact that most of the original residents could not afford to return caused more ill will toward the University. In the east campus area, the University also made a commitment to upgrade and preserve the remaining homes that it planned to keep—in order to maintain the unique blend of town and gown in the neighborhood.[81]

Another facet of Patterson's approach to physical expansion was fresh attention to older buildings. In the decades since World War II, Carolina had focused most of its attention on constructing new buildings on the edges of the campus, while the older buildings in the heart of the historic area had been allowed to deteriorate to the point that some were uninhabitable. Graffiti covered walls, and the gray-green paint that covered Horseshoe buildings was in need of replacement. In one incident, a shower stall in a Horseshoe dormitory fell through the floor while a student was showering in it. There were serious proposals in the late 1960s and early 1970s to demolish the most dilapidated buildings on the Horseshoe one by one—starting with the McCutchen House. However, new sensibilities toward historic buildings led to new attention for the old campus. In 1972, Tom Jones and Hal Brunton secured $2,800,000 ($9,122,400) from the legislature to restore the decaying buildings on the Horseshoe. They began preliminary planning for an intensive historic preservation project. In preparation for the restoration, in 1973 USC archaeologist Stanley South led a dig on the Horseshoe that yielded a wealth of information about the area's architectural history.[82]

When William Patterson became president, he continued the emphasis on resurrecting the Horseshoe and committed personnel and energy to the idea of completely restoring the area in accord with modern concepts in historic preservation. The comprehensive project was dedicated to bringing the physical conditions in the old buildings up to the standards of USC's new ones. Planners envisioned that the entire campus would be the attractive place that it had been before the onset of the unprecedented construction of the 1960s and early 1970s. With the aid of renowned architectural consultant Russell Wright, by mid-1975 a Horseshoe advisory committee, chaired by historian Walter B. Edgar, established guidelines for the restoration that aimed to restore the buildings' facades to their antebellum appearance and to make the grounds themselves more attractive than ever. The horseshoe-shaped drive was closed to cars and paved with salvaged bricks from the Booker T. Washington High School complex, facades were renovated and returned to their original color (from the gray-green they had been since just after World War II), and the interiors of the buildings were brought up to modern standards, including central air conditioning. Beginning with the McCutchen House— which was transformed into the Faculty House, an elegant dining facility—in 1974 the University began a comprehensive building-by-building restoration project that took more than ten years to complete. A cooperative effort led at different times by Tom Jones, Hal Brunton, William Patterson, Walter Edgar, and Patterson's successor James B. Holderman, the renovation left the heritage of the Horseshoe to the University of South Carolina and future generations of students in top condition. It is now the true heart of the Carolina campus.[83]

Elsewhere, new construction continued within the bounds of the master plan for campus development. In the east campus, private donations helped Carolina build badly needed modern facilities. A $500,000 ($1,380,509) gift from the estate of Martha Williams Brice aided the completion of a new six-story nursing complex, the Williams-Brice College of Nursing, in 1975. A $1 million ($2,761,017) gift from prominent alumnus E. Smythe Gambrell of Atlanta made possible a new social sciences building, Gambrell Hall. In the west campus area, a $5 million ($11,977,941) biological sciences complex, later named for renowned agriculturalist David R. Coker, was completed in 1976; an adjacent pharmacy building was finished a year later.[84]

Patterson's drive toward "consolidation" included evaluating the myriad innovative academic programs established in the previous decade; in some cases programs were recommended for cancellation, others were restructured, and still others were retained. The Patterson years represented Thermidor for the innovative programs of the early 1970s, especially those designed for the "unmotivated" and "underachieving" student. Early in Patterson's term the Contemporary University program underwent restructuring, and became

Interdisciplinary Independent Study, directed by Phyllis Fleishel and later Thorne Compton.[85] Another program that came under review was the proposed cultural center. Only one month after Patterson took office, the center's director, Bert Dillon, resigned. The center, which had begun to take shape during President Jones's last years, was discontinued. The academic programs it included were given over to the colleges or schools to which they were appropriate.[86]

Administrators subjected the controversial College of General Studies to scrutiny as well. The University's new provost, Keith Davis, initially announced that the college would be restructured. The associate's degrees it offered would be merged into the existing four-year departments in the University's regular colleges. After an uproar from Dean Harry E. Varney and other College of General Studies supporters, administrators postponed and eventually canceled the restructuring.[87]

One example of consolidation that did take place was a reorganization of the three colleges that had once made up the College of Arts and Sciences. In the summer of 1975, the College of Arts and Letters and the College of Social and Behavioral Sciences were merged, creating the College of Humanities and Social Sciences. Political science professor Chester Bain became dean of the new college. Patterson cited reduced administrative costs as a chief reason for the consolidation, and he looked to the eventual merger of the new college with the College of Science and Mathematics, thus reconstituting the former College of Arts and Sciences.[88] The Patterson years also saw restructuring of the office of student affairs. The widespread reshuffling saw many top administrators in the Jones administration retire or leave Carolina for other universities.[89]

Another change concerned the University's grading system. While "NC" had originally been intended as a "non-prejudicial" grade, it became a problem for students applying to graduate schools, where the NC grade was often treated as an F, hurting the student's grade point ratio. By 1975, with the reaction to the 1960s calls for "relevant" education in full swing and with the Vietnam War over and the draft abolished, faculty opposition to the system grew to a point where the NC system was abandoned for a more traditional A through F grading scale.[90]

Restructuring and consolidation did not mean that the University of South Carolina had become static. There was continued growth in the number and types of academic programs available. In 1975 alone, the University added a range of programs in the media arts, as well as master's-level programs in computer science and applied history.[91]

Another important new program, begun in 1974, was the Master's in International Business Studies degree. Conceived and designed by USC's business administration faculty (led by Dean James Kane), it capitalized on the recognized strengths of both the College of Business Administration and the international studies program at USC. The program was an innovative way of preparing students for the increasingly global nature of business in South Carolina and the world. It included intensive language training and a mandatory six-month internship in a foreign country, along with standard business courses. Admitting its first students in the summer of 1974, M.I.B.S. soon became one of the best known and respected graduate degree programs offered at Carolina.[92]

Carolina added several entirely new academic divisions during 1974 as a result of legislative requests. In that year, the University received a $150,000 ($414,153) appropriation to establish a program in criminal justice. The new College of Criminal Justice offered a curriculum leading to the Master in Criminal Justice degree, and a year later began a baccalaureate-level criminal justice program as well.[93] Also in 1974, legislative action mandated the formation of a public health program, and the University decided to develop it within a new college that would also contain speech pathology and audiology programs. In response to demands for increasing opportunities for health education in South Carolina, the new College of Public Health began offering graduate-level programs for administrators, educators, public health nurses, and other public health personnel.[94]

A third new academic division was the result of more than ten years of discussion and an acrimonious debate in South Carolina. The new University of South Carolina Medical School received CHE approval in 1974, but not before a protracted and complex political battle. Even after program approval, the medical school remained the subject of a bitter political struggle long after it admitted its first class in 1977.[95]

The prospect of establishing a second medical school in South Carolina went back at least as far as 1962, when the Greater Columbia Chamber of Commerce began a campaign to establish a two-year school in Columbia. After the USC board of trustees began studying the question, however, Governor Hollings pointed out that a consultant's study of the Medical College of South Carolina in Charleston indicated that it should be the recipient of any new state funds for medical training. Tom Jones then announced his opposition to a new medical school at Carolina.[96]

The Columbia Chamber of Commerce continued to push the program throughout the 1960s. By 1967, the new CHE, led by John K. Cauthen, hired a group of outside consultants (led by Vernon W. Lippard of Yale) who concluded that a projected shortage of physicians in South Carolina made the establishment of a second medical school an urgent necessity.[97] However, the 1968 Moody Report concluded that the state should spend any dollars available for medical education on upgrading the existing medical college, not building a new one (or establishing a medical university in Charleston as some were suggesting). The report recommended an affiliation between USC and the Medical College, and contained strong cautionary words for those who thought otherwise:

> If South Carolina now establishes a second medical school; or if South Carolina now establishes a third university at Charleston to upgrade the medical college; then South Carolina must abandon its hopes for quantum leaps forward in other areas. This is a matter of simple economics. . . . It would mean a severe slowdown in needed improvements and expansion at the existing colleges and universities. . . . It would subvert the state's intention to focus its resources in the areas of most needs and of multi-plier economic effect. It would make a mockery of the establishment of goals and priorities.[98]

The opposing recommendations of the Moody and Lippard Reports represented yet another difference of opinion between CHE chairman John Cauthen and Governor Robert McNair, and staked out political positions in a debate that would continue to rage for more than a decade.

By the early 1970s, in spite of the efforts of Governor John West to hold controversy at bay, the debate over a new medical school began to deteriorate into a name-calling exercise between Greenville and Charleston interests on one side and Columbia interests on the other. In the wake of the Lippard Report, Tom Jones became a proponent of a second medical school, and along with the Columbia Chamber of Commerce and Columbia doctors, they argued that the state urgently needed such a school to supply South Carolina with primary-care physicians. On the other side, the Medical University (the Charleston school became a university in 1969) and other Charleston interests, Clemson President Robert C. Edwards, the Greenville County Chamber of Commerce, the Greenville Hospital System, and Greenville doctors lined up against a second school, arguing that upgrading MUSC was the best use of scarce state dollars. The debate raged in the halls of the state house and in the newspapers of South Carolina as a study committee of the General Assembly considered the merits of the issue. When it became apparent that the Medical University could not expand fast enough to meet the state's critical need for physicians, in 1973, the General Assembly's health care study committee recommended that the state establish a second medical school, contingent on winning Veteran's Administration (VA) funding.[99]

The supporters of a second medical school (such as leading USC trustees Eston Marchant and William Brockington) cited the advantages of a central

location in Columbia and, more importantly, the availability of existing facilities at the old Columbia Veteran's Hospital (the VA was building a new facility adjacent to the old one). They stressed that the state would not have to
pay for facilities if federal funding could be secured—South Carolina would
thus get a "bargain" medical school to help supply the state with much-
needed doctors. Supporters envisioned that this school would concentrate on
training family practice physicians, of which there was a developing shortage
in South Carolina. Keys to initial passage of the USC medical school were the
support of Governor John West and State Senator Rembert Dennis, the winning of a seven-year, $25,058,841 ($69,187,885) grant from the VA (which
would pay for the majority of the new school's startup costs and ensure cooperation with the new Dorn Veterans Hospital), and finally an agreement with
Richland Memorial Hospital to use its clinical facilities for training, free of
charge for ten years. By a one-vote margin, during the spring of 1974 the CHE
approved the University's bid for a medical school. The General Assembly
then appropriated some $390,000 ($1,076,797) as a required match to the
Veterans Administration grant. The University of South Carolina thus had
official approval for its medical school, though it would be years before a faculty could be assembled, facilities secured, and students admitted. President
Patterson charged William N. Adams Smith, USC's vice president for health
affairs, with putting the new school together—including hiring faculty and
deans.[100]

Initially, the VA grant stipulated that the school should open in the fall of
1975, but delays in securing accreditation and funding postponed the opening. Political difficulties continued, such as when Adams Smith resigned,
charging that the administration aimed to hire a politically connected doctor
as permanent dean of the Medical School, instead of his own candidate
(Adams Smith's temporary replacement was USC physiology professor Francis L. Abel).[101]

Accreditation delays caused the General Assembly to reconsider the entire
issue in 1976, when the school's foes, including Governor James Edwards,
made a concerted effort to cut off state funding in an attempt to kill the new
school before it could get off the ground. An upstate newspaper editor wrote
of USC's medical school, "Taxpayers all over South Carolina are being robbed
blind by Columbia in the worst raid on the state treasury since the Car-
petbaggers were in power." However, through the efforts of Eston Marchant,
Sol Blatt Sr., Marion Gressette, and Richland County Senator Hyman Rubin,
funding was saved. However, accreditation delays continued as a result of the
uncertain financing and the consequent inability to hire faculty. However,
Carolina hired Roderick MacDonald as permanent dean of the school in September 1976, and on February 10, 1977, the University of South Carolina

Medical School earned accreditation from the American Medical Association and the Association of American Medical Colleges, clearing the way for its opening in the fall of 1977. When it opened, it welcomed 24 students—all from South Carolina.[102]

The new medical school eventually began to help the state address its shortage of physicians, but it added to the costs of higher education. It was possible to fund it, however, because the overall financial position of the University had improved markedly since the early 1960s. Financing public higher education in South Carolina underwent significant changes in the 1970s, including the institution of formula-based funding, which the CHE introduced beginning in 1971. The CHE declared that the formula was designed "for equitable sharing of state taxpayer support for South Carolina's public colleges and universities." Given the historic inequities in funding for the University of South Carolina, a CHE formula based primarily on full-time equivalent enrollment held promise for more equal financing on a per-student basis.[103] As long as the greater expense of graduate programs were taken into account, formula funding seemed a good idea to USC administrators, and Tom Jones and the USC board of trustees initially supported it.[104]

Formula funding did not take politics out of the funding equation, however, but instead added another layer of state oversight to the budget process. The CHE submitted its budget recommendations to the State Budget and Control Board, which then submitted its recommendations (still based on a formula but usually lower than the CHE recommendation) to the General Assembly, who most often approved an appropriation lower than both the Budget and Control Board and CHE recommendations.

By 1975, administrators began to believe that formula funding was not working to USC's advantage. In that year, a state financial crisis caused by a nationwide recession led the Senate finance committee to temporarily abandon the method of formula-based funding while also ordering an 8 percent across-the-board cut in state institution budgets. The University was forced to return some $4.4 million to the state as a result. USC's enrollments continued to rise and appropriations failed to keep up with the increases (in fact, they declined in real terms; see table 5.8). To compensate, the administration resorted to measures such as hiring and departmental budget freezes, tuition increases, deferral of preventive maintenance, curtailment of state-funded research, and reduction of graduate assistant pay to below the minimum wage level. The University managed to avoid cutting academic programs. However, a proposed Arts Center and a South Carolina Educational Television complex on the east campus were casualties of the recession.[105]

When changes to the CHE funding formula (a raise in the number of credit hours that constituted a full-time doctoral student) meant that USC's budgets would be cut even further while enrollment continued to rise, USC and Clemson teamed up to propose that the two universities be exempted from CHE jurisdiction. They proposed that the state form a special coordinating committee to oversee the budgets of the two research universities. USC and Clemson argued that the funding formula did not take sufficient account of the additional costs of graduate education and other special programs at these universities. CHE Chairman R. Cathcart Smith called the proposal "completely unheralded and somewhat shocking." CHE vice chairman Hugh M. Chapman argued that the universities would rather report directly to the Budget and Control Board and to the General Assembly, where political pressure could be brought to bear. Along with executive director Howard Boozer, CHE officials claimed that South Carolina's existing formula was comparable those in other states, and that both Clemson and USC's funding levels were similar to those of their peers. The latter arguments won the day, for the General Assembly refused to allow the two universities to escape CHE jurisdiction.[106]

The arguments of the CHE's leaders pointed to a remarkable change in South Carolina's funding of higher education since the early 1960s. In that period, South Carolina went from spending the least amount of any other southern state (as a percentage of tax revenues) on higher education to spending the most (see table 5.4). In the decades before 1975 South Carolina had

Table 5.4 Appropriations of State tax funds for operating expenses of higher education: as a percentage of tax revenue, 1963–63, 1973–74; per $1,000 of personal income, 1960, 1975–76

STATE	APPROPRIATIONS AS A % OF TAX REVENUE (RANKING)		APPROPRIATIONS PER $1,000 OF PERSONAL INCOME (RANKING)	
	1963–64	1973–74	1960	1975–76
South Carolina	6.2 (10)	17.4 (1)	$2.78 (9)	$17.75 (1)
Alabama	8.9 (4)	15.8 (5)	$4.36 (3)	$14.98 (3)
Florida	11.5 (1)	13.9 (8)	$2.41 (10)	$ 9.38 (9)
Georgia	8.0 (7)	16.1 (4)	$3.71 (5)	$10.37 (8)
Kentucky	8.1 (6)	11.9 (10)	$3.12 (7)	$12.45 (5)
Louisiana	11.0(2)	13.9 (9)	$7.42 (1)	$12.04 (6)
Mississippi	9.0 (3)	17.1 (3)	$5.74 (2)	$16.90 (2)
North Carolina	7.5 (8)	17.3 (2)	$3.98 (4)	$14.74 (4)
Tennessee	6.9 (9)	14.6 (7)	$3.08 (8)	$ 9.13 (10)
Virginia	8.2 (5)	14.7 (6)	$3.48 (6)	$10.58 (7)

Source: Fact Book on Higher Education in the South (Atlanta: Southern Regional Education Board), 1971–72, 62; 1973–74, 40; 1975–76, 48.

established a complex array of competing postsecondary educational institutions: two major centers for medical education (MUSC and USC's Medical School), a group of two-year colleges (USC and Clemson's extension campuses as well as the TEC system), a group of four-year colleges (USC's regional campuses and individual colleges such as Winthrop, The Citadel, Francis Marion, Lander, and the College of Charleston), and two research universities (Clemson and USC). The institutions began to meet the dire need for higher education in South Carolina. However, while the CHE was established to reduce or eliminate duplication in state-funded higher education, with so many competing interests, duplication was inevitable and the cost to run these systems expanded the state's higher education spending.

However, the cost of running the array of colleges was not the only reason for South Carolina's increased levels of spending. In comparison with its neighbors, by the mid-1970s the state was spending comparable amounts (or more) on its research universities on a per-student basis. This shift was indicative of the changed economy and the increasing influence of metropolitan elites in South Carolina's affairs. The Palmetto State was firmly a part of the emerging "Sunbelt South," and by 1975 the state's funding priorities included regionally competitive levels of funding for advanced education and research.

Unfortunately, the new level of higher educational funding in South Carolina provided a big political target for those who wanted to cut state

Table 5.5 State appropriations per full-time equivalent student, 1974–75, in selected southern state-supported institutions*
(conversions to 1991 dollars)

UNIVERSITY	STATE APPROPRIATION 1974–1975	FALL 1974 FTE STUDENTS	APPROP. PER FTE STUDENT, 1974–1975
USC (Columbia)	$41,221,526 ($113,813,331)	17,421	$2,366 ($6,533)
Clemson	$25,189,414 ($69,548,399)	10,172	$2,476 ($6,836)
Georgia Tech	$19,293,500 ($53,269,681)	8,958	$2,154 ($5,947)
University of Georgia	$51,735,000 ($142,841,212)	23,885	$2,166 ($5,980)
UNC (Chapel Hill)	$37,074,481 ($102,363,270)	17,890	$2,072 ($5,721)
NC State	$31,131,668 ($89,995,063)	12,585	$2,474 ($6,831)

Source: "Presentation to Special Committees on Formula," September 16, 1975, by Howard Boozer, executive director, South Carolina Commission on Higher Education, Patterson Papers, 22.

* State appropriations exclude medical and dental schools, agricultural and engineering experiment stations, and agricultural extension service. FTE students determined on SREB basis by dividing undergraduate credit hours by 15 and graduate credit hours by 12.

Table 5.6 State appropriations per full-time equivalent student to large
doctoral granting institutions, 1975–76, 1977–78 (ranking)
(conversion to 1991 dollars)*

STATE	APPROPRIATION PER FTE 1975–76	APPROPRIATION PER FTE 1977–78
South Carolina	2,304 (3) ($5,837)	2,721 (3) ($6,114)
Alabama	1,649 (7) ($4,178)	2,091 (7) ($4,698)
Florida	2,138 (5) ($5,416)	2,363 (5) ($5,309)
Georgia	2,242 (4) ($5,680)	3,042 (1) ($6,835)
Kentucky	1,745 (6) ($4,421)	2,228 (6) ($5,006)
Louisiana	1,628 (8) ($4,124)	1,714 (9) ($3,851)
North Carolina	2,368 (2) ($5,999)	2,819 (2) ($6,334)
Tennessee	1,548 (9) ($3,922)	1,822 (8) ($4,094)
Virginia	2,517 (1) ($6,377)	2,475 (4) ($5,561)

Source: Fact Book on Higher Education in the South (Atlanta: Southern Regional Education
Board), 1975–76, 49.
* It is unclear whether or not the 8 percent budget cut of 1975–76 budget cut was taken
into account in that year's SREB figures.

spending, such as Governor James B. Edwards. He pitted K–12 education
against the state's college's and universities in the annual budget battles, saying, "I think in the past we have put too much of our funding into higher
education; our priorities have to be shifted back to primary and secondary
education."[107] On another, more candid, occasion, he told a group of public
school teachers: "I'd rather have a hundred kids who read and write than four
Ph.D.s at the University of South Carolina. We have invested too much into
higher education."[108] These kinds of comments demonstrated that some state
leaders had little historical perspective when it came to the state's level of
higher education spending, since South Carolina had trailed most other southern states in this area for the majority of the twentieth century.

While the governor opposed the levels of higher education spending in
South Carolina, the University continued to feel the effects of the economic
recession and the high inflation of the mid-1970s. Reflecting the nationwide
fiscal crunch, appropriations stagnated. During 1976–77, the University
again had to return money to the state because of revenue shortfalls, this time
some $581,000 ($1,391,836). Skyrocketing energy use and natural gas shortages caused by a record cold winter led USC to join several other colleges and
universities in the region and unexpectedly close for fifteen days during February 1977. Continuing budgetary problems caused the University to lose good

professors, especially in the law school, where salary levels at other schools were more attractive.[109]

Such fiscal problems related to the state's economy highlighted a continuing weakness for the University of South Carolina. While state appropriation levels stagnated (though they were the equivalent of neighboring universities), Carolina still trailed far behind in the amount of private funds it could draw on to give it fiscal flexibility in times of economic downturn. The Business Partnership Foundation had success in aiding the College of Business Administration, but fund-raising for the University's overall endowment lagged far behind. For example, annual alumni giving stood at $289,000 ($972,688) in 1971, but in 1979, they gave but $227,820 ($427,556).[110] Economic recession and inflation took the momentum out of fund-raising among alumni, and despite several plans to start capital campaigns with large fund-raising goals, none was undertaken. As a result, the value of the University's endowment, like alumni contributions, barely grew at all (in real terms) during the 1970s. In fact, the endowment had grown little in the years since the "Greater University Fund" campaign of the early 1960s (see table 4.1).[111]

While Carolina suffered from low levels of private support for its academic operations, athletic director Paul Dietzel was a master promoter of USC's athletic teams and fans fervently supported their Gamecocks. Consequently, the USC athletic program had first-class athletic facilities, sporting an expanded football stadium, a new basketball coliseum, a modern baseball complex, and a new athletic dormitory. The third in Carolina's trilogy of prestige coaches, baseball coach Bobby Richardson, brought wins in a manner similar to those of Frank McGuire. In the early 1970s, Richardson (a former all-star for the New York Yankees) put Carolina baseball on the map. By the mid-1970s, Gamecock baseball teams were emerging as a national power. The 1974 team, led by pitcher Earl Bass, broke numerous school records on the way to a 48–8 record and an appearance in the NCAA playoffs—a first for a USC baseball team. The 1975 team broke almost all of the records that the 1974 team set.

Table 5.7 Market value of USC endowment, 1963, 1969, 1973, and 1978

DATE	MARKET VALUE OF ENDOWMENT
30 June 1963	1,353,249 ($6,023,067)
31 December 1969	2,264,954 ($8,180,954)
31 March 1973	2,904,496 ($8,910,403)
30 June 1978	3,962,250 ($8,275,007)

Source: Cartter, ed., *American Universities and Colleges,* 9th ed., 1052; BTM, 25 March 1970, 15 May 1973; Self-Study, 1980, table 4-16.

With two first team All-Americans on the team—prolific hitter Hank Small and Earl Bass—the Gamecocks compiled a 51–6–1 record and advanced to the finals of the College World Series, where they finished as NCAA runner-up. After a 38–14 record and another trip to the College World Series in 1976, Bobby Richardson resigned as head coach to run (unsuccessfully) for Congress. June Raines replaced him and maintained the success of Carolina baseball. His first team (1977), led by Randy Martz and future major league star Mookie Wilson, again went to the finals of the College World series, and again finished second in the nation. Raines's teams continued to win consistently, compiling thirty-one-win seasons in both 1978 and 1979.[112]

Another significant development in Carolina athletics was a 1972 federal law, Title IX, that required universities and colleges to end all sexual discrimination. A women's athletic program had begun in 1967 (known as the Women's Intercollegiate Athletic Association), and women's athletic teams were established as clubs funded in part by car washes and candy sales. As a result of Title IX, however, Carolina began to develop a comprehensive program of women's varsity sports under the direction of Helen Timmermans, the University's first assistant athletic director for women's sports. Carolina began fielding women's varsity teams in tennis, volleyball, gymnastics, softball, swimming, and basketball. While insufficient funding plagued women's sports in the early part of the decade, by 1976–77, the athletic department spent some $100,000 ($239,559) on women's teams. Frequent turnover of coaches in the early years of the women's program made building teams difficult, but in 1977, the University named Pam Parsons head basketball coach and assistant athletic director for women's sports. The women's programs grew steadily and Parsons set about making the Lady Gamecocks basketball team a national power.[113]

In men's basketball, the secession from the ACC took its toll. While Frank McGuire's teams continued to pile up wins, without ACC rivals on the schedule, the basketball euphoria in South Carolina that had burned so brightly in the early 1970s gradually subsided. Led by Tom Riker, the 1972 team went 24-5 and won more games than the previous year's ACC champion. They advanced to the NCAA tournament and lost in the second round to former ACC rival North Carolina. Both the 1973 and 1974 teams won twenty-two games and advanced to the NCAA tournament. Players such as Kevin Joyce and Danny Traylor were standouts on these teams. In spite of the excellent play of Mike Dunleavy and Columbia natives Alex English and Nate Davis, the 1975 team failed to win twenty games, the first Gamecock basketball team to do so since 1968. Dissension wracked the team and they failed to finish in the nation's top twenty for the first time in six years, and ended a streak of four straight NCAA tournament appearances. NCAA tournament bids for non-conference-affiliated basketball programs were becoming difficult to earn, and USC's average attendance at home games had fallen every year since the withdrawal from the ACC. With recruiting made more difficult without the promise of a conference tournament championship, McGuire began to lobby for a reentry into the ACC or another athletic conference.[114]

This development was made possible by Paul Dietzel's midseason 1974 resignation as USC head football coach. The charming "Pepsodent Paul" had promised the Gamecock faithful that nationally ranked teams were "just around the corner" throughout the early 1970s, but he could not deliver. Despite his charisma, the luster began to wear off his reputation and he became increasingly unpopular. Dietzel had been the prime mover behind USC's secession from the ACC and it had done less damage to the football program than basketball, but the wins failed to come in batches for Dietzel as they had for Frank McGuire. Dietzel's 1970 team, which returned many of the stand-outs from the 1969 ACC championship team, finished a disappointing 4–6–1. When subsequent teams—despite the predictions of the prognosticators—failed to challenge the nation's leading programs, fans became restless. On the campus, students began to bat about the phrase "GROD," short for "Get Rid of Dietzel." During 1973, Dietzel had a bout with diverticulitis and missed two games, but led by standouts Jeff Grantz and Steve Courson, the team compiled a seven-win season. After losing the first two games of the 1974 season (with a team that had been predicted to win a minimum of seven games), the embattled Dietzel announced he would step down as head coach at the end of the season. Though he cited health and family reasons for his resignation, rumors swirled that the board of trustees had pressured Dietzel into resigning, just as they had Tom Jones only a few months earlier.[115]

In the wake of Dietzel's resignation as head coach, he declared his intention to remain at Carolina. He initially hoped to be rehired as athletic director. Citing private conversations in which he claimed President Patterson assured him that the University "had a job for me to do when I quit coaching," Dietzel let it be known that he expected a job after the season. So the board of trustees created an entire office for Dietzel, the Division of University Relations, which he would head with a vice-president title, reporting directly to the president. The actual duties of the position were unclear. Dietzel initially accepted it, but then decided to leave the University for good, resigning his new job in February of 1975.[116]

The athletics situation became more complicated when the board of trustees went about hiring a new football coach. Their choice was Jim Carlen, a former Texas Tech head coach known as a successful program-builder, teacher, and devout Christian. Along with the head football coach's job, Carlen asked for total control of the athletic program. However, the board of trustees had decided in the wake of the Dietzel resignation that they would separate the jobs of head football coach and athletic director. Meanwhile, Frank McGuire's supporters all over South Carolina had lobbied the board to have him hired as athletic director. In order to maneuver around the tender egos in the athletic department, the board in essence created an athletic department organization in which President Patterson functioned as athletic director: Carlen and McGuire were both given the title associate athletic director and total control over their respective programs. Harold "Bo" Hagen, a former Gamecock football star, was given the nominal title of athletic director, but had no authority over football or basketball, only the so-called minor sports. The trustees had created an unorthodox three-headed athletic department. To make matters worse, relations between Carlen and McGuire deteriorated to the point that the two men did not speak.[117]

It was in this confused athletic situation that the University found itself when discussions began in early 1975 about reentering the ACC. The issue became the one of the hottest in Columbia. In the summer of 1975 some 60 percent of students supported rejoining the conference. Initially, all three athletic directors supported the move to reenter the conference. President Patterson made contacts with ACC officials in the spring of 1975, and the board of trustees instructed him to begin making arrangements for a formal application for readmission. Patterson and board chairman Eston Marchant supported reentry, citing low attendance figures at basketball games as well as the overall advantages of affiliation with like-minded institutions. After an initial flurry of activity in mid-1975, however, it became clear that reentering the ACC would not be a simple matter—indeed it appeared that at least a few member schools (such as the University of Maryland) were adamantly opposed to taking Carolina back. Nonetheless, board of trustees' secretary, George Curry, acted as intermediary between the ACC and the board's athletics committee, and by mid-1976 he managed to negotiate a firm but confidential offer laying out the ACC's terms for readmission. After considering the terms (which included a nonrefundable membership fee, reportedly as high as $400,000 [$958,235], and a requirement that a member school could have only one athletic director), in a sharply divided vote the board of trustees refused to swallow its pride and go back into the ACC. They rescinded their application to the conference, thus ending the possibility of reentry for the time being—but not closing the door to a return completely.[118]

The acrimonious atmosphere in the athletic department compounded confusion over the issue. The outspoken Jim Carlen, who initially supported conference affiliation in public, changed his mind. His football program had gained status as one of the most financially lucrative independent programs in the nation, and the prospect of sharing the wealth within a conference structure did not appeal to Carlen or his supporters. He still claimed to be "conference-oriented," but citing the costs to the athletic program of playing ACC schools whose programs failed to generate the revenues that USC did, he opposed reentry. In addition, his teams consistently won games without the conference (the Gamecocks went to the Tangerine Bowl in 1975). Frank McGuire, whose teams were suffering rather than prospering outside the ACC, publicly supported reentering the conference, but he understood the board's reluctance and agreed to abide by their decision.[119]

The ACC issue heated up once again in 1977 when the board revisited the issue, but by this time public disagreements between Carolina coaches (Carlen, who wanted to stay out of the conference, and McGuire, who wanted back in) as well as board members caused the University considerable embarrassment. Several board members, including vice-chairman Hugh H. Wells of Seneca, chairman Eston Marchant, and Othniel Wienges of St. Matthews were strong supporters of reentry into the ACC. Other trustees, such as the outspoken Michael Mungo of Irmo, James W. Cothran of Bishopville, and Paul S. Goldsmith of Greenville, were just as adamantly opposed. Opponents remained convinced that if Carolina supporters knew of the ACC's secret terms—primarily the membership fee, which they deemed outrageous for a conference charter member to have to pay—fans would disapprove of reentry as well. In spite of the public pronouncements from the mercurial Frank McGuire accusing the board of sacrificing the basketball program for the football program, the secret negotiations between George Curry and ACC commissioner Robert James were for naught. Strong arguments from board members who opposed having anything to do with the ACC carried the day; by the late 1970s the hopes of Carolina fans for reaffiliating with the conference they had helped to form faded away. Eston Marchant concluded that his "greatest mistake" as board chairman was allowing Paul Dietzel to lead the University out of the ACC. It hurt the University's reputation both athletically and academically, Marchant believed, severing an important relationship with some of the Southeast's finest universities.[120]

The ACC issue was one of many that swept up students during the 1970s. In the early 1970s, opposition to the Vietnam War continued to arouse student activism, but the riots in May of 1970 had left the chief activist group, AWARE, in disarray. In the wake of the unrest and with the decline of both the war and the draft in the early 1970s, on-campus student unrest gradually subsided, though it did not completely end until the American involvement in Vietnam was over. For example, Rita Fellers continued to lead antiwar activity, chairing the Moratorium Rally in October 1970, heading a February 1971 antiwar march, and in April 1971 traveling with a group of USC students to Washington to attend a major antiwar demonstration.[121] Students increasingly focused their activism on local concerns, including the ecology (environmental) movement, improving the University's academic atmosphere, increasing student responsibilities in self-government, and improving campus safety. The latter issue arose after an epidemic of violent attacks on campus—including three rapes—in the fall of 1970.[122]

One issue that aroused student passion during the 1970s was the parking situation. The dramatic expansion of the urban campus left little room for student automobiles, and the difficulties of parking their cars was a major complaint of resident and commuting students alike (it became a fact of life at Carolina, as the complaints continue into the twenty-first century). The *Garnet and Black* reported that 76 percent of students consistently had trouble parking, and called the issue "not a problem" but a "crisis." The campus had grown so large that by the end of the decade, the University established a bus system to get students from dormitories such as the Roost and Bates House to faraway areas such as the east campus.[123]

Another hot local issue among students was the question of closing Greene Street. The constant traffic and the danger of crossing the busy street that runs through the heart of the campus had been a problem since the construction of the Russell House in the 1950s. In 1961, an engineering study recommended closing the street, but the Columbia City Council refused to do so. In the 1970s, the closing of Greene Street became a focus of student activism. Student demonstrations in 1974 and 1975 highlighted their desire to close the street (in the latter incident, eighteen were arrested). In 1975 student body president Steve Hill introduced an intriguing proposal to turn the area into an attractive "greenway" with a pedestrian mall and an amphitheater. In spite of a trial closing in 1974 and the efforts of both board members and administrators to close the street, because of opposition from Five Points merchants the city council refused to close it permanently. In late 1977, they finally agreed to close it during selected hours on weekdays, but Greene Street remains an obstacle for pedestrians.[124]

Probably the most frightening aspect of student life was the serious rise in drug and alcohol abuse. In 1970, Tom Jones declared that it was impossible for drug use to get out of control on the Carolina campus because "if people are serious drug users, they won't be serious students for long." He was wrong. Administration estimates in 1970 put the level of drug use at about 10 percent for most drugs (excluding alcohol), but most students felt these figures were far too low. The *Garnet and Black* suggested that drug use by students was far more common than administrators believed. Their unscientific survey revealed that some 79 percent of students said that they knew someone who used marijuana, pep pills, barbiturates, heroin, morphine, or LSD. Forty-nine percent favored more lenient laws regarding the use of marijuana. The

Gamecock also reported instances of drug use and distribution on campus, and faculty members had been arrested for selling to students.[125]

By the mid-1970s it was apparent that more students than ever were using illegal drugs—especially marijuana. In 1974, 37.4 percent of students reported regular or semi-regular marijuana use. Others reported experimentation with amphetamines, cocaine, hallucinogens, and narcotics. Faculty members reported that students often came to classes while "high." All in all, the illegal drug problem—which was common to most American college campuses —presented a serious challenge to faculty and administrators, as well as to the basic mission of the University.[126]

The use and abuse of alcohol, a socially acceptable drug, continued to increase as well. Since it was legal and most students were of age, there was little the administration could do about casual student drinking. In late 1970, the board of trustees approved the sale of beer on the campus, citing the problem of "unhealthy and unwholesome night spots which surround the campus and which are pervaded by an atmosphere that exerts an undesirable influence upon the students." They allowed the University to develop an on-campus student lounge where students could drink in a space over which administrators exerted control. In 1973, the Golden Spur began selling beer to students in the Russell House, giving them an alternative to Columbia's bars. This development was symptomatic of alcohol use on campus, where nearly 80 percent of the student body claimed to be regular drinkers.[127]

The University's endorsement of on-campus beer sales was also indicative of the demise of the in loco parentis philosophy that had formerly governed University-student relations. Student Affairs officials struggled to make on-campus living attractive to students, to whom off-campus life offered nearly unlimited freedoms. Students themselves continued to seek greater autonomy in their lives. In 1970, they expressed a desire for the end of curfews in dormitories and sign-out policies for women students, for more opportunities to entertain members of the opposite sex, and for the abolition of housemothers. For the 40 percent of USC students who lived on campus, the 1970s saw new rules that further liberalized decades-old policies in the dormitories. In 1970 the board of trustees approved a dormitory visitation policy with three levels of supervision, from a level that included a housemother and strictly forbade in-room visitors, to one with limited supervision and daily open house to 11:30 P.M. All guests however, were still required to sign in when visiting. With the opening of the apartment-style Bates West dormitory in 1974, USC dorm life reached a watershed, for it was the first coeducational dormitory at USC and it also allowed twenty-four-hour visitation. In other dorms, a steady relaxation of visiting hours accompanied the end of the sign-in rule for guests (which had proven unenforceable) in 1975, and in loco parentis was, for all practical purposes, dead.[128]

Another barometer of life on campus was a college fad that swept the nation just as panty raids had in the 1950s: streaking. In early March 1974, the craze, which the *Garnet and Black* defined as "the art of shedding one's clothes and making a mad dash from one designated area of campus to another," came to Carolina. On March 3, rumors began to spread that fraternity members, athletes, and other students planned a mass streak. The news swept the Columbia area, and on that evening a crowd estimated as high as 5,000 gathered in anticipation of the spectacle and filled Greene Street in front of the Russell House, making it impassable. Among those in the crowd were an ABC-TV news crew and hundreds of curious Columbians—some elderly—in addition to USC students. The crowd was in a festive mood, with music and drinking marking the occasion, not tear gas as had been used on the crowds that gathered in the same area four years earlier. A homemade sign hung from Woodrow dormitory that proclaimed "USC's on the Winning Streak!"

To the delight of the crowd, at about 10:00 P.M. the mass of some 508 naked students (led by a torch bearer, some were dressed only in a tie and tennis shoes) raced from the Roost and Bates House up the Bates House ramp and through a cheering throng on Greene Street, headed toward Capstone House. The entourage ran through the Columbia Hall lobby and back to the Horseshoe, where they made an appearance in front of the President's Home. From there it was on to the Undergraduate Library (now Thomas Cooper), where they climbed the first floor stairway in front of the glass window, providing a clear view to the gathered spectators. After three hours of harmless exhibitionism, the crowd dispersed without incident. Sporadic instances of streaking on a smaller scale continued in the following weeks.[129]

The streaking craze demonstrated that campus life remained vital. However, through the mid-1970s the influence of the Greek system continued a decline that had begun in the mid-1960s. As the *Garnet and Black* put it, "Greeks no longer hold the lofty prominence they enjoyed in past decades. Their influence has waned." The yearbook declared in 1970: "It's happening at college campuses all over the nation . . . the greek system is slowly fading into that dismal portion of history known as the past." Though membership in Greek organizations dropped both absolutely and in percentage numbers, they continued to be an integral part of campus life and filled an important niche in Carolina's overall student life. The Beaux Arts Club, an exclusive dance club and a survivor from the 1930s, remained one of the most exclusive social organizations on campus. By the late 1970s, as student activism declined, the Greek system made a comeback, though it never regained the unchallenged status it had held as late as the mid-1960s.[130]

The diminishment of the Greek system was a sign of the fragmentation of the campus community into many subcultures within the "megaversity." With more than half the student body living off campus, USC student life was a far cry from the conformity of the 1950s. About a quarter of students surveyed in 1970 considered themselves "loners," with many citing the difficulties of meeting people on the large urban campus. George S. Duffie, United Methodist campus minister, noticed that the fragmentation of the university in the mid-1970s was causing serious problems. He wrote of a "growing and deeply disturbing recognition that the intensifying disciplinary fragmentation is only symptomatic of a fragmentation of the humanness of life itself at USC." While most students found homes within student organizations from religious groups to academic and purely social ones, aside from events like football or basketball games there had ceased to be such a thing as the "Carolina college experience" that could be commonly shared.[131]

One growing group on campus were black students, who grew in absolute numbers as well as proportionally during the 1970s but who reflected the increasing fragmentation of student life. The University, stung by charges of continuing racism in admissions by the federal government in 1970, worked hard to attract black students. In 1970, there were 279 black students at Carolina, less than 2 percent of the student body. By 1979, the 3,070 black students comprised nearly 12 percent. Black students became a more integral part of student leadership as well—Harry Walker's election as student body president in 1971 represented one of the first times in the United States a black student won such an office at a historically white university. Walker was elected with the support of a coalition that represented the Association of Afro-American Students as well a number of white student groups. The following year, Tim McConnell won election as vice-president, demonstrating that the earlier event was not a fluke. However, because of their relatively small number at Carolina, many of Carolina's African-American students still felt alienation on campus. They claimed that often they felt as if they were "outside looking in." When Gail Ransome became USC's first black homecoming queen in 1973 with the support of the Association of Afro-American Students, she was greeted by some boos from the USC stadium's student section. In 1976, black fraternities (of which there were four; Kappa Alpha Psi was the first, chartered at USC in 1970) withdrew from USC's Interfraternity Council (IFC) in a dispute over spending. They joined with USC's four black sororities to form a rival Panhellenic Council, an organization for black Greeks only. Charles McMillan, in USC's office of student affairs, commented about black students on campus, "There is no open arm of acceptance at the University. Black students are looking for acceptance as students and this takes time."[132]

One characteristic of the 1970s student was dissatisfaction with authority. In the wake of the resignation of Tom Jones, some students and faculty viewed President Patterson with suspicion—seeing him as a yes-man for more powerful interests in the state who wanted the administration to regain control of the University from students and faculty. Several subsequent issues raised student hackles, making for a tumultuous three-year presidency for Patterson. The reorganization of the Contemporary University program angered involved students; the consolidation of academic programs and the reorganization of the administrative structure alienated some long-time faculty and led to the resignation of a number of top administrators. The demise of the Center for Cultural Development upset students who had been involved in efforts to improve the academic atmosphere at Carolina. The botched reorganization of the College of General Studies alienated students and faculty in that division.[133]

A 1975 plan to allow the president and the board of trustees to admit seven percent of incoming law school classes (regardless of their academic credentials) resulted in the admission of fourteen students who were technically ineligible—including the sons of powerful state politicians. Students, faculty, and the law school dean reacted angrily. Under withering criticism both within and without the University, President Patterson and the board ultimately abandoned the plan when the American Bar Association warned that such action violated their standards and put the law school's accreditation at risk. Robert Foster, dean of the School of Law, resigned in protest of the board's action in the wake of the controversy.[134]

A similar controversy arose when William Adams Smith, vice president for health affairs and the administrator responsible for putting together Carolina's new medical school, resigned his post, charging that the University planned to name Sol Blatt's doctor as the first dean of the Medical School. An acrimonious and very public dispute arose between Adams Smith and Patterson, further solidifying the impression that the University was controlled by outside interests. The entire medical school issue was intensely political, and the continuing controversy over the role of USC's branch campuses vis-à-vis the TEC schools also embroiled the University. The clumsy handling of the ACC reentry issue caused controversy as well. A nationwide economic recession forced the administration to cut back on academic programs as well as routine maintenance, and led the administration to raise tuition fees (by $25 [$60]).[135]

The combination of all these factors led to a general loss of morale at Carolina and a sense that the institution had lost the momentum it seemed to have under Tom Jones during the 1960s. William Patterson expressed skepticism toward those who suggested that Carolina should seek to become nationally recognized for excellence. "I think the University should serve the state first and then from its statewide prominence it should move toward earning national and international prominence. I personally cannot see setting outlandish admission policies for schools and colleges which were originally designed to serve the best interests of the state."[136] Students charged that Patterson, as a sixty-three-year old career administrator, was out of touch with them. They cited his statement quoted in the *Gamecock*—"To tell you the truth, I haven't got much interest in young people"—as evidence. *Garnet and Black* writers Bob Baker and Ann Ross wrote, "It seems that USC is returning to a diploma mill status and people are again questioning the quality of education they are receiving under the direction of a man who shows such little concern." The pessimism was indicative of national trends. The mid-1970s, dubbed by historians the "era of limits," was a time of economic difficulty and reevaluation of the 1960s. This was the case at the University of South Carolina, where a degree of what would later be called "malaise" set in as the booming growth of the 1960s slowed and as the problems associated with this growth became more pronounced. Universities all over the country increasingly focused on more immediate problems rather than building for the future. Many Americans lost faith in their leaders in this period, and attitudes toward Carolina's leadership reflected the national mood.[137]

In September 1976, Patterson announced his intention to retire from the University, effective at the end of June 1977. Many faculty expressed their admiration for a man who had served the University in various positions for thirty-four years. While the consolidation of his administration had angered some whose programs were cut, Patterson had had the University's best interests at heart, and most appreciated it. A majority felt he had provided effective leadership, and under his leadership faculty gained a great deal more control over their affairs, including the establishment of a landmark policy that made faculty the primary judge in tenure and promotion issues. Faculty also gained a greater role in choosing department chairs and deans, and the USC faculty senate gained powers that few public universities in the nation granted their faculties. Also under Patterson's watch, the extensive renovations of McCutchen House turned the decrepit duplex into the Faculty House, with elaborate dining and meeting areas especially for faculty.[138]

Recalling his years as president, Patterson realized that his tenure had been filled with controversy and turbulence. As Columbia's *Record* put it, "Patterson has not been a happy university president." He realized that he would not be remembered as a dynamic leader who singlehandedly led the University to greatness. "All I've done is keep the ship afloat," he said, somewhat self-effacingly. "I've never done anything spectacular, anything you could

look back and say, 'Things were different after old Patterson came along.'"
One regret was that he never developed a close relationship with students.
But perhaps even Patterson had been too harsh a judge of his own legacy. As
assistant to the president and chief academic officer, he was known as a
behind-the-scenes operator who knew how to make things happen. Faculty
recall that Patterson was indeed "a better 'number two' man than a president," but so many of the problems Patterson dealt with as president were
not his doing, including the economic downturn of the mid-1970s that forced
the University to curtail its activities and sapped its morale. As he left office,
he expressed one final wish: "My hope," he said, "is that the state will realize
that higher education in South Carolina can be no better than its three leading universities—Clemson, the Medical University and the University of South
Carolina. These three institutions must be the pace-setters, but they must
have the support to set the pace."[139]

In the wake of Patterson's retirement announcement, the board of trustees
formed a set of committees to begin a search for his replacement. The presidential vacancy was accompanied by the usual rumors of possible candidates,
including former governor Robert E. McNair and board chairman Eston
Marchant. Neither man was interested. As usual, the search committee was
bombarded by those representing special interests. After going through the
search process once, the committee could not agree on a candidate. Upon the
recommendation of Senator Strom Thurmond and others, a primary candidate emerged in the second search process. James B. Holderman, forty-one
years old, was the former executive director of the Illinois Board of Higher
Education, former vice president of the Eli Lilly Foundation of Indiana, and
at the time he was hired, senior vice president of the Academy for Educational Development in Indianapolis, an educational consulting firm. Robert E.
McNair remembered that though Holderman was not at first at the top of the
list of candidates, he "charmed the daylights out of the board" and other University supporters. William H. Patterson spoke in favor of Holderman, declaring that he was "enormously impressed" with him, and did not feel that
Holderman "would let his ego get away with him." After a ten-month search,
on June 30, 1977, the USC board of trustees unanimously named Holderman
as USC's twenty-fifth president. Moving to Columbia with his wife Carolyn
and their three daughters, the charismatic young president assumed the duties
of the office on September 1, enthusiastic about improving the University of
South Carolina.[140]

Holderman immediately stressed what he believed should be the University's primary goals: excellence in undergraduate education and public service. Toward the first goal, he moved immediately to improve the quality of the
student body. He shook up undergraduate admissions, beginning a prospective

student touring program, adding ten new recruiters to the staff, and moving the admissions office from the supervision of the provost's office and having the admissions director report directly to the president. He stressed that the University must aggressively recruit outstanding students. Holderman noted that 80 percent of South Carolina high school students who scored 1200 or higher on the SAT went out of state to college. At Carolina in 1976, only 93 of 2,600 entering freshmen had scored over the 1200 mark on the test. These figures, he determined, must change.[141]

The new administration attracted outstanding students through a number of strategies, but the most visible was the establishment of an honors college, known as the South Carolina College. A separate administrative college with a unique curriculum for honors students had been under discussion since 1967. Such a program would be an expansion of the existing honors program that primarily offered "honors" sections of freshman- and sophomore-level courses. In the late years of Tom Jones's administration, the University's academic forward planning committee (chaired by Chester Bain and John M. Bryan) proposed the reestablishment of the South Carolina College using the concept of a "cluster college" that would integrate living and learning experiences on the Horseshoe. However, this initial plan envisioned that the South Carolina College would be open to all interested and motivated students, not just those with the highest SAT scores. Jones resigned as president, however, before any action could be taken on the committee's report.[142]

Under William H. Patterson the vision of a revived South Carolina College continued. Patterson's conception of the new South Carolina College was that it would be a cluster college, with dormitories, classrooms, and offices in the soon-to-be renovated facilities of the Horseshoe, and like the earlier plan, it would be open to all interested students. As one his first actions as president-elect, Patterson appointed a faculty committee to devise a plan for the new college. This committee was chaired by William Mould, the director of the existing honors program.[143]

Citing the same figures Holderman would later use regarding the low percentage of South Carolina students with high SAT scores who attended college in state, Mould and his committee argued that many of Carolina's best students were leaving the university for other colleges, largely because of USC's lack of academic atmosphere or a visible commitment to academic excellence. The committee's vision of the cluster college was as a selective honors college rather than one open to all students, combining a four-year program of small classes with attentive advisement and guidance, offering a curriculum incorporating all academic majors. In their vision, the honors college would provide the benefits of a small liberal arts college in the context of a large urban university. A Scholastic Aptitude Test score of 1250 (no lower than 600 on either verbal or math sections) was to be the minimum entrance requirement for the proposed college.[144]

When the committee presented its plan to the faculty, it was met with charges that an exclusive honors college smacked of elitism—"academic apartheid," some dubbed it. In the democratic atmosphere that had produced "wide-open" programs such as Contemporary University and the University Without Walls, a selective honors college was anathema to some. However, reaction to the all-inclusive programs of the early 1970s had set in. After concerted intra-University lobbying by committee members and supporters of the plan, the proposal for a separate South Carolina Honors College passed the faculty senate in early December 1975.[145]

Despite faculty approval, the University's board of trustees put the implementation of the new Honors College on hold. Patterson himself was not friendly to the idea of an exclusive honors college, and he was sensitive to the charges of elitism that the honors idea embodied. Citing the financial constraints that struck the University in the mid-1970s, the board voted to postpone implementation until either additional state funds or private financing for the plan could be secured.[146]

Soon after becoming president, James Holderman realized that the honors college idea was just the kind of program he was looking for to help improve undergraduate education and raise the profile of the University of South Carolina. He convinced the board to approve the program in December 1977, and immediately charged Mould and Peter Sederberg (who would serve as the Honors College's first "master") with implementing the plan—though at first there was little money available. Mould and Sederberg made plans for recruiting new students, securing facilities and developing a curriculum. However, the charges of elitism resurfaced, this time from students living on the Horseshoe who would be displaced by the new program. As result of this resistance, the Honors College was phased in over a three-year period. In the fall of 1978, the University of South Carolina Honors College welcomed its first freshman class, comprised of 167 students, 85 percent of whom were from South Carolina. The new program's name, the South Carolina College, and its location, the historic Horseshoe, were conscious attempts to establish links with the University's past.[147]

As the Carolina board of trustees looked to the future, they cited a history of inadequate long-term planning at the University, and within a month of James Holderman's taking office the board charged him with issuing a prospectus outlining his objectives and priorities over the next five years. Just over one hundred days after taking office, Holderman delivered to the board the first of his comprehensive planning documents, "The Carolina Plan." The major thrust of the Carolina Plan was that the University had to make a "paradigm shift" in how it conceived of itself. First, it proposed a fundamental change in the relationship between the Columbia campus of the University and its eight branch campuses.

Indeed, the problem of coordinating the sprawling, loose confederation of nine institutions known as the University of South Carolina "system" had been a chief concern of William Patterson in the latter days of his administration. Since the late 1950s, the University had developed eight extension campuses: Beaufort, Lancaster, Salkehatchie, Union, Aiken, Spartanburg, Coastal Carolina in Conway, and Sumter, the last of which the University inherited from Clemson in 1973. In response to the tremendous growth of these campuses, in 1972 the General Assembly authorized them to expand to a four-year program when their enrollment reached a student FTE of 1,000 or more. Three campuses, Aiken, Spartanburg, and Coastal Carolina, attained this mark and expanded to four-year status in 1974 and 1975, before the law allowing others to expand was repealed. Although most people referred to various campuses as a "system," it hardly functioned as one. Each campus submitted separate budget requests to the General Assembly. Improvements in physical facilities depended entirely on local support. The new four-year branches sought and had been given considerable autonomy over academics and curriculum, but in some cases, credit earned for courses on the regional campuses did not transfer to the Columbia campus, thus defeating the original purpose of the branch campuses as feeder institutions.[148] William Patterson wrote of the so-called system, "This tidy description is NOT reflected in the day-to-day realities of the President's control of the Columbia campus and his *endeavors* to control the eight others, particularly . . . the new four-year schools. (The 'system' described is one man, who is trying to exercise power over the entire operation.)"[149] In the wake of the state's decision not to establish a community college system in the late 1960s and early 1970s, the role of the USC branches in the state's overall program of higher education was still unclear and was muddied further by the creation of four-year branch campuses. The laws governing the operation of the University had been written long before the semi-autonomous regional campuses developed, and the state desperately needed to clarify the extent of the Columbia campus's jurisdiction over these rapidly expanding institutions. The relationship of the campuses with the "main" campus in Columbia was a continuing source of friction and hard feelings.[150]

Vice president for regional campuses Willard Davis and President Patterson recognized that the extension campuses, especially the new four-year campuses, were becoming increasingly successful competitors with the Columbia campus for students and scarce state funding. In response, they developed a plan under which the University's board of trustees would consolidate the system and take legal title to the regional campuses from the local commissions that had previously governed them. A single president would govern all campuses in the system. This included fiscal authority, meaning that the University would submit a lump-sum budget for the entire system. If such authority were not granted, wrote Patterson, the University might "have to get out of the Regional Campus business." Other aspects of the plan included a provision that the four-year colleges would avoid expansion into graduate studies and would remain exclusively non-residential—thus reducing the possibility that they would become competitors with the Columbia campus for programs, students, and funding. On the regional campuses, this centralization plan was seen as a counterattack on their attempts to gain more autonomy.[151] Nonetheless, in early 1977, the board decided to pursue the centralization program. When Holderman came on board in September of that year, the trustees charged him with developing a list of priorities for achieving academic excellence within the context of a centralized USC system. He submitted his list as the Carolina Plan.[152]

The Carolina Plan trumpeted the idea of a unified Carolina System—one that conceived of the University of South Carolina as more than just the Columbia campus. Holderman was an outspoken advocate of the branch and regional campus concept, and he attempted to smooth relations with the system campuses. However, following the wishes of the board, he stressed "control from the center," arguing that "the President needs to be able to exercise leadership throughout the system not only by influence and persuasion but by formal authority." The hallmark of the plan was the concept of a "unitary budget," one approved by the board of trustees, supported by local bodies, and presented to legislature on behalf of the whole. Despite the drive toward consolidation, Holderman was very conscious to not alienate the branch and regional campuses. He said, "I think that this University should be many things to many people. There is room . . . for two-year associate degree programs, for four-year bachelor's degree programs, master's level programs, Ph.D. programs, for public service and research. I don't buy the notion that one must necessarily beat out the other." He stressed that the system campuses could maintain considerable autonomy while at the same time he pushed for coordination among the branches, arguing that the various campuses should share resources, including faculty. One example was his initiative that allowed all system students to use the resources of the Thomas Cooper Library.[153]

The board of trustees promptly approved the Carolina Plan in December 1977, and Holderman set about implementing it. His first priority was the University's budget, and he set about using the "unified" approach. This approach made best use of the political ties of the various regional campuses

in their local areas for the benefit of the entire system. The goal was full funding for the entire University system under the CHE's appropriations formula,
something the University had never received from the General Assembly.[154]

The unified approach paid off, and for the first time since the CHE began
basing its budget recommendations on formulas, the University received the
full amount called for under the guidelines. The General Assembly passed
the budget over the veto of Governor James Edwards. The University community was ecstatic, since the budget represented a 13 percent increase over the
previous year. Included in the budget was money for faculty salary increases
that raised USC's average faculty salary by 13 percent—to a level that surpassed the average for all southern universities for the first time in history.[155]

The following year, the University system received nearly full-formula funding, and the levels of state support for the University were at historic highs.
From a financial standpoint, the unified system capitalized on the political
reach of the branch campuses into so many areas of the state. The system, as
a political entity, had become a reality, though as an academic system there
was more work ahead.[156]

While governmental appropriations were on the rise, Holderman and his
administration did their best to increase the University's private fund-raising

Table 5.8   State appropriations per full-time equivalent student, University of
South Carolina (Columbia campus), 1971–1980
(conversions to 1991 constant dollars)

FISCAL YEAR, ENDING JUNE 30	STATE APPROPRIATIONS (IN MILLIONS)	TOTAL FTE ENROLLMENT*	STATE APPROPRIATIONS PER FTE
1971	17.6 ($59.2)	12,954	1,361 ($4,580)
1972	22.8 ($74.3)	14,794	1,545 ($5,034)
1973	26.3 ($80.7)	16,929	1,554 ($4,767)
1974	33.7 ($93.0)	17,913	1,880 ($5,191)
1975	41.4 ($104.9)	18,341	2,258 ($5,721)
1976	43.1 ($103.2)	19,596	2,200 ($5,270)
1977	43.0 ($96.6)	19,091	2,251 ($5,057)
1978	53.9 ($112.6)	19,015	2,834 ($5,918)
1979	61.4 ($115.2)	19,910	3,082 ($5,784)
1980	71.9 ($118.9)	20,450	3,517 ($5,816)

Source: "Annual Report of the University of South Carolina," 1970–71; "Annual Report of the
South Carolina Commission on Higher Education," January 1973, January 1974, January
1975; "Self-Study, 1980, The University of South Carolina Columbia," table 4-5.
* Full-time equivalent enrollment for 1971–1973 is for fall term only.

as well. As he wrote in the Carolina Plan, "In an era of reduced flexibility of public dollars, public institutions have become increasingly dependent on the private dollar." The University had to expand the general endowment and the amount of money available for scholarships.[157] Holderman recognized that since Carolina's endowment resources were so small, he must take seriously his job as chief fund-raiser and give that issue a considerable amount of his time. He reorganized the USC Educational Foundation to include the regional campuses in not only its governance but its benefits as well. He reorganized the alumni association, restyling it the Greater USC Alumni Association, uniting the alumni groups at the branch campuses under one umbrella organization. The University also assumed control of the alumni association budget, ensuring greater cooperation between the University's own development efforts and those of the alumni association. Alumni Association membership increased from 5,400 in 1976 to 9,000 in 1978.[158] In time, the efforts of the Holderman administration to expand private resources would considerably increase the level of the University's endowment.

While developing plans and raising money, soon after taking the reigns of the University Holderman was forced to deal with a series of potentially explosive controversies in the complicated Carolina athletic department. Prior to his arrival, the board of trustees had attempted to get control of a confusing "three-headed" organization in the athletic department: in late 1976, they named Jim Carlen athletic director (a job they had allegedly promised him when he was hired in 1975), giving him control over all sports except the basketball program. Frank McGuire kept his associate athletic director title and authority over basketball, and Bo Hagen, formerly in charge of all sports save football and basketball, became the head of the newly reorganized alumni association. This new organizational structure, though an improvement, still left the president as the individual responsible for coordinating the athletic program, a difficult task since Jim Carlen and Frank McGuire were not close.[159]

In the meantime, the outspoken McGuire had developed a stormy relationship with Sol Blatt Sr. and Sol Blatt Jr. (the latter two had originally been staunch McGuire supporters). Despite the fact that Blatt Sr. was no longer Speaker of the House and Blatt Jr. was no longer on the board of trustees (he was named a federal judge in 1972), the father-son duo maintained a strong influence in Gamecock athletics. The deteriorating relationship between the Blatts and McGuire was compounded because the Blatts were friendly with McGuire's foe within the University, football coach Jim Carlen. To make matters worse for McGuire, the tremendous success of the early 1970s had ended for his teams, as had high attendance levels at basketball games. It appeared that the Blatts and other powerful decision makers were ready to see McGuire step down. Whether or not a new president could ease McGuire out of his job was a significant issue in the presidential search process during 1977.[160]

Into the tempest that raged in athletic affairs stepped an outsider, James B. Holderman. In the first months of his presidency he publicly announced a strategy to convince McGuire to step down. The coach was to cease his duties after the 1977–78 season and assume the position of athletic director of the branch campuses, with his headquarters at USC–Coastal Carolina in Conway —a move by the president not only to get McGuire out of Columbia but also to centralize control of the growing athletic programs of the USC system campuses.

The only problem with Holderman's announcement was that McGuire refused to accept the new position. The coach made his unhappiness with the situation well known. "All I want to do is coach basketball," he said, asking that he be allowed to stay on for at least two more years. The coach fumed about the Blatts, board members (particularly Marchant and Mungo), Holderman, and Carlen. Newspapers and sports pundits sided with McGuire, charging the administration and trustees with ungratefulness toward a legendary coach.[161] Students rabidly supported the coach as well, with the Gamecock's Sally Wilson writing, "As if McGuire hasn't had enough slaps in the face from University officials since the arrival of [Jim] Carlen, the offer of a Coastal Carolina job is adding insult to injury. If the board decides another coach could do a better job of improving USC's basketball program, then fire McGuire. But at least they could have the decency to make that decision instead of conniving behind the back of a coach and creating a demeaning alternative for a nationally prominent man."[162] In the face of McGuire's intransigence and overwhelming public support for the coach, Holderman retracted the offer of a "promotion" to McGuire.[163]

A month later, in January 1978, the president and board of trustees tried another strategy: they would force McGuire out by applying a newly lowered retirement age, which would ostensibly force the coach out at the end of the 1978 season. Only months previously, the board had lowered the University's mandatory retirement age from seventy to sixty-five. Fans revolted against this attempt to oust the coach. The Columbia Tip-Off Club took out a full page advertisement in the State supporting McGuire in the face of the administration's pressure and urging others to give the coach a vote of confidence. McGuire then claimed that he would not turn sixty-five in November 1978, as most had assumed, but a year later. Nonetheless, three USC professors, biologist Wade T. Batson, international studies professor Paul Blackstock, and historian Henry Lumpkin, successfully challenged the legality of the new retirement rule in court. Holderman's second attempt to force out McGuire failed, and the president committed to honoring McGuire's contract.[164]

Only weeks after this controversy simmered down, in the midst of the basketball season Holderman again tried to resolve the disarray in Carolina athletic department. This time, his strategy was to create a position with authority over the athletic programs of all USC campuses, vice president for athletic affairs, thus relieving himself of the responsibility of coordinating the athletic program. His choice to fill the position was James A. Morris, who had held numerous positions, including USC economics professor, dean of the USC College of Business Administration, vice president of the ACC, and executive director of the CHE. At the time of his appointment, Morris was acting as a labor mediator, a position that prepared him well for the acrimony in USC's athletic department. The new position reflected Holderman's vision of a unified USC system as expressed in the Carolina Plan, and even pleased Frank McGuire, who respected Morris.

The press supported Holderman's decision naming Morris, praising him as an ideal choice to rein in the conflicting egos in the department, and Holderman for finally taking decisive action to resolve the University's athletic organizational problems. However, the move did not solve the University's athletic problems, for an angry Jim Carlen insisted that his powers and authorities as athletic director were being usurped. In the ensuing dispute, Carlen hired an attorney to investigate whether Morris's appointment violated his contract. To add to the continuing controversy, the Gamecock Club, siding with Carlen, publicly disputed Morris's authority over its funds. Then, SLED and state auditors began an investigation of the athletic department's handling of concession funds. Holderman realized that the continuing athletic controversies threatened his fledgling administration. The faculty senate urged the president to "take all appropriate steps to resolve the continuing athletic controversy in such a manner that the faculty, the administration, and the public can be assured that the educational function of the University can not again be impaired by eruptions within the athletic department." Some board members were very dissatisfied with Holderman's handling of athletic matters and even considered firing the president during a contentious May 1978 trustees meeting to address the situation. The board ultimately affirmed Holderman's authority over athletic matters, but Morris's position was allowed to lapse after he resigned, handing Carlen a significant victory. Unfortunately for the new president, he had managed to alienate both Frank McGuire and Jim Carlen, as well as their supporters, in little more than six months at Carolina.[165]

In mid-1979, University officials began making inquiries to a respected all-sports athletic conference in the Southeast about joining (the board had previously voted not to join the Metro 7—a basketball-only conference— despite the wishes of many fans). The board had come to the conclusion that affiliation with an all-sports conference was in the University's best interest. However, it was also clear to them that if the University wanted to affiliate with such an organization, it would have to get its athletic house in order. To the board, this meant two things: separating the positions of athletic director and football coach, and convincing Frank McGuire to step down.[166]

In September 1979, they moved to make these two things happen. Three days before the first football game, the administration notified Jim Carlen that his contract as USC's athletic director would not be renewed when it expired at the end of 1982. Carlen responded in a controversial article in *Sports Illustrated* in which he accused the trustees of being "foolish" and disrespectfully called Holderman USC's "little ole president." Nonetheless, after Carlen's 1979 team won five straight games, the trustees extended his football coaching contract for another two years. The board then began negotiating with Frank McGuire to settle his contract and retire him from the basketball program. When word of the negotiations leaked, the entire basketball team threatened to quit if McGuire were fired. In late October, the board announced that it had reached a settlement with the coach: he would step down after the 1979–80 season and receive a settlement of $400,000 ($750,691). Students protested the move. The *Gamecock* printed a special edition covering the controversy and a crowd of some 500 students rallied in front of the President's Home in support of McGuire, but to no avail. The coach had agreed to the settlement, and at least one facet of the long-running problems in USC's athletic department was cleared up. However, the acrimony between Jim Carlen and the administration would linger into the next decade.[167]

Resolving the continuing controversies in the University's athletic administration was but one of the challenges facing President Holderman. In December 1978, Holderman presented the board of trustees with "Carolina Plan II," a more detailed five-year plan for University development built on the foundation set by the original Carolina Plan. He praised the efforts of the University community to develop system cohesion in his first year, including unitary budgeting, and faculty and library exchanges. Holderman committed the administration to continue efforts to strengthen Carolina as a university system.[168]

Carolina Plan II focused in part on improving the student body. Holderman pointed to efforts to improve the admissions office and recruiting, as well as to the new Honors College and the rising average SAT scores of USC's freshman classes. The plan stressed the University's commitment to expanding private support and fund-raising efforts as well. Holderman cited developments in the USC Educational Foundation and the Greater USC Alumni Association—such as the introduction of the Alumni Scholars program and the creation of a new national advisory committee (composed of distinguished alumni and South Carolinians who would help Carolina develop its untapped fund-raising potential) as examples of how the University would move forward in the area of private support.[169]

The most significant outcome of the 1978 "Carolina Plan II" was the articulation of the University's major mission as it moved toward the broad goal of academic excellence. In his first public comments after becoming president, Holderman noted that USC was "an excellent regional university." However, he wanted more for the institution. According to the plan, the primary mission of the University of South Carolina was to "achieve national recognition as a major public university with distinctive and high quality instructional, scholarly, and service programs."[170] Transcending its regional base and achieving national recognition was to be the most prominent theme of the University's next decade.

Carolina Plan II outlined one of the primary ways in which James Holderman would go about achieving national recognition. In it, he introduced the concept of 'Carolina as a Window to the World,' which meant that the University would make a special effort to attract eminent visitors both from home and from abroad and to develop a significant international dimension.[171] This focus on internationalism was not new to Carolina. It recalled Donald Russell's initiative to develop programs such as the department of international studies and his success in attracting the nation's leading foreign policy figures. Holderman capitalized on the foundation laid by his predecessors to again make the University of South Carolina a place with a prominent international focus. He declared that USC was on its way to becoming "a major international university."[172]

To say such things was one thing, but Holderman was able to combine the words with enormous charisma and personal charm that impressed almost everyone who met him in South Carolina. Renowned for his public speaking skills, Holderman "had an inimitable way of handling people and crowds," observers noted. "One on one, Jim Holderman could be one of the most charming people I've ever seen. . . . He made you feel like you were the only person in the room. . . . He had a dynamic personality, with what appeared to be great intellect and vision."[173]

With his charismatic personality, Holderman oozed confidence and optimism, and he used these characteristics to combat an institutional inferiority complex that had developed at the University since the early part of the century. In his 1971 inaugural address, South Carolina Governor John West had lashed out at "the tyranny of limited expectations" in the state. Clearly, though the University had made tremendous strides in the years since World War II, with exception of the growth of the 1960s, the changes had largely been incremental, not the "great leap forward" that some had proposed. More recently, withdrawing from the ACC because conference academic standards were too high hurt the University's academic reputation, and the controversies of the 1970s led to low morale—witness the student comments that Carolina was "returning to a diploma mill status." Holderman, on the other hand, told the University community *not* that it had a long way to go to become a great University, but that it already was one. He said to *Gamecock* writer Jan Easterling, "Unfortunately, some people feel that it [the University of South Carolina] isn't as good as it really is. There's some people who say we're not as good as Duke, Chapel Hill or Emory. But I think we're as good if not better than any school in the southeast. We just haven't done the best job we could of telling the story of Carolina."[174]

He made it a personal mission to tell that story. Holderman told the *Observer,* "For too long, we've had a perception of ourselves as not being a top-notch university. We didn't realize that we already had a great deal going for us."[175] After his first successful budget effort in the General Assembly, he told the alumni that the "the institution was already a quality place and now we're ready to talk about it."[176] Paraphrasing Franklin D. Roosevelt, he told the faculty, "We are on our way to greatness. Nothing can prevent that except our own reluctance."[177]

Meanwhile, the University had begun putting into action Holderman's "Window to the World" concept. Building on the prestige of the already well-known Institute for International Studies, in November 1978 the International Studies Association (the professional organization of scholars and government officials in that field) announced that it was moving its headquarters to the University of South Carolina. Holderman also trumpeted the excellence of the Master's in International Business Studies, one of the best programs of its kind in the nation.

In 1978 he began to turn his personal magnetism toward the goal of attracting prestigious international visitors to Carolina. With the one hundredth birthday of former secretary of state James F. Byrnes approaching in the spring of 1979, Holderman and USC officials seized on the anniversary as an ideal opportunity to bring world leaders to the campus. Capitalizing on personal acquaintances in the United Nations, Holderman managed to attract United Nations Secretary General Kurt Waldheim in April 1979, United States Secretary of Defense Harold Brown in May, and West German Chancellor Helmut Schmidt in June, all as part of the Byrnes Centennial celebration.[178]

These visits raised the University's profile, but Holderman scored potentially his biggest coup in late 1978 when he secured a commitment from Egyptian president and Nobel Peace Prize winner Anwar Sadat, near the zenith of his world stature and influence, to visit the campus at some point in 1979. Carolina scientists struck up a relationship with the Egyptian president as a result of an ongoing study by the Earth Sciences and Resources Institute. Since the mid-1970s, the Institute had been overseeing a geologic study of rock formations in North Africa with the help of a $5 million ($11,234,483) grant from the National Science Foundation. Through connections made during this project, a delegation of USC officials led by Provost Frank Borkowski visited Sadat and extended an invitation for him and his wife, Jihan, to come to Columbia to receive honorary degrees. They accepted. Holderman and the USC administration began to make plans for the visit, enlisting the help of prominent South Carolina leaders, including Governor Richard Riley. Holderman's strategy of using high-profile visits to promote the University worked. They not only generated publicity but secured the support of local officials. The proposed Sadat visit, Holderman said, would have "a tremendous effect on the University. It will put us on the map and underline what we are trying to do."[179] Anwar Sadat never made a visit—as a result of ongoing problems in the Middle East and, later, his 1981 assassination. However, along with the visits by Schmidt, Waldheim, and Brown, Sadat's acceptance of the USC invitation demonstrated that the institution was being recognized as "on the map."

The University had indeed come a long way to reach the point where it felt it was being recognized for excellence. A difficult decade of student, political, and athletic controversy culminated with these high-profile visits. The anxious period of adjustment had come to a conclusion on a high note. The University had grown so fast since 1960 that the institution needed time to adjust. By the end of the decade the institution and its people had learned how function as a "megaversity."

The last years of the 1970s were a turning point for Carolina. James B. Holderman's infectious enthusiasm led students and faculty to believe what he told them: they really were part of an excellent institution. In mid-1979, a *Gamecock* writer, noting the visits of foreign dignitaries, also wrote that "USC is rapidly becoming a leader in academics, and the educational opportunities have vastly improved from those of just a few years ago." She was "encouraged by the recent trend toward establishing academic excellence at what was once jokingly referred to as a 'party school.'"[180]

As of late 1979, though objective criteria really did not support the contention that the University had made any great leaps since the mid-1970s, the psychological upturn was indeed striking. The Carolina community had begun to believe in itself. It was learning to overcome "the tyranny of limited expectations." The "paradigm shift" that Holderman had begun to affect applied to more than just the new concept that the University's various campuses were a unified system; it also involved a reconceptualization of Carolina's place in the world of higher education in the minds of its faculty, its students, and the people of South Carolina. In the next decade Carolina would ride a roller coaster of success and embarrassment, and the entire University community would be confronted with a dilemma: was the paradigm shift that began on the late 1970s real, or was it merely created by the charisma of James B. Holderman?

6 | A GILDED DECADE?

1980–1990

I want us to roll off people's tongues automatically when they talk about the best universities. Michigan, Stanford, Harvard, Yale and the University of South Carolina. That's where I want to be.

James B. Holderman, 1986

For USC, the 1980s could be referred to as a remake of the old western movie *The Good, the Bad and the Ugly.*

Jeff Wilson, the *Gamecock,* 15 January 1990

■

The 1873 novel *The Gilded Age* by Mark Twain and Charles Dudley Warner ridiculed the graft and corruption of post–Civil War Washington, D.C. It described a period in which opportunists of all stripes sought to take financial advantage of the federal government's efforts to rebuild the South following the war—skimming off federal dollars meant to benefit destitute black southerners only recently freed from slavery. The novel gave its name to the era, a time, according to historian George Tindall, rife with "jobbery, profiteering and false glitter."

At the University of South Carolina in the 1980s, several scandals led some to conclude that the decade was a "gilded age"—a time of profiteering, superficiality, and false glitter. Highly publicized illegalities and financial excesses of USC's administration and athletic department left the University's reputation temporarily in tatters. As part of an era of excess that included national scandals such as Iran-Contra, insider trading on Wall Street, the collapse of the savings and loan industry, and the "Lost Trust" corruption scandal in South Carolina's own state house, the controversies involving the behavior of James B. Holderman and others in his administration were not isolated, but they unquestioningly left a black mark on the public's perception of the University of South Carolina.[1]

Despite Holderman's very public fall, there were those who adamantly defended his administration and insisted that the 1980s were the best decade in the University's history. His supporters cited unprecedented successes in fund-raising, the manifold increases in scholarships and endowed faculty chairs, the procession of national and international leaders and celebrities who visited the campus, the building of a unified University system, the raising of the University's international profile, and the overall sense of enthusiasm and confidence Holderman brought. He declared that the University of South Carolina could be one of the world's top ten universities. With flash and pomp, he taught the University of South Carolina to believe in itself and raise its aspirations, his defenders argued.[2]

There is no question that James Holderman was a dynamic, controversial figure who elicited intense emotion on the USC campus and in South Carolina. His administration left a lasting impact on the University. Was this merely a gilded decade, or was it a watershed period in which Carolina built the foundation necessary for the institution to join the ranks of the nation's prominent research universities? Whatever the passionate arguments of Holderman's defenders and detractors, it must be remembered that the University of South Carolina was far more than "Jim" Holderman, and that for better or worse the institution made strides during the 1980s that determined much of the direction it took as it looked toward the twenty-first century.

The University of South Carolina during the 1980s was shaped not only by the plans of the USC administration (as expressed in two Carolina Plans, and later, the 2001 Plan), but also in the context of the South Carolina Commission on Higher Education's *Master Plan for Higher Education,* which the General Assembly approved during the spring of 1980. The CHE's ultimate goal was to streamline higher education and eliminate duplication, a goal of state policymakers since the Peabody Report of 1946. The *Master Plan,* an overall blueprint for South Carolina's public colleges and universities, was a first for South Carolina. It called for a more activist CHE, closely involved in administration and governance. The General Assembly authorized the CHE to recommend the elimination of academic programs, and the *Master Plan* attempted to delineate the missions of each individual state-supported campus in South Carolina. According to the *Master Plan,* the Columbia campus of the University of South Carolina was "to place its major emphasis and resources on the improvement of its graduate and professional programs in business, law, education and the liberal arts and sciences."[3]

President Holderman and other USC leaders expressed serious reservations about the *Master Plan,* since in some ways it conflicted with their vision of what the University should be. They were uncomfortable with a more powerful CHE, now empowered to review degree programs at all public institutions with the authority to recommend elimination. The most immediate threat the *Master Plan* and an activist CHE presented to USC was a scaling back of programs that were duplicated at other institutions in South Carolina, most notably the School of Engineering, the School of Medicine, and the associate's degree programs in the College of General Studies—all of which had been notably absent from the *Master Plan*'s recommendations for emphasis and improvement at Carolina. Each of these programs had drawn considerable political attacks at various times in previous decades because of the apparent duplication of state effort they represented.[4]

Acting upon the recommendations of the *Master Plan* and a consultants' study, in late 1980 the CHE asserted that USC should terminate seven associate's degree programs in the College of General Studies. The programs were an unnecessary duplication of programs already offered at Midlands Technical College in Columbia, the CHE argued. Their consultants' report had noted the problems created when a flagship research university tried to provide both high-quality graduate and research programs while at the same time offering community college–level services.[5]

The proposal sparked a bruising political battle that pitted the University against the CHE. President Holderman and the supporters of the associate's programs opposed any trimming, claiming that to phase out the programs would lower the number of black students at Carolina, since they made up some 25 percent of the students in the associates degree programs. They appealed the CHE recommendation—testing for the first time the CHE's expanded powers—and unleashed the full force of the University's lobbying machine. The administration seized the opportunity presented when the General Assembly invited USC football star George Rogers to appear before a joint session in order to honor his accomplishments. Rogers won the prestigious Heisman Trophy in the fall of 1980, and was also a student in the College of General Studies. While accepting the congratulations of legislators, Rogers used the occasion to laud the General Studies program. "If it wasn't for General Studies," he told them, "there would be no George Rogers and no Heisman Trophy either." The CHE charged the University with spreading misinformation about its goals—it wanted to phase out only the associate's degrees, not the entire College of General Studies or any of the regional campuses, as some had claimed. Governor Richard Riley weighed in on the issue, supporting the CHE's position and its new powers, claiming that CHE decisions should be upheld for South Carolina to have a rational, coordinated system of higher education. In the end, the General Assembly instead upheld the University's appeal, saving the associate's degree programs.[6]

CHE Chairman James E. Bostic and member Fred Sheheen both blamed their defeat on the University's superior lobbying efforts. The incident demonstrated that despite the CHE's new powers, in dealing with the University its power to enforce rulings was limited. It also showed the ruthless determination of James B. Holderman when challenged. The episode foreshadowed a decade of acrimony between Holderman and the CHE over the authority to direct the future of the University of South Carolina. Ironically, only two years later the University agreed to phase out the associate's degree programs it had fought so hard to save, when severe budget constraints forced the University to cut back its academic programs. Nonetheless, Holderman had powerfully demonstrated the inherent weakness of South Carolina's Commission on Higher Education.[7]

The degree of the University of South Carolina's success in the 1980s had a great deal to do with the financial support the institution received. After a period of substantial growth in both student enrollment and state funding during the 1960s and early 1970s, the 1980s saw much slower increases in state appropriations and steady levels of FTE enrollment. While the CHE's funding formula determined budget requests, only once (1984–85) did the General Assembly fully fund the University according to the formula. In other years, the percentage of the full formula appropriated fluctuated between the low 80s to the high 90s, and for the decade it averaged 92 percent.[8]

As a result, the fiscal hallmark of the 1980s was a steady decrease in the percentage of the University's total revenue funded by state appropriations and a corresponding increase in the proportion funded by student tuition and fees. In 1981, state appropriations made up nearly 52 percent of the overall budget. By 1990, this figure had fallen to 45 percent. On the other hand, student fees, which comprised approximately 14.5 percent of the budget in 1981, made up nearly 23 percent in 1990. They led President Holderman to declare that the University of South Carolina was "in reality state *assisted* rather than state *supported*."[9]

There were tight financial years during the early 1980s as administrators strove to keep up momentum while state support failed to match the University's growth and ambitions. Nationwide, state appropriations for higher education declined in real terms in the late 1970s and early 1980s, and during the first four years of the decade USC's revenue stagnated, and actually declined in 1982–83 (in real terms). The following year, the University faced "the most severe fiscal crisis of modern times," according to President Holderman. Administrators claimed that USC faced a $13.5 million ($17.7 million) deficit. They chose to phase out certain programs rather than impose across-the-board cuts. Among the programs they eliminated were the undergraduate program in education (it was replaced with a five-year degree program), the seven associate's degree programs in the College of General Studies, and the undergraduate health education program, and a transfer of the degree programs in media arts to the College of Applied Professional Sciences (the new name for the College of General Studies—renamed in 1982). These cutbacks represented the first substantial program cuts since the runaway growth of the 1960s and early 1970s. An *Observer* headline read: "Heady Era Ends as USC Starts Cutting Back."[10]

The administration and the board of trustees resorted to one primary strategy to maintain revenue growth: raising student tuition and fees. Student fees increased three times faster than state appropriations in the 1980s. For in-state undergraduates, tuition and fees increased from $1,040 to $2,448 (63% in real terms). Meanwhile, state appropriations per FTE student increased from $3,407 to $5,900 (20.4% in real terms).[11]

While USC students and their parents were saddled with a larger share of the cost of operating the University of South Carolina, the Holderman administration moved forward with its plans for national and international prominence. One of the chief goals of the administration's planning documents, the Carolina Plans, had been a consolidation of the disparate university campuses into a system. In addition to unified system budgeting, internal reorganization stressed autonomy in local management but fostered system cohesion. Clear lines of authority were established. The titles of the senior administrators on the four-year campuses were redesignated from "vice president" to "chancellor," and they reported directly to the University president. The two-year campuses, formerly called "centers" or "branches," were now called "University campuses," and reported to a single vice president for regional campuses. The leaders of the various USC campuses began to meet regularly, and, combined with the steps taken during the late 1970s, by the middle of the decade the University of South Carolina had developed the hallmarks of a real University "system."[12]

While developing system cohesion was a primary interest in the late 1970s and early 1980s, President Holderman's most conspicuous impact at Carolina was his effort to raise the University of South Carolina's national profile. He sought to improve the institution's public perception, cast away a history of low expectations, and build the image of the University. His strategy for doing this was directly related to the declaration that USC would become a "window to the world." He told the faculty in 1982, "The international focus which we have sought to bring to Carolina has attracted attention both here and around the world."[13] He stressed that South Carolina was already an internationally-oriented state, with some 25 percent of the state's economy coming from international investment.[14] By linking the University's international curriculum with the state's existing foreign economic base, he set about building the University's image around its international programs. Continuing a trend begun in the late 1970s, a series of national and international visitors raised USC's profile and created an impression that the University was indeed "on the rise" and worthy of international attention. Holderman put his boundless energy and enormous charisma to work reaching his singular goal for the University of South Carolina: a national reputation as a top university.[15]

In January 1980, USC hosted Jiang Zemin, at the time Chinese ambassador to the U.S. (and future Chinese premier). In February, Carolina hosted a debate for Republican presidential hopefuls in the days before South Carolina's primary election, welcoming future presidents Ronald Reagan and George Bush among other presidential candidates.[16] The University's international focus took off with the establishment of the James F. Byrnes International Center in 1980 under the direction of Professor James A. Kuhlman. The office was designed to coordinate the international activities and programs of all nine USC campuses and extend USC's international outreach. As part of the Byrnes Center's inaugural year, Carolina hosted numerous diplomatic figures from around the world, including French ambassador H. E. F. De Laboulaye, Jihan Sadat (the wife of Egyptian president Anwar Sadat), British foreign minister Lord Carrington, and Australian prime minister Malcom Fraser. USC welcomed one international personality after another to speak at lectures and colloquia, among them former secretary of state Henry Kissinger, Japanese trade minister Shintaro Abe, West German ambassador Peter Hermes, Dominican Republic president Salvador Jorge Blanco, and Chaing Zemin for two additional visits. In late 1981, President Holderman was elected chairman of the U.S. national commission for the United Nations Educational, Scientific and Cultural Organization (UNESCO). He claimed that his election reflected the national and international stature of Carolina's academic programs and outstanding students and faculty. In June 1982, USC hosted a special meeting of the UNESCO national commission, welcoming ninety-three leaders from around the world to evaluate the future of the organization. The international dimension had brought a new atmosphere to the University.[17]

An early high-water mark in this lineup of world leaders was the visit to USC by President Ronald Reagan in September of 1983, when former USC president and then federal judge Donald S. Russell presented Reagan with an honorary degree. In front of an estimated crowd of 8,500 gathered on the Horseshoe, President Holderman called the occasion "one of the most important and cherished moments in our [USC's] history." It was, declared Holderman, "the first time in our 182 years that an incumbent president of the United States has been given an honorary degree by the University."[18]

By this time Carolina had begun sponsoring high-profile conferences of national and world leaders. In May 1983, a conference of leading journalists brought U.S. trade representative William Brock, Sir Roy Denman (the head of a delegation from the Commission of the European Community), Yoshio Okawara (Japanese ambassador to the U.S.), and Allan Gottlieb (Canadian ambassador to the U.S.). In September 1983, another conference on the security of democratic nations brought another round of visits from western ambassadors.[19]

More conferences brought more big names to the University. A major July 1984 conference of Caribbean heads of state brought President Reagan back to the campus for the second time in a year.[20] A November 1984 conference on nuclear arms control brought the leaders in that field to Columbia. In October 1985, a USC-sponsored conference on strengthening the NATO Alliance brought vice president George Bush and NATO secretary-general Lord Carrington. At that conference Bush declared that USC was the United States' equivalent of Vienna or Geneva. The USC community was proud of the recognition these conferences and visits brought; Charles Kegley, chairman of the USC advisory council, said in the wake of the Bush visit, "Coming out of this conference these people will have USC on their minds and that can be invaluable in terms of improving the stature of our university."[21] George Bush made a return visit to the campus in May of 1990, this time as president, to deliver the commencement address.

The effort to bring attention to the University through international exposure also manifested itself in the creation of distinguished visiting professorships that attracted national and international figures to USC's classrooms. Among those who taught in the distinguished visiting professor program were Lyn Nofziger (a former top aide to President Reagan), William Brock (U.S. trade representative), Jihan Sadat (wife of the slain Egyptian president Anwar Sadat), Yoshio Okawara (former Japanese ambassador to the U.S.), journalists Robert MacNeil and James Lehrer (co-anchors of the PBS news program "The MacNeil/Lehrer News Hour") and Howard Simons (a former managing editor of the *Washington Post*).[22] Lawrence Eagleberger, a veteran diplomat and future secretary of state in the Bush administration, served as a distinguished visiting professor before accepting the post of chief executive officer of the Byrnes International Center in 1985, a job created so that he could help bring even more international exposure to the campus.[23]

Another facet of the effort to increase international exposure was the development of international exchange programs. The University signed some 52 foreign exchange agreements between 1978 and 1986. They included a much-publicized agreement with Shanxi University in China, the first between a U.S. university and a Chinese provincial university (a relationship begun as a result of the USC visits by Jiang Zemin, a Shanxi native).[24]

International exchanges and guest diplomats brought exposure for the University, and paralleled Holderman's attraction of celebrities from cultural realms as well. He struck up relationships with actors Helen Hayes, Jimmy Stewart, Michael York, Richard Thomas, Michael Keaton, and Cicely Tyson;

composers John Williams and Andrew Lloyd-Webber; comedians Bill Cosby and Danny Kaye; journalists Walter Cronkite, Robert McNeil, and Jim Lehrer; and media mogul Michael Eisner—all of whom made visits to the USC campus (many for honorary degrees or to participate in classes). Holderman attracted Hollywood actor Robby Benson, who taught film at USC for two years in the late 1980s. He also brought intellectual celebrities such as William F. Buckley, Alex Haley, and Carl Sagan to the campus.[25]

While visits by diplomats and celebrities exhilarated many in the University community, the apex of Holderman's efforts to attract prestigious guests was the September 1987 visit by Pope John Paul II. Holderman had sought a papal visit since he first arrived on campus. By cultivating a relationship with Columbia native and Chicago archbishop Cardinal Joseph Bernardin (who received a USC honorary degree in 1982), he was able to work out a Columbia stop on the Pope's 1987 U.S. visit. In preparation, the University held a year-long observance of an "ecumenical year," and welcomed world religious leaders such as the Reverend Billy Graham, the Most Reverend Robert Runcie (archbishop of Canterbury), and Archbishop Iakovos (head of the Greek Orthodox Church in North and South America).

The Pope's visit was the highlight of the ecumenical year observance. Appearing on the Horseshoe in front of a crowd of more than 10,000, John Paul II told the crowd, "It is wonderful to be young, it is wonderful to be a student in the university, it is wonderful to be young and a student at the University of South Carolina." After an hour-long meeting with twenty-six American Protestant and Eastern Orthodox leaders in the President's House (a meeting which the Pope declared would have the effect, "with God's grace, of breaking down the barriers of misunderstanding that have plagued us for centuries"), the Pope proceeded to Williams-Brice Stadium for a service, which also included Protestant leaders, in front of a crowd of some 60,000. The papal visit brought more worldwide attention to the University of South Carolina than any other single event in its history.[26]

Holderman's international focus had USC "riding high." David H. Rembert, USC faculty senate chairman, said that as a result of all the visits, USC had been exposed to the international community, "but more importantly, the international community now knows something about the University of South Carolina." Charles A. Brooks, who in late 1986 was the acting executive director of the CHE, said, "Jim Holderman has succeeded in making the country and the world aware that USC exists. If you're going to make the institution more than a regional institution, you've got to do the things Holderman's done."[27]

As dramatic as these visits were, the University was making strides in other areas. Among the most notable changes came in its demographics. Beginning in 1981, women began to make up a majority of USC's overall student body, and by 1990 nearly 56 percent of Columbia campus students were female. In addition, as Holderman attempted to lead Carolina into the ranks of the nation's major research universities, the percentage of the total student body who were graduate students rose some 34 percent, while the number of undergraduates declined more than 15 percent. The decrease in the proportion of undergraduate students was due to several factors, including increased emphasis on graduate study and research, elimination of the associate's degree programs, and the overall demographic trend in student-age population (which had begun to decline for the first time since the early 1950s). Nonetheless USC proved popular with prospective students, and despite the demographic changes, by 1989 the University received some 52 percent more undergraduate applications than it did in 1984.[28]

As the size of the undergraduate population shrank, the quality of the students themselves gradually improved. This was due in part to an agreement struck in 1984 between the CHE and all eight of South Carolina's senior colleges to set minimum admissions requirements for entering freshmen, and in part due to the larger applicant pools.[29] Between 1975 and 1986, the average high school class rank of incoming freshman rose from the top 31 percent to the top 18 percent. The average SAT score for all entering freshmen increased from 928 in 1979 to 974 in 1988. Still, USC's average SAT score trailed that of other state schools such as Clemson (which had an average SAT score in 1988 of 1020 for entering in-state freshmen), but as one presidential report described the Carolina's approach to admissions: "It is not the University's policy to play 'catch-up' to other schools on the matter of SAT averages. Average scores tend to be higher at smaller institutions that cater to a select segment of the population. USC however, encompasses a large and diverse student body, serving the disadvantaged as well as the gifted."[30]

Table 6.1   Student population at the University of South Carolina, 1980–1990 (total headcount figures)

YEAR (FALL)	TOTAL ENROLLMENT	UNDERGRAD. ENROLLMENT	% OF TOTAL UNDERGRAD.	GRADUATE ENROLLMENT*	% OF TOTAL ENROLL GRADUATE
1980	26,135	18,969	73%	7,166	27%
1985	23,263	15,089	65%	8,174	35%
1990	25,613	16,017	63%	9,596	37%

Source: Denham, ed., The University of South Carolina Statistical Profiles, 1984–85, 24; 1991–92, 28.

* Includes law, doctor of pharmacy, and medical students as well as graduate school.

The highly touted South Carolina College (the University's honors college) was one way the University served the gifted. Participants in the program had average SAT scores of 1252 by 1990. The honors college grew from 396 students in 1980–81 to 687 in 1989–90. The proportion of South Carolina College students from South Carolina increased from 73 percent in 1984–85 (earliest data) to 86 percent in 1989–90, indicating that the college was fulfilling its purpose, that of keeping more of South Carolina's best students in the state. The honors college, with its "Ivy League" standards, had begun to develop a strong reputation.[31]

South Carolina College indeed attracted outstanding students. Among them was Arthur Tai, a native of Taiwan who moved to Lugoff at age five and grew up in that town. He entered USC as a Carolina Scholar in 1978, a member of the Honors College's first class. Graduating in 1981 with a degree in international studies, Tai became USC's eighth recipient of a Rhodes Scholarship, in 1982. He said that USC's international emphasis was very important to him. "I feel like it's gone a long way toward giving Carolina a cogent identity. One thing I've always been concerned about is that people have a sense at Carolina that they're not good enough. We are a good school. We just have to have people who believe in that and work toward it."[32] Tai was not the only USC Rhodes scholar in the 1980s; USC-Spartanburg graduate Daniel Dreisbach won a Rhodes Scholarship in 1980. These were the first USC students to win the prestigious scholarships since 1924, and were proof that the quality of Carolina's students was improving.[33]

While South Carolina College served USC's gifted students, the 1980s saw the development of a new program to encourage the development of students who had the ability to do college-level work but who failed to meet the University's minimum entrance requirements. Through the new Provisional Year program, underachieving students were given remedial training and close faculty attention. Established in the College of Applied Professional Sciences in 1984 and limited to 250 students per year, the Provisional Year helped between 70 and 80 percent of its students successfully enter a degree-granting program in their sophomore year, students who otherwise would not have been admitted to Carolina.[34]

Other new programs broadened the possibilities of a Carolina undergraduate education. New bachelor's degree programs in the College of Applied Professional Sciences included hotel, restaurant and tourism administration, and retailing. New offerings in the University's other schools and colleges included undergraduate degrees in statistics, real estate, pharmacy, computer science, and computer engineering.[35]

A new Bachelor of Fine Arts degree in theatre complemented much improved offerings in that field. After a critical 1985 report from the CHE on the state of USC's theatre program, administrators launched a drive to improve it. The report noted that USC's theatre program lacked anything unique or unusual that made it especially attractive, and it lacked an affiliation with a professional theatre. If USC's program in theatre was to earn accreditation from the National Association of Student Theaters, affiliation was essential.

With the help of actress Helen Hayes (a Washington, D.C. native and a close friend of President Holderman), in 1986 the University announced a partnership with the Folger Shakespeare Theatre in Washington. The program was mutually beneficial, as the Folger Theatre was in financial difficulty and in danger of closing. In return for their affiliation, USC would pay the theatre some $300,000 ($372,769) per year for eight years. For USC's part, its students received the opportunity to apprentice or intern at the theatre, and Folger professionals would regularly teach as adjunct faculty at Carolina. Despite significant financial problems, the program was a rousing success. Thomas P. Cooke, chairman of the Department of Theatre and Speech, wrote in 1987, "I cannot stress adequately the importance of our association with the Shakespeare Theatre at the Folger. . . . This kind of bold and imaginative action has made it possible for us to gain national attention and respect." By mid-1989, some 29 students had done internships with the Folger and 11 had participated in at least one full professional performance. Many of these students returned to USC to teach. The program improved the USC theatre program to such a degree that some of the nation's best theatre students began to seek out USC's classical theatre training.[36]

The subject of undergraduate education received special attention during the mid-1980s as questions arose about the University's commitment to teaching while it was striving to become a prominent research university. One college dean expressed the worry that undergraduate education had become "a poor step child" as Carolina moved to expand research and advanced study. Nonetheless, many faculty remained committed to undergraduate teaching. A department chair wrote anonymously that many supported undergraduate education, even though "in many instances" to do so was "dangerous to their professional career."[37]

A special presidential commission appointed in 1984 and chaired by law school dean Harry Lightsey agreed that this sentiment was a problem, stating that "the lack of rewards for excellent teaching has placed research in direct competition with teaching," but that both teaching and research were "essential to the vitality of the institution." It concluded that USC should take steps to improve the quality of undergraduate education (in part by instituting a common core for all academic programs, implemented in the fall of 1988) while at the same time maintaining broad access for South Carolina's citizens.[38]

The University continued to be a national leader in the development of programs to improve undergraduates' freshman year of college. In 1986 Carolina established the National Center for the Study of the Freshman Year Experience as a clearinghouse for information on the freshman year. Under the direction of John N. Gardner, the program hosted annual national and international conferences, spreading the knowledge gained through fifteen years of experience in the University 101 course.[39]

For all of USC's undergraduates, the 1980s brought significant changes to student life. One of the biggest changes came with the nationwide movement in the mid-1980s to raise the minimum legal drinking age from 18 to 21. With the new law, more than 70 percent of Carolina undergraduates were not old enough to drink, and the campus had to adjust. The legal change meant that University officials had to become as actively involved with enforcement of alcohol laws as they had been with drug laws. Dean of student affairs Dennis Pruitt put into place strict new rules regarding alcohol consumption and possession on campus. This action eliminated University-sanctioned events at which underage drinking could occur, such as the concerts and outdoor parties that had become staples of Carolina student life. *Gamecock* editor Linda Taylor wrote, "In the past, on campus, a party generally wasn't a party without alcohol." After the mid-1980s, any party on campus at which alcohol was served was subject to strict regulations, including registration with the office of student affairs and the University police. The Golden Spur in the Russell House, home to on-campus beer sales since 1973, closed in the wake of the drinking-age change. With the closing of the Golden Spur and the elimination of the public parties and outdoor concerts that had brought the University community together, students went behind closed doors to drink surreptitiously, or in other cases obtained fake IDs that gained them entrance into local bars. The drinking-age change further fragmented the University campus community, as it drove a great deal of student socializing off-campus.[40]

The new drinking age affected Greek social life profoundly. Rush parties were now "dry," and the new regulations ended a tradition of Thursday night parties on McBryde Quadrangle. To avoid the University's strict regulations, Greek organizations, like independents, began to move their parties off-campus to local bars, which then assumed legal responsibility for enforcing drinking laws. Dean of student life Jerry Brewer admitted that he was concerned about the off-campus drinking but commented that if the organizations were "going to engage in illegal activity, I'm glad they're gone." Because of the expense of renting a local establishment, Greek organizations held fewer parties than they had had before the legal change.[41]

In spite of the changes in laws, during the 1980s the Greek system showed strong signs of recovery from the decline of the late 1960s and early 1970s.

In the early 1980s, the Greeks made a comeback in campus politics (from which they had been shut out since the early 1970s). The Interfraternity Council (IFC) and Panhellenic Association established a "primary system" to produce a slate of Greek candidates for office, which ensured that Greek organizations voted as a bloc. Though this primary system did not ensure election for Greek candidates, it did mean that Greeks once again became active in campus politics.[42]

Another important development in Carolina's Greek system was racial desegregation of the primary governing bodies for Greeks. The IFC and Panhellenic Association had been whites-only organizations since 1976, when the black fraternities and sororities left those organizations to form the Panhellenic Council. Through the efforts of Greek leaders, student body president Kelvin Stroble and Dean Pruitt, by the fall of 1986 the Greek governing bodies, if not the chapters themselves, once again became fully integrated. For a university that had one of the highest black populations among the nation's historically white state institutions (some 15 percent of undergraduates and 9 percent of graduate students in 1991), this was a significant development.[43]

Changes in visitation arrangements in the dormitories became a hot issue in the late 1980s. Though only 7,000 of Carolina's nearly 25,000 students (28 percent) lived on campus, the issue of the University's permissive visitation regulations became intertwined with the rise of the Christian Coalition in state politics. In the late 1980s, Mike Fair, an ex officio trustee and state legislator from Greenville (and a self-described religious conservative), recommended that the University eliminate all overnight opposite-sex visitation in USC dormitories. He believed that unlimited visitation encouraged sex outside of marriage; USC's liberal visitation rules, Fair said, encouraged an "open, promiscuous environment." As a result of such conservative activism, in spite of student protests, in April 1989 the board of trustees approved a plan that banned all overnight opposite-sex visitation for freshmen, and would ultimately eliminate it for all students by the 1992–93 school year.[44]

The new visitation regulations initially applied to two freshman dormitories, one each for men and women (Burney and Douglas), where all opposite-sex visitation was prohibited; students were given a voluntary choice of living in these dorms. However, only 36 of the 2,900 incoming freshmen opted to live there, and the dorms were subsequently filled with some 465 students who had requested other arrangements but were offered no other option. These students protested loudly, and by the spring semester 1990 the board relented, liberalizing the rules in all except one floor in each dorm. The ban on overnight visitation in all dorms stood, however, further encouraging students to move off-campus. The board ultimately returned to the president the authority to set dormitory visitation regulations. The effort to bring back in loco parentis at Carolina met with only limited success.[45]

For the University's graduate students, on-campus student life issues were not as pressing a concern. Carolina was committed to developing strong graduate programs in a wide range of fields. Throughout the 1980s, as USC sought to develop a national reputation as a graduate research institution, the Graduate School continued the phenomenal growth that began in the early 1960s (see table 6.2). Carolina added some twenty-five new graduate degrees during the decade. Twelve were master's-level programs in subjects including hotel, restaurant and tourism administration, creative writing, religious studies, theatre, electrical and computer engineering, genetic counseling, and earth resources management. Thirteen doctoral-level programs were added as well, in fields such as health, sociology, geography, music education, biomedical science, social work, and computer science. Overall, by 1990 the University offered master's degrees in eighty-nine fields and doctorates in fifty-four. No other state university in the Southeast had as large a graduate school or as high a proportion of graduate students as Carolina (see table 6.3) This was largely due to the high number of part-time graduate students in the College of Education. In FTE comparisons of numbers of graduate students, Carolina still trailed many of its peers (including the Universities of North Carolina and Virginia). Nonetheless, these figures demonstrate the transformation of the University of South Carolina in the post–World War II period. Prior to World War II, Carolina had had one of the smallest graduate schools in the South, but with the shift to an industrial economy, graduate programs took on increased importance as the University's role as a service center for the economy expanded (see table 1.1).[46]

Table 6.2 Growth of the University of South Carolina's Graduate School, 1940–1990 (total headcount figures)*

YEAR	GRADUATE SCHOOL ENROLLMENT	% OF OVERALL ENROLLMENT
1940	75	4
1950	586	16
1960	318	6
1970	2,006	14
1980	6,274	24
1990	8,453	33

Source: Denham, ed., The University of South Carolina Statistical Profiles, 1991–92, 3–4.
* Figures do not include students in postbaccalaureate professional schools in law, medicine, or doctor of pharmacy.

Table 6.3 Graduate enrollment in selected southern universities, fall 1991
(total headcount figures; includes both part-time and full-time students)*

UNIVERSITY	GRADUATE SCHOOL ENROLLMENT	PERCENT OF OVERALL ENROLLMENT
Univ. of South Carolina (Columbia)	8,886	34
Univ. of Virginia	4,615	26
Univ. of North Carolina (Chapel Hill)	5,710	24
Univ. of Kentucky	4,814	20
Univ. of Georgia	5,315	19
Univ. of Florida	6,757	19
Louisiana State Univ. (Baton Rouge)	4,643	17
Univ. of Alabama (Tuscaloosa)	3,222	16
Univ. of Mississippi	1,741	16

Source: American Universities and Colleges, 14th ed. (New York: Walter De Gruyer and the American Council on Education, 1992).
* Figures do not include students in postbaccalaureate professional schools.

Among Carolina's graduate programs, probably the most highly praised was the Master's in International Business Studies, which consistently placed among the top programs of its kind in the country. In rankings of such programs, USC's M.I.B.S. frequently bested those from Harvard, Columbia, the University of Pennsylvania, and New York University. Another graduate program receiving recognition was chemistry, which in 1989 ranked 17th in the nation in the number of Ph.D.s produced and 33d in federal support for research. It far surpassed any other USC department in the production of Ph.D.s. In the early 1980s the department was cited by the National Academy of Sciences and the American Council on Education as one of the six most improved in the country. USC's marine science program also earned high praise, helping it to earn a place among the top five such programs nationwide. Other Carolina programs receiving recognition for excellence were English, public health, geosciences, mathematics, physics, economics, history, international studies, and psychology.[47]

The drive to become a major graduate research university meant the institution had to significantly increase its funding for research and sponsored programs. With the help of the Office of Sponsored Programs and Research (SPAR), the University's faculty did just that. Between 1979–80 and 1988–89, total funding for all research, training, and service projects more than doubled (going from $19 million [$31.4 million] to nearly $41 million [$45 million] and increasing some 42 percent in real terms). The growth of research and scholarly activity was also reflected in a 72.4 percent increase in the number of active grants (580 in 1979–80 to 1000 in 1988–89). Federal funding for University-based projects increased 98 percent in real terms and made up some 71 percent of total research funding in 1988–89. Federal funding remained the major source for research grants, and included agencies such as the National Science Foundation, the National Institutes of Health, the Department of Defense, and the Department of Education.[48]

In addition, internal sources of funding for research grew as well. The Carolina Venture Fund was one new source. The Venture Fund began in 1984 as a project of the Carolina Research and Development Foundation, which began to sell off its remaining real estate properties and made a concerted move to become more involved with supporting research at USC. The Venture Fund awarded approximately $100,000 ($131,054) per year for research. Venture Fund grants were intended to be used as seed money to nurture scholarly activity that had the potential to later tap larger funding sources.[49]

Another important new source of funding came from the state-sponsored Cutting Edge legislation passed in 1988. Among the provisions of the Cutting Edge program were a Governor's Professor of the Year award for faculty from state-supported colleges, funding for endowed faculty chairs, a new merit-based scholarship program for the state's brightest students (the Palmetto Fellows), and most importantly, a Research Investment Fund that supported research in South Carolina's research universities. It was compared to the landmark Educational Improvement Act legislation of 1984 that improved the state's primary and secondary schools, and the Cutting Edge legislation was an attempt to improve the quality of South Carolina's state-funded colleges. The Research Investment Fund began awarding grants in 1988, and that year USC received eight awards totaling over $1 million ($1.15 million); in 1989, nine awards totaled nearly $1.4 million ($1.54 million).[50]

While increases in funded research were indeed impressive, competition for these funds was intense nationwide. The University of South Carolina

Table 6.4 Externally sponsored research at the University of South Carolina, 1979–80, 1984–85, 1988–89

YEAR	TOTAL FUNDING FOR EXTERNALLY SPONSORED RESEARCH (IN MILLIONS)	% CHANGE (CONSTANT DOLLARS)
1979–80	8.56 ($14.15)	–
1984–85	19.21 ($24.31)	72%
1988–89	25.34 ($27.83)	14%

Source: Self-Study, 1991, 4-16, table 6.

continued to trail many of its peers in national rankings of amounts of research and development expenditures, although it did manage to improve its relative position somewhat between 1984 and 1988. The road leading to national prominence as a research university was a challenging one.

The research dollars USC managed to attract funded major projects that joined two of the University's primary missions—research and public service. The Baruch Institute for Marine Biology and Coastal Research (founded in 1969 and located near Georgetown) and the International Institute for Public Health Research (also located near Georgetown) were leaders in their fields. The Baruch Institute, headed by John Vernberg, participated in major National Science Foundation and National Oceanic and Atmospheric Administration studies in ecological and estuarine research. The nearby International Institute for Public Health Research, led by Mac Tidwell and supported by grants from the U.S. Agency for International Development, among others, was a world leader in the study and control of vector-borne diseases such as malaria. The Earth Sciences and Resource Institute, funded by private industry as well as the U.S. and foreign governments, conducted worldwide studies in the search for new oil reserves. These institutes directly contributed to the outstanding reputations of Carolina's marine science, public health, and geoscience programs.[51]

Other prominent programs included the Technology Transfer Cooperative, funded by the U.S. Department of Commerce. Carolina was one of three nationwide sites selected to establish a center to deliver advanced technology to small- and medium-sized companies in the region. USC entered the age of supercomputing in 1988 with the installation of a powerful parallel computer

Table 6.5 Relative national ranking in research and development
         expenditures, 1984, 1988

UNIVERSITY	NATIONAL RANKING, R&D	
	1984	1988
Univ. of Wisconsin (Madison)	4	3
Penn. State Univ.	21	15
Georgia Institute of Tech.	23	27
Univ. of N.C. (Chapel Hill)	47	37
Clemson	88	91
Florida State	89	87
Univ. of S.C. (Columbia)	121	113
Univ. of Alabama (Tuscaloosa)	181	151

Source: Self-Study, 1991, 4-18.

capable of 2,000 MIPS (millions of instructions per second), purchased from the Perceptics Corporation, and the establishment of the Center for Parallel Supercomputing Applications, directed by George Johnson. While the center's main focus was the development of software, the new computing resources expanded the research possibilities and further strengthened the University's ties with state industry. Other such partnerships were the Savannah River Research and Education Foundation, founded in cooperation with Clemson and MUSC in late 1988, which worked alongside the Westinghouse Corporation (the Savannah River Plant's operator) to address the problems of chemical and hazardous waste disposal. USC scientists also became participants in exciting new developments in biotechnology through the efforts of the Institute for Biological Research and Technology.[52]

The faculty who conducted the research and taught Carolina's undergraduates and graduates continued to compile an impressive record of personal and scholarly achievement. In the English department, Carolina's poet-in-residence, James Dickey, was inducted into the prestigious American Academy of Arts and Letters in May of 1988, occupying a chair once held by John Steinbeck. Literary scholar Matthew J. Bruccoli continued his own output of distinguished literary criticism and with his publishing firm, Bruccoli Clark Layman, Inc., oversaw the monumental reference series *Dictionary of Literary Biography*. In the department of Government and International Studies, political scientist Merle Black continued to produce landmark studies of southern politics, and Richard L. Walker, the founder of the USC's department of international studies, served as U.S. ambassador to South Korea from 1981–1987. In the department of history, professor Robert Herzstein's 1988 book *Waldheim: The Missing Years* created an international sensation when it revealed that Kurt Waldheim, Austrian President and former secretary-general of the United Nations (and 1979 visitor to USC), had served in Nazi military units in World War II—a fact he had concealed—thus ending his political career.

In the sciences, pathbreaking physicist Yakir Aharonov, who held endowed chairs at both USC and Tel Aviv University, won several prestigious awards, including the Rothschild Prize and the Israel Prize in Exact Sciences, both awarded by the Israeli government. Physicist Fred Myhrer won the His Majesty the King Gold Medal for Scientific Research, one of Norway's highest scientific honors. Chemist Steven Burke was one of thirteen chemists nationwide named by the National Science Foundation as a Presidential Young Investigator in 1984, and later Michael Sutton of the College of Engineering won a similar award. Computer engineer Hideaki Kobayashi produced cutting-edge research in microchip technology. These faculty were but a few of the scholars who called Carolina home in the 1980s and who contributed to the improving reputation of Carolina's research and teaching capabilities.[53]

Despite these marks of progress, faculty salaries at Carolina continued to lag behind national averages as well as the averages of many of USC's peers in the region; keeping outstanding faculty at Carolina was an ongoing challenge in a competitive marketplace (see table 6.6). A 1987 survey of thirteen of the university's major departments showed that some 80 of 101 faculty who left the school in the previous year had done so for higher-paying jobs at other institutions. Among those who left were some of the University brightest stars, including chemist Steven D. Burke, who had won the NSF's Presidential Young Investigator Award, a $500,000 ($655,269) research grant, and an Alfred P. Sloan Fellowship while at USC. Burke left USC for the University of Wisconsin. E. Aubrey Thompson, a biology professor with more than $1 million ($1.24 million) in grants from the National Cancer Institute, the American Cancer Society, and the National Institutes of Health, left

Table 6.6 Average faculty salaries (all ranks) at selected southern state universities, 1980–81, 1990–91

STATE UNIVERSITY	AVERAGE SALARY, ALL RANKS, 1980–81 (IN $1,000S)	AVERAGE SALARY, ALL RANKS, 1990–91 (IN $1,000S)
USC–Columbia	25.2 (41.6)	45.5 (47.4)
Clemson	25.7 (42.5)	43.3 (45.1)
U. Georgia	26.3 (43.5)	44.7 (46.6)
U. Florida	25.0 (41.3)	45.8 (47.7)
U. Alabama	23.9 (39.5)	42.7 (44.5)
U. Mississippi	22.9 (37.9)	38.0 (39.6)
Louisiana State	25.6 (42.3)	43.7 (45.5)
U. Tennessee	24.1 (39.9)	46.1 (48.0)
UNC–Chapel Hill	29.6 (49.0)	50.2 (52.3)
U. Virginia	27.9 (46.1)	55.6 (57.9)
National average (Public Universities)	25.7 (42.5)	47.7 (49.7)
South Atlantic average*	Not Available	48.5 (50.5)

Source: "Annual Report on the Economic Status of the Profession," *Academe: Bulletin of the AAUP* 67, no. 4 (August 1981), 210–93; "The Annual Report on the Economic Status of the Profession," *Academe: Bulletin of the AAUP* 77, no. 2 (March–April 1991), 9–91. For similar information by rank, see Self-Study 1991, appendix 5-D, p. 63.

* South Atlantic region included Delaware, Washington, D.C., Florida, Georgia, Maryland, North Carolina, and South Carolina.

Carolina for a position at the University of Texas. English professor Gregory Jay, who had been named by the Modern Language Association as one of fifteen scholars who would "reshape English," left USC for a job at the University of Wisconsin, complete with a 54 percent pay raise. These were but a few examples of the promising scholars who left for more financially rewarding universities.[54]

Faculty salaries at USC in fact did increase in real terms during the 1980s, but Carolina lost ground to national universities in comparative ratings of faculty salaries, as did most other southern state universities (see table 6.6). President Holderman pointed out the large gap between USC salaries and those at universities such as North Carolina and Virginia, the very institutions whose company the University sought. "The average salaries paid at the University of South Carolina do not paint a pretty picture," he told the board of trustees. ". . . We cannot let the faculty down by offering below average awards."[55]

In a list of USC's priority items, the medical school was among the highest. After surviving the political battles of the 1970s and admitting its first class in 1977, the school conferred its first degrees on a class of 22 in 1981. That same year, the school received full accreditation from the American Medical Association. In the 1983–84 academic year, the school completed a move from temporary quarters on the downtown Columbia campus to a spacious facility adjacent to the new Dorn Veterans Hospital on Garner's Ferry Road. The new facility was financed by $14 million ($19.15 million) in federal funds.[56]

However, efforts to cooperate with the Medical University of South Carolina in the delivery of health education in the state had been unsuccessful. Across South Carolina the USC medical school still had skeptics who were convinced, nearly ten years after the General Assembly first approved the school, that funding two medical schools was a waste of taxpayers' money. As part of its *Master Plan* mandate, the Commission on Higher Education appointed a twenty-one-member "Blue Ribbon Committee on Medical Doctor Education" to evaluate medical education in South Carolina. The committee's report reopened the seemingly neverending debate over the USC School of Medicine—a debate made even more intense because the Veterans Administration's funding commitment to the school had ended. The committee recommended that the USC School of Medicine and the Medical University of South Carolina merge, and that the state limit medical school admissions to 200 students per year, thus saving money and eliminating a rivalry that had made it difficult to coordinate medical education. MUSC President James B. Edwards supported the merger, putting the issue this way: "Either we have one school dedicated to excellence, or two schools that will always be mediocre because the resources are divided."[57]

President Holderman fiercely opposed the merger proposal. "We are not mediocre and have no plans to be," he responded to Edwards. "I don't see how the people of the state are positively affected by a merger. Our infant mortality rate is among the highest in the nation and we're sitting around arguing over whether we ought to have two medical schools." Many, including Holderman, saw the merger proposal as a power grab by MUSC. "The real objective here isn't merger," he charged, "it's the abolition of this medical program. And it ought to be called for what it is."[58]

As in the earlier associate's degree controversy, Carolina defeated its rival and won the political battle. The CHE voted not to merge the two schools but instead approved a USC-backed plan to establish a "Joint Board Committee on Health and Medical Education" charged with coordinating the two medical schools. The board, with an equal number of representatives from USC, MUSC, and the CHE, was created in 1984. Soon thereafter, it agreed to the 200-student-per-year cap (125 at MUSC, 75 at USC). The USC School of Medicine survived and has since been a success story at Carolina.[59]

The medical school controversy was not the only one for USC during the early 1980s. The Gamecock athletic department provided a continuing saga of coach resignations and firings, as well as significant successes. The football program provided most of the excitement and controversy. In late 1979, in an attempt to establish order in the athletic department and ease Carolina's entry into an all-sports athletic conference, the board of trustees notified head football coach and athletic director Jim Carlen that when his contract expired in 1982, the positions of coach and athletic director would be separated. This move was widely interpreted as stripping Carlen of his leadership of the athletic department. The coach's blunt manner had earlier led him into conflict with board members, but his difficulties were nothing that a few wins would not cure.

Both the 1979 and 1980 Gamecocks provided wins in the form of 8–3 regular seasons (the 1979 team notched the first eight-win season for Carolina football since 1903) and bowl berths. The highlight of the 1980 season, and perhaps the entire prior history of USC football, was a 17–14 victory over the University of Michigan in front of over 104,000 fans in Ann Arbor. This win focused national attention on running back George Rogers, a Duluth, Georgia, native who had been second in the nation in rushing and a first team All-America player in 1979. In 1980, Rogers won unprecedented honors for a Gamecock player, including the Heisman Trophy, the most prestigious award in college football. He was also named College Football Player of the Year and a consensus All-America. Rogers led the nation in rushing in 1980, and his career rushing total (excluding bowl games) ranked fourth all-time in NCAA history. In 1980, Rogers became the most honored player in nearly a century of Gamecock football.[60]

The success of the 1979 and 1980 seasons paid dividends for Jim Carlen. Despite what the board of trustees had told Carlen a year earlier regarding their intention to separate the positions of head coach and athletic director, in the wake of the 1980 season they changed their minds. In December, they extended Carlen's contracts as both football coach *and* athletic director. Board of trustees chairman R. Markley Dennis, a Carlen supporter, admitted that two consecutive eight-win football seasons had influenced their decision. The board maintained that they still intended to keep the positions of head coach and athletic director separate, but ruled with questionable logic that one individual could hold both positions.[61] The mercurial board then changed their minds again a year later. After a 6–6 football season that included both a monumental victory over third-ranked North Carolina and a humiliating defeat to lowly Pacific, they fired Carlen from both positions in a contentious meeting marked by the absence of one of Carlen's strongest supporters, chairman Markley Dennis.[62]

In the wake of the Carlen firing, the board stuck to its previous commitment to separate the jobs of head coach and athletic director. They brought in Bob Marcum, the former athletic director at the University of Kansas, as Carolina's athletic director, an action they thought would bring order to the athletic department.[63] The athletic controversies persisted, however. One day prior to the announcement that Marcum had been hired, President Holderman announced the resignation of women's basketball coach Pam Parsons. The temperamental Parsons had been at USC since 1977 and had quickly molded the Lady Gamecocks into a national power. Her team was 30–6 during the 1979–80 season (finishing third in the nation) and 21–9 in 1980–81. Parsons managed to recruit some of the nation's most highly sought players and seemed to be doing for women's basketball what Frank McGuire had done for the men's program in the 1960s and early 1970s.

However, in the spring of 1980, serious problems appeared. Several players quit the team and the program was put on probation for recruiting violations. The 1980–81 team was wracked with dissension. Even more players left, bringing the total to some 15 over a three-year period. An anonymous letter to the *Gamecock* asked rhetorically, "Why did these valuable players feel it necessary to leave a strong and growing program?" The writer answered that Parsons was "an aggressive, power hungry tyrant." Soon thereafter, two assistant coaches quit, and soon after that, two more players quit. The NCAA declared that one of these players had been ineligible, and the team forfeited eight games of the 1980–81 season. Although the 1981–82 team started 7–0 and boasted a number-two national ranking, Parsons stepped down at mid-season amid charges of recruiting violations and other misdeeds. A sensational story in *Sports Illustrated* brought national attention to the problems under Parsons. Assistant coach Terry Kelly took over the team for the remainder of the season. Despite the adversity, the Lady Gamecocks finished with a 23–8 record and advanced to the semifinals of the NCAA Tournament. The Women's Sports Federation named Sheila Foster first-team All-America, Brantley Southers freshman All-America, and Terry Kelly rookie coach of the year.[64]

In the meantime, the trustees hired Richard Bell, a longtime assistant under Jim Carlen, as head football coach. After a disappointing first season as head coach in 1982 (the Gamecocks were 4–7 and suffered a humiliating 20–23 defeat to Furman), athletic director Marcum fired Bell. Marcum ostensibly let Bell go because the coach had refused to fire four of his assistant coaches, but most understood that the dismissal was due largely to the team's on-the-field performance and blamed it at least partly on the comparative national success of the Clemson program at the same time. Florida State coach Bobby Bowden believed that the firing was evidence of intense pressure to win at all costs, which led coaches to cut corners and eventually to abuses such as those that eventually showed up at both Carolina and Clemson. He commented on the Bell firing, "One year is not fair. . . . People wonder why coaches cheat. I think its because of the pressure from being fired."[65]

The successive firings of coaches Carlen and Bell, along with the Parsons resignation, cost the University more than just its reputation. Both Carlen and Bell sued, claiming wrongful termination. The University eventually settled with Carlen, agreeing to pay him over $500,000 ($683,879) to end his suit. Bell took his case to federal court, where a jury awarded him more than $171,000 ($224,102). Parsons agreed to a $20,000 ($28,232) settlement at the time of her resignation, and in the wake of the *Sports Illustrated* story, she too, sued, charging President Holderman, his top assistant, Chris Vlahoplus, and *Sports Illustrated* with libel. Though she later dropped the case against Holderman, she won an additional $20,000 ($27,355) settlement from the charge against Vlahoplus. In all, the lawsuits by the three former coaches cost Carolina over $1 million ($1.36 million) in settlements and legal fees.[66]

In spite of the ongoing upheaval, there were positive developments in the athletic program. In 1983, Carolina at last affiliated with an athletic conference, although its choice was not the all-sports conference it had hoped for. It was the Metro Conference, one that did not include conference football. However, with members such as Louisville and Memphis State it did boast strong basketball programs, and schools such as Florida State and Virginia Tech were noted for their baseball teams. The Gamecock basketball program had been under the direction of former Duke head coach Bill Foster since Frank McGuire's retirement, and the baseball team continued its success under June Raines. The Gamecock baseball team advanced to the College World Series in 1981, 1982, and 1985, and by 1990, Gamecock baseball teams had posted twenty straight winning seasons.[67]

The success of these teams was impressive, but the 1984 Gamecock football season captured the hearts of Carolina fans. Second-year head coach Joe Morrison, a former NFL star known for his all-black attire on game day, led a team that few expected to win more than seven games to a remarkable 10–2 record, the best in University of South Carolina history. The so-called season of "Black Magic" and the "Fire Ant" defense featured two All-Americans, offensive lineman Dell Wilkes and linebacker James Seawright. It was an unforgettable season for longsuffering Carolina fans, and their reaction reflected the shock of unexpected success. *Observer* writer Henry Eichel called the season "so magical we can hardly believe it happened." Later, he wrote that the Gamecocks "finally shook the Chicken Curse and paid us back for all those years of broken dreams." The magical season eventually became the subject of two full-length books. Despite losing in the Gator Bowl (the Gamecock's sixth bowl loss in six games), the team finished 11th in the nation, the highest finish ever for a Carolina football team.[68]

The year 1984 was truly an exciting one for the University of South Carolina, featuring a presidential visit, the conference of Caribbean heads of state, and "Black Magic." These successes did nothing to hurt one of the University's major initiatives, a capital campaign called the "Summit Fund," which sought to raise some $35 million ($47.87 million) in private contributions.[69]

As state appropriations declined, private funding grew ever more important—and Jim Holderman was a master fund-raiser. Actress Helen Hayes said of him, "[He] charms the birds right out of the tree, to say nothing of the money right out of the pocket." Only once before in its history had Carolina made a major drive to raise private funds (the "Greater University Fund" of the early 1960s), and its levels of private support showed its lack of effort. USC's private endowment was well below the average of institutions it considered its peers. There was simply not a culture among Carolina supporters of large-scale private giving. Former governor Robert McNair, one of the University's most influential supporters, later said of the Summit Fund's $35 million ($47.87 million) goal, "We all said to [Holderman], 'it can't be done. People are not going to support a public institution.' They're going to give their money to private schools." But James B. Holderman set out to show them that, indeed, it could be done.[70]

Beginning in January of 1981, Holderman and the administration began to raise money in the private phase of the Summit Fund campaign. By the time the campaign (headed by Helen Hayes and Allied Corporation chairman Edward Hennessy) entered its public phase in October 1983, they had raised approximately $17 million ($23.25 million). Completed at the end of 1984, the Summit Fund exceeded its goal, raising a total of $38.8 million ($50.8 million) in gifts and pledges. The fund was used to help the University in six major areas: scholarships and fellowships, faculty, academic programs, equipment, libraries, and research. McNair said later, "I was surprised that you could get that much money, because we had never been able to do it before."[71]

Among the Summit Fund's achievements were 19 new endowed chairs (the University total went from 26 in 1981 to 45 at the end of 1984), an increase in scholarship funds from $456,000 ($683,370) to $1.2 million ($1.31 million), and an increase in the University's overall endowment from $8.3 million ($12.44 million) in 1981 to $23.4 million ($30.6 million) by the end of 1984. The fund aided research by helping start the Carolina Venture Fund. The donation to the University of an entire barrier island in Beaufort County, Pritchard's Island, benefited Carolina's already outstanding marine science program.[72]

In the mid-1980s the University of South Carolina was truly riding high on a wave of self-confidence largely inspired by Jim Holderman's charisma and desire to "reach for the stars." In 1984 the *Christian Science Monitor* ran a front-page story on Holderman's success, calling him "a 'diplomat' who puts the University of South Carolina on the map." The article reported on rumors that Holderman would seek an ambassadorship or cabinet-level position in the Reagan administration, with which he had close ties.[73] He had impressed the state's power structure with his ability to raise money and attract national figures, and he had become recognized as one of the most powerful men in South Carolina. He was even credited with helping attract new industries to the state, including Pirelli and Mack Trucks. State Senator Heyward McDonald called the times "a real joyride for those who loved the University and wanted to see it grow."[74]

Near the zenith of his success, Holderman announced a truly ambitious vision for the University that became the hallmark of the remainder of his administration. On September 4, 1985, in his annual speech to the USC system faculty (broadcast live, as his annual year-opening speeches had been since the late 1970s, on closed-circuit television to all USC campuses), he announced his "2001 Plan" for Carolina. He told them, in the inspiring and challenging style that was typical of his public speaking: "My principal purpose today is to propose that we set our sights at [the] highest level. . . . By 2001 I believe it is possible for our University to be among the very best universities in the nation and the world; to jump to people's minds automatically when they consider the very best; a mystically conceived top ten if you will. That is the league, the company with which we can and should be associated. It is not an impossible dream. In fact, we are clearly on our way."[75]

That a Carolina president would so boldly proclaim that the University could, and indeed *would* be among the top ten in the world if they would follow his plan was a true break with the past; he was proclaiming a lofty ambition for the institution. "Our goal is to be a truly great research university," he declared. To do so, Carolina had to increase its emphasis on research. He told the faculty, "For the University of South Carolina to find itself, once and for all, in the company of the best, we will need a dramatic plan to increase our research funding." He proposed a state-sponsored fund for research, not unlike that created in 1988 by the Cutting Edge legislation. In addition, he emphasized that "our growing reputation as a center for learning will not be achieved at the expense of instruction." He insisted that Carolina must serve all its constituencies equally well. "Make no mistake about it," he said, "we will be among the very top centers of research and scholarship, but we will also remain at the forefront in instruction and service."[76]

Holderman's plan offered something for everyone and Carolina would be among the world's best. To those familiar with the history of the state and the University, for the University to achieve such exalted goals in a such a short time, in a relatively poor state with low overall educational achievement, without setting priorities, must have seemed improbable. Holderman was not deterred. The University of South Carolina had never seen anyone with aspirations like these. From appearances, Holderman might just be able achieve his goal in time for the University's bicentennial in 2001. It is a testimony to Holderman's charismatic ability that at first, relatively few in South Carolina questioned whether he could make this goal a reality.

For most of his first nine years as president, Holderman received near-unanimous approval from the business and political leaders in Columbia and South Carolina; they saw Holderman's efforts on behalf of the University as good for business and the state's development. He was an active participant in efforts to lure industry to the state. Businessmen heard his rhetoric about achieving prominence and liked it. Moreover, they saw his ability to raise money and liked that even more. Some faculty had been dissatisfied with his flamboyant methods, but most appreciated the opportunity to work at an institution with lofty aims; the University of South Carolina was thinking big.[77]

Holderman's golden halo eventually tarnished, but not all at once. His decline began simply enough: with a disgruntled journalism student, Paul Perkins, who was upset with his ever-increasing tuition bill. In the summer of 1986, Perkins asked the administration to provide him with the financial details of Jihan Sadat's position as distinguished visiting professor; she had taught a three-hour-per-week course at Carolina ("Women in Egyptian Culture") since the spring of 1985. The course and its teacher had given the University considerable notoriety, and the retinue of security personnel that accompanied her every visit to Gambrell Hall, where she taught her course, attracted attention on campus. Out of curiosity, Perkins asked what it cost the University to employ Sadat; he thought the topic might make an interesting freelance story. When the administration refused to tell him, he and his wife Cheryl, a local attorney, filed a Freedom of Information Act (FOIA) request, demanding that the University release Sadat's salary and expenses. On the last day allowed for a response, Holderman replied to Perkins, but he refused to disclose the salary figures, claiming that such information for faculty below the level of department head was privileged information.[78]

Holderman's refusal established a pattern that he and his aides would repeat in the years to come. In the wake of his refusal to disclose the information, Paul and Cheryl Perkins sued the University for its release under the FOIA. The suit brought considerable media attention, and for the first time in his administration, Holderman's methods were being publicly scrutinized. Holderman adamantly resisted calls to disclose the information, claiming that to reveal Sadat's salary would hamper efforts to attract other distinguished visiting professors, who, he said, "lend a tremendous stature and breadth to the institution." Holderman told television reporters, "If we were to begin to reveal faculty salaries, whether they be distinguished visiting lecturers or regular full-time faculty, we would begin to lose the best ones in rapid succession."[79] On another occasion, University officials argued against releasing Sadat's salary information because, they said, it "would be vital to terrorists and other persons seeking to endanger, injure, or assassinate Mrs. Sadat."[80]

In the wake of the media scrutiny Sadat quit her position, doing so, she said, to avoid further embarrassing the University. But Paul and Cheryl Perkins refused to drop their lawsuit, and the University continued to fight it. In late October 1986, state judge James E. Moore ordered the University to release all information surrounding Sadat's salary and expenses while employed at USC. At a widely publicized press conference, President Holderman announced that Sadat had been paid some $314,586 ($390,892) in salary and expenses to teach her one class for three semesters. Among the payments was $94,283 ($117,152) for forty-four round-trip chartered flights between Columbia and Washington, D.C. Despite the apparent extravagance, Holderman maintained that Sadat had "performed magnificently" and "helped the university achieve national attention way beyond our capacity to reimburse her."[81]

Upon learning of Sadat's salary, many faculty were incensed. They insisted that in his haste to raise the University's reputation, Holderman was pursuing personalities rather than talent. Chairman of the faculty senate Rufus Fellers said that faculty reaction was "one of indignation, that this is out of the question, ridiculous." While visiting professors like Sadat brought national recognition, their contributions to the academic program, said Fellers, were "not very significant." An anonymous faculty member said "If Sadat had been a person of known academic quality, that would have been one thing. She wasn't."[82] At a university whose average faculty salary was $34,100 (and falling further behind national averages), the high price of getting Sadat was especially galling to faculty. Students, who had just absorbed another tuition increase, were angry as well. "I'm ticked!," wrote Jeff Shrewsbury.[83]

The Perkins FOIA case opened a Pandora's box in Holderman's administration, and for the next five years, new, ever more startling information trickled out with regard to how he conducted his presidency. The story became an important one in regional newspapers, particularly the *Greenville News* and the *Charlotte Observer* (and notably not in the *State*). Reporters at the Greenville and Charlotte papers doggedly investigated the unfolding story, which the administration only fueled with its efforts at secrecy. Access to University records provided by the Perkins's FOIA suit revealed, along with Sadat's salary, that other distinguished visiting professors and speakers had been paid high salaries and honoraria for minimal work. Lyn Nofziger, Robert McNeil, James Lehrer, and Howard Simons, all distinguished visiting professors, received between $30,000 ($37,277) and $45,000 ($55,915) each per semester for appearing in classes from one to three times per month; Lawrence Eagleberger alone received $64,499 ($80,144). Henry Kissinger and Bill Cosby received honoraria of $25,000 ($31,064) each for one appearance on campus. This information generated a media feeding frenzy, including an editorial in the *New York Times*. The *Times* wrote, "The University of South Carolina shells out hundreds of thousands of dollars for token appearances by what seems to be the entire cast of 'Lifestyles of the Rich and Famous.'" The *Times* editor labeled Holderman's strategy "hucksterism," but actually stopped well short of condemning the practice of hiring distinguished visiting professors as a shortcut to national prominence. Nonetheless, as student Jeff Shrewsbury put it, "the only recognition USC is getting from Jihan Sadat is a snicker from around the USA that we were stupid enough to shell out all those bucks, and even more dumb to cover it up."[84]

In response to the Sadat controversy, the board of trustees limited the salaries of visiting professors to be no higher than the average salary for USC's full professors.[85] However, this belated move did not satisfy critics or reporters, who sensed that this story was only the tip of an iceberg. As Jerrold Footlick wrote, "If paying Jihan Sadat that kind of money was Holderman's idea of building the University's reputation, how else was he utilizing its resources?"[86] Among the documents released to quell the Sadat story had been records of the president's discretionary fund, which showed that Holderman's excessive spending had not been confined to visiting professor's salaries. News organizations sought full access to the records of the remainder of the discretionary funds account though which part of Sadat's expenses had been paid. The board of trustees, citing a clause in the freedom of information act that allowed them to withhold anything that three-fourths of the board agreed was not in the public interest, refused to disclose how President Holderman spent half of his $729,000 ($905,828) 1985–86 discretionary account. The portion they kept secret contained records of travel expenses and gifts related to fund-raising, and the nature of these records elicited a suspicion that the board was attempting to hide information. More FOIA suits followed, and the board set itself up in a adversarial relationship with the press that continued for more than four years; they gave the impression that they were concealing impor-tant information. Their defense was simply that to disclose the records would embarrass donors and harm fund-raising.[87]

Throughout the winter and spring of 1986–87, the *News,* the *Observer,* the Associated Press, and WIS-TV in Columbia pursued the story, trumpet-ing each new detail in page-one, above-the-fold stories. News outlets insisted that they were upholding the public's right to know about an important state institution, while Holderman attacked them for using the story to sell news-papers. Nonetheless, he and his aides kept to their strategy of secrecy. Reports began to leak about lavish spending on things other than visiting professors, including expensive gifts to influential state officials and USC trustees, char-tered jets, and exorbitant hotel stays—all paid for with public money—at a University that had all along been pleading poverty to the General Assembly, its students, and faculty.

For two and half months following the media FOIA requests to view the records of the University's discretionary account, the board of trustees refused to disclose the information. In late January 1987, heightened media pressure forced the trustees to reverse course and disclose some of the records, but they chose to redact the names of about 200 prominent donors and gift recip-ients, ostensibly to protect their privacy and the University's interest in keep-ing these individuals as viable donors. Columbia real estate developer and board of trustees vice chairman Michael Mungo (chairman of the board's newly established fiscal oversight committee) maintained that he had been through the records in question "meticulously" three different times, and that there was nothing amiss. Nonetheless, Mungo determined, continued secrecy was a must. "It is essential that we respect the confidentiality of these people because it is in the public interest," he said. "We cannot kill our Golden Geese . . . . We are on the verge of greatness. . . . Hopefully, we will now be allowed to continue our pursuit of excellence in the public interest without needless outside frivolity."[88]

If Mungo, Holderman, and the board thought that this limited release would satisfy the public, they were off the mark. The incomplete records whetted appetites for information and gave the public a glimpse of Holder-man's extravagant style: for example, $2,000 ($2,485) Steuben glass fig-urines were a frequent gift to the dignitaries and celebrities who visited USC.

Celebrities were not the only recipients of the various kinds of gifts bought with public funds: a number of state and federal legislators and high-ranking state government officials, including Oregon Senator Mark Hatfield, Governor Richard Riley, and House Speaker Bob Sheheen received expensive gifts. Between 1983 and 1986, Holderman spent a total of some $80,000 ($99,405) on Steuben glass and $27,000 ($33,549) on porcelain. Other gifts included a $5,000 ($6,327) manuscript letter from Abraham Lincoln, as well as expensive artwork (John James Audubon prints were a favorite) and rare documents. According to those who worked with him, Holderman took great satisfaction in giving gifts to all types of people, and the giving of expensive gifts was a hallmark of his personality. The newly released records also revealed equally extravagant travel. A four-day 1984 trip to Haiti and Barbados by Holderman and two aides cost more than $20,000 ($24,851); among the gifts associated with the visit was a $473 figurine given to Haitian dictator Jean-Claude "Baby Doc" Duvalier. The administration's travel budget averaged more than $12,000 ($15,726) a month between 1983 and 1985—surpassing even that of the governor's office. Holderman maintained that such was the cost of doing business at a research university that was trying to do great things.[89]

Despite the spending controversy and calls for Holderman's resignation, the president maintained the staunch support of distinguished South Carolinians such as Governor Carroll Campbell, businessmen Francis Hipp, W. W. "Hootie" Johnson, Robert Royall, James Self, and Craig Wall, the *State* newspaper, and most importantly, members of the University's board of trustees. The *State's* editorialist insisted, "Holderman's successes override his excesses." Hipp called the critical media stories "cheap shot attacks," while former governor Robert McNair accused Holderman's media critics of having a "vendetta" against the University. "All of us are angry that they are trying to destroy the best thing that's ever happened to South Carolina," McNair said of them. "The real story is that all of the sudden here is this sleepy university that's always been overshadowed by Chapel Hill and Georgia Tech and Virginia suddenly emerging with national recognition." Holderman had capitalized on what he called South Carolina's "inhibiting inferiority complex" with his "dare-to-be-great" rhetoric.[90]

The press did not back down, and by March 1987 public officials were asking more serious questions about Holderman and the University's finances. In particular, the state ethics panel and fifth circuit solicitor Jim Anders inquired whether gift-giving to state officials violated ethics laws. Others, such as state senator Glenn McConnell, sought to learn the details of the relationship between the University's foundations, particularly the CRDF, and the University. McConnell requested a legislative audit. His interest had been piqued when the records revealed that USC's foundations had given

Holderman a $200,000 ($248,512) loan on a home at Lake Murray, as well
as $87,500 ($108,724) per year in supplemental compensation, in addition
to his $92,428 ($114,848)-per-year state salary and access to a $729,000
($905,828) discretionary fund.[91] The USC story took on a life of its own in
the press. Even the CBS-TV news program "60 Minutes" investigated.[92]

In the face of the media barrage, Holderman demonstrated a characteristic that would become typical of the last years of his presidency: in the words
of board chairman Othniel Wienges, "Holderman would rather ask for forgiveness than permission." The president issued a carefully worded mea culpa
for his gift-giving extravagance. He claimed that while the gift-giving was
"done with the single purpose of moving this institution forward very rapidly," he realized that it was "in some instances excessive and I am sorry for
this error." He pointed to new disclosure rules the board had instituted on
future discretionary spending and the limits they had placed on the salaries
of visiting professors. "Moreover," he said, "I have ended the practice of giving gifts from any source except for tokens of recognition similar to those traditionally given by colleges and universities." He concluded with what must
have been a truly sincere wish: "I hope that we can put these matters behind
us." Two months later, the board announced a new policy on discretionary
spending. They assured the public that funds raised from sources such as
concession sales at athletic events and on-campus vending machines (which
funded the discretionary account that the president had spent on gifts and
travel) would now be spent on academic programs. The president's contrition
put off the reporters from "60 Minutes," who then lost interest in the story.[93]
Nonetheless, despite the apology, Holderman maintained that nothing was
out of the ordinary. He told students and faculty, "Why there has been such
a string of negativism, I don't understand. I'm not doing anything now that I
haven't done in the past 10 years."[94]

For a while, it looked as though Holderman and the University would
indeed put the controversies behind them. After a one-month investigation,
solicitor Jim Anders reported on the president's spending practices, declaring
that he found "more than marginal excesses" but no crimes. Though newspapers claimed that Anders had missed key evidence, the criminal investigation
ended there.[95] The state ethics commission, which investigated Holderman
for his gift-giving to legislators and public officials, ruled that the practice
"had the appearance, if not the effect, of impropriety" and demanded that it
end immediately. However, the commission did not recommend any disciplinary action, and Holderman and his administration viewed their ruling as
a victory.[96]

Despite Holderman's wishes, these rulings did not end the controversies during the spring of 1987. Another uproar surrounded the financial arrangements

on the highest-profile capital construction projects of his administration, the Swearingen Engineering Center and the Koger Center for the Arts. The $15 million ($20.5 million) Swearingen Center was announced with great fanfare in 1983. It was to be named for John E. Swearingen, a 1938 graduate of the University and then-chairman of the board of the Standard Oil Company of Indiana. The center, when completed, was to be one of the finest facilities of its kind in the Southeast, a major addition to the University's physical plant and academic capacity, and it was initially claimed that the building would be entirely funded by private gifts raised primarily from donors in the petroleum industry.[97]

The building was controversial from the start, with the *Greenville News* claiming that it represented "private giving to change public higher education policy, in this instance to seize for USC a major engineering and research role traditionally assigned to Clemson University as the state's academic center for applied science and technology."[98] The fact that it was to be privately funded meant that the center did not have to be approved by the CHE or the Budget and Control Board. Private funding also meant that the construction did not have to follow the state's procurement code, which required competitive bidding for building projects.

However, it was the unorthodox financing of the project that eventually drew most of the fire from the University's critics. The Carolina Research and Development Foundation (CRDF) would borrow the money to build the building and the University would lease it from the foundation, paying the lease with money it received from pledges of private funds that USC raised. At the end of the lease, the foundation would then turn the building over to the University. Holderman insisted that the project was "fully funded by pledges on the facility to the Research and Development Foundation."[99]

The University broke ground on the ambitious project in early 1985. Soon, the plans for USC's science and engineering programs grew. Carolina subsequently proposed a $48 million ($64.2 million) multi-building "Energy Research Complex," which included not only the Swearingen Center, but the refurbishing of a former South Carolina Electric and Gas building adjacent to the Swearingen Center (a gift to the University), and the construction of a graduate science center elsewhere on campus (the latter building had previously been disapproved by the CHE in 1985). Denied funding for this expanded project by the state, Holderman went to Washington to find the money. With the help of Senate appropriations committee chairman Mark Hatfield (whose son attended USC) and members of South Carolina's congressional delegation, he secured a $16.3 million ($20.25 million) federal grant for the project. Holderman assured Congress that this money would supplement $15 million ($18.6 million) in private funds already raised. Like the other funds that were used to pay for the building, instead of going to the University, the federal grant was deposited with the CRDF.[100]

It soon became clear why Holderman had found it necessary to make his Washington pitch. Not only would the Swearingen Center cost more than originally planned (estimates ran to $20.1 million [$24 million]), but the money that Holderman claimed to have raised for the project was not actually available. To secure federal funding, he had told the U.S. House appropriations committee in April 1986 that he was "pleased to say that our fundraising efforts to date have generated approximately $15 million ($18.6 million) from private sources for construction costs." However, when state legislators began to question the financing arrangements in the wake of the gift-giving controversy, Holderman admitted that the $15 million represented pledges, not cash actually on hand to make lease payments. In fact USC had received only $4.6 million ($5.71 million) of the funds from his pledges. "Who is left holding the bag if the [private] funding is not in place?" asked State Senator Verne Smith.[101]

In May 1987, Holderman asked the South Carolina General Assembly to finance the revenue shortfall in order to make the University's lease payments to the CRDF. State Senator Joe Wilson vigorously opposed the University, declaring that if the legislature was told a project would be privately funded, "then indeed it ought to be funded privately." After an intense lobbying effort by USC supporters, the State Senate approved $1.9 million ($2.28 million) to pay the University's Swearingen Center lease. Later, the vast majority of the federal grant, some $14.1 million ($16.9 million), was used to pay off the CRDF's Swearingen Center loan instead of equipping the expanded Energy Research Complex. Most of the pledges of private funding that Holderman had claimed to have received never came to the University or to the foundation.[102]

As the financial arrangements for financing the Swearingen Center began to come to light, similar criticism arose respecting the financing of the Koger Center for the Arts. A major arts center had been in the works at USC since the late 1960s, but funding problems had delayed it; Holderman revived the project in the late 1970s. One planned function of the building was as a home to the Movietone newsreel archive, a 1980 gift to USC from the 20th Century Fox Corporation valued at $100 million ($165.38 million)—billed as the largest gift in U.S. corporate history. Receipt of the valuable newsreels had been a coup for the University, and Holderman called them "a priceless national treasure and academic resource." Scholars who had a chance to work with them agreed. However, Carolina had no good place to store the volatile old film, and Holderman proposed that the new Arts Center fill that role. However, economic hard times during the early 1980s ended hope that the new facility could house the film archive.[103]

But they did not end plans for a performing arts building. By 1986, plans for the 2,000-plus-seat fine arts center were finalized, complete with an "acoustically flawless" performance hall that would, in Holderman's words, be "the most comprehensive arts complex . . . perhaps in this country." The $15 million ($18.6 million) center would be built adjacent to the Carolina Coliseum using a combination of public and private funds: with a $4 million ($4.97 million) gift from alumnus and Florida real estate developer Ira Koger, Richland County agreed to contribute $3.75 million ($4.65 million), the city of Columbia anted up $2 million ($2.5 million), and the University would fund the remainder. As in the case of the Swearingen Center, the CRDF was the vehicle used to handle the various sources of construction funding, and the University would lease the building from the foundation until their loan was paid off.[104]

This seemed reasonable, but the arrangement began to draw fire. Critics complained that, as with the Swearingen Center, the Koger Center construction had avoided competitive public bidding because the CRDF was a private foundation (even though well over half of the building's financing would come from public money). State Senator David Thomas labeled this arrangement a "sweetheart deal" for selected local contractors. Additional complaints arose when the University went to the General Assembly to ask for appropriations covering its share of the cost: the CRDF had borrowed some $9.25 million ($11.49 million) to cover both the University's share and much of the $4 million ($4.97 million) Koger gift, which, like many of the gifts for the Swearingen Center, turned out to be only a pledge. The University was obligated to pay the foundation some $800,000 ($994,050) a year (for ten years) in lease payments, but in the absence of the pledges had no way to finance its portion. Another development dumbfounded local officials who had committed their city and county funds to the project: Holderman revealed that half of the Koger gift was a part of a trust that would be received only upon the donor's death—a fact officials claimed Holderman did not tell them in his original pitch for their funds.

Thus, as in the case of the Swearingen Center, the state government was asked to step in and cover a funding shortfall well after construction on the project had begun, a situation that angered a number of legislators. The controversies surrounding the Koger and Swearingen Centers and discretionary spending made for a difficult public relations year for USC between the summer of 1986 and the summer of 1987. However, as the University's leaders had managed to do during the entire episode, they survived. In 1988, the Columbia descendants of Ambrose and Narciso Gonzales, the founders of the *State,* gave the University $1.5 million ($1.7 million) in honor of the two men to help finance the arts center. In addition, at the same time the General

Assembly approved the controversial Swearingen Center appropriation it approved an $802,000 ($964,887) lease payment for the Koger Center. By mid-1990, the state had paid the foundation about $2 million to fund the University's portion of the lease. The Koger Center financing remained controversial, and through the early 1990s critics continued to charge that it had been "completely misrepresented to the legislature." Ultimately, the Carolina Research and Development Foundation, which had originally been involved in the project only as a vehicle to arrange financing, became the largest contributor to the Koger Center when it used $5.8 million from its principal to pay off the Koger Center loan. The full amount of Ira Koger's pledge never materialized, as in the 1990s the stock that formed the core of his trust became essentially worthless. Nonetheless, in spite of the controversy, the Koger Center for the Arts became a reality.[105]

The Swearingen and Koger Centers flaps raised serious questions from even staunch USC supporters. Some trustees, including Eddie Floyd of Florence, asked the legislature to audit the financing of both buildings. In 1987, the CHE investigated, but because so much of the financing centered around private pledges to the CRDF (which were beyond the reach of state scrutiny and for which USC officials refused to provide detailed records) the Commission was forced to take Holderman's word that the pledges would come in and that funding for both projects was sound. "The only other step we can do is assume Jim [Holderman] is lying and go look at the pledges, and I'm not willing to do that," said CHE commissioner Fred Sheheen. "I don't believe that the whole top tier of university officials would submit false information to the commission," he said. The CHE cleared the University of any wrongdoing in funding either project, and Holderman escaped censure for the controversy.[106] However, after the foundation's records were finally opened to the public in 1991, it turned out that many of the pledges for both buildings had been oral promises to Holderman, and they never materialized. In early 1991 University officials were still looking for some $12.5 million in pledges for the Swearingen and Koger Centers, and by the end of that year they had given up hope of ever getting nearly $10 million in pledges that were still outstanding.[107] Though these developments were still in the future, in 1987 the controversies reinforced a growing public perception that Holderman was not a conscientious steward of public dollars.

In the end, the University of South Carolina and the state ended up with two gleaming modern facilities which were tremendous additions to the physical plant, and as a result of the various funding sources involved, they cost state government relatively little. The ultramodern Swearingen Center, opened in 1987, consisted of a 210,000-square-foot triangular main building with an additional 100,000 square feet of classroom and office space in the donated SCE&G building across the street. It housed traditional engineering laboratories as well as up-to-date laboratories for research in computer technology and machine intelligence. The Swearingen Center quickly became an important engine for the growth of the University's research capacity. Located on the south edge of the campus, it represented the further movement of the campus in the direction that Donald Russell had begun moving it in the 1950s. The Koger Center, built adjacent to the Carolina Coliseum, opened in January 1989 to a performance by the London Philharmonic Orchestra. It featured a modern concert hall appropriate for symphony and theatrical performances, as well as rehearsal rooms. It finally filled the University's need for a large auditorium for special events—a need that dated from the antebellum period. At the outset of the twenty-first century, it ranks as one of the Midlands region's most important cultural assets.[108]

Meanwhile, the legal battles between the University's board of trustees and the media continued. In a FOIA suit, the *Observer* sought full access to records of how some $3.5 million ($4.35 million) in USC discretionary funds had been spent between 1977 and 1986. The board of trustees delegated to President Holderman the authority to handle all FOIA suits, and the administration fought desperately to avoid having to disclose the records, which were covered by the state's weak FOIA law. Eventually, Carolina won this battle on a technicality when the state supreme court ruled that the *Observer* had filed its FOIA suit too late. Nonetheless, the University board announced that the records of the discretionary account would be open to public inspection after January 1, 1987.[109]

The *Greenville News* and the Associated Press (AP) focused their FOIA legal battle against the University by seeking full access to the records of USC's private foundations. In the wake of the discretionary funds controversy, Holderman announced that he would use these foundations as a funding source for his efforts to promote the University. As private entities, under existing state law their records were closed to the public, though the news organizations argued that since the foundations had received federal, state, and local funds, they were in actuality public entities and their records were thus subject to the FOIA.[110]

The functioning of the University's foundations had been a topic of concern since the early 1980s. The General Assembly worried enough about their operations that in 1982 they launched a Legislative Audit Council investigation of all private endowments of state institutions. The council's report criticized the way state resources were used to support the private foundations. Public and private funds were routinely intermingled in the endowments, which were technically private and unaccountable to taxpayers. In addition, they criticized the practice of state agency administrators (such as college presidents and vice presidents) serving on the boards of directors of the foundations, as it represented a possible conflict of interest.[111] In response to the report, lawmakers such as Alex Harvin of Williamsburg County called for legislation to ensure better oversight of these foundations, but none was forthcoming.[112] The controversies over the financing of the Swearingen and Koger Centers demonstrated the dangers of commingling public and private money, but the University consistently argued in court that the foundations were private and their records thus confidential.

While the FOIA lawsuit brought by the *News* and the AP made its way through the courts, life went on at the University. Holderman determined that the tribulations of 1987 would not get in his way, and in the fall of that year, with what appeared to be the worst of the controversies behind him, he drove forward with his ambitious goal of national prominence for USC. In fact, the high point of his presidency came on September 11, 1987, when he welcomed Pope John Paul II to the Horseshoe. Despite rumors that he would resign after the Pope's visit, Holderman countered that he meant to stay at USC until he retired at age sixty-five—an event which would coincide with the University's bicentennial year, 2001. "Why would I go now? My gosh, we're on a tremendous climb," he said. "I don't think last year hurt us at all." He spoke of 1987 as "a year of controversy" but maintained that "weathering it was important." Equally important, he retained the support of the most influential Carolina supporters, who continued to hail him as the man who would lead the University to greatness.[113]

Soon after the papal visit, in December 1987 Holderman announced more grand plans for the University, embodied in a report to the board of trustees titled *2001: The New Dimension*. The new document set forth the goals his administration sought to reach by the University's bicentennial. "We will become the *prototype university* of the 21st century," it stated. The primary objective in the document represented a modification of Holderman's earlier vision for USC. He had claimed in 1985 that the University of South Carolina would be among the top ten universities in the world by 2001. In 1987, the University's primary goal was to rank among the top ten *systems* of higher education in the United States by 2001—an important distinction.[114]

Prominent goals in *2001: The New Dimension* were to raise the University's endowment to over $200 million ($239,735,000) and to become one of the top Carnegie Research I universities in the nation, with more than $150 million ($180 million) in research per year. The goals called for top-level excellence in almost every area of academic study: USC would maintain a megacomputing complex unequaled in the world; it would be a major center for medical and health research; it would have one of the nation's top research libraries; and it would become one the leading secular universities in the world in ecumenical studies and the humanities.[115] By 2001, Holder-man predicted, "we should be the best university in the South. We can rival, if not surpass, Duke, Chapel Hill—even Princeton."[116]

With the announcement of the ambitious goals of *2001: The New Dimension*, USC seemed to have regained the momentum it possessed before the controversies of 1986–87 temporarily derailed Holderman's plans. Passage of the Cutting Edge initiative in the spring of 1988 added to the sense that the state was ready for a "quantum leap" toward building quality universities. Private fund-raising for the University increased from $17.7 million ($21.29 million) to $19.6 million ($22.56 million) between the 1986–87 and 1987–88 fiscal years, despite the negative publicity of the Holderman spending controversies. Research funding from outside sources increased as well, spurred in part by the resources in the new Swearingen Center (see table 6.5). The controversies surrounding construction of the Swearingen and Koger Centers were largely forgotten as the new facilities began to fulfill their missions.[117]

To coincide with the opening of the Koger Center, President Holderman declared 1988–89 to be the "Year of the Arts," focusing attention on the University's cultural programs. Carolina hosted performances from dancer Rudolf Nureyev and the Vienna Boy Choir, among many other artists; it also welcomed lectures and residencies by movie stars such as Richard Thomas and Robby Benson. In other areas, ongoing academic and research programs in computer science, geology, and engineering brought more attention to Carolina. Administrators began a push to secure more state funding in order to raise faculty salaries to the average at the top southern universities. In 1988, Holderman unveiled a new logotype for Carolina, a design promoting the nomenclature "The USC," which he claimed symbolized "the unity and strength of the nine-campus system." He redoubled his calls for national prominence at "The USC" and insisted that because of advancements under his administration, "Carolina's peer group of higher education institutions includes some of the nation's major universities."[118]

Despite the new momentum, difficulties remained. One was a problem that had plagued the University long before Holderman's arrival—trouble within the athletic department. In 1986, basketball coach Bill Foster, who had survived a 1982 midseason heart attack, resigned under pressure; he later received a $240,000 ($298,215) settlement. In the spring of 1987, the NCAA placed USC's basketball program on two years' probation for rules violations ranging from the sale of complimentary player tickets to serious recruiting misdeeds.[119]

The probation was unfortunate, but a controversy that began in 1988 brought even more unfavorable national attention to Carolina. In March 1988, President Holderman fired athletic director Bob Marcum amid charges of financial improprieties and the failure to adequately monitor the University's drug-testing program for athletes. Marcum disputed the firing, suing in court to recover the balance of his salary. He was eventually awarded some $234,000 ($269,389), the sixth USC athletic official in a decade to secure a financial settlement after being fired or forced to resign.[120]

New athletic director King Dixon instituted a strict, comprehensive drug-testing program, and in October 1988 the University community learned why such a program was necessary. Former Gamecock football player Tommy Chaikin alleged in a sensational *Sports Illustrated* article that he had been heavily involved with steroids during his playing career from 1983 to 1987; he claimed that as many as half of his teammates were involved as well, and that coaches and team doctors knew of and condoned the drug use. Several former coaches and players backed up Chaikin's story, including former offensive lineman Woody Myers, who said, "I personally used steroids and would use them again." Another former offensive lineman, Deron Farina, said that coaches "never directly . . . told you to [take steroids], you just understood what they want. They stressed the weight room so much." Other players adamantly denied knowledge of drug use, as did coaches. Coach Joe Morrison said, "We have never condoned the use of steroids or any other illegal substance," and charged Chaikin with being a troublemaker. Nonetheless, a subsequent criminal investigation revealed that four coaches had indeed been involved in a steroids scheme, resulting in guilty pleas from three. A jury acquitted the fourth. Head coach Joe Morrison, beloved by most Gamecock fans because his teams won, died of a heart attack only fourteen weeks after Chaikin made his allegations. In April 1990, the NCAA placed the USC program on probation as a result of the steroid scandal.[121]

In spite of the adverse publicity, Jim Holderman did not let the athletic department's troubles interrupt his drive for top-ten status. "We know that the University will be prepared for 2001 precisely because we have developed an ambitious, realistic vision," he said in 1989. "By all accounts, we're doing fantastically well," he assured USC's constituencies.[122]

Holderman and his supporters cited area after area in which the University was making strides toward its 2001 goal. USC's annual private fund-raising had increased from $3.19 million ($5.26 million) in 1979–80 to $21.49 ($22.40 million) in 1989–90.[123] He cited other areas for success as well: Merit-based scholarship programs, which increased from $250,000 ($561,724), aiding 500 students in 1976–77, to $3.6 million ($3.75 million) in 1989–90, aiding 3,576 students. Twenty Carolina scholars each year received four-year scholarships paying $5,000 ($5,211) per year; the average SAT score of the 1989–90 Carolina scholars was 1339. The University's total endowment funds grew from $3.9 million ($8.76 million) to over $50 million ($52 million).

Alumni Association membership went from 5,000 in 1976–77 to 22,000 in 1989–90. The number of endowed faculty chairs in the USC system increased from 19 in 1977 to 110 in 1990. The South Carolina Honors College had "Ivy League" standards, with students in the college scoring an average of 1252 on the benchmark SAT, ahead of the overall averages at schools such as Notre Dame, Vanderbilt, and the University of California at Berkeley. USC's Master's in International Business Studies ranked number one in the nation according to *U.S. News and World Report.* Sponsored programs and research topped $40 million ($41.6 million) in 1989–90, up 90 percent from only five years earlier. The "parade of stars" to come to USC was ongoing, with Michael Eisner (CEO of the Walt Disney Corporation), prominent composer Andrew Lloyd Webber, and President George Bush scheduled to attend commencement ceremonies in May 1990—visits that reinforced the impression that Holderman was raising USC's national profile.[124]

The list of accomplishments was indeed impressive and was one for which Holderman, his administration, the faculty and USC's students could be justly proud. But by the late 1980s there were critics who challenged Holderman's claims to putting USC on the road to "top ten" status. They pointed to broader measures of the University's quality and found it wanting, especially in areas outside of the select programs upon which Holderman showered praise. Critics complained that while emphasis was put on a few specialized programs, the basic undergraduate program had gone begging for resources. Overall faculty salaries were below the regional average (which was $37,058 [$38,623], while USC's overall average was $35,950 [$37,468]); USC placed 9th among 15 southeastern state universities in measures of average faculty salary. USC's in-state tuition costs were high, second only to those of the University of Virginia when compared to all southeastern state universities. Only once in the 1980s had the University received full formula funding from the General Assembly. Average SAT scores for entering freshmen at USC trailed those at both Clemson and The Citadel and were far behind those at the nation's best universities. The only southeastern state university with a lower freshman average SAT score was the University of Alabama.

USC was not in the nation's top 100 in annual expenditures for research and development. It was still a Carnegie Research II institution, an important measure of the size and breadth of a university's research program (Carnegie Research I status was held by the nation's top doctoral-granting universities). In addition, the University's library had suffered during the 1980s, slipping from 57th nationally in library acquisition expenditures in 1974 to 91st in 1986. The library collection ranked 75th out of 107 research libraries in the nation in overall holdings in 1990–91 and trailed state universities in Virginia, North Carolina, Georgia, and Florida in this vital category. As John

Olsgaard of USC's College of Library and Information Science said, "A university's library tends to be a measure of how the school ranks as a research institution." Some observed that while the University was busy fighting public relations battles in the press, the academic infrastructure was adrift.[125]

These criticisms were legitimate, and they underscored the difficulties the administration would have moving the University of South Carolina to the "top ten" in little more than a decade. They largely reflected a legacy of underfunding that failed to give state institutions a fighting chance to achieve excellence. For that reason, they were as much criticisms of the state's leadership in general as of USC's administration or board of trustees. However, much of the blame could be placed on the administration, which publicly proclaimed lofty goals but failed to follow through by building the basic infrastructure that would help make the goals a reality. Critics charged that the administration instead focused attention on narrow, relatively superficial accomplishments that had limited long-term benefit for the institution. In addition, with its profligate spending the administration continued to provide fuel to its most vocal critics—especially the *News* and the *Observer*—and the air of suspicion and extravagance surrounding it never disappeared.

For instance, a new controversy arose in mid-1988 when the *Observer* revealed details of Holderman's unique student intern program. Students he selected privately—without a formal nomination and interview process— traveled with him all over the country and to Asia, the Caribbean, and Europe. Holderman rarely traveled alone (he usually had a bodyguard), and his retinue stayed in the most luxurious hotels and ate in the best restaurants along their way. The interns were paid handsomely. Holderman arranged for some to receive University credit for their travels and experiences. Like others with whom Holderman had contact, some interns received expensive gifts, and some even accompanied the president on shopping sprees. The *Observer* concluded that hundreds of interns had traveled on the trips, costing the University hundreds of thousands of dollars. Several interns moved into high-paying administration jobs after graduation—jobs that paid well more than starting salaries for assistant professors with earned doctorates. Carolina students who did not have the opportunity to participate had long referred to the handpicked interns as "Holderclones." Many were incensed about the secretive program, asking, "How do you join all the president's boys?" The *Gamecock's* editor called the program "exclusionary and elitist" and complained that such lavish sums of public money were spent on a few students while the rest suffered ever-increasing tuition charges. Some members of the faculty were concerned that the academic credit offered to the interns did not meet accreditation standards, but an internal investigation later cleared the president's office of any wrongdoing. Holderman's supporters on the board and in the state's business community stood by him, arguing that the intern program was a fantastic opportunity for the students selected and that the sums spent on the program were "chicken feed" compared to the amounts of money Holderman was raising. "To a business person," said one, "that's the bottom line."[126]

Sensational stories in the media, fueled by the air of secrecy surrounding the president's office, continued to haunt the University. The *News* persisted with its FOIA case seeking to open the records of the University's foundations, and in July 1989 a state judge ruled that the records should be subject to public scrutiny. The foundations, furthering the perception that they had something to hide, appealed the decision, again delaying the opening of their records.[127]

The following month the General Assembly's legislative audit committee (LAC) released a report on the relationship between the University, its foundations, and discretionary spending—a report many at the University saw as politically motivated. The LAC report was a scathing indictment of the University's management of public funds, confirming many doubts about the administration's activities. It addressed questions involved in the financing of the Koger and Swearingen Centers, which the University had initially claimed would require no state funding but which by July 1, 1988, had cost taxpayers some $4.5 million. The LAC also found that University officials had continued to mislead the Budget and Control Board about the status of private pledges on the two buildings.

Auditors were critical of the close relationship between USC's foundation directors and top university administrators, who were in several cases the same people. The LAC's criticism was that such dual office holding by public officials could potentially represent a conflict of interest. The LAC also found that these University officials received salary supplements from the foundations—in addition to their state-funded salary—ranging from $15,000 ($16,476) to $54,000 ($59,316), a finding that strengthened the impression that conflicts of interest existed between the University and the foundations. The committee also criticized the board of trustees for its handling of some $3.4 million ($3.7 million) in public discretionary funds, showing that it had kept confidential the names of some gift recipients in violation of their own disclosure policies. Overall, the LAC report depicted an administration at risk of conflicts of interest and willing to cut corners when it came to public disclosure, and a board of trustees failing to exercise proper oversight. Whether or not the report was politically motivated, the circumstances that had led to the study were undeniably the University's own doing. The report had come from the General Assembly's own audit committee and had to be taken seriously. In its aftermath, USC's credibility with the general public was, in the words of University spokesman Russ McKinney, "completely shot."[128]

To compound matters, just after the release of the LAC report, the CRDF was forced to release records detailing more expensive travel by University officials—this time on the CRDF's private jet—at public expense. At a cost to taxpayers of some $423,000 ($464,644), Holderman, his family, and University officials had flown on the jet in the company of the celebrities and diplomats brought to USC.[129] While such allegations were not new, the media frenzy that surrounded the new revelations combined with the conclusions of the Legislative Audit Committee to forcefully and clearly demonstrate that there were still significant problems with the way the University handled public money. These reports prodded the board of trustees to begin to take some action to reign in the president's spending practices; they realized that the criticisms of Holderman's administration had done significant damage to the University's public credibility, the lifeblood of any publicly supported institution. The board began to require regular reports from President Holderman on the spending of the University's discretionary fund. They later appointed an internal auditor to oversee the discretionary spending, but the auditor reported to Holderman, not the board, thus diluting the benefits of independent oversight.[130]

In the spring of 1990, a new series of FOIA requests from the *Observer* revealed that Holderman continued to misuse public funds after years of public rebukes for similar behavior. He spent some $534,000 ($556,549) from the University's discretionary fund during an eighteen-month period prior to May 1990, including $90,000 ($93,800) for travel and $162,000 ($168,840) on meals. He spent up to $724 ($755) a night on hotel rooms and hired $35 ($36)-an-hour chauffeurs to drive him. Other examples of extravagance with public funds further undermined the University's credibility, such as when he used a University credit card to buy two bronze statues for his offices at a cost of $6,900 ($7191), and expensive clothing and electronic equipment for himself and others (including student interns).[131] In spite of the controversy over his extravagant gift-giving in 1987, Holderman had continued give expensive gifts as a way of ingratiating himself to others. Critics pointed out that this type of profligate spending was not essential to fund-raising success, as Holderman argued when such spending was challenged. "You have to spend money to raise money," the president and his supporters repeatedly argued. However, the University was raising amounts comparable to peer universities whose presidents had no comparable expense account to pay for expensive gifts and shopping trips. As he had done in the midst of the first media frenzy surrounding his spending habits, Holderman issued another mea culpa, this time to the faculty; instead of apologizing for his excessive spending, however, he apologized for not better communicating the reasons why such spending was necessary.[132]

For many of Holderman's former supporters, this new round of spending revelations was too much. "He had deceived me," said USC board chair Michael J. Mungo, a man who had once defended Holderman's spending but who now became one of the president's most vocal and aggressive critics. The media interest in the story continued; even the *State*, the paper that was once one of Holderman's fiercest defenders but which had been sold to newspaper conglomerate Knight-Ridder, was now aggressively covering the story. Along with the *Greenville News* and the *Observer*, they ratcheted up the pressure on Holderman and the administration, running a series of front-page stories critical of his spending habits. In response to the new round of allegations, in late May 1990 the board of trustees passed strict limits on discretionary spending, declaring, "All expenditures by University personnel . . . will be reasonable, appropriate and justifiable." Among the limits they imposed were that hotel rooms were not to exceed $300 ($313) a night, University credit cards could not be used for personal purchases, and that the board chairman had to be informed of any large sums of money spent entertaining potential donors. Board chairman Michael J. Mungo stated that the intent of the rules was "to eliminate extravagance."[133]

In spite of the new revelations, Holderman retained the firm support of many of the most influential members of Columbia's business and political community. The Columbia Chamber of Commerce planned a public relations blitz to demonstrate their support for Holderman, and other prominent Columbians discussed underwriting Holderman's fund-raising expenses. The city's leadership insisted that his positive contributions to the city outweighed any negative perceptions his spending habits brought to the University. In the midst of this new storm of criticism, in mid-May 1990 USC welcomed President George Bush and Walt Disney Productions head Michael Eisner to deliver commencement addresses, bearing out the accolades of those who praised Holderman for raising the University's national profile. However, the media criticisms continued through the month of May. Facing increasing pressure from the board's new rules, the *State*'s new aggressive reporting, and threats of still more revelations, nine days after the board curbed his spending Holderman resigned.

The University community gave him a hero's sendoff. Said former South Carolina governor Robert McNair, "Jim Holderman meant more to the University of South Carolina and this community than any other president in modern history." USC trustee Charles Simons of Aiken said of Holderman's resignation, "It's a sad day for the state of South Carolina. It leaves us without probably the ablest president in [USC's] history." An unscientific poll by the *State* showed that some 61 percent of Columbians continued to support Holderman, and many believed the media had driven him from office. He had made Carolina's supporters and Columbians proud of their University. In a farewell speech, Holderman claimed to have lifted the University of South Carolina "from regional presence to national prominence." He asked, "Have we not conquered once and for all the false image of reactionary and xeno-phobic provincialism? Who can deny that this university is a respected citizen of the world today?" "If I leave anything behind," he said before his final exit, "I want it to be the realization that this University does indeed have the capacity to aim high and make it." Faculty senate chair Gunther Holst said that Holderman had "lifted this university from academic mediocrity and obscurity and put it in a place of national prominence." Governor Carroll Campbell presented Holderman with the Order of the Palmetto, South Carolina's highest civilian award. The board of trustees conferred on him the title "distinguished president emeritus" and bestowed honorary degrees on both him and his wife, Carolyn. They named provost Arthur K. Smith interim president.[134]

The widespread acclaim for James B. Holderman soon faded. His resignation did not end the damage that his administration would do to the public's perception of the University of South Carolina, nor did it end his connection to the institution. He remained a tenured professor in the Department of Government and International Studies, and indicated that he intended to eventually return to Carolina to teach. However, soon after he left office, investigations revealed that while president he had run a secretive scholarship program in which he awarded some $1.4 million of discretionary funds over a period of nearly ten years (beginning in 1981) to 381 students. Many recipients were in the controversial student intern program or were the children of influential politicians and other officials, such as Oregon Senator Mark Hatfield (who was Senate Appropriations Committee chairman when USC received the Swearingen Center grant). Others were the sons and daughters of celebrities, local businessmen, state officials, university trustees, and high-level USC staff. The scholarship program was without a formal application process or reviews of financial aid forms. Holderman defended it as a valuable tool to advance the University, but the revelation added to the sense that he had created conflicts of interest for those who should have been overseeing his administration.[135]

Shortly thereafter, the *News* and the AP finally won their FOIA lawsuit seeking access to the records of the CRDF—as a result of Holderman's having routed state and federal money through the private foundation—and the courts forced the CRDF to disclose its long-guarded records. A series of sensational media stories followed throughout the spring of 1991. After the courts ordered the foundation records opened to public scrutiny, foundation executives announced that some four years worth of records, covering 1981 to 1984, were "missing" and concluded that they had been inadvertently thrown out. The records had been the subject of a contentious lawsuit for nearly four years, and the sudden revelation that now some of the records were missing inspired conspiracy theories. When a former student worker for the foundation led reporters for the *Greenville News* to the "lost" records in the Richland County landfill (where the student claimed he had been ordered to dispose of them), the worst suspicions of USC's critics were borne out. The newly opened records suggested that Holderman had misused a corporate donation intended for a University foundation to instead pay for personal travel, and had another donation deposited into his own account. In May 1991, he pled guilty to using his office for personal gain and no contest to a charge of tax evasion. His pleas were a direct result of the information garnered from the long-concealed foundation records.[136]

The final chapter of Holderman's career at the University of South Carolina played out in the closing months of 1991. In October, the *Observer* published a front-page story detailing allegations that Holderman had made sexual advances toward students in the controversial presidential intern program. While Holderman categorically denied the allegations, the University administration, led by John M. Palms (hired in early 1991 as the twenty-sixth president), took the charges seriously and conducted their own investigtion. Their internal investigation corroborated the nature of the allegations reported by the *Observer,* and Palms immediately took steps to institute tenure revocation procedures against Holderman. Before the process could begin in earnest, in December 1991 Holderman resigned his faculty tenure in the Department of Government and International Studies, ending his fourteen-year connection with the University of South Carolina. The board of trustees took a final step, deciding by a one-vote margin to revoke Holderman's title of distinguished president emeritus.[137]

When Arthur K. Smith took over as interim president in June 1990, he was determined to reestablish the momentum that had existed at Carolina before the crush of events had sidetracked the University. He declared "an era of openness and accountability" to restore public trust in the institution. His first major act as interim president was to cancel the controversial scholarship program that had been directed out of the president's office. Smith acknowledged that the institution's image had taken a beating in the last years of the Holderman term, declaring, "Correcting some of the damage that the university's image has suffered must be a very important priority for me and others in the university system."[138] He also reaffirmed that the "2001 vision" lived on, despite Holderman's resignation. Smith's most significant accomplishment as interim president was to affiliate the University with an all-sports conference. In August 1990, the board gave him the authority to accept a conference invitation if one could be secured. In September, the Southeastern Conference (SEC) extended Carolina an invitation to join, and Smith accepted it. Supporters of Carolina athletics were ecstatic to have the opportunity to compete in a nationally prestigious athletic conference nearly twenty years after seceding from the ACC. After almost two decades in a comparative athletic wilderness, with the SEC membership the University of South Carolina enjoyed a new identity and found a new peer group in the southeast's leading collegiate athletic conference. The conference membership brought immense public relations value.[139]

Many observers believed that Arthur Smith, who acknowledged that he was a candidate for the permanent job as president, had thus sealed this position at the University. However, the board of trustees opted to look elsewhere, and in January 1991 announced that they had chosen the University of South Carolina's next president: John M. Palms, a distinguished nuclear physicist, former professor, and provost at Emory University who had been president of Georgia State University for some eighteen months before coming to Carolina. Palms readily accepted the challenge of directing the University toward the general goals of excellence outlined in *2001: The New Dimension*, with a focus on developing specific criteria to measure the University's progress.[140]

With the appointment of John Palms, the University entered a new era, but one with some continuities from the previous decade. The 1980s had been filled with noteworthy events and some of the highest levels of enthusiasm and optimism in the University's history. Holderman's administration had brought the University increased international visibility, filled its accounts, and boosted its self-esteem and expectations for itself. In many ways, his administration had created a sense of momentum and a real opportunity for the University of South Carolina to markedly improve. It was a stronger institution at the end of the decade than it had been at the beginning. The 1980s marked a new era when Carolina began to overcome "the tyranny of limited expectations" and have the confidence that it could achieve a status as a leading American research university. James B. Holderman taught the University to aim high. But he left the institution in turmoil, and the public image that he had worked so hard to create was shattered. The many-faceted controversies of Holderman's precipitous fall inflicted significant harm to the integrity of the institution and overshadowed many of the good things he had accomplished. The University's credibility as a steward of state tax dollars suffered serious damage, and as a state institution dependent on taxpayer dollars for nearly half of its operating revenue, such damage was indeed severe.

Few in the modern world of higher education would doubt the importance of achieving favorable public attention for the good things happening
at an institution. It is widely accepted that, for a public university president,
these are nearly imperative if the institution is to appeal to its many constituencies and obtain the resources it requires to meet the needs of the state
it serves. From this perspective, what Jim Holderman did in attracting favorable attention to the University of South Carolina was an important part of
his job, and he was quite successful. However, the style in which he went
about attracting public attention and the way in which he handled the University's assets stepped over a dimly defined line of what was considered
acceptable behavior for a public official. His personal behavior with students,
publicly revealed well after his resignation, clearly crossed that boundary.

In the wake of the debacle, many observers pointed to the board of
trustees and asked how they could have been so lax in exercising oversight.
Several board members claimed that with his disarming charm and over-
powering charisma, Holderman had intimidated and manipulated them. He
had assured them that nothing was amiss and that the media simply had a
grudge against him. Even after his departure, he retained the support of the
university's most powerful supporters, who liked the results he brought and
as a result the rest gave him the benefit of the doubt. The effectiveness of their
"hands-off" approach was reinforced by the high-profile successes of the
administration, such as presidential and papal visits. As a result, few dared
ask for an inquiry into his methods for fear of ridicule, intimidation, or of
being labeled an enemy of Holderman, and by implication of the University
of South Carolina. The board of trustees, as a body, never publicly admon-
ished him for his spending habits, and no board member lost his seat as a
result of the controversy. One trustee said of the response to his few attempts
to audit Holderman's financial records: "Senior trustees made statements like,
'you're hurting the university; Jim Holderman's a great man; he's brought us
up from mediocrity.'"[141] Trustee Herbert Adams of Laurens put it this way:
"If you ever questioned anything, I felt like I was stepping on hallowed
ground."[142] In later years, Holderman admitted that he had overpowered the
board. "I overwhelmed them," he said, "with the gee-whiz factor. Gee whiz,
they would say, he's gonna do that? They were knocked out by it. They liked
all the things we were doing."[143]

Whether Holderman beguiled or intimidated those who would have questioned his behavior, there was an overall absence of self-scrutiny and healthy
self-criticism that might have helped those in responsible positions understand what was being accomplished in comparison with Carolina's peers.
In addition, Holderman's style undermined public faith in the University's
credibility. Years later, he unapologetically admitted as much, while still

defending his behavior. "I overdid it. I did not keep in mind what this state could afford and understand. But I don't know that I'd do it differently if I had to do it all over again, because I think we made a difference." He insisted that he was misunderstood and that the public did not comprehend what it took to make a university great. He labeled his opponents "neanderthals" who cared only how the University of South Carolina was perceived in small-town South Carolina. "I did not care how we were perceived in Newberry. I was interested in how we were perceived in Washington, D.C. and New York. That is why I got criticized."[144] His attitude toward the state holds an important lesson for the University of South Carolina. As board of trustees Michael Mungo said just after Holderman's resignation, "The pursuit of excellence does not excuse not listening to your constituencies."[145] It was the University *of* South Carolina, not simply a university *in* South Carolina.

7 | STILL THE
FAITHFUL INDEX

UNIVERSITY OF SOUTH CAROLINA

Chartered in 1801 as the S.C. College. Opened January 10, 1805. Entire Student Body Volunteered For Confederate Service 1861. Soldier's Hospital 1862–65. Rechartered as U. of S.C. 1865. Radical Control 1873–77. Closed 1877–80. College of Agriculture and Mechanic Arts 1880–82. S.C. College 1882–87. U. of S.C. 1887–90. S.C. College 1890–1905. U. of S.C. 1906. FAITHFUL INDEX TO THE AMBITIONS AND FORTUNES OF THE STATE.

Text of historical marker, Sumter Street entrance to the University
of South Carolina, erected by the City of Columbia, 1936

The striking advances of the University of South Carolina have an intimate relationship to the post–World War II metamorphosis of the State economy. As the tax base of the State has improved the funding of the University has improved, and more and more South Carolinians have felt themselves economically capable of supporting their young people through a college of education. These highly educated young people will find it unnecessary to leave here for other regions upon graduation, because they will find suitable opportunities in industries, business, and professions within the State. The economy is destined to flourish and educational opportunities will continue to develop.

Thomas F. Jones, 1963

■

In his classic *The Mind of the South,* South Carolina native Wilbur J. Cash decried the irrelevance of the region's intellectual and educational leaders in 1940. "Here was the final great tragedy of the South as it stood in 1940," he wrote. Cash argued that the South's intellectual and educational leadership "was almost wholly inarticulated within the body of the South. If the people of the region were not entirely unaffected" by the region's intellectual leadership, "they were still affected by it only remotely and sporadically."[1]

Despite Cash's gloomy evaluation, in the years after he wrote his pessimistic treatise the South and southern higher education underwent a transformation. World War II unleashed powerful forces that remade the region and the state of South Carolina in the years after 1945, lessening the stifling impact of the twin evils of the post–Civil War South, racism and poverty. The forces set in motion by World War II transformed southern higher education, bringing it into a position of relative parity with colleges and universities in other regions and remaking the relationship between universities and the larger society.[2] The University of South Carolina was fully a part of these changes. That USC participated in nationwide changes was a break with the past, for in the early decades of the twentieth century Carolina had been confined to a relative backwater when compared to its peers across the nation. In the post–World War II era, the University, like South Carolina and the rest of the South, rejoined the mainstream of the nation. Likewise, the University of South Carolina moved from the periphery of life in South Carolina to a central role in the economic, cultural, social, and intellectual life of the state. The irrelevance that Cash had noted of southern intellectual leadership in 1940 was largely gone. By 1990, USC was tightly woven into the fabric of modern South Carolina, and each could not successfully exist without the other.

Among the revolutionary changes that swept the University of South Carolina in the period between 1940 and 1990 was a new conception about whom the University of South Carolina would serve. World War II and the GI Bill made college education accessible and desirable for unprecedented numbers of young South Carolinians, and the "tidal wave" of baby boomers during the 1960s and early 1970s transformed the University of South Carolina from a small institution of fewer than 3,000 students in 1950 to one of more than 26,000 by the late 1980s. This growth was more than a function of a simple population increase. In 1940, 31 percent of South Carolinians who graduated from high school entered college in the fall of the same year. Aided by new programs to help students attend college, such as federally subsidized student loans and direct grants, by 1988, that number was 50 percent.[3] A university education became an attainable goal for almost any motivated young person in South Carolina.

The most significant social movement in modern American history, the civil rights movement, also revolutionized access to the University of South Carolina. After decades of intransigent defense of white supremacy and racial segregation, South Carolina's white leadership acknowledged the inevitable and peacefully desegregated when Henrie Montieth, James Solomon, and Robert Anderson broke the University's eighty-six-year-old color barrier in 1963. By 1991, there were nearly 3,300 African American students at the University of South Carolina, representing some 15 percent of undergraduate and 9 percent of graduate students—one of the highest percentages of African American students at a historically white state university in the nation.[4]

USC's racial integration, while not without its tense moments, was peaceful and reflected the state's overall desire to maintain peace and harmony in its race relations.[5] Desegregation ended wasteful duplication of educational effort and offered the University a far wider pool from which to draw excellent students. Furthermore, it allowed the University to have an impact on a broader proportion of South Carolina's population, helping shape the new South Carolina that emerged in the postwar decades. Finally, by abandoning its costly defense of white supremacy, the leadership of the state and the University were free to develop the institution into a complete research university with national standards that could serve the burgeoning industrial economy of South Carolina.

Where these students could choose to go to college changed dramatically as well, as South Carolina and other southern states provided far more publicly-funded post–high school educational opportunities in the postwar period than ever before. South Carolina's government stepped in to provide these opportunities, creating a 26,000-student research university in Columbia and a nine-campus University of South Carolina "system," in addition to an expanded Clemson University, new technical colleges, and new state-supported four-year colleges. In 1950, some 50 percent of South Carolina's college students attended publicly-supported colleges and universities. By 1988, nearly 80 percent did.[6]

World War II brought significant changes to the University of South Carolina, embodied in the veterans who took advantage of the federally-funded GI Bill of Rights to attend college. More veterans attended the University of South Carolina than any other college or university in the state. The GI Bill and the veterans' use of it to enroll at the University of South Carolina cemented the institution's place as the largest, most comprehensive university in the state, a place it had not held before the war. Writing of the changes in higher education across the United States in the post–World War II period, Thomas N. Bonner called the GI Bill "the first of the great events that sparked the unintended revolution in higher education" in the United States. There is no better example of that revolution than the University of South Carolina.[7]

World War II and the GI Bill began a chain of events that revolutionized life for USC students. By 1990, restrictive rules governing student behavior—rules that had been the standard at USC since its founding—had all but disappeared. World War II veterans were generally older, more serious students concerned about quickly finishing their degrees and earning a living, and they were far different from any other generation of college students before them—they had earned the right to be treated as adults. The students of the 1950s and the early 1960s turned the veterans' approach on its head: they largely fit the stereotype of the complacent, conforming student, and the essence of the decade was captured in the most popular activity for male students, the panty raid. For USC's women, the 1950s reflected a continuation of the societal values that steered them into traditional roles.

By the late 1960s, however, student life began a dramatic, and seemingly permanent, change. With a rapidly expanding student body, more and more students began to live off-campus, beyond the limitations that a University-enforced system of in loco parentis could impose upon them. The advancing women's movement led to changes in the University's treatment of women, and new societal norms about the treatment of all young people led to an erosion of in loco parentis. By the middle 1970s, USC's on-campus students were free from most of the old restrictions on their behavior; their newfound freedom reflected similar developments on other southern college campuses.[8] A related development was the changing gender balance of students at the University. Exclusively male for most of its first century, Carolina began accepting women in 1895, and in 1940 women made up some 35 percent of the student body. However, by 1981 women were in the majority and by 1989 they made up nearly 56 percent of the student body.[9]

The astounding overall enrollment growth of the era had negative consequences. One of the casualties of the University's transformation was the close, family-like relationship of the student body. Like it or not, as a research "multiversity," the University of South Carolina in many ways became a less intimate and more impersonal and bureaucratic place in the years after 1960.

The period after World War II saw substantial change in the University's financial circumstances. For the first half of the twentieth century, USC was crippled by paltry state appropriations. In fact, South Carolina consistently funded its institutions of higher education at a rate lower than that of any other southern state. In the 1950s the state established a policy that allowed state institutions to borrow against future revenues to fund construction projects, enabling them to modernize their physical plants and leading to a college building boom. In addition, federally-funded projects in the 1960s such as urban renewal and federal loans and grants made even more rapid campus expansion possible. This unprecedented physical growth continued through the mid-1970s.

Another fiscal revolution concerned annual state appropriations. Through the mid-1960s, South Carolina continued to underfund its colleges and universities. However, by the mid-1970s, South Carolina had gone from spending the lowest percentage of its tax dollars on higher education of any southern state to spending the most. By the late 1980s, while South Carolina no longer spent more than any other southern state (as a percentage of total expenditures) on higher education, it was above both the regional and U.S. averages in higher education spending as a percentage of overall expenditures.[10] In the

South as a whole, by the early 1970s, the region's states provided public higher education funding (as a percentage of state taxes) at a level higher than the U.S. average—certainly a significant development for a region that had trailed the nation in education since the Civil War.[11] This new emphasis on higher education partly reflected the values brought by a new economy in the South. Though most states in the region were still controlled by an elite, the new urban elite placed far greater value on higher education than had the rural elite that controlled the state until the 1970s.[12] Desegregation was another factor, as the federal aid that became available during the 1960s was tied to nondiscrimination clauses.

While spending on higher education vastly increased, by the late 1980s the variety of advanced educational opportunities available at the University of South Carolina expanded to a level unimaginable in 1940. From a university that offered no doctoral programs in 1940, USC offered Ph.D.s in some 54 fields in 1990. From a graduate school of 78 students representing less than 4 percent of the student body in 1940, Carolina's graduate school of 9,596 (nearly four times Carolina's entire enrollment in 1940) made up 37 percent of the student body in 1990. Much of the expansion of USC's graduate programs was a result of the influx of students and federal dollars during the 1960s. A staggering array of degree programs in fields as varied as computer engineering and hotel, restaurant and tourism administration reflected fundamental changes in the state's economy. The University of South Carolina was filling the needs of a diverse economy that increasingly relied on the highly educated, and its expanded degree offerings mirrored similar developments at universities across the region.[13]

While graduate programs grew in response to the changing economy, research as a function of the University of South Carolina took on a new importance. Again, the federal government took the lead in sponsoring academic research, which had been virtually nonexistent at USC until the mid-1950s. By the late 1960s, USC attracted considerable amounts of federal research dollars, as well as funds from state, local, and private sources. Though by the late 1980s the institution ranked below the nation's leaders in research expenditures, Carolina was a genuine research university committed to a public service mission in addition to teaching. Other southern universities developed similar research programs and benefited greatly from federal funding. Though in 1988 no southern university ranked among the top twenty in the nation in the amount of federal support for research, over 27 percent of federal research expenditures went to southern institutions.[14]

The postwar years saw important changes in the nature of the University's faculty. The 1940 faculty had been almost solely interested in teaching, but by the 1970s research had become an important measure of a faculty member's worth to the institution. Faculty preparation for their careers reflected nationwide changes in higher education, where the doctoral research degree became a virtual sine qua non for university-level teaching across the nation. In 1940, only 29 percent of USC's faculty held the Ph.D. By 1991, that figure was 80 percent, and 90 percent of faculty in the liberal arts and sciences held the degree.[15] The faculty gained more power within the University's administrative structure, with a faculty senate holding important policy-making responsibilities and considerable control over faculty tenure decisions. The challenge for Carolina was to attract and hold outstanding faculty, a task made difficult by historically low faculty salaries. Between 1940 and 1990, though USC fought its way out of the cellar in faculty salary rankings among southern universities, its salaries still remained well below the leading public institutions in the region. Salaries in southern institutions as a region trailed national averages, as they had for the entire twentieth century.[16]

Faculty salaries were largely a function of state support for the University, but during the post–World War II period Carolina began to rely more and more on outside sources of income for operating revenue. During the late 1970s and 1980s, student tuition and fees began to make up a larger proportion of that revenue, as did research grants and contracts from outside sources. These trends reflected national changes in the way states funded higher education, with an increasing proportion of institutional revenues deriving from sources other than direct state appropriations.[17] Raising private funds for endowments that supplemented these sources of funding became increasingly important as well, and became another important measure of the University's success. By the 1980s, fund-raising was a high-profile mission of Carolina's administrators, particularly the University president, who was now more of a manager and goodwill ambassador for the institution than a practicing scholar.

The overall role of the University of South Carolina in the context of South Carolina's structure of higher educational institutions was a bone of contention throughout the post–World War II period. Should USC have a school of engineering? Should it have a medical school? Were such programs wasteful duplication or a necessity in a small state seeking to improve the quality of life and educational level of its citizens? What was the relation of the state university to technical education and/or community colleges? Other southern states, notably Georgia and North Carolina (both more populous and prosperous states than South Carolina), opted for different routes than the one chosen in the Palmetto State. South Carolina's leaders chose their route consciously, and the University continues to face similar questions as it enters its third century. Consequently, in spite of monumental improvements in the quality, diversity, and availability of higher education, South Carolina's public research universities and colleges remain competitors for scarce state funding.

Nonetheless, the state's commitment to developing two comprehensive research universities indicated the extent of change in the Palmetto State in the period between 1940 and 1990. An overwhelmingly agricultural economy had been transformed; by the 1980s South Carolina's economy was committed to industry. Likewise, the state's leaders had once been primarily committed to maintaining a system of white supremacy; by the 1980s they were firmly committed to economic development as their primary goal. The remarkable development of the University of South Carolina from a small, primarily undergraduate institution to a modern research university was a direct reflection of this transformation.

Despite the overwhelming change, there remained a strong strand of continuity. Though the University of South Carolina of 1990 was a very different place from the University of South Carolina of 1940, USC was still what the people of South Carolina wanted it to be. Free from the restraints brought by racism and poverty, it could now strive for genuine excellence on a national model. The University of South Carolina had become an integral part of the emergence of a new South Carolina in the post–World War II period. The historical marker on Sumter Street briefly summarizes the institution's first century, but in its second, Carolina remained the "Faithful Index to the Ambitions and Fortunes" of South Carolina.

Postscript | BUILDING UPON
A GRAND TRADITION

1991–2001

Could the attention of the legislature be directed to this important object, and a State college be raised and fostered by its hand at Columbia . . . there could be no doubt of its rising into eminence, because being supported at first by the public funds, the means could not be wanting of inviting and providing for learned and respectable Professors in the various branches of science. Well chosen libraries would be procured, and philosophical apparatus lead the pursuits of our youth from theory to practice.

Governor John Drayton, 1801

Our potential for the state compels us to believe that USC's students must soon find here the same caliber of institution that their nineteenth-century forebears did—one of the great universities in America.

John M. Palms, 1997

■

The events of 1990 and 1991 made for two of the most difficult years in the history of the University of South Carolina. As University leaders dealt with the aftermath of the Holderman debacle, they also faced economic recession and budget cuts. However, they kept an eye on the future, looking toward a day when, with the setbacks of those years behind it, they might again proclaim ambitious goals. The board of trustees and John Palms remained committed to the goals of national excellence that had been announced with such fanfare in the 1980s. The 1990s saw the institution build on the accomplishments of previous years while proclaiming a lofty vision of what it should be in the twenty-first century.[1]

However, the institution's first priority in the months and years immediately after James B. Holderman resigned his faculty tenure was reestablishing the credibility and integrity of the institution, which had been so gravely undermined. Restructuring of the administration and the University's foundations streamlined areas that had been the focus of intense media and legislative attention and ensured that they supported the institution's overall academic priorities. New deans of colleges and schools gradually replaced those held over from the 1980s. The board of trustees took steps to ensure that Carolina was completely open and accountable to the public. John Palms insisted that the University must recommit itself to fundamental ethical values, and his inaugural address and subsequent public speeches stressed the University's motto, *Emollit mores nec sinit esse feros* ("Learning humanizes character and does not permit it to be cruel") as one basis for those values. The Division of Student Affairs initiated an effort to establish a code of ethics for students, embodied in the "Carolinian Creed," which describes a "code of civilized behavior," including personal and academic integrity, respecting the rights and property of others, eschewing bigotry, and demonstrating concern for others. With the exception of serious problems at the University's Lancaster campus (when the academic credibility of certain degree programs on that campus was challenged), the memories of the University's years of controversy between 1986 and 1991 have faded, replaced by a sense of momentum and optimism for the future. The University's integrity as a steward of the state's dollars and its ambitions has been restored.

Even as University leaders worked to reestablish institutional credibility, they continued to work toward a goal of overall academic excellence. The board of trustees has remained committed to advancing Carolina's standing relative to state universities in neighboring states, and to the recognition of USC as an institution of national quality. However, much of the work of University leaders in the 1990s involved a continuing struggle to overcome the "tyranny of limited expectations" in South Carolina. Their challenge has been to create a collective consensus among the University's constituencies that the rightful place of the University of South Carolina is among the best research universities in America. Accurate measures of the quality or relative level of excellence of a university are difficult to devise and nearly always subjective. Nonetheless, John Palms determined that membership in the Association of American Universities (AAU), the highly select group of the nation's very best universities, was an appropriate measure of whether this goal was achieved. Early in his tenure President Palms declared the overarching institutional goal of AAU membership, and in 1997 the board of trustees formally endorsed his vision along with a set of ten major goals it would take to move Carolina into the ranks of the AAU. In 2000, the board went further and established specific, measurable criteria for the first five years of the twenty-first century that they hope will carry the University to AAU membership, while balancing that vision with the imperative of continued service to South Carolina.

During the 1990s, the University achieved a number of milestones that indicate that there are indeed reasons for optimism. University leaders returned to the idea that in order to build institutional excellence, improving the faculty had to be the primary focus. Part of the strategy has been to hire young faculty from AAU-caliber institutions, and some 70% of the 500 faculty hired during the 1990s were from these types of institutions. The University has also made a concerted effort to diversify the faculty by hiring increasing numbers of minorities and women. As another way to improve the faculty, promotion and tenure standards were overhauled in order to ensure that the University was keeping and promoting its best. The faculty have had increasing success attracting competitive research grants from federal and private sources, an important indicator of the esteem and potential of an institution's faculty. Outside research funding topped $121 million in 2000, up from $40 million 1990. In 2000, the board of trustees reached an agreement with the boards of the state's two other research universities, Clemson and the Medical University of South Carolina, to collaborate on projects that compete for research grants, further increasing the chances that South Carolina's universities will be in an even more favorable competitive position to attract coveted research dollars.

The ambitious vision of the University in the 1990s has attracted unprecedented amounts of private support for a state institution in South Carolina. In 1995, the University upgraded and expanded its development office in preparation for its bicentennial capital campaign. The campaign goal, announced in that year, was $200 million. Because of quick success and the booming economy of the late 1990s, that target was soon increased to $300 million, and in 2000, to $500 million. As a result, the University's overall private endowment rose from $57 million in 1990 to about $275 million in 2000. In addition, the overall quality of USC's student body has continued to improve, allowing USC's highly regarded Honors College steady growth. Over 90% of Carolina's students hail from South Carolina, and the University attracts diverse students from around the nation and world. Nearly one-fifth of USC students are African American, the highest proportion of any formerly all-white state university in the nation. The board of trustees has pressed hard to maintain the University's commitment to the Palmetto state and its students, and they have emphasized improvements in the living-learning atmosphere for those who live on campus. The 1990s saw a construction boom that rivaled that of the 1960s and 1970s, a surge of activity that has continued into the bicentennial year. That phase of construction has been guided by a master plan for campus development that puts improving student life near the top of the priority list.

The optimism surrounding the University as it enters its bicentennial year of 2001 is palpable. For one of the few times in its history, there is a consensus among Carolina's trustees, administrators, faculty, students, and alumni about the direction of the University. At the beginning of its third century, the University of South Carolina appears to be on the verge of conquering a legacy of limited expectations. However, to accomplish the University's ambitious goals, there is one piece of the puzzle still missing: adequate state support. While there is no consensus among the state's leaders to make a major investment in its research universities, there is agreement that increased levels of public funding are the only way to make USC's goals a reality. At this writing, the University's bicentennial celebration has begun, and thoughts of the University's future are at center stage. As the University community ponders its next century, it is also useful to consider the past, particularly the post–World War II era, when the research university emerged. In these years, the University was transformed into the institution that now aspires to inclusion among the nation's greatest universities. It is upon a foundation of two centuries of growth and change that future visions of excellence for the University of South Carolina will be built.

NOTES

PREFACE

1. Daniel Walker Hollis, *University of South Carolina,* vol. 1, *The South Carolina College* (Columbia: University of South Carolina Press, 1951), vol. 2, *College to University* (Columbia: University of South Carolina Press, 1956). Hollis's history was the first written by a professional historian trained in "scientific history." The earlier histories of the institution are Maximilian LaBorde, *History of the South Carolina College, from Its Incorporation, Dec. 19, 1801 to Dec. 19, 1865* (Charleston, S.C.: Evans and Cogswell, 1874) and Edwin L. Green, *A History of the University of South Carolina* (Columbia: The State Co., 1916). In addition, the Institute for Southern Studies at the University of South Carolina published a useful pictorial history of the University titled *Remembering the Days: An Illustrated History of the University of South Carolina* (Columbia: R. L. Bryan, 1982).

2. The idea that World War II was an important watershed in southern history has gained increasing acceptance as historians have come to more fully understand the long-term impact of the war on southern life in general. See especially Clarence L. Mohr, "World War II and the Transformation of Southern Higher Education," in Neil R. McMillen, ed., *Remaking Dixie: The Impact of World War II on the American South* (Jackson: University Press of Mississippi, 1997), 33–55, as well as other essays in that volume; see also Numan Bartley, *The New South, 1945–1980: The Story of the South's Modernization* (Baton Rouge: Louisiana State University Press, 1995); Morton Sosna, "More Important Than the Civil War? The Impact of World War II on the South," in James C. Cobb and Charles R. Wilson, eds., *Perspectives on the American South: An Annual Review of Society, Politics and Culture* 4 (New York and London: Gordon and Breach Science Publishers, 1987), 145–61; and David R. Goldfield, *Promised Land: The South Since 1945* (Arlington Heights, Ill.: Harlan Davidson, 1987).

3. For some critiques of the "house history" genre, particularly with regard to southern colleges and universities, see John Thelin, "Southern Exposure: House Histories with Room for a View," *The Review of Higher Education* 10, no. 4 (summer 1987), 357–68; Thelin, "Supplemental Bibliography," in Frederick Rudolph, *The American College and University: A History* (reprinted Athens: University of Georgia Press, 1990), 517–25; Thomas Dyer, "Higher Education in the South Since the Civil War: Historiographical Issues and Trends," in Walter Fraser, R. Frank Saunders, Jr., and Jon L. Wakelyn, *The Web of Southern Social Relations: Women, Family and Education* (Athens: University of Georgia Press, 1985), 127–45; Dyer, "On the Writing of College and University History," *The Pennsylvania Magazine of History and Biography* 113, no. 3 (July 1989), 439–46.

4. Among the recent wave of southern house histories published in the last fifteen years, the most notable are James R. Montgomery, et. al., *To Foster Knowledge: A History of the University of Tennessee, 1794–1970* (Knoxville: University of Tennessee Press, 1984); Paul K. Conkin, *Gone With the Ivy: A Biography of Vanderbilt University* (Knoxville: University of Tennessee Press, 1985); Thomas G. Dyer, *The University of Georgia: A Bicentennial History, 1785–1985* (Athens: University of Georgia Press, 1985); Robert C. McMath Jr., et. al., *Engineering the New South: Georgia Tech, 1885–1985* (Athens: University of Georgia Press, 1985); William D. Snider, *Light on the Hill: A History of the University of North Carolina at Chapel Hill* (Chapel Hill: University of North Carolina Press, 1992); Robert F. Durden, *The Launching of Duke University, 1924–1949* (Durham: Duke University Press, 1993); David G. Sansing, *The University of Mississippi: A Sesquicentennial History* (Jackson: University of Mississippi Press, 1999); Clarence L. Mohr and Joseph E. Gordon, *Tulane: The Emergence of a Modern University, 1945–1980* (Baton Rouge: Louisiana State University Press, 2000).

5. See histories listed above, especially Mohr and Gordon, and Durden, as well as Amy T. McCandless, *The Past in the Present: Women's Higher Education in the Twentieth Century South* (Tuscaloosa: University of Alabama Press, 1999); and the entire *History of Higher Education Annual* 19 (1999), a theme issue dealing specifically with southern higher education in the twentieth century.

6. Paul Conkin, *Gone With the Ivy: A Biography of Vanderbilt University* (Knoxville: University of Tennessee Press, 1985), 737.

7. Merle Curti and Vernon Carstensen, *The University of Wisconsin: A History, 1848–1925* (Madison: University of Wisconsin Press, 1949), vol. 1, ix.

8. Hollis, vol. 2, 20.

PROLOGUE—THE UNIVERSITY OF SOUTH CAROLINA, 1801–1940

1. Daniel W. Hollis, "Samuel Chiles Mitchell, Social Reformer in Blease's South Carolina," *South Carolina Historical Magazine* 70, no. 1 (January 1969), 20.

2. Michael Sugrue, "South Carolina College: The Education of an Antebellum White Elite," Ph.D. dissertation, Columbia University, 1993; Hollis, *University of South Carolina*, vol. 1, *The South Carolina College* (Columbia: University of South Carolina Press, 1951); Edwin L. Green, *A History of the University of South Carolina* (Columbia: The State Company, 1916); Maximilian LaBorde, *History of the South Carolina College, from its Incorporation, Dec. 19, 1801 to Dec. 19, 1865,* 2d ed. (Charleston: Walker, Evans and Cogswell, 1874). For a good, short synopsis of the history of the University, see Hollis's "A Brief History of the University," in *Remembering the Days: An Illustrated History of the University of South Carolina* (Columbia: R. L. Bryan Company, 1982), ix–xxviii; Walter B. Edgar, "2001: Building on a Grand Tradition," unpublished paper in Walter B. Edgar Papers, Manuscripts Division, South Caroliniana Library, University of South Carolina, Columbia (repository hereafter referred to as SCL). References to "Hollis" followed by volume number but no other title will be to his *University of South Carolina.*

3. Hollis, vol. 1, ch. 7; Hollis, *University of South Carolina,* vol. 2, *College to University* (Columbia: University of South Carolina Press, 1956), 3–79; see also Pamela Mercedes White, "'Free and Open': The Radical University of South Carolina, 1873–1877," M.A. thesis, University of South Carolina, 1975; John Herbert Roper, "A Reconsideration: The University of South Carolina During Reconstruction," *Proceedings of the South Carolina Historical Association* (1974), 46–57; W. Lewis Burke Jr., "The Radical Law School: The University of South Carolina School of Law and Its African American Graduates," and Michael Robert Mounter, "Richard Theodore Greener and the African American Individual in a Black and White World," in James Lowell Underwood and W. Lewis Burke Jr., *At Freedom's Door: African American Founding Fathers in Reconstruction South Carolina* (Columbia: University of South Carolina Press, 2000), 90–115 and 130–65.

4. Hollis, "A Brief History," xx–xxii; Ernest M. Lander Jr., *A History of South Carolina, 1865–1960,* 2d ed. (Columbia: University of South Carolina Press, 1970), 139–40.

5. Walter B. Edgar, *South Carolina in the Modern Age* (Columbia: University of South Carolina Press, 1992), 22–24; Hollis, vol. 2, 148–96. By comparison, in the 1893–94 academic year, Clemson had over 400 freshmen while Carolina had but 18.

   Throughout this work I have used the conversion tables devised by John J. McCusker in "How Much Is That in Real Money? A Historical Price Index for Use as a Deflator of Money Values in the Economy of the United States," *Proceedings of the American Antiquarian Society* 101, pt. 2 (October 1991): 297–373. McCusker's price index tables allowed me to convert all dollar figures to 1991 constant dollar equivalents. All dollar figures are given in contemporary values, followed by the 1991 value in parentheses.

   As McCusker notes, these monetary conversions should be considered "hypothetical rather than definitive." They are intended to give the reader a sense of what the approximate value of dollars spent in 1940 or 1960 were in 1991. To convert these numbers from 1991 dollars to current dollars, the reader must consider the inflation rate between 1991 and the current date and convert from these figures.

6. Hollis, vol. 2, 160–61, 170–76, 197–221, 239–40, 269–70; Lander, 140–41; "Annual Report of the Superintendent of Education, 1910," in *Reports and Resolutions of the General Assembly of South Carolina, 1911,* 130–31; Edgar, "2001," Edgar Papers.

7. Hollis, vol. 2, vii–viii, 177, 240; Hollis, "A Brief History," xxii–xxiii; Allan M. Cartter, "The Role of Higher Education in the Changing South," in John C. McKinney and Edgar T. Thompson, eds., *The South in Continuity and Change* (Durham, N.C.: Duke University Press, 1965), 289.

8. Hollis, vol. 2, ch. 12, especially 295; see also Michael John Dennis, "Educating the 'Advancing' South: State Universities and Progressivism in the New South, 1887–1915," Ph.D. dissertation, Queen's University at Kingston, 1996.

9. Hollis, vol. 2, 296–322.
10. Hollis, vol. 2, 303.
11. *Report of the University of South Carolina for 1948–1949, Prepared by Norman M. Smith, President, at the Request of the Board of Trustees* (serial is contained in *Reports and Resolutions of the General Assembly of South Carolina* and is hereafter referred to as "Annual Report, *year*"), 13.
12. Hollis, vol. 2, 332–34.
13. Hollis, vol. 2, 336–37; Annual Report, 1948–49, 12.
14. Hollis, vol. 2, 333–34, 338.

CHAPTER 1—"ON THE BRINK OF A NEW ERA," 1940–1945

1. H. Clarence Nixon, "Colleges and Universities," in W. T. Couch, ed., *Culture in the South* (Chapel Hill: University of North Carolina Press, 1934), 229–47. Nixon had been a contributor to the landmark book *I'll Take My Stand: The South and the Agrarian Tradition* (1930) that led its writers, most of whom had a connection to Vanderbilt University in Nashville, Tennessee, to be labeled the "Nashville Agrarians." For a closer look at H. Clarence Nixon, see Sarah Newman Shouse, *Hillbilly Realist: Herman Clarence Nixon of Possum Trot* (Tuscaloosa: University of Alabama Press, 1986); on the Agrarian movement, see Paul Conkin, *The Southern Agrarians* (Knoxville: University of Tennessee Press, 1988) and Daniel Joseph Singal, *The War Within: From Victorian to Modernist Thought in the South, 1919–1945* (Chapel Hill: University of North Carolina Press, 1982).
2. The volume that included Nixon's essay also included essays by South Carolinians as well as graduates of the University of South Carolina. John D. Allen, a Latta native, contributed "Journalism in the South." H. C. Brearley, from St. Charles, a 1916 graduate of the University of South Carolina and professor of sociology at Clemson, contributed "The Pattern of Violence." Brearley himself was a close associate of Odum and helped prepare the *Manual for Southern Regions*, a study guide to accompany Odum's magnum opus, *Southern Regions of the United States*. Broadus Mitchell, a 1913 graduate of the University of South Carolina (and son of Carolina's fourteenth president, Samuel Chiles Mitchell), contributed "A Survey of Industry." Josephine Pinckney, a Charleston native and noted poet and novelist, contributed "Bulwarks Against Change." No USC faculty members contributed to the volume.
3. For an evaluation of Howard Odum and the regionalist movement in Chapel Hill, see Singal; Michael O'Brien, *The Idea of the American South, 1920–1941* (Baltimore: Johns Hopkins University Press, 1979); and Dewey W. Grantham, *The South in Modern America* (New York: HarperCollins, 1994), 139–69.
4. G. Croft Williams, a professor of sociology at the University of South Carolina, had contributed to the emerging sociological literature on the South with his 1928 book *Social Problems of South Carolina* (Columbia: The State Company, 1928). This book preceded most of the work of the "regionalists" that followed Howard Odum, but they nonetheless ignored the book, and it was not cited in

Odum's 1936 masterpiece *Southern Regions of the United States*. Williams's next book, *A Social Interpretation of South Carolina* (Columbia: University of South Carolina Press, 1946) attacked regionalism head on, asserting that it was essentially meaningless. Williams argued that state, rather than regional, study was the only kind of sociological research that could bring about material improvements, because states were political entities that were equipped to bring tangible power to bear on social problems. See his preface, viii.

5. Hollis, vol. 2, vii–viii.

6. James C. Cobb, "World War II and the Mind of the Modern South," in Neil R. McMillen, ed., *Remaking Dixie: The Impact of World War II on the American South* (Jackson: University Press of Mississippi, 1997), 9.

7. Clarence L. Mohr, "World War II and the Transformation of Southern Higher Education," in McMillen, ed., *Remaking Dixie*, 34.

8. Annual Report, 1940, 3,6,9; "Annual Report of the Board of Trustees of Clemson Agricultural College to the General Assembly" (in *Reports and Resolutions of the General Assembly of South Carolina*, report hereafter "Clemson Annual Report, *year*"), 1940, 4, 6–8; Hollis, vol. 2, 239. Because Clemson annually received the entire receipts from a state tax on fertilizer, special appropriations for its agricultural extension and research work, and a portion of the state's federal Morrill Act funds (all in addition to its regular state appropriation), it is difficult to directly compare the total state appropriations of Clemson and the University. For example, in 1939–40, USC's total appropriation (maintenance only) amounted to $299,875 ($2,942,749). In the same year, Clemson's total state appropriation for collegiate activities (maintenance only) was $272,585 ($2,674,946). However, Clemson received $51,385 ($504,254) in federal Morrill Act funds. Clemson also received another $306,704 ($3,009,764) state appropriation for its agricultural extension and research work. This additional funding allowed Clemson to fund administrative costs common to both collegiate and research/extension work. See also *Public Higher Education in South Carolina* (Nashville: George Peabody College For Teachers, 1946), 42–52.

9. *Reports and Resolutions of the General Assembly of South Carolina*, 1941, vol. 2, "Report of the State Treasurer of South Carolina, July 1, 1939 to June 30, 1940," passim. USC received 25 percent of the total state spending on higher education.

10. Ibid., 1939–40, 9, 1940–41, 7; *Bulletin of the University of South Carolina, Announcements for 1939–40* (title varies; hereafter "USC Catalog, *year*"), 239–40.

11. Annual Report, 1939–40, 3, 1940–41, 7.

12. Allan M. Cartter, "Qualitative Aspects of Southern University Education," *Southern Economic Journal* 32, no. 1, part 2 (July 1965), 39–47.

13. Tindall, *The Emergence of the New South, 1913–1945* (Baton Rouge: Louisiana State University Press, 1967), 498; Cartter, "Qualitative Aspects," 39–69.

14. Clarence Stephen Marsh, ed., *American Universities and Colleges*, 4th ed., (Washington, D.C.: American Council on Education, 1940), 1040.

15. Faculty Minutes, 1 September 1943, 239–40; V. R. Cardozier, *Colleges and Universities in World War II* (Westport Conn.: Praeger Publishers, 1993), 118; Hollis, vol. 2, 216–17; USC Catalog, 1947–48, 25–39; *Garnet and Black*, 1942, 22; author interview with Rufus G. Fellers, 4 February 1997. Callcott's Albert Shaw lectures were published by the Johns Hopkins University Press as *The Caribbean Policy of the United States*.
16. Marsh, *American Universities*, 1940, 845.
17. *Public Higher Education*, 113.
18. Annual Report, 1940, 6–7; *Public Higher Education*, 129; Frank H. Wardlaw, ed., *Men and Women of Carolina: Selected Addresses and Papers by J. Rion McKissick* (Columbia: University of South Carolina Press, 1948), 96–97.
19. Hollis, vol. 2, 307–8.
20. Frederick Rudolph, *The American College and University: A History* (New York: Knopf, 1962; reprint, Athens: University of Georgia Press, 1990), 394–99; John S. Brubacher and Willis Rudy, *Higher Education in Transition: A History of American Colleges and Universities, 1636–1968*, 2d ed. (New York: Harper & Row, 1968), 216–17; Joseph M. Stetar, "In Search of a Direction: Southern Higher Education after the Civil War," *History of Education Quarterly* 29 (fall 1985). For an extended discussion of this evolution at the University of South Carolina in the post–World War II period, see Elsie Watts, "The Freshman Year Experience, 1962–1990: An Experiment in Humanistic Higher Education," Ph.D. dissertation, Queen's University, 1999.
21. *Garnet and Black*, 1938, 25; Author interviews with Rhett Jackson, 29 November 1999, Palmer McArthur, 25 January 2000. Interview with Helen A. Tovey, by Sally McKay, Carolyn Matalene, and Katherine Reynolds, 26 January 2000; Greene Street had been known as "Green" Street since the founding of Columbia. However, in 1976, in commemoration of the nation's bicentennial, the spelling of the street was changed to Greene Street to honor Revolutionary War General Nathaniel Greene. In this work, the street will be referred to as "Greene" Street.
22. Jackson interview; McArthur interview; Lauren Currie McArthur Jr., *Growing Up in Bennettsville, Student Days* (Greenville, S.C.: Furman University, 1998).
23. McArthur interview; Wardlaw, ed., *Men and Women of Carolina*, 1–20; James B. Meriwether, "Preface," in Mary M. Dunlap, Leland H. Cox, and George F. Hayhoe, comp., *A Catalog of the South Caroliniana Collection of J. Rion McKissick*, (Spartanburg: Reprint Company, 1977), ix.
24. Wardlaw, ed., *Men and Women of Carolina*, 24.
25. Wardlaw, ed., *Men and Women of Carolina*, 84–89.
26. Wardlaw, ed., *Men and Women of Carolina*, 107; Author interview with Daniel W. Hollis, 21 February 1997. On the controversies surrounding Thomas Cooper, see Hollis, vol. 1, 74–118.
27. Wardlaw, ed., *Men and Women of Carolina*, 84–89, 107; Annual Report, 1939–40, 3–4; 1940–41, 9; *Gamecock*, 28 November 1941, 12 December 1941, 11 January 1948; Hollis, vol. 2, 337; McArthur interview.

28. Annual Report, 1939–40, 9; USC Catalog, 1940–41, 16. The deans of the various colleges and schools in 1940 were Francis W. Bradley, College of Arts and Science; Orin F. Crow, School of Education; Samuel C. DePass, School of Journalism; James N. Frierson, School of Law; Emery T. Motley, School of Pharmacy; George E. Olson, School of Commerce; Walter E. Rowe, School of Engineering; Reed Smith, Graduate School; W. H. Ward, Extension Division.

29. Hollis, vol. 2, 337; *Public Higher Education,* 125; Callcott interview.

30. *Garnet and Black* (Columbia: Yearbook of the University of South Carolina), 1930, 259.

31. Carolina was one of only seven South Carolina colleges on the AAU's approved list. They were the College of Charleston, The Citadel, Converse College, Furman University, The University of South Carolina, Winthrop College, and Wofford College. Marsh, *American Universities,* 1940, 18, 1040–43; Fellers interview; Hollis interview.

32. Leonard T. Baker to the president of the University of South Carolina, 1986, 23 March, 1936, "Modern Era" topical file, USC Archives.

33. Wilfred H. Callcott, ed., *South Carolina: Economic and Social Conditions in 1944,* (Columbia: University of South Carolina Press, 1945), 188–92; *Public Higher Education,* 179–81.

34. McArthur interview. Tovey interview.

35. Hollis, vol. 2, 334–36; McArthur interview; McArthur, *Growing Up in Bennettsville,* 51. A study of the vocations of parents of Carolina's 2,004 students in the 1940–41 school year, done to counteract the charge that Carolina was the college of South Carolina's elite, showed that a plurality, 214 students, were the sons or daughters of farmers. The list of parental occupations was interesting: according to the survey most parents of Carolina students did not hold "prestigious" jobs. Next on the list, behind farmers, were housewives (the vocation of the parents of 190 students), then merchants and grocers (145), retired and unemployed (128), salesmen (116), railroad employees (79), and teachers (77). These were followed by lawyers (66) and doctors (60). Twenty-six students were the children of textile workers, 23 of clerical workers, 21 of ministers, and 5 of legislators and jurists. Carolina's students included 16 children of real estate dealers, 14 of electricians, 13 of carpenters, 9 of dentists, 9 of cotton brokers, and 7 of general laborers. There was one child each of a janitor, a jeweler, a butcher, a social worker, a brick maker, a golf course owner, a baker, a nightwatchman, and a termite exterminator, among many others. Annual Report, 1940–41, 9–10.

36. *Garnet and Black,* 1939, 110.

37. Hollis, vol. 2, 335; USC Catalog, 1940–41, 86–87; Steven W. Lynn, "A History of Greek-Letter Social Fraternities at South Carolina College and University," USC Archives, 76–81; Wardlaw, ed., *Men and Women of Carolina,* passim; McArthur, *Growing Up in Bennettsville,* 32–51.

38. Hollis, vol. 2, 337–38; Annual report, 1939–40, 3. The restrictions on women's admission, housing, and higher tuition rates had been a cost-saving measure taken in 1933, in the midst of the Great Depression. For a detailed look at life

for women students at Carolina in the period before World War II, see Victoria Terhecte Kalemaris, "No Longer Second-Class Students: Women's Struggle for Recognition and Equity at the University of South Carolina, 1914–1935," M.A. thesis, University of South Carolina, 1998.

39. McArthur interview; *Gamecock,* 8 February 1946; Amy Thompson McCandless, *The Past in the Present: Women's Higher Education in the Twentieth Century South* (Tuscaloosa: University of Alabama Press, 1999), 155–56.

40. Annual Report, 1939–40, 5, 9. Some 408 women were enrolled in the College of Arts and Science in 1939–40, while there were only 6 in the School of Law, 2 in the School of Pharmacy, and none in the School of Engineering.

41. Calvin B. T. Lee, *The Campus Scene, 1900–1970: Changing Styles in Undergraduate Life* (New York: David McKay Company, 1970), 60.

42. Amy M. T. McCandless, "From Pedestal to Mortarboard: Higher Education for Women in South Carolina From 1920 to 1940," *Southern Studies* 23, no. 4 (winter 1984), 359.

43. Tovey interview; McArthur interview; Jackson interview; Wienges interview; John Andrew Rice quotation is from his autobiography, *I Came Out of the Eighteenth Century,* and is quoted in Hollis, vol. 2, 236.

44. Author interview with H. Willard Davis; Jackson interview; McArthur interview; *Garnet and Black,* 1939, 116–19 and passim; McArthur, *Growing Up in Bennettsville,* 43.

45. USC Catalog, 1940–41, 87–88; Hollis, vol. 2, 335–36; Jackson interview; Tovey interview; John Hammond Moore, *Columbia and Richland County: A South Carolina Community, 1740–1990* (Columbia: University of South Carolina Press, 1993), 365, 395.

46. Annual Report, 1948–49, 7; USC Catalog, 1940–41, 37; The next smallest state university campus in the South was the University of Kentucky, whose campus covered 94 acres, more than twice the size of Carolina. By comparison, the University of North Carolina had 222 acres of developed land, with 400 undeveloped acres for expansion, the University of Tennessee owned 2,266 acres, and the University of Georgia had some 4,000 acres. Marsh, *American Universities,* 407, 505, 676, 884.

47. Leonard T. Baker to the president of the University of South Carolina 1986, 23 March 1936, "Modern Era" topical file, USC Archives.

48. Marsh, *American Universities,* 1940, 845; Hollis, vol. 2, 333–34, 338–39. The New Deal also helped fund the paving of campus walkways (which had previously been dirt paths), but the labor was provided by professor Havilah Babcock and his students. Their effort is still visible in the brick walkways on the Horseshoe that have the initials of prominent faculty and student organizations in the paving stones.

49. Leonard T. Baker to the president of the University of South Carolina 1986, 23 March 1936, "Modern Era" topical file, USC Archives.

50. Ibid. Two wings had been added to the old building in 1927, but the library remained cramped. Before the construction of the new library at the head of

the Horseshoe, there were three libraries at Carolina: the general library collection, a law library located in old Petigru College (now Currell College), and the school of journalism library, located in Legare College.

51. Hollis, vol. 2, 338–39; Paul Conkin, *Gone with the Ivy: A Biography of Vanderbilt University* (Knoxville: The University of Tennessee Press, 1985), 411–14; *Garnet and Black*, 1941, 9.

52. Hollis, vol. 2, 339; *Public Higher Education*, 382–83; In the 1960s, a USC librarian called the building "the worst library that has ever been built in the United States." USC administrator Harold Brunton called the building "a bill of goods." The original plan for the building had been designed for an administration building at Davidson College. Architect Hibbs, however, convinced University officials that it could easily be converted to use as a library, and thus the state could save on architectural fees. Harold Brunton, interviewed by William Savage, 3 March 1987, USC Archives.

53. *Public Higher Education*, 382–91.

54. Hollis, vol. 1, 135–36; Hollis, vol. 2, 179–80, 217, 313–14.

55. Annual Report, 1940–41, 5–7; minutes of the board of trustees of the University of South Carolina, 1940–1961, Manuscripts Division, South Caroliniana Library (hereafter "BTM"), 11 December 1940, 9 December 1942, 15 December 1943.

56. BTM, 2 September 1940; Franklin D. Roosevelt letter to Paul V. McNutt, 20 August 1940, quoted in J. Rion McKissick to male undergraduate students, 4 September 1940, printed in BTM, 3 September 1940. Annual Report, 1940–41, 3–5; *Gamecock*, 26 September 1941, 10 October 1941, 30 October 1941, 28 November 1941; Cardozier, *Colleges and Universities*, 68.

57. Annual Report, 1940–41, 4; Cardozier, *Colleges and Universities*, 9–11. Those called to active duty with the National Guard in 1940–41 were Isadore Schayer (professor of hygiene), E. H. Law (University physician), E. B. Clippard (English instructor), and Sterling DuPree (physical education instructor).

58. Annual Report, 1940–41, 4–5; Cardozier, *Colleges and Universities*, 156–57, 168–82; BTM, 15 December 1943; See also Henry H. Armsby, "Engineering Science and Management War Training Program: Final Report," *U.S. Office of Education Bulletin* 1946, no. 9, (Washington, D.C.: U.S. Office of Education, 1946).

59. *Gamecock*, 26 September 1941.

60. Ibid., 12 December 1941.

61. Ibid., 13 February 1942.

62. Ibid., 9 January 1942. The University did not move to the accelerated schedule until 1943 because of the expense. The U.S. Navy funded the accelerated calendar.

63. Ibid., 12 December 1941; see President McKissick's similar sentiments in Wardlaw, ed., *Men and Women of Carolina*, 140–42.

64. McArthur interview; *Gamecock*, 9 January 1942; *Garnet and Black*, 1942, 56; Lee, *The Campus Scene*, 73.

65. *Gamecock*, 6 February 1942; 20 March 1942.

66. Ibid., 6 February 1942, 9 October 1942, 4 December 1942; BTM, 9 December 1942. The war was serious business, and the campus atmosphere reflected a community intending to do its part. President McKissick declared that "the University is not a playground, but a training ground for the utmost service all of us can render" (*Gamecock,* 25 September 1942). "Never before," McKissick said, "has our campus been so quiet. Never before has the attitude of our students toward their work and duty been so serious as now" (BTM, 15 December 1943).

67. BTM, 9 December 1942; *Gamecock,* 9 January 1942; Cardozier, *Colleges and Universities,* 112.

68. Annual Report, 1943–44, 9; *Gamecock,* 26 September 1941, 18 December 1942, 19 November 1943; Cardozier, *Colleges and Universities,* 116; Davis interview. Most civilian men left on campus were either 4-f's (not qualified for military service) or those not yet of age to be eligible for the draft.

69. Annual Report, 1944–45, 10.

70. Ibid., 4; "Faculty Members on Leave-of-Absence," 15 May 1945, Guy Fleming Lipscomb Papers, SCL. Faculty on leave of absence were Robert D. Bass, English; Howard E. Carr, physics; Orin F. Crow, education; Richard B. Davis, English; Sterling DuPree, physical education; Rex Enright, physical education; Christopher Fitzsimmons, commerce; T. Walter Herbert, English; A. S. Hodge, modern languages; Ruben Johnson, engineering; Leila G. Johnson, social work; Frank Johnson, physical education; Archibald R. Lewis, history; James O. Overby, Political Science; Nancy H. Pope, physical education; Alfred G. Smith Jr., economics; George W. Tomlin, economics; Charles Treadway, physical education; Ted Twomey, physical education; M. K. Walsh, psychology; W. S. Woods, modern languages; Wilbur C. Zeigler, modern languages; Edwin Clippard, English.

71. *Gamecock,* 26 September 1941, 19 November 1943; Annual Report, 1943–44, 9.

72. McCandless, *The Past in the Present,* 85–89, 195–208.

73. *Garnet and Black,* 1944, 53; BTM, 9 December 1942, 15 December 1942.

74. *Gamecock,* 18 December 1942.

75. Hollis, vol. 2, 339.

76. Author interview with Robert E. McNair, 11 September 2000.

77. BTM, 15 December 1943; *Gamecock,* 9 April 1943, 17 December 1943; *Garnet and Black,* 1944, 27.

78. Cardozier, *Colleges and Universities,* 109–10; Hollis, vol. 2, 339–40; *Gamecock,* 12 February 1943, 28 April 1944; USC Catalog, 1943–44, cover page; *Garnet and Black,* 1943, 22; The midyear graduations were the first in University history.

79. BTM, 9 December 1942, 10 November 1943, 15 December 1943; *Gamecock,* 8 January 1943.

80. BTM, 9 December 1942, 17 March 1943, 15 December 1943; *Gamecock,* 18 December 1942, 14 January 1944; Cardozier, *Colleges and Universities,* 155–56; USC Catalog, 1943–44, 11–17, 80. Among others who taught in the V-5 program

were W. C. McCall (education), John C. Ayers (biology), Joseph W. Bouknight (chemistry), Robert L. Jones (mathematics), William Y. Wagner (English), Merrill G. Christopherson (English), Louise J. DuBose (sociology), Benjamin Fishburne (modern languages), and William W. Weber (mathematics).

81. USC Catalog, 1943–44, 80; BTM, 10 November 1943, 13 December 1944; Cardozier, *Colleges and Universities,* 156–57, 179–82.

82. McArthur interview; Callcott interview; Cardozier, *Colleges and Universities,* 52–63; USC Catalog, 1943–44, 80; *Gamecock,* 9 April 1943, 13 August 1943, 26 May 1944; BTM, 17 March 1943, 10 November 1943, 13 December 1944, 18 June 1946; *The Salvo* (USC NROTC news magazine), October 1944, 5; For an extended treatment of the V-12 program nationwide, see James G. Schneider, *The Navy V-12 Program: Leadership for a Lifetime* (Champaign, Ill.: Marlow Books, 1987). Rebecca Callcott pointed out that she and the other women who were hired as instructors during the war were forced out of their positions once the war was over. See also McCandless, *The Past in the Present,* 209–10.

83. BTM, 10 November 1943; 23 June 1944.

84. Annual Report, 1942–43, 11–12; *Charlotte Observer,* 26 October 1941; *Faithful Index: The University of South Carolina Campus* (Columbia: University of South Carolina, 1976), 38; Andrew W. Chandler, "'Dialogue with the Past': J. Carroll Johnson and the University of South Carolina, 1912–1956," master's thesis, University of South Carolina, 1993, 209–10.

85. BTM, 23 June 1944, 13 December 1944; *Gamecock,* 18 December 1942, 8 January 1943, 22 September 1944. One example of this was Wauchope House, later the University's president's home, which had served since the 1850s as a faculty residence. When J. Rion McKissick died in September 1944, the faculty duplex became home to the Alpha Delta Pi Sorority.

86. *Garnet and Black,* 1944, 54–55.

87. *Garnet and Black,* 1944, 116; *Gamecock,* 25 September 1942; Cardozier, *Colleges and Universities,* 132–33.

88. Jackson interview; McArthur interview; *Garnet and Black,* 1944, 58, 64, 225, 232–33 and passim.

89. *Gamecock,* 28 April 1944, 18 October 1944, 29 October 1948; Cardozier, *Colleges and Universities,* 123–24; Lynn, 85–87; Schneider, *The Navy V-12 Program,* 434.

90. George Greichen Caughman, interviewed by Jane E. Hutchison, 6 October 1994, in "University of South Carolina Archives Oral Histories," USC Archives.

91. *Garnet and Black,* 1942, 14.

92. *Garnet and Black,* 1944, 53; For a similar sentiment, see editorial in *Gamecock,* 17 September 1943.

93. *Gamecock,* 28 April 1944, 6 October 1944, 29 October 1948.

94. *Garnet and Black,* 1944, 18–19.

95. Leonard T. Baker to the president of the University of South Carolina, 1986, 23 March 1936, "Modern Era" topical file, USC Archives.

96. Hollis, vol. 2, 336; John Chandler Griffin, *The First Hundred Years: A History of South Carolina Football* (Marietta, Georgia: Longstreet Press, 1992), 69–70.

97. *Gamecock,* 11 December 1942, 8 January 1943; Walter B. Edgar, *South Carolina: A History* (Columbia: University of South Carolina Press, 1998), 515; *Garnet and Black,* 1942, 149, 161; Griffin, *The First Hundred Years,* 71.

98. BTM, 16 March 1943; Griffin, *The First Hundred Years,* 71; Don Barton, *The Carolina-Clemson Game, 1896–1966* (Columbia: The State Printing Company, 1967), 209.

99. Griffin, *The First Hundred Years,* 71–74; Barton, *The Carolina-Clemson Game,* 182–83.

100. Griffin, *The First Hundred Years,* 71–74; Barton, *The Carolina-Clemson Game,* 182–83; *Gamecock,* 18 October 1944, 12 May 1944; Tom Price, *A Century of Gamecocks: Memorable Baseball Moments* (Columbia: Summerhouse Press, 1996), 38; *Garnet and Black,* 1944, 160–71 and passim; Hollis, vol. 2, 336; Schneider, *The Navy V-12 Program,* 434.

101. Annual Report, 1943–44, 12; BTM, 10 November 1943, 13 December 1944, and passim, 1943–1944; The prosperous wartime economy brought increased revenues to the state treasury, and during the war the state assumed the University's bonded indebtedness, relieving the University of $564,000 of debt left from the construction of buildings during the New Deal. Hollis, vol. 2, 340; for more detail on the University's finances during the war, see Table 1.4.

102. *Public Higher Education,* 129–34; BTM, 24 August 1943, 10 November 1943, 27 May 1947.

103. Cardozier, *Colleges and Universities,* 118–19; *Gamecock,* 25 September 1942; BTM, 10 November 1943; Davis interview.

104. *Gamecock,* 25 September 1942, 8 January 1943, 5 January 1945; "Wartime Program: University of South Carolina," "World War II" file, topical files, USC Archives; *Garnet and Black,* 1942, 129; "Institutional Self-Study of the University of South Carolina, Submitted to the Commission on Colleges and Universities of the Southern Association of Colleges and Secondary Schools, March 15, 1961," USC Archives, 457–58.

105. *Gamecock,* 28 April 1944.

106. BTM, 15 December 1943; 13 December 1944.

107. Annual Report, 1943–44, 3–5; USC Catalog, 1944–45, 106–7, 119–21, 126–27; BTM, 13 December 1944.

108. Annual Report, 1944–45, 10–11.

109. Ibid., 1943–44, 4–5, 1944–45, 10–11, 23; the *State* (Columbia), 21 January 1945; *Gamecock,* 11 May 1945.

110. Annual Report, 1943–44, 4–5, 1944–45, 11–12; BTM, 23 June 1944, 13 December 1944; Callcott, ed., passim; *Gamecock,* 7 December 1951; G. Croft Williams, *A Social Interpretation of South Carolina* (Columbia: University of South Carolina Press, 1946).

111. Annual Report, 1946–47, 17–19; *University of South Carolina Alumni News,* April 1947, 6.

112. BTM, March 1944 (p. 112), 13 December 1944; Allen H. Stokes, *Guide to the Manuscript Collection of the South Caroliniana Library* (Columbia: University

South Caroliniana Society, 1982), vi–x; Annual Report, 1943–44, 4–5; 1944–45, 11; *Record,* 25 May 1948.

113. Annual Report, 1943–44, 4–5; 1944–45, 11; *Record,* 25 May 1948; BTM, 13 December 1944. Wilfred Callcott became dean of the Graduate School in 1944 after the death of Reed Smith; he was approved for the job at the same board of trustees meeting that reauthorized the Ph.D.

114. BTM, 1 December 1944.

115. Edgar, *South Carolina: A History,* 516–17; Keith Olson, *The G.I. Bill, the Veterans, and the Colleges* (Lexington: University of Kentucky Press, 1974) 3–24; Michael J. Bennett, *When Dreams Came True: The G.I. Bill and the Making of America* (Washington and London: Brassey's, 1996), 76–193; "The Veteran and the University of South Carolina," pamphlet in SCL, c. 1944, 5–6.

116. Edgar, *South Carolina: A History,* 516; Annual Report, 1944–45, 6; BTM, 12 December 1945.

117. *Gamecock,* 8 September 1944, 19 January 1945; BTM 15 June 1945; Hollis, vol. 2, 340–41; Annual Report, 1944–45, 23; McArthur, *Growing Up in Bennettsville.* McKissick was the third president in twenty years to die in office. Some claimed that he had worked himself to death in addressing Carolina's wartime problems.

118. Wardlaw, 13–16; Dwight A. Dunbar, "A History of the University of South Carolina School of Music, 1920–1993," Ph.D. dissertation, University of South Carolina, 1995, 34–43; Mary M. Dunlap, Leland H. Cox, and George F. Hayhoe, comps., *A Catalog of the South Caroliniana Collection of J. Rion McKissick* (Spartanburg: Reprint Company, 1977), ix–xvi.

119. Wardlaw, 15.

120. Ibid., 16.

121. BTM, 13 December 1944; the *State,* 13 December 1944.

122. BTM, 13 December 1944.

123. Garnie William McGinty, *A History of Louisiana* (New York: Exposition Press, 1951), 280; William Ivey Hair, *The Kingfish and His Realm: The Life and Times of Huey P. Long* (Baton Rouge: Louisiana State University Press, 1991), 228–29; T. Harry Williams, *Huey Long* (New York: Alfred A. Knopf, 1969), 493–525.

124. BTM, 13 December 1944, 17 January 1945; *State,* 7 May 1945; Chandler, "Dialogue with the Past," 181–87.

125. John K. Cauthen, *Speaker Blatt: His Challenges Were Greater* (Columbia: R. L. Bryan, 1964), 16–52, 125–27, 203–09; V. O. Key, *Southern Politics in State and Nation* (New York: Alfred A. Knopf, 1949), 150–55; Roger M. Williams, "'Two Old Men:' In S.C., Brown and Blatt Are the Senior Partners," *South Today* 4, no. 8 (April 1971), 4; William D. Workman, *The Bishop From Barnwell: The Political Life and Times of Edgar J. Brown* (Columbia: R. L. Bryan, 1963), 46, 99–129; N. Louise Bailey, Mary L. Morgan, and Carolyn R. Taylor, *Biographical Directory of the South Carolina Senate, 1776–1985,* vol. 1 (Columbia: University of South Carolina Press, 1986), 203.

126. Jack Bass and Walter Devries, *The Transformation of Southern Politics: Social Change and Political Consequences Since 1945* (Athens and London: University

of Georgia Press, 1995), 277; Key, *Southern Politics,* 150–5. In the 1940s, the Budget Commission was composed of only three members: the governor, the chairman of the senate finance committee, and the chairman of the House Ways and Means Committee.

127. Key, *Southern Politics,* 155.

128. Williams, "Two Old Men," 4; Workman, *Bishop from Barnwell,* 99–129; Cauthen, *Speaker Blatt,* 125–27.

129. Workman, *Bishop from Barnwell,* 276; Cauthen, *Speaker Blatt,* 204–5; USC Catalog, 1946–47, 13–14.

130. BTM, 5 September 1944; *Gamecock,* 8 September 1944; *Record* (Col, 12 December 1944; Sol Blatt to Ralph Lewis, 16 September 1944, Blatt biographical file, University of South Carolina Archives.

131. *Record,* 12 December 1944; *State,* 13, December 1944; *Daily Item,* 13 December 1944; BTM, 13 December 1944.

132. *State,* 14 December 1944; 7 January 1945; *State Magazine* (published in the Sunday edition of the *State*), 1 May 1949; Hollis, vol. 2, 341.

133. *Record,* 20 January 1945; *State Magazine,* 1 May 1949; Cauthen, *Speaker Blatt,* 125–27; Walter B. Edgar, ed., *Biographical Directory of the South Carolina House of Representatives,* vol. 1, *Session Lists, 1692–1973* (Columbia: University of South Carolina Press, 1974), 556, 561; James A. Hoyt to W. W. Ball, 22 December 1944, James A. Hoyt Papers, SCL. Author interview with Daniel Walker Hollis, 21 February 1997; author interview with Sol Blatt Jr., 30 May 1997.

134. See numerous letters to the editor of the *State,* 15–31 December 1944, 9 January 1945; Chandler, "Dialogue with the Past," 186–90.

135. *State,* 28 January 1945.

136. Mary Graydon Arial to the editor of the *State,* 19 December 1944.

137. *State,* 15 December 1944. See other hostile editorials in the *State* on 18 and 19 December 1944.

138. *Sumter Daily Item,* 16 December 1944.

139. *News and Courier,* 16 December 1944. William Watts Ball was also an 1887 graduate of USC and had been a supportive alumnus. However, he fell out with the University in the 1930s. As South Carolina's most bitter opponent of the New Deal, Ball became a critic of the University after the institution accepted WPA grant funds and then awarded Harry Hopkins (WPA director) an honorary degree in 1938. From then on, Ball decried the influence of politics in state-funded higher education. Upon his death, Ball bequeathed his valuable collection of personal manuscripts to Duke University rather than USC. See John D. Stark, *Damned Upcountryman: William Watts Ball, A Study in American Conservatism* (Durham, N.C.: Duke University Press, 1968), 176 and passim.

140. *Gamecock,* 15 December 1944.

141. *Gamecock,* 5 January 1945.

142. *State,* 21 December 1944; the four hundred students represented 35 percent of the civilians on campus in the fall of 1944, and Captain R. C. Needham, the

commander of the V-12 program, prohibited any V-12s from attended the politically charged meeting. Schneider, *The Navy V-12 Program,* 434.

143. *State,* 14 January 1945.

144. Ibid., 31 December 1944.

145. Ibid., 23 December 1944, 2 January 1945,.

146. *Spartanburg Herald,* 15 December 1944; *Sumter Daily Item,* 16 December 1944; *State,* 19, 21 December 1944, 11 January 1945; BTM, 15 January 1945.

147. BTM, 15 January 1945.

148. *Gamecock,* 16 February 1945, 20 February 1946; "University of South Carolina News Letter," 7 February 1945, Fitz Hugh McMaster Papers, SCL; "University of South Carolina Plot Plan, May 1945," Norman Murray Smith Papers, USC Archives, SCL; BTM, 12 December 1945.

149. *Gamecock,* 16 February 1945.

150. "University of South Carolina News Letter," 7 February 1945, Fitz Hugh McMaster Papers, SCL.

151. *Public Higher Education,* 9; *House Journal* 1945, 343, 459; *Senate Journal* 1945, 313; Manuscript Act, R690, 1946, South Carolina Department of Archives and History (hereafter SCDAH).

152. For a discussion of the South's ambivalence to modernization, see James C. Cobb, "Modernization and the Mind of the South," in his *Redefining Southern Culture: Mind and Identity in the Modern South* (Athens: University of Georgia Press, 1999), 187–210.

CHAPTER 2—"THE G.I. IS THE FINEST THING THAT COULD HAVE HAPPENED," 1945–1949

1. "Annual Report to the President of the University of South Carolina by the Registrar, 1958–1959," SCL, 3, 22; Annual Report, 1939–40, 3; 1943–44, 10; 1944–45, 5; 1946–1947, 15–16, 32; 1947–48, 24; *University of South Carolina Alumni News,* June 1947; Olsen, *G.I. Bill,* 44; for more detailed enrollment figures for the post-war period, see Table 2.1.

2. See pamphlet titled "The Veteran and the University of South Carolina," c. 1944, SCL.

3. Ibid.; quotation, Annual Report, 1947–48, 17, see also 25; BTM, 13 December 1944.

4. Annual Report, 1939–40, 9; "Annual Report to the President of the University of South Carolina by the Registrar, 1958–1959," 22; "University of South Carolina Statistical Data, July 1, 1946 to June 30, 1950," Smith Papers; Clemson Annual Report, 1940, 4, 1947, 8, SCL.

5. Annual Report, 1943–44, 4; 1944–45, 7–8; 1946–47, 8–9; 1947–48, 16–17; BTM, 13 December 1944; 15 June 1945; 12 December 1945; *Gamecock,* 11 May 1945; A. J. Brumbaugh, ed., *American Universities and Colleges,* 5th ed. (Washington, D.C.: 1948), 816.

6. Annual Report, 1946–47, 3.

7. Annual Report, 1946–1947, 8, 1948–49, 7; Hollis, vol. 2, 342; *State,* 17 January 1947; *Gamecock,* 20 February 1946, 15 March 1946, 22 March 1946, 3 May

1946, 25 September 1946; *University of South Carolina Alumni News,* December 1946; BTM, 18 June 1946, 22 August 1946, 11 December 1946; Author interview with Robert Ochs, 2 February 2000.

8. Annual Report, 1946–1947, 3–4.

9. Edgar, *South Carolina: A History,* 515–18; For a similar sentiment in neighboring Georgia, see Jennifer E. Brooks, "Winning the Peace: Georgia Veterans and the Struggle to Define the Political Legacy of World War II," *Journal of Southern History* 66, no. 3 (August 2000), 563–604.

10. *Gamecock,* 19 April 1946.

11. Jackson interview; McArthur interview; Author interview with Charles Wickenberg, 2 October 1999. Ironically, William Preston Horton went on to become a Naval admiral himself.

12. Author interview with Ernest F. Hollings, 19 December 2000.

13. *Carolinian,* March 1988, 10; Wickenberg interview.

14. *Record,* 7 September 1945, 29 April 1949; *Gamecock,* 20 December 1946, 14 January 1947; Hollis interview; Author interview with Professor Willard Davis, 26 February 1997; USC Catalog, 1946–47, 15–16.

15. BTM, 5 February 1946, 11 March 1946; *Gamecock,* 8 February 1946; 20 February 1946; 16 March 1946; Annual Report, 1948–49, 15; Hollings interview.

16. *Gamecock,* 15 October 1946.

17. *State,* 2 October 1946; *Gamecock,* 1 October, 5 October, 12 October 1946.

18. *Gamecock,* 10 December 1946; see also: *Gamecock,* 1 October 1946, 5 October 1946, 12 October 1946, 15 October 1946, 2 November 1946, 16 November 1946, 21 November 1946; 16 December 1946; author interview with Robert Sumwalt Jr., 25 February 1998.

19. *Gamecock,* 14 January 1947.

20. See *Gamecock,* 1 October 1946, 5 October 1946, 12 October 1946, 15 October 1946, 2 November 1946, 16 November 1946, 21 November 1946, 10 December 1946, 16 December 1946; Interview with Robert Sumwalt, Jr., 25 February 1998.

21. Nadine Cahodas, *Strom Thurmond and the Politics of Southern Change* (New York: Simon and Schuster, 1993), 86, 87; author interview with John Carl West, 3 February 2000; Hollings interview; see also Workman, *Bishop from Barnwell,* 105–16.

22. Workman, *Bishop from Barnwell,* 116.

23. *Observer,* reprinted in the *Gamecock,* 10 December 1946. See other discussions of Smith's relations with USC students in the *Gamecock,* 2 November 1946, and *Anderson Independent,* 25 January 1947.

24. BTM, 13 January 1947; *State,* 14 January , 19 January 1947.

25. *State,* 17 January 1947.

26. See Bruce J. Schulman, *From Cotton Belt to Sunbelt: Federal Policy, Economic Development and the Transformation of the South, 1938–1980* (New York: Oxford University Press, 1991), 124–26; Numan V. Bartley, *The New South,* vol. 10, *The History of the South,* Wendell Holmes Stephenson and E. Merton Coulter, eds.

(Baton Rouge: Louisiana State University Press), 21–22, 135; Brooks, "Winning the Peace," 563–604.

27. Bruce Littlejohn, *Littlejohn's Political Memoirs, 1934–1988*, (Spartanburg: privately printed, 1989), 146–52; West interview; *Legislative Manual of the 87th General Assembly of South Carolina*, 69–110; *Gamecock*, 12 October 1946.

28. *State*, 20 January 1947, 6 February 1947; *House Journal*, 1947, Resolution H. 17, introduced 21 January 1947.

29. *State*, 6 February 1947; Cauthen, *Speaker Blatt*, 208; Workman, *Bishop from Barnwell*, 115; *Code of Laws of South Carolina, 1976*, vol. 21, 148–49.

30. *State*, 6 February 1947.

31. Cauthen, *Speaker Blatt*, 128–29; Workman, *Bishop from Barnwell*, 117; Littlejohn, *Littlejohn's Political Memoirs*, 149–53.

32. Littlejohn, *Littlejohn's Political Memoirs*, 51–53; *Code of Laws of South Carolina, 1976*, vol. 21, Article 3, Section 24, 148; Workman, *Bishop from Barnwell*, 282–83.

33. Littlejohn, *Littlejohn's Political Memoirs*, 51–53; *State*, 6 February, 1 April, 10 April, 12 April, 15 April, and 25 April 1947; *Gamecock*, 11 February, 15 April, and 26 April 1947; Workman, *Bishop from Barnwell*, 282–85. In November 1939 John Bolt Culbertson, a USC alumnus and maverick legislator, had filed suit in the South Carolina Supreme Court against Sol Blatt and six other trustees who he claimed held office in violation of the state constitutional prohibition against dual office holding. The USC trustees vigorously opposed the suit, and the court dismissed it. BTM, 13 December 1939; *Culbertson v. Blatt et al.*, 15094 Supreme Court of South Carolina, 194 S.C. 105; 9 S.E. 2d 218; 1940 S.C. Lexis 99.

34. Sol Blatt to Ralph Lewis, 28 April 1947, Blatt Biographical File, USC Archives; *Gamecock*, 26 April 1947; *State*, 25 April 1947.

35. Cameron Fincher, *Historical Development of the University System of Georgia: 1932–1990* (Athens: Institute of Higher Education, University of Georgia, 1991), 1–10.

36. *State*, 21 January 1945; *Senate Journal*, 1945, 2 March 1945, p. 313; James V. Dreyfuss, "The Origin of Statewide Higher Education Coordination in South Carolina, 1945–1967: A Documentary History," Ph.D. dissertation, University of South Carolina, 1997, 85–86.

37. *Public Higher Education*, 12–18; *House Journal*, 1946, 7 February 1946, 343; Dreyfuss, "Origin of Statewide Higher Education Coordination," 85–94.

38. *House Journal*, 1947, p. 1489, 7 May 1947; *Senate Journal*, 1947, 1175; *Senate Journal*, 1948, p. 1544; *Gamecock*, 11 February, 22, February, 25 February, 1 March, 13 May, 24 May 1947; *State*, 7 February, 12 February, 20 February, 27 February, 3 April 1947; Dreyfuss, "Origin of Statewide Higher Education Coordination," 92–94.

39. Olson, *G.I. Bill*, 66–67; *Gamecock*, 8 February 1946, 29 March 1946, 23 November 1946, 9 January 1947, 21 January 1949; Annual Report, 1946–47, 7–8; Chandler, "Dialogue with the Past," 199–200; *State*, 22 December, 27 December, 31 December 1946; 22 August 1947; BTM, 18 June 1946.

40. Olson, *G.I. Bill,* 67–68; *Gamecock,* 19 November 1946, 19 March 1948; BTM, 18 June 1946, 22 October 1947; Chandler, "Dialogue with the Past," 199.

41. BTM, 27 May 1947; Chandler, "Dialogue with the Past," 193–98.

42. BTM, 24 June 1947, 22 October 1947, 12 December 1947; *Record,* 20 December 1947; Annual Report, 1946–47, 7.

43. Annual Report, 1944–45, 5, 16; 1946–47, 16, 28; BTM, 22 October 1947, 16 March 1948; Norman Smith to J. C. Long, 31 December 1947 and 17 June 1948, Smith Papers; Norman Smith to Donald Russell, 30 January 1948, Smith Papers; Chandler, "Dialogue with the Past," 209–11.

44. USC Catalog, 1947–48; *Gamecock,* 1 April 1947, 26 April 1947; *USC Alumni News,* February 1947; Sol Blatt Jr. to Rutledge L. Osborne, 5 March 1969, Thomas F. Jones Papers, USC Archives.

45. *State,* 2 April 1948; *Record,* 12 April 1948; Norman Smith to the president of the University of South Carolina, 29 August 1949, Smith Papers; Donald Russell to Norman Smith, 29 April 1948, Smith Papers.

46. Chandler, "Dialogue with the Past," 211–21; *Gamecock,* 10 February 1950; Hollis, vol. 2, 342.

47. Annual Report, 1947–48, 3–12, 1948–49, 4–12.

48. Annual Report, 1947–48, 8; *Gamecock,* 19 November 1948.

49. Sumwalt interview; *Gamecock,* 5 November, 19 November, 3 December, 10 December, 17 December 1948; BTM, 14 December 1948.

50. See *Public Higher Education.*

51. Key, *Southern Politics,* 131–35; *Public Higher Education,* 7–9, 49.

52. *Acts and Joint Resolutions of the General Assembly of the State of South Carolina,* 1947, vol. 45, part 1, 621–22; "Report of the Comptroller General of South Carolina, 1947–48," *Reports and Resolutions of South Carolina to the General Assembly of the State of South Carolina,* 1949, vol. 1, 8. By 1991–92, this figure had risen to 15.5 percent. See *SREB Fact Book on Higher Education* (Atlanta: Southern Regional Education Board, 1994/1995), 138; http://www.state.sc.us/osb/histanly.htm, "appropriations by functional group," accessed May 2001.

53. BTM, 11 March 1946.

54. Hollis, vol. 2, 343; Annual Report, 1947–48, 12–13.

55. Annual Report, 1948–49, 17; 1949–50, 12–13.

56. Hollis, vol. 2, 342–43; Annual Report, 1947–48, 47.

57. Annual Report, 1947–48, 47; author interview with Donald S. Russell, 20 March 1997, 25 March 1997.

58. "Comparative Statement of Requests and Actual Appropriations for the State Educational Institutions for the Years Beginning July 1 1940 and Ending June 30, 1952," Smith Papers.

59. E. Thomas Crowson, *The Winthrop Story, 1886–1960* (Baltimore: Gateway Press, 1987), 546.

60. "Statement of Per Capita Cost at Winthrop, Citadel, Clemson, and the University, As Reported in the Printed Budget Dated January 1948, Smith Papers (Budget,

1949–50 folder). The figure used to compare Clemson annual appropriation includes the special annual appropriation Clemson received from the state tax on fertilizer. See *Public Higher Education,* 42–52.

61. BTM, 15 March 1949.

62. Solomon Blatt to Norman Smith, 14 December 1949, Smith Papers.

63. Solomon Blatt to Ralph Lewis, 24 October 1950, Smith Papers.

64. Blatt to Smith, 14 December 1949, Smith Papers.

65. Annual Report, 1947–48, 13.

66. Ibid., 13–14; *Gamecock,* 1 April 1949; Solomon Blatt to Norman Smith, 11 February 1949, Smith Papers; Norman Smith to Solomon Blatt, 17 February 1949, Smith Papers.

67. Annual Report, 1947–48, 25, 38.

68. Brumbaugh, ed., *American Universities,* 816; Annual Report, 1946–47, 29; 1948–49, 20–22, 42; BTM, 22 August 1946; *Gamecock,* 11 May 1945; Dunbar, "A History," 43–46.

69. *Record,* 25 May 1948. Lesesne is the author's grandfather.

70. Annual Report, 1948–49, 32–33.

71. *Record,* 10 February 1950; Annual Report, 1947–48, 35; 1948–49, 18, 36; F. W. Bradley to Norman Smith, 11 January 1950, Smith Papers. In addition, there were only four states in which the state university's chemistry department was unaccredited: Mississippi, Montana, South Carolina, and Wyoming.

72. *Record,* 10 February 1950.

73. BTM, 12 December 1945; *USC Alumni News,* April 1947, 7; *Record,* 10 February 1950; Annual Report, 1939–40, 9–10.

74. Brubacher and Rudy, *Higher Education in Transition,* 236; *USC Perspective* (alumni association newsletter) 1, no. 3 (February 1961), 1.

75. Norman Smith to R. H. Wienefeld, 18 February 1950, Smith Papers; *USC Alumni News,* April 1947, 6; Annual Report, 1944–45, 5; 1946–47, 15, 16, 24–25; 1947–48, 24, 33; Dunbar, "A History," 53–54.

76. E. M. Billings to Norman M. Smith, 5 July 1949, Smith Papers; F. W. Bradley to Norman M. Smith, 11 January 1950, Smith Papers. Among the members of the chemistry department, all but one had a teaching load above fifteen hours per week. The American Chemistry Society considered this load "irregular" and "countenanced only as a makeshift in a crisis." Twelve to fifteen hours was considered normal, while "among the best schools" most had a load below twelve hours. Other critical needs to USC's accreditation were: additional equipment, better housing, and greater efforts to stimulate research.

77. Annual Report, 1948–49, 26–27; Norman Smith to J. M. Goddard, 14 September 1949, Smith Papers; BTM, 22 August 1946; 18 March 1947, 22 May 1947, 22 October 1947, 9 December 1947, 14 December 1948.

78. Davis interview.

79. BTM, 27 May 1947.

80. BTM, 18 March 1947.

81. BTM, 22 August 1946.
82. Ibid.; BTM, 24 June 1947, 14 December 1948, 21 March 1951, 8 June 1951.
83. Davis interview; BTM, 27 May 1947, 24 June 1947; unsigned letter addressed "To the Gentlemen of the Board of Trustees of the University of South Carolina," c. 1950–51, Smith Papers (Faculty and Staff Salaries file).
84. Samuel L. Prince to the Elective Trustees of the University of South Carolina and to President Smith, Dean Chase and Dean of the Faculty Bradley, 22 March 1951, Smith Papers.
85. Ibid.
86. Hollis interview.
87. Davis interview.
88. Ibid.
89. Ibid.
90. Ibid.
91. Thomas G. Dyer, University of Georgia: A Bicentennial History, 1785–1985 (Athens: University of Georgia Press, 1985), 251–55.
92. BTM, 1 June 1948.
93. Public Higher Education, ch. 1; Gamecock, 1 March 1947, 13 May 1947, 16 January 1948; In 1949, the Gamecock and the students agitated for a revival of the Peabody plan. In 1950, University student and state legislator Joseph Wise Jr. resubmitted the Peabody plan in the General Assembly, but it got nowhere. See Gamecock, 9 April 1948, 14 October 1949, 28 October 1949, 4 November 1949, 11 November 1949, 2 December 1949, 6 January 1950, 13 January 1950.
94. BTM, 14 March 1948.
95. Robert Maynard Hutchins, "Education in a Democracy," Gadfly 4 (August 1952), 1, quoted in Hollis, vol. 2, 304–5.
96. BTM, 14 March 1948; 1 June 1948.
97. Olson, G.I. Bill, 31–34.
98. Olson, G.I. Bill, 48–56; Bennett, 241.
99. USC Alumni News, June 1947; Annual Report, 1946–47, 4; McNair interview.
100. Author interview with Ernest F. Hollings, 19 December 2000.
101. Marion Star, 5 January 1948; Lee, The Campus Scene, 82–83; McNair interview.
102. The Carolina Handbook: University of South Carolina (Columbia: University YMCA and YWCA, 1949), 87 (copy in Smith Papers).
103. Gamecock, 25 February 1947; Carolina Handbook, 1949, 87.
104. McNair interview.
105. West interview.
106. USC Alumni News, June 1947.
107. Gamecock, 21 April 1950.
108. Hollings interview.
109. Carolina Handbook, 1949, 87.
110. Gamecock, 5 April 1950, 21 April 1950. See a similar sentiment in Stephen E. Ambrose, Citizen Soldiers (New York: Touchstone, 1997), 477–78.

111. *Gamecock,* 29 October 1948.

112. McArthur interview; author interview with Selden Smith, 31 January 2000.

113. BTM, 15 June 1945; *Carolina Handbook,* 1949, 21, 23, 42–43; *Gamecock,* 21 April 1950; Jackson interview; Smith interview. Some have suggested that the cosmopolitan culinary tastes veterans brought back from their world travels contributed to the growth of restaurants devoted to international cuisine in Columbia.

114. *Gamecock,* 30 September 1949, 14 October 1949; *USC Alumni News,* April 1949; *Carolina Handbook,* 1949, 11.

115. *Carolina Handbook,* 1949, 58; *Garnet and Black,* 1946–49, passim.

116. *Gamecock,* 23 October 1946, 13 May 1947, 19 March 1948, 18 February 1949.

117. *Gamecock,* 27 April 1946.

118. *Gamecock,* 29 April 1949.

119. BTM, 12 December 1945, 24 June 1947. A similar situation existed at the University of Georgia, where the booster club also wielded tremendous power and overshadowed the administration in athletic matters, although the board of trustees was not directly involved in athletics at that school. See Dyer, *University of Georgia,* 285–90.

120. BTM, 12 December 1945; See also BTM, 5 February 1946.

121. *Gamecock,* 21 December 1945.

122. *Gamecock,* 7 September 1945; BTM, 12 December 1945.

123. *State,* 24 October 1946.

124. *State,* 25 October 1946; Barton, *Carolina-Clemson Game,* 196–99.

125. *Gamecock,* 7 December 1947.

126. McArthur interview; *Gamecock,* 10 October 1947, 20 October 1947.

127. *State,* 7 February 1948, 23 August 1948; *Gamecock,* 13 February 1948.

128. BTM, 16 February 1949; Norman Smith to R. L. Osborne, n.d., Smith Papers (1947–48, Board of Trustees–Committees–Athletic file).

129. *Gamecock,* 19 November 1948.

130. *Gamecock,* 9 April 1949.

131. See, for example, *Gamecock,* 12 November 1948, 3 December 1948, 10 December 1948, 11 February 1949, 20 January 1950, 17 February 1950.

132. *Gamecock,* 18 February 1949; 29 April 1949; 13 May 1949, 20 May 1949, 27 May 1949.

133. *USC Alumni News,* August 1953, 4.

134. *Gamecock,* 13 May 1949.

135. Sam P. Wiggins, *The Desegregation Era in Higher Education* (Berkeley, Calif.: McCutchan Publishing, 1966), 2–3; Gil Kujovich, "Equal Opportunity in Higher Education and the Black Public College: The Era of Separate But Equal," *Minnesota Law Review* 72 (October 1987), 29. See especially Part III, "The Demise of the Separate But Equal Doctrine." John Boles, *The South Through Time: A History of an American Region,* 2d ed. (Upper Saddle River, N.J.: Simon and Schuster, 1999), 527; Robert R. Mayer, ed. *The United States Supreme Court,*

vol. 7, *The Court and the American Crises, 1930–1953* (Danbury, Conn.: Grolier Educational Corporation, 1995), 163–64; http://www.uky.edu/Law/library/commemoration/gaines.htm (accessed 24 May 2001).

136. BTM, 8 July 1938, 26 October 1938, 7 December 1938, 28 July 1939.

137. Edgar, *South Carolina: A History,* 518–19; I. A. Newby, *Black Carolinians: A History of Blacks in South Carolina from 1895 to 1968* (Columbia: University of South Carolina Press, 1973), 350.

138. Newby, *Black Carolinians,* 350; *Gamecock,* 6 December 1973.

139. *State,* 1 June 1947, 6 June 1947; See the account of this case in Cahodas, *Strom Thurmond,* 104–5, 112–13; Matthew Perry interview with Grace J. McFadden, 18 August 1980, in "The Quest for Civil Rights," USC Film Library; John H. Wrighten to the board of trustees, 17 August 1946, Smith Papers; Daniel George Sampson to the registrar, School of Law, 29 July 1946, Smith Papers.

140. *State,* 13 July 1947; Cahodas, *Strom Thurmond,* 113–14; Newby, *Black Carolinians,* 350–51; *John H. Wrighten v. Board of Trustees of the University of South Carolina et al.,* Civil Action #1670, U.S. District Court for the Eastern District of South Carolina, Columbia Division, 72 F. Supp. 948; 1947 U.S. Dist. LEXIS 2420, 12 July 1947.

141. *John H. Wrighten v. Board of Trustees of the University of South Carolina et. al.,* Civil Action #1670, findings of fact, Smith Papers (Negro Problem, Wrighten Case file).

142. Cahodas, *Strom Thurmond,* 113.

143. *John H. Wrighten v. Board of Trustees of the University of South Carolina et. al.,* Civil Action #1670, opinion, Smith Papers (Negro Problem, Wrighten Case file).

144. Newby, *Black Carolinians,* 351.

145. *John H. Wrighten v. Board of Trustees et. al.,* opinion, Smith Papers (Negro Problem, Wrighten Case file).

146. Edgar, *South Carolina: A History,* 528.

147. *John H. Wrighten v. Board of Trustees et. al.,* opinion, Smith Papers (Negro Problem, Wrighten Case file); *Record,* 18 June 1948.

148. Newby, *Black Carolinians,* 351; *John H. Wrighten v. Board of Trustees of the University of South Carolina et. al.,* Civil Action #1670, findings of fact, Smith Papers (Negro Problem, Wrighten Case file); Edgar, *South Carolina, A History,* 528.

149. *Gamecock,* 13 February 1948. See a response to this editorial, 25 March 1948.

150. Norman Smith to H. O. Strohecker, 30 August 1949, Smith Papers; W. H. Callcott to Camille C. Levy, 28 July 1949, Smith Papers.

151. *USC Magazine* 5, no. 3 (fall 1970), 3.

CHAPTER 3—AN EDUCATIONAL RENAISSANCE, 1950–1959

1. Annual Report, 1946–47, 16; 1948–49, 30; Annual Report to the President by the Registrar, 1958–59, 22; BTM, 20 March 1951; *Record,* 9 October 1952.

2. BTM, 20 March 1951.

3. USC Catalog, 1947–48, 7.
4. *Gamecock*, 5 April 1950.
5. Annual Report, 1949–50, 14; *State*, 20 October 1951; Lee, *The Campus Scene*, 88–89. For more on the draft and college students in this period, see George Q. Flynn, "The Draft and College Deferments During the Korean War," *Historian* 50, no. 3 (1988), 369–85.
6. Solomon Blatt to Norman Smith, 10 June 1950, Smith Papers.
7. BTM, 21 March 1950, 2 August 1950, 18 October 1950.
8. *Gamecock*, 16 February 1951.
9. BTM, 2 August 1950, 18 October 1950, 12 December 1950; *State*, 8 September 1951; "Construction Program, Order of Work," 28 May 1951, Smith Papers.
10. BTM, 18 March 1952; Chandler, "Dialogue with the Past," 226; *Faithful Index: The University of South Carolina Campus*, 39–40, 42.
11. Chandler, "Dialogue with the Past," 235–40; *Gamecock*, 11 February 1954.
12. Annual Report, 1950–51, 9; Chandler, "Dialogue with the Past," 241–50; "Bids Wanted," from "The Board of Trustees of the University of South Carolina," n.d., c. August 1952, Donald S. Russell Papers, USC Archives.
13. James F. Byrnes, *All In One Lifetime* (New York: Harper & Brothers, 1958), 407–9; *State*, 17 January 1953.
14. "Admiral Smith May Be on Way Out as USC Head," unidentified UPI news clipping, 28 June 1951, Smith biographical file, USC Archives; *News and Courier*, 26 October 1951.
15. BTM, 24 October 1951.
16. *Gamecock*, 2 November 1951, 9 November 1951, 30 November 1951.
17. *State*, 6 June 1952.
18. *State*, 19 March 1952; BTM, 27 May 1952.
19. BTM, 27 May 1952; "Some of the Accomplishments at the University of South Carolina in the Past Six Years, 1944–1951," Smith Papers.
20. BTM, 19 October 1949, 24 October 1951, 27 May 1952.
21. BTM, 19 October 1949, 24 October 1951; *Gamecock*, 2 November 1951, 21 March 1952; Chandler, "Dialogue with the Past," 251–56. For more on the University of South Carolina's original President's House, see Melissa Jean Haines, "A Lost Heritage: the Former President's House on the University of South Carolina Horseshoe," M.A. thesis, University of South Carolina, 1991.
22. *State*, 21 December 1951; *Gamecock*, 30 November 1951. Russell later admitted that he had sought the job, as he realized that the University was in turmoil. His ability and his close relationships with Governor Byrnes and influential trustee Rutledge L. Osborne helped him secure it. Author interview with John Edmunds, 7 March 2000.
23. *News and Courier*, 25 October 1951; "No Politics, Please!," undated clipping from the *Greenville News*, c. 25 October 1951, USC News Service Scrapbook, SCL.
24. *News and Courier*, 26 October 1951.
25. *Greenwood Index-Journal*, 5 December 1951.

26. *State,* 21 December 1951.

27. *Time,* 7 January 1952, 59.

28. *State,* 24 February 1998.

29. *State,* 21 December 1951; *USC Alumni News,* June 1952, 3–4; *Carolinian,* September 1987; John C. Moylan III, "Donald Stuart Russell—In Memoriam," *South Carolina Law Review* 49 (spring 1998), 353–57; *New York Times,* 25 February 1998, p. B-8; H. Emory Widener Jr., "Honorable Donald Stuart Russell (1971–1998)" from "Remembering the Fourth Circuit Judges: A History from 1941 to 1998," *Washington & Lee Law Review* 55 (spring 1998), 474–76; "Donald Stuart Russell," *The Complete Marquis Who's Who* (Chicago, Ill.: Reed Elsevier, 1999).

30. Ibid.

31. Ibid.; *State,* 21 December 1951, 27 February 1998; David Robertson, *Sly and Able: A Political Biography of James F. Byrnes* (New York and London: W. W. Norton, 1994), 492–93; BTM, 14 March 1948, 1 June 1948.

32. *State,* 17 January 1953.

33. *Gamecock,* 13 February 1953, 21 October 1953; *Carolinian,* September 1987, 6; Davis interview; Hollis interview; William Savage interview with Harold Brunton, 3 March 1987, USC Archives.

34. *Gamecock,* 13 February 1953, see also 20 March 1953.

35. Isadore Lourie to the editor of the *State,* 6 March 1998; *Gamecock,* 2 March 1951, 21 March 1952, 10 April 1952, 31 October 1953; *Record,* 1 June 1952; BTM, 27 May 1952; Chandler, "Dialogue with the Past," 251–62; Hollis interview.

36. *Gamecock,* 13 March 1953, 29 April 1955, 4 May 1956; Chandler, "Dialogue with the Past," 261–62; Hollis interview; Author interview with Donald Russell, 20 March 1997. Russell commented that he was "embarrassed" by the extravagance of the new president's home. The renovations eventually cost a total of more than $167,000 ($858,180), but the Russells made up the difference out of personal funds (Russell interview; "President's home–General Const. Co. Contractor," handwritten invoice, Russell Papers).

37. *State,* 10 October 1952. Even before he took office, Russell appointed a special faculty committee to do a complete evaluation of the University's operations and make specific recommendations about changes that should be made. See Donald Russell to W. H. Callcott et. al., 3 June 1952, Samuel Derrick Papers, SCL; "Preliminary Report of President's Special Reorganization Committee," 30 July 1952, Derrick Papers.

38. "Justification of Appropriation Request," BTM, 22 October 1953.

39. BTM, 1 June 1948.

40. Ibid.

41. *Florence Morning News,* 21 March 1956; draft budget request, 1953–54, beginning "Traditionally and basically," Russell Papers.

42. BTM, 14 March 1948.

43. BTM, 22 October 1953.

44. *State,* 17 January 1953.

45. *Gamecock,* 3 October 1953; BTM, 23 June 1953.

46. *State,* 13 November 1952; Davis interview; news release in Francis W. Bradley biographical file, 21 January 1960, USC Archives.

47. *State,* 3 October 1954, 25 October 1957; *Gamecock,* 2 October 1953, 16 October 1955, 21 September 1956; *USC Alumni News,* August 1953, 5; Self-Study, 1961, 529–38; USC Catalogs, 1952–1958, passim. Russell unsuccessfully tried to lure Clement Eaton (the noted historian of southern intellectual life in the antebellum period at the University of Kentucky) to Carolina in 1954. Eaton declined primarily because the salary offered was too low. See Donald Russell to Clement Eaton, 17 June 1954, Russell Papers.

48. Ibid; Mary Irwin, ed., *American Universities and Colleges,* 6th ed. (Washington, D.C.: American Council on Education, 1952), 880; Irwin, ed., *American Universities and Colleges,* 8th ed. (Washington, D.C.: American Council on Education, 1960), 958; Fellers interview; News Release, 21 January 1960, Francis W. Bradley biographical file, USC Archives.

49. Draft budget request, 1953–54, Russell Papers.

50. Donald Russell to Lewis L. Strauss, 27 June 1955, Russell Papers.

51. *Rock Hill Herald,* 8 October 1954.

52. BTM, 22 October 1953.

53. USC Catalog, 1951–52, 30, 172.

54. Ibid.

55. *USC Alumni News,* August 1953, 5; *Darlington News and Press,* 23 December 1954; BTM, 23 June 1953; *Gamecock,* 19 March 1954, 7 March 1958; *State,* 23 March 1954; F. T. Rogers to D. S. Russell, 15 November 1954, Russell Papers; Annual Report, 1952–53, 12; Self-Study, 1961, 533.

56. Edgar, *South Carolina: A History,* 522–23; *State,* 17 January 1953.

57. *USC Alumni News,* October 1953, 4.

58. "Justification of Appropriation Request . . . to the State Budget and Control Board," delivered 17 December 1952, Russell Papers.

59. Irwin, *American Universities* (1952), 880; Self-Study, 1961, 353; "School of Education Program," 22 May 1951, Smith Papers; Chester C. Travelstead to Harry Lesesne, 10 March 2000, letter in author's possession.

60. BTM, 22 October 1953.

61. BTM, 21 October 1952; *News,* 23 November 1952.

62. *Florence Morning News,* 12 November 1954; USC Catalog, 1954–55, School of Education, 5.

63. *News and Courier,* 21 July 1953; BTM, 8 July 1953; *USC Alumni News,* October 1953, 4; *State,* June 1 1956; Chester Travelstead, "'I Was There'—A Series of Autobiographical Vignettes," vol. 11, "The South Carolina Story," April 1983, 1–4, typescript in author's possession.

64. Author interview with Lawrence E. Giles, 23 February 2000; Lawrence E. Giles, "My Life and Times, 1914–?," manuscript autobiography in author's possession; Author interview with Johnnie McFadden, 22 February 2000. Many in the revamped School of Education earned a reputation as "integrationists," which would lead to considerable turnover in the school. Among those

branded as "integrationists" in the mid-1950s were Lawrence Giles, Warren Rudman, and Chester Travelstead.

65. *Charleston Evening Post,* 7 September 1954.

66. Frank S. Chase to Donald Russell, 4 March 1954, Russell Papers; *Gamecock,* 22 January 1954; *Morning News,* 19 November 1954; *USC Alumni News,* October 1953, 5; BTM, 22 October 1953.

67. *Record,* 13 November 1953; *State,* 10 January 1954; *Gamecock,* 15 January 1954; Frank S. Chase to Donald Russell, 4 March 1954, Russell Papers; Annual Report, 1954–55, 6; Chester Travelstead to Harry Lesesne, 10 March 2000, letter in author's possession.

68. *State,* 19 October 1951; 11 January 1957; *USC Alumni News,* February 1957, 4–6; Mary Still Coryell, *A Century of Excellence in Engineering: University of South Carolina College of Engineering, 1894–1994* (Columbia: College of Engineering, University of South Carolina, 1994), 31–36.

69. USC Catalog, 1951–52, 207–22; Coryell, 26–35.

70. Faculty Minutes, 7 December 1955; Russell interview. Russell later noted that it helped them that MIT's president, James R. Killian Jr., was a South Carolina native. MIT's leadership in engineeering is demonstrated in Roger Geiger, *Research and Relevant Knowledge: American Research Universities since World War II* (New York: Oxford University Press, 1993) 30–31.

71. Ibid.

72. Ibid.; *USC Alumni News,* February 1957, 4–6; BTM, 20 July 1955; Robert L. Sumwalt to Frank B. Gary, 15 December 1955, Russell Papers.

73. *State,* 17 July 1955; Fellers interview; *Gamecock,* 21 September 1956; Faculty Minutes, 7 December 1955; *USC Alumni News,* February 1957, 4–6.

74. Draft budget request, 1953–54, Russell Papers.

75. Self-Study, 1961, 15, 109, 457–60.

76. *Record,* 4 March 54.

77. Self-Study, 1961, 283.

78. *Record,* 10 May 1950.

79. *Gamecock,* 20 November 1953; Davis interview. The growth of the chemistry department had begun in the late 1940s. Chairman Davis attracted several quality chemists even before Russell's arrival, including O. D. Bonner (Ph.D., Kansas) and Peyton Teague (Ph.D., Texas). In addition, Davis brought the department up to national standards, receiving accreditation from the American Chemical Society in April 1951. See J. H. Howard to Norman M. Smith, 16 April 1951, Smith Papers.

80. BTM, 22 October 1953; *Gamecock,* 27 February 1953; *Greenwood Index-Journal,* 24 February 1953.

81. BTM, 20 July 1955.

82. USC Catalog, 1950–51; Commencement Programs, 17 August 1954, 6 June 1955, 8 August 1959 and 3 June 1960, USC Archives.

83. Donald Russell to Cleon O. Swayzee, 17 August 1954, Russell Papers; Richard L. Walker to Donald Russell, 1 February 1957, Russell Papers; Davis interview.

84. BTM, 26 June 1957; 4 June 1959; *Gamecock,* 29 March 1957, 18 September 1959. With the 1953 gift of more than $50,000 ($254,531) that made the Byrnes Chair possible, Russell had earlier in his administration tried to create other special professorships to lure prestigious scholars to the University. For instance, in 1955 the board of trustees authorized the creation of the Hugh Legare professorship in history and the George McDuffie professorship in English. The Russell gift, which by that time was worth nearly $60,000 ($305,437), was to be split between the two endowed chairs. However, attempts to bring in "star" professors to fill the provisional McDuffie and Legare chairs were unsuccessful. Hence, the initial Russell gift was used to fund the salary supplement to Walker and later the Byrnes Chair of International Studies, and the plans for the McDuffie and Legare professorships were abandoned (see BTM, 20 February 1953, 8 July 1953, 15 February 1955, 14 January 1956). For more on the turns in Walker's career that led him to the University of South Carolina, see Richard L. Walker, "China Studies in McCarthy's Shadow: A Personal Memoir," *The National Interest* 53 (fall 1998), 94–101.

85. Richard L. Walker to Donald Russell, 1 February 1957, Russell Papers; undated news release, circa fall 1957, Russell Papers; pamphlet, "The College of Arts and Sciences, University of South Carolina, International Studies," Russell Papers; pamphlet, "United States–Soviet Relations: An Age of Struggle, 1958–1959, Five Lectures," Russell Papers.

86. BTM, 21 October 1952.

87. *Gamecock,* 6 November 1953.

88. Donald Russell to "Dr. Ivey" of the Southern Regional Education Board, 23 February 1953, Russell Papers; *USC Alumni News,* August 1953, 5; *State,* 3 October 1954; *Evening Post,* 23 February 1959; Annual Report, 1952–53, 10–11.

89. Russell interview.

90. Russell interview; *Record,* 23 September 1958; *State,* 10 July 1955; *Gamecock,* 16 October 1959.

91. *News and Courier,* 22 January 1959.

92. Author interview with Robert Ochs, 2 February 2000; in the early 1990s the history department's faculty voted to abolish the Oxford exchange program in order to give itself a pay raise.

93. For the growth of federally funded research and the expansion of research universities in this era, see Roger Geiger, *Research and Relevant Knowledge,* especially chapters 1 and 2; Brubacher and Rudy, *Higher Education in Transition,* 236; Cartter, *Qualitative Aspects,* 50–51; BTM, 29 May 1951; Annual Report, 1950–51, 26–27; *State,* 21 December 1952; Annual Report, 1953–54, 8; "Report of the Visitation to the University of South Carolina, April 16–19, 1961, Submitted to the Commission of Colleges and Universities of the Southern Association of Colleges and Secondary Schools," SCL, 54. Between 1955 and 1961, the Faculty Research Committee allocated some $157,000 ($730,723) of University funds for research projects.

94. *Greenville News,* 7 December 1952.

95. *State,* 23 October 1955.
96. Annual Report, 1952–53, 13; *University of South Carolina Business and Economic Review,* SCL, passim; *Daily Item,* 20 October 1953.
97. *Daily Item,* 18 July 1950; BTM, 29 May 1951; *Gamecock,* 12 October 1951; Self-Study, 1961, 228.
98. Annual Report, 1950–51, 26, 52–53, 12; *Charleston News and Courier,* 6 December 1953; *Record,* 29 July 1954; *State,* 2 August 1954.
99. *USC Perspective,* February 1961, 1; *State,* 29 July 1954; *News and Courier,* 2 August 1959; *Greenville News,* 20 October 1958; Self-Study, 1961, 227.
100. Self-Study, 1961, 233.
101. "Report of the Visitation to the University of South Carolina, April 16–19...," 30–31, 54.
102. Draft budget request, 1953–54, Russell Papers.
103. Self-Study, 1961, 15; BTM, 20 January 1954, 2 October 1954; Wilfred Callcott, "Report to the Committee on Higher Education," 24 April 1961, Sumwalt Papers; *State Institutions of Higher Learning: Report No. 3 to the General Assembly of the State of South Carolina by the Fiscal Survey Commission, 1956,* 33.
104. Annual Report, 1952–53, 3–4, 1953–54, 4. Carter L. Burgess had a remarkable career both before and after his stint as assistant to the president. In World War II, he entered the army as a second lieutenant and rose to the rank of colonel, serving as secretary to the general staff of SHAEF—General Eisenhower's headquarters—where he met Donald Russell. After serving in the State Department and at Carolina, he became assistant secretary of defense for manpower in the Eisenhower administration. He then embarked on a business career, serving as president of Trans World Airlines and AMF, Inc. He served as ambassador to Argentina in the Johnson administration, and director of the Foreign Policy Association. He also served on the boards of directors of Ford Motor Company, J. P. Morgan & Co., and SmithKline Beecham. See *Fortune* 108 (31 October 1983), 140–56.
105. Annual Report, 1950–51, 51; Russell interview.
106. Russell interview; Byrnes, 409; *Statutes at Large of South Carolina* vol. 48, 169 (Act 139), 611 (Act 369); Annual Report, 1952–53, 4; *State,* 10 May 1954.
107. Irwin, *American Universities* (1952), 880; Annual Report, 1952–53, 4; Hollis, vol. 2, 344; *Record,* 18 August 1953; *Gamecock,* 24 April, 1953; "Building Program, Land," file, 1951–52, Smith Papers; "Memorandum for Special Advisory Committee on Land Acquisition," n.d., c. July 1953, Russell Papers; *State,* 6 November 1953, 10 May 1954, 14 October 1958; BTM, 10 April, 4 May, 23 June, 8 July, 5 August, 19 September, 22 October 1953; Donald Russell to the members of the Executive and Athletic Committees, 8 April 1954, Russell Papers.
108. Annual Report, 1953–54, 3; BTM, 13 January 1954, 20 January 1954.
109. Chandler, "Dialogue with the Past," 266–77; Donald Russell to State Budget and Control Board, 10 April 1953, Russell Papers; J. M. Smith to Donald Russell, 11 September 1953, Russell Papers; BTM, 13 January 1953, 27 May 1955; *Gamecock,* 6 May 1949, 16 November 1951, 6 March 1953, 21 March 1952, 21

October 1953, 18 February 1955, 22 April 1955, 29 April 1955, 23 September 1955, 16 October 1955; *State*, 10 June 1955, 17 October 1955; *News and Courier*, 15 May 1954; *Greenwood Index-Journal*, 26 September 1953.

110. Donald Russell to the Members of the Board of Trustees, 7 August 1954, Russell Papers; *USC Alumni News*, August 1955, 3–4; *Gamecock*, 12 November 1954; 10 December 1954, 23 September 1955; *Record*, 26 August 1954; *State*, 18 September 1955; *New York Times*, 7 August 1955; Chandler, "Dialogue with the Past," 267.

111. BTM, 27 May 1955; *Gamecock*, 16 October 1955, 21 September 1956; *Buildings of the Columbia Campus, The University of South Carolina* (Columbia: Division of University Relations, 1990), 51.

112. BTM, 18 September 1957; 19 April 1956; *State*, 2 February 1957; *Gamecock*, 8 February 1957; *Alumni News*, February 1957, 11; *Buildings of the Columbia Campus*, 37.

113. BTM, 12 January 1957; Donald Russell to J. M. Smith, 3 January 1957; *State*, 10 January 1958; *Buildings of the Columbia Campus*, 11; BTM, 19 April 1956, 17 January 1957, 3 June 1958; *Gamecock*, 18 April 1957.

114. BTM, 20 October 1955.

115. Ibid.; *State*, 29 October 1955, 14 May 1957, 12 June 1957, 1 December 1957, 26 June 1960; 4 April 1963; *Gamecock*, 20 January 1956, 10 May 1957; Donald Russell to Irving G. McNayr, 2 May 1957, Russell Papers; Donald Russell to J. M. Smith, 25 February 1957, Russell Papers.

116. Chandler, "Dialogue with the Past," 274; Leonard L. Long to Rutledge L. Osborne, 29 January 1954, Russell Papers.

117. BTM, 20 January 1954.

118. Chandler, "Dialogue with the Past," 274; See also W. G. Lyles to Sol Blatt Jr., 6 February 1954, Russell Papers; Sol Blatt. Jr. to Rutledge L. Osborne, 3 February 1954, Russell Papers; Michael M. Hare to Louis M. Wolff, 3 February 1954, Russell Papers.

119. BTM, 16 February 1954; William H. Patterson to Michael M. Hare, 17 February 1954, Russell Papers.

120. Paul Venable Turner, *Campus: An American Planning Tradition* (Cambridge, Mass.: MIT Press, 1984), 260, quoted in Chandler, "Dialogue with the Past," 276–77.

121. *News and Courier*, 6 March 1958.

122. *Record*, 4 March 1959.

123. *News and Courier*, 7 March 1958; See also *News and Courier*, 29 April 1958; *Record*, 6 May 1958.

124. *Gamecock*, 4 November 1955; 20 January 1956; *State*, 22 October 1958.

125. *State*, 13 March 1955.

126. *State*, 30 May 1954. When Wardlaw College was built in 1930 in a cornfield behind the row of faculty homes, the plan called for these houses to be demolished. However, the Depression struck and the homes remained. Most of these houses were built in 1907, but the cottage at the corner of Sumter and College

Streets had been built in 1858 and had an interesting history. Originally built as the "Marshall's House," after the Civil War the home was occupied by the Freedmen's Bureau; it then served as a home to law professor A. C. Haskell and later to despised carpetbagger professor Rudolph Vamphill during the "Radical University" period. Later in Reconstruction, the house served as army officers' quarters, and after Reconstruction it served as a faculty home, housing such distinguished personages as Frank C. Woodward (president of the South Carolina College, 1897–1902), Patterson Wardlaw, longtime dean of the school of education, and Leonard T. Baker, three times president of the University.

127. Havilah Babcock to Donald Russell, 3 March 1954, Russell Papers.

128. Annual Report, 1950–51, 49, 1958–59, 4; *State Institutions of Higher Learning,* 22; BTM, 19 April 1956, 15 November 1956; "Annual Report to the President by the Registrar, 1958–59," SCL, 10.

129. Clemson Annual Report, 1951, 6, 1959–60, 28.

130. *State Institutions of Higher Learning,* 26–27; Donald M. McKale, ed., *Tradition: A History of the Presidency of Clemson University* (Macon, Ga.: Mercer University Press, 1988), 176; Wright Bryan, *Clemson: An Informal History of the University, 1889–1979* (Columbia: R. L. Bryan, 1979), 131. Reacting to the diminished attractiveness of military and single-gender education, in 1955 Clemson's board of trustees decided to abolish compulsory ROTC and open up to women.

131. *State Institutions of Higher Learning,* 8–9, 21, 25–27; BTM, 19 April 1956, 15 November 1956; *Greenwood Index-Journal,* 6 February 1956.

132. Self-Study, 1961, 23. Tuition fees were committed to amortizing bonds. The remaining 30 percent of operating revenue came from miscellaneous fees such as the University fee, room fees, and summer course fees.

133. Annual Report, 1950–51, 51; Self-Study, 1961, 23.

134. E. F. Schietinger, *Fact Book on Higher Education in the South, 1965* (Atlanta: Southern Regional Education Board, 1965), 34.

135. "Report of the Visitation to the University of South Carolina, April 16–19...," 14–15.

136. "Student-Faculty Ratio For Selected Years," 31 October 1956, Russell Papers; "Faculty-Student Ratio—Southern Colleges," chart, 1956–57, Russell Papers; BTM, 15 November 1956; Irwin, *American Universities* (1952), 880; Irwin, *American Universities* (1960), 958.

137. BTM, 8 June 1951.

138. Annual Report, 1950–51, 53; "It's an Open Secret at USC—The Future Is 'Looking Up,'" undated newspaper clipping (c. March 1956) from the *Observer,* Russell Papers; BTM, 15 November 1956, 25 October 1957 .

139. Davis Interview; "Let's Get Going!: An Analysis of the Faculty Salary Situation at the University of South Carolina," pamphlet published by the University of South Carolina Alumni Association, 1956, USC Archives.

140. Geiger, *Research and Relevant Knowledge,* 43.

141. "Let's Get Going!"; *USC Alumni News,* February 1957; *State,* 7 January 1956.

142. Quoted in the *Greenwood Index-Journal,* 23 June 1952; Russell interview.

143. Kenneth M. Lynch to the presidents of the state institutions of higher learning, 8 July 1952, Russell Papers; "South Carolina Council of Higher Education . . . Articles of Agreement and Procedure," n.d., Russell Papers.

144. Lynch to presidents, 8 July 1952, Russell Papers; Donald Russell to Frank Poole, 29 August 1952, Russell Papers; "Presidents of State Institutions," 1 October 1952, Russell Papers; "South Carolina Council of Higher Education . . . Articles of Agreement and Procedure," n.d., Russell Papers. In 1951, the General Assembly created another committee to study the state's higher education system and consider eliminating duplication. They made their report in early 1952, and recommended that the state create a higher education commission. The General Assembly defeated their recommendations. See *House Journal*, 6 February 1951; BTM, 18 March 1952; J. A. Sprill Jr. to Norman Smith, 15 December 1951, Smith Papers.

145. *News*, 4 February 1955; *State Institutions of Higher Learning*, 3–8; Dreyfuss, "Origin of Statewide Higher Education Coordination," 95–109. The fiscal survey commission also recommended that the state make further study as to whether South Carolina should continue to support two schools of engineering—one at the University and the other at Clemson. See 9–10, 31–34.

146. *Garnet and Black*, 1955; *Gamecock*, 27 March 1953, 15 April 1953, 9 October 1953, 28 May 1954, 11 March 1955, 22 February 1957; *State*, 6 June 1955, 1 June 1957; *News and Courier*, 7 June 1955, 1 June 1957; *Citizen* (Tucson, Arizona), 6 June 1955, clipping, USC News Service Scrapbook, SCL.

147. *Gamecock*, 24 September 1954.

148. *Gamecock*, 16 October 1955.

149. *Gamecock*, 7 December 1956.

150. John Patrick Diggins, *The Proud Decades: America in War and Peace, 1941–1960* (New York: W. W. Norton, 1988), 203–4; see also Paul A. Carter, *Another Part of the Fifties* (New York: Columbia University Press, 1983), 168–78.

151. Philip E. Jacob, *Changing Values in College* (New York: Harper Brothers, 1957), 1.

152. Lee, *The Campus Scene*, 90.

153. *Gamecock*, 18 December 1959. For the rebellions of the early nineteenth century, see Hollis, vol. 1, index entry "Discipline."

154. *Gamecock*, 7 December 1956.

155. *USC Alumni News*, April 1949; *Gamecock*, 13 October 1950, 21 September 1951, 21 September 1956, 20 September 1957.

156. *Garnet and Black*, 1976, 38.

157. *Record*, 21 May 1952; *State*, 22 May 1952; *News and Courier*, 21 May 1952; *Daily Times* (Union) 21 May 1952; W. P. Boyleston to Norman Smith, 22 May 1952 (telegram), Smith Papers; Arney Childs to W. H. Patterson, 12 June 1952, Smith Papers; Lee, *The Campus Scene*, 96.

158. *Record*, 21 May 1952.

159. L. B. Jackson to Norman Smith, 21 May 1952, Smith Papers; BTM, 27 May 1952; W. H. Patterson to F. F. Welbourne, 12 June 1952, Smith Papers.

160. *Gamecock*, 1 April 1955, 7 April 1955.

161. *Gamecock*, 16 November 1956, 18 October 1957; *Morning News*, 11 April 1959.

162. Annual Report, 1953–54, 23.

163. *USC Alumni News,* May 1957, 2; "University of South Carolina Archives Oral Interviews," Frances Turkett Riley interviewed by Jane E. Hutchison, 6 October 1994, USC Archives.

164. Marty Jezer, *The Dark Ages: Life in the United States 1945–1960* (Boston: South End Press, 1982), 246–47; Diggins, *The Proud Decades,* 204; William Chafe, *The Unfinished Journey: America Since World War II,* 4th ed. (New York: Oxford University Press, 1999), 123–28.

165. *Garnet and Black,* 1955.

166. See any *Garnet and Black* from the 1950s, but especially 1955.

167. *Gamecock,* 20 February 1953, 2 October 1953, 1 October 1954, 15 October 1954, 18 March 1955; BTM, 19 September 1953, 4 March 1954; Donald Russell to the members of the Executive and Athletic Committees, 8 April 1954, Russell Papers; *Record,* 21 January 1955.

168. Pat Conroy, *Beach Music* (New York: Doubleday, 1995), 454. Despite his rich descriptions of student life at Carolina, Conroy was never a Carolina student.

169. Conroy, 454–59; *Gamecock,* 21 September 1951; *Garnet and Black* 1951–1959, passim.

170. *Garnet and Black,* 1958, 316–19.

171. McCandless, *The Past in the Present,* 222–24. A. W. Zelomek, *A Changing America: At Work and Play* (New York: John Wiley and Sons, 1959), 27–28; Diggins, *The Proud Decades,* 212.

172. *USC Alumni News,* May 1957, 2.

173. Hollis, vol. 2, 336.

174. *Gamecock,* 20 May 1955.

175. Edward M. Singleton, "A History of the Regional Campus System of the University of South Carolina," Ph.D. dissertation, University of South Carolina, 1971, 9–10.

176. Singleton, "A History of the Regional Campus System," 15–21; *Chronicle* (Augusta), 24 May 1959; BTM, 18 September 1957.

177. *Morning News,* 4 April 1957; *Gamecock,* 1 November 1957.

178. Singleton, "A History of the Regional Campus System," 22–34.

179. *Record,* 16 September 1977; Author interview with T. Eston Marchant, 6 May 1997.

180. *News and Courier,* 11 October 1957, 26 October 1957; BTM, 25 October 1957; *Record,* 26 October 1957.

181. BTM, 25 October 1957.

182. Ibid.

183. *News and Courier,* 26 October 1957.

184. *Gamecock,* 16 May 1958.

185. *Gamecock,* 1 November 1957.

186. BTM, 20 February 1953, 8 July 1953, 15 February 1955, 14 January 1956, 25 October 1957, 23 November 1957, 4 June 1959; Donald Russell to Lindsley F. Kimball, 4 October 1954, Russell Papers, "General Education Board" file; draft letter from Donald Russell beginning "I understand from Mr. Burgess," n.d., Russell Papers, "Russell, D. S." file, 1953–54.

187. BTM, 25 October 1957; *Gamecock*, 1 November 1957; *News and Courier*, 26 October 1957; author interview with Robert Sumwalt Jr., 25 February 1998.

188. Hollis interview; Fellers interview; Rebecca Callcott interview. Previous acting presidents who were the chief academic officer on campus included deans Leonard T. Baker, who served in the job three different times (1926, 1931–1936, and 1944), and Francis W. Bradley in 1952.

189. BTM, 25 October 1957, 23 November 1957. The board's search committee included the following members: Rutledge L. Osborne, A. C. Todd, James W. Cothran, J. Davis Kerr, and Douglas McKay.

190. *Spartanburg Herald*, 18 September 1958; *Evening Post*, 19 September 1958; *News and Courier*, 20 September 1958.

191. Littlejohn, *Littlejohn's Political Memoirs*, 176–77; *Independent*, 28 September 1958; *State*, 22 November 1958; Workman, *Bishop from Barnwell*, 118–24.

192. *News and Courier*, 8 February 1958; 19 April 1958.

193. *Gamecock*, 20 February 1958.

194. *State*, 11 April 1959; *Record*, 7 May 1959; BTM, 7 May 1959. Clemson had done the same thing—naming acting president Robert C. Edwards president only a month before, probably contributing to the board's ability to compromise on the decision. See Workman, *Bishop from Barnwell*, 280–82, McKale, 194–96.

195. *Gamecock*, 6 December 1957.

196. *State*, 21 November 1956; *Gamecock*, 11 January 1957; *News and Courier*, 31 October 1957.

197. Self-Study, 1961, 145; BTM, 6 March 1958.

198. BTM, 9 December 1957, 6 March 1958; Self-Study, 1961, 143, 145.

199. Hubert Spigner to Robert Sumwalt, 26 June 1958, Robert L. Sumwalt Papers, USC Archives.

200. By rank, the increases in median nine-month salary between 1956–57 and 1960–61 were: 1) assistant professors, $4,800 ($23,623) to $6,250 ($28,599); 2) associate professors, $5,400 ($26,576) to $7,100 ($32,488); and 3) professors, $5,850 ($28,790) to $7,700 ($35,234) (Self-Study, 1961, 143). For the salary levels responding to the AAUP ratings, as well as ratings and salary levels of other institutions in the U.S., see "The Economic Status of the Profession, 1959–60: Annual Report by Committee Z," *AAUP Bulletin* 46, no. 2 (summer 1960), 156–93.

201. BTM, 29 July 1959; See also Faculty Minutes, 7 October 1959.

202. BTM, 29 October 1959.

203. *State*, 2 June 1958.

204. USC Catalog, 1959–60, 349, 1960–61, 266; Faculty Minutes, 7 October 1959; *State*, 12 February 1959.

205. Faculty Minutes, 7 October 1959; USC Catalog, 1960–61, 266; *Record*, 27 January 1960.

206. "The Establishment of the University of South Carolina Institute of Science and Technology," 20 March 1958, Sumwalt Papers.

207. Memo to deans and heads of departments, from Robert L. Sumwalt, 25 November 1958, Sumwalt Papers.

208. "The Establishment of the University of South Carolina Institute of Science and Technology," 20 March 1958, Sumwalt Papers; Faculty Minutes, 7 May 1958; *USC Perspective*, February 1961, 1.

209. Giles, "My Life and Times," 151–52.

210. *USC Alumni News*, February 1957.

211. *State*, 4 May 1958.

212. "University of South Carolina Educational Foundation," Steering Committee, 17 November 1956, Russell Papers.

213. *State*, 4 May 1958; Henry H. Lesesne, "A History of the Alumni Association of the University of South Carolina, 1843–1996," pamphlet published by the Greater USC Alumni Association, 1996, 29–30; BTM, 28 August 1958; *Greenville Piedmont*, 7 May 1958.

214. In 1956, the South Carolina Bar Association established the law school endowment fund to benefit that school, and by 1960 it had raised $35,263 as well; Self-Study, 1961, 38; BTM, 9 December 1957.

215. Paul R. Lawrence, *Unsportsmanlike Conduct: The National Collegiate Athletic Association and the Business of College Football* (New York: Praeger, 1987), 41–47; Bruce A. Corrie, *The Atlantic Coast Conference, 1953–1978* (Durham, N.C.: Carolina Academic Press, 1978), 28–29.

216. Lawrence, *Unsportsmanlike Conduct*, 47–49; Corrie, *Atlantic Coast Conference*, 28–29; Clarence P. Houston to Norman M. Smith, 16 November 1949 and 19 June 1950, Smith Papers; H.C. Willet to Norman P. Smith, 6 September 1950, Smith Papers; BTM, 21 March 1950. For the trials and tribulations of an athletics program at a similar university, see Dyer, *University of Georgia*, 285–90.

217. *Gamecock*, 14 March 1952.

218. *Gamecock*, 3 December 1954; 8 March 1957. On the UPI All-America team with Grady Wallace was Wilt "the Stilt" Chamberlain of Kansas.

219. "It's An Open Secret at USC—The Future Is 'Looking Up,'" undated newspaper clipping (c. March 1956) from the *Charlotte Observer*, Russell Papers; BTM, 20 January 1954; *Greenwood Index-Journal*, 2 February 1954; *Anderson Independent*, 3 February 1954; quotations, *Greenville News*, 3 December 1957.

220. *State*, 7 April 1960, 8 April 1960; Corrie, *Atlantic Coast Conference*, 210; "Report of the Visitation to the University of South Carolina, April 16–19," 15; Director of Libraries, USC, Annual Report, 1960–61. For a short summary of Rex Enright's career at Carolina, see Barton, *Carolina-Clemson Game*, 321–24.

221. Corrie, *Atlantic Coast Conference*, 34–44; *USC Alumni News*, June 1953.

222. Barton, *Carolina-Clemson Game*, 271–72; Donald Russell to R. M. Cooper, 8 May 1956, Russell Papers; G. E. Metz to Donald Russell, 17 December 1956, Russell Papers; R. F. Poole to Donald Russell, 20 March 1957.

223. "Recent Supreme Court Opinions on Segregated Education," *Higher Education* 7, no. 1 (September 1, 1950), 3–5; Boles, *The South Through Time*, 527–28; http://ccwf.cc.utexas.edu/russell/seminar/sweatt/sweattindex.html; http://www.uky.edu/Law/library/commemoration/mclaurin.htm.

224. Among the board members voting to deny the applicants admission were Governor Strom Thurmond and state senator Marion Gressette—two men who played key roles in the 1950s in defending segregation. Jacob Joseph Martin to Registrar, School of Law, 14 June 1950, Smith Papers; *State,* 16 June 1950, 20 August 1950; Norman Smith to Rutledge L. Osborne, 12 July 1950, Smith Papers; BTM, 2 August 1950; Norman M. Smith to Cleveland Stevens, 19 August 1950, Smith Papers; Norman M. Smith to Samuel Herman Rubens, 19 August 1950, Smith Papers; Norman M. Smith to Jacob Joseph Martin, 19 August 1950, Smith Papers; misc. notes in "Negro Problem" file, Smith Papers.

225. BTM, 24 October 1951; W. H. Callcott to President's Office, 26 July 1952, Smith Papers.

226. Samuel Prince to Norman M. Smith, 15 December 1951, Smith Papers; F. D. G. Riddle to Norman M. Smith, 17 January 1952, Smith Papers; "Association of American Law Schools, Resolution Adopted at the Annual Meeting December 28–30, 1951, Smith Papers; "Interim Report for 1954 of the Special Committee on Racial Discrimination to the Association of American Law Schools," Russell Papers; "Final Report for 1954 of the Special Committee on Racial Discrimination to the Association of American Law Schools," Russell Papers.

227. Samuel Prince to Norman M. Smith, 8 January 1952, Smith Papers. The irony was that a South Carolina school case Marshall was pursuing even as Prince wrote this, *Briggs v. Elliott,* composed a key part of the *Brown v. Board of Education* ruling that overturned separate but equal for good.

228. Frank Edward Cain to Samuel L. Prince, 22 December 1951, Smith Papers; Samuel L. Prince to Norman Smith, 2 January 1952, Smith Papers; Norman M. Smith to Frank Edward Cain, 2 January 1952, Smith Papers; Frank Edward Cain to Norman M. Smith, 9 January 1952, Smith Papers; Miriam Holland to Pauline Bullard, 15 March 1952, Smith Papers; Samuel Prince to Donald Russell, 8 December 1954, Russell Papers; Newby, *Black Carolinians,* 351.

229. *Gamecock,* 18 September 1951; Statement of John Duffy, session 4, "The Origins of Desegregation at the University of South Carolina, 1963–1988," audio tape, 19 November 1988, in possession of Grace J. McFadden.

230. *Gamecock,* 6 November 1953.

231. *Gamecock,* 20 November 1953, 25 November 1953.

232. *Gamecock,* 4 December 1953.

233. *Gamecock,* 15 January 1954. See the entire discussion on segregation in the *Gamecock,* 20 November 1953–22 January 1954.

234. Edgar, *South Carolina: A History,* 522–23; Hollings interview.

235. T. C. Callison and James S. Verner to James F. Byrnes, 27 March 1951, Smith Papers; BTM, 29 May 1951, 24 October 1951; "Comments on the Recommendations of the Committee on College Testing Program, May 18, 1951, submitted by H. O. Strohecker, Registrar," Smith Papers.

236. T. C. Callison and James S. Verner to James F. Byrnes, 27 March 1951, Smith Papers; BTM, 29 May 1951, 24 October 1951; "Comments on the

Recommendations of the Committee on College Testing Program, May 18, 1951, submitted by H. O. Strohecker, Registrar," Smith Papers.

237. Statement of John Duffy, "The Origins of Desegregation at the University of South Carolina, 1963–1988," audio tape of conference held 19 November 1988 (Session 4), in possession of Grace J. McFadden; Chester C. Travelstead, "I Was There," 2, 8. Duffy remembered that Russell was attacked for his gradual-ist position during the 1958 gubernatorial campaign.

238. Donald Russell to R. F. Poole, 24 April 1954, Russell Papers; Donald Russell to Henry R. Sims, 14 May 1954, Russell Papers; Faculty Minutes, 27 May 1954.

239. Faculty minutes, 27 May 1954; BTM, 28 May 1954; Gamecock, 21 September 1956; Remembering the Days, xxvii. In 1955, Winthrop adopted the entrance examination policy, and in 1956 Wofford and Clemson did as well. An inter-esting note about the faculty meeting at which the exams were approved came from Chester C. Travelstead, then dean of the school of education. Travelstead recalled the exchange between Russell and a faculty member in this paragraph. When the meeting's minutes were distributed, the exchange appeared in the minutes as Travelstead remembered it. However, a week later, a message from the president's office requested that all copies of the minutes be returned. A few days later, a neatly revised set of minutes was distributed, and the exchange with Russell was left out. Travelstead speculated that such was done to main-tain Russell's political viability. See Travelstead, "I Was There," 9.

240. "Description of the Student Body of the University of South Carolina in Terms of Performances on Standardized Mental Tests, Annex III-1a," Russell Papers, c. 1954; Marcia G. Synott, The Half-Opened Door: Discrimination and Admis-sions at Harvard, Yale and Princeton, 1900–1970 (Westport, Conn: Greenwood Press, 1979), 199–231.

241. Faculty minutes, 27 May 1954.

242. News and Courier, 13 June 1954.

243. State, 14 June 1954; for others, see State, 18 June 1954; News and Courier, 6 June 1954; Greenville News, 13 June 1954; Observer, 16 June 1954.

244. John R. Williams to the editor of the State, undated clipping, Russell Papers.

245. Sol Blatt Jr. to Donald Russell, 10 June 1955, Russell Papers; Donald Russell to A. C. Todd, 19 August 1954, Russell Papers.

246. Russell interview.

247. John R. Williams to the editor of the Columbia State, undated clipping, Rus-sell Papers.

248. Earl Black, Southern Governors and Civil Rights: Racial Segregation as a Cam-paign Issue in the Second Reconstruction (Cambridge: Harvard University Press, 1976), 82.

249. News and Courier, 9 June 1954.

250. Watts, "The Freshman Year Experience," 82; Edgar, South Carolina: A History, 524–28.

251. Union Daily Times, 16 June 1954.

252. Sol Blatt Jr. to Donald Russell, 25 June 1954, Russell Papers.

253. Donald Russell to James F. Byrnes, 26 June 1954, Russell Papers.

254. Author interview with Lawrence F. Giles; Giles, "My Life and Times," chapter 13. The disappearance of free speech in the South as related to civil rights had parallels in the anticommunist hysteria of the same era. For the influence of anticommunism on American universities, see Ellen Schrecker, *No Ivory Tower: McCarthyism and the Universities* (New York: Oxford University Press, 1986), Geiger, *Research and Relevant Knowledge*, 37–40, and William J. Billingsley, *Communists on Campus: Race, Politics, and the Public University in Sixties North Carolina* (Athens: University of Georgia Press, 1999); For the atmosphere created by opposition to racial integration in the 1950s, see Howard H. Quint, *Profile in Black and White: A Frank Portrait of South Carolina* (Washington: Public Affairs Press, 1958).

255. Chester C. Travelstead, "Turmoil in the Deep South," *School and Society* 83, no. 2084 (April 28, 1956), 143–47; *News and Courier*, 4 May 1954; Travelstead, "I Was There," 2, 5–6, 8.

256. Frank S. Chase to Donald Russell, 4 March 1954, Russell Papers; Melvin Eugene Timmerman et. al. to Chester C. Travelstead, 1 January 1956, letter in author's possession.

257. Travelstead, "Turmoil," 143–47; see also Travelstead, "I Was There," 10–12.

258. Travelstead, "Turmoil," 143–47; Travelstead, "I Was There," 10–12; Chester C. Travelstead to George Bell Timmerman, Jr., 2 May 1955, Travelstead topical file, USC Archives.

259. George Bell Timmerman, Jr. to Donald Russell, 31 May 1955, Travelstead topical file, USC archives.

260. Travelstead, "Turmoil," 145; Travelstead, "I Was There," 19–20; Quint, *Profile in Black and White*, 176; Chester Travelstead to Harry Lesesne, 10 March 2000, letter in author's possession.

261. Chester C. Travelstead, "Today's Decisions for Tomorrow's Schools," 2 August 1955, Travelstead topical file, USC Archives.

262. Chester Travelstead to Harry Lesesne, 10 March 2000, letter in author's possession.

263. L. Marion Gressette to George Bell Timmerman Jr., 19 August 1955, Travelstead topical file, USC archives; Travelstead, "Turmoil," 143–47; Travelstead, "I Was There," 29.

264. Frank F. Welborne to Chester C. Travelstead, 19 August 1955, Travelstead topical file; Quint, *Profile in Black and White*, 176; Travelstead, "I Was There," 30–33.

265. Travelstead, "Turmoil," 143–47; Travelstead, "I Was There," 70–73; Maxie Myron Cox, "1963—The Year of Decision: Desegregation in South Carolina," Ph.D. dissertation, University of South Carolina, 1996, 77; Giles, "My Life and Times," 150–51. Even after moving from South Carolina, Travelstead maintained a love-hate relationship with the South. He took pride in being a southerner but remained a harsh critic of segregation. He wrote in 1960, "It is at this

point that something akin to shame characterizes the feeling of this observer for his homeland. Nothing short of shameful describes accurately or adequately conditions which deny any group of people in this country its 'unalienable rights' as provided by law in the Bill of Rights" (see Chester C. Travelstead, "Southern Attitudes Toward Racial Integration," *School and Society* 88, no. 2174 [May 7, 1960], 231–34).

266. Josephine Piekarz to Donald Russell, 17 February 1956, Russell Papers; Donald Russell to William Savage, 13 March 1956, Russell Papers; Sarah Drayton to Donald Russell, 15 March 1956, Russell Papers; Margaret Rauhof to Donald Russell, 19 January 1956, 9 February 1956, Russell Papers; Donald Russell to Margaret Rauhof, 2 February 1956, Russell Papers; Giles, "My Life and Times," 146–47; Giles interview.

267. *State,* 10 December 1955; typed notes, n.d., Russell Papers; Melvin Eugene Timmerman et. al. to Chester Travelstead, 1 January 1956, letter in author's possession. Donald Russell, later in his life, claimed that Travelstead was not fired for speaking out against segregation at all, but for insubordination. However, during the bitter 1958 gubernatorial campaign with Ernest Hollings in which Russell was attacked for his "weakness" on the integration issue, Russell bragged about his firing "a man named Travelstead." Travelstead himself held no grudges, and his judgement of Donald Russell is worth noting. Late in his life he wrote of Russell, "I felt he was inherently neither a racist nor a bigot . . . . He knew very well how opposed I was to segregation of the races . . . and yet never once did he disagree; nor did he caution me against working quietly and legally to help correct this deplorable custom in the South. As it turned out, Donald Russell would always, in the final analysis, say and do for public scrutiny only those things which he thought would enhance his own future— particularly in politics. I found out well before the Supreme Court decision on racial segregation that he wanted to be Governor of the state. He was finally successful in being elected to that office, but only at the expense of many others, including me" (Travelstead, "I Was There," 8).

268. Ralph Fuchs to Donald Russell, 16 January 1956, Russell Papers; Donald Russell to Ralph Fuchs, 23 January 1956, Russell Papers; Giles interview.

269. *Gamecock,* 2 December 1955.

270. Ibid.

271. *Gamecock,* 9 December 1955.

272. Ibid.

273. *News and Courier,* 25 November 1955; *Fresno (California) Bee* quoted in Travelstead, "I Was There," 59; for numerous editorials and letters that addressed the firing, see Travelstead, "I Was There," 34–69.

274. *News and Courier,* 15 January 1957, quoted in Quint, *Profile in Black and White,* 36–37.

275. Joseph Margolis, "The Role of the Segregationist," *Bulletin of the American Association of University Professors* 43, no. 4 (winter 1957), reprint in SCL.

276. *Barnwell People-Sentinel,* 9 January 1958.

277. *Summerville Scene,* 3 January 1958.
278. Sol Blatt to R. L. Sumwalt, 30 December 1957, Sumwalt Papers.
279. Sol Blatt to B. F. Hagood, Jr., 3 January 1958, Sumwalt Papers.
280. Handwritten notes titled "Margolis Case," Sumwalt Papers.
281. M. Kershaw Walsh to W. H. Callcott, 12 February 1958, Sumwalt Papers; Theodore T. Lafferty to Kershaw Walsh, 24 February 1958, Sumwalt Papers.
282. Handwritten notes titled "Margolis Case," Sumwalt Papers.
283. Ibid.
284. *News and Courier,* 13 April 1958.
285. Joseph Margolis to Robert Sumwalt, 1 June 1958, Sumwalt Papers.
286. Ibid.; Robert K. Carr to Robert Sumwalt, 13 June 1958, 8 July 1958, Sumwalt Papers; Robert Sumwalt to Robert K. Carr, 3 July 1958, Sumwalt Papers.
287. BTM, 3 June 1958.
288. *Gamecock,* 9 March 1956.
289. *Gamecock,* 16 March 1956, 29 March 1956.
290. Quint, *Profile in Black and White,* 116–25.
291. *State,* 16 January 1958, 17 January 1958, 18 January 1958; *News and Courier,* 16 January 1958, 17 January 1958, 18 January 1958.
292. Quint, *Profile in Black and White,* 123.
293. W. C. McCall to Thelma K. McClam, 20 January 1958, Sumwalt Papers; W. C. McCall to Mary Alston, 20 January 1958, Sumwalt Papers; W. C. McCall to Christine Thomas, 20 January 1958, Sumwalt Papers.
294. *Observer,* 23 January 1958.
295. "Application for Entrance Examination to Enter the University of South Carolina," Mitchell, Cornell Franklin and James Jones, 11 February 1958, Sumwalt Papers; handwritten notes titled "Negro Applications," Sumwalt Papers.
296. Resolution in Sumwalt Papers; handwritten notes titled "Negro Applications," Sumwalt Papers.
297. Handwritten notes titled "Negro Applications," Sumwalt Papers.
298. For the internal controversy within the NAACP, see John H. Bracey Jr. and August Meier, eds., *Papers of the NAACP, Part 3: The Campaign for Educational Equality. Series D: Central Office Records, 1956–1965. Group III, Series A, General Office File, Desegregation—Schools, South Carolina* (Bethesda, Maryland: University Publications of America), reel 8 of 13, frames 0296–0377; Bracey and Meier, eds., *Papers of the NAACP, Part 22: Legal Department Administrative Files, 1956–1965. Group V, Series B, Administrative Files. General Office File— Schools, South Carolina* (Bethesda, Maryland: University Publications of America), reel 26 of 27, frames 22–34; quotation, Modjeska M. Simkins to Roy Wilkins, 24 March 1958, Bracey and Meier, eds., *Papers of the NAACP, Part 3: The Campaign for Educational Equality. Series D: Central Office Records, 1956–1965. Group III, Series A, General Office File, Desegregation-Schools, South Carolina,* reel 8 of 13, frame 358; see also Barbara Woods Aba-Mecha, "Black Woman Activist in the Twentieth Century: Modjeska Monteith Simkins," Ph.D. dissertation, Emory University, 1978, 248–60.

299. *Greenville News,* 17 January 1958; *Acts and Joint Resolutions of the General Assembly of the State of South Carolina, Regular Session of 1956,* p. 1948.

300. *Cheraw Chronicle,* 30 January 1958.

301. See Quint, *Profile in Black and White; Gamecock,* 19 September 1958.

302. *News and Courier,* 9 September 1958.

303. *Gamecock,* 12 September 1958; "Student Congress Defeats USC Segregation Proposal," undated clipping from the *Evening Post,* c. August 25, 1958, USC News Service Scrapbook. For more about the NSA, see Angus Johnston, "A Brief History of the NSA and USSA," http://www.essential.org/ussa/org/html#civil (15 May 2000).

304. Angus Johnston, "A Brief History of the NSA"; *Gamecock,* 25 November 1959. In 1964, when Curry left the NSA, former USC graduate student Hayes Mizell took over the Southern Student Human Relations Project. See M. Hayes Mizell, "The Impact of the Civil Rights Movement on a White Activist," paper presented at the Southern Historical Association, Fort Worth, Texas, 4 November 1999, Wofford College Archives.

305. *Gamecock,* 18 December 1959.

306. *Gamecock,* 19 February 1960.

CHAPTER 4—THE GREAT TRANSFORMATION, 1960–1969

1. Edgar, *South Carolina: A History,* 552.

2. Clark Kerr, *The Great Transformation in Higher Education, 1960–1980* (Albany, N.Y.: State University of New York Press, 1991), xii–xiii; "To Keep Pace with America," *USC Magazine* 2, no. 1 (summer 1966); for more on this transformation, see Geiger, *Research and Relevant Knowledge,* especially chapters 7–9.

3. John K. Folger, *Future School and College Enrollments in the Southern Region* (Atlanta: Southern Regional Education Board, 1954), 8–9, 27–29, and passim; Robert W. Paterson, "The College Population in South Carolina, 1940–1980," *The University of South Carolina Business and Economic Review* 2, no. 4 (1 April 1955): 1–4; See also Ronald B. Thompson, *The Impending Tidal Wave of Students* (Columbus, Ohio: The Ohio State University; for the American Association of Collegiate Registrars and Admissions Officers, October 1954).

4. Paterson, 4.

5. BTM, 28 August 1958; Faculty minutes, 7 May 1958; "Preliminary Estimates of College Enrollment Trends and Prospects for the President's Special Committee on Long-Range Development," 8 November 1958, Sumwalt Papers.

6. Caroline Denham, ed., *The University of South Carolina Statistical Profiles, 1991–92* (Columbia: System Office of Institutional Research, The University of South Carolina, 1992): 3–4; *Self-Study 1980: The University of South Carolina, Columbia: Report of the Steering Committee to the Commission on Colleges, Southern Association of Colleges and Schools* (Columbia: University of South Carolina, 1981) (hereafter Self-Study, 1980), table 3–5.

7. *Fact Book on Higher Education in the South, 1970* (Atlanta: Southern Regional Education Board, 1970), 32.

8. Faculty minutes, 7 May 1958; see also *State,* 2 June 1958. Notable for its absence from Sumwalt's priority list was the most pressing problem facing the institution at the time, the future of racial segregation.

9. *Observer,* 23 December 1959.

10. *Gamecock,* 6 May 1960.

11. Quotation, William H. Robinson, "Desegregation in Higher Education in the South," *School and Society* 88, no. 2174 (May 7, 1960), 234–39; For a broad conceptual look at desegregating Southern higher education, see Peter Wallenstein, "Black Southerners and Non-Black Universities: Desegregating Higher Education, 1935–1967," *History of Higher Education Annual* 19 (1999), 121–48.

12. Draft letter to Gertrude Boatwright from Rollin E. Godfrey, n.d., c. March 1960, Sumwalt Papers; *Observer,* 27 April 1960.

13. Julie A. Wright to the President and Members of the Board of Trustees, University of South Carolina, 2 September 1960, Sumwalt Papers; Robert Sumwalt to Julie A. Wright, 12 September 1960, Sumwalt Papers; R.H. Wienefeld to Miss Essie Anne Duncan, 13 October 1960, Sumwalt Papers; Julie Wright to Robert Carter, 18 April 1961, Bracey and Meier, eds., *Papers of the NAACP, Part 22: Legal Department Administrative Files, 1956–1965. Group V, Series B, Administrative File, Carter, Robert L., Outgoing Correspondence* (Bethesda, Maryland: University Publications of America, 1997), reel 8 of 27, frames 756–757; Julie Wright to Gloster B. Curent, 21 February 1961, and Robert L. Carter to Julie Wright, 4 April 1961, Bracey and Meier, eds., *Papers of the NAACP, Part 22: Legal Department Administrative Files, 1956–1965. Group V, Series B, Administrative Files, General Office Files, Carter, Robert L., General Correspondence,* reel 5 of 27, frames 864 and 866.

14. *Gamecock,* 4 November 1960, 2 December 1960. Fraternity and sorority parties, not subject to the University's rule, often had black performers, as the music that students liked in the early 1960s, rock and roll, was at the time almost exclusively performed by black artists.

15. Author interview with Selden K. Smith, 31 January 2000; Mizell, "The Impact of the Civil Rights Movement on a White Activist."

16. Author interview with Selden K. Smith, 31 January 2000; Mizell, "The Impact of the Civil Rights Movement on a White Activist"; see documents in South Carolina Council on Human Relations Papers (SCCHR) Papers, "Admin, Student Council, 1961" file, SCL: "Student Program of the S.C. Council on Human Relations," 9 January 1961; "Announcing: A Workshop for College Students ," ca. 5 February 1961; "The Student Program of the Council," "The Situation in the Colleges in South Carolina," "The Purpose of the Student Program of the South Carolina Council on Human Relations," n.d., miscellaneous "Program Event" descriptions; "Evaluation of the Student Program"; "Summary Report on Student Workshop," 1961; "Planning Council," 1961; Elizabeth Ledeen to Constance Curry, ca. 5 May 1961. Among other USC students who attended the 1961 Penn Center conference were history students Charles Joyner and

Dan T. Carter (see notepad entries in "Admin, Student Council, 1961" file, SCCHR Papers, SCL).

17. *Gamecock,* 3 March 1961.

18. *Observer,* 8 March 1961; *Record,* 24 March 1961; *Gamecock,* 10 March 1961; Robert E. Landry to "Dear Sir," 20 March 1961, Sumwalt Papers.

19. Tom Wolfe, "The Artist the Art World Couldn't See," *New York Times Magazine,* 2 January 2000; see also the many essays and illustrations in *Frederick Hart: Sculptor* (New York: Hudson Hills Press, 1994); BTM, 6 April 1961. Hart was admitted to the University despite the fact that he never earned any high school credits. He was able to pass the entrance examination with an impressive enough score that his high school record did not matter.

20. Elizabeth Ledeen to Elizabeth McWhorter, 27 March 1961, SCCHR Papers, SCL; "Intercollegiate Council Mailing List, 1962" SCCHR Papers, SCL.

21. *Evening Post,* 3 August 1962; *News and Courier,* 29 August 1962; George McMillan, "Integration with Dignity," *Saturday Evening Post,* 16 March 1963, 15–21.

22. See Charlayne Hunter-Gault, *In My Place* (New York: Farrar Straus Giroux, 1992), and Calvin Trillin, *An Education in Georgia,* 3d ed. (Athens and London: University of Georgia Press, 1991).

23. Cox, "1963: The Year of Decision," 14–18. Cox is a good secondary source for detailed coverage of the desegregation of USC in 1963.

24. *Observer,* 27 July 1962. Harvey Gantt had sued for admission to Clemson in July as well. See Cox, "1963: The Year of Decision," 18.

25. "Memo to: Files, Subject: Integration and the Press," 4 September 1962, Jones Papers; David Abeel to Thomas F. Jones, "Report on I-Day," 7 December 1962, Jones Papers; Watts, "The Freshman Year Experience," 85–86; Fellers interview.

26. Cox, "1963: The Year of Decision," 78; *State,* 1 November 1962; *Gamecock,* 2 November 1962; *Observer,* 3 November 1962; Statement of Henrie Monteith Treadwell and Matthew Perry, "Origins of Desegregation at USC, 1963–1988," videotape of conference, 18 November 1988, in possession of Grace J. McFadden; Grace J. McFadden interview with Modjeska M. Simkins, 22 May 1979, in "The Quest for Civil Rights," USC Film Library; Grace J. McFadden interview with Matthew Perry, 18 August 1980, in "The Quest for Civil Rights," USC Film Library; McCandless, *The Past in the Present,* 106; Henrie M. Treadwell to Carolyn Matalene, "Recollections," May 2000, in author's possession. After registering for classes in the fall of 1963, Monteith told reporters, "I don't want people to feel I'm doing this just to be a symbol. I want an education" (see *Record,* 12 September 1963).

27. Cox, "1963: The Year of Decision," 81; *Record,* 28 September 1962; For the crisis at Ole Miss, see the following: Russell H. Barrett, *Integration at Ole Miss* (Chicago: Quadrangle Books, 1965); Nadine Cahodas, *The Band Played Dixie: Race and the Liberal Conscience at Ole Miss* (New York: Free Press, 1997), especially chapter 4; James Silver, *Mississippi: The Closed Society* (New York: Harcourt, Brace and World, 1964) and Silver, *Running Scared: Silver in Mississippi* (Jackson: University Press of Mississippi, 1984).

28. *Gamecock,* 5 October 1962, 12 October 1962, 19 October 1962, 30 November 1962; *Observer,* 5 October 1962.

29. *Gamecock,* 5 October 1962, 12 October 1962, 19 October 1962.

30. "They Don't Want Riots," undated *Time* clipping, c. 6 December 1962, USC News Service Scrapbook.

31. *Record,* 11 December 1964; See also *News and Courier,* 11 December 1962. For more on the efforts of South Carolina's leaders to prepare the state for integration, see, George McMillan, "Integration with Dignity," *Saturday Evening Post,* 16 March 1963.

32. Cox, "1963: The Year of Decision," 14–69; While Cox's is the most comprehensive treatment, for a brief account of the integration of Clemson, see Kirk K. Bast, "'As Different As Heaven and Hell': The Desegregation of Clemson College," *Proceedings of the South Carolina Historical Association* 1994, 38–44.

33. Cox, "1963: The Year of Decision," 45; *New York Times,* 30 January 1963; Wallenstein, "Black Southerners," 121–48. For a detailed look at the desegregation of the University of Alabama, see E. Culpepper Clark, *The Schoolhouse Door: Segregation's Last Stand at the University of Alabama* (New York and Oxford: Oxford University Press, 1993).

34. *Gamecock,* 11 January 1963, 1 February 1963, 8 February 1963.

35. *Spartanburg Herald,* 26 April 1963.

36. Preston Manning to Thomas F. Jones, 10 April 1963, Jones Papers, quoted in Watts, "The Freshman Year Experience," 86.

37. Broadcast editorial service . . . Frank B. Best, Orangeburg, S.C., 27 April 63, Jones Papers.

38. Watts, "The Freshman Year Experience," 85–86; *State,* 21 May 1963; John H. Martin, interviewed by William Savage, 3 March 1987, USC Archives.

39. *Gamecock,* 17 May 1963.

40. Cox, "1963: The Year of Decision," 82.

41. Mizell, "The Impact of the Civil Rights Movement on a White Activist"; McCandless, *The Past in the Present,* 229; "Student Program – June and July, 1963 Report" SCCHR Papers, SCL. For more on SCOOP, see Hayes Mizell Papers, SCL, and Mary King, *Freedom Song: A Personal Story of the 1960s Civil Rights Movement* (New York: William Morrow, 1987), 63.

42. Cox, "1963: The Year of Decision," 83–84.

43. Ibid., 84–85; BTM, 29 July 1963; memo to Dr. Paul Berg et. al., from Thomas F. Jones, 18 April 1963, letter in possession of Charles H. Witten; Fellers interview; "Mobilizing the University for Desegregation," audio tape from "The Origins of Desegregation at the University of South Carolina, 1963–1988," 19 November 1988, in possession of Grace J. McFadden. Dean Fellers's committee had the somewhat nondescript title "Ad Hoc Committee on University Affairs." For more on Maximilian LaBorde, see Hollis, vols. 1 and 2, especially vol. 2, pp. 66 and 358, note 26.

44. BTM, 29 July 1963.

45. Ibid.

46. Cox, "1963: The Year of Decision," 87–88, 92; BTM, 29 July 1963; USC Desegregation Plan, 26 July 1963, in possession of Charles H. Witten; Fellers interview; Statement of James Solomon, "Student Perspectives on Desegregation," videotape from conference, "The Origins of Desegregation at the University of South Carolina, 1963–1988," 18 November 1988, in possession of Grace J. McFadden.

47. Cox, "1963: The Year of Decision," 91; *Orangeburg Times and Democrat*, 3 September 1963; Solomon statement, "Origins of Desegregation"; "South Carolina Council Human Relations Report for September – November, 1963," SCCHR Papers, SCL.

48. *Observer*, 28 August 1963.

49. Henrie Monteith Treadwell to Carolyn Matalene, "Reminiscences," May 2000, in author's possession.

50. Cox, "1963: The Year of Decision," 87–92.

51. *Greenville News*, 12 July 1963, quoted in McCandless, *The Past in the Present*, 233.

52. *State*, 12 September 1963; *Record*, 11 September 1963, 12 September 1963; *Observer*, 12 September 1963; Cox, "1963: The Year of Decision," 93.

53. Fellers interview.

54. *Gamecock*, 13 September 1963.

55. Cox, "1963: The Year of Decision," 93; statement of Henrie Monteith, "The Origins of Desegregation at USC, 1963–1988," videotape of conference, 18 November 1988, in possession of Grace J. McFadden.

56. William Savage interview with John H. Martin, 3 March 1987, USC Archives.

57. Turk quote, *Gamecock*, 11 October 1963; there was a small story on page 30 of the *New York Times* (see issue for 12 September 1963).

58. Cox, "1963: The Year of Decision," 94.

59. Henrie Monteith Treadwell to Carolyn Matalene, "Recollections," May 2000.

60. Ibid; statements of Thorne Compton, James Solomon, and Robert Anderson, "Student Perspectives on Desegregation," videotape from conference, "The Origins of Desegregation at the University of South Carolina, 1963–1988," 18 November 1988, in possession of Grace J. McFadden; Robert Anderson interview with Grace J. McFadden, Grace J. McFadden oral history collection, in possession of Grace J. McFadden.

61. Cox, "1963: The Year of Decision," 93, 96–97; *Observer*, 12 September 1963; *Index-Journal*, 22 November 1963; *Spartanburg Herald*, 19 February 1964; *Record*, 12 September 1963; McCandless, *The Past in the Present*, 227.

62. Quoted in Cox, "1963: The Year of Decision," 98.

63. Ibid.

64. *News and Courier*, 10 November 1964, 22 August 1965; *Carolinian* 8, no. 2 (September 1983); Henrie Monteith, "Origins of Desegregation at USC " videotape; Robert Anderson interview with Grace J. McFadden.

65. Author interview with I. S. Leevy Johnson, 9 February 2000; Statement of Jasper M. Cureton, "Student Perspectives on Desegregation," videotape of conference, "The Origins of Desegregation at the University of South Carolina,

1963–1988, 18 November 1988, in possession of Grace J. McFadden; For more on Robert McC. Figg Jr., see Thomas Koehler-Shepley, "Robert McC. Figg, Jr.: South Carolina's Lawyers' Lawyer," M.A. thesis, University of South Carolina, 1994.

66. Self-Study, 1980, tables 3–5 and 3–8; Watts, "The Freshman Year Experience," 159; *Carolinian* 8, no. 2 (September 1983); statement of Grace J. McFadden, "Origins of Desegregation at USC, 1963–1988," videotape, 18 November 1988, in possession of Grace J. McFadden; statement of James Luck, "Integrating USC's Faculty," audiotape from conference, "Origins of Desegregation at USC, 1963–1988," 19 November 1988, in possession Grace J. McFadden; USC Magazine 4, no. 2 (spring 1969), 5; author interview with Harold White, 4 February 2000; *Gamecock,* 21 April 1967, 26 April 1968, 24 September 1968, 25 April 1969; *News and Courier,* 10 November 1964; McCandless, *The Past in the Present,* 227; "SCSCHR Report on the Enrollment of Negro Students," fall 1964, SCCHR Papers, SCL. Harold White proudly pointed to the fact that of the first sixteen black football players at Carolina who completed their eligibility, all earned a degree.

67. McKale, ed., 177–79.

68. BTM, 26 June 1959, 29 July 1959. The following specific areas were to be included in USC's final CMP report:

    1. Organization and Administration
    2. Space Utilization and Future building needs
    3. Academic salary levels and faculty utilization
    4. Budgetary and Financial control
    5. Development and Public relations
    6. Dormitory management
    7. Business management functions.

    Specifically excluded from the study were libraries, athletic administration, curriculum, teaching methods and evaluation of the faculty. Hollings was seemingly enamored with having Cresap, McCormick and Paget evaluate state institutions to judge their effectiveness and recommend improvements; Winthrop College, the Medical College, and the state departments of Education and Insurance also had CMP management surveys done during his administration. See *State of South Carolina: Organization and Administration of the Insurance Department* (New York: Cresap, McCormick and Paget, 1959), *Winthrop College: A Study of Organization and Administration* (New York: Cresap, McCormick and Paget, 1960), *State of South Carolina: Organization and Role of the State Department of Education* (New York: Cresap, McCormick and Paget, 1961), and *The Medical College of South Carolina: A Study of Organization and Management* (New York: Cresap, McCormick and Paget, 1962).

69. *University of South Carolina Administrative Survey Report,* vol. 1, *Organization and Top Administration* (New York: Cresap, McCormick and Paget, 1960), (hereafter referred to as "CMP Report"), II-3, II-6. The thirty-one included the eight deans who headed the schools and colleges of the University, the dean of

the faculty, the dean of administration, the director of the extension division, the commanders of the two military departments, the athletic director, and the heads of seventeen individual departments in the College of Arts and Sciences.

70. Ibid., II-4.

71. Ibid., II-4 and II-7.

72. CMP Report, II-13–II-18, II-22.

73. BTM, 1 March 1960; 17 May 1960; Faculty Minutes, 6 April 1960; letter "To the Members of the Faculty" from Robert L. Sumwalt, 18 May 1960, Sumwalt Papers; letter "To the Members of the Faculty and Staff" from Robert L. Sumwalt, 7 June 1960, Sumwalt Papers; *Gamecock,* 16 September 1960. There was additional administrative reshuffling as a result of the CMP report: R. H. Wienefeld (formerly dean of the College of Arts and Sciences and head of the department of history) became the new dean of the Graduate School; H. Willard Davis (former head of the department of chemistry) became the new dean of the College of Arts and Sciences; R. D. Ochs became head of the department of history; O. D. Bonner became head of the department of chemistry; and Rufus G. Fellers became dean of the School of Engineering.

74. CMP report, II-16–II-17; *State,* 1 June 1961, 10 September 1961; *Record,* 11 January 1961, 17 January 1961; *Gamecock,* 23 September 1960; Self-Study 1961, 38–42; quotation, "Address at Annual Alumni Meeting," 2 June 1961, Sumwalt Papers.

75. Though the Greater University Fund raised over $2 million, it never quite reached its goal. However, it did succeed in establishing the base for the University's endowment. BTM, 18 May 1961; *State,* 1 June 1961, 10 September 1961, 12 September 1961; *Gamecock,* 17 November 1961, 18 May 1962; Annual Report, 1962–63, 28; C. Wallace Martin to W. D. Workman, 10 November 1966, Jones Papers, USC Archives; Lesesne, "A History of the Alumni Association," 31; Annual Report, 1967–68, 25–26; *USC Perspective* 7, no. 1 (summer 1968).

76. Annual Report, 1967–68, 25–26; 1968–69, 26; *University of South Carolina Magazine* 4, no. 2 (spring 1969): 2–5. The first ten Carolina Scholars were James Russell Banks of Florence, John Michael Coxe of Bennettsville, Linda Diane Harvey of Woodruff, Stanley David Hudnall of Columbia, Cynthia Anne Lyle of North Augusta, Lewis Phillips Jr. of Greer, Robert Matthew Riley of Sumter, Richard Schwartz of Columbia, William Stokes Taylor of Spartanburg, and Betty Anne Williams of Orangeburg.

77. BTM, 4 November 1958.

78. BTM, 6 April 1961; *State,* 11 September 1960, 17 September 1962; *News and Courier,* 18 March 1961; *Gamecock,* 16 September 1960, 14 September 1962; Faculty Minutes, 5 October 1960.

79. *Gamecock,* 12 February 1960; *News and Courier,* 9 February 1964; BTM, 29 August 1960; *State,* 16 June 1960, 11 March 1961, 3 June 1964, 30 July 1964; author interview with Johnnie McFadden, 17 February 2000; author interview with Fannie Phelps Adams; for more on universities and urban renewal programs, see Charles G. Dobbins, ed., *The University, the City and Urban Renewal*

(Washington, D.C.: American Council on Education, 1964). Joe Darby, who grew up in the neighborhood destroyed by this urban renewal project, described its effect this way: "Urban renewal tore the heart out of a community that was modest but cohesive." In the 1990s, former Wheeler Hill residents began holding annual reunions to bring the community together again. Darby wrote that the reunions are "testimony that Wheeler Hill was more than an assortment of modest homes. Wheeler Hill was a place where families were built, pride was nurtured and where a sense of community (that could not be bulldozed) still survives. . . . Some may have called it an 'economically depressed' urban area, but it was home for many families who still cherish its memories" (see "Public Housing Improvements Must Not Destroy Communities," *State,* 30 May 1999).

80. *State,* 19 June 1961; Callcott interview; *Buildings of the Columbia Campus,* 40.

81. BTM, 17 May 1960, 31 October 1961, 20 March 1962; *Evening Post,* 18 January 1961; "Report to the Committee on Higher Education" by Robert L. Sumwalt, 24 February 1961, Sumwalt Papers; "Report to the Committee on Higher Education" by W. H. Callcott, 24 April 1961, Sumwalt Papers; *Gamecock,* 15 January 1960; *Journal of the House of Representatives of the Second Session of the 93rd General Assembly of the State of South Carolina,* 1960 (hereafter "House Journal,"), 25–26; CMP Report, III-3, III-5–6, III-11–13; Self-Study, 1961, 140–49. A comparison of the salaries of faculty of the highest rank, full professor, in 1959–60 is instructive: the median salary of professors from 74 public universities in the U.S. was $9,480 ($43,872); the median salary of professors in 19 public universities in the southeast was $8,870 ($41,049); the median salary of professors at USC was $7,250 ($33,552).

82. Faculty Minutes, 4 October 1961; *USC Perspective* 2, no. 10 (June 1962), 1–2; "Report of Governor's Advisory Committee on Higher Education," 6 March 1962. The number of teaching faculty increased from 227 in 1955 to 284 in 1960. See *Higher Education in South Carolina,* vol. 1, *Coordination of the State Supported System* (New York: Cresap, McCormick and Paget, 1962), IV-1.

83. Hollis interview; Hollings interview; Blatt interview; Duncan Lyle Kinnear, *The First 100 Years: A History of Virginia Polytechnic Institute and State University* (Blacksburg: Virginia Polytechnic Educational Foundation, Inc., 1972), 415–16. Hollings's criteria for a new president were guided in part by the recommendations of the Governor's Advisory Committee on Higher Education and the CMP report.

84. *State,* 12 March 1962, 13 March 1962; "New USC President Genial, Soft-Spoken," *Record,* c. 28 June 1962 (clipping in USC News Service Clippings, SCL); BTM, 10 March 1962.

85. For a discussion of the remarkable development of research universities in the post–World War II era, see Geiger, *Research and Relevant Knowledge,* chapters 1–5; for MIT in particular, see 63–73.

86. *State,* 29 March 1962; Thomas F. Jones, "The University of South Carolina: Faithful Index to the Ambitions and Fortunes of the State," (New York: The Newcomen Society of America, 1964), 6–7; Robert W. Topping, *A Century and*

Beyond: The History of Purdue University (West Lafayette, Indiana: Purdue Research Foundation, 1988), 375.

87. *State,* 13 March 1962.

88. BTM, 25 September 1962.

89. Jones, "The University of South Carolina," 13.

90. For an extended treatment of Jones's efforts to build USC on the research university model, see Watts, "The Freshman Year Experience," especially chapter 2.

91. *State,* 29 March 1962, 3 July 1962; *Record,* 3 July 1962, 24 July 1962.

92. *Observer,* 3 July 1963.

93. BTM, 13 October 1962; *State,* 14 November 1962; "Statement to the Ways and Means Committee," 30 January 1963, Thomas F. Jones Papers, USC Archives; *Morning News,* 31 January 1963.

94. BTM, 10 March 1962, 13 October 1962; *Observer,* 2 November 1962; *Gamecock,* 9 November 1962; *Morning News,* 28 November 1962; *USC Perspective* 3, no. 6 (February 1963)1, 3.

95. *Observer,* 7 November 1962.

96. *State,* 11 January 1963.

97. *House Journal,* 1963, 36. The reference to the NASA grant demonstrates the influence of Tom Jones on the speech, as Purdue had been a recipient of a prestigious NASA grant in the early 1960s while Jones was there. See Geiger, *Research and Relevant Knowledge,* 189.

98. *House Journal,* 1963, 36–37.

99. Ibid., 37.

100. *State,* 17 January 1953.

101. *State,* 13 November 1952.

102. *State,* 13 January 1963.

103. *Observer,* 22 January 1963.

104. Ibid., 10 January 1963.

105. Hollings interview; Author interview with Fred Sheheen, 7 February 2000.

106. *House Journal,* 1963, 39; *State,* 10 January 1963.

107. See Cox, "1963: The Year of Decision," 14–69.

108. *New York Times,* 30 January 1963.

109. *Observer,* 22 January 1963; *House Journal,* 1963, 61, 194–97; *State,* 30 January 1963; Cox, "1963: The Year of Decision," 217–31. Russell's stance had changed considerably since 1952 when, a USC president, he had claimed that "the university is the focal point for education in our state."

110. See Cox "1963: The Year of Decision."

111. Geiger, *Research and Relevant Knowledge,* 125; Mark D. Smith, "Guide to the University Archives," M.A. thesis, University of South Carolina, 1988, 50; BTM, 19 September 1964; *USC Perspective* 5, no. 3 (October 1964), 1; Thomas F. Jones to Solomon Blatt, 4 February 1969, Jones Papers; author interview with Harold Brunton. Jones purposefully avoided putting emphasis on engineering for several reasons. Since his background was in engineering, Jones wrote, "It became clear to me that my actions in that area were considered with suspicion

by the faculty," so departments were chosen "where the action was beyond suspicion of any personal bias." In addition, he avoided engineering because of
the possibility of duplicating what was being done at Clemson.

112. USC Catalog, 1962–63, 1969–70, passim.

113. Ibid; author interview with Jerome D. Odom, 21 March 2000.

114. Allan M. Cartter, *An Assessment of Quality In Graduate Education* (Washington,
D.C.: American Council on Education, 1966), 130 and passim; Kenneth D.
Roose and Charles J. Anderson, *A Rating of Graduate Programs* (Washington,
D.C.: American Council on Education, 1970), 40 and passim; Charles J. Ander-
son to Thomas F. Jones, 6 November 1970, Jones Papers (ACE file).

115. Irwin, *American Universities* (1960), 958; W. Todd Furniss, ed., *American Universities and Colleges,* 11th ed. (Washington, D.C.: American Council on Education, 1973), 1465. The numbers of faculty increased along with enrollment,
rising from 271 in 1958 to 627 in 1970.

116. *University of South Carolina Institutional Self-Study,* 1971, 270.

117. For example, the current (2000) provost, Jerry Odom (chemistry), and associate provost for undergraduate affairs, Donald Greiner (English) were hired in
the "localized leaps" in those departments. See "USC a Proud Institution Before
Holderman," *State,* 10 June 1990.

118. BTM, 23 October 1964; Annual Report, 1965–66, 3; *News and Courier,* 10
April 1965; *Record,* 13 April 1965; Self-Study, 1971, 274–84. The average
salaries for USC faculty in 1965–66 (9–10 month basis) were as follows: assistant professors, $8,233 ($35,062); associate professors, $10,013 ($42,644);
professors, $11,843 ($50,437). In 1969–70, average salaries were: assistant professors, $11,496 ($41,523); associate professors, $13,978 ($50,488); professors,
$17,621 ($63,646).

119. *State,* 1 January 1963; *Gamecock,* 11 January 1963. Carolina's seven professional
schools were the College of Engineering and the Schools of Journalism, Law,
Pharmacy, Education, Business Administration, and Nursing.

120. *Record,* 2 November 1964; *State,* 6 November 1964.

121. "The President's Newsletter," 17 November 1967, Jones Papers.

122. *Greenville News,* 29 September 1965; "Remarks by governor Robert McNair
to the Annual Meeting of the Greater Spartanburg Chamber of Commerce,
Spartanburg, South Carolina, March 31, 1969," Robert McNair Papers, Modern
Political Collections, SCL.

123. McNair interview.

124. C. Wallace Martin to Thomas F. Jones, 10 October 1963, quoted in Watts, "The
Freshman Year Experience," 96.

125. BTM, 8 December 1965; Annual Report, 1966–67, 9, 20. The following year,
the legislature approved a $607,000 ($2,478,203) appropriation for the Graduate School.

126. *USC Perspective* 4, no. 4 (November 1964), 1; *Gamecock,* 6 January 1961;
Geiger, *Research and Relevant Knowledge,* 220–29; Thomas F. Jones to Dean R.
H. Wienefeld, 29 January 1966 (draft), Jones Papers.

127. *USC Magazine* 1, no. 3 (winter 1966), 16.

128. BTM, 17 April 1967, 13 October 1967; *Gamecock,* 19 December 1966; Self-Study, 1971, 418–20; *USC Magazine* 3, no. 2 (April 1968), 19.

129. "Report of the Visitation Committee," 54; Watts, "The Freshman Year Experience," 35, 45–46.

130. Watts, "The Freshman Year Experience," 39–41.

131. *State,* 1 July 1960, 20 July 1960.

132. *Gamecock,* 2 February 1962, 11 January 1963; *USC Magazine* 1, no. 3 (winter 1966), 11–14; Hal Brunton interview with Bill Savage, 3 March 1987, USC Archives.

133. BTM, 2 October 1965; Annual Report, 1966–67, 11; 1968–69, 20; Geiger, *Research and Relevant Knowledge,* 157–97; *USC Magazine* 2, no. 1 (summer 1966), 9–10.

134. Watts, "The Freshman Year Experience," 47.

135. Self-Study, 1971, 724–25; *USC Magazine* 2, no. 1 (summer 1966), 9–10; *USC Magazine* 4, no. 2, (spring 1969), 10–11.

136. Geiger, *Research and Relevant Knowledge,* 173; Walker interview; Author interview with Jerome D. Odom, 21 March 2000; *USC Perspective* 7, no. 4, (September 1969); *USC Magazine* 2, no. 3 (winter 1967), 6; Annual Report, 1968–69, 20–21; *Gamecock,* 13 January 1967.

137. BTM, 18 October 1961, 10 November 1961, 12 December 1963, 9 September 1969, 8 September 1976; *USC Perspective* 7, no. 4 (September 1969); *Gamecock,* 8 December 1961; Annual Report, 1964–65, 4, 1967–68, 20, 1968–69, 32. By the time federal funding of the CEAA ended in 1976, the center had established some 188 texts by American writers; Walker interview.

138. BTM, 1 April 1966; 3 June 1966, 5 August 1966, 5 October 1968; *Gamecock,* 24 May 1966.

139. BTM, 31 October 1961.

140. BTM, 7 April 1964; *Record,* 18 May 1964; *USC Perspective* 4, no. 2 (September 1964), 1.

141. Self-Study, 1961, 82–83.

142. *USC Magazine* 1, no. 2 (fall 1965), 11; *Gamecock,* 14 October 1966, 7 March 1969; Peter G. Siochos and Kathy Aboe, "With Honors: A History of the South Carolina Honors College, 1977–1997," senior thesis, University of South Carolina, 1997, 11–15.

143. See Self-Study, 1971, 393–95; BTM, 9 February 1961, 6 April 1961; Watts, "The Freshman Year Experience," 46–47. Not all members of the board of trustees supported efforts to raise academic standards, especially those chiefly concerned with football. At a meeting of the board's athletic committee, committee chairman Sol Blatt Jr. said of the higher standards that "there is no real reason for the University to be placed on a pedestal and lead the academic world when the high school curriculum and instruction in South Carolina are below the average of other states." Blatt concluded that "it appears that we are catering to the exceptional student too much" (BTM, 9 February 1961; see also 6 April 1961).

144. Self Study, 1961, 109; Dunbar, "A History," 34–64.
145. *USC Perspective* 6, no. 3 (August 1966), 1.
146. Ibid.; *USC Magazine* 3, no. 2 (April 1968), 10–14; Dunbar, "A History," 65–103.
147. *USC Perspective* 6, no. 3 (August 1966), 1; *USC Magazine* 3, no. 2 (April 1968), 2–5.
148. *USC Perspective* 6, no. 3 (August 1966), 1; *USC Magazine* 3, no. 2 (April 1968), 6–9.
149. *Gamecock*, 27 September 1963; News Release #7026, 24 May 1963, Jones Papers; "Announcement of Engineering Science College," c. August 1963, Jones Papers; Rufus G. Fellers to Thomas F. Jones, 7 August 1965, Jones Papers.
150. *Gamecock*, 22 October 1968; informational pamphlet, "Opportunity Scholars Program, University of South Carolina, J. Manning Hiers, Ph.D., Director," pamphlet in Jones Papers; Self-Study, 1971, 132–40; Lucilla Von Kolnitz, *Studies of Two Special Freshman Programs at the University of South Carolina* (Columbia: University of South Carolina, 1969), 1–4; Von Kolnitz, *University of South Carolina Admissions and Registration, Opportunity Scholars, 1968–1969* (Columbia: University of South Carolina, 1970), passim.
151. Watts, "The Freshman Year Experience," 132; Charles H. Witten, "Organizational and Administrative Necessities for Culturally Disadvantaged Students," paper presented to American College Personnel Association, 16 March 1970, in Witten's possession.
152. Paterson, 4.
153. Hollings interview; James C. Cobb, *The Selling of the South: The Southern Crusade for Industrial Development, 1936–1980* (Baton Rouge, La.: Louisiana State University Press, 1982), 166–67.
154. "Report of the Joint Legislative Committee Created to Study Problems of Educating on the College Level the Increasing Number of Students of College Age in South Carolina," 8 May 1961, *House Journal*, 1961, 2118–30. The members of the committee included three from the South Carolina Senate: Edgar Brown, Edward Cushman, and Bruce Williams; three from the South Carolina House: Martha Fitzgerald, Paul McChesney, and Hall Yarborough; and three nonlegislative gubernatorial appointees: Nicholas Mitchell, Charles Palmer, and A. L. M. Wiggins, who served as committee chairman.
155. "Report of the Governor's Advisory Committee on Higher Education," 6 March 1962, 1, 11–13; *Higher Education in South Carolina*, 2 vols. (New York: Cresap, McCormick and Paget, 1962). The other members of the Wiggins Committee were: Harriett S. Mason, Thomas H. Pope, Huger Sinkler, Frank B. Gary, Jennie C. Henry, and Brown Mahon.
156. "Report of the Governor's Advisory Committee," 1.
157. Ibid., 5–7, 53–61.
158. Ibid., 53–56; *State*, 27 September 1962; *Observer*, 2 August 1963; James V. Dreyfuss, "Origin of Statewide Higher Education Coordination," 118–20.
159. Dreyfuss, "Origin of Statewide Higher Education Coordination," 122–23; *Observer*, 2 August 1963.

160. BTM, 20 March 1962; quote: Singleton, "A History of the Regional Campus System," 34.

161. BTM, 20 March 1962, 9 December 1964, 2 October 1965. Mitchell assumed the directorship of the extension division in 1957, taking over from the retiring Havilah Babcock.

162. BTM, 12 October 1963, 9 December 1964, 2 October 1965, 8 December 1965; *Gamecock*, 8 October 1963; *USC Perspective* 5, no. 6 (February 1965); *USC Magazine* 1, no. 3 (winter 1966), 15; *USC Magazine* 1, no. 4 (spring 1966), 10–12; *Index-Journal*, 19 February 1966; Self-Study, 1971, 609–29, 393–95; Watts, "The Freshman Year Experience," 37, 47, 56–57; Sheheen interview. The SAT minimum for admission to the associate's degree programs was a combined score of 600, as opposed to a sliding scale of between 750 and 900 for the regular degree programs (depending on high school class rank). USC had raised its admission standard along with other state schools in 1961.

163. Ruth J. Edens, *USC Sumter: A History, 1966–1992* (Sumter: USC Sumter, 1993), 7–8; Solomon Blatt to Thomas F. Jones, 30 January 1965, Jones Papers; *State*, 21 February 1965, 25 February 1965; author interview with T. Eston Marchant, 6 May 1997.

164. Singleton, "A History of the Regional Campus System," 31–38; BTM, 1 April 1966; *Evening Post*, 2 April 1966; Mary Lou Bryant, "The University of South Carolina at Spartanburg: the Early Years, 1967–1974," Ph.D. dissertation, University of South Carolina, 1993, 1–5, 25–28. The Charleston center operated briefly but was discontinued when the College of Charleston was taken over by the state.

165. BTM, 8 December 1965.

166. "A Report on South Carolina's Need for a Planned System of Public Education Beyond the High School" (Columbia: Office of the Governor, 1965), 3; *House Journal*, 1965, 982–92; *News and Courier*, 15 April 1965; For more on California's pioneering effort to combine high quality with widely available public higher education, see John A. Douglass, *The California Idea and American Higher Education: 1850 to the 1960 Master Plan* (Palo Alto, Calif.: Stanford University Press, 2000).

167. "A Report on South Carolina's Need."

168. "A Report on South Carolina's Need"; *News and Courier*, 15 April 1965; *Morning News*, 17 May 1965; *Record*, 27 January 1966.

169. *Morning News*, 17 May 1965.

170. *Lancaster News*, 24 August 1965; author interview with Phil Grose, 1 February 2000; author interview with Fred Sheheen, 7 February 2000; author interview with John Edmonds, 7 March 2000; McNair interview.

171. *State*, 21 January 1966; William Savage interview with Hal Brunton.

172. *Index-Journal*, 19 February 1966.

173. "Interim Report of Committee Created to Study the Feasibility of Establishing a State Supported System of Junior Colleges," March 1966.

174. *State,* 3 April 1966; *Morning News,* 18 April 1966; Dreyfuss, "Origin of Statewide Higher Education Coordination," 126–28; *South Carolina Commission on Higher Education Annual Report,* February 1968, 5–10; McNair interview.

175. Dreyfuss, "Origin of Statewide Higher Education Coordination," 127–29; *Opportunity and Growth in South Carolina, 1968–1985* (New York: Moody's Investors Service, Inc., 1968), 217–29; Singleton, "A History of the Regional Campus System," 164–68; "Report of Francis Marion College by the Board of Trustees of the State Colleges to the General Assembly," July 1, 1970–June 30, 1970, in *Reports and Resolutions,* 1972, 3–5.

176. Singleton, "A History of the Regional Campus System," 161–64, 167–68; Dreyfuss, "Origin of Statewide Higher Education Coordination," 127–31; *South Carolina Commission on Higher Education Annual Report,* January 1970, 3, 7–9; *Gamecock,* 27 September 1968. "Remarks by Governor Robert McNair," 31 March 1969, McNair Papers; McNair interview.

177. BTM, 1 March 1960; *Gamecock,* 14 April 1960; *South Carolina State Budget, Submitted to the General Assembly of South Carolina by the State Budget and Control Board* (hereafter "State Budget"), 1963–64, 82, 1970–71, vol. 1, 71; USC Catalog, 1970–71, A-31. An additional required fee, the so-called "university fee," for in-state students (except law) rose from $120 in 1959 to $400 ($552 to $1,404) in 1970. This fee covered "operating expenses, student activities, athletic, infirmary fees, and special building fees."

178. *State,* 13 September 1964.

179. *Gamecock,* 12 February 1965; *Record,* 16 February 1965, 1 March 1965; "Penalize Success?," undated memorandum, c. February 1965, Jones Papers.

180. *Gamecock,* 12 February 1965, 12 March 1965; *Record,* 16 February 1965, 1 March 1965, 16 March 1965; *Greenville News,* 4 March 1965, 9 March 1965, 11 March 1965, 16 March 1965; *News and Courier,* 10 March 1965.

181. BTM, 13 October 1966, 23 September 1967, 16 November 1968; Hal Brunton interview with Bill Savage, 3 March 1987, USC Archives.

182. *Buildings of the Columbia Campus,* 13; Thomas F. Jones to Ernest F. Hollings, 24 May 1967, Jones Papers; Hal Brunton interview with Bill Savage, 3 March 1987, USC Archives

183. *USC Perspective* 5, no. 4 (November 1964), 2; *USC Perspective* 6, no. 3 (August 1966), 1; BTM, 11 January 1963, 5 August 1966, 13 October 1966; *USC Magazine,* 1, no. 2 (fall 1965), 15; *Gamecock,* 24 September 1965, 23 September 1966; *Faithful Index,* 88, 106.

184. BTM, 30 March 1965; Peter D. Hyman to William H. Patterson, n.d. (c. 1974), William H. Patterson Papers, USC Archives (University Counsel file); David W. Robinson to James B. Holderman, 27 May 1980, James B. Holderman Papers, USC Archives; Hal Brunton interview with Bill Savage, 3 March 1987, USC Archives. The CRDF was based on a similar foundation that Tom Jones had used at Purdue. By borrowing from commercial banks, the CRDF purchased the Woodland Terrace Apartments and the Hotel Columbia, and played a key role in acquiring property in all of USC's expansion areas in the east, south and west.

185. BTM, 30 March 1965; *State*, 18 May 1965, 31 October 1965; *USC Magazine* 1, no. 4 (spring 1966), 13–20.

186. *Buildings of the Columbia Campus*, 54; *USC Magazine* 1, no. 4 (spring 1966), 19; *USC Perspective*, 5, no. 2 (September 1964); *USC Perspective* 6, no. 1 (spring 1966); *USC Perspective* 6, no. 7; *Gamecock*, 14 January 1966.

187. Julian H. Levi, "Ground Space for the University," in Dobbins, *University*, 10–11. See other articles in this volume emphasizing similar viewpoints by William L. Slayton, Francis J. Lammer, Harold Taubin, and Oliver Brooks.

188. BTM, 12 October 1963, 20 December 1963; *State*, 3 January 1964, 31 October 1965.

189. Mrs. J. A. McGeary to Thomas F. Jones, 3 March 1966, Jones Papers.

190. Marchant interview; Alva M. Lumpkin and H. Simmons Tate to Thomas F. Jones and Harold Brunton, 22 February 1966, Jones Papers; Mrs. Furman R. Bradham, Sr. to the editor of the Columbia *Record*, 11 March 1966, Jones Papers; Edgar A. Brown to Thomas F. Jones, 14 March 1966, Jones Papers; "Why is the University Building a Dormitory-Conference Center on Barnwell Street?," 16 March 1966, memorandum in Jones Papers; Thomas F. Jones to the board of trustees, 22 March 1966. The University's expansion in this neighborhood ran counter to the best available advice, and the advice was ignored not only here but in the Wheeler Hill neighborhood as well. Francis J. Lammer of Philadelphia wrote that residents surrounding an expanding university should be vital elements in the planning process. "The planning and interchange of ideas," he wrote, ". . . should include all segments of the population affected by the redevelopment program. If the people who surround the university do not understand what is going on, they have no incentive to cooperate in the program—they can only resist." The University of South Carolina failed to involve community residents in their plans, so resist they did. See Francis J. Lammer, "Municipal Concern for Campus Development," in Dobbins, *University*, 23.

191. *Buildings of the Columbia Campus*, 44; *Gamecock*, 23 September 1966; Hal Brunton interview with Bill Savage, 23 March 1987, USC Archives; *USC Magazine* 2, no. 4 (spring 1967), 13.

192. *Buildings of the Columbia Campus*, 41; *USC Magazine* 3, no. 4 (fall 1969), 14; H. Brunton to James B. Meriwether, 9 December 1966, Jones Papers; James B. Meriwether to Harold Brunton, 18 December 1966, Jones Papers; Marchant interview.

193. The urban renewal project covered an area bounded by Heyward Street on the south, on the west by Sumter Street, on the North by Catawba, and on the east by Marion Street. It also included open land north of Catawba extending to Rice Street. *State*, 23 September 1964, 31 October 1965; "The Housing Authority of the City of Columbia, South Carolina, University of South Carolina Extension Urban renewal Project no. 2 (Project no. S.C. R-5), Informational report Number Three," c. 1965, Jones Papers; *USC Magazine* 3, no. 4 (fall 1968), 14–16.

194. BTM, 30 March 1965; Harold Brunton Jr., "A Plan for Campus Development," *USC Magazine* 1, no. 4 (spring 1966) 13–20; *Gamecock*, 22 November 1968.

195. "The Housing Authority of the City of Columbia, S.C., East Glencoe Urban Renewal Project (Project no. S.C. R-11), Informational Report Number One," 6 April 1967, Jones Papers. The spelling of Green Street was changed in 1976 to "Greene" to honor Revolutionary War General Nathaniel Greene. In this case, since the church was named "Green Street" Methodist, I will refer to it with the older spelling.

196. Statement of Green Street United Methodist Church, n.d., c. 1968–69, Jones Papers (file Business Affairs, Building Projects, Law School); *Gamecock,* 15 October 1968, 17 October 1969.

197. BTM, 9 September 1969.

198. Statement of Green Street Methodist Church, Jones Papers; *Gamecock,* 10 December 1969.

199. *Gamecock,* 14 October 1966, 28 March 1969.

200. *Gamecock,* 13 May 1966, 14 October 1966, 17 February 1967; BTM, 27 July 1965; *Record,* 12 May 1965; *Buildings of the Columbia Campus,* 14–15, 58–59; *USC Magazine* 4, no. 1 (winter 1968), 2–5; Brunton interview.

201. Don Barton and Bob Fulton, *Frank McGuire: The Life and Times of a Basketball Legend* (Columbia: Summerhouse Press, 1995), 80–81.

202. Ibid., 77–82, 218; *Record,* 18 February 1964; Blatt interview; Daniel Klores, "Out of Bounds: Frank McGuire and Basketball Politics in South Carolina," *Southern Exposure* 7, no. 3 (fall 1979), 106.

203. Corrie, *Atlantic Coast Conference,* 83–84; *Gamecock,* 10 December 1965.

204. *USC Magazine* 1, no. 4 (spring 1966), 9, 29–30; BTM, 4 April 1966, 17 April 1968; Blatt interview; McNair interview; Benjamin B. Boyd to Thomas F. Jones, 30 March 1966, Jones Papers; Charles D. Myers et. al. to Tom Jones, 29 March 1966 (telegram), Jones Papers; Jack D. Morris, Jr. to Thomas F. Jones, 30 March 1966, Jones Papers; letter "To: Vice Presidents, Deans and Department Heads" from H. Brunton, 25 June 1968, Jones Papers. USC's management of its athletic department had earned censure from Cresap, McCormick and Paget in their study. The board of trustee's athletic committee functioned as an administrative committee. The director of athletics was employed by the committee and reported to it. The president was only sometimes consulted on athletic matters and the faculty's committee on athletics was responsible only for determining the eligibility of athletes. CMP had recommended that the board abolish the committee and turn over the day-to-day running of athletics to the president. The board refused. This decision earned the wrath of the Southern Association of Colleges and Schools (SACS), the University's accrediting body. In a 1961 study of the University's operations, SACS representatives called the athletic committee's continued micromanagement of the University's athletic program "a very unsatisfactory situation." The arrangement failed to conform to SACS standards, and like the CMP report, SACS recommended that the athletic director be responsible to the president and the faculty athletic committee— not the board of trustees. The board again declined to make this reform.

205. Rhett Jackson to Thomas Jones, 7 April 1966, Jones Papers.

206. Hampton Davis to Thomas F. Jones, 6 April 1966, Jones Papers.

207. Henry Ray Wengrow to Tom Jones, 7 April 1966, Jones Papers; see also James Hamilton to Dr. Jones, 7 April 1966, Jones Papers.

208. Corrie, *Atlantic Coast Conference*, 85; Thomas F. Jones to James H. Weaver, 21 June 1966, Jones Papers; "Re: Letter of June 4, 1966 to Dr. Thomas F. Jones for Commissioners James H. Weaver," 14 June 1966, Jones Papers; Paul F. Dietzel to Commissioner Weaver, 1 August 1966, Jones Papers.

209. Paul F. Dietzel to Commissioner Weaver, 1 August 1966, Jones Papers.

210. Corrie, *Atlantic Coast Conference*, 85–86; Barton and Fulton, *Frank McGuire*, 84–86; *Gamecock*, 16 December 1966; Klores, "Out of Bounds," 106–7.

211. Corrie, *Atlantic Coast Conference*, 86; Robert C. Thames Jr. to Thomas F. Jones, 7 November 1966, Jones Papers; *Gamecock*, 16 December 1966; Klores, "Out of Bounds," 107.

212. *News and Courier*, 24 November 1966, 1 December 1966, 9 December 1966, 16 December 1966; Edward E. Saleeby to Sol Blatt Jr., 6 December 1966, Jones Papers; John T. Caldwell to Thomas F. Jones, 1 December 1966, Jones Papers; Corrie, *Atlantic Coast Conference*, 86–87; *State*, 1 November 1966; Barton and Fulton, *Frank McGuire*, 85–86; Klores, "Out of Bounds," 107–8.

213. *News and Courier*, 16 December 1966; *Gamecock*, 16 December 1966.

214. Corrie, *Atlantic Coast Conference*, 87–88; *Atlanta Constitution*, 9 January 1967; *Gamecock*, 13 January 1967. The violations were as follows: (1) An athlete (presumably Grosso) was admitted contrary to the regular published entrance requirements. (2) Three athletes, ineligible to receive institutional financial assistance, were given assistance from a personal fund. This referred to the three football players who had caused USC to forfeit its games in 1965. (3) Financial assistance to athletes was not administered through the regular institutional channels. (4) A secret fund was created to entertain high school coaches. (5) A basketball tryout game was arranged at a summer camp in New Jersey. (6) The educational expenses of an athlete (Grosso) were paid by a corporation upon which the individual "was neither naturally nor legally dependent."

215. *Gamecock*, 13 January 1967; undated, unsigned memorandum beginning "These private, unofficial and highly confidential remarks...," c. January 1967, Jones Papers.

216. John Hamilton to Thomas F. Jones, 8 January 1967, Jones Papers.

217. *Gamecock*, 13 January 1967; Corrie, *Atlantic Coast Conference*, 88; Thomas F. Jones to Frank McGuire, 25 January 1967, Jones Papers; Klores, "Out of Bounds," 107–8. After the end of the spring 1967 semester, Mike Grosso transferred to the University of Louisville. The University's acceptance of the NCAA penalties without complaint infuriated McGuire, and he blasted Dietzel in private for not supporting the basketball program. Dietzel and McGuire's relationship was rocky from the start, when the athletic director moved McGuire's office from the Roundhouse complex to the trailer outside.

218. *USC Magazine*, 3, no. 2 (April 1968), 22–25; Barton and Fulton, *Frank McGuire*, 86–99.

219. Griffin, *The First Hundred Years*, 109–14.

220. *Garnet and Black*, 1960, 8; author interview with John D. Gregory, 16 November 2000.
221. Watts, "The Freshman Year Experience," 73–75; BTM, 19 September 1964.
222. Gregory interview; author interview with Thorne Compton, 16 November 2000.
223. *Gamecock*, 20 March 1964; Conroy, *Beach Music*, 454–55.
224. *Gamecock*, 12 November 1965, 16 March 1970; Denham, *University of South Carolina Statistical Profiles*, 4.
225. Gregory interview; Compton interview.
226. *Record*, 11 March 1965.
227. Conroy, *Beach Music*, 454.
228. Gregory interview; Compton interview.
229. *Record*, 11 March 1965.
230. Norman L. Rosenberg and Emily S. Rosenberg, *In Our Times: America Since World War II*, 6th ed. (Upper Saddle River, N.J.: Prentice-Hall, 1999), 78–81; Paul S. Boyer, *Promises to Keep: The United States Since World War II*, 2d ed. (New York and Boston: Houghton Mifflin, 1999), 136–41.
231. *Gamecock*, 4 November 1960.
232. BTM, 31 October 1961.
233. *Gamecock*, 4 November 1960; 2 December 1960.
234. *Gamecock*, 9 February 1968; "Campbell on Narcotic Arrests," 1 March 1968, WLTX videotape, RC 2672, USC Film Library.
235. Selden Smith interview; author interview with Walter B. Edgar; author interview with Joab M. Lesesne Jr.
236. *Gamecock*, 28 February 1964.
237. *Gamecock*, 11 April 1969.
238. *Gamecock*, 6 March 1964, 20 March 1964.
239. "The Revised Self-Study of the College of Arts and Sciences," 1970, 23, USC Archives.
240. Compton interview; Geiger, *Research and Relevant Knowledge*, 233–35; for a critical look at student life on a mid-1960s large university campus, see Nicholas von Hoffman, *The Multiversity: A Report on What Happens to Today's Students at American Universities* (New York: Holt, Rinehart, and Winston, 1966); see also Thomas N. Bonner, "The Unintended Revolution in Higher Education Since 1940," *Change* 18, no. 5 (September/October 1986), 49; Clark Kerr, *The Uses of the University*, 4th ed. (Harvard University Press, 1995), 48–49; and Christopher Jencks and David Riesman, *The Academic Revolution* (University of Chicago Press, 1977), 531–33.
241. *Gamecock*, 6 March 1964.
242. Quotation, *Gamecock*, 28 February 1964.
243. *Gamecock*, 30 October 1964.
244. *Gamecock*, 3 December 1969; Watts, "The Freshman Year Experience," 80.
245. Mrs. I. L. Jones, letter "To Whom It May Concern," 25 January 1963, Jones Papers, quoted in Watts, "The Freshman Year Experience," 80.

246. Watts, "The Freshman Year Experience," 95, 107–8, 138; author interview with Charles Witten, 26 January 2000.

247. Watts, "The Freshman Year Experience," 89–93.

248. Hollis, vol. 2, 317–8; *Gamecock*, 8 April 1960, 13 May 1960, 20 November 1964, 19 March 1965, 14 May 1965.

249. BTM, 27 September 1962; for a discussion of these trends nationwide, see Geiger, *Research and Relevant Knowledge*, 233–37; for a discussion of these trends at USC in more detail, see Watts, "The Freshman Year Experience," chapters 3 and 4.

250. *Gamecock*, 3 November 1967, 3 May 1968.

251. *Gamecock*, 9 May 1969, 12 September 1969, 7 November 1969.

252. USC Catalog, 1962–63, 9; State Budgets, 1960–1970, passim.

253. Watts, "The Freshman Year Experience," 95, 104.

254. *Annual Report of the South Carolina Commission of Higher Education* (hereafter "CHE Annual Report") January 1973, 41; *Gamecock*, 17 February 1967, 11 July 1974.

255. *Garnet and Black*, 1976, 26.

256. *Gamecock*, 20 September 1968, 29 October 1968, 29 October 1969, 7 November 1969, 19 November 1969, 5 December 1969; Watts, "The Freshman Year Experience," 156.

257. BTM, 13 May 1969; *Gamecock*, 25 October 1968, 19 November 1968.

258. Gregory interview.

259. *Gamecock*, 9 October 1964, 6 November 1964, and passim, fall 1964, 22 October 1968, 11 April 1969. A group of USC students made news when they heckled first lady Lady Bird Johnson at an airport stop in Columbia. See the *State*, 10 October 1964.

260. *State*, 15 July 1964.

261. Jones quoted in Watts, "The Freshman Year Experience," 98–99.

262. *Gamecock*, 5 November 1965; *State*, 28 October 1965; see also *Record*, 13 May 1965.

263. Conroy, *Beach Music*, 454, 532.

264. Watts, "The Freshman Year Experience," 99–101; "Preliminary Guidance Regarding Campus Gatherings in Public Places," 26 April 1965, Jones Papers; *Record*, 30 April 1965; "The WIS Seven O'Clock Report," 1 May 1965, Jones Papers; *News and Courier*, 1 May 1965; *Gamecock*, 7 May 1965; Thomas F. Jones to Gordon Hanes, 2 July 1965, Jones Papers; William J. Billingsley, *Communists on Campus: Race, Politics and the Public University in Sixties North Carolina* (Athens: University of Georgia Press, 1999). William J. Billingsley has argued that legislative efforts to stifle the speech of communists and leftists in 1960s North Carolina was directly related to opposition to the civil rights movement, and a similar dynamic was under way in South Carolina.

265. Brad Poston to President Jones, 3 May 1965, Jones Papers, quoted in Watts, "The Freshman Year Experience," 101.

266. Watts, "The Freshman Year Experience," 101–3; BTM, 5 August 1966, 13 October 1966; *Gamecock*, 11 November 1966.

267. BTM, 22 February 1967.

268. *Gamecock,* 23 March 1967 and passim, spring 1967; *News and Courier,* 18 February 1967; Sol Blatt to Thomas F. Jones, 4 February 1967, Jones Papers; Thomas F. Jones to Jerry M. Hughes, 1 March 1967, Jones Papers.

269. *Gamecock,* 28 April 1967, 5 May 1967, 19 May 1967; *Record,* 3 May 1967; Doris B. Giles, "The Antiwar Movement in Columbia, South Carolina, 1965–1972," unpublished paper in the Manuscripts Division, SCL, 6–7.

270. BTM, 7 June 1967; memorandum "To: University of South Carolina Faculty Committee to Investigate the Conduct of Dr. Thomas Tidwell, From: Ad Hoc Committee, University of South Carolina Chapter, American Association of University Professors," c. May 1967, Jones Papers; Odom interview; Ironically, Tidwell later received research support from a grant from the Army Research Office.

271. Robert Patterson et. al. to President Jones, 2 May 1967; *Record,* 3 May 1967; *Gamecock,* 5 May 1967, 19 May 1967; "Memorandum of office meeting on Tuesday, May 9 and telephone conversation of Wednesday, May 10, with Robert B. Patterson, faculty advisor to AWARE," c. May 1967, Jones Papers; James A. Torgeson and Trina P. Sahli to President Jones, 12 May 1967, Jones Papers; official statement of AWARE Free Speech Committee, 15 May 1967, Jones Papers; Giles, 7–8; Watts, "The Freshman Year Experience," 146. One year later, the board of trustees approved a "Policy on Unlawful and Violent Student Demonstrations," which committed the University to upholding academic freedom and promised protesters protection "to the limit of its resources." The board also reaffirmed the University president's authority to suspend any student "considered to be a threat to the safety or security of the University" (see BTM, 31 May 1968).

272. Gregory interview; Compton interview.

273. Giles, 8, 12, 20; Watts, "The Freshman Year Experience," 148, 156–60, 170–71; Annual report, 1968–69, 3; *Gamecock,* 3 November 1967, December 1967, 15 December 1967, 18 October 1968, 25 October 1968, 29 October 1968, 1 November 1968, 8 November 1968, 22 November 1968; 6 December 1968, 10 December 1968, 13 December 1968, 17 December 1968; BTM, 16 November 1968, 28 April 1971; unlabeled memos dated 24 March to 22 April 1968, apparently from AWARE informant, Jones Papers. AWARE's most vocal leader was Brett Bursey, who had come to Carolina in 1967 after transferring from the University of Georgia and had become involved in the Southern Student Organizing Committee, an independent organization with goals similar to the SDS; it had started as a civil rights organization but evolved into an antiwar group. Bursey served as that organization's state representative or "traveler," and he later became the most visible anti-establishment figure in South Carolina in the late 1960s and early 1970s.

274. Letter to President Jones, 30 October 1968, quoted in Carolyn Matalene and Katherine Reynolds, eds., *Carolina Voices: Two Hundred Years of Student Experiences* (Columbia: University of South Carolina Press, 2001), 190–91.

275. *Gamecock,* 16 February 1968; 23 February 1968; Watts, "The Freshman Year Experience," 144. For a complete account of the Orangeburg incident, see Jack

Bass and Jack Nelson, *The Orangeburg Massacre,* 2d ed. (Macon, Ga.: Mercer University Press, 1996); see also *Proceedings of the South Carolina Historical Association* 1999 for a thirty-year retrospective program.

276. Cleveland Sellers, *River of No Return: The Autobiography of a Black Militant and the Life and Death of SNCC* (New York: Morrow, 1973; reprint, Jackson and London: University Press of Mississippi, 1990;), 206–7 (page references are to reprint edition); Bass and Nelson, *Orangeburg Massacre,* 8–9; see special report, "'The New Mood of Blackness,' in *Southern Education Report* 4 no. 1 (July-August 1968), for growth of black consciousness movement in the South; Watts, "The Freshman Year Experience," 143; Ken Price, "Milestones in Desegregating USC," videotape from conference, "The Origins of Desegregation at the University of South Carolina," 19 November 1988, in possession of Grace J. McFadden.

277. "A Report by the Negro Students of the University of South Carolina," c. 1968, Jones Papers; Watts, "The Freshman Year Experience," 173–74.

278. *Gamecock,* 17 September 1968; Watts, "The Freshman Year Experience," 145–46.

279. *Gamecock,* 19 April 1968; Moore, *Columbia and Richland County,* 427.

280. *Gamecock,* 19 April 1968; 25 February 1969; Paul Clancy, "A Campus and Town Join Up to Cool It," *Southern Education Report* 4, no. 3 (October 1968), 20–23; Witten, "Organizational and Administrative Necessities," 8; Watts, "The Freshman Year Experience," 145; Statement of Robert Alexander, "Mobilizing the University for Desegregation," audiotape from the conference The Origins of Desegregation at the University of South Carolina, 1963–1988, 19 November 1988, in possession of Professor Grace J. McFadden; *USC Magazine* 5, no. 4 (winter 1971), 2–4.

281. In October 1968, when a USC police officer tried to arrest a black student in the Russell House, a crowd of black and white students gathered, and the officer dispersed them with tear gas because he believed they were "too unruly." A report on the incident showed that the officer had failed to use proper procedures and tried to arrest an innocent man. See *Gamecock,* 18 October 1968, 25 October 1968; G. A. Buchanan to Thomas F. Jones, 23 September 1968, Jones Papers.

282. *Gamecock,* 4 February 1969, 7 February 1969, 11 February 1969; "Black Rap," published by Association of Afro-American Students, U.S.C., c. February 1968, Jones Papers.

283. *Gamecock,* 11 February 1969; Watts, "The Freshman Year Experience," 162.

284. *Gamecock,* 14 February 1969; Giles, 20. Since flag burning was illegal in South Carolina, Bursey was arrested in the incident.

285. *Gamecock,* 18 February 1969; *Garnet and Black,* 1970, 46–49.

286. Ibid.

287. Ibid.

288. BTM, 13 May 1969.

289. "Black Rap," c. February 1968, Jones Papers.

290. Ibid.

291. *Gamecock,* 11 April 1969, 9 May 1969; Watts, "The Freshman Year Experience," 163.

292. *Gamecock,* 9 May 1969; BTM, 13 May 1969.

293. John Roy Harper, 21 November 1996, speech to "Dreams of Change: Remembering the Struggle for Civil Rights" symposium on USC Campus; *Garnet and Black,* 1970, 46–49.

294. *Gamecock,* 25 October 1968.

295. Kerr, *The Uses of the University,* 14–15.

296. Cartter, "Qualitative Aspects," 69; Cartter, "The Role of Higher Education in a Changing South," 295.

CHAPTER 5—ADJUSTING TO LIFE AS A "MULTIVERSITY," 1970–1979

1. Self-Study, 1971, 204; Self-Study, 1980, xxx, table 3–5, table 4–7; Denham, *University of South Carolina Statistical Profiles,* 4.

2. *Gamecock,* 29 October 1968, 27 October 1969, 11 November 1969, 9 December 1969, 12 December 1969, 17 December 1969, 9 January 1970, 11 January 1970; Watts, "The Freshman Year Experience," 184–85; Robert McC. Figg Jr. to Thomas F. Jones, 19 December 1969, Jones Papers; Hal Brunton to Sol Blatt Jr., 17 December 1969, Jones Papers; Faculty Minutes, 17 December 1969; BTM, 19 February 1970; *USC Magazine* 5, no. 2 (summer 1970), special section titled "The Months of May." This publication was the University's official report on the events of the spring of 1970; Sol Blatt to Thomas F. Jones, 23 March 1970, Jones Papers. Sol Blatt wrote to Tom Jones of the faculty unrest, "If we ever cave in and comply with some of their demands, then the University can kiss goodby some of [its] appropriations." Blatt wrote Jones that he had told legislators who had threatened to cut USC spending bills that "things would change at the University and that you will assert more leadership and a strong hand in controlling the faculty." He continued: "I don't care what the faculty said, if they don't love the University enough to want it to make progress and I mean every part of it, including the Athletic Department, then they have no business at the University and should be told to go elsewhere."

3. J. H. Moore, 408–9; Giles, 11–16; for a detailed look at the UFO Coffeehouse story, see William Shepard McAninch, "The UFO," *South Carolina Law Review* 46, no. 2 (winter 1995), 363–79; see film of protests at City Hall opposing UFO closing, "Protests over 'UFO' closing," WLTX videotape, RC 2672, USC Film Library.

4. Ibid.; *USC Magazine* 5, no. 2 (summer 1970), special section titled "The Months of May"; BTM, 25 April 1970, 22 May 1970; *Gamecock,* 13 April 1970; a good, complete account of the unrest is also in Watts, "The Freshman Year Experience," 184–99; "Jones on Drug Arrests," WLTX videotape, RC2685, USC Film Library.

5. *USC Magazine* 5, no. 2 (summer 1970), special section entitled "The Months of May"; BTM, 22 May 1970; *Record,* 30 April 1970, *Gamecock,* 29 April 1970, 4 May 1970; Moore, 408; Giles, 14–19; see Foard's account of the entire episode

in *Garnet and Black,* 1971, 47–49. At the trial of the five operators of the UFO Coffeehouse, most observers predicted an acquittal. Instead, the prosecution won a conviction. The sentence, a $10,000 fine and six years in jail, was so outrageous in light of the charge—"keeping and operating a public nuisance"—that USC students and faculty, who had followed the trial closely, were outraged. The incident raised levels of tension on campus even further. The convicted men claimed, with apparent validity, that the closure and convictions were a result of opposition to the political and cultural views represented by the UFO Coffeehouse.

6. *USC Magazine* 5, no. 2 (summer 1970), special section titled "The Months of May"; BTM, 22 May 1970.

7. *USC Magazine* 5, no. 2 (summer 1970), special section titled "The Months of May"; BTM, 22 May 1970. The USC news conference had been called to announce the board of trustees' decision about whether or not to withdraw from the ACC. While the board voted to remain in the conference this time, this uncertainty only added to the complex of emotions swirling around the University.

8. *USC Magazine* 5, no. 2 (summer 1970), special section titled "The Months of May"; BTM, 22 May 1970; Watts, "The Freshman Year Experience," 187–88. Brett Bursey's role in the events of May 1970 were as a non-student. In March, he had been banned from the campus after vandalizing the Columbia offices of the Selective Service. After Bursey was arrested for this act during the middle of an AWARE meeting in the Russell House, Sol Blatt wrote Tom Jones, "I cannot understand why the University would allow a fellow like Allen Bursey to continue to stay at the University when he is violating every law possible, creating a disturbance on campus, destroying goodwill for the University by his conduct and is doing everything he can to disrupt the orderly operation of the University. I wouldn't care what the Discipline Committee said, I would get rid of this fellow." Three days later, the administration suspended Bursey from USC and prohibited him from returning to the campus. Nonetheless, he was able to lead the student "Strike Coalition," since they held their meetings off-campus. Sol Blatt to Thomas F. Jones, 23 March 1970, Jones Papers; L. Eugene Cooper to Brett Bursey, 26 March 1970, Jones Papers.

9. *USC Magazine* 5, no. 2 (summer 1970), special section titled "The Months of May"; BTM, 22 May 1970; McNair interview. Among the crowd gathered outside the Russell House was activist leader Brett Bursey, obeying the order that barred him from campus but standing on a street corner near the edge of campus talking with other student activist leaders through a walkie-talkie.

10. *USC Magazine* 5, no. 2 (summer 1970), special section titled "The Months of May"; BTM, 22 May 1970.

11. *USC Magazine* 5, no. 2 (summer 1970), special section titled "The Months of May"; BTM, 22 May 1970; Marchant interview; Blatt interview; McNair interview; Watts, "The Freshman Year Experience," 191; Craig Colgan, "Fragments of the Months of May," *Carolinian* 26, vol. 2 (April 2000), 13. SLED Chief Pete

Strom was among those in attendance at the board meeting by virtue of his role in breaking up the Russell House takeover, and was among those trapped on the second floor. Remarkably, despite the riot on the first floor, the small contingent of University police officers and SLED agents were able to deter the rioters from attacking those on the second floor, though Strom and the other agents, who were armed, feared that they would have to use deadly force to stop the mob from assaulting the board members. Hugh Willcox, a board member from Florence, surprised his fellow board members when, in the midst of the riot, he decided to leave the building. He calmly walked past the SLED agents guarding the second floor, down the steps, past the rioting students, and got in his car and drove away—safely. Sol Blatt Jr., commented, "I wouldn't have done that for $100,000!" Several students arrested in the Russell House takeover were also involved in the administration building riot. All except Brett Bursey had been released from jail after spending the night there following the Russell House incident. After their release, they joined the protesting crowd on the Horseshoe. Damage to the administration building from the effects of the riots totaled $5,400.

12. *USC Magazine* 5, no. 2 (summer 1970), special section entitled "The Months of May"; BTM, 22 May 1970.

13. *USC Magazine* 5, no. 2 (summer 1970), special section titled "The Months of May"; BTM, 22 May 1970; news release, 12 May 1970, Vietnam Era subject file, USC Archives. The faculty met at Town Theater because the state of emergency prohibited large meetings on the campus.

14. *USC Magazine* 5, no. 2 (summer 1970), special section titled "The Months of May"; BTM, 22 May 1970; *Gamecock,* 18 May 1970; Giles, 26–28; McNair interview. Students rallied in Gregg Park because the state of emergency prevented rallies on the campus.

15. *USC Magazine* 5, no. 2 (summer 1970), special section titled "The Months of May"; BTM, 22 May 1970; *Gamecock,* 14 May 1970; Watts, "The Freshman Year Experience," 193; McNair interview.

16. *USC Magazine* 5, no. 2 (summer 1970), special section titled "The Months of May"; BTM, 22 May 1970; Giles, 26–28; Compton interview. Fonda fundamentally misunderstood the essentially local reasons for the violence in Columbia. She assumed that it was primarily antiwar agitation, when it in fact it was primarily in protest of local officials' interference in student life.

17. *USC Magazine* 5, no. 2 (summer 1970), special section titled "The Months of May"; BTM, 22 May 1970.

18. Cramer Crider et. al. to Dr. Jones, 18 May 1970, Jones Papers, quoted in Watts, "The Freshman Year Experience," 194.

19. Watts, "The Freshman Year Experience," 194.

20. BTM, 7 July 1970, 31 July 1970, 19 September 1970, 3 October 1970; Solomon Blatt to Hugh Gibson, 15 June 1970, Jones Papers; Solomon Blatt to John W. Foard Jr., 18 June 1970, Jones Papers; Solomon Blatt to Thomas F. Jones, 19 June 1970, Jones Papers; *Spartanburg Herald,* 4 September 1970; *Gamecock,* 28 September 1970, 13 November 1970; Moore, 410.

21. First quotation, Giles, 27 (see also 24–27); second quotation, USC Magazine 5, no. 3 (fall 1970), 12; third quotation, Moore, 410; BTM, 22 May 1970. An impartial review of the riots identified sixteen specific—eight internal and eight external—factors that led to the disturbances. See USC Magazine 5, no. 3 (fall 1970), "The Months of May." Ironically, SLED chief Pete Strom had been a key figure in helping maintain peace on the campus during the desegregation of the University seven years earlier.

22. Gamecock, 26 October 1970, 12 February 1971; Moore, 410; Giles, 29. Brett Bursey was the only person arrested during the spring 1970 disturbances to serve any jail time. After being betrayed by his roommate and fellow radical Jack Weatherford (who turned out to be a SLED informant), he served two years for his role in vandalizing the Columbia Selective Service office and later served time in Texas on drug charges. He was pardoned in South Carolina in 1981. See Giles, 20–22, 44–48, Doris Giles's interviews with Bursey in the South Caroliniana Library, and extended articles in the Gamecock, 28 April 1971, 12 October 1979.

23. BTM, 22 May 1970, 25 June 1970.

24. BTM, 19 September 1970; "Thank You, Mr. Rut," USC Magazine 5, no. 3 (fall 1970), 2–4; Buildings of the Columbia Campus, 31.

25. First quotation from clipping from a State University of New York at Buffalo publication, June 1978, Holderman Papers (University 101 File); second quotation, Gamecock, 8 February 1971; M. Ryan Graham, "University 101: Education's Aladdin's Lamp at the University of South Carolina, 1972–1979," seminar paper for SCCC 325G, in author's possession.

26. Author interview with Hal Brunton.

27. Watts, "The Freshman Year Experience," chapter 4, especially 139–40, 149–50, 166–69; Gamecock, 12 January 1968; Laurence S. Flaum, "The Meaning of Relevance in Higher Education," 10 January 1969, Jones Papers; Jay C. Smith to Robert T. Blackburn, 19 June 1974, Jones Papers; John N. Gardner, interview with M. Ryan Graham, 1 April 1999. The search for "relevant" education was an important nationwide response to the explosive growth of colleges and universities. See works such as William H. Morris, Effective College Teaching: The Quest for Relevance (Washington, D.C.: American Council on Education, 1970).

28. Self-Study, 1971, 120–30; "The Report of the Ad Hoc Committee in Arts and Sciences Appointed by Dean Nelson to Evaluate the Program of Contemporary University and Independent Study," n.d. (c. November 1970), Jones Papers; Watts, "The Freshman Year Experience," 160, 166–67.

29. "The Report of the Ad Hoc Committee"; Gamecock, 6 February 1970, 13 February 1970, 23 October 1970, 5 May 1971; David Stenmark and Michael Garet to Thomas F. Jones, 2 November 1970, Jones Papers.

30. Conrad Lodziak to Thomas F. Jones, 22 March 1971, Jones Papers.

31. Mary Stewart Lesslie, "Evaluation of Nontraditional College Programs: UWW at USC," M.A. thesis, University of South Carolina, 1974, 53–62; Gamecock, 30 November 1970, 27 September 1971; Thomas F. Jones to Samuel Baskin, 4 May

1970, Jones Papers; Conrad Lodziak to Thomas F. Jones, 22 March 1971, Jones Papers; John J. Duffy to Thomas F. Jones, 7 May 1971, Jones Papers. In the spring semester 1971, 55 students were involved in UWW; more than 50 percent were from low-income backgrounds and 30 percent were black.

32. *Gamecock,* 28 April 1972, 25 July 1974, 8 August 1974, 26 September 1974, 26 June 1975, 23 February 1976; Thomas F. Jones to Theodore Grossman, 26 June 1973, Jones Papers; Lesslie, "Evaluation," 57; Conrad Lodziak to Thomas Jones, 22 March 1971, Jones Papers; John J. Duffy to Thomas F. Jones, 7 May 1971, Jones Papers; Watts, "The Freshman Year Experience," 250. One description of the faculty's view of innovative course offerings was that they were "mercurial in their appearance. Such courses are viewed as being conceived suddenly, and often illicitly, passed by a docile senate and given to the faculty without reasoned consideration." See R. V. Heckel et. al., *University 101: An Educational Experiment* (Columbia, S.C.: Social Problems Research Institute, 1974), 8.

33. BTM, 13 May 1971; "Curricula and New Courses Committee Proposal for Baccalaureate in General Studies," 24 March 1972, Jones Papers; *CarolinaType* (campus community newspaper), May 1972; *Gamecock,* 7 April 1972, 1 October 1973; "Proposal for the Bachelor of General Studies As Part of the College of General Studies at the University of South Carolina," n.d. (c. 1972), Jones Papers; Thomas F. Jones to Theodore Grossman, 26 June 1973, Jones Papers; For an overview of the College of General Studies just before the institution of the B.G.S. degree, see "General Information Bulletin: Presentation of Academic Accomplishments and Plans, College of General Studies, University of South Carolina," 10 April 1972, Thomas Cooper Library.

34. "Proceedings of Hilton Head University of South Carolina Think Tank, September 25–27, 1970," Jones Papers; "Potential Problems/Solutions at USC," c. October 1970, Jones Papers; *Gamecock,* 4 October 1971; *CarolinaType,* November 1971; *Garnet and Black,* 1972, 186–87; "Report of Faculty Advisory Committee on the Gravatt Report," 3 May 1972; Watts, "The Freshman Year Experience," 239–41. Some faculty commented that the think tanks represented another example of what had become a hallmark of the University—ad hoc, piecemeal planning.

35. *Garnet and Black,* 1972, 186–87; *CarolinaType,* September 1972; Heckel et. al., *University 101,* 6–15. For a detailed account of the establishment of University 101, see Watts, "The Freshman Year Experience," especially chapter 5. The other members of the faculty committee who compiled the initial University 101 plan were Francis D. Atkinson, William H. Caldwell, Robert V. Heckel, J. Manning Hiers, and Richard A. Rempel.

36. Ibid.; Annual Report, 1975–76, 39; letter from John N. Gardner to "Entire University 101 Faculty," 15 November 1976, William H. Patterson Papers, USC Archives; John N. Gardner to James B. Holderman, 6 February 1979, Holderman Papers; M. Lee Upcraft et. al., *The Freshman Year Experience: Helping Students Survive and Succeed in College* (San Francisco: Jossey-Bass Publishers, 1989), chapters 15–19. In 1977, the program won the award for "Outstanding

Institutional Innovative Program" by the National Association of Student Personnel Administrators.

37. Thomas F. Jones to Robert Schmid, 16 March 1971, Jones Papers; *State*, 10 July 1971; *Ford Foundation Letter*, 15 July 1971, Jones Papers; *CarolinaType*, May 1973; "Ford Foundation Venture Fund Grant, Grant Number 710–0484, Narrative Report," 1974, 1975 and 1976, Patterson Papers; *State*, 15 April 1973.

38. *Gamecock*, 17 April 1970, 24 April 1970; "The Final Report of the Student Government Committee for Curriculum Review in the College of Arts and Sciences, April 1969–May 1971," Jones Papers.

39. *Gamecock*, 15 January 1971, 12 February 1971.

40. Faculty Minutes, 3 May 1961, 4 April 1962; BTM, 30 April 1963, 3 October 1970; Self-Study, 1971, 257–63.

41. BTM, 15 September 1970, 6 January 1971, 29 March 1971, 6 July 1972, 15 May 1973; CHE Annual Report, January 1973, 9–10, January 1974, 10.

42. *CarolinaType*, October 1971; BTM, 12 December 1970; D. Bruce Marshall to Acting Dean Robert D. Ochs, 18 May 1970, Jones Papers; *Gamecock*, 22 January 1973; "Some Information About the History of Women's Studies," timeline from USC Women's Studies Program, in possession of author.

43. BTM, 8 June 1972; Annual Report, 1971–72, 10–11; *Gamecock*, 22 June 1972; Self-Study, 1980, 17. The five vice-provosts were William N. Adams Smith, Health Sciences; H. Willard Davis, Regional Campuses; John C. Guilds, Liberal and Cultural Disciplines; Bruce W. Nelson, Advanced Studies and Research; Provost William H. Patterson served as acting head of the Professional Schools division.

44. John C. Guilds to Members of the Faculty, 17 October 1973, Jones Papers; *Gamecock*, 12 July 1973; "The Center for Cultural Development," report in Jones Papers, n.d. (c. 1973).

45. BTM, 16 October 1971, 29 September 1973; *Gamecock*, 27 October 1971, 15 October 1973; *CarolinaType*, December 1971.

46. Speech by William H. Patterson to Richland, Cayce-West Columbia and Columbia Kiwanis clubs, c. September 1974, Patterson Papers; Kenneth Toombs to Thomas F. Jones, 9 December 1969, Jones Papers; "Report of the Director of the University Libraries, University of South Carolina, July 1975 to July 1976," Patterson Papers, 24; *USC Magazine* 4, no. 4, (December 1969); *Buildings of the Columbia Campus*, 11–12.

47. *Carolina News*, 1 February 1970; "Report of the Director of the University Libraries, University of South Carolina, July 1975 to July 1976," Patterson Papers, 24–25; BTM, 4 March 1969, 4 December 1969, 19 February 1970; Sol Blatt Jr. to Hal Brunton 15 December 1969, Jones Papers; Hal Brunton to Sol Blatt Jr., 17 December 1969, Jones Papers; *Gamecock*, 12 December 1969, 17 December 1969, 19 December 1969, 9 January 1970, 11 January 1970, 23 February 1970; Faculty Minutes, 17 December 1969; Robert McC. Figg Jr. to Thomas F. Jones, 19 December 1969; Hal Brunton interview with Bill Savage, 3 March 1987, USC Archives.

48. "Report of the Director of the University Libraries, University of South Carolina, July 1975 to July 1976," Patterson Papers, 25–30; Kenneth Toombs, "The History of the University of South Carolina Libraries," 17 pp., n.d., Patterson Papers; *Buildings of the Columbia Campus*, 36; Hal Brunton interview with Bill Savage, 3 March 1987, USC Archives.

49. *Faithful Index*, 108 and passim; *CarolinaType*, May 1972; Marchant interview. The plans for the College Street portion of the campus included a new arts center and a new complex for South Carolina Educational Television, both of which were eventually built elsewhere in Columbia.

50. BTM, 15 September 1971; *Gamecock*, 22 March 1972, 21 April 1972, 26 April 1972, 28 April 1972 and elsewhere in spring of 1972; *Garnet and Black*, 1970, 28–35; Hal Brunton interview with Bill Savage, 23 March 1987. Similar debate accompanied the renovations of the Gibbes Green area into a pedestrian mall two years later. See *Gamecock*, 4 April 1974, 12 June 1974; Annual Report, 1974–75, 33.

51. *Faithful Index*, 108 and passim.

52. Barton and Fulton, *Frank McGuire*, 99–105; Klores, "Out of Bounds," 108–9.

53. Barton and Fulton, *Frank McGuire*, 105–11; Klores, "Out of Bounds," 109.

54. Corrie, *Atlantic Coast Conference*, 97; Klores, "Out of Bounds," 109; Barton and Fulton, *Frank McGuire*, 112–13; Blatt interview.

55. Corrie, *Atlantic Coast Conference*, 97, 102; *Gamecock*, 11 March 1970, 13 April 1970; BTM, 25 March 1970, 29 March 1970; author interview with Lawrence Giles.

56. Corrie, *Atlantic Coast Conference*, 102; BTM, 5 May 1970. This board meeting came a day after the killings at Kent State University, and at a press conference called to announce the board's decision, some two hundred students occupied the press room. Despite their presence, the press conference went off without incident. See *USC Magazine* 5, no. 2 (summer 1970).

57. Paul F. Dietzel to Thomas F. Jones, 25 September 1970, Jones Papers; Blatt interview.

58. BTM, 23 October 1970; *Gamecock*, 26 October 1970; Corrie, *Atlantic Coast Conference*, 104. Clemson, also unhappy with the ACC's SAT requirement, stated that their institution was also reconsidering its approach to recruiting standards.

59. Corrie, *Atlantic Coast Conference*, 106; "Introductory Remarks by Chairman Caldwell to ACC Institutional Heads, 9 December 1970, Greensboro, NC," Jones Papers; BTM, 12 December 1970.

60. BTM, 29 March 1971; Marchant interview; Blatt interview; Barton and Fulton, *Frank McGuire*, 112–13, 129–30; Klores, "Out of Bounds," 109.

61. Corrie, *Atlantic Coast Conference*, 109.

62. Marchant interview; Blatt interview; Corrie, *Atlantic Coast Conference*, 109–10; *Gamecock*, 31 March 1971; BTM, 14 September 1973.

63. Blatt interview; Marchant interview. Blatt particularly remembered that many board members were upset about Jones's ordering that the flag be lowered to half mast on the day of the Russell House takeover.

64. *Gamecock,* 28 April 1971; *Record,* 29 April 1971.
65. *State,* 19 May 1971; C. H. Witten to T. F. Jones, 30 April 1971, Jones Papers; *Record,* 18 May 1971; BTM, 27 May 1971, 15 September 1971, 16 October 1971; *Gamecock,* 19 May 1971; Sol Blatt to Thomas F. Jones, 24 May 1971, Jones Papers.
66. Sol Blatt to Thomas F. Jones, 24 May 1971, Jones Papers. Blatt wrote Jones that he had "gotten I don't know how many letters and telephone calls about The Gamecock" and that he "would not care if we had a riot the next moment and had to call out the National Guard."
67. Blatt interview; Marchant interview; Sheheen interview; Grose interview; *State,* 26 September 1971, 1 June 1975, 14 June 1975; *Gamecock,* 18 October 1971, 17 July 1975, 24 July 1975, 31 July 1971; Edens, 98–99. Only months later Jones announced the University would slow undergraduate enrollment growth—but it would maintain the Regional Campuses while doing it. Bartolozzo resigned after only ten weeks as TEC system head, charging that the USC lobbying machine was too powerful to overcome. He insisted that maintaining the dual system of TEC schools and regional campuses was discriminatory against poor Carolinians and that to maintain it was "economic suicide."
68. *State,* 26 September 1971; *Gamecock,* 29 October 1968, 27 October 1968, 29 September 1971, 1 October 1971, 6 October 1971, 18 October 1971, 27 October 1971; Blatt interview; Edgar interview; Blatt interview. Just after the controversy quieted, Sol Blatt Sr. retired from the legislature. The *Gamecock* greeted the news with an editorial titled "Goodbye Blatt," rejoicing over the retirement. Three legislative members wrote to Tom Jones that the editorial was "in the poorest taste, blatantly unfair, and served no useful purpose." They commented that it "could have a negative effect on the future programs at the University, including a second medical college." See *Gamecock,* 3 November 1971 and J. Clator Arrants, Tom G. Mangum, and O. H. Wienges Jr. to Thomas F. Jones, 4 November 1971, Jones Papers. Despite Blatt Jr.'s efforts to convince Jones to resign, he maintained that he personally liked Jones and gave him credit for vastly improving the University.
69. *Gamecock,* 2 February 1972.
70. *Gamecock,* 7 February 1972, 9 February 1972, 11 February 1972, 14 February 1972, 22 March 1972, 29 March 1973.
71. Marchant interview; West interview; author interview with Michael J. Mungo; *Gamecock,* 28 January 1974, 31 January 1974, 31 January 1971, 4 February 1974, 7 February 1971, 18 February 1971, 22 April 1974, 18 April 1974, 5 December 1974, 12 December 1974.
72. Author interview with Hal Brunton; interview by William Savage with Hal Brunton, USC Archives. Ironically, Jones's explanation of his own downfall also described the fate of one of his nineteenth-century predecessors, Thomas Cooper. During his term as president, Cooper was always opposed by leading sectarian Protestants, but by the 1830s he had accumulated enough enemies that despite support among the state's ardent nullifiers, he was forced to resign (see Hollis, vol. 1, ch. 6).

73. *Gamecock,* 28 January 1974, 31 January 1974, 31 January 1971, 4 February 1974, 7 February 1971, 18 February 1971, 22 April 1974, 18 April 1974, 5 December 1974, 12 December 1974; Edgar interview.

74. *Gamecock,* 28 January 1974; Denham, *University of South Carolina Statistical Profiles,* 4; Annual Report, 1962–63, 40; CHE Annual Report, 1976, 60; *Garnet and Black,* 1975, 460–61.

75. Marchant interview; West interview; BTM, 30 January 1974; *Gamecock,* 31 January 1974, 4 February 1974, 7 February 1974, 18 February 1974, 5 December 1974; *Garnet and Black,* 1974, 344–46, and 1976, 338–43. Governor West, who attended the board meeting at which Jones announced his resignation and Patterson was named president, later admitted, "[I] went to the board meeting because I thought Dr. Patterson should be the president. He wanted the job of interim president, but I thought he should be president period . . . full-fledged."

76. *Gamecock,* 31 January 1974, 4 February 1974; *State,* 6 July 1996.

77. Geiger, *Research and Relevant Knowledge,* 254.

78. BTM, 30 January 1974; *Gamecock,* 31 January 1974.

79. *Gamecock,* 18 July 1974. The reorganization called for six vice-presidents, with those presiding over academic areas reporting to Provost Keith Davis and the others reporting directly to the president. The major change involved the separation of operations from business affairs and giving the regional campuses a vice-president. The new officers were John Welsh, instruction; H. Willard Davis, regional campuses, research and continuing education; W. N. Adams Smith, health affairs; B. A. Deatwyler, finance; Harold Brunton, operations; Nicholas P. Mitchell, administrative services.

80. *Gamecock,* 18 July 1974; Speech by William H. Patterson to Richland, Cayce-West Columbia, and Columbia Kiwanis clubs, c. September 1974, Patterson Papers; *CarolinaType,* September 1974.

81. BTM, 11 September 1975, 17 September 1976; *CarolinaType,* January 1975; *State,* 20 January 1977; *Gamecock,* 18 April 1977, 25 April 1977; author interview with Fannie Phelps Adams; speech by William H. Patterson to Richland, Cayce-West Columbia, and Columbia Kiwanis clubs, c. September 1974, Patterson Papers; speech by William H. Patterson to the Rotary Club of Columbia, 18 February 1975, Patterson Papers; H. Simmons Tate, Jr. to Richard Rempel, 17 July 1974, Patterson Papers; H. Simmons Tate, Jr. to William H. Patterson, 7 October 1974, Patterson Papers; Richard Rempel to H. Simmons Tate, Jr., 8 October 1974, Patterson Papers; Harold Brunton to William H. Patterson, 10 October 1974, Patterson Papers; Mrs. Charles O. Jones Jr. to Robert MacNaughton, 17 October 1974, Patterson Papers; Joseph W. Bouknight to Robert MacNaughton, 19 August 1974, Patterson Papers; Richard Rempel and Elmer Schwartz to Members of the Facilities and Grounds Advisory Committee, 8 January 1975, Patterson Papers; H. Simmons Tate to William H. Patterson, 18 February 1975, Patterson Papers; William H. Patterson to H. Simmons Tate, 19 February 1975, Patterson Papers; Gayle O. Averyt to Harold Brunton,

9 April 1975, Patterson Papers; R. A. Rempel to The Buildings and Grounds Committee of the Board of Trustees, 22 May 1975, Patterson Papers; Harold Brunton to William R. Bruce, et. al., 28 May 1975, Patterson Papers; Harold Brunton to Richard Rempel, 12 May 1975, Patterson Papers; "Proposed Modified Development Plan," c. 1975, Patterson Papers; BTM, 20 September 1974, 24 January 1975, 25 January 1975.

82. BTM, 23 June 1972; State, 27 February 1974; *State* Magazine, November 25, 1979; Harold Brunton to W. S. Turbeville, 14 August 1975, Patterson Papers; Harold Brunton, "University of South Carolina—Columbia Campus, Horseshoe Restoration & Renovation, Project History," 13 January 1981, Holderman Papers; Stanley South and Carl Steen, "Archaeology on the Horseshoe," Research Manuscript Series 215, South Carolina Institute of Archaeology and Anthropology; Hal Brunton interview with Bill Savage, 3 March 1987, 23 March 1987, USC Archives.

83. Speech by William H. Patterson to Richland, Cayce-West Columbia, and Columbia Kiwanis clubs, c. September 1974, Patterson Papers; Harold Brunton to W. S. Turbeville, 14 August 1975, Patterson Papers; Harold Brunton, "University of South Carolina—Columbia Campus, Horseshoe Restoration & Renovation, Project History," 13 January 1981, Holderman Papers; Walter B. Edgar to William H. Patterson, 7 May 1975, Patterson Papers; Harold Brunton, "Horseshoe Restoration Project, Status as of September 26, 1975," Patterson Papers; BTM, 7 June 1974, 20 September 1974; *Southern Living,* June 1986, 39–40; Annual Report, 1974–75, 33; see also "Horseshoe Renovation" subject file, USC Archives, especially John W. Califf III, "Report on Restoration of the Horseshoe"; *Garnet and Black,* 1976, 374–75.

84. *Buildings of the Columbia Campus,* 42, 15.

85. Brunton interview; *Gamecock,* 25 July 1974, 8 August 1974, 26 September 1974, 26 June 1975, 23 February 1976.

86. *Gamecock,* 8 August 1974, 7 August 1975.

87. *Gamecock,* 30 January 1975, 28 August 1975, 2 December 1976.

88. *Gamecock,* 5 June 1975, 5 February 1976.

89. *Gamecock,* 3 July 1975, 28 August 1975; *Garnet and Black,* 1976, 338–43.

90. *Gamecock,* 4 November 1974, 7 November 1974, 20 February 1975; *Garnet and Black,* 1976, 260–63.

91. BTM, 28 May 1975; CHE Annual Report, 1977, 14.

92. *Gamecock,* 17 July 1975; BTM, 4 January 1974; CHE Annual Report, 1975, 18.

93. BTM, 20 September 1974, 5 December 1975; CHE Annual Report, 1976, 15, 1977, 15.

94. Annual Report, 1974–75, 56–57; CHE Annual Report, 18–19, 23.

95. CHE Annual Report, 1975, 19, 22–23.

96. *Index-Journal,* 17 August 1962; Ernest F. Hollings to The Members of the Board of Trustees, 24 October 1962, Jones Papers; *News and Courier,* 4 November 1962.

97. Telephone conversation record, John K. Cauthen and George Curry, 28 April 1966, Jones Papers; BTM, 14 September 1966; *Gamecock,* 18 November 1966;

Vernon W. Lippard, W. Reece Berryhill, and Joseph C. Hinsey, *Medical Education in South Carolina, Report of the Consultants to the Commission on Higher Education, 1967,* 1, Jones Papers.

98. *Opportunity and Growth in South Carolina,* 9, 338.

99. *State,* 26 September 1971 (pp. 2–B and 8–B); 15 August 1973; CHE Annual Report, 1973, 28–29, 1974, 33; "Report of the Survey of the University of South Carolina Medical School, Columbia South Carolina, April 7–9, 1976," Patterson Papers; West interview.

100. Marchant interview; Sheheen interview; BTM, 4 January 1974; CHE Annual Report, 1974, 33–34, 1975, 19, 22; Annual Report, 1974–75, 55–56; *Garnet and Black,* 1974, 434–35. The University's agreement with the Veterans Administration called for the state to fund 10 percent of the school's operational costs in the first two years. The state would pay a larger portion of the school's costs in following years, and after seven years the state would pay all operational costs. The grant was conditioned on the timely accreditation of the new medical school.

101. W. N. Adams Smith to W. H. Patterson, 8 December 1975; *Greenville News,* 14 December 1975; *Gamecock,* 12 January 1976.

102. *Piedmont,* 5 March 1976, 6 April 1976; *Greenville News,* 14 March 1976, 30 March 1976; *Gamecock,* 12 January 1976, 23 February 1976, 26 February 1976, 24 June 1976, 1 July 1976, 14 July 1977, 28 February 1977; upstate newspaper editor quoted in *State,* 3 April 1983; "Remarks by T. Eston Marchant . . . To House of Representatives," 16 March 1976, Patterson Papers.

103. CHE Annual Report, 1973, 37; Hal Brunton interview with Bill Savage, 3 March 1987, USC Archives.

104. CHE Annual Report, 1973, 22–23; BTM, 13 May 1971.

105. CHE Annual Report, 1976, 35; *State,* 6 June 1975, 19 June 1975; *Gamecock,* 5 June 1975, 19 June 1975, 28 August 1975; *CarolinaType,* spring 1976; Marchant interview; BTM, 4 August 1978.

106. BTM, 13 September 1975; *State,* 16 June 1975; *Gamecock,* 12 June 1975; "Draft of report submitted by Clemson and USC, 9/9/75, to Special Committee on Formula," 14 August 1975, Patterson Papers; *State,* 10 September 1975, 14 September 1975, 17 September 1975, 18 September 1975 ; *Record,* 17 September 1975; *Greenville News,* 19 September 1975; "Statement of R. Cathcart Smith, Chairman, South Carolina Commission on Higher Education," delivered 16 September 1975, Patterson Papers; "Statement of Hugh M. Chapman, Vice Chairman, South Carolina Commission on Higher Education," 16 September 1975, Patterson Papers; "Presentation to Special Committees on Formula . . . , September 16, 1975 by Howard Boozer, Executive Director, South Carolina Commission on Higher Education," Patterson Papers.

107. *Gamecock,* 31 July 1975.

108. Ibid., 19 June 1975.

109. BTM, 2 March 1976, 12 February 1977, 4 August 1978; Annual Report, 1976–77, 71–72; *Gamecock,* 3 July 1975, 26 July 1976, 3 February 1977, 24

February 1977; *State,* 20 April 1977. By the mid-1970s, USC's faculty salaries as compared to other Southern Regional Education Board (SREB) Group I schools (those awarding over 100 doctorates per year) were just below average. The SREB Group I average salary (all ranks) was $17,251 ($43,704) in 1975–76, while USC's average for all ranks was $16,939 ($42,914). See Self-study, 1980, table 4–11.

110. Lesesne, "A History of the Alumni Association," 33; *Carolinian,* fall 1979, 10.

111. *Gamecock,* 5 December 1969, 4 February 1970, 13 November 1970; *CarolinaType,* November 1971; BTM, 20 November 1971, 15 September 1973; *State,* 24 July 1975; Chris Vlahoplus to James B. Holderman, 27 October 1977, Holderman Papers.

112. *Gamecock,* 12 June 1975, 6 June 1975; Price, *A Century of Gamecocks,* 40–41, 68–138.

113. BTM, 7 June 1976; *Gamecock,* 22 November 1976, 21 April 1977; *Garnet and Black,* 1974, 432–33, and 1976, 110–17.

114. Barton and Fulton, *Frank McGuire,* 113–22; Klores, "Out of Bounds," 109; *Garnet and Black,* 1976, 118–19.

115. *Gamecock,* 15 March 1972, 4 December 1972, 16 September 1974, 23 September 1974; Paul Dietzel to William H. Patterson, 3 October 1974, Patterson Papers; BTM, 9 November 1972; Klores, "Out of Bounds," 109–10; Klores, *Roundball Culture: South Carolina Basketball* (Huntsville, Ala.: AM Press, 1980), 323–25.

116. *Gamecock,* 23 September 1974, 3 February 1975; Paul Dietzel to William H. Patterson, 27 November 1974, Patterson Papers; BTM, 13 December 1974; Klores, *Roundball Culture,* 324; Blatt interview.

117. *Independent,* 23 December 1974; Klores, "Out of Bounds," 110; Klores, *Roundball Culture,* 325–27.

118. BTM, 27 May 1975, 1 March 1976, 19 June 1976; *State,* 6 June 1975, 11 June 1975; *Gamecock,* 12 June 1975, 26 June 1975, 22 January 1976, 24 June 1976; Corrie, *Atlantic Coast Conference,* 131; Klores, *Roundball Culture,* 353; *Garnet and Black,* 1976, 118–19.

119. BTM, 1 March 1976, 19 June 1976; Corrie, *Atlantic Coast Conference,* 131; Klores, *Roundball Culture,* 353–54.

120. Barton and Fulton, *Frank McGuire,* 130; *Gamecock,* 24 June 1976, 7 March 1977; Corrie, *Atlantic Coast Conference,* 139; James W. Cothran to Hugh H. Wells, 23 March 1977, Patterson Papers; James W. Cothran to W. H. Patterson, 2 May 1977, Patterson Papers; Paul S. Goldsmith to William H. Patterson, 5 May 1977; Hugh L. Willcox to William H. Patterson, 6 May 1977, Patterson Papers; George Curry to Hugh H. Wells, 30 May 1977, Patterson Papers; Marchant interview; Klores, *Roundball Culture,* 354–58.

121. *Gamecock,* 23 September 1970, 4 November 1970, 5 February 1971, 8 February 1971, 12 February 1971, 14 May 1971, 20 September 1971, 28 April 1971; Watts, "The Freshman Year Experience," 198, 239; George Q. Flynn, *The Draft, 1940–1973* (Lawrence: University Press of Kansas, 1973), 225–58.

122. *Gamecock,* 30 September 1970, 4 November 1970, 9 November 1970; *CarolinaType,* December 1977; *USC Magazine* 5, no. 3 (fall 1970), 9–12.

123. *Garnet and Black,* 1970, 30–31, 1974, 428–29, 1979, 49; *Gamecock,* 23 September 1970.

124. *Garnet and Black,* 1974, 423, 1976, 366–69; *Gamecock,* 1 March 1973, 29 October 1973, 25 July 1974, 27 March 1975, 3 July 1975, 7 August 1975, 16 October 1975, 23 October 1975, 1 December 1977; BTM, 27 May 1975, 27 October 1975, 5 December 1975; Annual Report, 1977–78, 82.

125. *Garnet and Black,* 1970, 38–39, and 1973, 112–20; *Gamecock,* 7 January 1970, 14 December 1970, 2 February 1972, 29 March 1973.

126. *Gamecock,* 20 February 1975, 24 July 1975; *Garnet and Black,* 1976, 177; "The Scope of Student Drug Use at the University of South Carolina," December 1972, Jones Papers; Edgar interview.

127. BTM, 12 December 1970, 10 July 1973; *Gamecock,* 14 December 1970, 12 July 1973; *Garnet and Black,* 1976, 177.

128. *CarolinaType,* October 1972; BTM, 27 May 1971, 24 January 1975, 13 September 1975; *Gamecock,* 5 September 1974; *Garnet and Black,* 1970, 22–25, 230–33, and 1974, 102–4.

129. *Gamecock,* 7 March 1974; *Garnet and Black,* 1974, 110–11.

130. *Garnet and Black,* 1970, 82, 1976, 194–95; *CarolinaType,* March 1972.

131. *Garnet and Black,* 1970, 36–43; *Gamecock,* 26 February 1976.

132. Self Study, 1980, table 3–8; *Gamecock,* 9 March 1970, 26 March 1971, 30 November 1972, 5 March 1973, 2 October 1973, 10 December 1973, 28 July 1977; Dewey E. Dodds to Thomas J. Jones, 9 March 1970, Jones Papers; Thomas F. Jones to Dewey E. Dodds, 21 May 1970, Jones Papers; "Milestones in Desegregating USC's Student Body," videotape of conference session at USC, "Origins of Desegregation at USC, 1963–1988," 18 November 1988, in possession of Grace J. McFadden.

133. *Gamecock,* 7 June 1975, 28 August 1975; *Garnet and Black,* 1976, 338–43.

134. *Garnet and Black,* 1976, 338–43; *Gamecock,* 16 October 1975, 23 October 1975, 15 January 1976.

135. *Gamecock,* 19 June 1975; *Garnet and Black,* 1976, 338–43.

136. *Gamecock,* 12 June 1975

137. *Gamecock,* 12 June 1975, 30 September 1976; *Garnet and Black,* 1976, 340; *Garnet and Black,* 1977, 180–86. For a discussion of the "era of limits," see George D. Moss, *Moving On: The American People Since 1945* (Englewood Cliffs, N.J.: Prentice-Hall, 1994), 268–318. For the impact of this era in higher education, see Geiger, *Research and Relevant Knowledge,* chapter 9.

138. BTM, 4 June 1977; *Gamecock,* 12 June 1975, 2 September 1976; Self-Study, 1980, 169–73, 192–93 and appendix 5-A; Annual Report, 1976–77, 69–70. Patterson had been the author of the University's first *Faculty Manual* during the 1960s.

139. *Record,* 10 August 1977; Fellers interview; Brunton interview; *Carolinian,* spring 1977.

140. BTM, 18 September 1976, 4 June 1977, 24 June 1977, 30 June 1977; *Gamecock,* 11 April 1977, 7 June 1977; *CarolinaType,* summer 1972, 5; Marchant interview; McNair interview; author interview with James B. Holderman, 6 November 1998; author interview with Michael J. Mungo, 22 October 2000; Eston Marchant to Select Committee, 22 June 1977, Patterson Papers. The members of the select committee that chose Holderman were Othniel Wienges, Paul Goldsmith, Frampton Toole, and R. Markley Dennis. Other candidates considered were General DeWitt C. Smith of the U.S. Army War College and Richard Thigpen, the thirty-two-year-old vice chancellor of the University of Alabama.

141. BTM, 3 August 1977; *Gamecock,* 31 October 1977. The results of Holderman's emphasis on undergraduate programs can be seen in the University's enrollment figures. See Tables 5.1 and 5.2.

142. Peter G. Siachos and Kathy Aboe, "With Honors: A History of the South Carolina Honors College, 1977–1997," senior honors thesis, University of South Carolina, 1997, 15–19; BTM, 4 January 1974; *CarolinaType,* March 1975, 7.

143. *Gamecock,* 12 June 1975, 30 September 1974; Siachos and Aboe, "With Honors," 20–21; *Garnet and Black,* 1977, 186.

144. *Gamecock,* 12 June 1975, 30 September 1974; Siachos and Aboe, "With Honors," 20–21; *Garnet and Black,* 1977, 186; Faculty Minutes, 18 November 1975, 3 December 1975.

145. Faculty Minutes, 18 November 1975, 3 December 1975; Siachos and Aboe, "With Honors," 31–32.

146. BTM, 28 April 1976, 7 June 1976; William Savage interview with Hal Brunton.

147. Siachos and Aboe, "With Honors," 33–67; *Gamecock,* 10 October 1977, 13 February 1978; Annual Report, 1977–78, 59–60, 1978–79, 58–59; James B. Campbell to James B. Holderman, 23 November 1977, Holderman Papers; "The Carolina Plan: A Prospectus 1978–1983, A Report from the President To the Board of Trustees, The University of South Carolina, December 1977," 15; Self Study, 1991, 1–4. See Siachos and Aboe's appendixes for facsimiles of the documents relating to the founding of the Honors College.

148. Sheheen interview; Singleton, "A History of the Regional Campus System," 112–13; *State,* 6 June 1975; *Record,* 16 September 1977; CHE Annual Report, January 1976, 14.

149. "The University of South Carolina Today and Tomorrow," June 1976, Patterson Papers.

150. Annual Report, 1975–76, 54–55; *Record,* 16 September 1977; *Gamecock,* 23 September 1976, 28 March 1977; Edens, 82–104; *Garnet and Black,* 1977, 181–82.

151. BTM, 5 December 1975, 16 August 1976, 2 December 1976; "The University of South Carolina Today and Tomorrow," June 1976, Patterson Papers; "Presidential Recommendation for A University of South Carolina System," 1 September 1976, Patterson Papers; *Record,* 16 September 1977. Patterson's plan also included a provision by which the president of the University of South Carolina would be designated "system chancellor," four-year chief executives given the title "president" (reporting directly to the chancellor), and two-year

campus chief executives maintain the title "vice president" (reporting to a single president for two-year campuses). The board preferred the title "president" for the senior officer in the system. Patterson also suggested that the four-year campus faculties be given greater autonomy in academic planning.

152. *Gamecock*, 28 March 1977; BTM, 2 December 1976, 24 January 1977; Marchant interview.

153. "The Carolina Plan," passim; *Record*, 16 September 1977.

154. BTM, 4 August 1978; "The Carolina Plan," 24–25; *Carolinian*, fall 1978, 2.

155. Ibid.; "Carolina Plan II: A Prospectus 1979–1984, A Report From The President To The Board of Trustees, University of South Carolina, December 1978," 9; "University of South Carolina, President's Annual Report for 1978," USC Archives; *Gamecock*, 10 August 1978; *News*, 28 July 1978; *Record*, 27 July 1978; James B. Holderman to James B. Edwards, 19 July 1978, Holderman Papers. USC's average faculty salary in 1975–76 was $16,939 ($40,579) as compared to an average of all Group I universities in the SREB of $17,251 ($41,326). By 1978–79, USC's average was $21,282 ($39,940) as compared with a Group I SREB universities average of $21,262 ($39,903) (see Self-Study, 1980, table 4–11).

156. Sheheen interview; BTM, 9 August 1979; *Gamecock*, 14 September 1979.

157. "The Carolina Plan," 29.

158. Ibid., 29–30; Lesesne, "A History of the Alumni Association," 36; "Carolina Plan II," 18–22; "University of South Carolina, President's Annual Report for 1978."

159. BTM, 18 September 1976; Lesesne, "A History of the Alumni Association," 36; *Gamecock*, 10 November 1977.

160. Marchant interview; Holderman interview; Barton and Fulton, *Frank McGuire*, 130; Klores, *Roundball Culture*, 339–40, 368–69. Symptomatic of the University's declining relationships with McGuire were two events in mid-1977: first, McGuire was inducted to the College Basketball Hall of Fame, but the University sent no representative or message of appreciation to his induction ceremony. Then, the General Assembly overwhelmingly voted a resolution asking the USC board of trustees to rename the Carolina Coliseum after McGuire. The board tabled the resolution, deciding instead to name only the arena after McGuire.

161. *State*, 8, 9, 16 November 1977; *Record*, 8, 16 November 1977; *Gamecock*, 10 November 1977; Klores, *Roundball Culture*, 378–83.

162. *Gamecock*, 10 November 1977.

163. Klores, *Roundball Culture*, 379–82; *Record*, 16 November 1977.

164. Klores, *Roundball Culture*, 370–86, 403; Klores, "Out of Bounds," 109–10; Barton and Fulton, *Frank McGuire*, 130–31; *State*, 22 January 1978, 26 January 1978; *Record*, 25, 26 January 1978.

165. *Gamecock*, 2 March 1978, 6 March 1978, 10 April 1978; *State*, 2 March 1978, 5 March 1978, 7 March 1978, 7 April 1978, 4 May 1978, 11 May 1978, 18 May 1978, 28 May 1978; *Record*, 1 March 1978, 2 March 1978, 3 March 1978, 6 April

1978, 11 May 1978, 17 May 1978, 22 August 1978; Klores, *Roundball Culture,* 382–85; Holderman interview; Provost Frank Borkowski remembered that Holderman survived the May 1978 board meeting by a one-vote margin; Borkowski interview.

166. BTM, 4 September 1979; *Gamecock,* 5 October 1979; Klores, *Roundball Culture,* 402–6.

167. Douglas S. Looney, "Do not ignore all the signs," *Sports Illustrated,* 17 September 1979, 54–55; BTM, 4 September 1979, 26 October 1979; *Gamecock,* 25 October 1979, 29 October 1979; Klores, *Roundball Culture,* 402–6.

168. "Carolina Plan II," 8–13; BTM, 8 December 1978.

169. "Carolina Plan II," 13–28.

170. Ibid., 29.

171. Ibid., 32–33.

172. *Observer,* 14 January 1979.

173. Jerrold K. Footlick, *Truth and Consequences: How Colleges and Universities Meet Public Crises* (Phoenix, Ariz.: American Council on Education and Onyx Press, 1997), 90.

174. *Gamecock,* 1 September 1978, see also 16 February 1978.

175. *Observer,* 14 January 1978.

176. *Carolinian,* fall 1978, 1.

177. Quotation, *Carolinian,* fall 1979, 1; *Gamecock,* 7 June 1979, 7 June 1979; BTM, 5 February 1979.

178. Undated clipping from the *Observer,* titled "Schmidt's Visit Is USC's Latest Coup," c. June 1979, Holderman Papers.

179. Author interview with Frank Borkowski, 22 March 2000; *Record,* 11 January 1979; *Piedmont,* 10 January 1979; *Gamecock,* 24 September 1979, 5 October 1979; *Observer,* 14 January 1979; BTM, 5 February 1979.

180. *Gamecock,* 7 June 1979.

CHAPTER 6—A GILDED DECADE? 1980–1990

1. For a critical overview of the Holderman administration and its scandals, see Footlick, *Truth and Consequences,* 89–105, and the less scholarly and more sensational article by Alison Cook, "Magna Cum Fraud," *Gentleman's Quarterly,* August 1992, 185–92, 197–202.

2. Statement of Professor Gunther Holst, BTM, 31 May 1990; McNair interview.

3. CHE Annual Report, 1981, 11; *The South Carolina Master Plan for Higher Education* (Columbia: South Carolina Commission on Higher Education, 1979), 87.

4. BTM, 26 October 1979; See *Public Higher Education* and *State Institutions of Higher Learning* for questions about the necessity for two schools of engineering in South Carolina, and chapters 4 and 5 of this work for discussion of criticisms of USC's medical schools and associate's degree programs.

5. CHE Annual Report, 1982, 14–16; "Background information on the USC College of General Studies and the CHE Recommendation to Discontinue Two-Year Occupational Programs," 27 January 1981, enclosure in letter from James

E. Bostic to Bill Atchley et al., 29 January 1981, Holderman Papers; *Gamecock,* 16 January 1981; "Governor's Remarks On Commission's Recommendations on Two-Year Occupational Programs At USC," news release, 20 February 1981, Holderman Papers.

6. *Gamecock,* 28 January 1981, 6 February 1981, 23 February 1981, 4 March 1981, 6 March 1981; "Background information on the USC College of General Studies and the CHE Recommendation to Discontinue Two-Year Occupational Programs," 27 January 1981, enclosure in letter from James E. Bostic to Bill Atchley et al., 29 January 1981, Holderman Papers; "Information on USC's College of General Studies, Future South Carolina Citizens Need Your Help," n.d., Holderman Papers; press release, "Governor's remarks on Commission's Recommendations On Two-Year Occupational Programs at USC," 20 February 1981, Holderman Papers; "Black Student Enrollment College of General Studies," n.d., Holderman Papers; "Questions and Answers About Associates Degree programs Offered at USC-Columbia and Commission Recommendations," n.d., Holderman Papers; *Allendale County News Leader,* 4 February 1981; Holderman interview.

7. *Gamecock,* 6 March 1981; Footlick, *Truth and Consequences,* 91–92; BTM, 12 April 1983; Sheheen interview.

8. *The University of South Carolina, Columbia: Institutional Self-Study for Reaffirmation of Accreditation by the Southern Association of Colleges and Schools* (Columbia: University of South Carolina, 1991) (hereafter Self-Study, 1991), 9-1–9-2, appendix 9-B; "The University of South Carolina, Report of the President, 1977–1986," 31; "Target 2001: Report of the President of the University of South Carolina System, July 1987–December 1988," 42.

9. Self-Study, 1991, 9-1–9-2, appendix 9-B, 9-G; "The University of South Carolina, Report of the President, 1977–1986," 32.

10. Ellie McGrath, "Cash Squeeze on Campus," *Time,* 5 September 1983, 50–51; Self-Study, 1991, appendix 9-C; *News,* 12 December 1983, *Carolinian,* December 1982; BTM, 10 December 1982, 12 April 1983; *Observer,* 21 March 1983. There were skeptics about how much the money shortage was really hurting USC. Of the program cuts, State Senator Bob Lake of Newberry said, "It's bureaucratic defense. When the legislature and the budget and control board demand that they cut back a little bit, they immediately go to the most sensitive program they've got. . . . One of the best attended programs they've got is education, so they figured they'd cut it out just to hear the people scream."

11. CHE Annual Report, 1982, 69; Michael Brown, ed., *1995 South Carolina Higher Education Statistical Abstract* (Columbia: Commission on Higher Education, 1995), 86; Self Study, 1991, Appendix 9–B.

12. "The University of South Carolina, Report of the President, 1977–1986," 4–5; Holderman interview.

13. *Carolinian,* September 1982.

14. "The University of South Carolina, Report of the President, 1977–1986," 22.

15. Manuel Justiz, Kenneth L. Schwab, and Marilyn C. Kameen, "The University of South Carolina: Turning Small Strengths into Major Assets," *Educational Record* 67, no. 4 (fall 1986), 26–27.

16. *Gamecock,* 29 February 1980.

17. *Gamecock,* 4 September 1981, 11 December 1981, 6 October 1982, 22 September 1982, 16 October 1984; *Carolinian,* December 1982; "The University of South Carolina, Report of the President, 1977–1986," 23; Holderman interview. Holderman's tenure as chairman of the U.S. national commission of UNESCO coincided with the Reagan administration's efforts to withdraw from the organization. Despite Holderman's efforts to keep the U.S. in UNESCO, the Reagan administration withdrew in December 1984. See William Preston Jr., Edward S. Herman, and Herbert I. Schiller, *Hope and Folly: The United States and UNESCO, 1945–1985* (Minneapolis, Minn.: University of Minnesota Press, 1989), 1954–85.

18. *Carolinian,* September 1983.

19. *Carolinian,* December 1984.

20. *Gamecock,* 25 July 1984, 31 August 1984; *Carolinian,* September 1984.

21. *Gamecock,* 11 October 1985; *Carolinian,* December 1985.

22. "The University of South Carolina, Report of the President, 1977–1986," 23; *Gamecock,* 4 April 1986; *New York Times,* 12 November 1986; *Garnet and Black,* 1985, 143.

23. BTM, 14 February 1985; *Gamecock,* 15 February 1985; *Carolinian,* March 1985

24. "The University of South Carolina, Report of the President, 1977–1986," 7, 23; *Gamecock,* 10 October 1980, 7 November 1980; Self-Study, 1991, 10-16–10-19, Appendix 10-D; author interview with Francis Borkowski. Upon signing the Shanxi agreement, President Holderman asserted, "USC is now at the forefront of U.S.–Chinese relations."

25. *State,* 26 May 1990; *New York Times,* 12 November 1986; Footlick, *Truth and Consequences,* 89.

26. *Wall Street Journal,* 11 September 1987; *Gamecock,* 14 September 1987; *Carolinian,* September 1987; "Target 2001: Report of the President, The University of South Carolina System, July 1987–December 1988," 32–33.

27. *State,* 7 December 1986.

28. Self-Study, 1991, 2-1–2-3; Denham, *University of South Carolina Statistical Profiles,* 5, 27.

29. *Gamecock,* 9 April 1984; *Directions for Academic Excellence: Building on Tradition, Report of the Presidential Commission on Undergraduate Education* (Columbia: University of South Carolina, 1985), 14. The minimum standards were four units of English, thee units of mathematics, two units of laboratory science, three units of social studies, and two units of foreign language.

30. Self-Study, 1991, 2–14; *Higher Education Statistical Abstract,* 14th ed. (Columbia, S.C.: Commission on Higher Education, 1992), 123–24; "The University of South Carolina, Report of the President, 1977–1986," 9.

31. Self-Study, 1991, 2-14, 2-16, 2-29–2-30; *Carolinian,* March 1989.

32. *State,* 21 December 1982; *Gamecock,* 17 January 1983.
33. Ibid.; "The University of South Carolina, Report of the President, 1977–1986," 9; *Remembering the Days,* 54. William Reese Smith Jr. graduated from USC in 1946 and won a Rhodes Scholarship in 1949 after attending Florida law school.
34. Self-Study, 1991, 2-30–2-31; *Gamecock,* 20 February 1985.
35. CHE Annual Report, 1983, 11; 1985, 12–13; 1986, 14; "The University of South Carolina, Report of the President, 1977–1986," 13.
36. CHE Annual Report, 1986–87, 3–4; BTM, 31 May 1990; *"Asides," A Quarterly Publication of the Shakespeare Theatre at the Folger* (summer 1986), 1–6, in Holderman Papers; *Carolinian,* September 1986; Thomas P. Cooke to Carol McGinnis Kay, 18 May 1987, Holderman Papers; James B. Holderman to Charles W. Coker, 19 June 1989, Holderman Papers; "Statement by Dr. Holderman at Press Conference, Shakespeare Theatre at the Folger, Thursday, July 26 [1986], 3:30 P.M." Holderman Papers; *Gamecock,* 13 April 1987, 24 February 1988.
37. Self Study, 1991, 2-1, 2-31–2-32.
38. *Directions for Academic Excellence,* 89–90 and passim. See also Self Study, 1991, 2-31–2-43.
39. BTM, 30 January 1986; "Target 2001," 17.
40. *Gamecock,* 1 August 1984, 29 August 1984, 19 September 1986, 4 February 1987.
41. *Gamecock,* 4 February 1987, 19 October 1987.
42. *Gamecock,* 24 February 1984.
43. BTM, 10 October 1985; *Gamecock,* 22 February 1984, 20 November 1985, 2 April 1990; *Higher Education Statistical Abstract, 1992,* 19, 21.
44. *Observer,* 26 March 1988; BTM, 7 April 1989, 13 April 1989; *Gamecock,* 3 April 1989, 14 April 1989; *New York Times ,* 19 April 1989.
45. *New York Times,* 20 August 1989, 19 November 1989.
46. "The University of South Carolina, Report of the President, 1977–1986," 16; Self Study, 1991, 3-1–3-3, Appendix 3-A; CHE Annual Report, 1985–86, 2; for FTE comparative figures, see *Higher Education in South Carolina: An Agenda for the Future* (Denver, Colo.: Augenblick, Van de Water & Associates, 1986), table C-3, part E, p. 219.
47. "The University of South Carolina: The Report of the President, 1977–86," 16; *Gamecock,* 2 April 1990; *Carolinian,* January 1989; BTM, 8 December 1989; Richard W. Riley to James B. Holderman, 10 December 1986, Holderman Papers.
48. Self Study, 1991, 4-15–4-17.
49. "The University of South Carolina: The Report of the President, 1977–86," 19; *Gamecock,* 18 July 1984; Self Study, 1991, 4-14–4-15.
50. Self Study, 1991, 4-14–4-15; Stephen L. Elliot, *Origins, Elements, and Implications of The Cutting Edge Initiatives for Research and Academic Excellence in Higher Education* (Columbia, S.C.: Commission on Higher Education, 1988), passim; *Observer,* 20 May 1988; *News,* 2 June 1988; *Carolinian,* January 1989.

51. BTM, 8 December 1989; *Gamecock*, 29 December 1986; "The University of South Carolina: The Report of the President, 1977–86," 17–22.

52. BTM, 2 November 1988; *News*, 23 December 1987; John A. Warren, "Research and Development in Higher Education," *South Carolina Business* 9 (1989), 74–77; "Target 2001," 20–23; *Carolinian*, January 1989.

53. "The University of South Carolina: The Report of the President, 1977–86," 11–12; "Target 2001," 6–11.

54. *Gamecock*, 17 October 1980; *Greenville News*, 11 August 1987.

55. BTM, 9 December 1988.

56. Annual Report, 1980–81; *Gamecock*, 3 October 1983; "The University of South Carolina: The Report of the President, 1977–86," 17.

57. BTM, 12 August 1982; CHE Annual Report, 1984, 11–12; *Spartanburg Herald*, 8 February 1983; *State*, 13 February 1983, 3 April 1983, 4 April 1983, 5 April 1983, 6 April 1983, 7 April 1983, 8 April 1983; *Gamecock*, 23 March 1983.

58. *State*, 6 April 1983; See also BTM, 12 April 1983.

59. *State*, 5 April 1983, 7 April 1983; CHE Annual Report, 1984, 11–12; 1985, 12; BTM, 24 March 1983; "The University of South Carolina: The Report of the President, 1977–86," 17. The new board was not statutory and had no power to enforce agreements, relying instead on the good faith of USC and MUSC.

60. Price, *A Century of Gamecocks*, 92–98; Griffin, *The First Hundred Years*, 127–29; Don Barton, *They Wore Garnet and Black: Inside Carolina's Quest for Gridiron Glory* (Columbia, S.C.: Spur Publishers, 1985), 246–59. Rogers followed up his sensational senior season by becoming the first player chosen in the National Football League draft, winning rookie-of-the-year honors, and leading the NFL in rushing in 1982. He was the first football player in history to lead the NCAA and NFL in rushing in consecutive seasons.

61. BTM, 4 September 1979, 5 December 1980; *State*, 6 December 1980; *Gamecock*, 8 December 1980.

62. BTM, 12 December 1981; *State*, 13 December 1981; author interview with Othniel H. Wienges, 31 January 2000.

63. *State*, 3 January 1982.

64. *State*, 2 January 1982; *Gamecock*, 11 April 1980, 25 April 1980, 21 November 1980, 16 January 1981, 26 April 1982; *Garnet and Black*, 1982, 308–315; Jill Lieber and Jerry Kirshenbaum, "Stormy Weather at South Carolina," *Sports Illustrated*, 8 February 1982, 30–37. The most sensational allegation against Parsons was that she had had sexual relationships with players.

65. *State*, 2 December 1982; *Gamecock*, 3 December 1982.

66. *Gamecock*, 21 February 1983, 8 June 1983, 14 November 1983, 27 August 1984, 31 August 1984. As result of her libel suit against *Sports Illustrated*, Parsons was convicted of perjury, stemming from her false testimony about her sexual relationships with players. Nearly eighteen years later, she testified in the U.S. House of Representatives' impeachment trial of President Bill Clinton.

67. BTM, 12 April 1983; *Carolinian*, June 1983; *Gamecock*, 15 April 1983; Price, *A Century of Gamecocks*, 41, 138–81.

68. Tom Price, *The '84 Gamecocks: Fire Ants and Black Magic* (Columbia: University of South Carolina, 1984), 192 and passim; William Price Fox and Franklin Ashley, *How 'Bout Them Gamecocks!* (Columbia: University of South Carolina Press, 1985), passim.

69. "The Carolina Plan," 12.

70. *Gamecock,* 10 October 1983; *Higher Education in South Carolina: An Agenda for the Future,* table C-3, part I, p. 223; *Atlanta Constitution,* 6 June 1987; Holderman interview.

71. "Remarks: USC President James B. Holderman Summit Fund Luncheon, October 7, 1983," speech in Holderman Papers; *Gamecock,* 10 October 1983, 4 November 1983, 20 June 1984, 20 March 1985; "Summit Fund, The University of South Carolina," campaign literature, question and answer sheet, n.d., Holderman Papers; *Carolinian,* March 1985; *News,* 25 March 1985; *State,* 18 October 1983; "The University of South Carolina, The Report of the President, 1977–1986," 32–33.

72. *Carolinian,* March 1985; "The University of South Carolina, The Report of the President, 1977–1986," 33; *Gamecock,* 25 January 1984.

73. *Christian Science Monitor,* 29 October 1984.

74. Cook, "Magna Cum Fraud," 187.

75. Text of speech reprinted in *Carolinian,* September 1985.

76. Ibid.

77. Footlick, *Truth and Consequences,* 100–1; Cook, "Magna Cum Fraud," 187–89; *Constitution,* 8 June 1987; *State,* 7 December 1986.

78. Footlick, *Truth and Consequences,* 92–93; *New York Times,* 18 September 1986; *Gamecock,* 12 October 1984, 23 January 1985, 29 August 1986, 8 September 1986, 16 September 1986; Paul R. Perkins and Cheryl F. Perkins to James B. Holderman, 11 June 1985, Holderman Papers.

79. *New York Times,* 18 September 1986; Footlick, *Truth and Consequences,* 92–93; Paul R. Perkins and Cheryl F. Perkins to James B. Holderman, 11 June 1985, Holderman Papers; *Gamecock,* 8 September 1986, 15 September 1986, 19 September 1986;.

80. *New York Times,* 12 November 1986.

81. *New York Times,* 18 September 1986, 22 October 1986, 29 October 1986; *Gamecock,* 10 September 1986, 15 September 1986, 19 September 1986, 17 October 1986, 29 October 1986; Footlick, *Truth and Consequences,* 93; "Paul R. Perkins and Cheryl F. Perkins, Plaintiffs v. The University of South Carolina, Defendant, Order (86-CP-40-3405)," 27 October 1986, Holderman Papers.

82. *New York Times,* 12 November 1986; *Gamecock,* 31 October 1986, 7 November 1986; *Observer,* 13 December 1987. Sadat's course had no requirements other than a research paper turned in on the last day of the class. Of the academic rigor of Sadat's course, journalist Alison Cook wrote that it had "a Mickey Mouse aura," and that it "overflowed with Columbia society ladies." Cook quoted one of these women as saying of the class, "It was so poor. . . . [Sadat]

was trying, but she didn't have anything to say." See *Garnet and Black*, 1985, 143, and Cook, "Magna Cum Fraud," 189.

83. *New York Times*, 12 November 1986; *Gamecock*, 7 November 1986.

84. *New York Times*, 12 November 1986, 17 November 1986; *Washington Post*, 13 November 1986; *Gamecock*, 7 November 1986.

85. BTM, 21 November 1986.

86. Footlick, *Truth and Consequences*, 93.

87. BTM, 21 November 1986; *Observer*, 22 November 1986; *Greenville News*, 27 November 1986, 29 November 1986; *Gamecock*, 3 December 1986; *News and Courier*, 8 December 1986; Cook, "Magna Cum Fraud," 190.

88. BTM, 23 January 1987, quotation 12 February 1987; John Monk to Harry Lesesne, 19 July 2000, collection of the author; *Greenville News*, 24 January 1987, 25 January 1987; *Observer*, 24 January 1987. The *News* and *Observer* kept up constant coverage of the story after November 1986. The above references point to the specific articles cited, but the entire run of both papers for eight months following that date should be seen for more detail.

89. *Greenville News*, 18 December 1986, 13 February 1987; *Observer*, 11 December 1986, 12 December 1986, 13 December 1986, 17 December 1986, 19 December 1986, 23 December 1986, 1 February 1987, 6 February 1987, 14 February 1987, 24 September 1987, 20 February 1991; *State*, 27 February 1991, 21 June 1991; author interview with George Terry, 14 July 2000. As executive director of the Illinois Board of Higher Education during the early 1970s, Holderman had angered Illinois officials when he spent at least $22,000 ($74,045) on meals during a seventeen-month period. As USC president, he drew criticism when he flew trustees and other influential supporters to a 1977 football game in Hawaii at University expense, while students—even the USC cheerleaders— were forced to pay their own way. In 1980, the South Carolina Comptroller General's office had investigated him for using state money to buy and send gifts to legislators. See the *State*, 7 December 1986; *Gamecock*, 1 February 1980; Klores, *Roundball Culture*, 374.

90. Joseph P. Griffith Sr. et. al. to Addison Graves Wilson, 23 January 1987, Holderman Papers; Francis M. Hipp to Arthur M. Williams, 16 June 1987, Holderman Papers; BTM, 2 April 1987; *State*, 20 February 1987, 19 June 1990; *Constitution*, 8 June 1987; *Observer*, 30 January 1987.

91. *State*, 20 February 1987; *Observer*, 21 December 1986, 6 February 1987, 21 February 1987; *News*, 28 February 1987; *Gamecock*, 19 January 1987.

92. Cook, "Magna Cum Fraud," 190–91.

93. Othniel Wienges interview; BTM, 2 April 1987, 23 July 1987; author interview with John Monk, 20 January 2000.

94. *Gamecock*, 24 April 1987.

95. *Observer*, 9 April 1987; *News*, 9 April 1987; Cook, "Magna Cum Fraud," 191.

96. *News*, 24 September 1987; *Gamecock*, 25 September 1987.

97. *Gamecock*, 25 February 1983, 30 January 1984; *Carolinian*, March 1983.

98. *News*, 25 September 1986.

99. BTM, 6 December 1985; James B. Holderman to Robert E. Graham, 19 June 1985, Holderman Papers; James B. Holderman to Robert C. Gallager, 1 July 1985, Holderman Papers.

100. *Carolinian*, December 1986; *Gamecock*, 22 October 1986; *State*, 21 October 1986; *News*, 25 September 1986; South Carolina Legislative Audit Council, "Report to the General Assembly: A Review of the Relationship Between USC and its Foundations and USC Discretionary Spending" (Columbia: Legislative Audit Council, 1989), 23–24 (hereafter cited as "LAC Report"). Senator Mark Hatfield's relationship with the University of South Carolina was later investigated by the Senate Ethics Committee and a federal grand jury. In all, Hatfield received nearly $36,000 in gifts, honoraria, and travel expenses from the University of South Carolina during the 1980s, some of which was given during the lobbying effort for the Swearingen Engineering Center grant. In addition, Hatfield's son was a recipient of a controversial scholarship from Holderman. In 1992, the Senate Ethics Committee reprimanded Hatfield for his failure to report the gifts while being asked to consider the grant, but concluded that there was no "linkage" between USC's gifts to Hatfield and the Swearingen Center grant. A five-term senator, Hatfield declined to run for reelection in 1996. See the *State*, 18 May 1991, 21 May 1991, 3 June 1991, 5 June 1991, 17 June 1991, 26 September 1991; *Observer*, 1 May 1991, 17 June 1991, 10 March 1992, 13 August 1992; *Wall Street Journal*, 13 August 1992.

101. *State*, 10 May 1987; *Observer*, 7 May 1987; *News* 7 May 1987; *Gamecock*, 24 April 1987; *Constitution*, 8 June 1987. Much of the pledged money was in the form of oil futures which precipitously declined in value after the gifts had been made.

102. *Observer*, 15 May 1987; *News*, 15 May 1987; *State*, 1 November 1991; BTM, 11 June 1987; LAC Report, 24. A 1991 Department of Energy investigation of USC's use of the federal grant concluded that the funds were "spent appropriately" and that records indicated no improprieties in the expenditure of federal funds relating to the Swearingen grant. See the *Observer*, 6 April 1991, 31 May 1991.

103. *Gamecock*, 9 April 1990, 11 April 1980, 29 August 1980, 7 November 1980, 21 November 1980; *Observer*, 27 March 1983; Zane Knauss to William H. Patterson and George Curry, 18 March 1975, Patterson Papers.

104. *News*, 9 April 1987; *Observer*, 11 August 1995 "Statement by Dr. Holderman at Press Conference, Shakespeare Theatre at the Folger, Thursday, July 26 [1986], 3:30 p.m.," Holderman Papers.

105. BTM, 11 August 1986; *News*, 5 April 1987, 7 April 1987, 9 April 1987, 1 May 1987, 8 May 1987, 12 May 1987; *Gamecock*, 13 April 1987, 24 April 1987, 24 June 1987; *Record*, 7 April 1987, 7 May 1987; *State*, 18 April 1988, 21 June 1990, 17 February 1991, 2 March 1991, 1 November 1991, 11 August 1995; Chris Vlahoplus to Joe Wilson, 27 April 1987, Holderman Papers; John O'Donnell to Chris Vlahoplus, 30 April 1987, Holderman Papers.

106. *Observer*, 14 May 1987, 16 May 1987; *News*, 14 May 1987, 16 May 1987.

107. *Observer,* 11 August 1995; *State,* 17 February 1991, 2 March 1991, 1 November 1995.
108. *Buildings of the Columbia Campus,* 16, 60.
109. Richard A. Oppel to James B. Holderman and Othniel Wienges, 18 December 1986, Holderman Papers; *Gamecock,* 10 June 1987, 22 July 1987; *News,* 3 February 1988, 6 June 1987; *Observer,* 18 July 1987, 29 March 1988; BTM, 2 April 1987; author interview with William Hubbard, 19 January 2000.
110. Both President Holderman and Executive Vice President Chris Vlahoplus served on the board of directors of both the USC Educational Foundation and the Carolina Research and Development Foundation.
111. South Carolina General Assembly: Legislative Audit Council, *A Review of the Relationship Between State Agencies and Associated Endowments,* 2 March 1983 (Columbia: South Carolina General Assembly, 1983), passim.
112. *News,* 13 October 1985.
113. *State,* 17 September 1987, 22 September 1987; *Atlanta Constitution,* 8 June 1987; *Observer,* 13 December 1987.
114. *2001: The New Dimension* (Columbia: University of South Carolina, 1987), 3, 6.
115. Ibid., 3–6.
116. *Wall Street Journal,* 11 September 1987.
117. "Target 2001," 2–3; Stephen L. Elliott, *Origins, Elements, and Implications of the Cutting Edge Initiatives for Research and Academic Excellence in Higher Education* (Columbia, S.C.: Commission on Higher Education, 1988), passim; *Carolinian,* September 1988.
118. "Target 2001," 2–4, 16–27; BTM, 9 December 1988; *State,* 10 December 1988.
119. Price, *A Century of Gamecocks,* 159–66; *Gamecock,* 4 March 1987.
120. *New York Times,* 3 November 1989; *Gamecock,* 2 March 1988, 21 March 1988, 3 November 1989; *Observer,* 26 March 1988.
121. Tommy Chaikin and Rick Telander, "The Nightmare of Steroids," *Sports Illustrated,* 24 October 1988), 84–102; BTM, 24 March 1988; *Gamecock,* 21 October 1988, 26 October 1988, 21 April 1989, 21 February 1990; *State,* 21 October 1988; *News,* 20 October 1988; *Observer,* 20 October 1988; "University of South Carolina Releases Information on Steroid Inquiry," press release, 19 February 1990, Holderman Papers.
122. "University Associates Address," delivered by President James B. Holderman, 13 September 1989, speech text in author's possession.
123. "The USC Brag," 12 April 1990, speech text in author's possession; "USC Total Private Support," 3 November 1986, Holderman Papers (FOIA Folder); Annual Report, 1989–90, 21.
124. Ibid.; *State,* 31 May 1990.
125. *News and Courier,* 1 April 1990, 2 April 1990, 3 April 1990; *State,* 3 June 1990; *Carolinian,* June 1986; *Gamecock,* 21 November 1986; Self-Study, 1991, 9–3; *SREB Fact Book on Higher Education, 1990* (Atlanta: Southern Regional Education Board, 1990), 93; *The Almanac of Higher Education, 1993* (Chicago: University of Chicago Press, 1993), 77–79; Hugh Davis Graham and Nancy

Diamond, *The Rise of American Research Universities* (Baltimore and London: The Johns Hopkins University Press, 1997), 226; author interview with Russ McKinney. Graham and Diamond used their own categories, and USC ranked as a "Research 3" institution under their criteria. See Graham and Diamond, chap. 6.

126. *Observer,* 21 August 1988, 22 August 1988, 24 August 1988, 29 August 1988, 9 September 1988, 17 September 1988; Dennis Pruitt to James B. Holderman, 21 July 1988, Holderman Papers; *News,* 23 August 1988; *Gamecock,* 26 August 1988, 29 August 1988; *State,* 6 May 1989.

127. *News,* 14 June 1989, 19 September 1989.

128. South Carolina Legislative Audit Council, *Report to the General Assembly: A Review of the Relationship Between USC and Its Foundations and USC Discretionary Spending* (Columbia, S.C.: Legislative Audit Committee, 1989), 1–5, passim; *State,* 2 March 1991; Footlick, *Truth and Consequences,* 102.

129. *Gamecock,* 26 July 1989.

130. BTM, 11 August 1989, 20 October 1989, 28 November 1989, 25 January 1990, 15 February 1990; Othniel Wienges interview.

131. Cook, "Magna Cum Fraud," 192; BTM, 12 April 1990; *State,* 7 May 1990; *Spartanburg Herald,* 10 May 1990; *Observer,* 6 May 1990, 25 May 1990, 31 May 1990; *Gamecock,* 6 June 1990.

132. *State,* 10 May 1990, 29 May 1990, 12 September 1996; The editors of the Chronicle of Higher Education, *The Almanac of Higher Education, 1991* (Chicago: University of Chicago Press, 1991); George Terry interview.

133. Cook, "Magna Cum Fraud," 192; Footlick, *Truth and Consequences,* 96; BTM, 12 April 1990, 21 May 1990; *State,* 17 May 1990, 19 May 1990, 25 May 1990, 26 May 1990, 27 May 1990.

134. BTM, 31 May 1990, 27 June 1990; *State,* 31 May 1990, 1 June 1990, 28 June 1990, 30 June 1990, 12 August 1990; *Observer,* 31 May 1990; *Gamecock,* 6 June 1990; Cook, "Magna Cum Fraud," 192; Footlick, *Truth and Consequences,* 96, 99–100; *Carolinian,* June 1990.

135. *Observer,* 19 June 1991, 28 June 1990, 7 September 1991; *State,* 19 June 1990, 7 September 1991, 8 September 1991; BTM, 27 June 1990; Cook, "Magna Cum Fraud," 192; Holderman interview.

136. *State,* 15 February 1991, 25 February 1991, 1 March 1991; *Observer,* 23 February 1991, 23 March 1991; Cook, "Magna Cum Fraud." As a result of his pleas, USC President John M. Palms informed Holderman that if he attempted to return to the University to teach, then tenure revocation procedures would be initiated against him. John M. Palms to Faculty Colleagues, 21 October 1991, FOIA Request Cartons, USC Archives; BTM, 13 December 1991.

137. *Observer,* 20 October 1991, 22 October 1991, 2 December 1991, 5 December 1991, 7 December 1991, 14 December 1991; Cook, "Magna Cum Fraud," 192–202; Footlick, *Truth and Consequences,* 96–99; John M. Palms to Faculty Colleagues, 21 October 1991, FOIA Requests, USC Archives; "Statement by Dr. John Palms, USC Board of Trustees Meeting," 13 December 1991, FOIA

Requests, USC Archives; James Bowker Holderman to Thomas L. Stepp, 5 December 1991, FOIA Requests, USC Archives; author interview with John M. Palms, 19 January 2001.

138. *Observer,* 3 July 1990.

139. *Observer,* 3 July 1990; *State,* 23 August 1990; BTM, 19 October 1990; *Gamecock,* 18 July 1990, 3 August 1990; *Carolinian,* September 1990.

140. BTM, 6 June 1990, 10 January 1991; *Gamecock,* 14 January 1991, 21 January 1991.

141. McKinney interview; Wienges interview; author interview with William Hubbard, 19 January 2001; Footlick, *Truth and Consequences,* 99–100; *Observer,* 17 November 1991; *State,* 21 April 1991.

142. *State,* 21 April 1991.

143. Holderman interview.

144. Ibid.

145. *State,* 1 June 1990.

CHAPTER 7—STILL THE FAITHFUL INDEX

1. W. J. Cash, *The Mind of the South* (New York: A. A. Knopf, 1941), 429.

2. See Mohr, "World War II and the Transformation of Southern Higher Education."

3. *Public Higher Education,* 177; *SREB Fact Book on Higher Education, 1990,* 31.

4. *South Carolina Higher Education Statistical Abstract,* 1992, 19, 21; *SREB Fact Book on Higher Education 1990,* 46–47. Nationwide, black students made up just over 9 percent of undergraduate enrollment and just over 4 percent of graduate enrollment.

5. See Cox, "1963: The Year of Decision," ch. 1.

6. Schietinger, *Fact Book on Higher Education in the South 1965,* 20; *SREB Fact Book on Higher Education 1990,* 40. The national figures for the proportion of students in public colleges were nearly identical to South Carolina's figures for both 1950 and 1988.

7. Bonner, 45.

8. See Dyer, *University of Georgia,* 351–52 on the disappearance of in loco parentis at the University of Georgia.

9. Hollis, vol. 2, 170–73; Caroline Denham, The University of South Carolina Statistical Profiles, 1989–90, 23.

10. *SREB Fact Book on Higher Education 1990,* 3, 82, 85.

11. *Fact Book on Higher Education in the South 1971 and 1972,* 56.

12. The triumph of urban elites in the South in the post–World War II era is a theme of Numan V. Bartley's *The New South, 1945–1980,* 293–97 and passim.

13. For the expansion of degree offerings at another southern state university, see Dyer, *University of Georgia,* 341.

14. *SREB Fact Book on Higher Education 1990,* 92.

15. See table 1.2; Denham, *University of South Carolina Statistical Profiles,* 1991–92, 43; Self-Study, 1991, 5–17.

16. See, for example, *SREB Fact Book on Higher Education 1990,* 109; Scheitinger, *Fact Book on Higher Education in the South 1965,* 47.

17. See, for example, *SREB Fact Book on Higher Education 1990,* 81.

EPILOGUE—BUILDING UPON A GRAND TRADITION

1. The discussion in this epilogue makes no attempt to be comprehensive, but to briefly survey the University in the period 1991–2001. It is based on my conversations with John M. Palms and William Hubbard, along with the following key documents: Jerrold K. Footlick, *Truth and Consequences;* Annual Report, 1990–1991; "Investing in USC's Future: The University of South Carolina Columbia Future Committee Report to the President," May 1993, USC Archives; "To Be a Great University: The President's Vision for the University of South Carolina As It Enters Its Third Century," 1997, USC President's Office; BTM, 19 October 2000; John Monk, "Piecing Together a Great University: What USC Could Be," special report, *State,* 24 September 2000; *State,* 20 October 2000.

BIBLIOGRAPHY

PRIMARY SOURCES

Oral History

Interviews by Author, 1997–2000

Fannie Phelps Adams

Sol Blatt Jr.

Francis T. Borkowski

Harold Brunton

Rebecca Callcott

H. Thorne Compton

H. Willard Davis

Walter B. Edgar

John Edmunds

Rufus G. Fellers

J. Lyles Glenn

Lawrence E. Giles

John D. Gregory

Philip Grose

James B. Holderman

Ernest F. Hollings

Daniel W. Hollis

William Hubbard

Rhett Jackson

I. S. Leevy Johnson

Joab M. Lesesne Jr.

T. Eston Marchant

Palmer McArthur

W. Russell McKinney Jr.

John McFadden

Grace Jordan McFadden

Robert E. McNair

John Monk

Michael J. Mungo

Robert Ochs

Jerome D. Odom

John M. Palms

Donald S. Russell

Oswald F. Schuette

Fred Sheheen

Selden K. Smith

Robert L. Sumwalt Jr.

George D. Terry

Cameron Todd

Richard L. Walker

Othniel H. Wienges Jr.

John C. West

Harold White

Charles H. Wickenberg

Charles H. Witten

University of South Carolina Archives Oral Interview Collection, USC Archives

George Greichen Caughman, interviewed by Jane E. Hutchison, 6 October 1994.

Frances Turkett Riley, interviewed by Jane E. Hutchison, 6 October 1994.

Harold Brunton, interviewed by William Savage, 3 March 1987.

John H. Martin, interviewed by William Savage, 3 March 1987.

Other Oral Interviews

Matthew J. Perry, interviewed by Grace J. McFadden, 18 August 1980, in "The Quest for Civil Rights," videotape in USC Film Library.

Modjeska Monteith Simkins, interviewed by Grace J. McFadden, 22 May 1979, in "The Quest for Civil Rights," videotape in USC Film Library.

Helen A. Tovey, interviewed by Sally McKay, Carolyn Matalene, and Katherine Reynolds, 26 January 2000, transcript in possession of Sally McKay.

Speeches/Conferences

"The Origins of Contemporary Desegregation at the University of South Carolina, A Twenty-Five Year Retrospective, 1963–1988." Video and audio tape of conference held 18–19 November 1988 on USC campus. In possession of Grace Jordan McFadden, University of South Carolina.

John Roy Harper, speech to "Dreams of Change: Remembering the Struggle for Civil Rights," symposium on USC campus, 21 November 1996.

Manuscripts and Letters

Office of the Board of Trustees, University of South Carolina. Minutes of the Board of Trustees of the University of South Carolina, 1962–1991.

South Carolina Department of Archives and History, Columbia, South Carolina, Manuscript Act, R690, 1946.

South Caroliniana Library, University of South Carolina

Samuel P. Derrick Papers

Walter B. Edgar Papers

James L. Hoyt Papers

Guy F. Lipscomb Papers

Fitz Hugh McMaster Papers

Robert E. McNair Papers

Minutes of the Board of Trustees of the University of South Carolina, 1940–1961

Minutes of the Faculty of the University of South Carolina

South Carolina Council on Human Relations Papers

University of South Carolina News Service Scrapbook, 1947–1966

University of South Carolina Archives

Biographical files

FOIA Requests

James B. Holderman Presidential Papers

Thomas F. Jones Presidential Papers

J. Rion McKissick Presidential Papers

Minutes of the Faculty of the University of the South Carolina

William H. Patterson Presidential Papers

Donald S. Russell Presidential Papers

Norman M. Smith Presidential Papers
Robert L. Sumwalt Presidential Papers
Vertical files
Wofford College Archives, Sandor Teszler Library, Spartanburg, South Carolina
  Mizell, M. Hayes. "The Impact of the Civil Rights Movement on a White
  Activist." Paper Delivered at the 65th Annual Meeting of the Southern
  Historical Association, Fort Worth, Texas, November 4, 1999.
Private Collections
Giles, Lawrence E. "My Life and Times, 1914–?," manuscript autobiography
  in possession of Lawrence E. Giles, Columbia, S.C.
Charles H. Witten papers, in possession of Charles H. Witten, Columbia,
  South Carolina.
Author's Possession
Holderman, James B. Selected speeches.
Chester C. Travelstead. *"I Was There," A Series of Autobiographical Vignettes,
  Volume XI, The South Carolina Story.*
Chester C. Travelstead to Harry Lesesne, 10 March 2000.
Henrie M. Treadwell to Carolyn Matalene, "Recollections," May 2000.

Newspapers and Periodicals
South Carolina
Anderson Independent
Barnwell People-Sentinel
Charleston Evening Post
Charleston News and Courier
Cheraw Chronicle
Columbia Record
Darlington News and Press
Florence Morning News
Gamecock (University of South Carolina)
Garnet and Black (yearbook of the University of South Carolina)
Greenville News
Greenville Piedmont
Greenwood Index-Journal
Island Packet (Beaufort County, S.C.)
Lancaster News
Marion Star
News Leader (Allendale County, S.C.)
Orangeburg Times and Democrat
Rock Hill Herald
South Carolina Business

Spartanburg Herald
The State (Columbia, S.C.)
Summerville Scene
Sumter Daily Item
Union Daily Times
Other
Atlanta Constitution
Augusta (Ga.) Chronicle
Charlotte (N.C.) Observer
Fortune
New York Times
Sports Illustrated
Time
Wall Street Journal
Washington Post

Government and University of South Carolina Publications

"A Report on South Carolina's Need for a Planned System of Public Education Beyond the High School." Columbia: Office of the Governor, 1965.

Acts and Joint Resolutions of the General Assembly of the State of South Carolina, Vol. 45, part 1. Columbia: State Printer, 1947.

Annual Report of the South Carolina Commission on Higher Education. Columbia: State Printer, 1968, 1970, 1973–1991.

"Annual Report to the President of the University of South Carolina by the Registrar, 1958–1959." South Caroliniana Library.

Bulletin of the University of South Carolina: Announcements. Columbia: University of South Carolina, 1939–1991. Published under various titles, but accessible through online catalog at the above title. In footnotes, referred to as "Catalog, *year.*"

The Carolina Handbook: University of South Carolina. Columbia: University YMCA and YWCA, 1949.

Carolina News.

"The Carolina Plan: A Prospectus 1978–1983, A Report from the President To the Board of Trustees, The University of South Carolina, December 1977." Columbia: University of South Carolina 1977. Available at the South Caroliniana Library.

"Carolina Plan II: A Prospectus 1979–1984, A Report From The President To The Board of Trustees, University of South Carolina, December 1978." Columbia: University of South Carolina, 1978.

Carolinian, 1976–1991.

CarolinaType, 1970–1976.

Commencement Programs, 17 August 1954, 6 June 1955, 8 August 1959 and 3 June 1960, USC Archives.

Denham, Caroline, ed. *The University of South Carolina Statistical Profiles, 1984–85*. Columbia: Office of System Research, The University of South Carolina, 1985.

———. *The University of South Carolina Statistical Profiles, 1991–92*. Columbia: System Office of Institutional Research, The University of South Carolina, 1992.

Directions for Academic Excellence: Building on Tradition, Report of the Presidential Commission on Undergraduate Education. Columbia: University of South Carolina, 1985.

"Director of Libraries, USC, Annual Report, 1960–61."

Elliot, Stephen L. *Origins, Elements, and Implications of The Cutting Edge Initiatives for Research and Academic Excellence in Higher Education*. Columbia: South Carolina Commission on Higher Education, 1988.

"General Information Bulletin: Presentation of Academic Accomplishments and Plans, College of General Studies, University of South Carolina." Columbia: College of General Studies, 1972. Available at Thomas Cooper Library, University of South Carolina.

Higher Education in South Carolina, 2 Vols. New York: Cresap, McCormick and Paget, 1962.

Higher Education in South Carolina: An Agenda for the Future. Denver: Augenblick, Van de Water & Associates, 1986.

Higher Education Statistical Abstract, 14th ed. Columbia: Commission on Higher Education, 1992.

Journal of the House of the House of Representatives of the General Assembly of South Carolina. Columbia: State Printer. Published annually, various volumes cited.

Journal of the Senate of the General Assembly of South Carolina. Columbia: State Printer. Published annually, various volumes cited.

"Institutional Self-Study of the University of South Carolina." Columbia: University of South Carolina. Published under varying titles, 1961, 1971, 1981, 1991. These were published for the purpose of reaffirmation of the University's accreditation by the Southern Association of Secondary Schools.

"Interim Report of Committee Created to Study the Feasibility of Establishing a State Supported System of Junior Colleges." Columbia: State Printer, 1966.

Legislative Manual of the 87th General Assembly of South Carolina. Columbia: The State Commercial Printing Company, 1948.

"Let's Get Going!: An Analysis of the Faculty Salary Situation at the University of South Carolina," pamphlet published by the University of South Carolina Alumni Association, 1956, USC Archives.

Opportunity and Growth in South Carolina, 1968–1985. New York: Moody's Investors Service, Inc., 1968.

Paterson, Robert W. "The College Population in South Carolina, 1940–1980." *The University of South Carolina Business and Economic Review* 2, No. 4 (April 1, 1955): 1–4.

"Report of the Governor's Advisory Committee on Higher Education." Columbia: State Printer, 1962.

Reports and Resolutions of the General Assembly of South Carolina. Columbia: State Printer, 1939–1991. These volumes contain all the annual reports of various state institutions, including colleges and universities. The reports of the University of South Carolina are available bound together with other reports, and separately at the South Caroliniana Library.

"The Revised Self-Study of the College of Arts and Sciences." Columbia: University of South Carolina, 1970.

Salvo. Magazine of the Naval ROTC at the University of South Carolina, 1943–1945. University of South Carolina Archives.

South Carolina General Assembly: Legislative Audit Council. *A Review of the Relationship Between State Agencies and Associated Endowments.* Columbia: South Carolina General Assembly, 1983.

South Carolina Legislative Audit Council. *Report to the General Assembly: A Review of the Relationship Between USC and its Foundations and USC Discretionary Spending.* Columbia: Legislative Audit Committee, 1989.

The South Carolina Master Plan for Higher Education. Columbia: The South Carolina Commission on Higher Education, 1979.

South Carolina State Budget, Submitted to the General Assembly of South Carolina by the State Budget and Control Board. Columbia: State Printer, 1963–64, 1970–71.

State Institutions of Higher Learning: Report No.3 to the General Assembly of the State of South Carolina by the Fiscal Survey Commission, 1956. Columbia: State Printer, 1956.

The Statutes At Large of South Carolina vol. 48: 169 (Act 139), 611 (Act 369).

"Target 2001: Report of the President of the University of South Carolina System, July 1987–December 1988."

2001: The New Dimension. Columbia: the University of South Carolina, 1987.

"The Veteran and the University of South Carolina," c. 1945, pamphlet in the South Caroliniana Library.

University of South Carolina Administrative Survey Report, Vol. 1, *Organization and Top Administration.* New York: Cresap, McCormick and Paget, 1960.

University of South Carolina Alumni News, 1941–1961.

University of South Carolina Magazine, 1965–1971.

"University of South Carolina, President's Annual Report for 1978." Colum-
bia: University of South Carolina, 1978. Available at USC Archives.
"The University of South Carolina, Report of the President, 1977–1986."
USC Perspective.
U.S. Bureau of the Census. *State Finances, 1942,* Vol. 3, *Statistical Compendium.*
Washington: U.S. Government Printing Office, 1943.

Other Published Primary Sources

The Almanac of Higher Education, 1993. University of Chicago Press, 1993.
Armsby, Henry H. "Engineering Science and Management War Training Pro-
gram: Final Report." *U.S. Office of Education Bulletin* 1946, No. 9.
Bracey, John H. Jr. and August Meier, eds., *Papers of the NAACP.* Bethesda, Md.:
University Publications of America, 1995.
Brumbaugh, A.J., ed. *American Universities and Colleges,* 5th ed. Washington,
D.C.: 1948.
Byrnes, James F. *All In One Lifetime.* New York: Harper & Brothers, 1958.
Cash, Wilbur J. *The Mind of the South.* New York: Vintage Books, 1941.
Cartter, Allan M., ed. *American Universities and Colleges,* 9th ed. Washington,
D.C.: American Council on Education, 1964.
"The Economic Status of the Profession, 1959–60." *AAUP Bulletin* 46, no. 2
(Summer 1960): 156–93.
"The Economic Status of the Profession, 1962–63." *AAUP Bulletin* 49, no. 2
(Summer 1963), 141–87.
Fact Book on Higher Education in the South, 1970 (Atlanta: Southern Regional
Education Board, 1970.
Fact Book on Higher Education in the South, 1971 and 1972 (Atlanta: Southern
Regional Education Board, 1972).
Folger, John K. *Future School and College Enrollments in the Southern Region.*
Atlanta: Southern Regional Education Board, 1954.
Furniss, W. Todd, ed. *American Universities and Colleges,* 11th ed. Washing-
ton, D.C.: American Council on Education, 1973.
Irwin, Mary, ed. *American Universities and Colleges,* 6th ed. Washington,
D.C.: American Council on Education, 1952.
———, ed., *American Universities and Colleges,* 8th ed. Washington, D.C.:
American Council on Education, 1960.
Jacob, Philip E. *Changing Values in College.* New York: Harper Brothers, 1957.
Littlejohn, Bruce. *Littlejohn's Political Memoirs (1934–1988).* Spartanburg: Bruce
Littlejohn, 1989.
Margolis, Joseph. "The Role of the Segregationist," *Bulletin of the American
Association of University Professors* 43, no. 4 (Winter 1957). Reprint in the
South Caroliniana Library.

Marsh, Clarence Stephen, ed. *American Universities and Colleges,* 4th. ed. Washington, D.C.: American Council on Education, 1940.

McArthur, Lauren Currie Jr. *Growing Up in Bennettsville, Student Days.* Privately published memoir in South Caroliniana Library, 1998.

"The New Mood of Blackness." *Southern Education Report* 4, no. 1 (July-August 1968).

Nixon, H. Clarence. "Colleges and Universities." In *Culture in the South,* ed. W.T. Couch, 229–47. Chapel Hill: University of North Carolina Press, 1934.

"Recent Supreme Court Opinions on Segregated Education." *Higher Education* 7, no. 1 (September 1, 1950): 3–5.

"Report of the Visitation To the University of South Carolina, April 16–19, 1961, Submitted to the Commission of Colleges and Universities of the Southern Association of Colleges and Secondary Schools." South Caroliniana Library.

"Rising Costs and the Public Institutions: The Annual Report on the Economic Status of the Profession, 1969–70," *AAUP Bulletin* 56, no. 2 (Summer 1970), 175–239.

Robinson, William H. "Desegregation in Higher Education in the South." *School and Society* 88, no. 2174 (7 May 1960): 234–39.

Schietinger, E. F. *Fact Book On Higher Education in the South, 1965.* Atlanta: Southern Regional Education Board, 1965.

———. *Fact Book on Higher Education in the South, 1968.* Atlanta: Southern Regional Education Board, 1968.

Sellers, Cleveland. *River of No Return: The Autobiography of a Black Militant and the Life and Death of SNCC.* Jackson and London: University Press of Mississippi, 1990.

SREB Fact Book on Higher Education, 1990. Atlanta: Southern Regional Education Board, 1990.

SREB Fact Book On Higher Education, 1994–1995. Atlanta: Southern Regional Education Board, 1994–1995.

Thompson, Ronald B. *The Impending Tidal Wave of Students.* Columbus, Ohio: The Ohio State University; for the American Association of Collegiate Registrars and Admissions Officers, October 1954.

Travelstead, Chester C. "Turmoil in the Deep South." *School and Society* 83, no. 2084 (28 April 1956): 143–47.

———. "Southern Attitudes Toward Racial Integration." *School and Society* 88, no. 2174 (May 1960): 231–34.

Jones, Thomas F. *The University of South Carolina: Faithful Index to the Ambitions and Fortunes of the State.* New York: The Newcomen Society in North America, 1964.

Von Kolnitz, Lucilla. "Studies of Two Special Freshman Programs at the University of South Carolina." June 1969. Available at Thomas Cooper Library, USC.

———. "University of South Carolina Admissions and Registration, Opportunity Scholars, 1968–1969." Dated March 1970. Available at Thomas Cooper Library, USC.

SECONDARY SOURCES

Published Works

Bailey, N. Louise, Mary L. Morgan and Carolyn R. Taylor. *Biographical Directory of the South Carolina Senate, 1776–1985*, vol. 1. Columbia: University of South Carolina Press, 1986.

Bartley, Numan V. *The New South.* Vol. 10, *The History of the South*, Wendell Holmes Stephenson and E. Merton Coulter, eds. Baton Rouge: Louisiana State University Press, 1996.

Barton, Don. *The Carolina-Clemson Game, 1896–1966.* Columbia: The State Printing Company, 1967.

———. *They Wore Garnet and Black: Inside Carolina's Quest for Gridiron Glory.* Columbia: Spur Publishers, 1985.

Barton, Don, and Bob Fulton. *Frank McGuire: The Life and Times of a Basketball Legend.* Columbia: Summerhouse Press, 1995.

Bass, Jack and Walter Devries. *The Transformation of Southern Politics: Social Change and Political Consequences Since 1945.* Athens and London: University of Georgia Press, 1995.

Bass, Jack and Jack Nelson. *The Orangeburg Massacre*, 2d ed. Macon, Ga.: Mercer University Press, 1996.

Bennett, Michael J. *When Dreams Came True: The G.I. Bill and the Making of America.* Washington and London: Brassey's, 1996.

Billingsley, William J. *Communists on Campus: Race, Politics and the Public University in Sixties North Carolina.* Athens: University of Georgia Press, 1999.

Black, Earl. *Southern Governors and Civil Rights: Racial Segregation as a Campaign Issue in the Second Reconstruction.* Cambridge: Harvard University Press, 1976.

Boles, John B. *The South Through Time: A History of an American Region.* 2d ed. Upper Saddle River, New Jersey: Prentice Hall, 1999.

Bonner, Thomas N. "The Unintended Revolution in Higher Education Since 1940." *Change* 18, no. 5 (September/October 1986): 44–51.

Brooks, Jennifer E. "Winning the Peace: Georgia Veterans and the Struggle to Define the Political Legacy of World War II." *Journal of Southern History* 66, no. 3 (August 2000), 563–604.

Brown, Michael L., ed. *Higher Education Statistical Abstract, 1995.* Columbia: South Carolina Commission on Higher Education, 1995.

Brubacher, John S. and Willis Rudy. *Higher Education in Transition: A History of American Colleges and Universities, 1636–1968,* 2d ed. New York: Harper and Row, 1968.

Bryan, Wright. *Clemson: An Informal History of the University, 1889–1979.* Columbia: R. L. Bryan, 1979.

Buildings of the Columbia Campus, The University of South Carolina. Columbia: Division of University Relations, 1990.

Cahodas, Nadine. *Strom Thurmond and the Politics of Southern Change.* New York: Simon and Schuster, 1993.

Callcott, Wilfred H., ed. *South Carolina: Economic and Social Conditions in 1944.* Columbia: University of South Carolina Press, 1945.

Cardozier, V. R. *Colleges and Universities in World War II.* Westport Conn.: Praeger Publishers, 1993.

Carter, Paul A. *Another Part of the Fifties.* New York: Columbia University Press, 1983.

Cartter, Allan M. *An Assessment of Quality In Graduate Education.* Washington, D.C.: American Council on Education, 1966.

———. "The Role of Higher Education in the Changing South." In *The South In Continuity and Change,* eds. John C. McKinney and Edgar T. Thompson. Durham, N.C.: Duke University Press, 1965.

———. "Qualitative Aspects of Southern University Education." *Southern Economic Journal* 32, no. 1, Part 2 (July 1965): 39–69.

Cauthen, John K. *Speaker Blatt: His Challenges Were Greater.* Columbia: R. L. Bryan, 1964.

Clancy, Paul. "A Campus and Town Join Up to Cool It." *Southern Education Report* 4, no. 3 (October 1968): 20–23.

Conkin, Paul. *Gone With the Ivy: A Biography of Vanderbilt University.* Knoxville: The University of Tennessee Press, 1985.

Conroy, Pat. *Beach Music.* New York: Doubleday, 1995.

Cook, Alison. "Magna Cum Fraud." *Gentleman's Quarterly* 62, no. 8 (August 1992): 185–92, 197–202.

Corrie, Bruce A. *The Atlantic Coast Conference, 1953–1978.* Durham, N.C.: Carolina Academic Press, 1978.

Coryell, Mary Still. *A Century of Excellence in Engineering: University of South Carolina College of Engineering, 1894–1994.* Columbia: College of Engineering, University of South Carolina, 1994.

Crowson, E. Thomas. *The Winthrop Story, 1886–1960.* Baltimore: Gateway Press, 1987.

Diggins, John Patrick. *The Proud Decades: America in War and Peace, 1941–1960.* New York: W. W. Norton, 1988.

Dobbins, Charles G., ed. *The University, the City and Urban Renewal.* Washington, D.C.: American Council on Education, 1964.

Dunlap, Mary M., Leland H. Cox, and George F. Hayhoe, compilers. *A Catalog of the South Caroliniana Collection of J. Rion McKissick.* Spartanburg: Reprint Company, 1977.

Dyer, Thomas G. *The University of Georgia: A Bicentennial History, 1785–1985.* Athens: The University of Georgia Press, 1985.

Edens, Ruth J. *USC Sumter: A History, 1966–1992.* Sumter: USC Sumter, 1993.

Edgar, Walter B. *South Carolina: A History.* Columbia: University of South Carolina Press, 1998.

———. *South Carolina in the Modern Age.* Columbia: University of South Carolina Press, 1992.

———, ed. *Biographical Directory of the South Carolina House of Representatives,* Vol. 1, *Session Lists, 1692–1973.* Columbia: University of South Carolina Press, 1974.

Egerton, John. *Shades of Gray: Dispatches from the Modern South.* Louisiana State University Press, 1991.

Faithful Index: The University of South Carolina Campus. Columbia: University of South Carolina, 1976.

Fincher, Cameron. *Historical Development of the University System of Georgia: 1932–1990.* Athens: Institute of Higher Education, University of Georgia, 1991.

Flynn, George Q. "The Draft and College Deferments During the Korean War." *Historian* 50, no. 3 (1988): 369–85.

Footlick, Jerrold K. *Truth and Consequences: How Colleges and Universities Meet Public Crises.* Phoenix Arizona: American Council on Education and Onyx Press, 1997.

Fox, William Price and Franklin Ashley. *How 'Bout Them Gamecocks!* Columbia: University of South Carolina Press, 1985.

Freeland, Richard M. "The World Transformed: A Golden Age for American Universities, 1945–1970." In *The History of Higher Education,* 2d ed., ed. Lester F. Goodchild and Harold S. Weschler (Needham Heights, Mass.: Simon and Schuster, 1997), 587–606.

Geiger, Roger L. *Research and Relevant Knowledge: American Research Universities Since World War II.* New York: Oxford University Press, 1993.

Graham, Hugh Davis and Nancy Diamond. *The Rise of American Research Universities.* Baltimore and London: The Johns Hopkins University Press, 1997.

Griffin, John Chandler. *The First Hundred Years: A History of South Carolina Football.* Marietta, Georgia: Longstreet Press, 1992.

Heckel, R.V., J. Manning Hiers, Barbara Finegold and John Zuidema. *University 101: An Educational Experiment.* Columbia: Social Problems Research Institute, 1974.

Hollis, Daniel Walker. *University of South Carolina*. Vol. 1, *The South Carolina College*. Columbia: University of South Carolina Press, 1951.

———. *The University of South Carolina*. Vol. 2, *College to University.* Columbia: University of South Carolina Press, 1956.

Horowitz, Helen Lefkowitz. *Campus Life: Undergraduate Cultures from the End of the Eighteenth Century to the Present.* New York: Knopf, 1987.

Jencks, Christopher and David Reisman. *The Academic Revolution.* University of Chicago Press, 1977.

Jezer, Marty. *The Dark Ages: Life in the United States 1945–1960.* Boston: South End Press, 1982.

Kerr, Clark. *The Great Transformation in Higher Education, 1960–1980.* Albany, N.Y.: State University of New York Press, 1991.

———. *The Uses of the University,* 4th ed. Harvard University Press, 1995.

Key, V. O. *Southern Politics in State and Nation.* New York: Alfred A. Knopf, 1949.

Kinnear, Duncan Lyle. *The First 100 Years: A History of Virginia Polytechnic Institute and State University* (Blacksburg, Virginia: Virginia Polytechnic Educational Foundation, Inc., 1972).

Klores, Daniel. *Roundball Culture: South Carolina Basketball.* Huntsville, Ala.: AM Press, 1980.

———. "Out of Bounds: Frank McGuire and Basketball Politics in South Carolina." *Southern Exposure* 7, no. 3 (Fall 1979).

Kujovich, Gil. "Equal Opportunity in Higher Education and the Black Public College: The Era of Separate But Equal." *Minnesota Law Review* 72 (October 1987): 29.

Lander, Ernest M., Jr. *A History of South Carolina, 1865–1960.* 2d ed. Columbia: University of South Carolina Press, 1970.

Lawrence, Paul R. *Unsportsmanlike Conduct: The National Collegiate Athletic Association and the Business of College Football.* New York: Praeger, 1987.

Lee, Calvin B.T. *The Campus Scene, 1900–1970: Changing Styles in Undergraduate Life.* New York: David McKay Company, 1970.

Lesesne, Henry H. "A History of the Alumni Association of the University of South Carolina, 1843–1996." Columbia: Greater USC Alumni Association, 1996.

Mayer, Robert, ed. *The United States Supreme Court,* vol. 7, *The Court and the American Crises, 1930–1953.* Danbury, Conn.: Grolier Eduational Corporation, 1995.

McAninch, William Shepard. "The UFO." *South Carolina Law Review* 46, no. 2 (Winter 1995): 363–79.

McCandless, Amy M. T. "From Pedestal to Mortarboard: Higher Education for Women in South Carolina From 1920 to 1940." *Southern Studies* 23, no. 4 (Winter 1984): 359.

———. *The Past in the Present: Women's Higher Education in the Twentieth Century South.* Tuscaloosa: University of Alabama Press, 1999.

McKale, Donald M., ed. *Tradition: A History of the Presidency of Clemson University.* Macon, Ga.: Mercer University Press, 1988.

McMillan, George. "Integration With Dignity." *Saturday Evening Post* 236, no. 10 (March 16, 1963): 16–22.

Mohr, Clarence. "World War II and the Transformation of Southern Higher Education." In *Remaking Dixie: The Impact of World War II on the American South,* ed. Neil R. McMillen, 33–55. Jackson: University Press of Mississippi, 1997.

Moore, John Hammond. *Columbia and Richland County: A South Carolina Community, 1740–1990.* Columbia: University of South Carolina Press, 1993.

Morris, William H. *Effective College Teaching: The Quest for Relevance.* Washington, D.C.: American Council on Education, 1970.

Newby, I. A. *Black Carolinians: A History of Blacks in South Carolina from 1895 to 1968.* Columbia: University of South Carolina Press, 1973.

Olson, Keith. *The G.I. Bill, the Veterans, and the Colleges.* Lexington, Kentucky: University of Kentucky Press, 1974.

Price, Tom. *A Century of Gamecocks: Memorable Baseball Moments.* Columbia: Summerhouse Press, 1996.

———. *A Century of Gamecocks: Memorable Basketball Moments.* Columbia: Summerhouse Press, 1996.

———. *A Century of Gamecocks: Memorable Football Moments.* Columbia: Summerhouse Press, 1995.

———. *The '84 Gamecocks: Fire Ants and Black Magic.* Columbia: University of South Carolina, 1984.

Public Higher Education in South Carolina. Nashville: George Peabody College For Teachers, 1946.

Quint, Howard H. *Profile in Black and White: A Frank Portrait of South Carolina.* Washington: Public Affairs Press, 1958.

Remembering the Days: An Illustrated History of the University of South Carolina. Columbia: R. L. Bryan Company, 1982.

Robertson, David. *Sly and Able: A Political Biography of James F. Byrnes.* New York and London: W. W. Norton and Company, 1994.

Roose, Kenneth D. and Charles J. Anderson, *A Rating of Graduate Programs.* Washington, D.C.: American Council on Education, 1970.

Rudolph, Frederick. *The American College and University: A History.* New York: A. Knopf, 1962; reprint, Athens: University of Georgia Press, 1990.

Schneider, James G. *The Navy V-12 Program: Leadership for a Lifetime.* Champaign, Ill.: Marlow Books, 1987.

Schulman, Bruce J. *From Cotton Belt to Sunbelt: Federal Policy, Economic Development and the Transformation of the South, 1938–1980.* New York: Oxford University Press, 1991.

South, Stanley and Carl Steen. *Archeology on the Horseshoe at the University of South Carolina.* Columbia: The South Carolina Institute of Archeology and Anthropology, The University of South Carolina, 1992.

Stark, John D. *Damned Upcountryman: William Watts Ball, A Study in American Conservatism.* Durham, N.C.: Duke University Press, 1968.

Stokes, Allen H. *Guide to the Manuscript Collection of the South Caroliniana Library.* Columbia: University South Caroliniana Society, 1982.

Synnott, Marcia. "Federalism Vindicated: University Desegregation in South Carolina and Alabama, 1962–1963." *Journal of Policy History* 1, no. 3 (1989).

Tindall, George B. *The Emergence of the New South, 1913–1945.* Volume 10, *The History of the South,* Wendell Holmes Stephenson and E. Merton Coulter, eds. Baton Rouge: Louisiana State University Press, 1967.

————. *America: A Narrative History.* New York: W. W. Norton and Company, 1984.

Topping, Robert W. *A Century and Beyond: The History of Purdue University.* West Lafayette, Ind.: Purdue Research Foundation, 1988.

Trillin, Calvin. *An Education in Georgia,* 3d ed. Athens and London: University of Georgia Press, 1991.

Twain, Mark, and Charles Dudley Warner. (1873.) *The Gilded Age.* New York: Oxford University Press, 1996.

Upcraft, M. Lee, John N. Gardner and Associates. *The Freshman Year Experience: Helping Students Survive and Succeed in College.* San Francisco: Jossey-Bass, 1989.

von Hoffman, Nicholas. *The Multiversity: A Report on What Happens to Today's Students at American Universities.* New York: Holt, Rinehart, Winston, 1966.

Wallenstein, Peter. "Black Southerners and Non-Black Universities: Desegregating Higher Education, 1935–1967." *History of Higher Education Annual* 19 (1999), 121–48.

Wardlaw, Frank H., ed. *"Men and Women of Carolina:" Selected Addresses and Papers by J. Rion McKissick.* Columbia: University of South Carolina Press, 1948.

Williams, G. Croft. *A Social Interpretation of South Carolina.* Columbia: University of South Carolina Press, 1946.

Williams, Roger M. "'Two Old Men:' In S.C., Brown and Blatt are the Senior Partners." *South Today* 4, no. 8 (April 1971), 4–5.

Workman, William D. *The Bishop From Barnwell: The Political Life and Times of Edgar J. Brown.* Columbia: R. L. Bryan, 1963.

Wiggins, Sam P. *The Desegregation Era in Higher Education.* Berkeley, Calif.: McCutchan Publishing, 1966.

Zelomek, A.W. *A Changing America: at Work and Play.* New York: John Wiley and Sons, 1959.

Unpublished Works

Aba-Mecha, Barbara Woods. "Black Woman Activist in the Twentieth Century: Modjeska Monteith Simkins." Ph.D. Dissertation, Emory University, 1978.

Bryant, Mary Lou. "The University of South Carolina at Spartanburg: The Early Years, 1967–1974." Ph.D. dissertation, University of South Carolina, 1993.

Chandler, Andrew W. "'Dialogue With the Past': J. Carroll Johnson and the University of South Carolina, 1912–1956." M.A. thesis, University of South Carolina, 1993.

Cox, Maxie Myron. "1963—The Year of Decision: Desegregation in South Carolina." Ph.D. dissertation, University of South Carolina, 1996.

Dreyfuss, James V. "Statewide Higher Education Coordination in South Carolina: 1945 to 1973." Unpublished paper in the Constance B. Schulz Papers, South Caroliniana Library.

———. "The Origin of Statewide Higher Education Coordination in South Carolina, 1945–1967: A Documentary History." Ph.D. Dissertation, University of South Carolina, 1997.

Dunbar, Dwight A. "A History of the University of South Carolina School of Music, 1920–1993." Ph.D. dissertation, University of South Carolina, 1995.

Giles, Doris B. "The Antiwar Movement in Columbia, South Carolina, 1965–1972." Unpublished paper in the Doris B. Giles Collection, Manuscripts Division, South Caroliniana Library.

Graham, M. Ryan. "University 101: Education's Aladdin's Lamp at the University of South Carolina, 1972–1999." Unpublished seminar paper, SCCC 325G, Spring 1999, in author's possession.

Kalemaris, Victoria Terhecte. "No Longer Second-Class Students: Women's Struggle for Recognition and Equity at the University of South Carolina, 1914–1935." M.A. thesis, University of South Carolina, 1998.

Lesslie, Mary Stewart. "Evaluation of Nontraditional College Programs: UWW at USC." M.A. thesis, University of South Carolina, 1974.

Lynn, Steven W. "A History of Greek-Letter Social Fraternities at South Carolina College and University." Unpublished paper in USC Archives.

Singleton, Edward M. "A History of the Regional Campus System of the University of South Carolina." Ph.D. dissertation, University of South Carolina, 1971.

Siochos, Peter G., and Kathy Aboe. "With Honors: A History of the South Carolina Honors College, 1977–1997." Senior thesis, University of South Carolina, 1997.

Smith, Mark D. "Guide to the University Archives." M.A. thesis, University of South Carolina, 1988.

Watts, Elsie. "The Freshman Year Experience, 1962–1990: An Experiment in Humanistic Higher Education." Ph.D. dissertation, Queen's University, 1999.

White, Pamela Mercedes. "'Free and Open': The Radical University of South Carolina, 1873–1877." M.A. thesis, University of South Carolina, 1975.

INDEX

Page numbers in italic indicate figures; page numbers in italic followed by t indicate tabular material.